190 million-year-old Jurassic ammonites from Yeovil, Somerset, England.

EARTHSCOPE

Ayers Rock, Australia, at sunrise.

1983 eruption of Kilauea Volcano, Hawaii.

EARTHSCOPE

Consultant Editor: Chris Pellant

A comprehensive survey of the processes that shape our planet,
as revealed by the latest scientific theories
and up-to-the minute technology

Uncle Bill and Auntie May

with much love

Chris

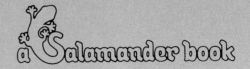
a Salamander book

Published by Salamander Books Limited
LONDON

A SALAMANDER BOOK

Published by Salamander Books Ltd
Salamander House
27 Old Gloucester Street
London WC1N 3AF
United Kingdom

© Salamander Books Ltd 1985

ISBN 0 86101 144 9

Distributed by Hodder & Stoughton
Services, PO Box 6, Mill Road,
Dunton Green, Sevenoaks,
Kent TN13 2XX

All correspondence concerning
the content of this volume should
be addressed to Salamander Books Ltd

CREDITS

Editor:
Jonathan Elphick
Editor, *Eyes in the Sky:*
Philip de Ste. Croix
Designers:
Roger Hyde
Nick Buzzard
Mark Holt

Picture Researcher:
Vickie Walters

Picture Assistant:
Sue Willcock

Colour reproductions:
Rodney Howe Ltd, England
David Bruce Graphics, England

Filmset:
Modern Text Typesetting Ltd,
England

Printed in Belgium by
Henri Proost et Cie, Turnhout

The 475ft (145m) San Raphael Falls, Ecuador.

CONTENTS

CONTRIBUTING AUTHORS

ROBERT BLACKBURN studied at Leicester and Teesside Polytechnics and Durham University, UK, where he obtained an MSc. He lectures in both higher and further education, and his current research interests include the history of ideas about the evolution of Man. Robert Blackburn wrote the section *The Arrival of Man* in the chapter *Fossils and Evolution*.

DR BASIL BOOTH gained a PhD from Keele University, UK, after graduating from London University. He is a world authority on volcanoes, and has led expeditions to all the Earth's major volcanic regions, including 22 different countries and 18 islands. He now runs an extensive picture library and consultancy service, and broadcasts on TV and radio. Basil Booth has made major contributions to the following chapters: *How Rocks are Formed*, *The Ocean Frontier*, *The Atmosphere*, and supplied advice and information for *The Arid Lands*, and for *Microfossils* in *Fossils and Evolution*.

DUNCAN BREWER is a freelance journalist with a particular interest in environmental issues. Over the years, he has contributed to major critical surveys of the mining, chemical, oil, nuclear and automobile industries, and has published many articles. Duncan wrote all of the last chapter, *The Mark of Man*, except for *The Exploitation of Antarctica*.

PROF JOHN COLLINSON spent two years as a Research Fellow in Sweden after gaining a BA and PhD at Oxford University, UK. After lecturing at Keele University, UK, he became Senior Exploration Geologist with Britoil in Glasgow. He is now Professor of Basin Analysis at Bergen University, Norway. John Collinson wrote the last six pages of *How Rocks are Formed*.

DR JOHN GOULD is a Physical Oceanographer at the UK Institute of Oceanographic Sciences. Since the late 1960s he has taken part in major studies of the circulation of the North Atlantic Ocean and has acted as Chief Scientist on a large number of oceanographic cruises. He has taken part in multinational experiments and is currently Chairman of the Oceanic Hydrography Working Group of the International Council for the Exploration of the Sea. He wrote *Ocean Currents and Circulation* in *The Ocean Frontier*.

ROBERT HEADLAND is a Research Scholar at the Scott Polar Institute, Cambridge, UK, and has served with the British Antarctic Survey for several years. He is investigating the history, exploitation, conservation and politics of Antarctica. In 1982 he was taken prisoner with twelve of his colleagues by the Argentine Navy when they attacked the island of South Georgia. He has written an account of all aspects of the island and is presently editing a comprehensive history of Antarctic expeditions. He wrote the section on *The Exploitation of Antarctica* in *The Mark of Man*.

DR TOM KEMP gained a PhD at Cambridge University, UK, specializing in mammal-like reptiles. He became Curator of the University Museum at Oxford in 1972, and also lectures in vertebrate zoology and evolution at Oxford University. He is the author of the book *Mammal-like Reptiles and the Origin of Mammals* and of many papers on fossil reptiles. Tom Kemp wrote the vertebrate sections in *Fossils and Evolution*.

Death Valley, California, seen through the thematic mapping unit of Landsat 4.

PROF JOHN LATHAM carried out PhD studies at Imperial College, London, then became a lecturer at the University of Manchester Institute of Science and Technology, where he now holds a Chair in Physics. Awarded a DSc by the University of Manchester, he has also received several awards from the Royal Meteorological Society. He is President of the International Commission on Atmospheric Electricity and a member of the Commission on Cloud Physics. John Latham wrote the sections on *Clouds and Rain* and *Thunder and Lightning* in *The Atmosphere*.

RICHARD S LEWIS is a journalist specializing in science and technology, who has made many in-depth studies of space exploration and space technology. He contributed to Salamander's *Space Technology* and was principal author of *Space Exploration*, also from Salamander. Richard Lewis wrote *Eyes in the Sky*.

DR DAVID PEEL has been a glaciologist with the British Antarctic Survey since 1969. His main research interests are concerned with the record of past environmental change preserved in the ice and snow layers of the Antarctic ice sheet. He has spent about 2½ years in Antarctica collecting evidence for global pollution by organochlorine pesticides and heavy metals and is currently engaged on an ice-core drilling project to trace past climate. He wrote the section *Antarctica: A Natural Laboratory* in *The World of Ice*.

CHRIS PELLANT graduated from Keele University, UK, in Geology and Geography, and has lectured in the Earth Sciences for many years in both higher and further education. He has written many articles for books and periodicals on various Earth Sciences topics. His main interests are the ancient rocks of northern Scotland and invertebrate palaeontology. As well as acting as Consultant Editor, he has written the introductory chapter, *Setting the Scene*, and contributed to the following chapters: *How Rocks are Formed*, *The Ocean Frontier*, *The Arid Lands*, *The Atmosphere* and *Fossils and Evolution*.

DR JOHN REYNOLDS was for several years a glaciologist with the British Antarctic Survey, and after working for an oil company, is currently lecturing in Geophysics at Plymouth Polytechnic, UK. He wrote the chapter *The World of Ice*, apart from the section on *Antarctica: A Natural Laboratory*.

DR DON TARLING graduated from Keele University, UK, going on to complete his MSc at Imperial College, London, and then a PhD at the Australian National University. He has recently received a DSc from Keele University. Most of his research has been concerned with continental drift and plate tectonics, chiefly based on palaeomagnetic studies in many areas of the world. He has published seven books and over 170 scientific papers. Don Tarling wrote the third chapter, *The Dynamic Earth*.

GABY VAGO, who was born in Hungary, read Geology at Durham University, UK, before embarking on a teaching career in the West Indies. He developed a deep interest in geomorphology and went on to make studies of weathering and erosion of arid regions. He now teaches Geology and Geography at Norton Knatchbull School, Ashford, Kent. He contributed to *The Arid Lands*.

PREFACE
—Chris Pellant—

Over the last few years, mainly because of a
number of revolutionary advances in both theory
and technology which have coloured our view of
the Earth, there has been an increasing need for an
informative, topical book which covers these developments and links them to the existing fund of knowledge
about our planet. My awareness of the desire for
such a book has been heightened by the requirements
of higher and further education students and members of
the general public who attend my informal talks and
lectures. Such a book must be exciting, both to read
and to look at, reflecting the dynamic nature of the
Earth itself, and must meet the needs of the non-
specialist reader.

The Earth sciences embrace a variety of scientific
fields of study. In order to produce a book that is
accurate, up-to-date and expertly written, an impressive
group of authors has been brought together to contribute
the text and captions. They are researchers in such
wide-ranging fields as volcanology, geophysics,
palaeontology, glaciology, cloud physics, oceanography,
space technology and sedimentology. I am indebted to
all of them for their expert contributions, completed
with attention to detail to meet exacting deadlines.

The text has been arranged so that it is possible to
refer to a single double-page 'spread' as a self-contained
unit within a chapter. *Earthscope* is not a book that
has to be read from cover to cover. The comprehensive
index enables rapid reference to be made to related
passages in other parts of the book. A glossary has also
been included with this aim in view.

Here I must take the opportunity of thanking my
wife, Helen, for her support, inspiration and untiring
help throughout the project, and for the many hours
she has spent proofreading and compiling the index.

The visual impact of *Earthscope* reflects the hard
work of the artists who drew or painted the many
original diagrams, charts and maps, and to the numerous

Sunset over Signy Island, Antarctica

photographers whose skills are represented here. The daunting task of obtaining and sorting through many thousands of transparencies from sources the world over has been expertly accomplished by Vickie Walters, with help from Sue Willcock. Without them, *Earthscope* would not be the beautiful book it is.

Earthscope is attractive not only because of the photographs and artwork it contains but also because of the skill of the design team, especially the chief designer, Roger Hyde, who, aided by Nick Buzzard and Mark Holt, patiently and expertly coped with all the problems of interpreting, commissioning and checking every stage in the assembly of text and visual elements, to produce a fresh and appealing design on every page.

Many other people have been influential in the production of *Earthscope*. I must first thank Nicole Bechirian for originally putting me in touch with the editor, Jonathan Elphick. He deserves my thanks and admiration for his skill in commissioning authors, moulding a variety of writing styles into coherent uniformity and supervising the whole project from its inception to the final product. I must also thank Professor Gordon Leedale of the Plant Sciences Department at Leeds University, UK, for much valuable advice and information during the project, Queen for their inspirational music and my wife Helen and children Daniel, Adam and Emily for managing without my full attention for the past eighteen months.

MAJOR EVENTS IN EARTH HISTORY

May 1984
First direct measurements of continental drift
released by NASA, USA
20 July 1969
Man reaches the moon (Apollo 11 Mission, USA)
4 Oct 1957
First artificial satellite launched (Sputnik 1, USSR)
16 July 1945
First nuclear weapon tested, Alamogordo, USA

20,000 m.y.
Formation of the Universe

5,000 m.y.
Formation of the Sun

2.5 m.y.
Onset of present ice age

2 m.y.
First humans

4,600 m.y.
Formation of the Earth and Moon

40 m.y.
Himalayas start to form

4,300 m.y.
The first rain

65 m.y.
Extinction of many groups
including dinosaurs

110 m.y.
Dinosaurs rule
Present-day continents forming
Modern Atlantic Ocean splits open

200 m.y.
Oxygen reaches
modern levels

300 m.y.
Coal deposited

400 m.y.
Vertebrates evolve
Plants clothe the land

600 m.y.
Animals evolve
hard shells

1,500 m.y.
Continents begin to drift
First mountains produced by folding

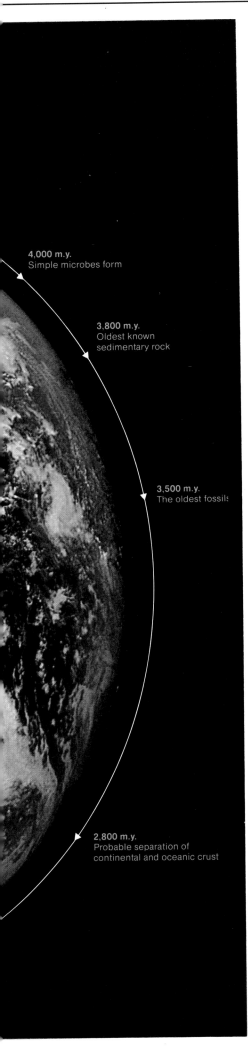

4,000 m.y.
Simple microbes form

3,800 m.y.
Oldest known
sedimentary rock

3,500 m.y.
The oldest fossils

2,800 m.y.
Probable separation of
continental and oceanic crust

Remote-sensing satellites orbiting the Earth reveal our planet as we have never seen it before. Geologists can detect patterns formed by rock structures which extend for thousands of miles over the Earth's surface. Possible sites of mineral wealth can be examined and weather systems monitored. Deep space probes reveal the secrets of the other planets.

The classical methods of geological enquiry have been aided by modern technology on land, too. Earth Scientists can now measure the rate of continental drift, give an absolute age to rocks, and trace the threads of organic evolution. But it is vital that along with such gains in knowledge, we develop a greater respect for our fragile, complex and beautiful home.

SETTING THE SCENE

The Earth's crust can be read like a history book, reaching back 4,600 million years. Space probes and Earth-based technology unravel secrets of our planet's origin and development

In the last few decades, our understanding of the processes shaping our planet has increased by leaps and bounds, thanks to painstaking scientific research aided by sophisticated modern technology. We are aware of the Earth as never before, through television and other mass-communication systems and the huge increase in global travel. The Earth Sciences have been revolutionized in many ways during this short time.

Time—its passing and its record—is the real essence of geological science. The rocks of the Earth's crust are the pages of Earth History. Pioneering geologists in the last century put forward ideas about using fossils to place strata in a correct relative sequence. They proposed the principle of Uniformitarianism, which assumes that the present is a yardstick against which we can interpret evidence from the past. Such ideas still form the basis of much geological enquiry.

Today, we can measure the real age of the Earth because of a subtle revolution, evidence for which has built up in the scientific literature for many years. By measuring the decay of radioactive isotopes in common rocks, absolute geological ages can be calculated. The Earth was born 4,600 million years ago! Scientists also know that the Moon and neighbouring planets are the same age. Despite this, much remains mysterious, and the past events which are preserved are often freak happenings and not the everyday occurrences about which Earth Scientists would like to know.

Space is like time in its vastness. Recent years have seen a revolution in the Earth Sciences through the many programmes of manned and unmanned space missions. Man has even played golf on the Moon! The Martian landscape has been photographed by a camera gently floated through that planet's hostile atmosphere to land on the desolate rocky surface. Probes have reached the depths of our Solar System and beyond. By hanging satellites high above the Earth, we can monitor its fickle weather systems. In two far-reaching ways the space programme has affected our concept of the Earth. The vast stores of information gained have coloured our views of the Earth's evolution. Also, for the first time, we have a real image of our globe.

Man has always been fascinated by the regular patterns formed by major features of the Earth's surface, such as the long lines of volcanoes and earthquakes. For over a hundred years, a few independent thinkers suggested that the continents have drifted apart, originally having been a single giant land-mass. Many geologists scorned these ideas. Today it would be almost impossible to find an Earth Scientist who does not believe in drifting of the continents as an active process. Less than two decades ago the all-embracing theory of Plate Tectonics, for which geologists had been searching for many years, was postulated. By logically relating the large-scale surface features of the Earth to a dynamic mechanism driven by heat from below, this theory suggests that the continents are carried along on rigid mobile plates, each about 60 miles (100km) thick. As the plates move apart, oceans form; when they collide, mountains are built.

Anyone who has found a sparkling pebble on the beach, seen a glaciated mountain range or a desert with shifting dunes, or been the first living being to uncover a fossil trapped in layers of rock millions of years earlier, must have been filled with wonder. Just as we realize how beautiful the Earth is, so we see how vulnerable it is, too. We are destroying our own life-support system by releasing poisonous wastes into our rivers and oceans, and into the very air we breathe. Until recently, most of us were ignorant of this destruction and abuse. This is no longer the case. We all share the responsibility for safeguarding our world for ourselves and countless other species. Earthscope aims to produce a profound and long-lasting respect for the Earth which will help to ensure our planet's future.

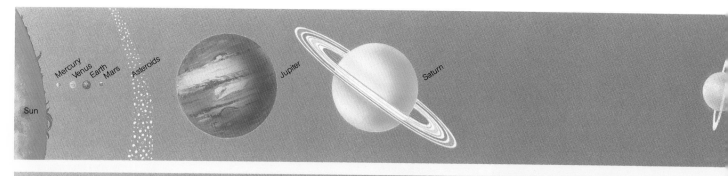

Major Space Probes

Mercury	Venus	Earth	Mars	Jupiter	Saturn	
Mariner 10 (US)	Venera 16 (USSR)	Numerous satellites	Viking 1 & 2 (US)	Pioneer 10 & 11 (US)	Pioneer 10 & 11 (US) ▶	Voyager 2 going on to probe ▶
	Pioneer Venus (US)			Voyager 1 & 2 (US)	Voyager 1 & 2 (US)	Uranus and Neptune

Only very recently has it been possible to journey away from the Earth, our home, and view her beauty. From space, our planet is a blue sphere rich in the variety of its shades and textures. Swirling cloud systems move above a surface covered largely with water. The outlines of the continents can be seen, through breaks in the clouds, as can the polar ice-caps. However, its serene appearance from afar belies the other, more violent aspect of our world.

Dynamic Earth generates immensely powerful and sometimes catastrophic events which move and disrupt the thin crust on which we live. The continents wander and collide, producing great mountain ranges such as the Himalayas. Volcanoes belch forth vast quantities of incandescent molten lava, earthquakes destroy whole cities in a matter of hours. Luckily, these are events by which many of us are not directly affected, and, compared with our near neighbours in space, the Earth has provided just the right conditions for the evolution of a wonderful variety of living things.

The Earth in Space

Ours is a small planet in a solar system which itself is a mere speck near the edge of one of the spiralling arms of the Milky Way Galaxy, a vast spinning disc of gas, dust and stars. Over 400 million galaxies have been detected from the Earth. Our Galaxy is some 80,000 light-years in diameter, and the nearest star to our Sun is Proxima-Centauri, 4.2 light-years away. (A light-year is the distance light travels in one year, about 6 million million miles, or 9.5 million million kilometres.)

Any theory about the origin of our Solar System must consider all the planets it contains, and their physical and chemical features. Four features are of particular relevance here. The first is that all the planets revolve around the Sun in the same direction. The second is that many planets have moons, and most of these move around their planets in this same direction, held by the planet's gravitational pull. The Sun itself spins this way, too. Thirdly, the 92 chemical elements found on Earth exist throughout the Solar System, in different proportions in different regions: astronomers have detected 70 of these elements in the Sun, using light-splitting spectroscopes. Finally, the inner planets, Mercury, Venus, Earth and Mars, are small and very dense. Most of the outer planets are of enormous size and low density.

The 'Big Bang' theory

The most plausible explanation of these, and other, features of our Solar System looks back

through time some 20,000 million years. It was then that the so-called 'Big Bang', an unimaginably immense explosion, scattered all the energy and matter in the Universe out from a very small volume into the vastness of space. Today, the Universe can still be seen to be expanding at a tremendous rate. Astronomers can measure the speed and extent of this expansion by looking at the 'red shift', or 'Doppler shift', of distant stars: this is the increase in the wavelength of light, so that it becomes more red, of stars or galaxies travelling away from the Earth at great speed.

Formation of the Solar System

About 1,000 million years after the Big Bang, dust and gas began to gather into isolated clouds, and, as gravity around these clouds increased with their increase in mass, they were able to attract yet more matter, and grew even bigger. In this way, galaxies were born. Within

these swirling, primitive galaxies, sun-centred systems may have been formed in various ways. Localized masses of dust and gas may have contracted to such an extent that, under conditions of greatly increased gravity, temperature and pressure increases promoted nuclear reactions near the centre, and a star began to shine. If another star passed through the swirling dust of the infant solar system, close enough for fragments to be torn off both stars, these fragments might have condensed to form planets.

This 'close-encounter' idea does not, however, account for many of the important features of our Solar System outlined above. An alternative theory suggests that the continued gravitational accretion of dust and gas which forms a star was arrested when the star's heat reached a certain level and stability. The dust and gas still spinning round the star would condense into planets and moons. The distribution of higher-

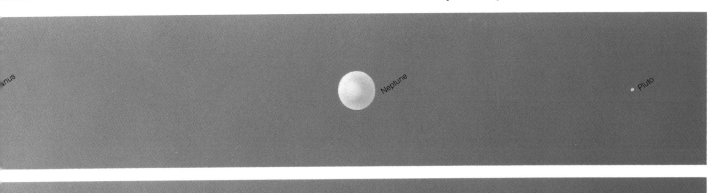

Left The Horsehead Nebula in Orion. Our solar system condensed from a similar cloud of dust and gas.
Below Maps of Venus based on information from space probes show two main 'continents' (brown), rolling plains (blue) and high mountains (white).

Above Over a million times bigger than Earth, the Sun holds the Solar System together. Here it is shown at the same scale as the planets. The inner planets, Mercury (a rocky, baking-hot dust bowl), Venus (clothed in a thick, noxious atmosphere), the Earth, and Mars (ice-capped and red-cratered) all lie inside the asteroid belt. The asteroids are chunks of rock and dust, some pebble-sized, others large enough to build towns on. Beyond them lie the giant planets: Jupiter (a dense mass of gas and liquid) and Saturn (another gas giant with its glorious ring system, made largely of ice and dust, maybe the fragments of a still-born moon). In the remoteness of deep space lie two more gas giants, Uranus and Neptune, and little, enigmatic Pluto.

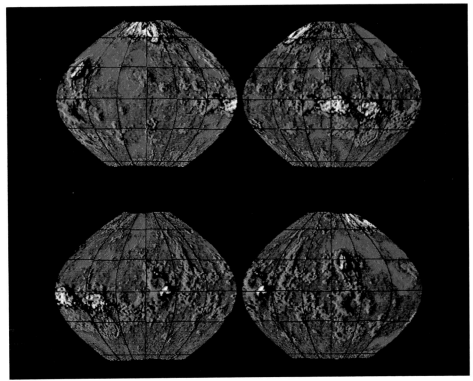

density planets near the centre and less dense ones further away, and the similar chemistry and direction of rotation through the system was produced in this way. A single planet, such as the Earth, would be differentiated into a shelled structure by the heat from radioactive decay at its centre. This radioactive decay, of isotopes of uranium, thorium and potassium, still produces heat today.

The age of the Solar System
The Earth and her Moon are both the same age, some 4,600 million years old. Scientists think that the other planets and moons in the Solar System are about the same age. The oldest rocks on the Earth's surface have been dated (by measuring their rate of radioactive decay) at 3,800 million years, and rock from the Moon's surface has been dated at between 4,600 and 3,150 million years old. The Moon's surface—unlike the Earth's—has not been recycled through time, so no younger dates than these have been estimated.

Origin of water and the atmosphere
Much of the reworking of the rocks on the Earth's surface has been done by its atmosphere and by the hydrosphere (the oceans, rivers and lakes). When the primitive Earth consolidated, water was probably produced by volcanic eruptions. An alternative theory suggests that all the water in the oceans could have arisen from the crystallization of the granitic continental crust. The atmosphere today is very different from the primitive layer of gases which existed when the Earth first formed. Today, oxygen is abundant, as are nitrogen and carbon dioxide. The newborn atmosphere was rich in hydrogen, ammonia, water, methane, hydrogen sulphide and other gases found today surrounding the planets Jupiter and Saturn. These low-density gases have been lost from Earth to space; oxygen is abundant because of photosynthesis by green plants.

Evidence from the Moon
On 20 July 1969, men first stepped out onto the lunar surface. This politically motivated space programme has provided exciting geological information, not only about the Moon, but also about the early history of the Earth and the changes in the Sun's radiation through time. To date, some 850 lb (385 kg) of lunar rock has been brought back to Earth by the American and Soviet missions. This basaltic rock appears to be very like that from the Earth's ocean floor, but there is evidence to suggest that the lunar basalts may have formed differently. The Moon gives us a picture of the past; it is as if frozen in time, because by a chance of size, its gravity is only one-sixth that of the Earth, insufficient to retain an atmosphere, and so its surface has never been recycled.

Beneath the crust, temperatures and pressures increase so dramatically that rock which we would recognize on the surface becomes utterly changed and eventually melted. Here is an environment so alien to us that no surface organism could hope to survive in it. It would be easier to build a city on the Moon, a quarter of a million miles away, than to live only 15 miles beneath London or New York.

Project Mohole

There are various ways of finding out what it is like inside the Earth. A direct method is to drill and sample the subsurface rock. As long ago as 1957, an ambitious American project was launched. This was Project Mohole, named after the Mohorovičić Discontinuity (understandably, usually abbreviated to 'Moho'), the zone separating the Earth's crust from the underlying mantle. The name honours the Yugoslav geologist Andrija Mohorovičić, who discovered this zone in 1909, after analysing the behaviour of earthquake waves passing through the crust.

The Mohole Project was a bold attempt to drill a hole through the crust to sample directly the rocks beneath. Tremendous technological problems were overcome, and, in 1961, using the drilling ship *CUSS 1*, the drill reached a depth of almost 650 ft (197 m) in the floor of the Atlantic Ocean east of Guadalupe Island in the West Indies. Unfortunately, because the financial and political bases of the project were ill-founded, it was curtailed in 1966.

International co-operation

In May 1964, four major US oceanographic institutions joined forces to set up the Joint Oceanographic Institutions Deep Earth Sampling (JOIDES) group, and were later joined by other teams from several US universities. The first leg of the Deep Sea Drilling Project (DSDP) began in August 1968. The history of JOIDES and the DSDP proved a welcome success compared with the aborted Mohole Project, and was able to expand its scope considerably in 1975, when five other nations—the UK, France, West Germany, the USSR and Japan—joined in. This phase was named the International Programme of Ocean Drilling (IPOD). The DSDP uses the 10,500-ton, specially converted oil-exploration drilling ship *Glomar Challenger*. Although important knowledge has been gained, drilling has been relatively shallow and restricted to non-hazardous areas. Future phases of ocean drilling, such as the Advanced Ocean Drilling Programme (AODP), beginning early in 1985, will use the advanced drilling ship *SEDCO/BP 471*.

Clues from volcanoes

Another direct way of studying rocks from the lower crust and mantle is to investigate those that have been forced to the surface from great depths by volcanoes and during orogenies—periods of mountain-building. Earth scientists face many problems in interpreting such rocks. Those in volcanic areas will have been heated and possibly altered, as will the rocks brought to higher regions of the crust by orogenies. Nevertheless, from the evidence of these deep materials, geologists have discovered that the layer beneath the crust, the mantle, is of ultrabasic composition—deficient in free silica and rich in the ferro-magnesian minerals (containing iron and/or magnesium), such as olivine and pyroxene.

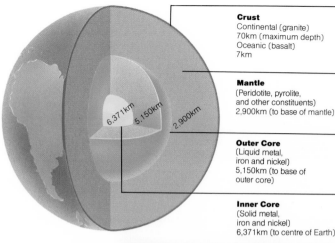

6,371km 5,150km 2,900km

Crust
Continental (granite)
70km (maximum depth)
Oceanic (basalt)
7km

Mantle
(Peridotite, pyrolite, and other constituents)
2,900km (to base of mantle)

Outer Core
(Liquid metal, iron and nickel)
5,150km (to base of outer core)

Inner Core
(Solid metal, iron and nickel)
6,371km (to centre of Earth)

Left The Earth's crust is the rocky surface on which we live. Dark, denser rock from the mantle has been found in the crust where huge faults and volcanic upheavals occur. Temperatures in the inner core approach 14,500°F. Ultimately, the heat generated by radioactivity at depth in the Earth is felt on the surface as it produces convection cells and currents in the mantle. These drive giant plate tectonics movements in the crust that cause earthquakes and volcanoes, form vast oceans and great mountain ranges, and move whole continents.

Right Three meteoroids appear as long pinkish streaks against a backdrop of stars (curved coloured lines) in a long-exposure photo of part of the Leonid meteor shower. Most meteoroids are tiny, dust-like particles that burn up by friction as they hit our atmosphere, causing the bright streaks of light we call 'shooting stars'. A few survive their violent journey to hit the Earth. These 'meteorites' are of great interest to the geologist: they may represent samples of material from primitive planets, and so reveal important details of internal planetary structure.

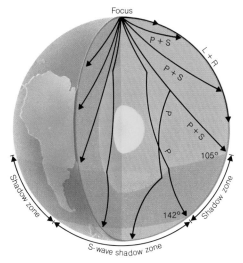

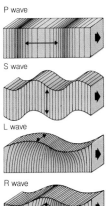

Above Study of different types of seismic waves and how they travel in the Earth reveals secrets of its internal structure. P waves travel more slowly in the core than in the mantle, and S waves are not transmitted at all, indicating that the outer core at least is liquid.
Left The large arrows show the direction of wave travel and the small ones the plane of vibration.
Below The surface L and R waves cause most damage, as seen in these two views of Anchorage, Alaska, after a 1964 earthquake.

Evidence from outer space
An unlikely method of finding out about the Earth's interior is by studying objects from outer space. Each year, the Earth is bombarded by thousands of meteoroids. Most of these are burnt up in our protective atmosphere, and very, very few do any damage. Meteoroids have been dubbed 'poor man's space probes', and they probably contain significant information about internal planetary matter, and even the origin of the Solar System. These extraterrestrial fragments have a composition very different from that of the Earth's crust.

They are classified according to their composition. The siderites are made of nickel and iron, and may represent typical dense, non-volatile galactic matter. The stony-irons are less dense, containing silicate and metallic components, while the stones are especially rich in silicates. The latter two groups contain material not unlike that thought to occur near the boundary between the Earth's mantle and core.

Studying shock waves
The best, though least direct, way of understanding the composition and structure of the Earth's interior is through the study of shock-waves generated by earthquakes and man-made disturbances, such as underground nuclear weapons tests. The study of these shock-waves and the way they behave as they pass through the different rock layers is called seismology. In recent decades, the techniques of seismology have become highly sophisticated. Seismic tomography uses the velocity of shock-waves to scan the Earth, providing 3-D images of the mantle, in a similar way to a medical scan.

The shock-waves fall into four main categories. The L-waves are of long wavelength and low frequency, and remain in the Earth's crust. It is these which can cause great destruction to human lives and property. From the geophysical standpoint, the P-waves, which oscillate to-and-fro in the direction of transmission, and the S-waves, which oscillate at right angles to the direction of transmission, are of fundamental significance. Less important are the R-waves, which oscillate in the vertical plane in the direction of transmission.

The P-waves can pass through both solid and liquid rock, whereas the S-waves will not travel through liquids. These waves can be recorded, for any given 'quake, on seismographs at stations all around the Earth's surface. Their velocity depends on the composition of the rocks through which they pass. So different recording stations will receive waves from a given 'quake at different times, depending not only on distance, but also on the densities of the intervening rocks. The speed of the waves can be computed experimentally for rocks of known densities, and, by comparison, the type of rock the real waves have passed through can be deduced.

The many records of earthquakes around the crust show that there is a zone on the surface, the shadow zone, extending from 105° to 142° of arc from the epicentre of the earthquake—the point on the Earth's surface directly above the focus, where the waves are generated. The S-waves are not recorded in this shadow zone. By plotting the zone, using data from many earthquakes, geologists were able to define the limits of a sphere inside the Earth, whose outer part is liquid enough to prevent the S-waves from passing directly through it. It also happens that the P-waves are considerably slowed down in this zone. This is the Earth's core. Seismologists have further revealed fairly sudden changes in density between the crust and mantle (at the Moho) and within the core itself. These discontinuities represent changes of state from one material to another.

If we could travel through the Earth's crust like Jules Verne's heroes in *Journey to the Centre of the Earth*, we would encounter the first discontinuity, the Mohorivičić Discontinuity, at a depth of between 3 ml (5 km) in the ocean basins to as much as 40 ml (60 km) in the continents. At the Moho, there is an increase in the velocity of the P- and S-waves, and we then enter the mantle. The mantle rocks are denser than those of the crust, and as we approach the outer core, they become denser still. At a depth of 1,800 ml (2,900 km), we meet the Gutenberg Discontinuity. Here, the density of the rocks jumps from 5.5 to 10.00, as we enter the outer core, until, at 3,200 ml (5,150 km), we reach the solid inner core with a density of over 13.00. Here, deep within the bowels of the Earth, temperatures are of the order of 14,500°F (8,000°C), and pressures about 3.5 million atmospheres.

Studying aurorae
It is possible that study of the aurorae will provide yet more information about the Earth's hidden core. These are the high-latitude spectral displays, the Northern Lights, or Aurora Borealis, and the Southern Lights, or Aurora Australis, which are produced by the interaction of electrically charged particles from the Sun with the Earth's magnetic field.

The surface of the Earth is a very thin skin of relatively cool rock, soil and water. In the great continental areas this skin is up to 40 miles (60 km) thick, very stable and tremendously old. In the ocean basins, by contrast, a mere 3 miles (5 km) separates the sea-bed from the great temperatures and pressures of the Earth's mantle.

The continental areas are regions with vast interior plains and high, snow-capped mountain ranges. The very high mountains such as the Andes, Rockies, Alps and Himalayas are not in the central parts of the land masses; in fact, they are near their margins. The centres of the continents tend to be relatively flat regions, which are occasionally interrupted by the stumps of formerly high mountain ranges, such as the Urals.

The continental crust

The continental crust is made up of two distinct structural units. There are long, linear orogenic belts, where deformation and metamorphism occur, and there are regions where vast thicknesses of relatively undeformed sediments and volcanic rocks accumulate. The complexity of structure and rock-type is a result of the continual reworking which the ancient land areas have undergone throughout geological time. Beneath the upper acidic layer of granite and high-grade metamorphic rocks which forms the upper continental crust is a lower layer of ultrabasic amphibolite and eclogite. These two layers are separated by the Conrad Discontinuity, about 25 miles (40 km) from the surface of each continent.

The oceanic crust

The changeover from continental to oceanic crust takes place at the base of the continental slope, where the continental shelves plunge steeply to the abyssal depths of the ocean.

In stark contrast to the ancient continental crust, the ocean crust is mobile and very young. In no area is the ocean crust older than 200 million years, and it becomes progressively younger towards the impressive ranges of submarine volcanic mountains which are still forming in the central zones of many ocean basins. The ocean floor covers some 66 per cent of the Earth's surface, but it has only recently been extensively investigated by geophysical and submersible techniques. The mountain ranges on the ocean floor are in places higher than any on dry land; Mauna Loa, a shield

volcano, rises 33,000 ft (10,000 m) from the sea-bed to its summit in the Hawaiian Islands.

The oceanic mountains form continuously, not in cycles of orogenic activity like those on the continental land masses.

Sea-floor spreading

In the central regions of the oceans, crustal rock is forming all the time; as the sea floor splits apart, lava from below plugs the fracture, and the sea floor spreads outwards, carrying the continents with it. At their margins the ocean floors are often destroyed and re-melted as they move down beneath the less dense continental crust along subduction zones. This process allows the ocean floors to spread without any increase in the size of the crust.

The ocean floors are covered by a veneer of sediment. This may be up to two-thirds of a mile (1 km) thick, and towards its base it is interbedded with basaltic lavas. When lava is erupted under water a skin immediately forms

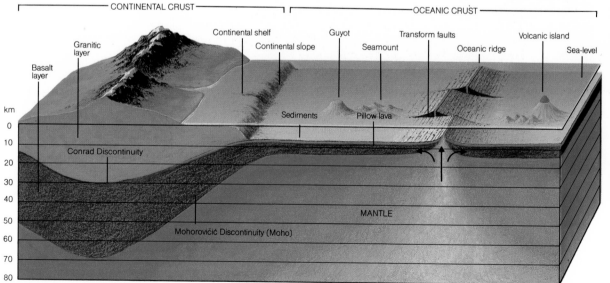

Left The crust beneath the continents is thick, supporting the bulk of mountain ranges. The young oceanic crust is thin and overlain by sediment. Seamounts are submerged volcanoes. Some have their summits eroded; these flat-topped types are called guyots. At an ocean ridge, the sea-bed is splitting and spreading, new rock forcing its way up from below to form new crust. The Conrad Discontinuity marks the junction of an upper granitic layer and a lower basaltic one; it occurs only beneath the continents since the upper layer is missing from the oceanic crust. The Mohorovičić Discontinuity separates the crust and the mantle.

Above This false-colour Landsat image shows part of the Canadian Rockies where complex folds have twisted the landscape. Snow (white) covers the high peaks, vegetation (red) clothes the slopes and fog (grey) fills some of the valleys.
Above right Sedimentary rock layers in south-west Britain strongly folded by compression of the crust.

Below Granite forms most of the continental crust. In this example, large brownish felspar crystals stand out from a felspar (white), quartz (grey) and mica (black) mass.
Bottom Basalt, forming the ocean crust, is dark, less silica-rich and denser than granite. The large crystals may have formed while the rock was molten underground.

around the molten rock. It continues to flow and forms large pillow-like masses. These basaltic pillow-lavas are known from many parts of the geological record and are interpreted as marine, sea-bed rocks. The deepest layer on the sea-bed is basaltic in composition. This is probably gabbro, a chemically similar rock to basalt lava, but coarser grained because of its slower rate of cooling.

Plate tectonics
The differences between the ocean crust and the continental crust, both physical and chemical, have posed many problems of interpretation for geologists. How are mountains formed? Why and how do the continents move? Why are the volcanic and earthquake zones in and around the ocean basins? Questions such as these proved difficult to answer with conviction until the all-embracing theory of plate tectonics was postulated. This theory brings together all aspects of geology with beautiful simplicity. It suggests that the crust is made of a series of rigid but mobile plates, each about 60 miles (100 km) thick. Seven, such as the Pacific Plate, are very large; the rest are much smaller. The plate margins are the volcanic and earthquake zones. Movement of the plates is caused by convection currents generated in the mantle. Structural activity is concentrated where the plates move apart, pass each other or collide.

This revolutionary theory changed the Earth sciences because never before had so many

geological phenomena, of world-wide occurrence, been explained so elegantly.

Plate tectonics manifests itself by large-scale, spectacular changes in the Earth's crust, such as volcanic eruptions and drifting of the continents. There are many structures such as folding and faulting, readily observed in the landscape, which can, with an understanding of plate tectonics theory, be related to various large-scale processes.

Folds and faults
Sedimentary rocks exposed in cliffs and quarries rarely lie horizontally. Instead, these rocks usually exhibit a slope or dip on their bedding surfaces. Dip (the greatest angle from the horizontal that can be measured down an inclined rock surface) is produced when strata are subjected to tectonic forces and become either tilted or folded. Folding is an expression of compression within the crust, rocks being squashed and buckled by lateral forces. If the forces are equal from both sides the fold will be neat and symmetrical, but when unequal forces are involved, an asymmetrical fold, with a leaning fold axis, occurs.

Rocks do not bend easily and very often fractures or faults form during earth movements. Stretching of the crust will produce 'normal' faults with steep fault planes. Compression and shortening of the crust leads to reverse and thrust fault formation, the latter moving huge slices of rock many miles.

The geological processes that shape our planet take place inconceivably slowly. Mountain ranges rise over tens of millions of years, only to be slowly, but inevitably, weathered and eroded over an equally long period of time. It has taken some 3,000 million years of evolution to produce the wonderful variety of complex organisms which live on the Earth today. Some geological processes—for example, volcanic eruptions, earthquakes and the deposition of mud and sand at the mouths of rivers—are obvious to us, but they will have no great impact on the geological record unless they continue for millions of years. This they are able to do. Geological time is for ever.

The length of geological time, like the enormity of the Universe, is almost incomprehensible in human terms. Our record of events which have taken place on the Earth is hidden in the rock of the crust. Time is locked away here, as layers of mud and sand; as fossilized animals and plants; as crystalline granite; all represent part of the chronological evolution of the Earth. To interpret past events and put them in the correct order, geologists consider time in two ways. Relative time places events in sequence. Absolute time gives a date, in years.

Relative time

The Relative Time Scale has been established over the past 150 years of geological research. It forms a standard scheme against which rock layers, or strata, in any part of the crust can be measured. Certain fundamental principles of stratigraphy (the science of placing the strata in the correct sequence and interpreting the events which formed them) were used to establish this relative scale. Possibly the most important of these is the principle of Superposition of Strata. This states that in a given sequence of rocks, the oldest layers lie beneath the younger ones, provided that no large-scale faulting or folding has upturned the rocks. Other principles suggest that an igneous dyke (a sheet-like intrusion of molten rock that is squeezed into fractures between pre-existing rocks) must be younger than the rock through which it cuts, and fragments of rock in a conglomerate (made up of rounded pebbles cemented together), for example, must come from an older formation.

During the late 18th and early 19th centuries, the great British amateur geologist William Smith, and other pioneering stratigraphers, realized the value of fossils as a stratigraphic tool. Smith was a canal engineer, and so had ready access to rock sections in southern Britain. He recognized that a sequence could be established, characterized by fossils, and that strata could be correlated over wide areas when they contained the same fossils.

Today, a detailed sequence of time zones is the basis of the relative time scale. Each zone is defined by the occurrence in the strata of a particular zone fossil. The time zone is, in effect, the life-span of the chosen zone fossil. This may be less than a million years. The fossils best suited for this purpose are widespread geographically (to give good correlation between areas far apart) and of limited vertical range (that is, with a short life-span). A jellyfish or other soft-bodied creature may fulfil these two criteria, but is not readily fossilized, so only common, easily identified organisms with hard shells are of real use.

Unconformities

Time zones are the basic components of the relative time scale. A group of zones is called a time period, and periods are grouped into eras. The divisions between periods and eras made by the stratigraphers often feature great changes in the sequence of the rocks, which may be marked by unconformities.

These represent one of the most intriguing

Left Over 1,500 million years ago these mountains (**1**) formed in north-west Scotland with highly metamorphosed gneiss in their deep roots. Later (**2**) the gneisses were laid bare by weathering and erosion to form a low-lying land surface. Rivers flowed across the exposed roots of the mountains, depositing sand, mud and pebbles. The sedimentary rocks formed by these river deposits (**3**) rest with an angular unconformity on the older gneisses. Geologists use the term 'unconformity' to describe any such break in their record of geological time.

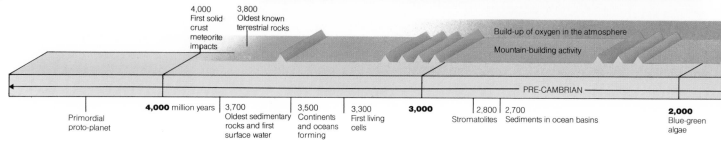

4,000
First solid crust meteorite impacts

3,800
Oldest known terrestrial rocks

Build-up of oxygen in the atmosphere

Mountain-building activity

PRE-CAMBRIAN

Primordial proto-planet

4,000 million years

3,700
Oldest sedimentary rocks and first surface water

3,500
Continents and oceans forming

3,300
First living cells

3,000

2,800
Stromatolites

2,700
Sediments in ocean basins

2,000
Blue-green algae

problems which confront stratigraphers. Essentially, an unconformity is a time-gap, where, in a certain place, the rock sequence is interrupted and the record of events is missing. Strata may have been deposited here, but have since been removed by erosion, other more recent strata being deposited above the unconformity surface. Unfortunately, such breaks in the succession of geological time are all too common. In north-west Scotland, for example, there is a major unconformity between the Lewisian basement complex and the overlying Torridonian sediments. Both formations are Pre-Cambrian in age, but the unconformity between them represents a time-gap of some 500 million years. To put this into perspective, a similar length of time from the end of the Cambrian period to the present day has seen three major periods of mountain-building, and also the evolution of animals from primitive invertebrates to Man!

Absolute time and radiometric dating

During the last few decades, a quiet revolution has taken place in the understanding of absolute time. The refinement of the techniques of radiometric dating has shown how old the Earth really is. A figure of 4,600 million years can be given to the time since the formation of the Earth; Pre-Cambrian rocks from Canada have an age of 3,500 million years; the base of the Cambrian period is dated at 600 million years ago, and so on.

The technique of radiometric dating is quite straightforward in principle. Radioactive elements trapped in minerals in the rocks of the crust decay spontaneously through time into more stable elements, releasing energy in the form of radiation. This happens at a constant rate. If the rate of decay from the 'parent' element to the 'daughter' element is known, and the present proportions of parent to daughter are calculated, then the time during which decay has occurred (in other words, the age of the rock containing the radioactive elements) can be measured.

There are, however, problems with this method of dating. Decay products may leak or become leached from the rock. The original rock may have been altered by metamorphism or weathering. Great accuracy is needed when measuring amounts of atoms. Also, it is not possible to apply this dating method to all types of rocks. Those such as lava or intrusive igneous rocks, which have crystallized at a sharp point in time, give the best results. Metamorphic rocks, such as gneiss, also give reliable results, but sediments are of little use because the minerals in them may have been derived from older formations, and weathering is part of the sedimentary process.

The rate of decay of a radioactive element is measured in terms of its 'half-life'. This is the time taken for *half* of the parent element's atoms to decay. The half-life may be a few seconds or millions of years, depending on the element. The most favoured methods for geological timekeeping are the potassium to argon system (half-life 11,850 million years) and rubidium to strontium system (half-life 50,000 million years). The carbon-14 system, with a half-life of only 5,570 years, is of use for dating only relatively recent material, up to about 70,000 years old.

The geological time scale used by geologists today is a composite scale of reference built up by using both relative and absolute dating. The two approaches are complementary. For example, a geologist might be investigating the age of a granite intrusion which has forced its way from deep below into slates of Silurian age. This granite is radiometrically dated at 390 million years old, which from the absolute time scale the geologist knows is a Devonian age. When the geologist then finds weathered fragments of the same granite in a nearby Carboniferous conglomerate, he or she can accept the radiometric age, because the granite, in relative terms, was formed later than the Silurian but before the Carboniferous: that is, during the Devonian period.

Above The unconformity analysed in the diagram, top left. Brown sandstones, part of the Torridonian sediment layer, can be seen lying on top of pink and grey gneiss. There is a huge time gap of 500 million years between the two layers.
Left Here, in the Grand Canyon of Arizona, USA, the pages of Earth history are revealed as the Colorado River cuts its way through strata laid down over millions of years. To travel down into the gorge is to journey back into the remote past.

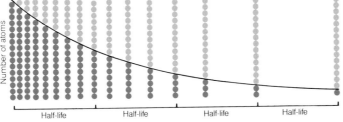

Above Radioactive decay of different forms, or isotopes, of some elements is used to measure geological time. Minerals like felspar and mica contain radioactive isotopes such as potassium.

The decay of the isotope forms a new element with the release of radioactive energy. Different elements take different times to break down. The time taken for half the number of parents atoms (brown) to

decay is its 'half-life'. After one half-life there is the same number of daughter atoms (yellow) as parent atoms. After two half-lives there are three times as many daughters as parent atoms.

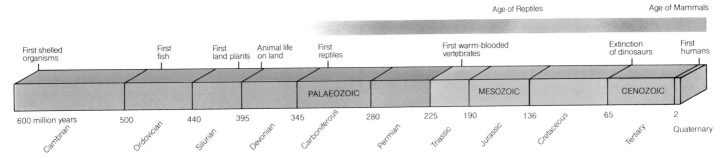

Age of Reptiles   Age of Mammals

First shelled organisms | First fish | First land plants | Animal life on land | First reptiles | First warm-blooded vertebrates | Extinction of dinosaurs | First humans

PALAEOZOIC   MESOZOIC   CENOZOIC

600 million years — 500 — 440 — 395 — 345 — 280 — 225 — 190 — 136 — 65 — 2

Cambrian / Ordovician / Silurian / Devonian / Carboniferous / Permian / Triassic / Jurassic / Cretaceous / Tertiary / Quaternary

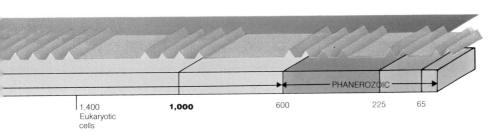

1,400 Eukaryotic cells | 1,000 | 600 | 225 | 65

PHANEROZOIC

Left The Pre-Cambrian era spans some seven-eighths of geological time. We know very little about the Earth's early history. During this immense era, the crust, atmosphere and oceans slowly developed. Mountains grew and were destroyed, life began to stir and the air gradually became richer in oxygen.

Above The last 600 million years is called the Phanerozoic ('obvious life') because the rocks laid down then contain visible evidence of life. We know much about this relatively short part of the Earth's history, including the rapid evolution of life and the wandering of the continents.

19

Since its formation some 4,600 million years ago, the Earth's surface has been shaped and changed by the various agents of geological activity. The evidence for all these changes during this enormous time-span is locked away in the rocks of the crust. By analysing these rocks carefully, geologists can reconstruct past environments and follow the wandering of the continents and the changing shapes of the oceans. Such studies form the science of palaeogeography.

The fundamental principle of Uniformitarianism is the basis of much of this paleogeographic detective work. This principle suggests that events which we can observe taking place to form rocks today have *always* been producing the same effects. In other words, if a rock many million of years old has the same characteristics of bedding (pattern of the layers in sedimentary rocks), chemistry, grain size and shape and mineralogy as a modern one that can be observed forming, then it can be assumed that the ancient rock was made by the same processes acting in the past. This idea that 'the present is the key to the past' works well—up to a point. Igneous intrusions and metamorphic processes that go on beneath the surface cannot be observed. Also, far back in the Pre-Cambrian era, the Earth's surface and atmosphere were very different from how they appear today. It is conceivable that events took place which have never been repeated. For the vast majority of sedimentary rocks, however, Uniformitarianism is a valuable key which geologists can use to unlock the past.

The Pre-Cambrian era

The oldest, longest and most mysterious part of the Earth's evolution is the Pre-Cambrian era. This represents some seven-eighths of geological time, from the Earth's formation to the beginning of the Cambrian period, 600 million years ago. Because much of the rock formed during this time is highly metamorphosed, broken by enormous faults, cut into by igneous intrusions and devoid of any fossils that can be used for dating, it is very difficult to interpret.

During the earlier part of the Pre-Cambrian era, the crust consolidated and became stable. These initial stages involved a great deal of volcanic activity, with the outpouring of huge amounts of molten lava, as well as metamorphism and structural alterations on a grand scale. Much of the rock dating from this time is high-grade gneiss, a coarse-grained banded metamorphic rock formed in the depths of the mountain chains. Vast areas of this rock occur in Canada, Greenland and north-west Britain. Between the episodes of mountain formation, sedimentary rocks, now altered by metamorphism, were formed. Those which retain some sedimentary characteristics resemble sandstones, limestones and shales. Anorthosite and granulite are also found in the highly metamorphosed areas. These are probably materials brought up to the surface from the deepest parts of the primitive crust by major earth movements. Granulite, for example, is formed at very high temperatures where its component anhydrous minerals are developed. In parts of southern Africa, in Canada and Australia, there are areas rich in pillow lavas, greywackes and cherts. Today, such rocks are typical of deep ocean areas.

The more recent part of the Pre-Cambrian is less difficult to understand. By this time, the

continental and oceanic crusts were recognizable. Great river systems flowed over the land, depositing vast thicknesses of sediment on the continental shelves and surfaces. Deltas and swamps built up, and in the oceans deep sedimentary basins developed. Apart from the lack of vegetation, it was a world we would recognize as our own: the scarcity of oxygen would, however, have literally made us gasp!

By the end of the Pre-Cambrian, the Earth's surface was ready for the start of the gradual, cyclic reworking which continues to this day.

The Palaeozoic era

The next great era of Earth history, the Palaeozoic, began with a series of scattered continental masses separated by deep-sea areas. The first major event was a marine transgression—the invasion of a large land area by the sea in a relatively short time (from a geologist's viewpoint). This resulted in much of the world's low-lying land becoming covered with sea-water, and here shelf sediments formed. Great thicknesses of shales and greywacke, often deposited by turbidity currents, accumu-

lated in the oceans. The continents may have been arid areas during the first period of the Palaeozoic, the Cambrian, but towards the end of the Lower Palaeozoic, glaciers started to grow and move. Evidence of this ice age is found in the Sahara desert today.

The continents slowly but surely moved towards each other during the late Lower Palaeozoic, buckling the sedimentary basins to produce mountain ranges of Alpine proportions. In some regions, mountain development, associated with volcanic activity and intrusions of granitic rocks forcing their way into other rock strata, lasted into the first period of the Upper Palaeozoic, the Devonian. Also during the Devonian, new marine basins were established, helping to pave the way for another wave of mountain-building. Much of the rock formed during the Devonian, known to geologists as 'red beds', results from the wearing down of the mountain ranges formed earlier.

Ancient supercontinents

The Upper Palaeozoic continents consisted of a northern supercontinent, Laurasia, formed from

Left Durham, north-east England, as it would have appeared during the Permian period. The shifting, ripple-marked sand dunes stretched eastwards towards the very salty Zechstein Sea.
Above This is what Pittsburg, USA, would have looked like during the Carboniferous period. The luxuriant rainforest vegetation accumulated as thick layers of peat, which later formed the coal seams mined in Pennsylvania today.
Right Zurich, Switzerland, as it would have appeared during the Triassic period. Corals and other shallow-water marine creatures flourished in the warm seas.

what is now North America, Greenland and Europe combined; an Arctic continent, Angaraland, made up of present-day Siberia, China and Korea; and the huge continent of Gondwanaland in the south, comprising modern India, Africa, South America, Australia and Antarctica. Between these were deep mobile belts, destined to become either mountain chains or shallow shelf-sea areas on which limestone and, later, great thicknesses of delta-top coal-swamps built up. While Laurasia was basking in equatorial heat during the Carboniferous period, Gondwanaland, lying near the South Pole, was covered with huge glaciers. The filling-in of the Laurasian-Gondwanaland ocean and the Hercynian mountain-building phase during the Permian period produced the continent from which the modern land masses are derived.

The Mesozoic era

The Mesozoic era opens with an episode very similar to that during the Devonian. Large areas of land were exposed and their surfaces were covered with the eroded fragments of high mountain chains. Salts, such as common salt and potassium chloride, were precipitated in these land-locked seas. In the Northern Hemisphere, Laurasia split away from Gondwanaland to form the Tethyan Ocean.

Worldwide sea-levels at this time were high, and shallow seas extended over much of the continental margins. This displacement of ocean water, both at the beginning of the Jurassic period and again during the Cretaceous, was probably the result of developing mid-ocean ridge systems. The modern North Atlantic was now developing, and a shallow sea extended into the western interior of North America.

Towards the end of the Mesozoic era, about 100 million years ago, the South Atlantic opened, resulting in the separation of South America from Africa. The initial disruption caused widespread evaporation of salts in the land-locked sea that was formed, before independent east and west sedimentary shelves were established on the east coast of Africa and the west coast of South America.

With the separation and rotation of Africa towards Eurasia, the Tethyan Ocean became greatly reduced in area, and the sea retreated from many land areas—a process geologists call regression. As Africa moved round to collide with Eurasia, small fragments of continental crust were crushed and sheared, together with compression of Tethyan Ocean sediments, to form great mountain chains, notably the Alps. In North and South America, the line of orogeny from the Rockies to the Andes was established.

The Cenozoic era

Throughout the Tertiary and Quaternary periods of the last era, the Cenozoic, there was a general widening of the modern oceans and development of present-day mountain ranges. The Alps and Himalayas continued to rise as the Tethyan Ocean dwindled even further and India moved inexorably northwards. All that remains of the once great Tethyan Ocean today is the Mediterranean Sea. Continental movement, especially at high latitudes in the Northern Hemisphere, provided sites for widespread development of ice-sheets, and glaciation occurred on a vast scale.

Mountaineers climbing the World's highest peaks, whether they are in the Andes, Alps, Rockies or Himalayas, may notice that amidst the ice and snow, the rocks are in layers and are sedimentary. These strata often contain the fossilized remains of marine shell-fish, indicating that they were formed in or near the sea. It took prodigious forces to uplift these sediments many thousands of feet above sea-level and build great mountain ranges. Geologists call this process orogenesis.

Orogenic cycles

An orogeny, or period of mountain-building, is an extremely protracted sequence of events, taking many tens of millions of years to develop fully. Orogenies tend to follow one another in cycles, often with the rocks of an earlier orogeny being involved in a subsequent episode of mountain formation. Orogenesis can be a worldwide event, and the areas affected are usually long, linear belts where the Earth's crust is moving. Such mobile belts have been recognized from rocks of Pre-Cambrian age and are a significant feature of the Earth's crust today. Even the very ancient belts have features similar to the recent ones, and it seems that orogenic cycles have been a feature of crustal development throughout much of geological time.

Initially the mobile belt is a downwarp of the Earth's crust (still often referred to as a geosyncline) in which vast thicknesses of deep-sea sediments accumulate. At this time the mobile belt is probably at its widest and least active. The sediments, derived from previously formed mountains on nearby continents, accumulate in a deep trough and consist of shales, mudstones and most commonly a poorly sorted mixture (that is, made up of grains of different sizes) of sand and clay called greywacke.

The rate at which sediment accumulates is difficult to estimate, but it may be of the order of 2in (5cm) per century. During a single geological period, as much as 4.3 miles (7 km) may be formed in a mobile belt. In several Pre-Cambrian deposits, for example in East Greenland and Spitsbergen, up to 9·3 miles (15km) of sediment accumulated before being folded and metamorphosed. This sedimentation is not continuous, and does not occur in all parts of the belt at the same time.

During the Late Pre-Cambrian and Lower Palaeozoic (Caledonian) Orogeny, which affected Northern Europe and what is now Eastern Greenland and North America, a great deal of sedimentation occurred while metamorphism and folding were going on elsewhere in the belt.

Deep-sea sediments

Greywacke is formed when masses of unconsolidated sediment slump off the continental shelf, possibly loosened by earth tremors. This sediment may stream down the continental slope through a submarine canyon and flow out across the deep-sea floor to settle as a graded greywacke—that is, composed of grains of many different sizes, arranged with the largest at the bottom grading up to the smallest at the top. While such deep-sea sedimentation continues, volcanic activity, which is related to plate movement, occurs. Many deep-sea sediments from typical orogenic situations contain pillow lavas, characteristic rocks from underwater volcanoes.

Strong folding and deformation of the rocks involved in an orogeny are their most characteristic features. As the mobile belt becomes narrow and the ocean trench sediments are compressed and buried against a foreland, the features of the original sediments and associated volcanic rocks are considerably altered.

Forelands

The foreland—a stable area of older rocks next to an orogenic belt—is often a mass of continental crust which initially is outside the area of orogenic activity. During the Caledonian Orogeny, the western foreland was made up of what is now Greenland and part of eastern Canada, and a fragment remains in north-west Scotland. The eastern foreland comprised present-day Scandinavia and central Britain. In north-west Scotland huge thrust faults show the compression and movement of late Pre-Cambrian and Lower Palaeozoic rocks against the north-west foreland. In Australia similar structures occur where the Lower Palaeozoic rocks are thrust over the Pre-Cambrian, while in the European Alps thrusting on a huge scale occurred during the Tertiary Alpine Orogeny.

Giant folds

Intimately associated with large-scale faulting is folding on an enormous scale. The major folds often lean over towards the foreland and break near their axial planes to form thrust faults, the upper limb of the fold moving forwards along the fault plane. Geologists use the term 'nappe' to describe folded rocks where the axis is horizontal and thrusting develops. Strata are often upturned when recumbent folding occurs. When deformation of this type takes place, rounded grains of sediment, such as small pebbles, become stretched, and may even end up looking like rods.

Grades of metamorphism

Metamorphism on a grand scale normally accompanies thrusting and large-scale folding. The extent to which the sediments are changed by metamorphism depends on the depth to which they are buried and the degree of folding they undergo. Geologists refer to the different stages of metamorphism as grades: the higher the grade, the more the rock has been metamorphosed. Low-grade rocks are produced by low temperatures and pressures; high-grade rocks form at high temperatures and pressures.

Hot fluids buried deep within the mountain roots are another agent which can alter rocks. In the deepest zones gneiss is formed. Higher in the crust, schist and slate are the metamorphic rocks formed by alteration of the mobile belt sediments. These rocks are less deformed than gneiss and may show original features such as bedding. These regionally metamorphosed rocks often occur in zones arranged in linear belts parallel to the axes of folding, the highest grades occurring towards the centre.

Igneous activity and mountain-building

Deep igneous activity usually reaches its zenith towards the end of a mountain-building episode.

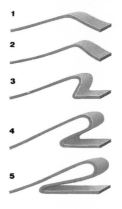

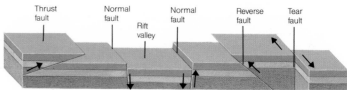

Left Compression and squeezing of rock strata in the crust leads to folding. If the compression is unequal on each side simple anticlinal folds (**1** and **2**) can become asymmetrical folds (**3**), with one limb steeper than the other. Eventually, overfolds (**4**) and nappes, or recumbent folds (**5**) are the result.
Below Movement along the many fractures in the crust is called faulting. Compression leads to shortening by the displacement of rocks upwards along thrust and reverse faults. Stretching with the downward movement of rock is possible along normal faults. Tear faults allow sideways movement, often over distances of many hundreds of miles.

Thrust fault · Normal fault · Rift valley · Normal fault · Reverse fault · Tear fault

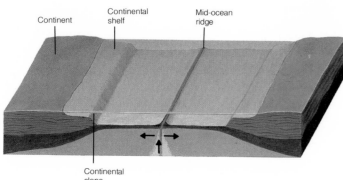

Continent · Continental shelf · Mid-ocean ridge · Continental slope

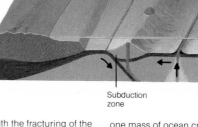

Trench · Island arc · Trench · Volcanic mountains · Subduction zone · Subduction zone

Above Modern ideas on mountain building apply plate tectonics theory. When continental masses split through rifting, new ocean basins can develop by sea-floor spreading. The new crust formed is of basalt, a dense rock, on which great thicknesses of muddy sediment can become accumulated. With the fracturing of the ocean crust, after millions of years of sea-floor spreading, subduction of one mass of ocean crust leads to island arc development, as in the Western Pacific. The ocean crust is consumed both beneath this arc and where a trench develops on a continental margin.

Enormous bulbous masses of granite, called batholiths, seep upwards into the mountain roots, sometimes reaching to within a few miles of the surface.

The acidic magma from which these are formed may be produced by melting of crustal rocks and sediment, during subduction of the sea-bed on the margin of a mobile belt. Migmatite, a mixed rock with both acid and basic characteristics, is also typically found in orogenic zones where sheets of acidic material have been injected along the structural planes in gneiss and other highly deformed rocks. Migmatite is contorted and banded, reflecting this process. If the magma finds its way to the surface, violent explosive volcanic activity can result, as with the volcanic cones of the South American Andes.

Today, the actively forming mountain chains, earthquake zones and volcanic regions of the Earth can be explained by the theory of plate tectonics. As continental plates move away from each other, new mobile belts may develop between them; when the oceans and their thick sedimentary deposits are crushed between converging plates, new mountains form.

After a period of mountain-building, impressive thicknesses of sedimentary rocks form as the mountains are weathered and eroded. Great heaps of scree and other detrital fragments

Above The high snow-capped Andes are within a short distance of the Chilean coast in this Landsat image. Beneath the deep blue water of the Pacific Ocean the sea-bed is being forced towards and under South America. The Andes were formed as the crust was buckled by this process of subduction.

pile up against and around the mountains. Sandstones, conglomerates and breccias are typical of this environment. One of the characteristic features of strata formed in these conditions is their red colour, due to oxidized iron. 'Red Beds' are common in the Devonian rocks of Northern Europe and the Arctic and resulted from the weathering and erosion of the Caledonian mountain range.

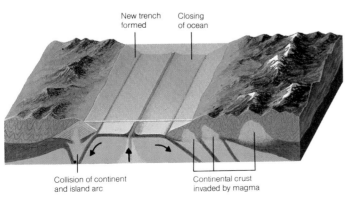

Continual movement of the zone of sea-floor spreading may carry the island arc into collision with the continent to produce folded and metamorphosed mountains. Mountains are also formed on the other side of the ocean, as the subduction of several plate 'slices' produces violent earth movements.

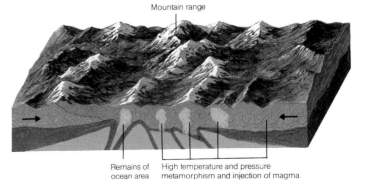

Closing of the ocean welds the two mountain areas together to produce peaks of Himalayan scale. Beneath them, the remains of the old ocean lie buried among the ancient sediments. In the mountain roots, granites are injected, and at higher levels the strata are folded into complex patterns.

Life has existed on the Earth for over three hundred thousand million years. It could not have appeared at all without the support of the unique chemical and physical properties of the Earth's surface and atmosphere. These have dictated the different forms which life has adopted, and the plants and animals have, in their turn, changed the atmosphere and the surface skin of the Earth. On other planets in some remote solar system, different conditions may have encouraged evolution's chance steps to produce organisms which to us would seem utterly bizarre. Even a planet similar to Earth, if one exists somewhere in the depths of space, may support very different life-forms, because evolution can lead in many directions.

The fossil record is a store of past life-forms. A fossil is any evidence of an organism that lived in the past, from totally preserved animals, trapped in amber, tar or ice, to the footprints left on wet sand—now hard sandstone—which record a dinosaur's afternoon stroll. Often, mineralogical changes take place to ensure preservation. These changes maintain a chemical balance between the shell or bone and its new environment within the rock strata.

A matter of chance

Of all the countless millions of organisms which have inhabited the Earth, only a mere handful are preserved as fossils. Those that lived on the land, for example, stood a much poorer chance of becoming preserved than those that lived in the sea. The land is the region where erosion by wind and water can relentlessly destroy all traces of life; by contrast, in the sea, great thicknesses of sediment can build up, preserving fossils in intricate detail.

By far the greater part of the fossil record is preserved in marine sedimentary rocks. The nature of the organism has much bearing on its

chances of becoming a fossil. The main requirement is a hard shell or skeleton, which will survive long enough to become covered with sediment. There are some amazing exceptions, however, such as the strange-looking, beautifully delicate invertebrates (animals without backbones) from the Burgess shales of the Middle Cambrian period in Canada, or the exquisitely preserved feathers of the primitive bird *Archaeopteryx* from the late Jurassic Solnhofen limestones in Germany. Even when a fossil has been preserved, it may be destroyed millions of years later by the intense heat or pressure of metamorphism.

Scientists who study fossils are called palaeontologists. They are often able to work out many details of the lifestyles of fossilized organisms and their ecology (relationships with each other, with other organisms and with their environment) by making a detailed analysis of the rock in which they occur, and by analogy with similar modern species. Many creatures which live on the sea-bed are very particular about factors in the environment such as the salinity of the water, the amount of light filtering down to the sea-bed, the nature of the sea-bed and the turbulence of the water. Palaeontologists use information such as this about modern species to suggest how the ancient ones might have lived.

The uses of fossils

Fossils have many uses. They provide evidence for evolution and past environments. As we have seen earlier, they can be used to place the pages of Earth history into their correct order. The classical principles of dating and correlating rocks using fossils were based on the collection and examination of the larger 'macro-fossils', such as molluscs and trilobites. In recent years, advanced techniques have been developed to enable geologists to use tiny micro-fossils to interpret borehole cores. Such work has revolutionized the search for oil and other economically important minerals. A borehole rarely

contains much useful macro-fossil evidence, but the cores obtained from it are crowded with the remains of minute organisms. Many of these valuable deposits are themselves fossil remains. Fossil fuels such as oil and coal are stores of energy accumulated by organisms which lived hundreds of millions of years ago. When these fuels are burnt today, in a power station or a car engine, this fossil energy is released. Light from an electric bulb can be thought of as fossil sunshine!

Fossils and evolution

Possibly the greatest contribution the fossil record makes is to our knowledge of the evolution of life on Earth. Fossils are biological material, and must be studied as such to understand best what they can tell us. However, palaeontologists face certain problems if they apply strict biological principles to fossils.

In order to name and classify organisms, biologists the world over use the binomial ('two name') system. Each organism is given a generic and a specific name. For example, because of anatomical and other similarities, the lion, leopard and tiger are all assigned to the genus *Panthera*. Each is distinguished by a different specific name: the lion is *Panthera leo*, the leopard *Panthera pardus* and the tiger *Panthera tigris*. The cat and the puma, on the other hand, are placed in a different genus,

The fossil record contains remains of all types of organisms, sometimes preserved entire, but usually incomplete.
Left Tree fern leaves preserved as a thin film of carbon, all that remains of the original plant.
Right An ammonite (*Dactylioceras*) preserved in a calcareous nodule.
Far right Beautiful preservation of the fish *Dapaus* gives palaeontologists much information.

The Evolution of Life

Below The chart shows the evolution of plants and animals over the past 4,000 million years, from primitive algae and worms to whales and Man.

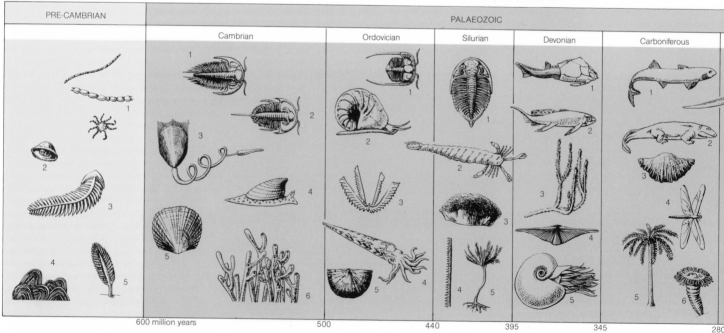

PRE-CAMBRIAN	PALAEOZOIC				
	Cambrian	Ordovician	Silurian	Devonian	Carboniferous

600 million years — 500 — 440 — 395 — 345 — 280

Pre-Cambrian
First traces of life include stromatolites (4), dated at up to 4,000 million years. Blue-green algae (1) are in rocks 2,000 my old. The Ediacara fauna (700 my) includes worms (3), jellyfish (2) and sea-pens (5).

Cambrian
The sea teemed with shelled invertebrates, such as trilobites (1,2), brachiopods (3,5), molluscs (4) and sponges (6). The evolution of shells allowed them to colonize new marine habitats and become fossilized easily.

Ordovician
Shelled marine invertebrates evolved new forms, like the trilobite (1), cephalopod mollusc (4) and sea-snail (2). Brachiopods (5) continued to flourish in shallow seas, while free-floating graptolites (3) first appeared.

Silurian
Life first invaded the land, in the form of spore-bearing plants and small fish-like vertebrates. In the sea, trilobites (1) still thrived, along with corals (3), crinoids (5), eurypterids (2) and graptolites (4).

Devonian
Armoured fish (1,2) lived in lakes and rivers. Brachiopods (4) and coiled cephalopods (5) lived in the sea. The trilobites dwindled and graptolites became extinct. Simple plants (3) continued to invade the land.

Carboniferous
Sluggish amphibians (2) lived in the vast swamps, and large insects, such as dragonflies (4), hawked among the giant tree-ferns. In the sea, corals (6) and brachiopods (3) flourished. Sharks (1) hunted in the warm waters.

Felis. Their specific names are *Felis catus* and *Felis concolor* respectively. The particular combination of generic and specific names is unique for each species.

Biologists classifying modern organisms are fortunate in having the whole animal or plant at their disposal. They can study its exact relationship with other living organisms, and any of the theories about species can be tested by artificial breeding. Palaeontologists have none of these advantages. They often have only fragments of bone or shell to work with, and will never be able to persuade two similar fossils to mate, even if they think they can distinguish a male from a female!

So a palaeontologist's theories about what constitutes a species may differ from those of a biologist. For example, a group of similar shells found in the same layer of rock may be assigned to one species, and a group of different shells from the same bed to another species. This is generally sound practice, but it can result in misleading conclusions if the males and females have shells of different shapes or sizes. Today, palaeontologists can use many sophisticated statistical techniques, aided by computers, to overcome such problems.

The origin of life
Four thousand million years ago, the Earth's surface and atmosphere were very different from those of today. The atmosphere contained a poisonous mixture of hydrogen, nitrogen, carbon dioxide, carbon monoxide, water vapour and hydrogen sulphide, with traces of methane and ammonia. The blazing ultra-violet radiation from the Sun was not filtered by these gases and it burnt its way through the thick clouds of water vapour swirling above the volcanically violent surface.

Back in the early 1950s, a series of elegantly simple experiments by the American scientists Stanley Miller and Harold Urey showed that complex organic molecules could be made by passing a high-voltage electric spark through a mixture of gases which mimicked the primitive Earth's atmosphere. The organic 'soup' which they produced was rich in molecules such as amino-acids, the 'building-blocks' from which living cells are made. Although Miller and Urey's 'soup' was far from being alive, subsequent similar experiments have shown that with different mixtures of gases, a whole range of organic molecules can be synthesized from inorganic chemicals. It is conceivable that the primitive Earth was rich in these easily manufactured organic molecules, but time was needed for them to combine to produce living cells. Single-celled organisms and bacteria could develop when these molecules combined. This profound step, which involved the production of the heredity-controlling nucleic acid DNA, has led to the huge variety of organisms, both extinct and living.

The oldest fossils
The oldest known fossils are the remains of micro-organisms from the Onverwacht formation, in South Africa, some 3,000 million years old. These, and the stromatolite reefs from rocks in Bulawayo, Zimbabwe, are probably the remains of blue-green algae. About 2,000 million years ago, the Gunflint rocks in North America preserved, in silica gels, complex microbial structures which have some cell components similar to those of modern blue-green algae. The thick-walled cells hint at the development of larger cells, whose division depends on the presence of oxygen. By about 1,400 million years ago, there was a definite increase in cell size. The steady, but initially slow, increase in the oxygen content of the atmosphere from two per cent of its present level 2,000 million years ago to six per cent 1,000 million years ago, and 50 per cent 400 million years ago, is largely a result of the photosynthetic activities of the blue-green algae and, later, the more advanced green plants. With this increase in oxygen, evolution had a vital new stimulus enabling large, complex organisms to appear.

Mutation and evolution
Living cells contain strands of nucleic acid. DNA (deoxyribonucleic acid) is able to make copies of itself, but if a mistake is made, or the process is changed by radiation or chemical and physical interference, then mutation may occur. These subtle changes may be devastating or revolutionary for the life forms concerned. Evolution, which has produced the huge variety of organisms on the Earth today, has proceeded because of mutation and because of natural selection, which allows adaptations to flourish if they are suited to their environment. An organism which is well adapted to its surroundings stands a good chance of surviving and reproducing, to pass on its genes to future generations. Individuals within a species differ, and these differences will be passed on to the offspring. Any influence which makes certain individuals better able to reproduce and rear young than others will lead to evolution, which is a change in the balance of genes in a species from one generation to the next.

The fossil record tells us that evolution seems to have really gathered pace during the late Pre-Cambrian. In the Ediacara Hills of South Australia, there is a rich and varied assemblage of fossils, the Ediacara Fauna, which is about 670 million years old. Similar fossils are found in other parts of the world, and are the remains of complex soft-bodied marine animals. Hard shells first appear in the rocks of Cambrian age, 600 million years ago. Apart from the obvious advantages to the organisms, hard shells provide a much more detailed fossil record from this time onwards. With the continued increase in the vital gas oxygen, from ten per cent of today's level during the Cambrian period, larger and more complex organisms could evolve.

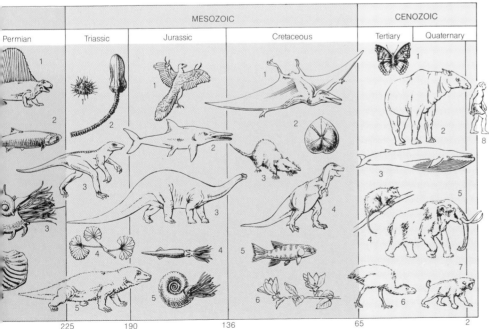

Permian
The dominant land animals were large reptiles, such as *Dimetrodon* (1). Giant ferns developed. Marine molluscs, such as cephalopods (3) and bivalves (4) thrived, as did fishes (2). The trilobites finally disappeared forever.

Triassic
The ancestral mammal-like reptile *Cynognathus* (5) and *Euparkeria* (3), a forerunner of the dinosaurs, appeared on land among ginkgos (4) and other plants. Echinoids (1) and crinoids (2) lived in the shallower regions of the sea.

Jurassic
Huge dinosaurs, such as *Brontosaurus* (3), dominated the land, and the first bird, *Archaeopteryx* (1), appeared. The seas swarmed with belemnites (4) and ammonites (5), the prey of large marine reptiles such as ichthyosaurs (2).

Cretaceous
Dinosaurs, including *Tyrannosaurus* (4) continued to evolve. Small mammals (3), flying reptiles called Pterosaurs (1) and flowering plants, such as magnolias (6) appeared. In the sea, echinoids (2) and modern fishes (5) abounded.

Tertiary & Quaternary
Mammals took over on land, including giants such as *Baluchitherium* (2) and small climbing forms like *Thylacodon* (4). Mastodons (5) and sabre-toothed tigers (7) evolved later. Birds dominated the air; there were also some huge flightless forms (6) on land. Butterflies (1) and other insects evolved with the flowering plants. In the sea, modern fishes and whales (3) flourished. By the end of this era, present-day organisms evolved, including Man (8).

The vast majority of the rocks of the Earth's crust are aggregates of mineral particles. Minerals are the building-blocks of these rocks, and exist in a bewildering variety of shapes, colour and chemical composition. Some are of considerable economic importance, whole civilizations having been founded on the wealth obtained from precious minerals such as gold. Today, gold, diamonds and other prized minerals form the basis of international currency. Museums the world over house fine collections of precious gemstones, whose great beauty often lies in their combination of crystalline precision and wonderful colouring. In mines deep within the Earth's crust, men and machines strive to win minerals which can be smelted to yield metals such as iron, copper and zinc.

The physical and chemical properties of all these minerals vary only within certain known limits, and they are formed entirely by natural inorganic processes. Geologists use a number of straightforward methods to identify a mineral.

Crystal symmetry and mineral habit

Many minerals form as crystals which can be classified according to their symmetry. Depending on the relative development of the various types of crystal faces, a mineral can be placed in one of six crystal systems: cubic, tetragonal, orthorhombic, monoclinic, triclinic and hexagonal. Quartz, for example, forms six-sided prisms, and is thus placed in the hexagonal system. Fluorite forms cubes and octahedra, which both have the symmetry of the cubic system.

Mineral habit is the actual shape of the specimen, which may be a delicate crystal, a rounded (reniform) shape, as in haematite, or a fibrous structure, as in gypsum.

The six basic crystal symmetry groups

Cubic
Fluorite
Garnet
Pyrite

Tetragonal
Chalcopyrite
Apophyllite
Zircon

Orthorhombic
Olivine
Barite
Andalusite

Monoclinic
Augite
Gypsum
Sphene

Triclinic
Plagioclase
Chalcanthite
Axinite

Hexagonal
and **Trigonal**
Beryl
Calcite
Quartz

Left The naturally formed crystals of minerals are classified according to their symmetry. There are six main systems, from the cubic, with a very high degree of symmetry, to the more complex hexagonal, which has less symmetry. Axes of symmetry (imaginary lines through the centre of a crystal, around which it can be rotated to produce the same view at least once) are used to define the systems. Within each of the symmetry groups, many different shapes, or 'habits', are possible, but all these can be referred to the same chosen axes of symmetry as the model for that group. The examples shown in the photographs on these pages illustrate this point.
Below Two crystals of iron sulphide (also called pyrites), which is classified in the cubic system, show the perfection of nature in crystal building. The cube, on the right of the picture, and the pyritohedron, on the left, are both commonly found forms of iron sulphide.
Bottom The Antarctic continent has great mineral wealth. Here, in the rock of Horseshoe Island, green veins of copper ramify the land. Veins like these often form in pre-existing rock fractures when hot fluids containing mineral components seep through the rock.

Identifying minerals

According to the way in which the atoms combine within a crystal, the crystal may split, or cleave, when broken, along predetermined planes. Different cleavage shapes are produced by different minerals; for example, calcite cleaves into rhombs (formed from equilateral parallelograms) and galena breaks up into small cubes.

Depending on the way light falling on the crystal is absorbed, or because of impurities in the crystal structure, the mineral will have a certain colour. This property alone is often fairly diagnostic. Malachite is a brilliant green colour, for instance, amethyst a rich purple, and galena dull grey.

The atoms from which different minerals are made vary in size, so minerals vary in their specific gravity—their density compared with that of water, arbitrarily given the value 1.0. Gold has a specific gravity (SG) of 19, while the SG of galena (lead sulphide) is 7.5, and that of quartz, typical of much of the Earth's crust, is 2.7. Halite is a mere 2·2.

When minerals are scratched, they resist being marked by different amounts. It is easy to scratch gypsum with a fingernail, but quartz cannot be scratched, even with a steel blade. By placing all minerals on a known relative scale of hardness, they can be separated from one another fairly easily.

Using all these and other properties, such as lustre (the way light is reflected, to give a vitreous or metallic sheen, for example) and transparency, a comprehensive picture of any mineral can be built up. Occasionally, as with

minerals found in Moon-rock, special techniques have to be used, including the use of an electron microscope, but with most minerals a hand specimen can be readily identified using the methods described above.

How minerals are formed

The Earth has many mineral-forming systems. When red-hot magma cools (providing its cooling is not so rapid that it forms a non-crystalline glass) mineral crystals form, and build an interlocking mosaic that is an igneous rock. Nearly all these crystals are silicate minerals, and they crystallize in a definite sequence, depending on their freezing points. The first to form are the dense ferro-magnesians, and the last are the quartzes.

If the cooling period is long, as in a large deep mass of granite, then very large crystals will form. Magma which cools rapidly produces small crystals. When the molten magma remains at the same temperature for some time, large crystals of one mineral may form. If the temperature then drops, the rest of the rock will crystallize out, producing minerals of smaller size. These form a matrix around the larger, previously formed crystals, producing the characteristic porphyritic texture of many igneous rocks. These have a beautiful interlocking patchwork of mineral crystals, often used for the decorative frontage of banks and insurance offices.

After uplift, weathering and erosion, these igneous minerals may find their way into layers of sediment. However, there are minerals which are exclusively sedimentary in their origin.

Above left Agate usually forms beautiful concentric layers which line cavities in igneous rocks. It is a form of quartz

Above Calcium sulphate in its hydrated form (gypsum) often crystallizes in a flower-like 'desert rose' form. Such patterns are common in arid areas where salts are precipitated.

Left Thin, delicate crystals of sodium aluminium silicate (also called natrolite) are commonly found in cavities in some igneous rocks.

Right Quartz, one of the commonest minerals, can form exquisite hexagonal crystals. If crystals form inside a sizeable rock cavity, they can grow quite large, but they are rarely as big or as fine as this splendid specimen.

Below left The bubbly habit of the iron oxide mineral haematite is called reniform (kidney-shaped): this mineral is often called 'kidney ore' because of its shape.

These include the evaporites gypsum, halite and potash, which are precipitated from salt lakes or lagoons when they dry up, especially in hot climates. Weathering of preformed mineral veins may leave a residual deposit, called 'gossan', in the higher levels of the vein, and produce a concentration of minerals lower down. In a similar way, weathering and transportation can concentrate heavy metallic minerals as 'placers' in river or beach sediment. Black beaches of ilmenite (an oxide of iron and titanium) are found in many parts of the world. Other placer minerals include gold, platinum, diamond and magnetite.

Minerals such as garnet, asbestos, graphite and talc are commonly formed by metamorphism—the alteration by high temperatures or pressures of rocks formed earlier.

Mineral veins

Most of the beautiful and economically valuable minerals are found in veins or lodes. These are faults or fractures in the crustal rocks, sometimes many yards wide and extending for many miles. In California, quartz veins extend for 50 miles (80 km), and in the Harz Mountains in north Germany, ore veins over 10 miles (16 km) long have been found. Within the fault zone there is a mass of jumbled and broken rock, full of cavities and hollows—ideal sites for minerals to crystallize from fluids seeping through the crust. These fluids, mainly very hot water and brine, are called hydrothermal solutions, and contain the component parts of a great variety of minerals, especially metallic ores. The hydrothermal solutions may come

from magma bodies or water trapped in deep sedimentary rocks. The minerals which form in these veins grow outwards into the fault cavities, and if there is enough space, beautiful large crystals will form.

Around many of the large granitic batholiths (masses of igneous rock that intrude into other rocks) in the continental crust lie concentric 'suites' of hydrothermal minerals. Typical of these are cassiterite (tin ore), chalcopyrite (copper ore), sphalerite (zinc ore) and galena (lead ore). The mineral which forms at the highest temperature is found nearest the granite. As well as useful metallic minerals, there are also 'gangue' minerals which were originally of no economic use, but are now in some cases valuable in their own right. These include fluorite, calcite, barite and quartz. There often seems to be an obvious link between the concentrically zoned minerals and the granite mass they surround. The hydrothermal fluids appear to have emanated from the granitic magma at a late stage during its cooling, when much residual water would have been present. Often joints in the granite are mineralized.

However, the link between the minerals and the igneous mass may not be quite so intimate. In northern England, the Weardale granite, which does not today appear on the surface, was investigated by a deep borehole, after a thorough survey of the associated mineral field and a geophysical survey, involving the analysis of magnetic, electrical and gravitational fields. The granite was encountered 1,280 ft (390 m) below the surface, and was found to be deeply weathered. The overlying Carboniferous sediments which contain the minerals were separated from the granite by an unconformity of some 100 million years! This is by no means the only case of its type. Hydrothermal mineral fields may be only indirectly linked with the granitic masses they surround. It may be that granite, a rock which allows high heat-flow from the depths towards the upper parts of the crust, helps to concentrate mineralizing fluids around the margin of the intrusion.

Similar fluids, as well as forming veins, can replace whole rock strata with ore minerals. In the Rio Tinto pyrite deposits in Spain replacement of this sort has yielded over 500 million tons of iron ore. The mineralizing fluids permeate the rock structure and effect a molecule-by-molecule replacement. This is often on so delicate a scale that fossils remain preserved in the new mineral. For example, fossil corals originally made of calcite can be found in the West Cumbrian haematite (iron ore) deposits of north-west England.

Ocean nodules

Precipitation of various metallic minerals around a nucleus has produced million of nodules on the deep ocean beds. Modern submersible technology has proved that they may occupy up to 50 per cent of the ocean floor; the visible tonnage on the Pacific Ocean bed is almost 100,000 million tons. The nodules may be rounded or quite flat, and as well as manganese (up to 40 per cent) they contain copper, iron, nickel and cobalt. These nodule fields are thus of great economic potential. It remains to be seen whether this rich harvest can be wrested from the deep sea-floor by dredging or some other means. The nodules occur in areas which are designated as international waters, and obvious political problems will almost certainly arise over their exploitation.

All over the Earth's surface, the readily observable processes of denudation, transportation and deposition ceaselessly recycle earlier formed rocks to produce layers of sedimentary rock. Even rocks such as granite and gneiss, originally formed deep underground, will ultimately be brought to the surface by earth movements, and here, in response to a new set of environmental conditions, they will be changed into new rocks.

Mechanical weathering

The efficiency of weathering, the breakdown of rock *in situ*, depends on the interaction of climate with rock structure and chemistry. Mechanical weathering produces rock fragments which are not chemically altered. When water freezes in the joints and cavities in rocks, expanding in volume by nine per cent, huge stresses build up, causing rock particles to break off and accumulate as scree at the base of steep cliffs. In arid regions, large temperature differences between day and night cause the different minerals in crystalline rocks to expand and contract at differing rates. The stresses this causes split off thin sheets of the rock: geologists call the process exfoliation, or 'onion-skin' weathering. Internal stresses also fragment rocks in arid regions when salt crystals form within rock cavities: this process is known as flaking. Sometimes, curved fractures appear in rocks, often over large areas, that have been under great pressure due to thousands of feet of overlying rock; when the rocks beneath are relieved of the burden, they expand upwards and crack. Geologists call this 'unloading'.

Chemical weathering

When combined with the carbon dioxide in the atmosphere, rain-water becomes weak carbonic acid. Other acids from the soil and atmospheric pollution increase the effectiveness of rain as an agent of chemical weathering. Felspar in granite can be reduced to clay by these acids, and even granite itself, the epitome of enduring rock, is eventually reduced to a loose mass of sand. In warm, humid climates, this process can be relatively rapid. In West Africa, for instance, a 3 ft (1 m) thick layer of granite has been removed in 22,000 years. These same acids attack limestone, forming soluble calcium bicarbonate, which is then carried away, dissolved in the water. In the north of England, 2 ft (60 cm) of Carboniferous limestone has been worn away over the last 8,000 years.

Some rocks, like those in the deserts of south-western USA, have a kind of natural 'cement' of minerals, which holds the grains together. This can be removed by chemical weathering, allowing the grains to be blown for great distances by the wind.

Above Here, on the Devil's Golf Course, Death Valley, south-west USA, columns of salt are pushed up during crystallization, only to be cut into weird shapes by weathering processes.
Left The striking red sandstones in Zion National Park, Utah, USA, are carved into amazing sculptures by the elements.
Right Enormous gorges and towering waterfalls, such as the Iguazu Falls in Brazil, occur in many regions where large river systems develop below high mountain ranges. The waterfall's sharp edge cuts the gorge out of the rock.

Over the past 200 years, particularly in the industrialized West, atmospheric pollution from the burning of coal and other fossil fuels has produced the notorious 'acid rain', which in some areas is strong enough to sting bare skin and corrode buildings and statues.

Erosion

Weathering, which produces fragments of rocks, is the first of a number of intimately related processes leading to sedimentation. The weathered fragments are carried by running water, moving ice and the wind, or fall under gravity down mountain-sides. The effect of this relentless movement on the land is called erosion. In both hot and cold deserts, the wind is the chief agent of transportation, picking up sand grains and hurling them at rock faces in a natural sandblasting process. Weak rock strata are picked out, producing the typically sculptured desert landforms, such as the bizarre pinnacles

of the Painted Desert in Arizona, USA. This sandblasting action can easily strip the paint from cars and buildings within hours. The size of the wind-blown grains is reduced, and they become rounded and 'frosted' by continual movement against each other. Under the electron microscope, these features can even be recognized on grains from ancient sandstones 250 million years old.

Water, either in rivers or running in sheets down hillsides, moves vast quantities of loose sediment. Spectacular valleys may be carved deep into the landscape by the process of corrosion, the relentless, downward, file-like action of water armed with rock particles. In the cold heights of Canada's Mackenzie Mountains, the South Nahanni River has cut its way 4,000 ft (1,200 m) down through thick layers of limestone and dolomite.

When a glacier moves, large boulders falling onto the river of ice high in the mountains are

Glacier Moraine   Lake   Salt lake   Pebble beach Lagoon   Submarine   Continental rise
                                                                          canyon
              Scree   Sand dunes   Delta   Continental   Turbidity
                                                                  slope   current

Abyssal
plain

Left Sedimentary processes continually remove old rocks to produce new strata. In hot regions, salt lakes with crystalline evaporites develop and, where rain is too sparse to support sediment-binding plants, dunes form and migrate with the wind. Submarine canyons have similar profiles to many deep river valleys on land. Turbid slurries of sediment are funnelled through them, carrying coarse material out to the deep ocean bed.

the sediment that is formed. In arid conditions, even the chemically vulnerable minerals, mica and felspar, may survive as fragments of detritus and be deposited as sandstone, which, when rich in felspar, is called arkose.

The speed of transport will also influence the mineralogy of the accumulating sediment. If a very rapid, turbulent river flowing down a steep mountainside carries and deposits a mass of sediment in an alluvial fan (where the river divides into a fan-shaped pattern of tributaries at the mountain's base), the sediment may contain a great deal of felspar, because chemical weathering has not had time to destroy it. Rocks such as the Torridonian arkoses in north-west Scotland are pink because of their high felspar content, due to rapid deposition and, possibly, an arid climate when they were formed about 900 million years ago.

Other chemicals may feature in sedimentary environments. A kind of natural 'cement' often forms, binding the grains together. Depending on the nature of fluids in the crust which seep through the sediment, this may be made of quartz, calcite, iron oxide or other minerals.

Organic and chemical sediments

As well as the oozes, clays, shales, sandstones and conglomerates formed by the processes described above, geologists distinguish two other classes of sedimentary rocks.

The organic sediments include limestone and coal, formed by the accumulation of material from dead animals and plants. Many limestones are actually fossil coral reefs, with lime-rich mud forming the cement-like matrix between the coral animals.

Coal is found only at certain times during the geological record, notably in the Carboniferous rocks of much of the Northern Hemisphere. The coal seams are found among rhythmically repeated layers of shale, sandstone and clay, evidence of the delta-top environment in which the coal-forming swamps originally developed about 300 million years ago.

The most important chemically formed rocks are the thick layers of evaporite minerals that are precipitated when salt lakes dry out. These layers of rock salt, gypsum and potash may alternate with marl and limestone, forming a definite sequence, the least soluble evaporite coming out of solution first. Rock salt, because it becomes plastic when under great pressure underground, can flow upwards like toothpaste being squeezed out of a tube, and break through the overlying layers of sediment, forming salt domes, which can help to trap oil. In eastern Louisiana, USA, the salt has found its way towards the surface through 30,000 ft (9,000 m) of sediment!

Clearly, sedimentary rocks exhibit a great variety of structure, grain size and chemistry. These features are controlled to a great extent by the environmental conditions which prevailed when they were forming. A number of distinct rock types and assemblages characteristically form in certain environments, and when these are found in the rocks of a given geological period, the environment of that time can be reconstructed. The sum total of all the features of a sedimentary rock (bedding form, colour, grain size, shape and so on) is called its facies. For example, a deep-ocean facies contains fine-grained sediment consisting of uniformly sized particles, while a continental shelf facies may be made of limestone, with shallow water creatures fossilized among its strata.

reduced to a fine rock 'flour' by the time they reach the glacier's snout in the valley far below. Rocks frozen into the base of the glacier ice gouge deep grooves in the solid bedrock. These striations, which are in the direction of the ice movement, help geologists work out, millions of years after the ice melted, the paths followed by ancient glaciers.

The sea alters the coastlines by hurling water, often containing rocks, at cliff-faces with explosive force. The compressed air trapped between wave and cliff-face can excavate large cavities. Storm waves can create pressures equivalent to those of exploding bombs.

Sedimentary rocks

Weathering and erosion produce the fragments, ranging from fine clay particles to large boulders (collectively called detritus), which, when organized and deposited in various environments, produce what geologists call sedimentary rocks. These are characterized by bedding, which is a pattern of distinct, sheet-like layers. There are various forms of bedding, depending on the dynamics of the fluid which carried and deposited the particles of detritus. Wind-deposited detritus produces large-scale 'dune bedding', with curved, sweeping layers. Turbidity currents in the sea, thundering down the continental slope, give rise to the repeated layers in which sediment size is graded, with coarse grains at the base and finer particles at the top, formed as the turbulent mass of water and sediments settles onto the sea-bed.

Grain size and shape

The size and shape of the grains of sediment depend on the way they have been eroded and transported. In contrast to the rounded desert sand grains, those carried and jostled in running water are angular. Large pebbles, on the other hand, will become rounded in a river bed or sea beach, in contrast to those in arid areas, which have sharp, angular corners. The more powerful the current, the larger are the fragments which can be carried. A swift mountain stream can move large boulders, but a wide river meandering across a flood plain carries its load as very fine silt and mud. When a river laden with sediment reaches the sea, the coarser material is dumped first, and the finer particles may be carried out into deeper water, to form layers on the continental shelf. In very deep oceans, remarkably little water-borne sediment is found. The ooze which accumulates on the ocean bed thousands of miles from land contains wind-blown volcanic dust and the bodies of oceanic animals and plants, which fall slowly like a fine rain from above. Occasionally, large boulders, rafted on icebergs, may be encountered in the abyssal depths.

Chemistry and mineralogy of sediments

The chemistry of the fragments of detritus is often very simple. This is because they are derived from preformed rocks, so that only the more durable of the minerals in these rocks can withstand erosion and transport. If a mountain made of granite is weathered in humid conditions, the mica and felspar will be broken down by chemical weathering, to form fine-grained clay particles. The quartz from granite will withstand both chemical and physical destruction, so that it makes up a high percentage of

Rocks at the Earth's surface are subjected to a variety of processes of alteration, such as weathering and erosion, which are very obvious to us and which can be observed taking place, even if very slowly—in human terms. Metamorphism involves processes of rock alteration which go on deep within the crust, where awesome forces, involving great pressures, searing temperatures and migrating fluids, totally change any rock. Metamorphic change does not involve melting; rather it entails subtle chemical and physical changes which produce a new rock, in equilibrium with a completely different environment from that in which it originally formed. By analysing the minerals in the metamorphic rock, geologists can often work out the temperatures and pressures at which these profound changes took place.

Thermal metamorphism

Geologists recognize two basic types of metamorphism—thermal (or contact) metamorphism and regional metamorphism. During thermal metamorphism, direct contact with magma causes dramatic changes in existing rocks. The molten magma may be at temperatures approaching 1,800°F (1,000°C). Geologists call the zone around the igneous rock which is altered by the intense heat the 'metamorphic aureole'. Here, pressure has virtually no influence. The aureole envelops the magma body, and its extent depends on both the size of the igneous mass and the nature of the surrounding rock (the 'country' rock) which forms the aureole. The metamorphic influence is most extreme next to the magma and fades away outwards.

When granitic magma, at a temperature of nearly 1,800°F (1,000°C), invades sedimentary strata such as shales and mudstones, the minerals in these strata recrystallize, removing the pattern of bedding and any fossils. The grains in the rock grow, and new metamorphic minerals develop, often giving the rock a spotted appearance, as with chiastolite and andalusite. The original shale or mudstone contains quartz, clay minerals and chlorite. The stable quartz grains remain and grow, but the others disappear or are changed into mica. Next to the granite, hornfels, a tough, flinty rock, is produced. Outside this, spotted slate grades into unmetamorphosed shales. Different country rocks, such as sandstone and limestone, change into metaquartzite and marble, their exact mineralogy being largely dependent on impurities in the original sediment.

Regional metamorphism

In orogenic zones, the mobile belts of crustal activity where mountains form, regional metamorphism occurs, often over many hundreds

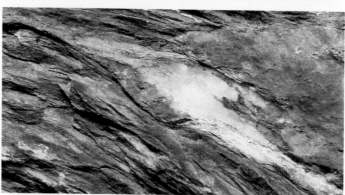

Top left Slate is formed in the lower temperature and pressure conditions near the surface of thick sedimentary rock sequences. Only weaker sediments like shale and mudstone are altered to produce a fine-grained dark rock, characterized by easily broken cleavage planes. The rock is often contorted by folding, and this example is riddled with thin quartz veins, which follow the rock's structure.
Centre left Schist is produced with an increase in temperature and pressure. This rock has a wavy, mica-rich banding. The sheen on the broken surfaces is due to the abundant mica. The conditions for schist formation are found deep within fold mountains. This specimen has a large 'eye' of quartz in it.
Bottom left In the deepest roots of fold mountain belts, where temperatures and pressures are extreme, coarsely crystalline gneiss is formed. The lighter bands are quartz and felspar rich and the dark ones contain hornblende and mica. The granitic composition of gneiss can result from high-grade metamorphism of almost any rock, so extreme are the conditions. Mudstone can form slate, which, with increasing pressure, forms schist and ultimately gneiss.
Right Coastal exposures of Pre-Cambrian gneisses in north-west Britain show the rugged features typical of this silica-rich, highly altered metamorphic rock.

of square miles. Here, the agents of metamorphism are often stress, high pressure and high temperature. Deep in the mountain roots, migrating fluids are also influential.

Regionally metamorphosed rocks can be recognized by structural features which reflect the influence of pressure and stress. The alignment of minerals in rocks which have been subjected to these conditions produces structures such as cleavage (where fine-grained minerals lie in parallel planes, allowing the rock to split into thin sheets) and schistosity (a structure of coarser mineral grains which form a wavy banding). As with thermal metamorphism, geologists can learn about the tempera-

tures and other conditions involved by examining groups of minerals in the rock.

At great depths in orogenic zones, where temperatures and pressures are extremely high, gneiss is formed. This rock is banded and made up of coarse grains. The banding (often alternating layers of light-coloured quartz- and felspar-rich rock and darker ferro-magnesian-rich rock) is a product of the movement of chemicals influenced by the very high temperatures. Gneiss will form from the high-temperature-and-pressure metamorphism of any pre-existing rock. The mineralogy of gneiss may be influenced by the composition of the original rock. Shales may become acid gneisses,

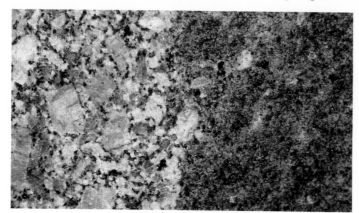
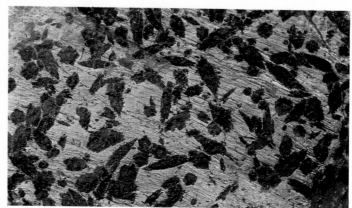

with garnet and kyanite; sandstones develop into gneisses rich in quartz and felspar; calcium-rich felspar and pyroxene are typical of gneisses formed from limestones.

At shallower depths, temperatures and pressures are less extreme, and here the rocks formed are medium-grained with wavy banding, or foliation. Mica is very common in rocks such as schist, lying parallel to the rock structures. Garnet, cordierite and kyanite are also formed during these medium-grade (medium temperature and pressure) changes, different minerals representing different temperature conditions. The foliated schists develop mainly from shales and other fine-grained

rocks. Sandstone and limestone become granular quartzites and marbles, with new minerals such as garnet and epidote forming from original impurities.

The least altered of the regionally metamorphosed rocks are phyllites and slates. These occur nearer the surface in the orogenic belts, and only weak rocks, such as shales and mudstones, are much altered. Temperatures are low and chemical changes very slight. Low to moderate pressures produce a typical slaty cleavage, in which mica and clay minerals are aligned at right angles to the direction of pressure. Tougher rocks, such as sandstones, limestones and basic igneous rocks, develop

only a very weak cleavage, since the flaky minerals are not as abundant in these rocks as in the shales.

Dislocation metamorphism

During major earth movements, large-scale faulting occurs deep within the rocks of the crust. Near to the fault plane, where temperature and pressure is increased, dislocation metamorphism occurs. Fragmentation of the rocks near the fault plane and the subsequent welding together of the fragments forms the rock mylonite. The rock fragments and dust are drawn out, with a texture reminiscent of schistosity, in the direction of fault movement.

Right Hot molten rock (magma) invades surrounding country rocks to produce new metamorphic rocks.
Far left Felspar-pink granite, in contact with hornfels, a crystalline flinty rock which, before intense heating from the granite, was volcanic ash.
Left Further from the magma, the country rocks are less altered, becoming 'spotted' by heating of new minerals, as with this specimen of cordierite.
Far right When altered by heat, limestone becomes solid crystalline marble.

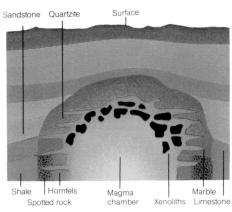

From its lofty orbit, the remote-sensing satellite trains its electronic "eyes" on our world; it can measure its shape, determine its geological properties, sound its atmosphere, record changing ocean conditions, assist in accurate weather prediction, give timely warning of fire and flood, and monitor worldwide patterns of resource management. For the first time, man can observe natural phenomena on a global basis across a far wider band of electromagnetic radiation than the narrow optical slot to which our eyes are tuned. The advent of the space age has not only opened up the wonders of the Solar System, the Milky Way and deep space to us; above all it has revealed the magnificence and complexity of our own planet.

EYES IN THE SKY

Packed with advanced sensors, a constellation of satellites constantly monitor conditions on Earth, feeding scientists new data on the changing face of our planet

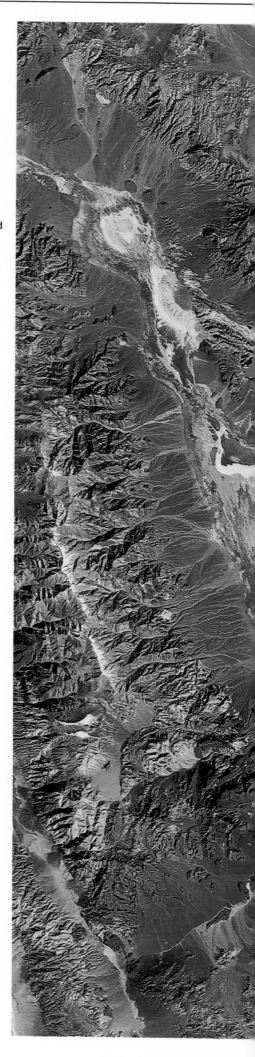

Our visual conception of the planet Earth is largely the product of images returned from manned spacecraft and satellites. Perhaps the most impressive of these was the first colour photograph of the Earth taken from lunar orbit by the crew of Apollo-8 on Christmas Day 1968. It showed us our habitat as the sunlit disc of a blue and white sphere, floating serenely in a velvet cosmos, a fragile, unique haven for life as we know it.

Nearer the Earth, astronauts and cosmonauts flying spacecraft in low orbits photographed coastlines, cities, deserts, seascapes, mountain ranges, storms, all with hand-held cameras peering through the windows of their capsules. These provided new perceptions of our planet's surface, its cloud forms, the violence of hurricanes and minuteness of the works of man compared with the forms of nature. From the hand-held camera pictures, essentially an extension of aerial photography, evolved a technology of remote sensing from space. It has provided the means not only of monitoring the Earth but also of reconnoitring the surfaces and meteorology of other planets.

Operational systems

Here, however, we will deal with Earth. As of November 1984, the United States has two meteorological satellites, NOAA-6 and -7, in polar orbits and the Soviet Union operates two Meteor class weather satellites covering the USSR's Eurasian land mass and the north Pacific Ocean. In geosynchronous orbit, 22,300 miles (35,880 km) over the equator, where they appear to be stationary relative to the Earth, are seven meteorological satellites in a circle 165,000 miles (265,500 km) in circumference. Five were fully operational late in 1984. They were the United States GOES-2 and -6 at 113° and 108° west longitude (GOES: Geostationary Operational Environmental Satellite); the European Space Agency's Meteosat-2 hovering on station at 0°; India's Insat-1B at 74° east longitude and Japan's GMS-2 (Himawari-2) at 140° east longitude. (Himawari—sunflower—is the Japanese name of the satellite; GMS stands for Geostationary Meteorological Satellite.)

These satellites, with the earlier Meteosat-1 and GMS-1 (Himawari-1) which are producing some data but no imagery, form a World Weather Watch system. They also contribute to the international Global Atmospheric Research Program, the most extensive effort in history to understand the behaviour of Earth's atmosphere.

Beyond weather observation, two systems of satellites have been placed in polar and near polar orbits by the United States and the Soviet Union to monitor conditions on the surface of the Earth and locate its resources of minerals and hydrocarbon fuels. The US National Aeronautics & Space Administration (NASA) developed a series of Earth Resources Technology Satellites named 'Landsat'. Operating in near polar orbit as of 1984 were Landsat-4 and Landsat-5, the most advanced of the series. The USSR developed Earth observation versions of its Meteor-1 and -2 satellites, starting with Meteor-Priroda launched in 1981. These large and heavy machines do double duty, observing the atmosphere as well as the ground.

Other nations are also involved in the developing field of remote sensing: France is building a Landsat-type Earth resources satellite called SPOT (*Satellite Probatoire d'Observation de la Terre*), to be launched in 1985; the European Space Agency (ESA) has been authorized by member states to develop the first of a family of ESA Remote-Sensing Satellites (ERS-1), an Earth resources spacecraft due for

Right Death Valley, California: a thermal infra-red Thematic Mapper image taken by Landsat-4, one of the most advanced remote-sensing spacecraft yet developed. The image has been processed with a false-colour technique so that specific spectral characteristics of the terrain show up as distinct colours. Such instruments offer totally new capabilities in the science of spectrally "deciphering" the constituent materials of the Earth.

launch in 1988; and Japan is building a marine resources observer called MOS-1 (Marine Observation Satellite-1) to monitor ecological conditions of coastal areas and states of the surrounding seas. It will be launched about 1986 into a near polar orbit. Japan also plans to orbit an Earth resources satellite in 1989. ERS-1 is being developed by the Japanese National Space Development Agency (NASDA), with instrumentation similar to that of ESA'S ERS: synthetic aperture radar, radar altimeter and microwave scatterometer. Although ocean scanning is an important objective, the satellite is designed to observe geological features of the Japanese islands, land use, agriculture, forestry, fisheries, general environmental conditions and the coastal zone.

Radar imagery

Starting with Tiros-1, the first Television and Infra-red Observation Satellite in 1961, NASA has steadily widened the regions of the electro-magnetic spectrum from which images can be formed, from visible light, through infra-red bands to microwaves. Remote sensing by radar has provided spectacular results. Thus, remote sensing technology has moved from the visible range, useful only in daylight, to the infra-red, for night imaging. With microwave radar, however, it is possible to acquire high resolution images day or night, whether or not the target is overcast by clouds. Radar imaging now is the most advanced state of the art.

This evolution has been clearly seen in the sequence of meteorological and Earth observation satellites developed in the United States. The early Tiros satellites of the first half of the 1960s relied mainly on television cameras that took daily cloud pictures in daylight and relayed them to ground stations for distribution to weather forecast centres. Improved Tiros machines used infra-red radiometers that scanned the clouds at night and created images from heat radiation. Improvements continued with advanced vidicon camera systems, infra-red scanners capable of sensing temperature and moisture at various levels of the atmosphere, infra-red radiometers providing higher resolution of cloud and surface images, and sensors that recorded the Earth's budget of incoming and outgoing solar energy. To these were added instruments that sensed the intensity of high-energy nuclear particles entering the atmosphere from the Sun: protons, electrons and alpha particles (helium nuclei).

Twenty years after Tiros-1, there exist four species of remote sensing satellites looking at Earth: the polar-orbiting weather satellites flying at 503 to 528 miles (810 to 850km), each covering the entire planet twice every 24 hours; the geostationary satellites which view nearly one third of the planet from their positions high above the equator; the Earth resources satellites that observe the conditions of farms, fields, forests, cities, rivers, lakes, coastal zones, deserts, jungles and ice sheets; and the geodetic-navigation satellites that survey the planet's shape and the distribution of mass on and within it. In the United States and Western Europe, these machines are designed for civil services. A military version of the US civil polar orbiters serves US defence needs. These machines flying at about 515 miles (831km) in near polar orbits in the US Defense Meteorological Satellite Program provide global weather information and also tactical weather data.

Remote sensing by satellites extends beyond observations of the appearance of the Earth's surface and the behaviour of the atmosphere; it also helps us define the planet's shape, the arrangement of mass on and within it and the precise relationship of points on the surface. The scientific discipline encompassing these geometric features is geodesy, a branch of applied mathematics that has been revolutionized by satellites.

In the United States, satellite geodesy initially grew out of an effort to develop a satellite Doppler navigation system for the Navy. When Sputnik-1 was launched on 4 October 1957, analysis of its radio signal showed that its orbit could be determined by the signal's Doppler (frequency) shift. This was confirmed by experiments with the 40MHz broadcast from Sputnik-2 and the 108MHz signals from Explorer-1 and Vanguard-1 satellites.

If a satellite's orbit could be determined from the Doppler shift of its signal at a ground station of known position, the obverse must be true: it would also be possible to determine the position of the station if the satellite's position was known. The application of the Doppler principle served another purpose. Because the frequency shift is a function of satellite motion, it enables observers to detect minute accelerations caused by variations in the strength of the Earth's gravitational field acting upon an orbiting object. Inasmuch as gravitational force is proportional to mass, variations in the force reflect the arrangement of mass in the Earth. Thus, the development of satellite Doppler navigation gave birth to satellite geodesy, opening a new era in solid Earth physics.

For example, in 1957-58 the tracking of Sputnik-2 and of Explorer-1 provided data from which the Earth's polar flattening value, 2/298·3, was derived. Later, data from Vanguard-1 showed that the Earth is slightly pear-shaped, with the 'stem' towards the North Pole. As a result of this configuration and of polar flattening, the Earth's equatorial diameter is 26·6 miles (42·7km) greater than its polar diameter; furthermore, the North Pole is slightly more distant from the centre of the Earth than the South Pole. All of these features of the Earth, hitherto unknown, were revealed by tracking the early satellites.

NASA and the Department of Defense worked jointly on navigation and geodetic satellites until 1965 when the programmes were divided. NASA pursued geodetic satellite and the Department of Defense navigation satellite development. Current US navigation and geodetic satellite technology was developed mainly with six satellites: Transit-1B, ANNA-1B, Beacon-Explorer B and Beacon-Explorer C (equipped with corner cube reflectors for distance measurements with laser beams, as well as radio transmitters), and GEOS-1, -2 and -3. The GEOS satellites (Geodynamic Experimental Ocean Satellite) were designed for NASA by the Applied Physics Laboratory of Johns Hopkins University, Baltimore. They carried flashing lights, a SECOR (sequential collation of range) transponder, a new range and range-rate tracking system developed by NASA's Goddard SFC, radio transmitters for Doppler tracking and a laser corner reflector array developed by the General Electric Co.

Geodetic measurements were made also with space balloons which carried radio beacons. The first were the two Echo passive communications satellites, launched respectively on 12 August 1960 and 25 January 1964 from Cape Canaveral. The most elaborate orbital balloon target was the 244lb (111kg) PAGEOS-1 (Passive GEOS) which was launched from Vandenberg on 24 June 1966. It was about the same size as

Above The 135ft (41m) diameter Echo-2 undergoes inflation testing before launch in 1964.

Geodetic scientists used these reflective communications satellites as orbiting mapping beacons.

Echo-1, but lacked radio beacons. PAGEOS with a highly reflective surface was tracked photographically. At its mean altitude, 2,640 miles (4,250km), it was as bright as a plus 2 magnitude star and could be seen by observers 1,800 miles (2,896km) apart using telephoto Baker-Nunn cameras. Its main purpose was to establish a worldwide triangulation network by optical sightings.

Laser reflectors
Last of the GEOS series was LAGEOS (laser geodynamic satellite), a 906lb (411kg) aluminium sphere only 23·6in (60cm) in diameter. The sphere with a heavy brass core was covered by 426 fused silica retroreflectors which lent it the appearance of an oversized golf ball. LAGEOS was launched from Vandenberg on 4 May 1976 into a near polar orbit 3,625 x 3,693 miles (5,835 x 5,944km). Its main purpose is to provide a means of measuring motions of the Earth's crustal plates and major fault systems with an accuracy of about 0·79in (2cm). The satellite reflects laser beams emitted from mobile ground stations. Plate motion studies have shown a requirement for at least two mobile laser stations on adjacent plates which are believed to be moving in relation to each other. Monitoring their rate and direction of movement may contribute to earthquake predictions, especially in the circum-Pacific earthquake belt or "zone of fire". The National Research Council of Italy and NASA are collaborating in the development of a second LAGEOS which will be launched in 1987 into an orbit particularly suited to advancing studies of crustal deformation in the Mediterranean area.

Geodetic satellites may be the most numerous of all orbiting vehicles. More than 60 of them launched by the US Department of Defense, NASA, the European Space Agency (ESA) and the USSR have been identified by NASA's National Geodetic Satellite Program. Many more designed to refine missile guidance programs are not specifically identified.

France has been a pioneer in laser satellite tracking and geodesy, starting with the launch of two 50lb (22·7kg) laser reflector satellites, Diademe-1 and -2, from Hammaguir in February 1967. They were followed by Péole, a 154lb (70kg) laser beam-reflecting satellite launched on 12 December 1970 from Kourou into a 385 x 465 miles (621 x 748km) orbit. Two more small tracking payloads with geodetic applications were launched in 1975 from Kourou by the French space agency, *Centre National d'Études Spatiales* (CNES). On 6 February, Starlette, a 104lb (47kg) machine covered with laser reflectors, was placed in a 500 x 688 miles (806 x 1,108km) orbit by an improved Diamant rocket—for which Starlette was billed as a test payload. On 12 May, two small satellites, Castor and Pollux, were launched, Castor with a mass of 170lb (77kg) into a 167 x 797 miles (269 x 1,283km) orbit and Pollux, riding piggyback with Castor, into a similar path.

Castor carried an accelerometer experiment called CACTUS which was designed to measure accelerations between one hundred thousandth and one thousand millionth of the acceleration of gravity at the Earth's surface. Orbital changes measured to that degree of precision can indicate the density of the upper atmosphere, the effect on the satellite of radiation pressure of sunlight both from the Sun and reflected by Earth, and variations of Earth's gravitational field so precise as to indicate the presence of mineral deposits.

ESA has recently announced a feasibility study of a high performance geodetic satellite called POPSAT (Precise Orbit Positioning Satellite) that would combine Doppler shift and laser measuring methods to track motions of Earth's crustal plates to an accuracy of 0·39in (1cm)—about twice the resolution of LAGEOS. POPSAT would also monitor components of the Earth's polar motion (precession, nutation) and variations in the planet's rate of rotation which affect the length of the day.

Left The reflective properties of LAGEOS are tested by scientists at NASA's Goddard Space Flight Center. The detection of laser pulses reflected by LAGEOS' 426 fused silica prisms permits extremely accurate measurement of the planet's crustal movements; it is thus a valuable tool in earthquake prediction.

Right France's Starlette: only 10in (25·4cm) in diameter, the compact size and high density offset the effects of atmospheric drag.

Laser Ranging
The two diagrams show how satellites are used as geodetic references to determine very precisely the position of tracking stations around the Earth. Comparison of these positions over a period of time then allows scientists to observe whether any movements of the Earth's tectonic plates have taken place. In the top drawing a geometric method of tri-lateration is used whereby simultaneous range observations of a satellite from three stations at known positions (**A**), taken at intervals in its orbit, fix the satellite's position and allow the relative position of the station (**B**) to be computed. In the lower drawing the precise orbit is calculated by taking successive readings of the time elapse between beaming a laser pulse at it and receiving its reflection. From the known orbit, the position of **B** can be determined.

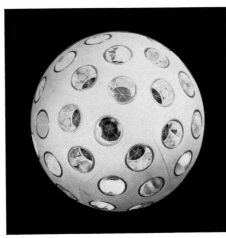
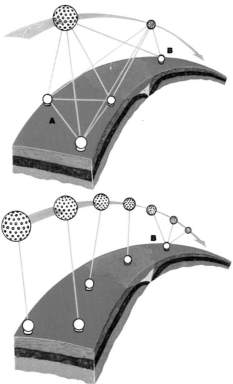
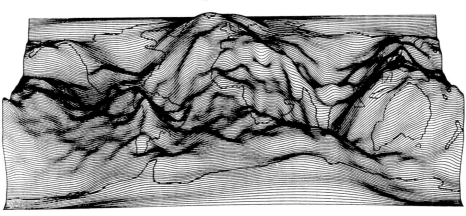

Left The Earth's gravity field is not homogeneous, and a satellite in orbit reacts to variations it experiences. This schematic illustrates how the gravity field of the geoid might look as determined by applying the principle of satellite-to-satellite tracking: measurement of the relative velocity and local accelerations of the two craft during their orbits permits the computation of gravity field intensities.

The first extensive NASA collection of Earth scenes from orbit was acquired during the Gemini and Apollo flight programmes, 1965–1972. Most of the pictures were made by astronauts holding 70mm cameras and pointing them at scenes visible through the spacecraft windows. In sum, these missions yielded about 4,000 black and white and colour images. Each generally covered an area of 100 by 100 miles.

Gemini crews were instructed to photograph storms, especially hurricanes and typhoons when they could see them, but their lenses saw much more—the panorama from space of the Earth's oceans, mountains, deserts, prairies, rivers and the chequerboard pattern of farms in the American middle west demonstrated the potential of space photography in discerning patterns of changing land use and of observing forest fires, floods and volcanic eruptions.

NASA's most extensive engineering tests of remote sensing instruments were conducted on Skylab, the first United States space station. Launched on 14 May 1973 by a Saturn V rocket, Skylab was operated for 171 days by three crews of three men each, who spent 28, 59 and 84 days respectively aboard the 86ft (26·2m) long station. Skylab was closed down when the third crew departed on 8 February 1974. The station's orbit decayed more rapidly than expected and it re-entered the atmosphere on 11 July 1979, breaking up off the southwest coast of Australia after frantic efforts by NASA to control its plunge into the Pacific.

The EREP equipment

Five Earth resources remote sensing experiments—collectively known as the Earth Resources Experiment Package (EREP)—were mounted in the station's multiple docking adapter. They were a multi-spectral photographic facility, an infra-red spectrometer, a multi-spectral scanner, a microwave radiometer/altimeter/scatterometer and an L-band microwave radiometer.

The multi-spectral photographic facility was designed to take pictures of the Earth in visible and near infra-red light with sufficient resolution to allow detailed assessment of the moisture content of the soils, of the identity and health of crops, of blight, of insect infestations of forests and of general patterns of land use, especially urban spread. This facility used two camera systems. One set consisted of six 70mm cameras with resolutions of 100ft (30m) and a 100 miles square (161km square) field of view. The camera types had been flown extensively on aircraft, and each was loaded with film sensitive to a different wavelength. One object of the experiment was to assess their performance in orbit, which was initially 262 x 274 miles (422 x 441km). The second camera system was an "Earth Terrain" camera, an instrument adapted from the Lunar Topographic Camera flown around the Moon on Apollo-14. Its field of view was 69 miles (112km) on a side, with a resolution of 35ft (11·5m). The images were produced in black and white, colour and infra-red sensitive colour (in which certain infra-red bands were depicted in false colour).

The infra-red spectrometer had also been tested as a remote sensing device at aircraft altitudes. The experimenters wanted to know whether it could identify ground features from orbit as well as it could from high flying airplanes. "This technique," said a NASA technical memorandum prophetically, "has the potential of providing a means of monitoring from space the extent and health of surface vegetation without the need for spatial resolution of individual plants. Geological information and precision sea surface temperature measurements will also be obtained." The data were recorded on magnetic tape which was returned, as was all the experimental photography film, by astronauts to laboratories on the ground for analysis and processing. In this way Skylab served as a test bed for advanced remote sensing instruments later flown on satellites.

Above left Four Earth resources synchronized cameras aboard Apollo-9 acquired this infra-red view of the Salton Sea, a shallow saline lake, and the intensively cultivated Imperial Valley in S. California in March 1969.

Above Astronauts wielding hand-held cameras in orbit can often secure spectacular pictures of natural phenomena. Here, a member of the Skylab-4 crew has captured the vortex of a typhoon over the south central Pacific Ocean in early 1974.

Above right Skylab in Earth orbit, 265 miles (426km) up. The EREP experiments were carried in the docking adapter—at the far end of the station in this view, beneath the Apollo Telescope Mount with its four solar panels.

Right A high definition view of Chicago and Lake Michigan recorded by Skylab's Earth Terrain camera using an 18in (457mm) focal length lens with 5in film.

EREP Spectral Coverage

1-3 Multi-spectral photography: (**1**) 0·5-0·9μm, b and w; (**2**) 0·5-0·88μm, IR colour; (**3**) 0·4-0·7μm, high resolution colour:
4 Earth Terrain camera: 0·4-0·7 μm, colour.
5 IR spectrometer: 0·4-2·4μm and 6·2-15·5μm.
6 Multi-spectral scanner: 13 bands—0·4-12·5μm.
7 Microwave system: 2·2cm
8 L-band radiometer: 21cm

EREP Spectral Coverage

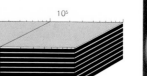

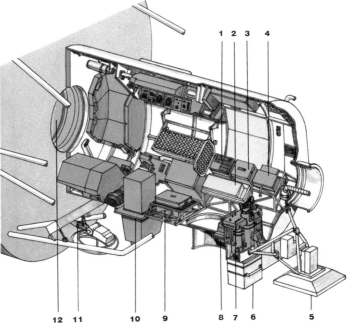

Skylab EREP Layout
1 Multi-spectral scanner electronics.
2 Film stowage.
3 EREP tape recorder.
4 Control and display panel.
5 L-band microwave radiometer.
6 Infra-red spectrometer.
7 Infra-red spectrometer viewfinder tracking system.
8 Multi-spectral photographic facility.
9 Back-up EREP tape recorder.
10 Multi-spectral scanner.
11 Microwave radiometer/ altimeter/scatterometer.
12 Hatch leading to airlock module.

EREP consisted of six remote sensing systems which were centrally managed from a control and display panel; all were sited in and around the Multiple Docking Adapter.

The multi-spectral scanner was put aboard to assess its feasibility as a spacecraft sensor; again, it had already proved successful on aircraft. The scanner recorded in 13 bands in the visible, near infra-red and thermal infra-red regions of the spectrum, each responsive to spectral signatures of specific surface features. On aircraft, it produced good results in surveying croplands, forests and urban areas, and displayed some utility for geologic mapping. It would be later developed for the Landsat series of spacecraft.

The microwave radiometer/scatterometer/ altimeter was an experiment in measuring microwave scatter from land and sea on a global scale. It provided engineering data for the design of a radar altimeter, and provided data complementary to those of the infra-red spectrometer and multi-spectral scanner. The L-band microwave radiometer, a passive microwave sensor, measured the brightness (temperature) of surfaces to an accuracy of 1° Kelvin.

These instruments were used in a survey of volcanic activity at five sites in Nicaragua and at Mount Etna, in Sicily. The sensors were activated during each of the manned periods aboard Skylab. Persistent cloud cover hampered the identification of volcanic hot spots which the thermal instruments were seeing in Nicaragua. Later in the mission, a very important hot spot was located. It turned out to be Mount Etna which could be seen smoking, even from orbit.

Soviet developments

Manned spacecraft also took part in the development of remote sensing instruments in the Soviet Union's space programme. The crew of Soyuz-9, launched on 1 June 1970 on an 18 day "endurance" flight, made photographic maps of the Caucasus, Central Asia and the Caspian Sea. Soyuz-12, launched on 27 September 1973, carried multi-spectral cameras for Earth observation. According to Soviet reports, they identified oil- and gas-bearing geological structures, discovered previously unknown crustal fractures and found new sources of ground-water in deserts. The crew of Soyuz-22, launched on 15 September 1976, tested cameras that produced large-scale photomaps with a scale of 1:50,000 during a flight that lasted 7 days 21 hours 54 minutes.

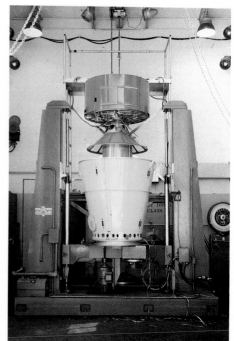

Left This was the first television picture to be taken of the Earth from space. It was returned by Tiros-1 in April 1960. Although crude by today's standards, it did show the feasibility of using satellites for weather observation.

Right ESSA-6 undergoes spin testing at the Western Test Range, Lompoc, California in 1967. This satellite became part of the Tiros Operational System. Its APT cameras provided direct real-time readout of data to ground stations.

Below right One of the most valuable features of a weather satellite is its ability to provide advance warning of hurricanes. This is a NOAA-3 VHRR visible light image of Hurricanes Ione and Kirsten taken on 24 August 1974.

In President John F. Kennedy's special message to Congress on 25 July 1961 calling for a manned landing on the Moon, there was another, less dramatic plea. It was a request to Congress for funds to enable the Weather Bureau to establish a National Operational Meteorological Satellite System under the aegis of the Department of Commerce.

Congress authorized the first appropriation for the system in September. The technology had been demonstrated by NASA's experimental weather satellite, Tiros-1. Launched on 1 April 1960 from Cape Canaveral, it began transmitting cloud pictures to ground stations a few days after it reached its orbit of 427 x 465 miles (687 x 748km) x 48·3°.

Formed in response to President Kennedy's plea, an interagency panel of officials of the Department of Commerce, the Department of Defense, NASA and the Federal Aviation Administration recommended establishment of a National Operational Meteorological Satellite System. Its objectives are summarised in the accompanying table.

Following the success of Tiros-1, nine more Tiros spacecraft were launched in high inclination orbits from Cape Canaveral (i.e., 48·5° to 98·6°). Although the programme was essentially experimental, these satellites provided usable data from their 0·5in (1·27cm) vidicon imaging systems. Experimental infra-red sensors were added to Tiros-2, -3, -4 and -7 for thermal data, but did not provide images.

Tiros in operation

The experimental period ended in February 1966 with the inauguration of the Tiros Operational System (TOS). These machines carried advanced one inch (2·54cm) vidicon systems which provided more detail and higher resolution of cloud scenes. The TOS satellites at first were designated as ASS (Advanced Survey Satellites) but later acquired another acronym, ESSA, the initials of the Environmental Science Services Administration which encompassed the Weather Bureau. The first of the operational satellites, ESSA-1, was launched from Cape Canaveral on 3 February 1966 in a near polar orbit, 421 x 598 miles (677 x 965km). In addition to the vidicon camera system, it

Objectives of a National Meteorological Satellite System

1 To view the atmosphere, day and night, on a global basis.
2 To transmit meteorological data to ground stations.
3 To provide continuous viewing of weather features over large areas of the planet.
4 To collect environmental data from remote and automatic weather stations, and relay them to ground stations.
5 To make regular temperature and humidity soundings of the atmosphere.
6 To measure the intensity of solar protons, electrons and alpha particles impinging on the ionosphere.
7 To observe activity on the Sun, and provide early warning of oncoming magnetic storms.
8 To participate in international meteorological investigations aimed at creating models of atmospheric behaviour.

carried a flat plate radiometer which provided data on the Earth's heat balance. This measurement of the budget of incoming and outgoing radiation was made only by the odd-numbered ESSA machines (1, 3, 5, 7 and 9). ESSA-2, launched from the Cape on 28 February 1966 into a higher, near polar orbit, 843 x 881 miles (1,356 x 1,418km), was equipped with an automatic picture transmission (APT) system (as were all the even-numbered machines) which dumped its imaging data as it came into view of a ground station. Nine ESSA satellites were launched between 1966 and 1969. They returned a total of 1,006,140 pictures.

Nimbus experiments (see following spread) provided the technological assurance for the development of an advanced series of weather satellites called ITOS (Improved Tiros Operational Satellites). The prime contractor was RCA, who had built the Tiros and ESSA machines. ITOS was equipped with three-axis stabilization, automatic picture transmitters, two advanced vidicon camera systems, dual scanning radiometers and the flat plate radiometer pioneered on ESSA for heat balance measurements.

When the Environmental Science Services Administration was retitled the National Oceanic and Atmospheric Administration in 1970, the ITOS acronym was changed to NOAA. NOAA-1, second of the ITOS design, was launched on 11 December 1970 with the same instrumentation as ITOS-1 except for the inclusion of a solar proton detector. New

radiometers, developed for night imaging of clouds, were installed in NOAA-2, launched on 15 October 1972. NOAA-2 was an advanced ITOS that relied on scanning radiometers to produce cloud images night and day. It was the first operational satellite equipped to make temperature profiles of the atmosphere on a global basis. It carried two new vertical temperature profile radiometers.

From the start, the NOAA satellites were launched into polar or near-polar orbits, from which they could cover the entire planet. The five ITOS-type satellites satisfied NASA's operational objectives of sounding the atmosphere regularly on a global basis and then gave way to a new generation of weather observers called Tiros-N. The first of these spacecraft was launched on 13 October 1978 into a medium high polar orbit, 527 x 537 miles (849 x 864km), and became immediately operational.

NOAA-7 is the currently operating Tiros-N polar-orbiting satellite for the Department of Commerce. Like all Tiros-N satellites, the complement of data-gathering instruments comprises an Advanced Very High Resolution Radiometer (AVHRR) providing visible and infra-red data for real-time automatic transmission and storage for later playback, which allows for more accurate sea-surface temperature mapping and identification of snow and ice, as well as day and night imaging; a vertical sounder which combines data from several instruments to record

Above Technicians assemble four giant Tiros-N satellites in high-bay areas at RCA's plant in Princeton, New Jersey. The circular components on the side of the craft are thermal control pinwheel louvres. The sensing instruments are carried on the platform above the central bus.

Left A Tiros-N high resolution visible image showing the western US states around California, and the Baja California peninsula in Mexico (at the bottom of the picture). Cloud formations can be readily tracked by such polar-orbiting spacecraft.

The Soviet Meteors

The USSR's first fully operational meteorological satellite was Meteor-1. It was launched from Plesetsk on 26 March 1969 into a 393 x 427 miles (633 x 687km) orbit. Its launch weight was listed as 4,850lb (2,200kg), and it was described as having three-axis stabilization by electrically driven, magnetically controlled momentum wheels, which allowed day-and-night precision imaging by television cameras and infra-red scanners.

By the end of 1970, three Meteor satellites were operating in near-polar orbits. Since then, the Soviets have operated the Meteor-1 satellites in pairs or trios at an average altitude of 528 miles (850km) in high inclination (81°) orbits. They are particularly important in monitoring ice conditions in the north polar basin.

Because of their fairly short lifetimes, Meteor satellites have to be replaced often. Soviet listings show that at least 40 were orbited between 1969 and 1982, including eight of the advanced Meteor-2 machines (see below) which are also equipped for sensing Earth resources. The Meteor system was an outgrowth of remote sensing experiments carried out by several classes of spacecraft. In addition to the Cosmos series, some Molniya communication satellites carried cameras as well as communication relay electronics. Since 1977, the USSR has operated its second generation meteorological satellite: Meteor-2. The operational system comprises two or three of these machines at 560 miles (900km) altitude. The Soviets have compared Meteor-2 with the US NOAA satellites and their instruments seem to have analagous capabilities.

The Meteor-2 instruments are a scanning telephotometer for direct image transmission (APT) in visible light; a television-type scanner which stores images made in visible light; a scanning infra-red radiometer that stores infra-red light images; and a scanning, 8-channel infra-red radiometer. The Meteor-2 satellite also carries a solar proton and electron monitor and transmits these data along with atmospheric observations.

Tiros-N Spectral Sensitivity: Right
Tiros-N's Advanced Very High Resolution Radiometer (AVHRR) responds in four channels in the visible and IR parts of the spectrum (**1-4**). AVHRR/2, an advanced version first flown on NOAA-8, added a fifth IR channel (**5**). The Tiros Operational Vertical Sounder (TOVS) comprises: stratospheric subsystem (**6**); tropospheric subsystem (**7**); and microwave subsystem (**8**).

Above To date, the Soviet Union has not orbited a geostationary weather satellite; instead it relies on polar-orbiters such as this Meteor-2, which observes in the visible and IR portions of the spectrum.

temperature and water vapour profiles and total ozone concentration; a data collection system called ARGOS, provided by the French *Centre National d'Études Spatiales* (at no cost to the United States) and the solar environmental monitor which measures solar particle flux near the Earth.

NOAA-8 was the first of three NOAA satellites—it failed while in orbit in July 1984—to carry search and rescue equipment which can receive, locate and track Emergency Locator Transmitters (ELTs) and radio beacons on aircraft and ships in distress. It joined the similarly equipped Soviet satellite, Cosmos 1383, which was launched on 20 June 1982. In addition to the vertical sounder, NOAA-8 carried a stratospheric sounding unit provided by the United Kingdom's Ministry of Defence Meteorological Office. This instrument extends temperature measurements to the stratosphere. In addition, Advanced Tiros-N satellites carry a solar backscatter ultraviolet radiometer for ozone mapping, and Earth radiation budget instruments. The second is due for launch in November 1984; the third is scheduled for March 1985.

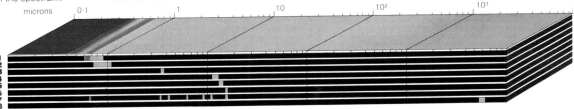

microns   0·1   1   10 10^2 10^3

During the early phase of weather satellite development, NASA experimented with an advanced class of satellites called Nimbus. The programme began with the launch of the 830lb (377kg) Nimbus-1 on 28 August 1964 into a near polar, Sun-synchronous orbit of 575 by 261 miles (926 by 420km) from NASA's Western Test Range near Lompoc, California, adjacent to Vandenberg Air Force Base. In an orbit synchronous with the Sun a remote sensing satellite can view the same areas of the planet under similar lighting conditions. Nimbus carried three improved vidicon cameras, improved automatic picture transmission and a high resolution infra-red radiometer which provided cloud images at night. Day and night imaging represented an advance on the ESSA machines which operated only in daylight.

A main objective of the Nimbus programme was to develop data that could be used to construct a numerical model of the atmosphere for GARP (Global Atmospheric Research Program). Nimbus was a butterfly-shaped satellite 10ft (3·05m) tall and six feet (1·82m) in diameter. Power was supplied by photovoltaic (solar) cells arranged in two paddles that were deployed, wing-like, in orbit and generated about 550 watts. On Nimbus-3, launched on 4 April 1969, NASA experimented with a nuclear isotope power generator (SNAP-19). Instead of using spin-stabilization, like the Tiros-ESSA machines, Nimbus tested three-axis stabilization (by momentum wheels and magnetic torque devices) as a means of enhancing viewing precision, especially of some ground features.

Because of a failure of its solar array drive system, Nimbus-1 operated only for one month, but it succeeded in providing high resolution television and infra-red weather photos. On its first day, it photographed Hurricane Cleo and later took spectacular pictures of Hurricane Dora and Typhoon Ruby. Its ground photos of Antarctica enabled mapmakers to correct the location of Mount Siple, a 10,000ft (3,050m) high Antarctic landmark used by pilots flying across the continental ice sheet. The mountain was then repositioned on maps 45 miles (72km) west of its earlier map location.

Nimbus-2, launched on 15 May 1966, was the first satellite to measure the Earth's heat balance with high and medium resolution infra-red radiometers. Nimbus-4, launched on 8 April 1970, extended soundings of temperature, water vapour and ozone inaugurated by Nimbus-3, and acquired imagery that differentiated between ice and water clouds. Nimbus-5, launched on 11 December 1972, carried an electrically scanning microwave radiometer which made it possible to distinguish ice boundaries for the first time. Nimbus-6, launched on 12 June 1975, carried a data processor which enabled it to transmit directly or to store data on a high-speed tape recorder. This satellite also was equipped with a prototype tracking and data relay system. It was designed to demonstrate how a polar orbiting satellite could send data to an out-of-view ground station via a satellite in geostationary orbit (ATS-6). The experiment was ancestral in the development of NASA's Tracking and Data Relay Satellite System (TDRSS) which is designed to replace most of NASA's ground stations by 1986.

Nimbus-6 was equipped also with a high resolution infra-red radiation sounder. The instrument measured Earth's emitted radiances, reflected solar radiation and global vertical

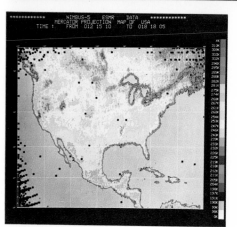

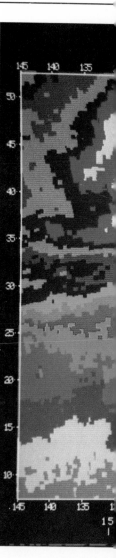

temperature and water vapour profiles to an altitude of 25 miles (40km). In addition, a pressure modulated radiometer obtained temperature data in the upper stratosphere and mesosphere; a scanning microwave spectrometer mapped temperature profiles in the troposphere (the lower atmosphere) along with water vapour and the water content of clouds; a temperature-humidity infra-red radiometer measured heat radiated from the surface day and night, and a Tropical Wind, Energy Conversion and Reference Level, known as "Twerle", monitored data from balloon-borne sensors.

Nimbus-7 and TOMS

The Nimbus prime contractor was the General Electric Company, and it produced, as the last of the series, a highly versatile satellite in remote sensing technology—Nimbus-7. This advanced machine was launched on 24 October 1978 into a 586 by 592 miles (943 by 953km) polar orbit, carrying in addition to the earlier Nimbus instruments a mesosphere-stratosphere sounder, a stratospheric aerosol counter, a total ozone mapping spectrometer and a coastal zone colour scanner. It was the first satellite to show a variation in the totality of solar radiation reaching the top of the atmosphere — the so-called solar constant.

Nimbus-7's total ozone mapping spectrometer (TOMS) made the first comprehensive measurements of ozone concentration and distribution in the upper atmosphere. The data enabled scientists at the Goddard Space Flight Center to construct false colour images of the planet's ozone field. Black and red represented

Above The TOMS experiment on Nimbus-7 was designed to measure and map the vertical and global distribution of atmospheric ozone; this image is a total ozone map of the North Pole.

Left A map of the United States derived from Nimbus-5's electrically scanning microwave radiometer data. In the false colour representation, green denotes soil moisture, yellow and brown higher surface temperatures, and dark blue partial ice cover.

low ozone values and blue and white, high concentrations. Yellow and green indicated medium concentrations. Applied to a Mercator map of the Earth, the colour code showed low values throughout the tropics, an abrupt increase at mid-latitudes in the southern hemisphere and patchy ozone highs and lows in the northern hemisphere. The tropics showed a general rise in ozone over the Atlantic Ocean and Africa.

Lowest ozone concentrations are not at the equator as supposed but rather over the central United States, Western Europe and the Western Pacific Ocean off the coast of China. The highest amounts of ozone were shown in the South Atlantic and south of Australia, but the major high ozone region appears from Nimbus-7 data to be centred near the South Pole. The northern hemisphere chart shows an ozone ridge aligned northeast and southwest across central California. Another high ozone concentration region stretches from Hudson Bay across Maine into the western Atlantic Ocean. Because it screens the Earth's surface from lethal ultraviolet radiation, ozone plays a critical role as an environmental safeguard. Some extinctions of life forms in the geologic record have been attributed to sudden catastrophic ozone depletion. Modern pollutants that create a similar depletion as they spread through the atmosphere have been identified as public health hazards.

Nimbus-7's ozone mapping spectrometer also measured the abundance of sulphur dioxide in the gas cloud emitted by eruptions of the El Chichon volcano in Mexico in March and

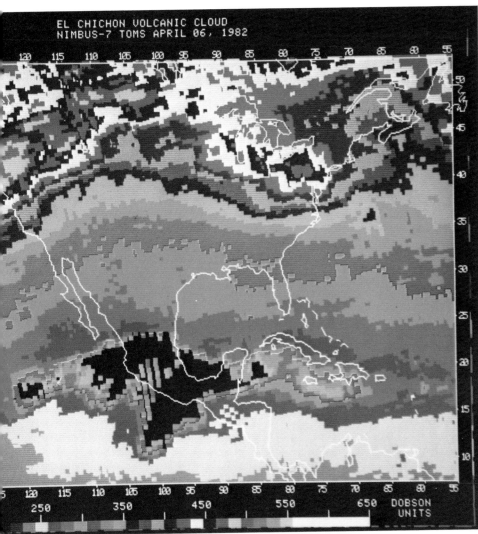

EL CHICHON VOLCANIC CLOUD
NIMBUS-7 TOMS APRIL 06, 1982

DOBSON UNITS

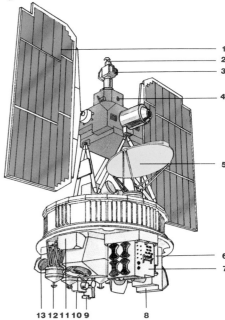

Nimbus-7
1 Solar array.
2 S-band antenna.
3 Digital Sun sensor.
4 Attitude control subsystem.
5 Scanning multichannel microwave radiometer.
6 Stratospheric aerosol counter.
7 Earth radiation budget experiment.
8 Coastal zone colour scanner.
9 Solar backscatter UV radiometer.
10 Total ozone mapping spectrometer.
11 Stratospheric and mesospheric sounder.

12 S-band antenna.
13 Temperature-humidity infra-red radiometer.

The family of Nimbus satellites have played a major role in providing data from which a systematic body of knowledge concerning the atmosphere has been built up. Nimbus-7, the most advanced of the series, was launched in 1978. As well as returning data on global weather patterns, it can track oil spills, monitor air pollution, and locate areas with good fishing potential.

Above The vast gas cloud emanating from the eruption of El Chichon volcano in Mexico in March 1982 is clearly visible in this TOMS image. Satellites are invaluable when it comes to monitoring the effects of such phenomena. **Below** The total ozone pattern over North America as recorded by Nimbus-7's TOMS in March 1979. The white diagonal bar marks the path of a jet stream; the yellow/tan oval in the western states is a tropospheric ridge.

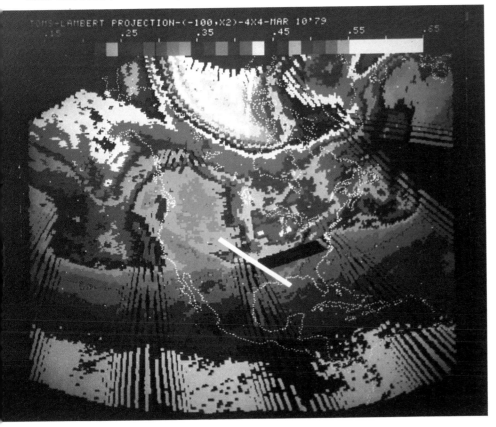

TOMS-LAMBERT PROJECTION-(-100,X2)-4X4-MAR 10'79

April 1982. The satellite was able to observe the entire cloud which within a few days of the April eruptions covered an area of a million square miles. Measurements by the TOMS instrument showed that the cloud contained 3·3 million tons of sulphur dioxide—less than many scientists expected, according to the Goddard Space Flight Center. The sulphur dioxide forms sulphuric acid droplets in the high atmosphere and reflects sunshine away from the Earth, a process generally believed to create cooling of global climate. Goddard reported that the cloud which floated 16 miles (26km) above the ground was tracked by Nimbus-7 for 10 days before drifting out of continuous tracking range.

Using first generation Meteor satellites, the USSR set up an experimental meteorological satellite programme in which advanced imaging instruments were tested. It was somewhat analogous to NASA's Nimbus programme. Called Meteor-Priroda, it evaluated two channel and four channel multi-spectral television systems (MRTVK). The Meteor-Priroda satellites were launched into near-polar, Sun-synchronous orbits of 404 miles (650km) altitude. Their television systems were designed to capture a field of view ranging from 745 to 1,180 miles (1,200 to 1,900km) with a resolution ranging from 0·62 to 0·18 miles (1-0·3km).

Data from these and from similarly equipped Meteor-2 machines were transmitted for processing and analysis to acquisition centres of the USSR State Committee for Hydrometeorology and Control of the Natural Environment in Moscow, Novosibirsk and Khabarovsk.

Left 10 November 1967, ATS-3, in geostationary orbit over Brazil, returns the first colour image of the Earth disc. The ability of such satellites to reveal large scale weather patterns is dramatically shown — a cold front stretches over the central USA, while a tropical storm extends into Argentina.

SMS/GOES Coverage The typical arcs of coverage of the data collection instruments of a weather satellite situated in geostationary orbit at 100° west longitude are shown in this diagram. The largest ellipse shows the total area — approximately a 20° window of azimuth and elevation — that is imaged by the spacecraft's visible and infra-red spin-scan radiometer. The inner ellipses show areas within which wind vectors can be measured: the smaller the area, the more accurate the assessment of wind speed, from 10 knots within the outer ring to 5 knots in the smallest zone delineated.

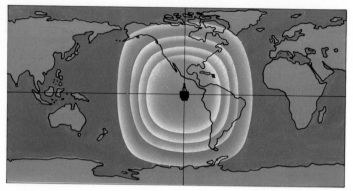

In order to meet the national objective of providing continuous viewing of large-scale, changing weather patterns, in 1965 NASA began to develop a new class of remote sensing satellites. They were designed to hover in longitude over one point on the Earth's surface by circling the globe in geostationary orbit 22,300 miles (35,800km) above the equator. This region of near-Earth space was to become well populated with communications relay satellites; by mid-1960s, the remote sensing machines were headed there.

The forerunner of the geostationary meteorological satellites was a series of experimental applications technology vehicles which NASA conceived as multiple test beds for communications and remote sensing of weather and ground features. Goddard Space Flight Center managed the programme.

The first of these machines, ATS-1, was launched into geostationary orbit from Cape Canaveral on 7 December 1966. Its mass in orbit was 775lb (352kg). It was stationed at 150° west longitude, over Hawaii. From its perch, the spin-scan cloud camera it carried managed to take the first picture covering nearly all of the Earth's disc on 9 December 1966. The ATS prime contractor was Fairchild Industries.

Satellites in this series steadily grew in complexity and mass. ATS-5, launched on 12 August 1969, had a launch weight of 950lb (431kg), while Fairchild's ATS-6, the last, largest and most complex of the series, had an on-orbit mass of 2,050lb (930kg). It was launched to geostationary orbit on 30 May 1974 by Titan-IIIC, the largest rocket in NASA's expendable launch vehicle inventory.

ATS-1 and -5 were the precursors of the geosynchronous meteorological satellites. ATS-5 had a primary mission of testing a theory that satellites in geostationary orbit could be stabilized by gravity gradient, a technique, first tried in 1966 with Gemini-11, of aligning the long axis of a satellite with the centre of the Earth. On ATS-5, as on Gemini-11, attempts to stabilize a satellite in this way were not successful, although theory predicted that they should be. As a result, geostationary satellites subsequently developed for remote sensing were either spin-stabilized or controlled in

attitude by momentum wheels, magnetic torque and/or thrusters.

ATS-6 was one of the most diversified experimental spacecraft in history. Its primary mission was the testing of a large, high-gain, steerable antenna which could be erected in orbit and provide good quality television to simple ground receivers. This versatile machine also demonstrated visual and infra-red mapping imagery, remote sensing with radiometric instruments, a laser communications system and techniques of relaying data from weather and scientific satellites to ground terminals. ATS-6 was stabilised and manoeuvred in orbit by a hydrazine and ammonia thruster system.

SMS and GOES

Based in part on ATS technology, a new generation of Geostationary Operational Environmental Satellites (GOES) was then developed by the Goddard Space Flight Center. Ford Aerospace and the Hughes Aircraft Company were prime contractors. Ford built two prototypes, Synchronous Météorological Satellites (SMS)-1 and -2. They were launched from Cape Canaveral on 17 May 1974 and 6 February 1975 and boosted into geostationary orbit. SMS-1 was stationed over the equator at 75° west longitude and SMS-2 at 135° west. From

Left ATS-3 at Cape Canaveral just before installation into its payload fairing. The large opening in the lower cylinder is the aperture leading to the mirror of the spin-scan cloud camera; the rods at the top of the spacecraft are VHF whip antennas.

Below GOES-1 monitors climatic conditions in Florida during a February 1977 freeze that menaced the citrus and vegetable crops. The colour code (black, yellow, light blue, pink, dark blue, orange) relates to ground temperatures expressed in degrees Fahrenheit.

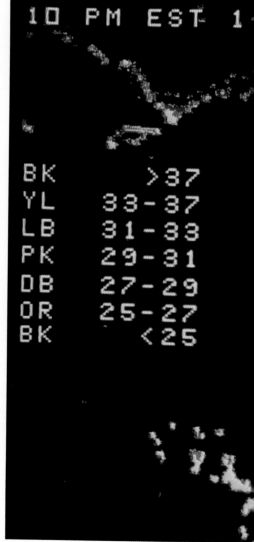

10 PM EST	
BK	>37
YL	33-37
LB	31-33
PK	29-31
DB	27-29
OR	25-27
BK	<25

these perches, they viewed the entire western hemisphere, excluding the polar regions.

The SMS machines were drum-shaped, 7·55ft (2·3m) long and 6·23ft (1·9m) in diameter, with a mass on orbit of 536lb (243kg). They comprised the first two-satellite system for continuous viewing of weather patterns over the United States and Canada and adjacent waters. They soon were supplanted by nearly identical but somewhat larger operational machines, the GOES series. GOES-1 and GOES-2 were launched from Cape Canaveral on 16 October 1975 and 16 June 1977 respectively, followed by GOES-3 on 16 June 1978.

The two SMS and first three GOES vehicles viewed the clouds through a pair of telescopes in an imaging unit called the Visible/Infra-red Spin-Scan Radiometer (VISSR). One telescope collected visible light and the other, infra-red light for night scenes. Visible light images—relayed to photomultiplier tube detectors through optical fibres—were recorded with a resolution of 0·6 miles (0·9km), and infra-red imagery—relayed to detectors by infra-red relay optics—at 4·3 miles (6·9km). The telescopes scanned a small strip of the Earth scene as the satellite spun at 100 revolutions a minute. Approximately 1,800 strips, acquired by 1,800 revolutions of the machine, made up a full scene. The scenes were converted to electronic data and formed images when transmitted to Earth in the same manner as a television signal does when transmitted to a receiver. The GOES machines photographed a complete disc of the Earth and transmitted the data every 30 minutes.

In addition to this imaging system, GOES-1, -2 and -3 carried a space environment monitor (SEM) consisting of a solar X-ray telescope, magnetometer and energetic particle sensors, and a data collection and transmission radio capable of picking up signals and relaying them to ground stations from 10,000 remote meteorological platforms every six hours. The GOES series not only observed weather on the Earth, but also weather on the Sun and the effect of solar storms on the atmosphere.

Temperature and moisture measurement
The first three GOES satellites were built by Ford. They were succeeded by three advanced machines built by Hughes: GOES-4, launched on 9 September 1980; GOES-5, launched on 22 May 1981 and GOES-6, launched on 28 April 1983. These satellites were 11·9ft (3·62m) high and 7·05ft (2·15m) in diameter. GOES-5 failed in orbit on 29 July 1984. The advanced GOES carried the imaging systems of the earlier series but added to it atmospheric sounding instruments. The combination (called Visible/Infra-red Spin-Scan Radiometer—Atmospheric Sounding System or VAS for short) added a third dimension to cloud imagery by measuring temperature and moisture at various altitudes. From these profiles, a three dimensional representation of cloud distribution could be constructed for forecast centres.

As of November 1984, two GOES machines were keeping watch over the western hemisphere, GOES-2 at 113° west longitude and GOES-6 at 108° west. They are controlled and operated from NASA's Wallops Island, Virginia station which is in sight of both of them. (The geostationary weather satellites of other nations are described on the following spread.) Each GOES transmits to a dedicated ground antenna at the station. The data are processed in a computer where information on the geographic location of the data are added. The total information is then transmitted back to the satellite at a slowed transmission rate, producing a mode called "stretched data". The stretched or processed data are then transmitted from the satellite once more to the ground, this time to a 26ft (8m) antenna mounted on the roof of the GOES data processing center at Suitland, Maryland.

There, the data are divided into two streams. One is stored in weather archives. The other is transmitted by microwave to the World Weather Building (of the Department of Commerce) at Camp Springs, Maryland. From there, the data stream is converted to a facsimile format and distributed by telephone lines to field service stations in Washington DC, Miami, Slidell (Louisiana), Kansas City, San Francisco, Anchorage (Alaska) and Honolulu.

At the field stations, data representing weather conditions at specific places are copied on a video disc system. Successive cloud images are melded together on the disc to form images of moving clouds when the disc is rapidly sequenced. The "movie" shows the dynamics of the atmosphere at a particular time of the day at a particular geographic location. It is a widely used display on television news shows.

Right A GOES-2 VISSR enhanced infra-red image shows severe storms moving inland from the Gulf of Mexico.

Below The eye of Hurricane David straddles the coast of Florida north of Miami in September 1979. The course of this hurricane was tracked by SMS-2, and data from this satellite were the prime means of giving advance storm warning and so saving many lives through prompt evacuation.

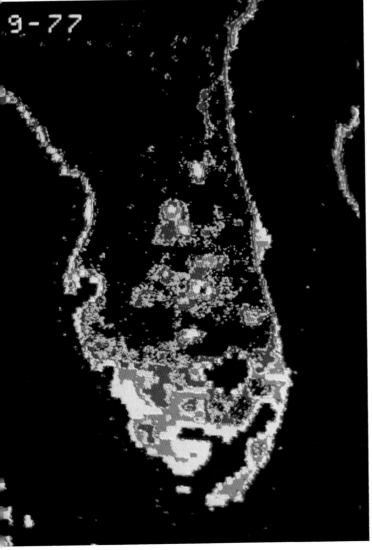

With two GOES observatories covering the western hemisphere, an equatorial ring of geostationary meteorological satellites has been completed by the European Space Agency Meteosat-1 and -2 hovering off the west coast of Africa, India's multi-purpose meteorological and communications satellite, Insat-1B, at 74° east longitude over the Indian Ocean south of Cape Comorin, and Japan's GMS-1 and -2 (Himawari) at 140° east longitude over the western Pacific Ocean. The Soviet Union has planned a geostationary weather satellite called GOMS (Geostationary Orbit Meteorological Satellite) at 60° east, but had not launched it as of July 1984.

Meteosat is a drum-shaped machine with the horn-shaped sunshade protecting the imaging radiometer that is characteristic of all these satellites. Meteosat consists of two cylinders, the smaller sited above the larger. Its overall height is 10·5ft (3·2m) and its maximum

diameter, 6·9ft (2·1m). In orbit, its mass is about 661lb (300kg). Power is supplied by photovoltaic cells covering the surface of the larger cylinder except for the aperture for the telescope and mirrors of the imaging radiometer. The upper cylinder carries transmitting and receiving electronics. Like GOES, Meteosat is spin-stabilized at 100 revolutions a minute, so that images, in visible and infra-red light, are built up of scans—5,000 lines for the visible and 2,500 for the infra-red. Image resolution is 1·55 miles (2·5km) in visible light and 3·1 miles (5km) in infra-red.

Meteosat-1 was launched on 23 November 1977 by a Delta rocket from Cape Canaveral, and Meteosat-2 on 19 June 1981 by the ESA launcher, Ariane, from Kourou, French Guiana. Meteosat-1 was stationed at 10° east longitude in early 1984, providing data on sea surface temperature, wind velocity, water vapour distribution and atmospheric radiation balance,

while Meteosat-2 was at 0° longitude over the Gulf of Guinea providing cloud images as well as temperature and humidity data. Meteosat imagery is displayed on European television channels in much the same way as GOES imagery is shown on American television. Both machines were built by the European COSMOS consortium, for which France's Aérospatiale was prime contractor. Both are equipped with systems for collecting and relaying data from remote weather stations. All Meteosat data are processed by the European Space Operations Centre at Darmstadt, West Germany. Processed data are transmitted back to the satellite which retransmits them to ESA ground stations for distribution.

Insat enters service

The ring of geostationary weather satellites around the Earth was closed on 31 August 1983 when India's multi-purpose weather and com-

Meteosat's Imaging Radiometer

1 Folding mirror 2.
2 Primary mirror.
3 Secondary mirror.
4 Folding mirror 1.
5 Folding mirror 4.
6 Refocusing mirrors 3 and 3'.
7 VIS detectors.
8 Cooled IR detectors.
9 Optical cone.
10 Separation mirror.

The principal instrument on Meteosat, this scanning radiometer provides basic data as visible, infra-red and water vapour radiances from which images can be generated simultaneously in three spectral channels. It comprises a Ritchey-Chretien 400mm telescope, focusing mirrors, scanning mechanisms, and electronic detectors distributed across the telescope's focal plane.

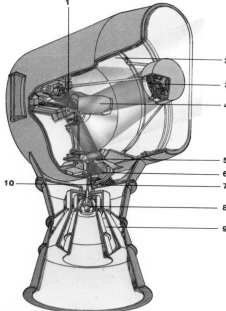

Left Insat-1B, with its Payload Assist Module boost motor attached, rises gently past Space Shuttle *Challenger's* rudder on 31 August 1983 on its way to geostationary orbit. This unique craft combines telecommunications, TV broadcasting and meteorological services in one satellite.

Right As this VISSR infra-red image reveals, from a vantage point of 140° east longitude GMS-1's scanning camera views all of the Far East, Australia and New Zealand, and even a substantial part of India. Japan's GMS satellites also serve as repeater stations for the collection and distribution of weather data, and monitor solar particles impinging on the Earth's atmosphere.

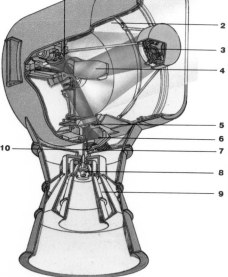

Left From its lofty viewpoint 22,300 miles (35,800km) above the Gulf of Guinea, this is how Meteosat-2 sees the world in its visible light spectral band. Such a scan consists of 5,000 lines of data, and takes 25 minutes to generate.

Right In contrast to the picture left, this is an example of a Meteosat colour-enhanced infra-red image. IR data can be used to determine sea surface temperatures and marine thermal gradients in cloud-free regions of the globe.

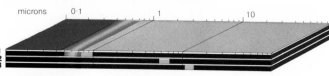

Meteosat Radiometer Waveband Coverage

Meteosat's radiometer is responsive in the three spectral bands shown here. The visible channel (**1**) extends from 0·5 to 1·0μm; the water vapour

absorption channel (**2**) from 5·7 to 7·1μm; and the thermal infra-red (**3**) from 10·5 to 12·5μm. The two detectors in the visible channel are special purpose photodiodes, while the infra-red

detectors (which must be cooled to less than −178°C to function properly) are made of mercury-cadmium-telluride. Each of the three infra-red detectors is 70μm square.

munications satellite, Insat-1B, was deployed by the Space Shuttle *Challenger* in low Earth orbit and boosted from there by upper stage into geostationary orbit. It was established on station at 74° east longitude. Insat is the second machine of its type. An earlier one, Insat-1A, was launched on 8 April 1982 by a Delta rocket, but was shut down when its attitude control system failed.

In addition to providing voice and video transmissions to India's thousands of rural communities as well as to large cities, Insat's Very High Resolution Radiometer photographs a complete disc of the Earth every 30 minutes. Insat collects information from 110 weather stations, processes and relays it to forecast centres throughout the subcontinent and provides early warning of tropical cyclones for much of southeast Asia.

The satellite was built by Ford Aerospace's Western Development Laboratories Division and has a unique feature to stabilize it—a solar sail. The sail is a parasol-like structure at the end of a 64ft (19·5m) boom which was extended when the satellite reached orbit. The sail was designed to balance the pressure of sunlight on the large solar cell array, and was deployed on the opposite side of the main bus. Insat's main body is a box, 7·15 x 5·08 x 4·66ft (2·18 x 1·55 x 1·42m). Its launch weight was 2,385lb (1,082kg).

Japanese spacecraft

Japan's geostationary meteorological satellites, GMS-1 and -2, are about the same size as GOES and similar in basic design. GMS-1, the smaller of the two geostationary meteorological satellites, has the typical drum configuration and horn sunshade. It is 7·08ft (2·16m) in diameter and 8·85ft high (2·7m), with an on-orbit mass of 670lb (304kg). Hughes built them under contract to the Nippon Electric Company, prime contractor to the National Space Develop-

ment Agency of Japan. GMS-1 was launched from Cape Canaveral by a Delta rocket on 14 July 1977 and inserted into geostationary orbit at 140° east longitude where it could observe weather over one third of the planet. Its range included Japan, Korea, Taiwan, the Philippines, Australia, New Zealand, Indonesia, Malaysia, Vietnam, Thailand, Burma, Laos, Tibet, China and part of Mongolia. The satellite carried the Hughes-developed Visible/Infra-red Spin-Scan Radiometer (VISSR) and acquired full disc images every 30 minutes. It also mounted the space environment monitor to watch the Sun.

GMS-2, also 7·08ft (2·16m) in diameter, but 9·84ft (3m) tall, was launched on 10 August 1981 from Japan's Tanegashima Space Center by a Japanese N-II rocket, a Delta-type launcher. It carries the same imaging system and related sensing instruments as its predecessor. GMS-3 is currently under development, and is scheduled to be launched in summer 1984.

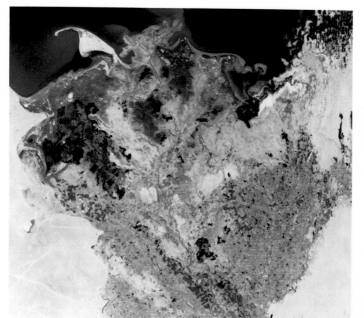

Left The southern part of the Aral Sea, a huge saline lake in Uzbekistan, was photographed by Landsat-1's MSS in May 1973. The scene is dominated by the fertile delta of the heavily sedimented Amu Dar'ya.

Right A Landsat-1 MSS colour composite of the San Francisco, Oakland, San Jose area in California. Compare the image clarity with that achieved by Landsat-4's TM viewing the same scene in 1982 (far right).

Below Landsat-3's MSS is inspected at Hughes' plant in El Segundo, California. The technician in the foreground is examining the aperture which houses the 13in (33cm) oscillating scan mirror and telescope optics.

The technique of remote sensing, developed for the meteorological satellites in the 1960s, was extended in the 1970s to allow surveys of the Earth's surface to be made from space, which would help man to monitor the resources of the planet. Not only would the gross physical characteristics of the surface provide geological information but the chemical assemblages of the surface rocks could be identified by the wavelengths of energy they reflected as clues to hidden wealth in the ground.

Radiometric scans of the Moon by Apollo-15 and -16 missions had revealed unsuspected concentrations of industrial metals. It was probable that terrestrial mineral, oil and gas deposits could be located from orbit by sensing geological structures that are commonly associated with the deposits.

Under the direction of NASA's Goddard Space Flight Center, a series of polar orbiting satellites designed to produce images of the Earth's surface in vivid detail was developed by the General Electric Company. The first was Earth Resources Technology Satellite-1 (ERTS-1). It was launched into a 559 x 567 miles (899 x 912km) orbit from the Western Test Range on 23 July 1972. It carried a Return Beam Vidicon system consisting of three cameras which each sensed a different spectral band between 0·48 and 0·83 micrometres, and a multi-spectral scanner (MSS), a line-scanning radiometer that sensed reflected solar energy in four spectral bands from 0·5 to 1·1 micrometres.

Although designed to operate for only one year, ERTS-1, renamed Landsat-1, proved remarkably durable and kept working for five and a half years until it was turned off on 6 January 1978. The video system had failed, but the MSS produced such high grade imagery that the camera was not missed, and later in the series this sort of video imaging was dropped from the spacecraft's mission. Landsat-2 was launched on 22 January 1975 and Landsat-3 on 5 March 1978. Each weighed 2,100lb (953kg) in orbit and was 10ft (3·05m) high and 13ft (3·96m) in width with photovoltaic cell solar panels extended. Landsat-3's Return Beam Vidicon system was different—it used two panchromatic cameras that produced side-by-side images—while the MSS was modified to include a fifth spectral band in the thermal infra-red region.

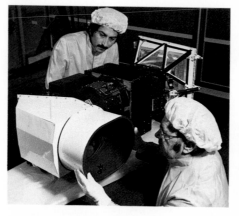

The Multi-spectral Scanner

The MSS produced images in which it was possible to distinguish features that were not readily distinguishable at vidicon camera resolution. The MSS sensed reflected sunlight in green, red and two infra-red bands. These wavelengths characteristically were reflected by certain features, such as forests, fields of grain, urban areas, open-pit coal mines, scrub timber. MSS imagery was processed and presented as a photograph with false colours used to distinguish features reflecting infra-red light. The false colour mosaics resembled non-representational art forms, but became clearly representational when interpreted. The system was effective in showing changes in the spectral pattern due to blight, pollution, water or frost.

The first Landsats were succeeded by an improved machine, Landsat-4. At launch, 16 July 1982, it weighed two metric tons (4,409lb) and was injected into a 483 miles (705km) polar orbit from the Western Test Range by a thrust-augmented Delta 3920 rocket. The orbit was planned to be low enough to be within reach of a Space Shuttle mission in the event that Landsat-4 should have to be retrieved for repair. Such a repair became necessary in 1983 when a transponder relaying imagery from the Thematic Mapper to the ground failed, and problems with the solar cell, power generating system also became apparent. However, in order to retrieve Landsat-4, a Shuttle would have to be launched from Vandenberg Air Force Base into polar orbit. Shuttle launch facilities at Vandenberg are not expected to be ready before 1985.

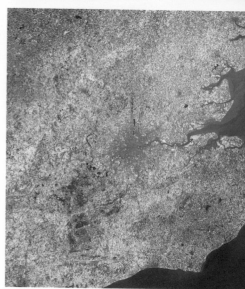

The new Thematic Mapper

Landsat-4 produced images of 115 mile (185km) wide swaths of the Earth's surface which it orbited 14·5 times a day. It imaged the entire Earth, except for the poles, every 16 days, when the cycle repeated. In addition to the MSS, it carried a more powerful radiometer, the Thematic Mapper (TM). This device read the surface in seven bands of the spectrum with an improved resolution of 98ft (30m). It was able to show more detail than the MSS with higher resolution.

Landsat-4 transmits image data to NASA ground stations in Fairbanks, Alaska, and Goldstone, California. The data are relayed to Goddard via an RCA communications satellite and distributed worldwide. Landsat-4 was the first NASA spacecraft to carry a Global Positioning System to receive signals defining its absolute position in three dimensions from US Department of Defense navigation (NAVSTAR) satellites. The system calculates Landsat-4's position in latitude, longitude and

Left London and the southern part of England came in view of Landsat-2's MSS on 29 July 1975. Bands 4,5 and 7 have been processed to show vegetation as red, and urban features as blue. Heathrow Airport is visible (middle left).

Right San Francisco again: this time the image is composed from spectral bands 3, 4 and 7 of Landsat-4's Thematic Mapper, operating at 438 miles (705km) altitude. Ground resolution shows a marked improvement: note the Golden Gate Bridge (upper left), the tiny island of Alcatraz to its right, and San Francisco Airport (middle left).

altitude every 6 seconds at a precise time. These data are transmitted to ground stations with imaging data.

With the enhanced sensitivity of the TM, analysts can distinguish among crops such as corn, wheat, rye, soybeans, tobacco, and observe their health. Blight would show up instantly because it alters reflected radiation. The satellite monitors renewable resources, such as food and fibre crops, soils, forests and rangelands and such features as volcanoes, geologic structures, and its orbit responds to variations in the Earth's gravitational field. It provides data on the expansion and decline of urban areas, the spread of blight and of insect swarms, the onset of floods and forest fires, coastal zone erosion and the effects of large oil spills in the ocean. It monitors the movements of herds of animals, the effects of earthquakes, and tracks massive icebergs breaking off the ice shelves of West Antarctica.

Detailed geologic mapping can be performed by the Thematic Mapper, but because of the

Thematic Mapper
This instrument, developed at the Santa Barbara Research Center of Hughes Aircraft Co, is an object-space line scanner that collects radiometric data in seven spectral bands. It uses a scan mirror and a Ritchey-Chretien type telescope to focus reflected light and thermal energy directly onto the prime focal plane assembly, and via a set of relay mirrors onto the cooled focal plane assembly. The prime focal plane assembly has four sets of 16 silicon detectors and registers TM bands 1-4. The cooled array consists of two sets of 16 monolithic indium antimonide detectors (bands 5 and 7), and 4 mercury-cadmium-telluride detectors (band 6).

1 Thermal control louvres.
2 Relay optics assembly.
3 Electronics module.
4 Calibration shutter.
5 Central baffle.
6 Scan mirror.
7 Secondary mirror.
8 Primary mirror.
9 Alignment and focus mechanisms.
10 Radiative cooler.
11 Earth shield.

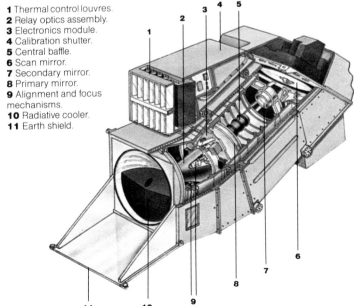

transponder failure, the instrument cannot now communicate with NASA's ground stations. However, it does transmit TM data at a frequency that the new Tracking and Data Relay Satellites (TDRS) can receive (via Ku-band) and relay to a ground station at White Sands, New Mexico. By mid-1983, the first of these new relay satellites, TDRS-1, was established in geostationary orbit and began to receive Thematic Mapper Ku-band transmissions from Landsat-4.

However, a partial power failure caused by the loss of two of the satellite's four solar cell panels threatened to extinguish all transmissions from Landsat-4. NASA moved quickly to launch its back-up satellite, Landsat-5, on 1 March 1984 into a nearly circular, 510 miles (820km) near-polar orbit from Vandenberg Air Force Base, California.

Landsat-5's instruments

The new, fifth Landsat carries multi-spectral scanner and thematic mapper sensing instruments similar to those of Landsat-4. Both were reported to be in working order on 6 April. MSS data are transmitted directly to ground stations in the United States and other countries by S-band, as on Landsat-4. However, Landsat-5 thematic mapper imagery can be sent directly to ground stations on the X-band transmission system which had failed on Landsat-4. These images could also be sent by Ku-band through TDRS-1 to the ground station at White Sands, for relay to and processing at Goddard.

The main advantage of the thematic mapper (TM) is its ability to sense electromagnetic radiation in narrower visible and near infra-red bands of the spectrum than the MSS and other types of multi-spectral scanning devices. In addition to near infra-red, the TM perceives bands in the middle and thermal infra-red regions. The narrower visible (0·52-0·60 microns) and near infra-red (0·76 and 0·90 microns) bands allow more exact measurements of increased reflectance from green vegetation. Variable reflectances indicate water content and general health. A narrower near infra-red band reduces the masking effect of absorption due to atmospheric water vapour and a narrower red band (0·63-0·69 microns) makes possible better chlorophyll measurements.

A new band measuring reflected sunlight in the blue-green (0·45-0·52 microns) allows more accurate observation of marine phytoplankton (sea plant life), based on chlorophyll absorption, and observations to greater depths. This band produces images in natural rather than false colour. New middle infra-red bands (1·55-1·75 and 2·08-2·35 microns) will improve vegetation sensing by assessing leaf water volume.

The middle infra-red portion of the spectrum indicates absorption by snow. This band is expected to be useful in distinguishing clouds from snow cover, a persistent remote sensing problem. The TM also senses in a thermal infra-red band (10·4-12·5 microns), a band useful in mineral and petroleum prospecting.

Landsat-5's multi-spectral scanner is the same as that on Landsat-4. It senses light in four bands of the visible and near infra-red portions of the spectrum. Scanning along the satellite's ground track is produced by the satellite's orbital motion (4·23 miles or 6·81km a second). The instantaneous field of view (resolution)—262ft (80m) of the MSS and 98·4ft (30m) of the TM—is located geographically by data provided by the satellite's Global Positioning System.

Above TM image of the Mississippi Delta where the river flows into the Gulf of Mexico near New Orleans. The mass of sediment evident in the water around the river mouth vividly illustrates the process of delta formation.

Below This infra-red TM picture of the region around Medicine Hat, Alberta graphically reveals the plains topography around the South Saskatchewan river. Cultivated fields are red; barren fields are green.

Right Landsat-4 registered this image of Keeweenaw Peninsula in northern Michigan on 30 September 1982. The folded terrain of this copper-rich area jutting into Lake Superior is clearly shown in this false-colour composite.

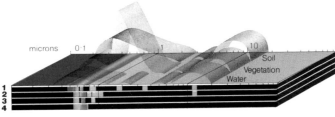

Spectral Responses
1 Thematic Mapper: responsive in 7 bands in the visible and IR region.
2 Landsat MSS: responsive in 4 bands in the visible and near IR wavelengths. Landsat-3's MSS also senses in a fifth thermal IR band.

3 SPOT HRV: three CCD arrays operate in narrow visible and IR bands.
4 SPOT HRV: one CCD array makes a panchromatic wide-band image. Grey curves show the wavelengths at which water, vegetation and soil exhibit peak response.

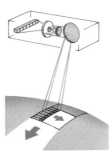

"Push-Broom" Scanner/MSS
The diagram above shows how SPOT's HRV imaging system differs from the conventional line-scanning MSS carried by the Landsats (below). A wide-field optical system forms a simultaneous image of all the points along a line of the ground track, and this is sensed by a row of photosensitive elements called charge coupled devices. SPOT's plane mirror can be angled to allow 475km off-track viewing.

Other nations join in

Earth observation satellites of the order of Landsat-4 are being developed by France, the European Space Agency and Japan. The French machine, called SPOT, has a main bus 6·56ft (2m) wide and 11·5ft (3·5m) long, from which projects a 51·2ft (15·6m) long solar array. It will carry two identical High Resolution Visible (HRV) imaging systems, each responsive in the visible and near infra-red wavelengths. Ground resolution is to be 65·6ft (20m) in the three spectral bands, and 32·8ft (10m) in the panchromatic mode, and the use of the two HRVs will allow the possibility of taking stereoscopic photographs and so reconstructing relief of land areas overflown. This machine is to be launched into a 522 miles (840km) near-polar orbit by Ariane booster in 1985. It will offer services in oil and mineral exploration, topographic surveys and land use, crop surveillance and environmental monitoring to governments and private enterprise. The prime contractor is Matra. On-orbit weight is said to be 3,858lb (1,750kg).

Japan is building a Marine Observation Satellite (MOS-1) for ocean observation which will be based on a smaller bus, 4·1 by 6·56ft (1·25 by 2m), with a total weight of 1,653lb (750kg). Its imaging system is an advanced Multi-spectral Electronic Self-Scanning Radiometer (MESSR) operating in four spectral bands, supplemented by a Visible and Thermal Infra-red Radiometer (VTIR) and a Microwave Scanning Radiometer (MSR). It is to be launched into a near polar orbit at 565 miles (909km).

ESA's Earth observation satellite, ERS-1, was approved by member states in 1982. It is being manufactured by an industrial consortium led by Dornier GmbH of West Germany. Launch is scheduled for 1987. The spacecraft will employ a bus similar to that developed for the French SPOT and a similar solar power array. It is to be launched by Ariane from Kourou into a 483 miles (777km) orbit. It will carry an array of active microwave instruments, including a synthetic aperture radar (SAR) which is being designed to generate 3 x 3 miles (5 x 5km) scenes in a swath 49 miles (80km) wide. Other sensing instruments are a wind scatterometer designed to measure wind velocity to an accuracy of 6·5ft (2m) a second and wind direction with an accuracy of 20 degrees; and a radar altimeter calibrated to measure significant wave height, the height of sea and grounded ice, and major ocean currents.

According to ESA reports, the main objectives of ERS-1 are to observe surface winds and wave structure over the oceans with the scatterometer and altimeter. The SAR is to be used to acquire images of the ocean surface and ocean wave fields. Additionally, the report states, land objectives will be addressed using the SAR. ERS-1 will be equipped with an along-track radiometer to sense sea surface temperature; a laser reflector system to back up the altimeter, and a precise range and range-rate experiment to provide back-up tracking and altimetry data. The ocean data are expected to contribute to weather research and forecasting.

Below Several simulations of SPOT imagery have been produced by CNES. This one shows farming areas on the Lauragais plain near Toulouse. Vegetation is mapped in red and orange; bare soil in blue and green. Though small the fields are mappable.

Above An impression of ESA's ERS-1 as it will look in orbit after launch in 1986. The long array is the synthetic aperture radar antenna, while the circular dish is the radar altimeter, accurate to 3·9in (10cm) over the oceans.

Synthetic Aperture Radar

Seasat's SAR worked by employing a side-looking planar antenna to radiate microwave signals and sense returned radar echoes across a 62 mile (100km) wide ground swath, much as an optical lens collects light. As the satellite was moving during this process, the radar "lens" was effectively elongated by the along-track motion— hence the term "synthetic aperture". From the radar echoes a high resolution image could be generated. A similar radar experiment, SIR-A, was flown aboard the Space Shuttle in 1981 with spectacular results (see pages 52-3).

The oceanic counterpart of NASA's Landsat was Seasat, a remote sensing machine designed primarily to observe the oceans. Its development was managed by the Jet Propulsion Laboratory. The satellite was constructed by the Lockheed Missiles & Space Company. It was launched into a 482 x 500 miles (776 x 800km) polar orbit from the Western Test Range on 27 June 1978. Its weight, 5,070lb (2,300kg), required an Atlas F-Agena launch vehicle. The main bus of this unusual satellite was the Agena stage (of the launch vehicle) and, with a module containing the remote sensing equipment, it was 40ft (12·2m) long and 4·92ft (1·5m) in diameter. In orbit, it resembled a pencil standing on end.

Seasat was the first satellite to carry an experimental radar imaging system called Synthetic Aperture Radar (SAR). This was an imaging system that photographed the surface in microwaves (the radio portion of the spectrum) instead of light. Although Seasat transmitted for only 100 days before it was silenced by a short circuit in the electrical system, the SAR image quality was impressive. It indicated that radar imaging would lead to a genuine breakthrough in the technology of remote sensing.

SAR creates its own illumination and thus is as effective an imaging system at night as during daylight. Moreover, the microwaves penetrate clouds so that overcast skies are no barrier to landscape pictures.

The imaging radar system consisted of a solid state transmitter and low noise receiver, a digital controller, a data transmission device and a large antenna. Folded during launch, the antenna was deployed in orbit to a length of 35·1ft (10·7m) and width of 6·9ft (2·1m). It functioned like the lens of an optical camera, but its effective aperture in flight was many times greater than the physical length of the antenna because of the motion of the satellite. As Seasat sped around the Earth at 5 miles (8km) a second, the aperture of the radar camera "lens" was synthesized or extended to 10 miles (16·1km). This "camera" thus could record a continuous image of the ground track 62 miles (100km) wide while operating with a resolution of 82ft (25m).

Seasat also carried a radar altimeter to measure ocean wave height and satellite altitude relative to the sea surface, a microwave scatterometer to measure wind speed and direction, a scanning microwave radiometer that could read sea surface temperature to within one degree C, and visual and infra-red radiometers to provide feature recognition support for the microwave sensors. The satellite was stabilized

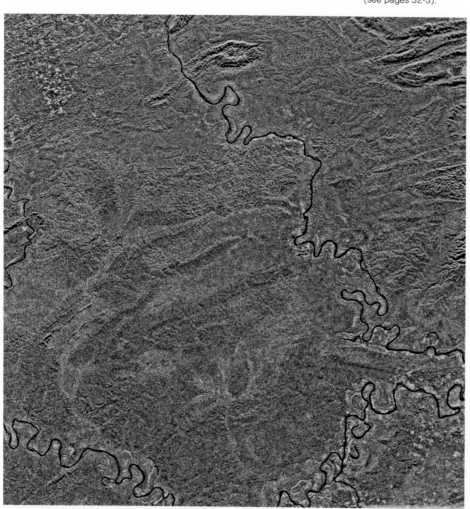

Above From its 500 mile (800km) orbit, Seasat's radar penetrated the dense forests of southern Mexico near the border with Guatemala, the region of confluence of the rivers Lacanatum and Salinas. The image has been colour enhanced to emphasise otherwise inconspicuous geological features, such as faults.

Left A Seasat SAR picture of the 14,162ft (4,317m) extinct volcano, Mt Shasta in N. California. Topographic detail of the flanks of the volcano is exceptional.

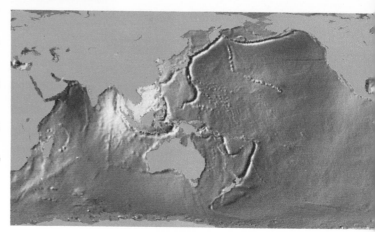

in three axes by momentum wheels and hydrazine thrusters. Its electrical power was supplied by two arrays of photovoltaic cells, supplemented during periods of darkness by nickel-cadmium storage batteries.

Some parts of the polar orbit had an adverse effect on image quality. It appeared degraded when the satellite passed over or near the Earth's magnetic poles and during periods of intensified auroral activity. SAR apparently was sensitive to changes in the intensity of the geomagnetic field; the higher the intensity, the poorer became image resolution. Rain-soaked ground occasionally created long, bright streaks in the images. Analysts decided that the system could depict topographic relief more clearly by changing the look angle to enhance the dimension of height.

During this period, NASA also launched an experimental Heat Capacity Mapping Mission (HCMM) satellite from the Western Test Range aboard a small Scout rocket. The satellite was modestly instrumented to measure temperature gradients on the surface that were characteristic of certain features. The data were converted by ground computers into false colour images in which urban heat islands would appear bright while the ocean and clouds would be dark. Temperature gradients were shown in coastal waters and tidal estuaries, and could be assembled into thermal maps of a region. The satellite was a preliminary experiment in the discrimination of rock types, mineral resources, vegetation, moist and dry soils and snow.

Experiments with Cosmos
The Soviet Union is also actively pursuing remote sensing technologies, and starting on 22 August 1980, a series of heavy Cosmos satellites were launched into low Earth orbits to test surface temperature sensing instruments. These machines, Cosmos-1207, -1209, -1212 and -1220, had military as well as civil missions. They carried multi-spectral scanners with high resolution capability and a new type of instrument for what the Soviets called "quick-look" sensing—immediate localized imagery. Although the USSR has no operational Earth resources satellite system like Landsat, it uses experimental satellites, Meteor-2 and Salyut space stations in much the same way. Of particular significance to the USSR is the Arctic basin. The twice daily television readout is used by the Soviet Polar Fleet to determine routes in the Arctic Ocean and to use this information to extend the navigation season. The USSR Marine Ministry estimated that using satellite data saved lost transit time with a value of 40 million rubles ($60 million).

The experimental Earth resources data from all satellite and manned spacecraft sources have been used to evaluate forest conditions and look out for forest fires. The satellites have completed geological mapping of the entire country at scales of 1:2·5 and 1:5 million. The photomapping has disclosed linear and ring structures of potential interest as clues to mineral deposits. In Central Asia, ground prospecting has shown that tungsten, tin, antimony and mercury deposits were characteristic of mobile, interstitial zones and that copper and molybdenum deposits were typical of stable blocks. The mobile zones where one geologic formation was intruding into another and the more stable regions consisting of stationary blocks could be identified from satellite photos. They thus provided a basis for selecting mineral prospecting sites.

Circular faults in the crust were identified in a Central Asian region called the Chatkalskiy Ridge. It was known from ground prospecting that copper deposits were associated with the intersection of two circular faults. It could be assumed, a Soviet report said, that a second intersection of circular faults might be ore-bearing. This was later confirmed by ground exploration.

The USSR has announced that it plans to develop remote sensing satellites in a future operational system with resolutions of 165 to 262ft (50 to 80m) and a narrow field of view of 112 to 124 miles (180 to 200km). In the Soviet view, equipment used on the US Landsats is "insufficient" for the type of Earth resources research planned by the USSR. Future remote sensing machines used for Earth resources assessment will have side-looking radars, microwave scatterometers and altimeters, UHF (ultra-high frequency) scanning radiometers and advanced infra-red scanners which would be capable of sensing in eight spectral bands.

Left A topographic relief map of the world's ocean surface produced from Seasat radar altimeter data. It is dominated by features indicative of sea floor spreading: the mid-ocean ridges, trenches, fracture zones and seamount chains.

Right A thermal map of the east coast of the USA processed from Heat Capacity Mapping Mission data. Cities—heat islands—appear as white dots: New York is top right. Temperature gradients are visible in coastal waters and tidal estuaries.

The most comprehensive array of remote sensing experiments in the United States space programme was carried on the second flight of the Space Shuttle *Columbia* (STS-2) between 12 and 14 November 1981. The mission was flown by Joseph H. Engle, commander, and Richard H. Truly, pilot. Although it was shortened from five to two days by a partial power failure, it was singularly productive in demonstrating the imaging capacity of synthetic aperture radar.

The SAR system carried on *Columbia* was a slightly modified version of the system on Seasat and was designated as SIR-A (Shuttle imaging radar). The antenna, carried with the electronics on a pallet in the cargo bay, was 30·7ft (9·35m) long and 7·08ft (2·16m) wide.

The OSTA-1 payload

OSTA-1 (NASA's Office of Space and Terrestrial Applications) included in addition to SIR-A: a multi-spectral infra-red radiometer designed for geologic mapping; an electronic feature identification and locating system which automatically selected certain scenes to be imaged and rejected others; an air pollution monitor which measured the distribution of carbon monoxide in the atmosphere to an altitude of 13 miles (21km); an ocean colour detector which scanned the sea for concentrations of chlorophyll-bearing algae where large populations of fish could be expected; and an optical survey of lightning which was made by the crew, photographing thunderstorms with a 70mm camera as *Columbia* passed over them.

The Shuttle multi-spectral infra-red radiometer (SMIRR) was designed to supplement SIR-A ground scenes. It was an experiment in identifying rock types by their reflectance of certain wavelengths of light. The instrument had potential value in locating mineral and hydrocarbon deposits by identifying rocks often found with them. Preliminary results showed that SMIRR could discriminate carbonate minerals from hydroxyl-bearing clays and certain types of clay could be distinguished.

The feature identification and locating experiment (FILE) measured surface reflections in red

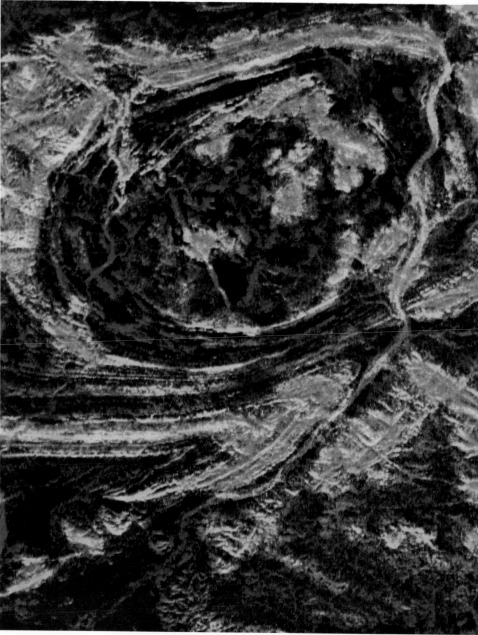

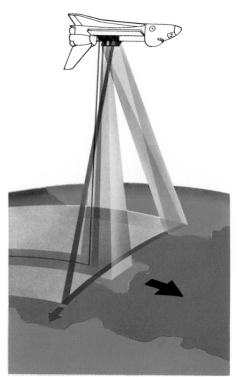

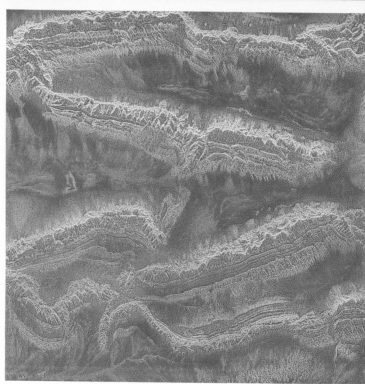

OSTA-1 Payload
This diagram shows the relative sizes of the ground sensing swaths of the OSTA-1 instruments.

■ SMIRR
Designed to identify the best spectral bands for future scanners, SMIRR zeroed in on 328ft (100m) diameter areas.

■ MAPS
This measured the amount of carbon monoxide in the troposphere: it had a 13 mile (21km) resolution.

■ SIR-A
A radar image 31 miles (50km) wide was recorded along the ground track. Resolution: 131ft (40m).

■ FILE
Essentially a data management device, FILE scanned 70 x 70 mile (113 x 113km) areas with a resolution of 0·7 miles (1·13km).

■ OCE
OCE scanned 345 mile (555km) swaths; resolution was 1·9 miles (3km).

Above A SIR-A false colour image of part of the Hamersley Range in Western Australia. The oval feature is a large granite and gneiss dome to the right of which runs the Hardey River. Red signifies rough terrain; yellow is textured; green and blue are smoother areas.

Left Considerable folding and stratification of the rock is visible in this false-colour SIR-A image of the Kelpin Tagh mountain range in Sinkiang province, China. The alluvial fans on the mountain sides return a strongly backscattered radar signal.

Right The Salyut space stations have been a vital component in the USSR's remote sensing programme. This is a cosmonaut's view through the porthole of Salyut 6's docking tunnel; the antenna is part of the IGLA rendezvous system.

and near infra-red bands and determined the ratios of these measurements in certain types of scenes. The ratio varied from vegetation to bare ground to water to snow. Sensing the variations, the system could discriminate among certain categories of scenes and could be programmed to accept some for imaging and reject others. The purpose of the device was to avoid the collection of reams of unwanted or repetitious data.

The incidence of carbon monoxide as an indicator of atmospheric pollution was measured in the middle and upper troposphere with a gas filter radiometer as a part of the measurement of air pollution from satellites (MAPS) experiment. It was a sensor designed to be flown regularly to monitor pollution trends. The ocean colour experiment (OCE) scanner scanned across the direction of flight with a mirror that reflected light into a telescope. The light was passed through a diffraction grating that separated the beam into its component colours which were sensed by photodiodes. Since a concentration of chlorophyll-bearing plankton in the sea gives a green colour to the water (by absorbing blue light), the detection of green indicated fish food and, hence, fish. The instrument was focused on the Atlantic Ocean region between the Canary Islands current and the equatorial counter-current and on the Pacific Ocean off the coast of Peru.

SIR-A produced spectacular results, fulfilling the promise of Seasat that synthetic aperture radar was a major advance in remote sensing. As *Columbia* passed over the Eastern Sahara on 14 November 1981, the radar camera acquired images of the Arabian Desert, considered the driest region on Earth. When geologists inspected the imagery, they found that instead of the smooth, undulating sand sheet which had previously been imaged by Landsat-2, an entirely different scene appeared. It revealed a vast drainage system with river valleys as large as that of the contemporary Nile underlying the sand. Unexpectedly, the radar beamed down at the desert had penetrated six to 10 feet (1·8 to 3m) of sand to uncover a buried landscape formed 40 million years ago, in the

Tertiary Period of geologic time. The actuality of this ancient landscape was confirmed by American and Egyptian geologists who visited the region to verify the imagery.

SIR-A imaged more than 3,860 square miles (10 million km²) of the planet in Africa, Australia, North and South America, Europe, the Mediterranean Basin, India, Indonesia and Southeast Asia. One imaging pass covered a 31 mile (50km) swath 15,500 miles (25,000km) long. The images were recorded on a roll of film 3,610 feet (1,100m) long. Analysts at the Jet Propulsion Laboratory expect that it will take years to develop this roll.

Remote sensing aboard Salyut

Remote sensing experiments have been conducted on all the Salyut space station missions, beginning with Salyut-1 in 1971. Although remote sensing was not the main activity aboard the Salyuts, studies of the geological-geographical nature of the Earth's surface and observations of the atmosphere have formed part of every mission.

Sustained remote sensing aboard a space station began with the Soyuz-11 mission to Salyut-1 in June 1971. For geophysical studies, this and later crews used portable cameras, electronic scanners and telescopes. Continuing studies were carried out aboard Salyut-3, launched on 25 June 1974; Salyut-4, launched on 26 December 1974; and Salyut-5, launched on 22 June 1976.

Salyut-6, first of the second generation of space stations, was launched on 29 September 1977 in a low Earth orbit of 133 x 159 miles (214 x 256km) inclined at 51·6° to the equator —like its predecessors. At this inclination, polar observation, so important to the Soviet economy, was limited and remote sensing was confined to lower latitudes. The principal instrument that Salyut crews used was the MKF-6M multi-spectral space camera, developed jointly by the USSR and East German (GDR) experts and built at the Carl Zeiss Optical Works, Jena. Salyut-6 also carried an infra-red telescope with a mirror 4·92ft (1·5m) in diameter. It measured heat radiation from the surface and from clouds and enabled measurements to be made in the spectral band of ozone absorption as indications of ozone concentrations. Earth observations reportedly accounted for one-third of the cosmonauts' work schedule aboard Salyut-6. The second crew on Salyut-6 took 20,000 pictures of various parts of the Earth, apparently a record.

Salyut-7, launched on 19 April 1982 into the standard Salyut orbit, carried a MKF-6M advanced multi-spectral camera, a KT-140 topographical camera and undisclosed experimental sensing instruments. Geophysical studies were carried on as on the earlier missions. Soviet sources have hinted at the development of agricultural inventory sensing on a large scale, possibly similar to the US AGRISTARS program (Agriculture and Resources Inventory Survey Through Aerospace Remote Sensing). AGRISTARS seeks to determine the effectiveness of remote sensing of croplands. It is currently being tested at NASA's National Space Technology Laboratory (NSTL) at Bay St Louis, Mississippi in conjunction with research at other centres. The programme compares the performance of remote sensing instrumentation on aircraft and satellites—much in the same way as the crew of Soyuz-11 tested it on Salyut-1 in 1971.

Essentially, all satellites and probes observing stars and planets are remote sensing machines. The link between those that look at stars and those that sense the nature of the Earth, the Moon and other planets is the 5,104lb (2,315kg) Solar Maximum Mission (SMM) satellite. It was launched on 14 February, 1980 into a roughly circular 353 miles (569km) orbit from Cape Canaveral. It was the first satellite equipped with a docking device so that it could be retrieved for repair by the Shuttle if necessary. Repair did become necessary in December 1980 when the SMM's instrument pointing system and one instrument failed. The Space Shuttle *Challenger* with a crew of five men was launched on 6 April 1984 to retrieve the satellite, fix it and replace it in orbit, a mission that was successfully achieved.

Solar Max, 13·12ft (4m) long and 7·55ft (2·3m) in diameter, was instrumented to observe solar flares at the maximum of the 11-year sunspot cycle. It was primarily a solar observatory, but it had a second mission of critical importance to weather and climate prediction on Earth. This was to observe the totality of solar radiation and record any changes in it.

For nearly a century, the intensity of sunshine reaching the top of the atmosphere has been assumed to be constant and because of that assumption, it is called the "solar constant". The energy value has been established at 1·37 kilowatts per square metre. However, some short-term variation in this value has been detected by Nimbus-7 and also by Solar Max. A drop of several per cent over a period of years would result in worldwide cooling, and possibly the onset of a new ice age.

Observing the solar constant

Three short-term experiments, following up the observations of Nimbus-7 in 1978 and of Solar Max in 1980, observed the solar constant in 1983 aboard Spacelab, the ESA-built laboratory module and pallet system flown for the first time in the cargo bay of *Columbia* from 28 November to 8 December 1983. The most ambitious scientific sortie into low Earth orbit since Skylab a decade earlier, Spacelab carried 38 experiment facilities that provided instrumentation for 71 investigations. Most of them dealt with materials science and physiology, but the solar constant studies and Earth observations also played a significant role. Aboard Spacelab, the effort to find variation in the Sun's total radiation was international in scope. The Jet Propulsion Laboratory supplied an Active Cavity Radiometer, designed to measure total solar radiance from the far ultraviolet through the far infra-red bands of the spectrum. The rationale for this and two European experiments was that small variations in total radiation might have significant climate effects. The instrument measured solar output with three heat detectors (pyrheliometers) mounted on the instrument pallet behind the laboratory module. Changes in radiance could be determined by comparing its heating effect with a known heat value.

A second experiment seeking the same information was provided by the *Institut Royal Météorologique de Belgique*, Belgium, using a pyrheliometer to sense total solar radiation. The data were compared with those from the Active Cavity Radiometer and a third experiment provided by the *Service d'Aéronomie du Centre National de la Recherche Scientifique*, France. The French experiment used a set of

Right The Metric Camera aboard Spacelab obtained this superb view of the Nan Shan mountains in Tsinghai province, NW China. The frozen lake, Ha-la Hu, is about 13,100ft (4,000m) above sea level. The only railway line connecting this region with the coast is faintly visible in the top right.

Below The splendour of the Himalayas from the Ganges plain (lower right) across Nepal into Tibet (top) is captured by the ESA/DFVLR Metric Camera on 2 December 1983 during the STS-9 flight. Huge glaciers such as Ngojumba and Khumbu are evident (top left) while a cloud-covered Mt Everest is top right.

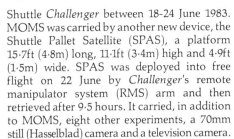

Stereo Imagery

At present there is an acute shortage of accurate topographical maps of the world. The Metric Camera experiment is the first phase of an ESA project called ATLAS which aims to produce such maps on a worldwide basis. In order to produce 1:50,000 scale maps certain accuracy requirements have to be met, among them elevation accuracy of ±10m. To determine terrain elevation, pairs of images are compared in photogrammetric stereo-scopic devices. Images with an 80% overlap are obtained by the camera working with an exposure frequency of 4-6sec along the flight path. Pictures 1 and 5 of any sequence would have a 20% overlap, and accurate elevation data for this strip should be obtainable by comparative evaluation.

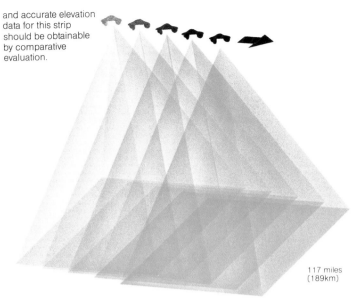

117 miles (189km)

three instruments called monochromators mounted on the pallet to measure radiation in ultraviolet, visible and infra-red light. It sought to determine which wavelengths of light might tend to be variable.

The Metric Camera

Only two instruments observed the Earth directly, both provided by ESA. One was the German-made Metric Camera mounted in the optical window of the Spacelab module. It was designed by the Zeiss Company to photograph the surface with a resolution ten times better than that of the meteorological satellites or Landsat-4, and thus test the mapping capabilities of high-resolution photography from space. The other instrument consisted of a synthetic aperture radar camera and two supporting microwave instruments. This experiment was a precursor to an SAR to be flown on ESA's ERS-1 (see page 49).

A number of European scientists regarded the Metric Camera as a landmark in remote sensing because it provided the first NASA-ESA opportunity to take photographs of the Earth from orbit as far as 58° of latitude north and south and return them to the ground for processing. In the last 100 years, it was said, only 35 per cent of the Earth's land area has been mapped adequately by conventional photomapping. The balance of the land area may be mapped from space, a project considered for later Spacelab missions.

A "push-broom" scanner

A new type of remote sensing instrument called MOMS (Modular Optoelectronic Multi-spectral Scanner) was also demonstrated during the earlier STS-7 mission flown by Space

Right The MBB-developed MOMS, first flown on the SPAS platform in June 1983, employs a new "push-broom" scanning technique in which each ground track pixel is detected by a discrete photo-sensitive diode, so that a whole image line (made up of 6,912 pixels) is generated instantaneously. This geologically detailed MOMS image shows the Andes declining from the Bolivian highlands towards the city of Cochabamba.

Shuttle *Challenger* between 18-24 June 1983. MOMS was carried by another new device, the Shuttle Pallet Satellite (SPAS), a platform 15·7ft (4·8m) long, 11·1ft (3·4m) high and 4·9ft (1·5m) wide. SPAS was deployed into free flight on 22 June by *Challenger*'s remote manipulator system (RMS) arm and then retrieved after 9·5 hours. It carried, in addition to MOMS, eight other experiments, a 70mm still (Hasselblad) camera and a television camera.

MOMS, as well as SPAS itself, was the product of the West German firm of Messerschmitt-Bölkow-Blohm (MBB), which expects to market MOMS output. The new "push-broom" type scanner functioned as a thematic mapper for about 30 minutes under radio control from Mission Control, Houston. It acquired images in visible and infra-red light of portions of Africa, South America, India, Southeast Asia and Australia in co-ordination with clear weather reports from the US GOES, ESA Meteosat and Japan's GMS-2. MOMS consists of two optical modules, a power box, logic box and recording system. It senses in two spectral channels in the visible and near infra-red range and is designed to achieve a 65·6ft (20m) pixel (picture element) size in a swath 87 miles (140km) wide from an orbital altitude of 186 miles (300km).

Following the STS-7 mission, MBB formed a consortium with the Communications Satellite Corporation (Comsat) and a New York investment group, the Steinbeck Reassurance Company, to exploit MOMS commercially. A corporation called Sparx was formed with the expectation of competing with Landsats-4 and -5 and France's projected SPOT satellite in providing remote sensing services for agricultural, environmental, marine and forestry agencies and industries. Comsat later withdrew from the venture, but Sparx reserved space for a repeat performance of MOMS (as a commercial payload) on a future Shuttle mission.

Another significant payload was flown aboard *Challenger* during the thirteenth Shuttle mission, -41G, 5-13 October 1984. It included the OSTA-3 experiments: SIR-B, the SAR-based imaging radar camera first flown on STS-2, the MAPS and FILE apparatus, also flown on STS-2, and a new topographical mapping instrument, the 948lb (430kg) Large Format Camera. This huge camera is designed for large scale geological imaging and environmental monitoring. Its 305mm focal length lens is expected to achieve very high resolution. The camera carries 4,000ft (1,220m) of film, and achieved 100 per cent of its desired coverage on the mission. Also deployed was an Earth Radiation Budget Satellite, part of a three-satellite system designed to measure the planet's incoming and outgoing radiation balance and the value of the solar constant.

The solid crust of the Earth beneath us is a dynamic, moving surface, powered by heat from the fiery interior. The mantle contains hot plumes of molten rock that reach up to drag the cold crust along. That the crust moves was suspected by Earth scientists for many years, but ultimate proof of this as a continuing event has only been found very recently in the theory of plate tectonics.

The Earth's crust is made up of rigid mobile plates that carry the continents on their backs. As the plates move apart, oceans are formed. The resulting scars quickly heal as lava spreads onto the new sea-bed, congealing as pillow-shaped masses (*left*). When plates collide, ocean sediments are compressed and altered as mountain ranges rise, topped by volcanoes.

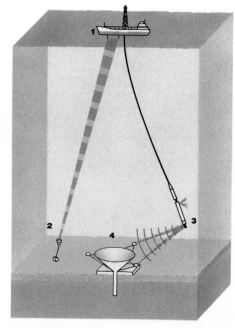

Above Drilling of the ocean floor from ships such as *Glomar Challenger* has yielded vital evidence of sea-floor spreading and continental drift. The diagram shows the computer-controlled positioning system (**1**), linked to a sonar beacon (**2**) on the sea-bed. A sonar scanner (**3**) allows the drill to enter a cone (**4**) for relocation of drill holes. **Below** Drill pipes aboard *Glomar Challenger*.

THE DYNAMIC EARTH

The concept of Plate Tectonics has revolutionized the Earth Sciences, accounting for many features of our planet, from earthquake distribution to the location of mineral wealth

Two-thirds of the Earth's surface has been studied in detail only during the last three decades. This is the part of the surface covered by sea-water and ocean sediment. An understanding of the solid rock of the ocean floor is crucial to our concept of how the sea-floor spreads apart and continents move.

The ocean floors are dominated by immense ridges which stand some 1-2 miles (2-3km) above the ocean bed and extend for over 50,000 miles (80,000km) as a continuous submarine mountain chain. The ridges are broken at intervals by enormous cracks or faults, which offset the ridge crests by as much as 185 miles (300km), but usually by only a few tens of miles. These ridges were originally mapped using the position of the earthquakes that occur in a narrow zone precisely along their crests. These earthquakes are caused by movements of the faults which offset the ridges, and the zones in which they occur is a few miles wide and between 1 mile (2km) and 7½ miles (12km) deep.

Magnetic stripes

It was not long before geophysicists discovered that the ridge crests were strongly magnetized. Instruments called magnetometers towed behind ships or aircraft always showed peak readings within a belt some 12-30 miles (20-50km) wide,

as they crossed the ridge crest. On either side of these strong readings, an area of lower than average magnetism was found, and further still from the crests was another strong zone. These sets of alternating strong and weak 'stripes' of magnetism, running parallel to the ridge crests, and on either side of them, extend for several thousand miles on each side. They are called magnetic anomaly stripes. Successive stripes have different widths, but the sequence of anomaly widths is exactly the same on each side of the ridge crest—in other words, the eastern side is a mirror image of the western.

By matching the anomaly sequence on either side of a fault zone, the degree of offset could be measured exactly. Even more remarkable was the discovery that when the sequence of magnetic anomaly widths is mapped away from the ridge, the pattern matches precisely the sequence, through time, of the reversals undergone by the Earth's magnetic field (the geomagnetic field). In other words, every time the geomagnetic field changes polarity, that is, whenever the north and south magnetic poles change over, then these changes are recorded in the rocks of the ocean floor.

Dating the ocean floor

This also means that, quite incredibly, the age of the ocean floor can be dated simply by measuring the magnetism of the ocean rocks, from ships, and matching the observed anomaly sequences with those of changes in the geomagnetic field recorded in dateable rocks exposed on the continents. These studies showed that the oldest rocks of the ocean floor were a mere 200 million years old—very young indeed when compared with the age of the oldest rocks of the continents, some 3,800 million years old. This maximum age for the ocean floor and the very recent age for the rocks at the ridge crests were later confirmed by drilling through the oceanic sediments, down to the solid rocks beneath. The technology of this drilling operation was a major advance, compar-

able with achievements of the space programme, but revealed puzzling features.

There are, for example, virtually no sediments on the crests of the ridges, and then they thicken very slowly towards the continents, often being more than 1-2 miles (2-3km) thick on the ocean floor immediately next to the continental rocks. Until drilling became possible, the only way the deeper sediments could be sampled was in anomalous areas (those showing a difference between observed and computed values), such as those where erosion had removed the upper layers. Such areas are rare, and, in any case, the fact that they are anomalous also made it uncertain whether such results could be extrapolated to more normal regions. Otherwise all samples of the sediments were obtained in dredge hauls or using steel cores which were dropped vertically into the sediments and then retrieved with the sediments inside them. Such methods only

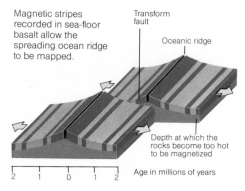

Magnetic stripes recorded in sea-floor basalt allow the spreading ocean ridge to be mapped.

Transform fault

Oceanic ridge

Depth at which the rocks become too hot to be magnetized

Age in millions of years

2 1 0 1 2

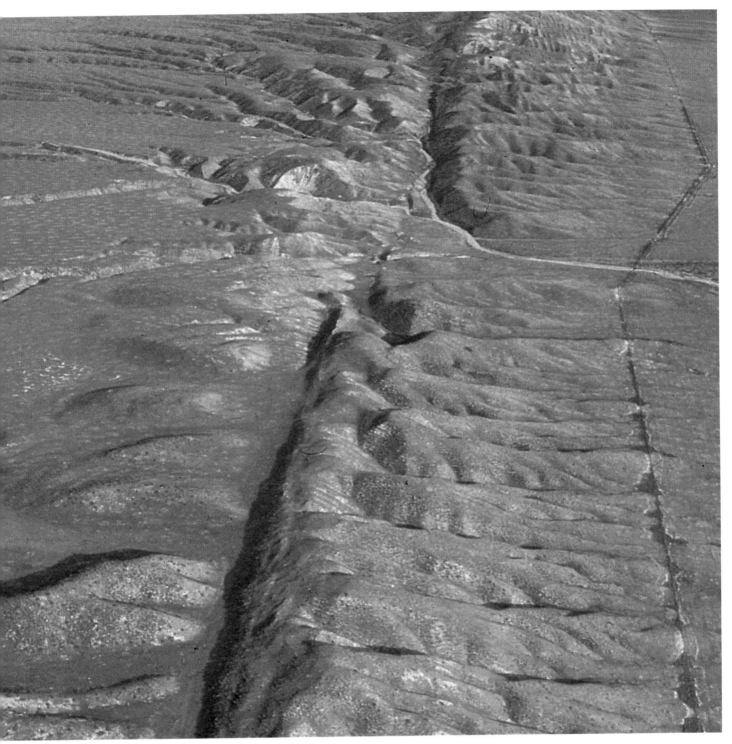

provided information on the uppermost 15-30ft (5-10m) of sediment and therefore only represented the last few million years of the oceanic sedimentary record. Drilling, however, allowed the sediments to be sampled down to depths of many hundreds of feet.

Ancient ocean circulation patterns

Samples of sediment obtained in this way revealed major changes in past oceanic circulation patterns and depths. The changing depths could be determined to some extent by their fossil content—those creatures that lived and died near the seashore are confined to the shallowest areas, while free-floating organisms can be found throughout the world's oceanic sediments as they are carried around the world by the surface currents. However, one

unexpected feature was the complexity of oceanic circulation patterns; only the surface ones are controlled by the wind patterns. Studies of the different depositional patterns therefore allow reconstructions to be made of the past current patterns. It had been thought that few currents disturbed the tranquillity of the oceanic depths, so that the oceans should have contained a complete record of sedimentation from their birth onwards. The reality turned out to be much more complex. The oceans were very shallow during their early formation and increased in depth with age, but there also appear to have been times of major changes in sea-level, with some periods where few, if any, sediments accumulated on the ocean floor. The reasons for this are unclear.

The distribution of some sediments is particularly interesting. Near the Equator, for example, the formation of calcium carbonate shells takes place so rapidly that a rain of

calcareous debris reaches the sea-floor where it forms a deposit. Away from the Equator, organic productivity is slower and the skeletons, as they sink below some 1-2 miles (2-3km), become dissolved in the oceanic waters so that such deposits cannot normally accumulate except near the Equator or in shallower waters. It is thus possible to trace the location of the past Equatorial zone by finding calcareous oozes in the cores of sediments drilled at different locations. In the Pacific, the older the age of the sediments, the further north are the Equatorial calcareous deposits, clearly demonstrating that the Pacific ocean floor has been drifting northwards, through the Equatorial zone, during at least the last 45 million years. The age of the basal sediments was also seen to increase systematically away from the ridge crests, confirming the increasing age of the ocean floor away from the ridge that had already been indicated by the magnetic studies.

The fact that an oceanic ridge crest is always the youngest feature of an ocean floor means that this is where new oceanic rocks must still be forming. This is also suggested by the occurrence of earthquakes and the fact that recent volcanoes are still forming in this region—for example those in Iceland, Tristan da Cunha and other volcanic islands along oceanic ridges. As such new, hot volcanic rocks are added to the older oceanic crustal rocks, they become magnetized as they cool. After solidification, these rocks are then carried perpendicularly away from the oceanic ridge crest, at equal rates in opposite directions, making way for new rocks to form and become magnetized. Each time that the field changes polarity, the direction of the magnetization of the volcanic rocks then forming at the ridge also changes. The oceanic rocks thus act as a magnetic 'tape-recorder' of the changing polarity of the Earth's magnetic field.

Such a model of new ocean-floor creation is also supported by the nature of the earthquakes at the ridge crests, as these show that the region

Above A view over Surtsey Island, Iceland, towards Little Surtsey. Basaltic volcanoes make new land where the sea-floor is actively spreading. Dark basaltic lava and ash show up around the craters, which billow with gas and steam.

Top right Surtsey first appeared from beneath the waves in 1963, and continued erupting until 1967.

Bottom right Fuelled by heat that rises along the spreading ocean ridge, geysers vent hot steam into the cold Icelandic air.

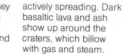

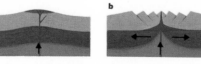

Continental margin (sediments)
Mid-ocean ridge-rift
Sediments
New sea-floor ocean crust
Transform fault
Sediments

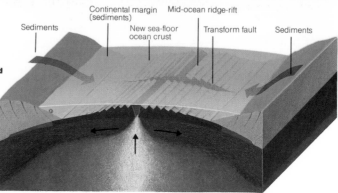

Left As the continental crust starts to arch and fracture (**a**), magma escapes and volcanic activity is produced. Faulting and downward collapse follow (**b**), and sea-water floods over the region (**c**). Soon a fundamental split develops, and the ocean ridge system gradually forms as the two land masses separate. The large diagram (**d**) shows the main features of the ocean basin when spreading of the sea floor has been active for tens of millions of years. Mountains of the central ridge, offset by transverse faults and separated land masses, can be seen.

is under tension, so that molten volcanic rocks will rise up tensional cracks, feeding the volcanoes along the ridge and then solidifying. After a few thousand years, the continuing tensional forces again separate the two sides, allowing new rocks to rise and also carrying the solidified rocks, with their magnetic patterns, away from the ridge crests. The ocean floor thus spreads slowly away from the ridges. This motion is at rates of about ½in (1·25cm) per year in the Atlantic, and up to 3-4in (8-10cm) per year in parts of the Pacific. The maximum rate of such sea-floor spreading appears to have been 8-9½in (20-24cm) per year during some phases of the opening of the Indian Ocean. As each ridge flank is spreading at this rate, it means that, in the Atlantic Ocean, Europe and North America are now separating at twice the spreading rate of the individual crest flanks, at ¾-1in (2-3cm) per year. Such rates of continental motion are only just becoming measurable, using precise satellite positioning by means of laser ranging.

Seismic studies of the oceanic rocks beneath the sediments have shown that there are three successive layers which overlie the normal mantle rocks of the Earth's interior. These crustal layers are labelled 2, 3 and 4, with the sediments themselves forming seismic layer 1. The upper crustal layer comprises the intruded volcanic rocks (dykes), which filled the tensional cracks, together with the lavas which flowed from them when they originally reached the surface. Immediately below this layer, which is uniformly 1¼ miles (2km) thick, lies a 3-4 mile (5-6km) thick layer of coarse-grained basic rocks, gabbros, which represent the now-solidified rocks which were the original source of the molten rocks that fed both the overlying dykes and lavas. A layer, less than half a mile (0·8km) thick, lies beneath the gabbros. Being so thin, its existence was not certain until recently and it is thought to be formed from the denser minerals which segregated out of the gabbros while they were molten.

Drilling in the oceans also confirmed the volcanic nature of layer 2, but the reliability of the interpretations of the seismic data for the deeper layers has not yet been checked directly. However, the seismic crustal model is exactly what would be expected from comparisons with areas where previous oceanic rocks have become trapped within continental rocks. Such rocks are rare as oceanic rocks are rich in iron and titanium, making them heavier than most continental rocks, so that they tend to sink back into the Earth, rather than being thrust onto the lighter continental rocks—except under unusual circumstances. Much useful information has come from studies of such rocks in the deserts of the Middle East where the outcrops are not obscured by vegetation, although these areas have only recently become accessible. Oceanic rocks are also known in Cyprus, New Guinea, southern Scotland, Newfoundland, and elsewhere. All such areas show oceanic sediments overlying lavas and dykes, which are in turn lying on top of a thick layer of gabbro. These rocks are also important sources of minerals, such as copper and nickel, and therefore the processes by which they have formed has additional economic interest.

Earthquakes can take place anywhere on the Earth's surface as they occur wherever the local strength of the rocks is exceeded by stress forces. These forces may arise in a wide variety of ways. For example, the rocks may simply collapse over a cavity, or there may be an avalanche due to the action of gravitational forces on a cliff edge. Such earthquakes are extremely weak on a global scale and so are only locally important. The main stress forces, and hence the major earthquakes, are related to the movements of the Earth's tectonic plates and, to a lesser extent, the motion of liquid rocks as they rise to feed volcanic activity. This means that all major earthquake (seismic) activity is located in specific zones. The narrowest of these bands lies along the crests of the oceanic ridges where new ocean crust is forming, and in the fracture zones where the oceanic ridge crests are offset from each other. Along the crests, the earthquakes are so weak that they are often difficult to detect, while those along the fracture zones can be very strong. In both cases, the earthquakes are shallow, generally less than 6 miles (10km) below the surface, and along fracture zones they are confined to a band only 6-7¾ miles (10-12km) wide. It is possible that along the ridges the activity is confined to an even narrower zone, but the weakness of the earthquakes and the distance from land-based detecting stations (seismic observatories) means that their location is less precise than for the stronger earthquakes along the fracture zones.

Analysing earthquake activity

The location of earthquakes is theoretically quite simple to calculate. The failure of the rocks generates two types of sound waves that radiate through the body of the Earth. One of these travels faster than the other, so that the faster P waves arrive first and the slower S waves arrive afterwards. The distance from the earthquake is thus simply determined from the time delay between these two arrivals, as both waves started to travel out at the same instant, and so the delay time between them is directly proportional to the distance between the earthquake and the recording station. Any one record only gives the distance away from that station, but if three records are available, then these precisely define the location as only one point will be at exactly the observed distance from all three stations.

The magnitude of the earthquake can be determined according to the energy of the seismic wave. The stronger the earthquake, the greater the amplitude of the seismic wave, but allowance must be made for the loss of energy as the seismic wave travels through the Earth. Using more sophisticated studies, preferably using recordings near to the earthquake, it is also possible to determine the directions of first motion as the rocks fail. Different first motions characterize different mechanisms. Tensional forces, for example, generate quite different first motions to those caused as one block of rocks grinds past another block.

On the ridge crests, the earthquakes show tensional features and appear to be caused as the ridge flanks on either side move, slowly but inexorably, in opposite directions to each other. This movement creates tension at the ridge which lowers the pressure on the underlying rocks, allowing them to become molten, and also eventually cracks the solid rocks nearer the surface so that the molten rocks can rise to the surface and solidify. This zone is therefore also associated with volcanic activity, such as that in Iceland, with each successive volcanic eruption being followed by a period of quiescence as the movements continue, until the breaking point of the surface rocks is again exceeded.

The magnitude of seismic activity along the fracture zones between the ridge crests is often several hundred times greater than on the ridge crests. The earthquakes in this location also have different source mechanisms, as these are caused by the two oceanic plates on either side of the fracture moving at the same rate as each other, but in exactly opposite directions. The rocks between therefore become severely broken and fractured. There is rarely much volcanic activity associated with such earthquakes, as the areas are mostly compressed, preventing the rise of any molten rocks which may have formed beneath them.

The Benioff Zone

The broadest zones of major earthquake activity are also where all of the world's deep earthquakes occur, at depths of 125-375 miles (200-600km). These zones occur in one of two localities, either where new mountains are still forming (for example, the Alps and Himalayas) by the collision of continents, or near to the deep oceanic trenches. In fact, these two localities are related, since mountains formed in this way can only occur where the intervening ocean has been destroyed by descending at a previous oceanic trench. These trenches are narrow V-shaped areas, often 5-6 miles (8-10km) deep and over 600 miles (1,000km) long. All of the largest trenches are in the Pacific, with the exception of the Java Trench in the eastern Indian Ocean. Only small trenches occur elsewhere—for example, the Antilles (Caribbean), Scotia (between South America and Antarctica) and Hellenic (Mediterranean) Trenches. The trenches are themselves bordered by very active volcanic island arcs, with the

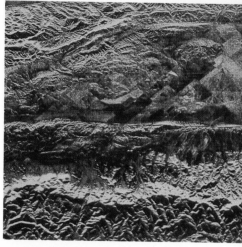

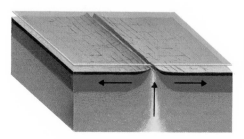

Above Where the sea floor spreads apart, as along the Mid-Atlantic ridge molten rock from below fills the fracture. New crust is constantly made at this constructive boundary plate.

When two unlike plates meet, the ocean plate, made of heavier, denser rock, is subducted. It melts at great depth and a range of volcanic mountains result along the destructive boundary.

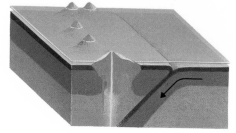

A destructive boundary may also occur where two ocean plates collide. One plate is subducted and destroyed. The molten rock produced rises up to make a curving arc of volcanic islands.

Above Los Angeles has suffered from repeated earthquake damage, related to the San Andreas Fault line which runs north-west along the west coast of North America. This highly active fault line occurs along the boundary between the North American Plate and the Pacific Plate. These two plates are slipping past each other: the earthquakes indicate times of activity. Earthquakes affect many densely populated areas, for example in the Middle East, China, Italy and western America.

Left An aerial photograph of the San Andreas Fault.

deepest earthquakes bordering the volcanoes on the side furthest from the trench. There is thus a systematic increase in the depth of the deepest earthquakes away from the trench, and the plane on which these increasingly deeper earthquakes occur is termed the Benioff Zone, named after an American geophysicist.

More detailed study of the Benioff Zone earthquakes show that they are not restricted to a single plane, as previously thought, but are confined within two parallel zones, only 6-12 miles (10-20km) apart, which dip at shallow angles, 30 to 45°, beneath the volcanoes, and then more steeply into the Earth, with no recorded earthquakes occurring deeper than 441 miles (710km). The Benioff Zone is itself overlain by some earthquake activity, mostly thought to be associated with molten rocks

rising to feed the volcanoes, although there is still uncertainty about many of their origins.

Mechanisms of subduction

The earthquakes within the Benioff Zone itself show variable characteristics. Near the oceanic trench they tend to be tensional in the upper part of the Benioff Zone and compressional in the lower part, while they seem to be mostly tensional from the trench down to depths of about 125 miles (200km), as if the rocks are being stretched. The earthquake activity is therefore thought to result from the descent of oceanic rocks, originally formed at the oceanic ridges, down into the mantle. This descent, which geophysicists call subduction, results in the bending of the oceanic rocks as they enter the trench—the upper surface being stretched around the bend, thereby giving tensional earthquakes, and the lower parts being compressed. As these cold oceanic rocks descend to greater depths, they become increasingly heated and squeezed, resulting in the brittle failure of these cold rocks at depths within the mantle. However this region of the Earth is so complex that it is still difficult to determine the source mechanisms of the deeper earthquakes, although these are being intensively studied. The available seismic information is most simply explained in terms of the gradual subduction of the cold oceanic lithospheric plate into the Earth's interior. Such a model also offers an explanation for the major volcanic activity which is associated with such subduction zones.

Continental masses can collide when oceans close. The Himalayas were formed by the movement of India into Asia. Crumpled strata and fold mountains are typical products at these collision zones.

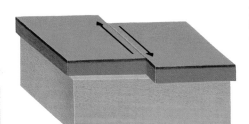

A conservative plate margin is where new crust is not created and little destruction takes place. One plate moves past the other, as along the San Andreas Fault line, with sudden jerks.

As the cold oceanic rocks descend, the pressure on them increases and also their temperatures slowly rise. These changes, particularly the increasing temperature, make many of their minerals unstable. Some of the first minerals to be affected are those that contain water as part of their crystal structure. These hydrous minerals, such as serpentines and amphiboles, then begin to dehydrate—expelling their water. This water migrates upwards because it is less dense than the rocks, and permeates into the mantle rocks overlying the Benioff Zone. These mantle rocks are hotter than the rocks in the Benioff Zone, which are still warming up to ambient mantle temperatures, and are close to their melting temperatures. However, the addition of water and other volatiles has the effect of lowering their melting temperature so that the mantle rocks in this region begin to melt. The molten rocks are themselves less dense than the more solid rocks, so these begin to ascend, eventually reaching the surface where they form explosive volcanic arcs.

The composition of the volcanoes in the island arcs also changes systematically according to the depth of the Benioff Zone. For example, the content of potassium increases relative to the amount of sodium and calcium as the depth of the earthquakes increases, so that near the trench the volcanic rocks are predominantly calcic, but become increasingly alkaline at greater distances. The generally high volatile content of these volcanoes, presumably reflecting the nature of the fluids which initiated the igneous activity, causes them to be highly explosive, such as the eruptions which destroyed Krakatoa in 1883 and Pompeii in AD 79, and was recently demonstrated by the relatively minor eruption at Mount St. Helens, USA.

Ore deposits and earthquake activity
However, not only do the major chemical elements vary, but there are also systematic changes in the rarer elements, such as the lanthanide series, as well as in the composition of the associated metallic ore minerals. Many of these ore deposits are of great economic importance. The copper sulphides, for example, represent about one-third of the world's known copper reserves. These economically important deposits change from being predominantly manganese and iron rich near the trench, to copper and molybdenum sulphides, with gold, when the earthquakes are at some 75-90 miles (120-150km) depth, and then to lead and zinc sulphides, with silver, when the earthquake activity is some 90-110 miles (150-180km) deep. This relationship to the maximum depth of earthquake activity is not fully understood, although the observation has already been used to predict and then discover new metallic ores in several parts of the world. It does, however, appear to be an absolutely fundamental factor, being modified only by the nature of the surface rocks into which the volcanoes are erupted.

Testing the theory
While the model of oceanic plates being subducted back into the interior of the Earth appears to be consistent with many geological and geophysical observations, it is difficult to test its physical reality. Only recently has the precise depth of earthquakes been determined, unexpectedly showing two planes of earthquakes, and the mechanism of earthquake generation is still difficult to examine. This is

partially because many seismic areas are remote, but even in areas such as Japan, the local seismic velocity structure is complex and varies from one location to another, making unambiguous analysis of any individual earthquake event difficult. Nonetheless, the present model provides a working explanation of most observed features, even though further investigations are essential to determine the actual mechanisms involved.

Irrespective of the mechanism, the subduction of oceanic rocks is essential unless the Earth is increasing its surface area at the same rate as new oceanic rocks are created at the world's ridges. An expansion of the Earth's radius by one third during the last 200 million years

would be necessary to account for the present size of the oceans if no subduction had occurred. On that basis, the Earth would have been pinhead-sized only some 1,000 million years ago unless the Earth was sometimes expanding, sometimes contracting. Such a concept would only be possible if, for example, the gravitational 'constant' fluctuated with time—but such effects would then be visible on other planetary surfaces, yet none of these show any signs of such changes. Most lunar craters, for example, were formed over 4,000 million years ago, even earlier than the oldest parts of the continents of the Earth, dated at 3,800 million years. Yet the lunar craters still show their original circular patterns, with no evidence for expansions or

Above The havoc caused by plate movement can be seen in the photo of Vestmannaeyjar town after a huge lava flow from Heimaey Volcano erupted in 1973. Here, astride the mid-Atlantic Ridge, plates move apart and molten rock wells up through the fracture.
Left At Salaparuta, Sicily, earthquake damage in 1968 resulted as two plates converged on each other.
Top right A stunning aerial view from Skylab 3 shows the Andes mountains and the South American continent curving south towards the top of the picture. These mountains are a classic case—built above a subduction zone where the ocean plate material dives below the continental crust. The Nazca Plate below the Pacific plunges beneath the continental rocks of Chile and Argentina.

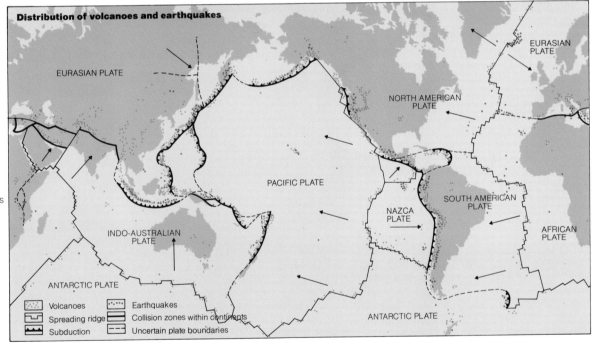

contractions since their creation. Similarly, both Venus and Mars show surfaces that appear to have remained virtually unchanged during the last 3,000 million years or more.

Plates and plate movement

Plate tectonics is therefore a theory by which the vast majority of the world's earthquake and volcanic activity is explained in terms of the relative motion of some six major surface plates (the Pacific, American, Europe-Asia, India-Australia and the Antarctic) and another dozen or so smaller plates, such as the Caribbean. These plates comprise both crustal rocks, continental and oceanic, together with the colder, upper parts of the Earth's mantle rocks.

They are some 75 miles (120km) thick in most of the oceanic areas and over 125 miles (200km) thick in the continental regions. The mantle rocks beneath the plates are warm enough to yield plastically when stressed. Therefore, no strain accumulates, and no earthquakes can occur below the plates. As the cold, rigid brittle plates move relative to each other, they create earthquakes. These are shallow and generally weak where the plates are moving apart, but strong and complex where the plates are colliding at subduction zones. Volcanoes are also formed where new plates are being generated or old plates destroyed.

In this view of the Earth's surface, each plate contains some oceanic parts, but they do not

necessarily include continental areas, as in the case of the Pacific plate. However, where continents are involved, their rocks are lighter than those of the oceanic rocks, and so these remain at the Earth's surface as the denser oceanic rocks are subducted. The continents therefore continue to accrete, but the oceanic rocks are continually recycled, largely destroying the evidence for their previous existence. As the continents cannot be subducted, they must move about the Earth's surface as plate motions change with time. A major test of the plate tectonic model is therefore to see whether the continents have, during the last few hundred millions of years, actually moved relative to each other across the Earth's surface.

The idea that the continents may be capable of drifting very slowly over the Earth's surface at rates of a few inches a year, but adding up to thousands of miles over geological time, is a very old concept. It was largely stimulated from geological observations which indicated that different areas of the world were previously in radically different climatic zones. Some 280 million years ago, for example, Britain was accumulating desert sandstones with all the characteristics of the present-day Sahara desert, and also great thicknesses of salts. At the same time, in places like India and Australia, glaciers were laying down ice-formed debris. However, it was then thought that the continents could not actually move as the intervening oceans were thought to be merely sunken continents and at least the upper parts of the Earth were solid. Such ancient climatic evidence was therefore thought to indicate that the Earth's rotational pole moved so that India and Australia were near to the pole at the same time as Britain lay on the Equator. Such an interpretation became increasingly difficult as further studies began to show that not only were India and Australia close to the pole, but so were the land-masses that are now southern Africa, Antarctica and South America.

Early controversies

By the early 20th century, there was considerable controversy about "continental drift", with many of the early fossil hunters becoming increasingly convinced that ancient life forms on different continents were so similar that it was difficult to see how this could have occurred unless the continents were immediately adjacent to each other at the time when the fossil plants and animals were alive. However, it was then thought that the Earth's mantle and oceanic rocks were so rigid that the continents could not plough through them without having left clear evidence of their passage. The evidence for this rigidity was simply based on the passage of earthquake waves through the Earth. The study of these waves soon showed that the Earth has a liquid core, with a radius almost half of that of the Earth itself, but the rocks above the core (the mantle) are seismically solid. Clearly, taken at its face value, such observations meant that the continents could not possibly move relative to each other.

The slow-moving mantle

It is now known that only the upper 60 miles (100km) or so of the Earth remain rigid over geological time. Most of the mantle beneath has a rigidity which is the same as that of sheet glass at normal surface pressures and temperatures. Sheet glass is, of course, both rigid and brittle when hit and certainly transmits both P and S seismic waves. However, studies of medieval glass windows show that they are usually thicker at their bases than at their tops. This is because their viscosities still allow a very slow flow of the glass during the last few hundred years. In the same way, P and S waves pass through the mantle rocks but these are still capable of flow if stressed for many thousands or millions of years. It is thus possible for slow movements to take place within the mantle. However, this does not resolve the problem of how the continents seem to move through the oceanic rocks without apparently disturbing them. The explanation is that the continents do not actually move through the oceans. Where the continents are separating, new oceanic

rocks form and spread to fill the intervening space. Where the continents are approaching each other, the intervening oceanic rocks are subducted back into the mantle. As the continents move, therefore, new oceanic areas form and older ones are destroyed to allow such motions to continue. The continents do not actually travel through the oceanic floor, but travel with it.

The role of new technology

The proof of this model for the Earth still lies largely with the evidence that such continental movements actually occur. Within the next year or two it is probable that sufficiently precise measurements, such as those made by laser ranging, will be available, so that present-day movements can be measured. The precision required is extremely high, as the continental motions only average some ½-2in (1-5cm) per year and may be irregular, and such changes must be measured over several thousand miles, so that a minimum accuracy of 1 in 100,000,000 is required. This is at the limits of existing

technology, but should be attainable over a period of five to ten years when the total separation between North America and Europe will have increased by some 10in (25cm). The geological evidence for earlier motions comprises not only fossil plant and animal distributions, but the matching of entire sequences of rocks on now separated continents. The geological history of eastern South America and western Africa are absolutely identical for most of the last 550 million years because they were then combined as just one part of a huge continent, Gondwana, and it is only since their separation during the last 100 million years that their geological records differ.

Evidence from past climates

Even more convincing is the ancient climatic evidence which was so persuasive to geologists in the last century. The coal mines of North America and Europe are now exploiting the remains of vast fern forests some 300 million years old. These ferns have all the characteristics of equatorial rain forests—the stems do not

Left This open-cast coal mine in Cumbria, England, proves that during the Carboniferous period this region was a tropical swamp forest where the coal-forming trees flourished. Since then, Britain has drifted far north of the Equator.
Right *Alethopteris lonchitica* is a typical delicate fossil from the coal-bearing rocks of the Carboniferous system.
Centre right *Glossopteris* is a plant fossil whose distribution supports the idea of continental drift.
Below Computer-drawn globes show the way in which the continents have moved over the Earth's surface during the last 300 m.y. In the Permian period, the southern continents were joined in a huge super-continent called Gondwanaland. About 100 m.y. ago the present Atlantic Ocean began to open; this trend continues.
Bottom The map shows evidence supporting the idea of continental drift. The distribution of fossil reptiles *Mesosaurus* and *Lystrosaurus* suggests a single land-mass in the Permian period. There is evidence in the rocks of the southern continents proving that in the Carboniferous period they were united and near the South Pole, suffering very extensive glaciation. Since then they have drifted to warmer latitudes.

100 million years ago

50 million years ago

0 million years ago

show seasonal growth rings, there is a rich variety of species, drip leaves are common, and so forth. The associated sediments, thick limestones and coral reefs, also indicate low, equatorial latitudes. These contrast strongly with the evidence from rocks of similar age in South America, Africa, India, Australia and Antarctica. These continents were being extensively glaciated and then covered by entirely different fern forests from those in North America and Europe. The 'southern' forests contained few species and show seasonal growth rings and other features indicative of high latitudes. Thin, very poor limestones and the virtual absence of corals again all suggest high latitudes at that time. The simplest explanation is that Europe and North America then formed a single continent, Laurasia, which straddled the Equator. The glaciated continents were combined to form another supercontinent, Gondwana, which then lay beneath the southern polar ice cap. However, much of this type of evidence tends to be subjective and difficult to quantify and hence has led to many disputes.

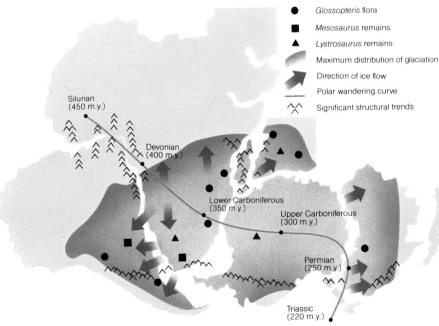

- ● *Glossopteris* flora
- ■ *Mesosaurus* remains
- ▲ *Lystrosaurus* remains
- Maximum distribution of glaciation
- ➤ Direction of ice flow
- ── Polar wandering curve
- ∧∧∧ Significant structural trends

Silurian (450 m.y.)
Devonian (400 m.y.)
Lower Carboniferous (350 m.y.)
Upper Carboniferous (300 m.y.)
Permian (250 m.y.)
Triassic (220 m.y.)

Such geological evidence has since been confirmed by more objective methods, mainly based on the study of the magnetization of rocks. Whenever a volcano erupts, then the molten rocks are non-magnetic, but as they solidify and cool further, they become magnetized in the direction of the Earth's magnetic field at that time and they are capable of retaining this direction for millions or even billions of years. Sedimentary rocks also contain magnetic grains and these also became aligned by the Earth's magnetic field during, and shortly after, the time of their deposition. Both rock types can therefore carry a 'magnetic memory' of the direction of the Earth's field at a specific time—the time that the rocks themselves formed. It is therefore possible to make records of changes in the Earth's magnetic field by studying the magnetization of rock samples of different ages. The main problems in such studies arise if the rocks have been chemically changed since their formation, such as during weathering processes, or if they have been reheated, such as by burial under thick layers of later sediments. In such circumstances, the original magnetization may be partially or totally overprinted.

It is not immediately obvious why such magnetic measurements should have any geological relevance, other than the fact that the oceanic rocks are able to record the changing polarity of the Earth's field—thereby allowing them to be dated. At the present day, the direction of the Earth's magnetic field gradually changes, averaging some 0·2° per year, but the changing directions tend to circulate around a mean direction. When such directional changes are averaged over an archaeological time scale of a few thousand years, then this mean direction is towards geographic north and the magnetic dip (the angle from horizontal) varies systematically from vertical near the present geographic poles to horizontal at the Equator. This means that the average position of the Earth's magnetic north pole during the last few thousand years corresponds with the location of the Earth's axis of rotation—the geographic pole of our planet.

Polar wandering

When the directions of magnetization in rocks of increasing age are examined from the same continent, their average magnetic pole position can be seen to gradually change away from the Earth's present rotational pole. This change, for most continents, is very slow and gradual, averaging some 0·3° per million years, and by plotting its position over several hundred million years, it is possible to construct a path showing the changing location of this average

magnetic pole position. Such polar wander paths are different for each continent. As the Earth's rotational pole remains fixed in space, the term 'polar wander path' is a misnomer as such paths do not arise because of the movement of the pole, but because the continents are moving relative to the pole. Although each continent has its own unique polar wander path, some of them are broadly similar in

shape, such as those of North America and Europe, or South America and Africa. If the continents are moved so that their polar paths match, then the resultant geographies are exactly those predicted by the geological matches.

While such matching of polar wander paths allows reconstructions of the ancient geographies, the inclination of the ancient magnetic field alone can be used to determine the ancient

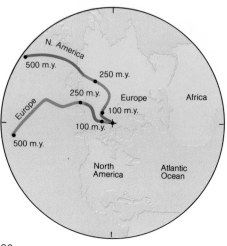

Left This map shows the apparent 'polar wander' curves for North America and Europe. The two lines meet only at the present-day pole, and are wide apart 500 m.y. ago. The curves are plotted according to rock magnetization, which records the position of the pole at the time the rock was magnetized. This magnetism is permanent in some rocks since their formation. The Earth's dipole magnetic field is thought to have remained throughout time, so to obtain these curves the continents must have moved relative to each other.

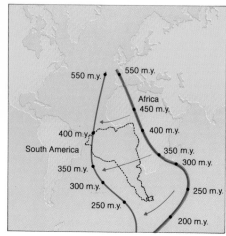

Left The polar wander curves for Africa and South America also diverge. A great deal of evidence (such as similar rock types) shows that these two land masses were joined for much of the Palaeozoic era. If this map is redrawn with the land-masses repositioned as they were in the Palaeozoic, the two curves follow a single line. This is further proof that the continents were joined. Since about 100 m.y. ago, South America and Africa have moved apart, forming the South Atlantic Ocean, and the frozen paths of polar wandering have diverged.

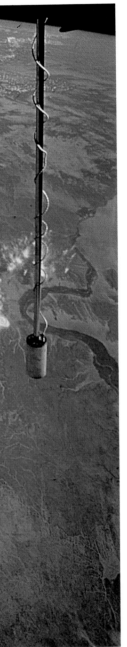

Left The Sinai Peninsula, the Red Sea, Arabia and Egypt are visible in this dramatic view from space. In many parts of Earth's crust, splitting of land areas is taking place to form new oceans, as occurred 100 m.y. ago when the present Atlantic first began to form, with the separation of what is now Africa and South America. The Red Sea is the site of a new ocean, which in 100 m.y. time may be of Atlantic proportions.
Right Taken by the crew of a *Gemini* spacecraft, this photo of the Red Sea and the Gulf of Aden shows the splitting off of a new ocean basin.
Below Along the west coast of USA further separation is taking place. Baja California, a peninsula reaching out parallel to the mainland, is gradually splitting off from the main part of California.

latitude in which the rocks lay when they were being magnetized. This means that it is also possible to test the reality of the ancient climatic evidence. When the continent lay near the Equator, then the magnetic inclinations in the rocks formed at that time will be low, while high latitudes will have steep inclinations. Such tests fully confirm that the 300 million-year-old fern forests of Europe and of Gondwana lay in respectively low and high latitudes.

The spreading oceans
At the moment, such observations, combined with the sea-floor spreading evidence, show that the Atlantic and Indian Oceans are still increasing their widths. North America began to separate from Africa some 180 million years ago—this spreading extending northwards and attempting to separate Greenland from Canada some 85 million years ago. However, after slightly separating these continents, the location of the oceanic spreading ridge changed and began to separate Greenland from Europe some 50 million years ago. Further south, the South Atlantic did not begin to form until 110 million years ago, when South America began to pivot away from Africa—the final link be-

tween the South and Central Atlantic not being established until some 90 million years ago. The Indian Ocean seems to have started opening only a little after the Central Atlantic, some 160 million years ago, when India and Antarctica began to separate from Africa. As India moved north, it collided with island arcs and then with Asia, forming the Himalayan mountains. Australia and New Zealand, however, remained attached to Antarctica until 80 million years ago, when New Zealand separated, with Australia separating only some 45 million years ago. The latest development was the spread of the Indian Ocean between Arabia and Africa as the Gulf of Aden and Red Sea were formed. This was only slightly older than the opening of the Gulf of California, some 10 million years ago, as Baja California began to move away from North America.

All of these new oceanic developments have occurred in areas where there have been no subduction zones—with the main exception of the Java Trench in the eastern Indian Ocean. This means that all of these new oceans must have expanded at the expense of the Pacific Ocean, where most of the subduction zones lie. Thus the area of the Pacific must have been

drastically reduced during the last 200 million years, despite this ocean being the site of the fastest sea-floor spreading rates during most of this great period of time.

The puzzle of the Arctic
One puzzling area is the Arctic. The Siberian side of the Arctic Basin is still opening, separating the continental Lomonosov Ridge away from Siberia, so this side of the Arctic Basin has been increasing in size. At the same time, it appears that North America, Europe and Asia are all moving northwards—which means that the total area of the Arctic Basin must be contracting —yet there is no evidence for active subduction in the Arctic. There are therefore several areas of the world where the plate tectonic model is apparently inadequate. However, most of these areas are where there is little information, and clearly these areas need more detailed study to determine their actual evolution or to assess the ways in which the present plate tectonic needs to be modified. The increasing application of new technology—including the bouncing of laser signals off satellites to measure continental drift—should soon begin to provide answers to some of these intriguing problems.

As with all new theories, it will be some time before the full significance of the plate tectonic concept can be really appreciated. Although it was essentially developed and tested by geophysical methods, its impact has been felt throughout the earth sciences. The fact that different continents can now be shown to have been either close together or separate at different times is obviously fundamental to any considerations of fossil plant and animal distributions, and hence to tests of theories of biological evolution. The impact on structural geology is similarly immense, indicating the way in which mountain belts can form and develop, although there are still problems of how stresses developed at collision zones between continents can be transmitted over immense distances. Another puzzle is what happens to cause sedimentary basins to form in one area and elevated blocks in another.

Economic benefits

It is equally difficult to evaluate the economic importance of plate tectonic theory. This is already proving fundamental in the planning of exploration programmes for both oil and mining companies. Oil, for example, appears to have only formed in vast quantities when the area concerned was lying within about 30° of the Equator, so that major deposits are unlikely to be found unless the area being studied was, at one time, in that latitudinal range. Even more pragmatically, the conditions for oil migration into reservoirs require the original organic materials to be gently warmed. Very fast heating will destroy the hydrocarbons, while very slow heating may mean that they have not yet accumulated into economic reservoirs. The actual degree of heating is largely controlled by their nearness to past and present oceanic spreading ridges, or the subduction zones—in other words, to past and present plate boundaries. Even the formation of the reservoirs is largely controlled by the way in which plate tectonic activity was operating at the time when the oil was migrating from its original sources. In a similar way, many of the metallic ore deposits found in sedimentary rocks also formed in low latitudes, while the volcanic metallic ores are clearly related to past plate tectonic boundaries, with the richest copper ores, such as those of Cyprus, having formed at previous sites of oceanic crustal formation. Other ores, such as those of the Andes of South America and the Western Cordillera of North America, formed in association with the subduction zones that still lie, or once lay, beneath them, giving rise to the zoned ore deposits at increasing distance from the previous subduction zone.

Problems of interpretation

An important feature of this model is that the continental rocks cannot be subducted, and therefore accumulate over subduction zones, although such continent blocks can then be split if new oceanic systems develop. This mean that the growth of the continents must be controlled by the creation of the lighter 'continental' rocks at the subduction zones. One of the major problems of Earth evolution is that the Earth, unlike the other planets which have so far been studied, has no preserved record of its earliest crustal rocks. The oldest continental rocks are only some 3,800-3,900 million years old, while the age of the Earth, Moon and planets is some 4,600 million years.

One possible explanation for this phenomenon is that no continental rocks could be created at such an early time. This would not be because subduction did not occur, as mantle convective motions must have happened at this time, but it is likely that the descending oceanic rocks were dehydrated at much shallower depths because of a more rapid increase of temperature with depth, and so the volcanic rocks could not be formed. As the Earth cooled, the first continental rocks began to form when cold oceanic rocks could be carried down to depths of some 60 miles (100km), after which continued, but very gradual, cooling allowed more and

more continental-type rocks to be generated. The explanation of the subsequent history of the continental crustal rocks is even more speculative, but there are distinct changes in their nature and scale some 2,500 million years ago, possibly associated with the formation of a single major continental block. This supercontinent has then been gradually broken down into different continental blocks, mainly during the last 1,000 million years. The details of this picture are, however, obscure, and even events during the last 500 million years are disputable, although it is generally agreed that continental splitting and closing have been

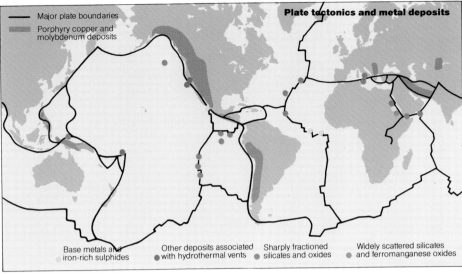

Plate tectonics and metal deposits

— Major plate boundaries
Porphyry copper and molybdenum deposits

Base metals and iron-rich sulphides • Other deposits associated with hydrothermal vents • Sharply fractioned silicates and oxides • Widely scattered silicates and ferromanganese oxides

Above Map of world distribution of metal ores in relation to modern plate margins. Looking for new metal deposits often involves applying plate-tectonics theory, as many of the richest metal ore deposits are connected with plate boundaries.
Left The Bingham Canyon copper mine is one of the Earth's largest human excavations, nearly half a mile deep and covering almost 3 square miles.
Right Lake Baikal in southern Siberia, near the border with Mongolia, is over 400 miles long and 50 miles wide. This 'lake' contains about 20 per cent of all the fresh water on the Earth's surface. Although this region is made up of continental crust, it is a very active zone, and here the crust may be splitting and a new ocean be starting to form.

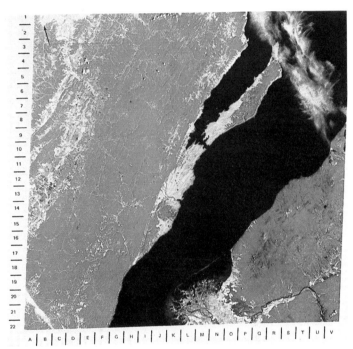

Right A computer projection of the configuration of land masses produced by continental drifting in 50 m.y. time. The South American continent will have split through the rift valley region. California and India will be separate 'islands', and there will be new mountain ranges—the Berings in the far north and another range in northern Australia. The Mediterranean will be part of the Atlantic.

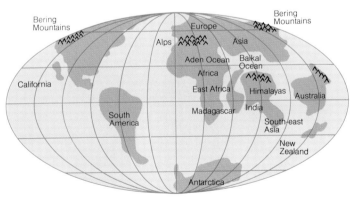

fundamental—the Atlantic, for example, having opened and closed along broadly similar lines at least three times during this period.

Future projections
Unless there is some drastic change within the next 50 million years or so, the Pacific Ocean must become smaller as the Atlantic and Indian oceans continue to grow. The growth should have finally split Arabia from Africa, and is likely to have extended down the East African Rift system. At the moment, this area is the site of earthquake and volcanic activity, possibly suggesting that a new oceanic ridge is already being initiated in this region. Similarly, parts of Siberia, such as the Lake Baikal area, may be the site of incipient ocean formation. In Europe, Asia and North America, new mountains may well be forming as these three continents approach each other across the north polar regions. However, by then northern Africa will have become strongly welded onto southern Europe as the Mediterranean develops into another Himalayan-like mountain system, and similarly, Australia will have developed a much more extensive mountain chain on its northern borders as it continues to plough through the island arcs of southeastern Asia.

As with any new theory, it is not the immediately obvious economic factors that are ultimately the most important. The main factor is that we now view the Earth from an entirely different angle. Features that were previously inexplicable now have an elegantly simple explanation, but many aspects of the Earth's surface still remain enigmatic. It seems unlikely, at this stage, that currently developing ideas will require drastic changes in the currently accepted theory, but it is certain that this theory has provided a major stimulus to all of the Earth Sciences, the effects of which will dominate our thinking for decades to come.

Since the young Earth's crust first solidified, new rock has been added from below. This molten rock, or magma, may remain deep in the crust, cooling slowly to form massive bloated batholiths and slender sheets called sills and dykes, or it may erupt as lava. Here, in Tequila, Mexico (*right*), the hard lava spine has remained after the rest of the volcano has been eroded.

Various processes, including wind and water action, reduce pre-formed rocks at the surface to eroded fragments, which are carried by rivers to form huge deltas. Sedimentary rocks, such as sandstones, form in this way. Rocks may be buried by dynamic forces such as plate tectonics and folding to depths where they are changed by heat and pressure or contact with magma, to form metamorphic rocks.

HOW ROCKS ARE FORMED

Probing material ejected by volcanoes, understanding the changes wrought deep underground, and analysing ancient sediments all teach geologists how rocks form and what treasures they may contain

Igneous rocks crystallize from molten magma under a great variety of conditions. Large masses of magma may intrude layers of rock deep in the crust, or magma may rise up and be extruded as lava, forming volcanoes. Depending on where the magma solidifies, both geographically and in relation to depth in the crust, a variety of igneous rocks may form.

The crystals which form from the freezing of the magma or lava will vary in size, shape and their relationship to each other, according to the cooling history of the rock they form. In a large, deep, intrusive body of magma, such as a batholith, cooling is slow, often taking tens of millions of years from initial injection to final consolidation. The crystals thus formed will be very large, and coarse-grained rocks such as granite and gabbro will result. In extreme cases, pegmatite forms, with exceptionally large crystals. When magma is forced along lines of weakness in the crustal rocks, often at no great depth, sheet-shaped sills and dykes are formed. These relatively narrow bodies cool quite rapidly and the grain size of the rock is therefore much smaller than in the deep plutonic masses. When lava flows out onto the surface, very small crystals form because cooling is swift; often a glass without recognizable crystals is produced. This rapid chilling is extreme when the lava is erupted in the sea.

Grain size

Rock texture is a product of the size of the grains and the relationships between them. A very common attractive texture found in the igneous rocks is that with large well-formed crystals set into a matrix of smaller crystals. This so-called 'porphyritic' texture is a result of two-stage cooling. Large crystals form first while cooling is slow. Then, for a variety of reasons, the magma, containing these large crystals in suspension, may be rapidly cooled, and the finer matrix is formed. The grain size, which is intimately related to the cooling history, is one of the criteria used in any classification of the various types of igneous rocks.

Different types of magma

Molten magma may have its origin hundreds of miles below the surface, in the Earth's mantle. The composition of the mantle at this depth is ultrabasic (consisting mainly of iron-magnesian minerals and having a low percentage of silica and felspar). Peridotite, which is sometimes brought from great depth by volcanoes, contains heavy, dense minerals such as olivine, an iron-magnesian silicate. It is possible for a great variety of igneous rocks to be derived from a magma which is rich in the so-called 'basic' components, containing a high proportion of silicates of iron and magnesium and generally deficient in silica. Recent research shows that even the 'acidic' (silica-rich) rocks can be derived from mantle material.

In a variety of places in the Earth's crust, solid rock melts to form magma. The materials with a low melting-point become liquid first. These are rich in elements such as silicon, calcium, magnesium, and iron oxides. Experimental work, in which a deep-seated rock was artificially melted, produced an initial melt composed of 68 per cent silicon dioxide, 10 per cent calcium oxide and 0.6 per cent magnesium oxide, with 1 per cent iron oxide and 13 per cent water. The melt derived in this way will be less dense than the rock from which it forms and so it will rise. At the mid-ocean ridges, basalt is extruded. This is of lower density than the mantle from which it is derived. At destructive boundaries more complex rocks form, because here sediment and other igneous rocks are subducted and mixed with the magma which has been generated at great depth.

Mineral formation

The silicate melt, which is magma, consists of chemical elements which form only a small number of minerals when it freezes into rock. Among these crystalline minerals the more common ones are quartz, felspars, amphiboles, pyroxenes and varying amounts of volatile substances such as water and various gases. There are definite sequences in which the minerals freeze out of the melt. At high temperatures the dark, denser minerals form. These are the silicates of iron and magnesium. Olivine forms first, followed by the pyroxenes, such as augite. These minerals, called 'pyrogenetic minerals', contain no water in their molecular structure. As the temperature of the melt falls, the water-rich 'hydratogenic minerals' such as hornblende and other amphiboles are formed.

Above Where igneous rocks cool determines their grain size. Their chemistry depends on their origin. Basic rocks (left), come from the lowest parts of the crust. Acid rocks (right) are made from the upper crust. Granite is in the magma chamber, micro-granite in smaller masses and rhyolite is erupted. The intermediate igneous rocks (centre) are diorite at depth, micro-diorite in the offshoots and andesite as lava.

GRAIN SIZE / CHEMISTRY	COARSE Over 2 mm (easy to see)	MEDIUM 0.2–2 mm (visible to naked eye)	FINE Less than 0.2 mm (visible only with a lens)	TYPICAL MINERALS
ACID	GRANITE	MICRO-GRANITE	RHYOLITE	Quartz Orthoclase Plagioclase Mica
INTERMEDIATE	DIORITE	MICRO-DIORITE	ANDESITE	Features of both Acid and Basic
BASIC	GABBRO	DOLERITE	BASALT	Plagioclase Pyroxene Olivine
ULTRABASIC	PERIDOTITE			Pyroxene Olivine
FIELD OCCURRENCE	PLUTONIC (Batholiths)	HYPABYSSAL (Sills and dykes)	VOLCANIC (Volcanoes)	

Diagram labels: RHYOLITE, ANDESITE, BASALT — VOLCANIC; Micro-granite, Micro-diorite, Dolerite — HYPABYSSAL; GRANITE, DIORITE, GABBRO — PLUTONIC; Melting No Mixing, Melting Mixing, Very little melting; CONTINENTAL CRUST, MANTLE, POSSIBLE ORIGINS

Chemically, these are similar to pyroxenes, apart from the presence of water. Finally, biotite mica crystallizes. This series of minerals increases in complexity, but the minerals do not grade one into another. For this reason, the sequence they form is referred to as a discontinuous series.

A contrast with these ferro-magnesians is shown by the pale, low-density mineral family known as the plagioclase felspars. At high temperatures, while olivine is forming, the calcium-rich plagioclase, anorthite, crystallizes. As cooling progresses, sodium replaces the calcium in the felspar structure and eventually albite, a sodium plagioclase, is formed. This substitution of calcium by sodium allows a whole series of plagioclases to form, with varying proportions of calcium and sodium between the two end-members. Eventually, if the melt still has enough potassium, aluminium and silica, orthoclase felspar and quartz appear.

As a silicate melt freezes and minerals form, elements are subtracted from the melt, and magmas which are initially low in silica may never produce quartz or orthoclase felspar. Magmas initially rich in sodium, potassium and aluminium will tend to produce rocks such as granite and rhyolite; those rich in magnesium, iron and calcium but deficient in silica will produce rocks such as gabbro and basalt.

However, as has been suggested earlier, it is possible for a 'basic' magma to produce acidic and ultra-basic rocks through differentiation. If, for example, a sheet of basic magma is injected among layers of cool sediments, its margins will freeze and produce a fine-grained basic rock such as dolerite or basalt. Within the still-molten body of magma olivine will form and, being of high density, will sink through the melt, forming a heavy, coarse-grained ultra-basic rock towards the base of the sheet. An example of this type of rock is dunite. As the

Above Volcanic landforms are not always masses of hard solid lava. Here, in Tenerife, in the Canary Islands, off north-west Africa, a volcanic eruption of cinders, dust and ash has produced a spectacular landscape which is in marked contrast to the classic cones of Japan and South America.

rest of the melt freezes, the upper parts of the body will form, assuming a generally basic composition. If cooling is slow and the conditions are favourable, a silica-rich layer may develop at a very late stage in the cooling history. This may have a composition approaching andesite.

Igneous rocks are classified and named according to the two criteria discussed above, grain size and chemistry. Granite and gabbro are both coarse-grained because they cool slowly but because they contain different minerals, granite is acidic and gabbro basic. Gabbro and basalt are made of the same minerals, but are classified as different rocks because basalt is fine-grained as a result of its rapid cooling.

71

In the depths of the Earth's crust, the molten rock, or magma, rises because it is less dense than the surrounding rock, and may eventually well out onto the surface. Very often, however, the magma solidifies at depth to form an intrusive body of crystalline rock. Such intrusions vary considerably in shape and size. Some are small, while others are of immense proportions, with surface areas of hundreds of square miles. When their exact base is unknown, these enormous underground blisters of igneous rock are called batholiths.

Anatomy of a batholith

The batholith in south-west Britain which stretches from Devon and Cornwall out into the Atlantic Ocean covers an area some 40 miles by 25 miles (65km by 40km). Although this is small when compared with the giant intrusions of South Africa and America, it has been so thoroughly investigated that its structure and composition are known in detail. For hundreds of years, the rich mineral veins, yielding tin and other valuable metals, have been mined, and the granite rock of which the batholith is made is ramified with mine workings. These have provided a wealth of information for geological researchers.

The batholith is exposed as a series of cupolas (dome-shaped upward extensions from the main body of the intrusion). Revealed by weathering and erosion of several miles of over-lying rock, these cupolas now form areas such as Dartmoor, Bodmin Moor and St Austell Moor. The outlying islands called the Scillies are a seaward extension of the batholith. Geophysical investigations, backed up by old mining records, show that the cupolas are linked at shallow depths. As the magma rose vertically in the south, then pushed horizontally northwards to crumple the overlying sedimentary rock strata, it carried with it small crystals of sodium-rich plagioclase felspar, which had crystallized from the magma melt. These crystals became orientated at right angles to the regional pressures. The magma was unable to push the overlying rocks upwards to any great extent, so the 'roof' of sedimentary rock cracked, and large blocks of rock fell into the magma, where they were dissolved.

As the magma cooled, a granite mass with uniformly sized crystals was produced. The magma contained volatiles—substances that would normally be gases at the high temperatures found in a magma, but which are dissolved because of the high pressures. These volatiles,

including water vapour, carried potassium and other elements which changed the crystals in the rock. Sodium atoms in the felspars were replaced by potassium atoms. The volatiles also penetrated the surrounding sedimentary rock strata, producing mineral veins rich in tin, copper, and wolfram (tungsten), and even altering the margins of the granite. Eventually, the volatile fluids accumulated under the domed-up roofs of the granite, to cool and crystallize slowly into a rock called pegmatite. This is notable for its very large crystals, which often contain precious gemstones.

Below Beneath S.W. England lies a gigantic batholith: much eroded, it is now exposed.

Top Vixen Tor on Dartmoor, England, shows well the effect of weathering on the joint systems of granite.

Electricity from the rocks?

Recent research on this batholith in south-west Britain has revealed that even now, 290 million years after the granite cooled, the rock may be a source of geothermal power (heat from the Earth's interior). Granite batholiths are regions of high heat-flow from the depths, and where there is an overlying area of insulating clay, as in the Paris basin in France, the heat is trapped near the surface. Such heat might possibly be used one day to produce electricity in a much cleaner and safer way than more conventional methods, but the high cost of extracting the heat is a major drawback.

Giant batholiths

The largest intrusions of all are invariably made of granite. One such intrusion in Malaya is 300 miles (480 km) long. The coastal batholiths of British Columbia, Canada, and Peru, South America, are over 1,000 miles long and 120 miles across (1,600km by 190km). The outcrops of batholiths at the surface often take the form of depressions, in which lie inclusions of dramatically altered sedimentary rock. This metamorphosed 'country' rock represents parts of the overlying roof of the intrusion which hung down like giant chandeliers into the molten magma chamber. Other fragments represent rock masses which have broken off the roof and walls of the magma chamber to fall into the melt and become assimilated.

Other major intrusions

As well as the batholiths, there are a number of other types of large intrusions. A lopolith is a saucer-shaped mass with a vertical feeder channel at its base. In the Transvaal region of

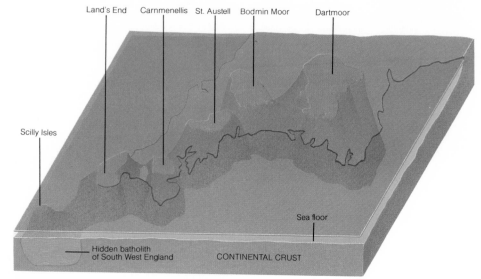

Land's End Carnmenellis St. Austell Bodmin Moor Dartmoor

Scilly Isles

Sea floor

Hidden batholith of South West England   CONTINENTAL CRUST

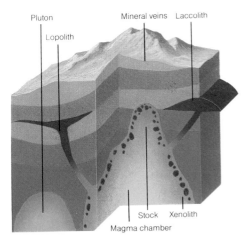

Pluton — Mineral veins — Laccolith — Lopolith — Stock — Xenolith — Magma chamber

Above Large igneous intrusions form a variety of structures, from saucer-shaped lopoliths to huge batholiths and smaller plutons.

Right Granite contains grey quartz, pale felspar and dark micas.
Below Gabbro is a mosaic of dark pyroxene and pale felspar.

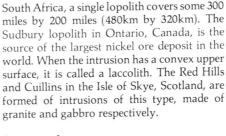

South Africa, a single lopolith covers some 300 miles by 200 miles (480km by 320km). The Sudbury lopolith in Ontario, Canada, is the source of the largest nickel ore deposit in the world. When the intrusion has a convex upper surface, it is called a laccolith. The Red Hills and Cuillins in the Isle of Skye, Scotland, are formed of intrusions of this type, made of granite and gabbro respectively.

A matter of controversy

The origin and means of emplacement of these gigantic volumes of originally molten rock have been a source of fierce arguments between geologists for many years. Some have argued that granite was made by a process in which the pre-existing rocks were invaded by low-melting fluids rich in silica, aluminium, sodium and potassium, and turned into granitic rock. Others believe that the igneous rock is formed by melting of the sedimentary rocks deep in the crust. Research has shown that both processes can occur, especially where continental collisions have folded and buckled buried sea-floor sediments containing large amounts of sea-water, which helps to lower their melting points. Whichever way the rock is altered, the overall process, which can lead from sediment to metamorphic and ultimately igneous rock, is called granitization.

Xenoliths

Whatever its origin, granitic magma is the least dense of the molten rock materials in the depths of the crust. It can rise towards the surface, sometimes breaking through overlying strata, as do the salt domes common in southern Iran. The sides of many large intrusions show a sharp contact with the surrounding country rocks, which are also buckled, suggesting this forceful means of intrusion. Around the margins of many large intrusions there are offshoots of igneous rock which invade and surround large blocks of country rock called xenoliths. These xenoliths become indistinct deeper in the intrusion where they have been altered by metamorphism. By surrounding masses of country rock in this way, the magma is able to force itself into the strata. It melts its way in and so takes over the volume occupied by the country rock in a more subtle fashion. This process, called stoping, is possibly what happens in many large intrusions, because enormous masses of rock have to be removed to make a space for the intrusion.

When molten magma invades the upper layers of the crust, it solidifies in a great variety of shapes, which are controlled by existing structures and weaknesses in the already formed rocks. Minor intrusions are those which, when compared with batholiths and plutons, are small and formed at high levels in the crust. The two best-known types of minor intrusions are sills (where the magma follows existing rock structures) and dykes (where the magma cuts across the strata or other structures at an angle). These two igneous features are parallel-sided sheet-shaped intrusions which may fill in joints, faults and other weaknesses in the crust. Where there is no obvious line of weakness in the crustal rocks, the pressure of the magma may be great enough to force its way into pre-formed rock. This hydrostatic pressure will usually take advantage of any slight weaknesses, so the magma may take on various shapes. Intrusions may begin as vertical dykes, then follow a horizontal weakness, then branch in various directions to produce a variety of complex structures.

Dyke swarms

Minor intrusions can form around large intrusions, such as batholiths, where offshoots from the main magma body find weaknesses in the surrounding country rocks, but they most commonly occur where the Earth's crust is being actively stretched, especially at spreading ridges. In Iceland, which straddles the Mid-Atlantic Ridge, continual spreading of the crust produces fissures which fill up with magma. This cools to form large 'swarms' of dykes. Such dyke swarms are well documented from the past, as, for example, in the Isle of Arran off the south-west coast of Scotland, where hundreds of dykes, intruded about 60 million years ago, during the Tertiary period, extended the crust by over six per cent. Dykes forming these swarms characteristically run

Above Here in Absaroka, USA, a hard andesite dyke still stands after erosion surrounding softer deposits has removed it.

Right Erosion has exposed a spectacular sill and feeder dyke in the Canary Isles off the north-west coast of Africa.

parallel to each other and are very numerous, frequently covering impressive distances.

Dyke swarms are occasionally radial when they are associated with volcanoes, as on the Hawaiian volcanoes of Oahu, and in the Absarokas volcanic region in western USA. Recent research has shown that dyke swarms feed magma into the volcanic magma chambers. Sills may often be fed from beneath by dykes. If there is a large enough supply of magma, the sill may reach a great thickness. The Palisades Sill in New Jersey, which is over 1,000ft (300m) thick, and the Mount Wellington Sill in Tasmania are large enough to show clear layering of their crystal structures. This helps geologists to work out the order in which the minerals in the

Above A thin section of dolerite shows the beautiful structure of this medium-grained basic rock. The crystals are randomly orientated, consisting of plagioclase felspar (thin lath-shaped, black and white crystals) and pyroxene (darker, colourful crystals). This rock is typically found in sills and dykes.

Left A dyke exposed by erosion at Lanzarote, in the Canary Isles off north-west Africa, where volcanic rocks and associated features are revealed.

Above right Minor intrusions can originate from magma chambers at depth as on this diagram. Usually they occur as sheets, either cutting across pre-formed rock strata or following bedding planes and other structures. Concordant sills follow the existing patterns; dykes, which are discordant, cut across earlier structures. Sheet intrusions are often associated with volcanic activity. Cone sheets and ring dykes usually lie below volcanoes, and are revealed by weathering.

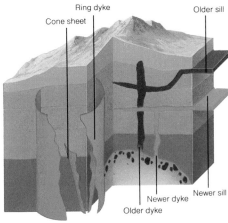

Ring dyke
Cone sheet
Older sill
Newer dyke
Newer sill
Older dyke

rock crystallize. The magma is molten when it is injected and the top and base of the sill is quickly solidified in contact with cool country rock to form a fine-grained rock. The Palisades Sill has a distinct layer just above its base which is very rich in the greenish-brown mineral olivine. Above this the sill is typical dolerite, with larger crystals in the centre, because of slower cooling. The explanation for the occurrence of the olivine-rich layer is that olivine is one of the first crystals to solidify in magma, and, because the rest of the magma was molten when the high-density olivine crystals formed, they sank through the melt to settle at its base. As well as this layered nature of many sills, they also characteristically trans-gress from one position among the layers of country rock to a higher level, through short steps or dykes. The Whin Sill in Northern England rises in this way through strata of Carboniferous age. Sills can occur as swarms, as in the Karoo dolerites of South Africa and in Antarctica and Tasmania. In the latter case, they cover an area of approximately 4,000sq miles (10,400sq km).

Resistant dolerite

Most sills and dykes are made of the dark heavy 'basic' rock of medium to fine grain-size called dolerite. This rock is very resistant to weathering, and the intrusions often stand above the surrounding countryside as ridges and escarpments. The rock is also often quarried for constructional use because of its durability and hardness. Because it is molten at temperatures of about 1,000°C (1,832°F), the magma has a marked effect on the country rock next to it. The extent of this effect depends on the size of the sill or dyke, but metamorphism may extend for tens of feet on either side of the intrusion. The shrinkage of the magma during consolidation produces cooling joints which sometimes form marked 'columnar' joint structures at right angles to the surfaces of the intrusive sheet.

Ring dykes and cone sheets

Associated with volcanoes are two special types of minor intrusions called ring dykes and cone sheets. When a violent strato-volcano erupts and collapses to form a caldera the magma rapidly releases its gas and within a few days, or even hours, millions of tons of pulverized rocks are ejected. The structure of the volcano is thus weakened and circular cracks develop. Magma fills these ring fractures as they form, solidifying to produce ring dykes. In Medicine Lake Volcano in California, there are nine steep-sided ring dykes. In Iceland, smaller parasitic cones develop on the Askja Volcano, where ring dykes break the surface. In the Isle of Mull off the west coast of Scotland, a centre of violent volcanic activity about 60 million years ago, there are classic ring dyke and cone sheet complexes. Cone sheets resemble concentric ice-cream cones. It is possible that before eruption a volcano can become inflated so that enough hydrostatic pressure is built up to make cone-shaped fractures, which are quickly filled with magma. After the explosive eruption, the volcano deflates; this is when the ring fractures are formed.

All these varied forms of minor intrusions are linked by the common factor of basaltic volcanism. (Acid igneous intrusions can also form sills and dykes but these are insignificant). New forms are often discovered, and it is difficult to catalogue these within the well-known types. 'Bell-jar'-shaped intrusions have been described from Iceland, and dykes plunging down from sills and back into the crust are also known from various localities.

From the elegant, symmetrical cone of Japan's Mount Fujiyama to the flattened craters of Iceland, and the ragged crescent of Santorin (Thera) in the Greek Aegean, volcanoes come in a wide variety of shapes and sizes. All are formed when magma from the Earth's mantle, heated to liquid mobility by pressure and friction, gains access to the Earth's surface, and is propelled outwards by expanding gases.

A volcano's shape is determined by the nature of its eruption, which in turn is governed by the related factors of magma type, gas content, and explosive intensity. Active volcanoes continue to change shape over the years— sometimes gradually, over centuries, and sometimes suddenly, in explosive eruptions. The most important factor determining the type of eruption is the consistency of the magma. Very fluid magma, with a low viscosity, usually produces relatively mild volcanic activity. The gas that powers the eruption is easily released from the magma, which then flows as lava from the "boccas" (mouths) and fissures through which it has forced an exit. The hot, destructive lava often travels considerable distances over the surface of the land.

Hawaiian-type volcanoes
The basaltic rock which forms magma of low viscosity has a silica content of less than 50 per cent. Volcanoes produced from this basaltic magma usually have a low profile, though the base can be wide. The dome-shaped mountains of the Hawaiian Islands have been raised by the gradual build-up over very many years of lava emissions. Iceland, the Azores, and Tristan da Cunha, all astride the spreading axis of the Mid-Atlantic Ridge, are also made up mainly of basalts. Although islands may take millions of years to grow from ocean floor lava vents, the process can be much faster. Capelinhos in the Azores has gradually grown from sea level to over 3,300ft (1,000m) high since first appearing out of the ocean in 1957.

Basaltic magma eruptions are not always gentle. Kilauea in the Hawaiian Islands threw hot lava to an altitude of over 600ft (180m) in its 1959 eruption. Iceland's Hekla, erupting in 1947 for the first time in 102 years, split its ridge wide open and emitted an ash cloud that eventually reached Finland, over 1,500 miles (2,400km) away. Violent volcanic activity is, however, rare in the case of basaltic magmas, and usually occurs only when water gains access to the molten interior of the volcano. The sudden conversion of water to steam generates violent explosions that fragment the magma into very fine rock particles. This type of volcanism is known as Surtseyan activity, after the island of Surtsey which grew swiftly out of the sea off the south coast of Iceland in 1963 (with intermittent eruptions to 1967).

Strombolian volcanoes
The island volcano of Stromboli, north of Sicily, is over 2,900ft (900m) high, the archetypal volcanic cone of popular imagination. Stromboli, like Vesuvius and Fujiyama, has acquired its regular shape from successive layers of lava and ejected, or 'pyroclastic', material, such as ash, volcanic glass, pumice and larger particles of fragmented magma. Strombolian activity, stemming from magmas with a higher silica content than basalt, though still less than 66 per cent, can vary in intensity from mild to violent. The lava flows are generally quietly released from boccas in the volcano's sides. Stromboli itself is in continuous mild eruption, with a red glow permanently visible over the cone at night. Such composite or strato-cone, volcanoes often have their shapes emphasized by massive ribs of solidified lava. There are two components in Strombolian eruptions, ballistic ejecta and non-ballistic ejecta. The former fall concentrically around the vent, being too heavy to be affected by the wind. The non-ballistic ejecta consists of windborne fragments and dusts which are deposited downwind. As they build up, they give the cone a windward side that slopes more steeply than the leeward side.

Andesite volcanoes
The 'ring of fire' surrounding the Pacific Ocean is made up of volcanoes produced by magmas of intermediate silica content and viscosity. Called 'Andesite' after the Andes mountain range, this magma type runs the full length of the West coast of the Americas, crosses to Asia via the Aleutian Islands, and runs south via Japan to split into a number of branches underlying the volcanic systems of Indonesia, Kermadec-Tonga, New Zealand and Antarctica.

Above Volcanic eruptions assume different forms. Fissure eruptions (**1**) produce the most voluminous flows of basic runny lava that may cover and lay waste huge areas. Hawaiian eruptions (**2**) produce a less-fluid lava and build up a low-angled volcano that often contains a lava lake. More violent Strombolian-type activity (**3**) produces fire fountains of red-hot ash that builds characteristic cones. Lava often flows from breaches in the cone. Water reacts explosively with molten rock to give Surtseyan cones (**4**) with wide craters and low walls. A Plinian eruption (**5**) is a constant gas blast that reaches immense heights. Plinian eruptions are the most violent, with huge volumes of material blasted out by deep-level explosive release of gas.

Left The 1983 Kilauea Rift eruption in Hawaii forms fire fountains where gases escape through basaltic lava. Moving slowly over a 'hot spot' in the Earth's mantle, the Hawaiian Islands are the youngest of a chain of ancient volcanoes.
Above Explosive activity along destructive plate margins is shown by New Zealand's Ngauruhoe, where nested summit craters formed during 1976.
Right Astride a spreading plate margin in the Danakil Depression, Ethiopia, the lava lake in Erta Elé Caldera vents gas clouds.

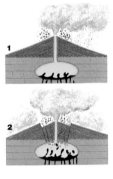

Left Caldera formation. A continuous or steadily reverberating Plinian eruption (**1**) discharges huge volumes of tephra from the magma chamber, which are dispersed over a wide area. Large ballistic blocks fall near the vent, while fine ash is borne away by the wind. With falling gas pressure, the eruption column may collapse to form nuées ardentes, while the summit of the volcano slowly sinks into the evacuating magma chamber (**2**) to form a circular depression called a caldera (**3**). This may contain a lake and post-collapse cones.

The greater viscosity of Andesitic magma retains the gases more persistently, so that pressure builds up, often blasting free through the overlying rock with explosive violence. The eruption of Mount Katmai in Alaska in 1912 excavated a crater 3,700ft (1,130m) deep. The explosion was heard 750 miles (1,200km) away, and even 100 miles (160km) away the dust deposited was up to 1ft (30cm) thick. In 1980, Mount St Helens, Washington, USA, part of the same Andesitic ring, became one of the most closely observed of modern eruptions, exploding with sufficient power to remove a large part of the mountain and to scythe 200 square miles (500sq km) of forest to the ground with its hot, debris-laden blast.

The most violent volcanoes

Acidic magmas contain high concentrations of silica—over 66 per cent—as well as higher levels of potassium, aluminium and sodium than are found in basalts. These very viscous magmas produce the most violent of all volcanic eruptions, often solidifying in the chimney of the volcano, to form a plug which allows enormous pressures to accumulate. The resulting explosion can be devastating, reducing the magma to dense clouds of fine fragments in a plume that can reach well over 12 miles (20km) in height, spreading ejecta over many thousands of square miles.

The most violent of our planet's eruptions have been so destructive that they have left only insignificant looking deposits. The explosion of Krakatoa in Java in 1883 sent a dust cloud right around the world, affected climatic conditions for more than three years, and killed over 36,000 people, many of whom were drowned in giant tidal waves. All that remained of the three-coned island was a huge caldera or crater reaching 900 feet (280m) below sea level. Crater Lake in Oregon, USA, is the caldera, 6 miles (9·6km) in diameter, of the eruption which destroyed the cone of Mount Mazama 7,000 years ago, covering an area of over 4,900,000 square miles (12,690,000sq km) with ash in the process.

Calderas are formed when the ground above a magma chamber complex settles into the space vacated by the magma. Recent research has shown the existence of volcanoes which have no cone and lie at normal ground level.

There is no material from which a cone can be built up, since the explosive eruption has been of such cataclysmic dimensions that the ejecta, being highly pulverized, is dispersed totally. When caldera collapse occurs in such cases, the caldera floor is depressed below normal ground level. Usually, calderas lie within the volcanic edifice well above normal ground level.

The largest active volcano on Earth is Mauna Loa in the Hawaiian group, 30,000ft (9,144m) high from its ocean floor base, and rising 13,677ft (4,158m) above sea level. Mauna Loa has a dome 30 miles (48km) wide and 60 miles (97km) long. Its crater is 600ft (183m) deep.

Volcanoes in outer space

Large though it is, Mauna Loa is dwarfed by some of the volcanoes discovered by recent space exploration programmes. Pictures taken by Viking orbiters in 1976 over Mars revealed, among others, a volcano named Olympus Mons standing some 14 miles (23km) above its surrounding plain, and having a diameter of 310 miles (500km). It is possible that even larger volcanoes exist on Venus. It has long been known that our own Moon has a volcanic history. Over a decade before the Apollo 11 mission numerous high resolution photographs transmitted to Earth by the Ranger, Surveyor and Orbiter spacecraft proved the existence of huge lava flows from volcanic fissures, as well as massive volcanic calderas among the multitude of meteor-impact craters. It is probable that meteor impacts have been instrumental in triggering large lunar volcanic eruptions.

When a volcano erupts, a wide variety of substances is vented from the earth, including many gases, solid fragments from varying depths, lava, dust, and water (usually in the form of steam). To help in the analysis of volcanic deposits, volcanologists have divided the ejected products into three main groups. In the initial explosive eruption, what are termed the pyroclastic fall deposits are blasted skywards. In a text-book eruption these would be followed, as gas pressure was reduced, by the pyroclastic flow deposits. The lava flow deposits, needing the least gas pressure to eject them, would come last.

Pyroclastic fall deposits

Pyroclastic fall deposits are both created and ejected by explosive eruptions, and fall back to the ground or settle through water to form layers over the landscape similar to a heavy snowfall. This regular layering is called mantle bedding, and the further away from the source vent, the thinner the layers and the smaller the grain sizes. Relatively close to the eruption vent, and distributed concentrically around it, are the heaviest fragments. Some are lumps of solid rock torn from the sides of the eruptive vent. These are called lithic fragments. All fragments large enough to be unaffected by the wind in their distribution are known as ballistic ejecta. As well as surface rock they also include large pieces of congealing lava, and most pyroclastic fall deposits contain a great deal of fresh lava called juvenile fragments. Volcanic bombs are large juvenile fragments with ballistic shapes ranging from spindles to spheres. The bread-crust bomb is a large glob of gas-rich magma of which the outer crust rapidly cools as it flies through the air. Inside, however, the molten rock is still releasing gas, causing the hard outer shell to crack, and the bomb to swell, to resemble the upper crust of a freshly baked loaf of bread.

The non-ballistic fragments which are light enough to be affected by wind currents are dragged downwind by the prevailing airstream. As the larger grains fall first, these wind-borne deposits build a tapering ellipse, dune-like in profile, with the vent at the higher end. The fresh lava fragments are often frothy with gas expansion cavities and escape holes, and very light-weight, floating where they land on water. The light-coloured fragments are called pumice, the dark are called scoria, and together they are known generally as tephra. Shards are the tiny slivers of glass formed when magma bubbles burst, and obsidian is the glass-like product of the eruption. It can be shattered into fragments by explosive activity.

In an explosive eruption, some or all of these pyroclastic fall components, together with huge amounts of volcanic dust released as old magma plugs are shattered, billow to high altitudes before spreading and falling. The amount of material released can be staggering. Mount St Helens produced 0·25 cubic kilometres of ejecta in the course of its 1980 eruption. The ash-cloud rose higher than 66,000ft (20,000m), with some of the airborne dust completely circling the globe within seventeen days. Yet earlier historical eruptions produced far greater quantities of ejecta. Krakatoa in Java produced 18 cubic kilometres in 1883, while the nearby Tambora produced an estimated 30 cubic kilometres in 1815, masking the sun sufficiently to cool the Earth and cause the 'year without summer' in 1816.

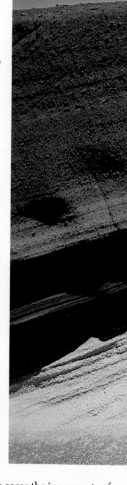

Left A breadcrust bomb at Vulcano, Italy, formed by hot pumice expanding inside after the crust had solidified.
Right Ash layers in the Canary Isles reveal the history of volcanic eruptions. Black basaltic bands represent Strombolian activity. White pumice bands represent an earlier Plinian eruption.
Below Columnar jointing in basalt, Mexico, caused by cracks formed due to shrinkage on cooling.

Pyroclastic flows

Pyroclastic flows and nuées ardentes (glowing clouds) consist of a dense suspension of fragments in a red-hot gas cloud that flows downhill at great speed, propelled by a volcanic explosion. When Mount Pelée in Martinique erupted in 1902 a nuée ardente destroyed the town of St Pierre, 5 miles (8km) below in a matter of seconds. The temperature of the ash and gas cloud on that occasion is estimated to have reached 1,800°F (980°C), and such flows are nearly always of high temperature. The deposits they leave are usually small in volume, rich in juvenile fragments or breadcrust bombs. Large pyroclastic flow deposits are made up mainly of pumice and glass shards, filling up valleys and depressions, sometimes

to great depths. In these cases the inner parts of the flow retain enough heat to weld the material into a dense mass under the weight of the overlying flow. Heavy rains can convert a pyroclastic flow into a volcanic mudflow, sometimes mobilizing deposits that have already come to rest. The ash cloud towering above an eruption can produce both rain and lightning. Heavy rain can flush ash out of the atmosphere and deposit it as a thin, even-grained layer. Sometimes ash accretes around falling raindrops to produce concentrically banded ash spheres. When lightning strikes fresh ash-falls, the ash melts to form a branching network of glass tubes coated with slightly fused ash and pumice. These are called fulgurites.

In the course of time, pyroclastic fall and

Stratopause

Tropopause

Km
— 50
— 40
— 30
— 20
—10

Left The diagram shows the volume of airborne debris (measured in dense rock equivalents, ignoring the air) of some major volcanoes over the past 9,000 years.
1 Mt St Helens, Washington State, USA produced 0·25cu km of debris in 1980.
2 El Chichon, Mexico produced 0·2cu km in 1982.
3 Vesuvius, Italy: 3cu km in AD 79.
4 Katmai, Alaska, USA: 10cu km in 1912.
5 Bezymianny, Kamchatka, USSR: 4cu km in 1956.
6 Mazama, Oregon, USA: 20cu km in 7,000 BC.
7 Tambora, Indonesia: 50cu km in 1815.

flow deposits become compressed into solid rock and are difficult to identify. Nearly all fall deposits harden to form a compact rock called tuff. Pyroclastic flows are recognizable from the plates of black obsidian resulting from pumice being compressed in thick deposits.

Viscous lava

Viscous lava flows are generally released in the later stages of explosive eruptions to form domes and spines in the volcano's chimney. Where the magma is more fluid the lava usually flows throughout the eruption. Flood basalts are the result of massive, and often repeated, releases of lava. Usually originating in steady fissure lava emissions, they can extend for miles in flat, layered plateaux, as in

Iceland. Lava streams usually occur where the emission is less, or the terrain steeper, as in the Hawaiian group. Both Mauna Loa and Kilauea regularly release lava flows which pour in slow rivers down the steep mountains, sometimes extending the islands by reaching the sea.

Lava forms itself into many shapes and textures as it cools, sometimes distorted into twisted ropes, sometimes cooling into irregular clinkers, occasionally into large blocks. Large gas bubbles form blisters, and converging lava streams build pressure ridges. Escaping gas can build up spatter cones like miniature volcanoes.

A key to the past

A careful study of volcanic deposits can give us a detailed account of early eruptions. A study

of one particular cross-section of volcanic strata on the island of Tenerife in the Canaries has revealed an opening eruptive sequence of fine ash still containing the leaf moulds it buried. The next layer, of pumice and reddened rock fragments, indicates a gas-blast stage involving high-pressure steam. Thunderstorms at this point fused glassy fulgurites into the ash layer. There followed massive pyroclastic flows, producing deposits tens of feet thick 15 miles (24km) from the source, completely filling some of the volcano's radial valleys. Overlying this is a fine ash layer washed out of the ash cloud by torrential rain. The sequence of fall deposit followed by flow deposit is repeated twice more. The magnitude of this ancient eruption was over ten times that of Krakatoa.

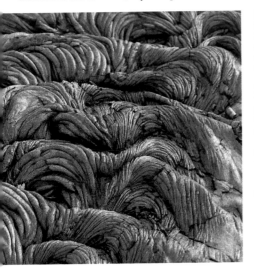

Left Pahoehoe, or ropy lava, is produced by basalt when special conditions allow the cooler surface crust to stretch and bend as the molten interior carries it along. Here, earlier formed simple folds have been refolded several times to produce a complex surface which resembles twisted ropes.
Right Upstream from the twisted ropes the pahoehoe lava is smooth, indicating a high-velocity flow. After the pahoehoe lava had solidified, a younger, more viscous magma formed the black aa lava, which flowed over the surface of the pahoehoe.

Throughout recorded history, volcanic eruptions have been responsible for some of the largest disasters known, taking many tens of thousands of human lives and destroying wildlife, crops, livestock and property. In economic terms, eruptions such as those of Krakatoa, in 1983, and Laki, in 1783, caused such widespread and long-term damage that the total loss can only be estimated.

In fact, the volcanic eruption at Krakatoa was not itself directly responsible for the great loss of life. This was largely the result of the massive waves, or tsunamis, produced by the seismic activity associated with the eruption. These inundated the coasts of Java and Sumatra, destroying villages and farmland, drowning thousands of the islands' inhabitants, and compounding the effects of widespread disease and famine. The details of these secondary effects of volcanism are, however, poorly documented for Krakatoa, and it is to Iceland that we must turn to seek such information.

Destruction in Iceland

On 8 June 1783, a fissure 15½ miles (25km) long opened across southern Iceland, accompanied by violent releases of gases and dramatic fountains of fire. The second day saw the beginning of one of the greatest outpourings of lava ever recorded. It was not until eight months later that the eruption finally ended, and during the intervening time over 12cu km of lava had spread over 220sq miles (565sq km) of Iceland's countryside, having been vented to the surface at rates as fast as 6,500cu yd (5,000cu m) per second. Volcanologists think that as much as 154 million tons of volcanic gases were released during the eruption, as well as huge volumes of fine dust. Rain falling through these gases became sufficiently acid to burn holes in vegetation and leave spots on the skin of new-born sheep. As the gas-cloud enveloped Iceland, large numbers of birds died, crops turned yellow and withered and grazing livestock perished, either through lack of food or by being poisoned by the fluorine that had contaminated the grass. Dead sheep lay huddled together in hollows, suffocated by the carbon dioxide that had accumulated there, in the very places they had sought shelter.

Contemporary reports tell of horses losing all their flesh, the hide rotting off the backs of cattle and their manes and tails falling off. One account includes such reports as:

"Cattle, also, were subjected to the same plague . . . the tail fell off with the tuft of hair . . . The hooves loosened and slipped off, or sometimes split in the middle. The ribs were deformed along the side and then broke apart in the middle, unable to support the weight of the beast when it must needs lie on its side." Some of the people of Iceland suffered a similar fate. Bumps and hard knobs appeared on their bones; their teeth, and in at least one case a tongue, dropped out. The fish stock in the surrounding sea was seriously affected, which, together with the loss of livestock and produce, reduced Iceland's population by over 10,000— about one-fifth of the total population.

The importance of climate

The effect of volcanic eruptions and soil fertility is, more than anything else, dependent on climate, for in tropical regions the high rainfall and constant humidity, together with high temperatures, encourage the decomposition of volcanic rock and allow weathering to

Above A ground surge (nuée ardente) cascades down the side of Ngauruohoe Volcano, New Zealand. As the eruption cloud collapses, a ring of hot debris piles up round the summit, then avalanches off under gravity to form a hot ash hurricane.

Right Thick flows of basalt aa lava bury a church during the 1949 eruption of San Juan on La Palma, Canary Isles. **Far right** Stricken houses burn on Heimaey, Iceland, as Eldjfell Volcano partly buries the town of Vestmannaeyjar.

extend to great depths. Ashfalls are quickly washed free of their poisonous components and vegetation rapidly becomes established. Lava flows take longer to break down but, where debris accumulates in the cracks and hollows of such flows, plants establish themselves and quickly begin the process of breaking up the underlying rocks by root action.

In higher latitudes and in arid regions the story is quite different. Lack of adequate rainfall and high temperature is not conducive to plant growth unless aided by Man. Lava fields remain desolate for many decades, or even centuries. Vegetation is slow to regenerate on fields of volcanic ash, which may be

savaged by destructive dust storms. However, where such ash can and does break down it forms some of the most fertile soils in the world readily colonized by plants.

Benefits from volcanoes

Tropical soils in volcanic areas such as Central America, Hawaii, Indonesia and the Philippines support an amazing variety of plant life. The nutrients leached from the ash or lava, usually basaltic or andesitic, are quickly absorbed by vegetation and put to good use in establishing luxuriant tropical growth.

Where lava flows into the sea, in the form of a lava delta, new land is established. On the

island of Heimaey, Iceland, the eruption from Eldjfell volcano in 1973 produced a lava flow that nearly closed the entrance to Vestmannaeyjar harbour, Iceland's most important fishing port. However, the lava stopped well before the entrance was sealed, and produced, instead, a larger harbour with a more sheltered approach.

Geothermal power

Geothermal energy is extracted from volcanic areas by trapping hydrothermal steam vents and using the steam to turn turbines and so provide cheap electricity. Major schemes are in use in Italy, New Zealand, Japan, America and Iceland. Much of Reykjavik, Iceland's capital, is heated by such geothermal power, and horticultural concerns rear pineapples in large greenhouses heated by geothermal steam.

Mineral riches

Other benefits of volcanism are mineral deposits, such as borax, sulphur and copper, which may be present in suffcient quantity to render mining them economically viable. Many mineral deposits occur around the sites of fumaroles, where hot steam has carried various elements to the surface and deposited them there. Large cavities are often filled with viable sulphur deposits. Borax is obtained as a by-product from geothermal power stations such as that at Lardarello in Italy. Initially the engineers at Lardarello found the pipes were being continually corroded by acid solutions, rich in boric acid,

ammonia, sodium perborate and various other chemicals. A modification which involved the extraction of these chemicals proved to be a double bonus. It yielded a series of valuable chemical by-products, amounting to thousands of tons per year, and low maintenance steam pipes into the bargain.

Copper ores which are closely associated with volcanism are found in such places as the ancient spreading ridge of Cyprus and the 'porphyry' deposits of the west coast of the USA. Deposited at concentrations as low as 0·3 per cent and as high as 2 per cent, these porphyry copper ores form some of the world's major deposits of this valuable metal and, as

extraction processes improve, even the mining of lower grade ores will eventually become a viable economic proposition.

From building blocks to toothpaste

Bulk volcanic products are used in the construction of buildings, road surfacing and in the preparation of many domestic products. Lava and ignimbrite blocks are still used to construct houses in many of the world's poorer countries, while pumice is one ingredient used in modern high-strength, lightweight building-blocks. Pumice, which is an abrasive volcanic glass, is used in scouring powders, and in some countries even as an ingredient of toothpaste!

Left Insurers valuing the vine crops during the 1971 eruption of Mt Etna, Italy. Compensation for crops ruined by lava flows is reported to be paid as much as ten years in arrears.

Right New Zealand's power station at Wairakei turns volcanic geothermal energy into high-pressure steam to drive turbines and produce relatively cheap electricity for nearby towns and cities.

Over sixty people died when Mount St Helens, a peak in the Cascade Mountains of Washington State, western USA, erupted in May 1980. Yet the death toll could have been in the thousands if scientists had not read the signs, realized that a major eruption was imminent, and persuaded state officials to declare a prohibited 'red zone' some 20 miles (30km) in diameter, barring entry to holiday makers and sightseers. The following year, a similar area was cleared around the active volcano on two separate occasions when instrument readings showed ground swelling within the crater, together with subterranean seismic activity. In both cases eruptions followed within two weeks.

Advances in monitoring technology have made the surveillance of active volcanoes an increasingly accurate science. The location of all of the Earth's active volcanoes—those which have erupted within historic times—is known. Most, though not all, are situated along tectonic plate boundaries. The prediction of future eruptions can be divided into two categories: general prediction, which aims to identify the characteristic type and frequency of activity of a volcano; and specific prediction, which uses physical instrumentation and chemical analysis to monitor the activities of volcanoes giving indications of imminent eruption.

General prediction

General prediction is based upon a meticulous study and interpretation of volcanic products. Deposits consisting of tephra falls, pyroclastic flows or volcanic mudflows are evidence of a violent eruption. If such deposits can be examined as stratified layers, and dated by radiometric techniques, then an accurate historical record of the volcano can be assembled. The rock type will indicate the viscosity of the magma, which is a governing factor in the explosive intensity of an eruption. The volcanologist also draws up maps showing the distribution, grain size and thickness of ejected ash and tephra. The explosiveness of the eruption, and the 'muzzle

velocity' of the volcano can be worked out from these maps. Further careful calculations, using all available measurements, can give some idea of the height of the eruption cloud, the extent of its spread, and hypothetical ash-fall areas for various wind directions.

Armed with the information accruing from such studies and analysis, general prediction can give us some idea of what to expect should a particular volcano give signs of new activity. By estimating the worst likely scale and type of eruption, given the volcano's history and nature, local authorities can decide on the extent of areas of evacuation, and the likely direction of flows and wind-borne falls. General prediction, through study of stratified sections, may also give an idea of a volcano's activity pattern over the years, and enable us to calculate roughly when the next period of activity might occur.

Above right A geologist plumbs the depths of the lava tube system from the roof of the volcano Mauna Loa, Hawaii, in 1973. Investigations such as this reveal much of the volcano's behaviour. In contrast to that of volcanoes such as El Chichon and Mt St Helens, the behaviour of Hawaiian volcanoes is highly predictable.
Above far right A geologist obtains a sample of lava on Mauna Loa for a density study.

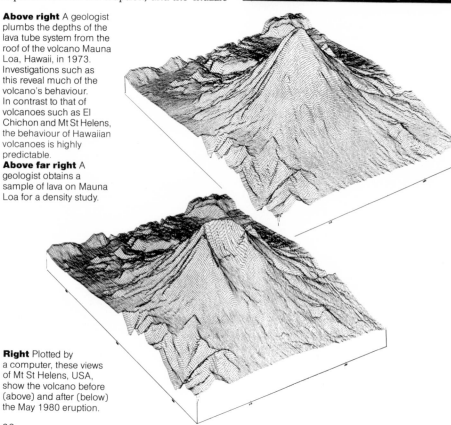

Right Plotted by a computer, these views of Mt St Helens, USA, show the volcano before (above) and after (below) the May 1980 eruption.

Specific prediction

Specific prediction is based on a very close examination of a subject volcano. It is both sophisticated and expensive. As a result, many volcanoes of high potential danger are without any form of surveillance. These volcanoes, erupting infrequently, often with dormant, or 'repose', periods of 5,000 years and more, pose the greatest risk. Many lie in Third World countries lacking both the resources and scientific base to mount costly monitoring schemes.

When El Chichon erupted at the end of March and again at the beginning of April, 1982, in a remote region of Mexico, it killed 100 or more people, wrecked property, and blanketed hundreds of square miles with ash. The force of the eruption took 0·2cu km of ash and gas as far as the stratosphere. Not connected to other Mexican volcanoes straddling the collision line between the Cocos and American tectonic plates, El Chichon had come under little or no scientific scrutiny, and was estimated not to have erupted for thousands of years. Yet a geologist had reported tremors and rumblings in the winter of 1980/1981, and local farmers had told of earthquakes since November 1981. Other warning signs had included the rising temperature of local rivers, together with a smell of sulphur. Finally alerted by further seismic activity, official geologic teams were mobilized far too

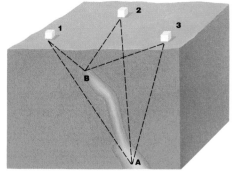

Above an array of seis-   of rising magma, measured
mograms (**1, 2, 3**) detects   at **A** and **B** reveals where
eruptions Depth and speed   and when it will erupt.

late, three or four days before the first eruption.

There are four principal physical techniques used in specific prediction: seismological (based on earthquakes); geodetic (based on ground measurements); gravimetric and electrical (based on variations in gravity, magnetization and electrical resistance); and thermal (based on ground temperature measurements).

Seismograms record the earthquake shocks created by rising magma as it pushes its way through rock, splitting a path for itself. An array of three or more seismograms can produce three-dimensional mapping of the earthquake foci, so that the progress of the magma can be closely monitored. Many eruptions on the island of Hawaii have been accurately predicted by this method.

Geodetic measurements record the changes in the Earth's surface caused by the magma pressure within the volcano's cone. Laser technology is employed in geodimeters. Laser pulses are timed to measure the distance between two ground stations with great accuracy. As the ground swells, the difference in the distance is immediately recorded. Tiltmeters record ground slope variations, and can indicate both the inflation of a volcanic cone as the magma rises, and its deflation as magma chambers are emptied. Both instruments are used to augment precise theodolite level surveys.

Gravimetry measures the effect of new magma bodies inside a volcano on gravity measurements, and depends on previous accurate gravity surveys. This technique can give a good idea of the volcano's internal structure. Geomagnetic monitoring reveals the change in a volcano's magnetic field as the rock loses magnetism in response to heating. In Japan this technique formed the basis for predicting the eruption of O-shima. In geoelectrical monitoring, high voltages are passed between sets of electrodes inserted in the ground, and the resistance measured. Different kinds of rock have different resistances, which are very sensitive to temperature changes.

Thermal surveillance can be as simple as noticing the premature melting of snow on a mountain, and as sophisticated as the computer assembly of infra-red thermographs made by orbiting satellites. Hot spots form where magma or hot gases approach the surface, and can be an accurate indicator of eruption points.

Chemical surveillance detects and measures the various gases released prior to an eruption, by means of gas sensors, both on the ground and carried aloft in aircraft. Established geological formations and hot springs may show a marked change in their gas chemistry, with an increase in sulphur dioxide, carbon dioxide, chlorine and fluorine as an eruption approaches. Radon gas increases rapidly just before an eruption, and falls just as quickly after it.

Most of this instrumentation can be monitored by remote control and the readings coordinated at a safe distance inside a volcanological observatory. The development of multipurpose satellite systems such as Landsat has greatly increased the efficiency and speed with which readings can be received, decoded, and retransmitted for correlation. We may never control volcanic eruptions, but as monitoring techniques become more sensitive and diverse we are able to predict them with ever-increasing accuracy.

Deep in the Earth's crust, where molten igneous material invades cooler surrounding 'country' rock, heat from the magma alters and bakes sedimentary, metamorphic and igneous rocks with which it comes into contact. Sedimentary rocks are the most susceptible to alteration by this direct heating. Previously formed metamorphic and igneous rocks usually withstand alteration until the temperatures involved are phenomenal and protracted. It is difficult to imagine an environment where solid rock can be altered by direct underground heating. The molten magma can penetrate and surround great masses of country rock, and in such situations it is possible for high temperature basalt and dolerite to alter granite which melts at lower temperatures. As well as direct heat, the magma contains gases and fluids. These can seep into the country rock, acting as fluxes, which lower the melting points of minerals. Where sandstone containing fossils of shells made of calcite is affected in this way, a new mineral called wollastonite (calcium silicate) is produced, with excess carbonate material being released as carbon dioxide gas. Fluids from granitic intrusions contain dissolved gases that can act upon surrounding rocks to break down minerals such as felspar to make clay. These fluids can seep though the delicate channels in the crustal rocks and produce a subtle and often complete recrystallization removing some elements which can be taken elsewhere to react with other rocks in the contact aureole. As well as in the unknown deep environment of contact metamorphism among the batholiths, sills and dykes, the searing heat of surface lava flows can alter rocks over which they flow. Masses of rock that get caught up in violent volcanic vents are similarly affected.

Hornfels

Clay and mudstone are fine-grained sediments which are deposited at low temperatures in the sea, or in lakes and rivers. With a gradual temperature increase, as in a metamorphic aureole near to a granitic batholith, a progression of mainly chemical changes takes place. Carbon, of organic origin, becomes segregated into discrete 'clots', producing the characteristic spotted rock of the outer zones of contact aureoles. As the temperature increases towards the magma, iron and iron oxide in the sediment are turned into magnetite. New silicate minerals, such as biotite mica (a rich brown or black, flaky mineral) and complex aluminium silicates, such as andalusite and cordierite, develop. The rock becomes hard, tough and flinty with no features of the original clay remaining. Geologists call such rocks hornfels, and it is characteristic of the inner zones of the contact aureoles of granites. In the English Lake District the Skiddaw granite has invaded shales and slates. If you were to walk from the rounded hills of slate 2 miles (3km) away towards the granite outcrops, you would see that the slates become spotted. Eventually, in the river valley, where the granite is exposed, tough, pale grey hornfels occurs next to the pale jointed granite.

Marble and minerals

When rocks such as limestones, which contain a great deal of calcium carbonate, are changed during contact metamorphism, they produce a wide variety of beautiful and much sought-after minerals. These include tourmaline, garnets and hornblende. Limestone, which is metamorphosed into marble, becomes progressively

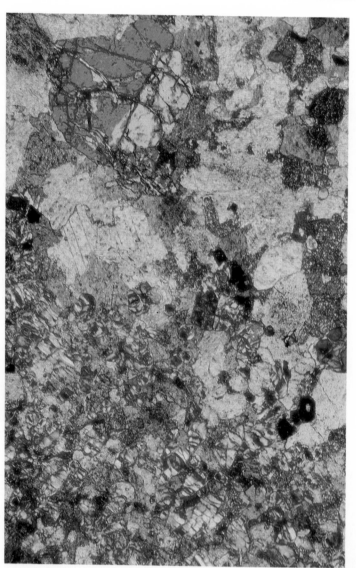

Right In the Canary Isles, a thick layer of dark basalt lava has been erupted over volcanic ash and soil. These have been heated and metamorphosed by the intense heat from the basalt (about 1,000°C), and the result is a red layer below the lava. Such effects are common in volcanic regions; red-hot lavas often burn and completely alter the soils and ash deposits below them. When limestone, which may contain impurities, is metamorphosed by direct heating, various metamorphic minerals grow from these impurities.
Left This highly magnified section of marble contains two such minerals. Diopside is a silicate of calcium , magnesium and iron and forsterite (large lumps) is a magnesium iron silicate.
Below In this close-up hornfels, a rock typical of the contact zones around granite, is shown. Typically a tough, flinty rock, hornfels results when direct heat is applied to rocks such as shale, mudstone and volcanic ash. As the magma body is approached, so the alteration of the country rock increases and new minerals develop in the hornfels. These include chiastolite (seen here) and garnet.
Bottom Table shows major metamorphic rocks, their relationships and origins.

recrystallized, and fossils and bedding structures are gradually removed as the magma is approached. The marble is veined by green and blue-grey patches of metamorphic minerals, often derived from impurities in the orginal limestone. Limestones often contain irregular patches of silica, called chert, and this alters to form pale wollastonite crystals. Green garnet and felspar are other attractive minerals formed from impure limestones.

A great number of characteristic minerals can be found in contact aureoles. The massive batholith in south-west England has altered a

Type of Metamorphism	Situation	Main Agents		Rocks before Metamorphism	Rocks after Metamorphism
CONTACT	AUREOLES	HEAT Plus Liquids and Gases		Basalt, Dolerite, Shale, Mudstone, Tuff	HORNFELS
				Sandstone	METAQUARTZITE
				Limestone	MARBLE
REGIONAL	OROGENIC BELTS	PRESSURE Low to High Temperature	Low Temp	Shale, Mudstone, Tuff	SLATE
			Med Temp	Slate, Phyllite, Sandstone, Basalt, Dolerite, Limestone	PHYLLITE SCHIST
			High Temp and Pressure	All types	GNEISS

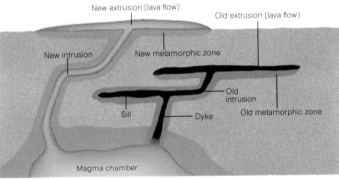

Right The metamorphic aureole of a large magma chamber is wide but minor intrusions such as sills and dykes are surrounded by a narrow metamorphic zone, and lava flows only heat and alter the rocks they rest upon.

Below This marble was originally limestone formed in a shallow sea 550 m.y. ago. It has been heated by a magma chamber of syenite, now exposed in the distant hills.

New extrusion (lava flow)
Old extrusion (lava flow)
New intrusion
New metamorphic zone
Old intrusion
Sill
Dyke
Old metamorphic zone
Magma chamber

wide variety of rocks, producing many beautiful minerals of fine crysalline shape. These include various colour varieties of quartz.

Long after their consolidation, igneous rocks can themselves be invaded by intrusions of magma. Rocks such as andesites and basalts are most susceptible to alteration. Near the Shap granite in northern England, andesites have been intruded and altered to make a beautiful mosaic of felspar, hornblende, chalcedony, iron pyrites and magnetite, often rich in garnet. Igneous pyroclastic rocks such as tuff and ash often behave like clays and mudstones, giving rise to hornfelses.

Occasionally very rare and precious minerals are formed by contact metamorphism. Clay intruded among basalts has been known to yield sapphire, and coal seams intruded by basic dolerite dykes contain diamonds where the carbon has been crystallized.

Analysing the changes

By a careful study of metamorphic rocks and their mineral assemblages geologists can reconstruct the history of the events which brought about the metamorphic changes. Garnet and wollastonite indicate the former presence of calcite while minerals such as andalusite and cordierite indicate muddy sediments. Spotted slates, with their carbon clots, and minerals such as chiastolite indicate lower temperatures. Flinty hornfels, containing minerals such as andalusite, suggest searing temperatures, of about 1,500°F (800°C) right next to the batholith.

Deep beneath the massive snow-capped ranges of fold mountains such as the Alps and Himalayas lie twisted and buckled sedimentary rocks, which are being subjected to extremes of temperature and pressure. Here, where mountains are formed by the collision of continents and the closure of oceans, the sediments of the ocean floor are regionally metamorphosed to form slates, schists and gneisses, very different from the clays and sandstones of the sea-bed. The deeper the sediments are buried, the higher the temperature and pressures to which they are subjected, and the more they become altered. Ultimately, they may even melt to form strangely banded and mixed rocks called migmatites. Granite may form as a result of this extreme alteration.

A classic example

In Scotland, the progressive regional metamorphism of the Pre-Cambrian Dalradian rocks has, for nearly a century, been a classic area of study. Here there once lay rocks, which were compressed, folded and altered by heat and pressure. The most highly deformed and metamorphosed rocks are in the centre of a wide area. On either side, to north and south, there is a gradient, from the highly altered ('high-grade') metamorphic rocks through 'lower grades' of metamorphism to the unaltered sediments at the edge of the region. The graded rocks are evidence of the heat gradient at the time of metamorphism. The different degrees of heat produced characteristic assemblages of minerals, by which geologists can recognize five zones of progressive regional metamorphism.

These metamorphic zones are identified by the place where a given mineral first appears in the rocks. Chlorite, the mineral formed at the lowest temperatures, gives way to biotite, garnet, kyanite and finally sillimanite as the temperature increases. In the chlorite zone, slates and phyllites, which show some structural alteration in the form of cleavage, reflect the low temperature and pressure on the margins of the metamorphic belt.

The biotite zone consists of schists with their characteristic wavy banding which contain black mica. Garnets are common, but the garnet zone is not defined until large red garnets appear in the schists, indicating a change in the temperature and pressure conditions. The kyanite zone is less easy to define because of its gradual rather subtle change

from the garnet zone. Kyanite, a blue-green, blade-shaped mineral, may occur within schists and even gneisses. Ultimately, sillimanite occurs in coarse-grained gneisses, which also contain biotite, and garnet.

These zones, originally described many years ago, are still of great practical use for field mapping, but modern geochemical techniques and research have led to their being generally discarded in favour of schemes relating to depth of burial and temperature/pressure conditions. Such schemes allow the inclusion of the mantle-derived rock eclogite, an attractive mixture of red garnet and shimmering green pyroxene. Recent research, using oxygen isotopes, has shown that these Scottish rocks were possibly subjected to temperatures of about 570°F (300°C) for the chlorite zone and 1,100°F (600°C) for the kyanite zone. Other work has shown that pressures of 5 kilobars were reached to produce garnet zone rocks and extremes of 9 to 12 kilobars may have been reached in the central parts of the metamorphic area. This corresponds to a depth of burial of between 20 and 25 miles (35 and 40km)!

Dynamic metamorphism

Dynamic, or cataclastic, metamorphism is another way in which rock subjected to pressures can be completely altered from its original form. The rock becomes crushed and sheared and drawn out into tightly packed 'lenticules'. The fracturing often begins at the boundaries between the individual crystals, when the stress exceeds the strength of the rock. The rocks resulting from this alteration are called mylonites. When the rock undergoing dynamic metamorphism is soft and yielding, 'cleavage' occurs, involving rotation of the minute individual grains in the rock so that they lie parallel to one another. Cleavage allows the rock to be split into thin flat sheets.

Metasomatism

In the deep mountain roots where regional and dynamic metamorphism occur, contact aureoles are also present, as this is the zone of granite injection. Metasomatism is a process by which new elements can be carried in solution by capillary action through seemingly solid rock and added to the composition of the rock. Many minerals, including fluorite, garnet and topaz, can be introduced and carried through rocks in this way.

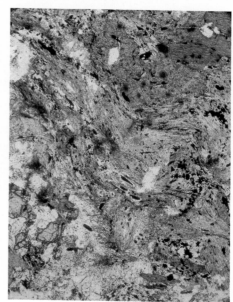

Where these processes are continued to their ultimate conclusion, gneiss is melted. This molten rock has minerals of low melting point and granitic material is formed. The rock melt forms veins in the higher-level gneisses, creating a mixed rock, migmatite, which may have acid and basic components. Continued melting may produce enough granitic liquid to form an intrusive body.

Minerals which are stable at high temperatures may be 'retrogressively' metamorphosed into an assemblage which is stable at much lower temperatures. When strong deformation and the injection of low-temperature fluids occurs, high-grade rocks may take on the characteristics of low grade alteration. In orogenic belts where the crust is active for very long periods, often as long as hundreds of millions of years, 'polymetamorphism' occurs. This involves more than one episode of alteration, with periods of quiescence between them. Geologists can sometimes interpret these repeated metamorphic episodes by studying 'relict' minerals and structures—those formed by the removal of surrounding materials.

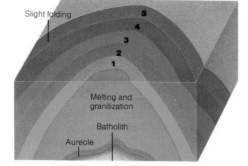

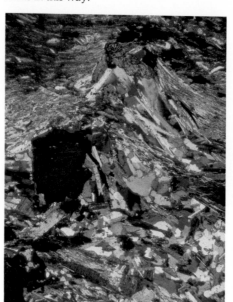

Above The diagram shows zones of progressive regional metamorphism, from highest (**1**) to lowest (**5**).

1 Sillimanite zone
2 Kyanite zone
3 Garnet zone
4 Biotite zone
5 Chlorite zone

Right Thin slices of highly metamorphosed rocks show their detailed mineral composition. This section of a schist reveals dark garnet and brown biotite.
Far right This more highly metamorphosed schist contains blades of kyanite and sillimanite.

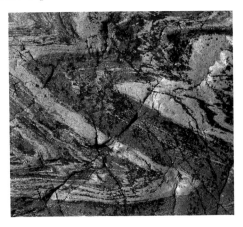

Above Metamorphic rocks often feature beautiful patterns and structures.
Left Canisp (on the left) and Suilven, in north-west Scotland, rise above the Lewisian basement, whose highly metamorphosed gneisses were formed deep beneath a mountain range of Himalayan proportions which existed some 2,000 million years ago — hundreds of millions of years before these two sandstone mountains were formed. This rugged, hummocky landscape is one of the oldest terrains on Earth.
Below The serene, snow-capped peaks of these mountains in Nepal are a far cry from the intense conditions deep in their roots, where rocks like the ancient gneisses of Scotland are forming today.

Lakes, in a sense, are amongst Nature's accidents. They provide exceptions and interruptions to the natural tendency of continental surface waters to run off via rivers to the sea. In doing so they contribute to some of the most beautiful landscapes and have been a fertile source of poetic and artistic inspiration. Only about one per cent of the Earth's continental surface is covered by lakes, and a high proportion of that is accounted for by a few very large lakes, notably the Caspian Sea and the Laurentian Great Lakes of North America. Lakes, however, range in size from these virtual inland seas down to small ponds and the variety of processes and products is enormous.

Open and closed lakes

A fundamental distinction which must be drawn in any account of present-day lakes is that between 'open' and 'closed' lakes. Open lakes are those where the inflowing river water is stored only temporarily before escaping to continue its flow to the sea. In closed lakes, however, the lake itself is the end of the drainage system. The water does not escape but is either lost by evaporation or sinks into the surrounding soil and rock to escape as groundwater.

How lakes form

In the mountains, lakes are commonly the products of glacial processes. In corries and glacial valleys, over-deepening has commonly led to cross-valley sills, which act as dams to river flow. Glacially scoured lakes go right down to sea level and many connect up with fjords. Other lakes, particularly in areas of high relief, are the result of damming by land-slides onto the valley floor. Such lakes tend to be relatively short-lived, since the barrier of debris is eventually eroded by the outflow. Evidence for a former lake of this type may be provided by beach terraces on valley walls. In low-relief areas in high latitudes, many lakes are also attributable to glacial processes. In Finland, a country famed for its lakes, the complex erosional and depositional landforms produced by the retreating ice of the last Ice Age have created a complex network of lakes, whilst the Laurentian Great Lakes of North America also owe something to the widespread glaciation of the area.

In warmer climates, most large lakes are attributable to tectonic causes. In the East African Rift Valleys, for example, which are areas of crustal extension and subsidence, the lakes form along the floor of the rifts, in some cases aided by volcanic damming. Lake Baikal in the Soviet Union is similarly associated with rifting, while the Dead Sea results from rapid subsidence due to the lateral relative movement of slabs of the lithosphere on either side of the Jordan Valley. In contrast to these rather elongated lakes associated with rifting are the large lakes of continental interiors, which tend much more to be circular in shape. Lake Eyre in Australia and Lake Chad and Lake Victoria in central Africa both occupy the centres of wide shallow depressions which are the result of a broad sagging subsidence of the continental crust. In addition, smaller lakes result from more unusual causes such as volcanic explosions (for instance, Crater Lake, Oregon, USA).

Expansion and contraction

Many of these tectonically controlled lakes in warm areas lie below sea level and are therefore

Above Lake Gokyo Tsho lies at almost 16,000ft beneath the peak of Cho Oyu in Nepal. Hollows in the bedrock or in ice allow such lakes to form.
Left Lakes like this one near Iquilos, Peru, form where changes in gradient are the result of hard rock strata or other irregularities.
Right Depressions caused by faults and volcanic eruptions form lakes such as Lake Rudolf, Africa, seen here. Lakes form in various other situations as well as those shown in these pictures.

Below The map of Equatorial East Africa shows the distribution of major lakes in relation to the dominant rift structures.

The narrow lakes, such as Lake Nyasa, occupy the rifts, while the more circular Lake Victoria fills a shallow depression outside the rifts.

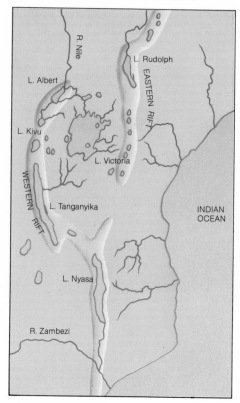

closed systems. Evaporation accounts for the water which flows in via rivers and streams. As a result such lakes are extremely sensitive to climatic changes and many expand and contract in area. Lakes Chad and Eyre have both been many times larger than their present size during more humid periods. Shifting of the shoreline is particularly spectacular when the lake sits in a very shallow depression. In addition to changes in area, closed lakes also show marked changes in the chemistry of their waters with changing climate. Where water loss is by evaporation, salts become concentrated in the residual water, in some cases to the point at which they precipitate out.

Open lakes, on the other hand, tend to fluctuate much less, both in size and in the chemistry of their water, with climatic change. Most of the material dissolved in the water passes through the system, and concentrations of dissolved matter seldom rise significantly. However, that is not to imply that open lakes are uniform in character, either between one another or through time. Two important factors influence the character of lakes enormously. One is the rate at which organic activity and, in particular, plant growth proceeds and the other is the distribution of temperature within the water mass of the lake. Where the lake waters are rich in nutrients, algae are abundant in the upper parts of the water body and as they die organic debris builds up on the lake floor. This leads to oxygen depletion in the lower part of the water and to a consequent reduction in fish and other life. Such a lake is

described as 'eutrophic'. Where nutrient levels are low, organic activity is reduced and the whole of the water column remains oxygenated —a condition termed 'oligotrophic'.

Associated with these differences, to some degree, is the phenomenon of thermal density stratification of the lake water. The Sun warms the surface waters of lakes, causing them to become less dense than the colder deeper water. This stratification inhibits vertical water movements and accentuates any tendency for bottom waters to become stagnant. The upper warmer waters are more mobile and are more readily renewed by inflow and outflow. In temperate areas, this stratification is generally seasonal, with mixing occurring when the surface waters cool in the autumn, but in tropical lakes the stratified state may be much more stable. There, rare overturning events can cause mass mortality of fish stocks when the poorly oxygenated waters reach the surface.

Lake sediments

The sediments laid down in lakes reflect these differences in chemistry and oxygenation. In open lakes the coarse material delivered by rivers tends to be laid down in lake deltas or to be redistributed close to the shore by waves, while the more central parts receive fine material from suspension, with the addition of organic matter generated in the lake itself. Seasonal variation in the supply of sediment may often give a clear and delicate lamination to these lake centre deposits, seen most clearly in the 'varves' of glacial lakes. Calcium carbonate is

also precipitated in some open lakes, largely as the result of the activity of shallow water plants and algae.

In closed lakes the sediments are much more variable, depending on the nature of the rocks in the catchment area. Where evaporation leads to high concentrations of dissolved salts, these may be precipitated both on the lake floor and around the margins. While the Dead Sea does not deposit sodium chloride naturally at the present day, it has done so in the past, and with a little human interference it readily does so in artificial salt pans. In East Africa the chemical composition of nearby volcanic rocks means that lakes such as Lake Magadi precipitate unusual sodium carbonate and sodium silicate minerals, which are exploited commercially for soda which they contain.

A clue to the past

Ancient lake deposits are quite common in the geological record and they are very valuable as indicators of past climates. Geologists can often detect episodes of expansion and contraction—periods of drying up, or desiccation, for example, leave tell-tale features such as mudcracks and salt crystal impressions. Sustained periods of eutrophic conditions leave thick and extensive deposits of organic-rich shales. These oil shales probably constitute an important energy resource for the future, while ancient chemical precipitates from closed lakes yield important deposits of gypsum and halite.

Below A temperate lake with density stratification of the water. Coarse material is deposited in deltas at the river mouth, while fine-grained sediment is dispersed in suspension.

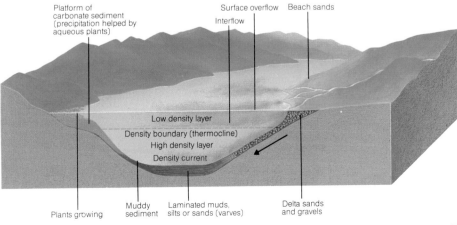

Platform of carbonate sediment (precipitation helped by aqueous plants)

Surface overflow   Beach sands
Interflow

Low density layer
Density boundary (thermocline)
High density layer
Density current

Plants growing

Muddy sediment   Laminated muds, silts or sands (varves)

Delta sands and gravels

Since the earliest days of modern geology, rivers have influenced the way in which Earth Scientists think about the Earth. In the 18th century, the large sizes of valleys produced by river erosion compared with the amounts of sediment actually transported by the streams influenced the great Scottish geologist James Hutton's appreciation of the large intervals of time involved in Earth history, and of the continuous and cyclic nature of erosion, deposition and the formation of new rocks. However, up until quite recently, most geologists tended to regard rivers merely as the agents by which weathered debris was transported from the land to the sea. Any sediment deposited on the way was thought to be held in temporary storage for subsequent erosion and transport.

Ancient sediments

More recently, geologists have realized that a great deal of sediment laid down directly by rivers, both in floodplains and on alluvial fans, has become incorporated into the geological record for long-term preservation. They now recognize ancient river deposits in some of the oldest sedimentary rocks in the world. Interest in these has increased not only because they can tell us a great deal about ancient geographies, climates and tectonic events, but also because they are associated with a wide range of economically important minerals.

Before the ancient sedimentary rocks could be interpreted in terms of their conditions of deposition and before geologists could make predictions about their likely occurrence in exploiting them, it was necessary to first understand the processes, behaviour and products of present-day settings. Rivers lend themselves very well to this uniformitarian approach, as their accessibility allows direct observation of their processes of erosion, transport and deposition. Geologists are able to observe the variety of forms developed on the river bed and on the surrounding banks, and also learn much about the associated internal structures by examining trenches and pits excavated in these areas. As a result, rivers are amongst the best understood sedimentary environments, especially in comparison to the less accessible marine environments where, until recently, only less direct methods of observation were possible.

Long-distance movements

Two main processes are responsible for the long-distance transport of material in rivers. Finer sediment—silt and clay—is transported in suspension, making the water turbid, particularly during floods. Coarser material—sand and gravel—moves as a bedload by the rolling and bouncing of grains close to the bed. Bedload transport causes the bed to become moulded into a variety of surface features. On sandy beds the channel floor is generally covered by small ripples, which are commonly superimposed on larger forms called 'dunes' or even larger ones termed 'bars'. Gravel-bed streams generally lack ripples and dunes but display a wide variety of bars. These various bedforms determine the frictional properties of the channel so that the flowing water and the bed adjust towards a dynamic equilibrium.

Classifying rivers

This adjustment or balance between the flow and the form of the channel extends to larger-scale features and indeed to the shape of the channel itself. Examination of maps or aerial

Above 'Braided' streams intertwine over a broad valley floor in Switzerland. The patterns which rivers make on the land surface vary greatly.
Right Dramatic waterfalls occur where great rivers plunge with awesome power over huge obstructions. Here, at Iguazu, Brazil, millions of tons of water rush headlong over

a hard rock obstruction, the formidable erosive power cutting a deep gorge downstream. When sea-level falls, or the land rises, rivers have to cut down to a new level, causing the river's features to become incised onto the landscape.
Far right The River Ardèche, France, has meanders which have cut deep into limestone.

photographs shows that rivers vary greatly in plan view. Geologists have made many attempts to classify this variety and to account for it. In broad terms, gravel-bed streams flowing on relatively steep slopes and often with little fine sediment in their banks show a 'braided' pattern where the flow splits and rejoins around lozenge-shaped bars at a whole range of scales. Such channels tend to be very unstable, and constantly shift their positions and pattern. Sand-bed streams on steep slopes and with readily eroded banks also tend to be braided, but the bars which split their flow are generally more extensive across the channel. On low slopes, or where the banks are less easily eroded due to the presence of fine, cohesive sediment or to the stabilizing effect of

growing plants, the channel commonly has a 'meandering' form. Such channels are much more stable and tend to shift their position only slowly and in a more predictable fashion. Erosion takes place on the outer concave bank while deposition is concentrated on the inner convex bank, the 'point bar'. Through time this channel shifting leads to the deposition of a tabular body of sand whose thickness is the same as the depth of the channel. Some meanders develop to the point where the flow cuts through the neck of the point bar, thereby creating an abandoned meander loop. The ends of the loop are plugged with sediment and it becomes an 'ox-bow lake', accumulating only fine and commonly organic-rich sediment. On very low slopes, as where a valley has been

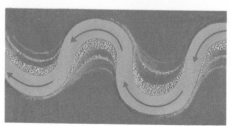

Above The river channel pattern in a pebbly braided river.
Below The pattern formed by a meandering river.

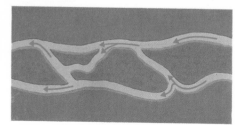

Above A sandy braided river has this channel pattern.
Below This type of channel is formed by an anastomosing river.

dammed or where the river flows over a silted-up lake floor, the channel pattern may be 'anastomosing'. Here the sluggish flow splits and rejoins on a long spacing, with the rather stable individual sectors showing either straight or sinuous traces.

Levees and floodplains

Outside the channels, on the river banks and the areas beyond, the surface is commonly dry for most of the time. Plants may grow and soils develop. During floods these areas become submerged and fine sediment carried in suspension by the floodwaters is laid down, causing a gradual build-up of the floodplain. This addition of new material helps account for the fertility of many river floodplains. Deposition during floods is most intense close to the channel and here sediment ridges, or 'levees', are built up. Beyond the levees the floodplain is normally dry, but some are swampy or even have permanent lakes. These can be sites of peat formation as the remains of plants accumulate.

Understanding ancient river deposits

In the geological record, river deposits are important in many rock sequences laid down under continental conditions. They are most commonly deposited after periods of mountain building in basins flanking the newly uplifted mountain-belts. Within such successions it is possible to recognize both ancient channel and floodplain deposits. The channel deposits are sandstones and conglomerates, which sometimes form extensive sheets, but in other cases are more restricted. The extensive sheets are most likely the products of freely migrating braided

Right Features of erosion and deposition associated with the migration of a meandering river channel. The outer, concave bank is gradually eroded, while sediment is deposited on the inner, concave bank (the point bar). In some meanders, this process continues until the river cuts across the point bar, isolating a loop of the water. Dunes may form on the point bar. Sediment dams the ends to form an oxbow lake, which gradually becomes filled with layers of fine sediments.

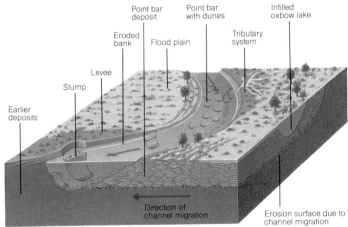

rivers, while restricted sand bodies are most likely the products of meandering or anastomosing streams. Within the sandstones and conglomerates the bedding can be related to the ripples, dunes and bars which were active in the channel.

Restricted sandstones and conglomerates commonly occur in channels cut into fine sediment, while finer sediment is generally found as extensive units between the sheet sandstones. These finer sediments are mainly the products of overband and floodplain deposition and their features give important clues to the climatic and drainage conditions under which they accumulated. Many examples are red, because of staining by hematite, and record oxidizing conditions due to a well-drained floodplain. Other examples are grey, with preservation of organic matter suggesting

reducing conditions and therefore poor drainage. Such sequences are important in the Coal Measures, where coals record the development of peat swamps and the soils upon which the plants grew are preserved beneath the coal seams as 'seat-earths'. Within these lie the preserved remains of the plants' roots, sometimes replaced by iron minerals.

Coal is only one of the important economic resources associated with ancient river sediments. Channel sandstones are, in some areas, important reservoir rocks for the accumulation of oil and gas, while in other areas they are the host rocks for uranium and copper mineralization. 'Placer' deposits of gold and other heavy minerals occur in both modern and ancient river deposits. At a more prosaic level, poorly cemented river deposits offer a major source of sands and gravel for the construction industry.

Most of the rock debris eroded from the land surface is transported by rivers, and the greater part of it finds its way to the sea, though some may be deposited in lakes and on river floodplains. As they enter the sea, rivers slow down and drop much of their load of sediment. The coastline is gradually built out into the sea and a delta develops. This area of low-lying land is generally traversed by several major branches of the river, which splits on reaching the low slope of the delta. These distributary channels fan out to feed sediment to the coast at several points. Delta-top areas between channels receive supplies of new, generally fine-grained material during floods. This addition, along with the availability of water for irrigation, makes delta plains very fertile, and it is no coincidence that the early civilizations of Egypt, Mesopotamia and north-western India were located in the delta regions of major rivers.

The fact that river mouths are such obvious sites of sediment accumulation means that they have long been used as modern analogues for ancient sedimentary rocks. In the 19th century, the English geologist Sir Charles Lyell used the Mississippi Delta as a model for certain Carboniferous rocks and such a comparative approach continues to the present day. Ancient sequences are interpreted in greater and greater detail as the complexities of modern deltas are better understood by geologists.

Deltas and oilfields

Much of the impetus for the study of deltas, both modern and ancient, has come from the oil industry. Many of the world's major oilfields are found in deltaic rocks. The oil wealth of Nigeria, the southern USA and the North Sea comes in large measure from rocks laid down in ancient deltas. Several of the major river systems of the world are very long-lived, and their mouth areas have been the sites of deposition for many millions of years. The deltas which we see on topographic maps are generally the products of only the last few thousand years of coastal advance, since the sea-level stopped rising after the amelioration of the most recent Ice Age. The modern deltas of the Niger and the Mississippi are building out over a pile of ancient deltaic sediments which date back to the Cretaceous period.

A delicate balance

The build-up of deltas into the sea is a very variable and complex business, and this is reflected in the variety of forms taken by modern deltas. A comparison of the mouth areas of, say, the Mississippi, the Nile, the Niger and the Gulf of Papua shows great differences, which can be accounted for by considering the processes which act in these settings. Deltas reflect a delicate balance between processes related to the river itself, in particular the rate at which it supplies material to the coast, and processes which relate to the basin. The two most important basin influences are tidal currents and waves, both of which serve to redistribute the sediment delivered by the river, in particular the coarser sandy portion.

The Mississippi delivers its load to the Gulf of Mexico, an area of very low tidal range and wave energy. As a result the delta builds forwards very rapidly as localized elongated 'fingers', each associated with a distributary channel. This 'birdfoot' delta pattern is diagnostic of low-basin energy. The Nile Delta, by contrast,

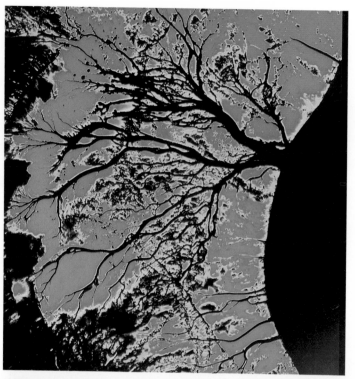

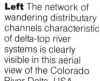
Left The network of wandering distributary channels characteristic of delta-top river systems is clearly visible in this aerial view of the Colorado River Delta, USA.
Below left A closer view of the mouth of the Colorado Delta, also from the air, reveals sediment in the water. This is carried away only sluggishly by the waters of the Gulf of Mexico, which has a low tidal range and wave energy.
Right The delta of the Paraiba River, Brazil, has meandering distributaries with deposits of sediment in between. As a river, laden with silt and mud, reaches a lake or the sea, the sediment is released and new land formed from the debris removed from older land areas. As the delta reaches further out into deeper water, the front becomes unstable and slumping occurs.

Below Four contrasting deltas, whose forms reflect the variety and balance of processes that deliver and redistribute the sediment. The Mississippi Delta has a 'birdfoot' pattern with long 'fingers' fed by distributary channels. In the case of the Nile, and to a lesser extent the Niger, the delta plain provides an area of high fertility compared with the surrounding area. The Gulf of Papua is a series of large estuary channels.

Mississippi

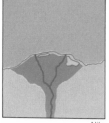
Nile

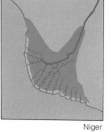
Niger

Gulf of Papua

has a smoother coastline with only minor protrusions at the channel mouths. This shape reflects the ability of waves in that part of the tideless Mediterranean to redistribute the river sands. Indeed at the present-day, the Nile has ceased to build forward its delta at all, and wave erosion has the upper hand, due to the starvation of sediment resulting from the building of the Aswan Dam.

The Niger Delta provides yet another illustration of the interplay of forces. The high wave-energy of the Atlantic redistributes sand into a smoothly curving beach front but, in addition, strong tidal currents have created a series of inlet channels which cut through the delta front. The Gulf of Papua Delta is, at first sight, hardly a delta at all but a series of large estuary channels. In this case the high tidal ranges and powerful tidal currents dominate the distribution of sediment.

Most of the world's major rivers carry by far the greater part of their load in suspension as fine-grained silts and muds. This material is distributed offshore, often for a considerable distance in front of the river mouths. Finer material is carried furthest, while coarser parts of the load are deposited closer to the mouth. In addition, the rate of deposition is greater near to the mouth, so that a gentle slope out to sea is created. The build-out of this delta slope therefore creates a body of sediment which coarsens upwards from offshore muds into sands laid down near the shore. This upward coarsening is common to most deltas, and the variability outlined above is confined to the delta top, whose deposits form a relatively thin interval on top of the coarsening unit. In addition to the rivermouth sand bars, the beaches and the tidal and river channels, most delta tops have extensive areas of swampy or marshy delta plain, where fine-grained and often organic-rich sediments accumulate.

Slumps and slides

The rapid rate at which deltaic sediments accumulate means that many of them are unstable because they are unable to undergo normal compaction. Water trapped within the sediment causes high pore pressures which weaken the sediment and cause it to fail. Large masses of material move *en masse* under gravity on low-angle slopes as slumps and slides. Clays, buried beneath the advancing delta front, may move upwards to penetrate the overlying sediment, producing 'mudlumps'.

Rivers without deltas

Examination of an atlas will show that not all major rivers have deltas. The Zaire River for example, one of the largest in the world, has no delta worthy of the name. Here the sediment is stored temporarily in the river-mouth area, but it then moves on by gravity-driven currents through a submarine canyon cut into the continental slope to build a huge submarine fan on the ocean floor. This process of 'sediment bypassing' occurs to a greater or lesser extent in front of other river-mouths, and the Niger, Mississippe and Brahmaputra all have major fans in the deeper water in front of them.

Ancient deltas

The variability of modern deltas is matched to a large extent in ancient sedimentary rocks.

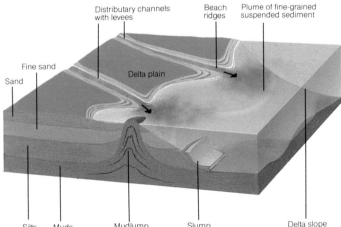

Distributary channels with levees — Beach ridges — Plume of fine-grained suspended sediment — Fine sand — Delta plain — Sand — Silts — Muds — Mudlump — Slump — Delta slope

Left This diagram shows some features of an advancing delta. The sediment plumes given off at the distributary mouths allow finer material to be carried out to sea. The fact that the finer material travels further while coarser sediment is trapped near the shore leads to a sequence of sediment which coarsens upwards. Instability of the sediments on the slopes causes them to slump, and overloaded sections of mud rise up through the water to the surface as 'mudlumps'.

Many sequences of a wide range of geological ages are regarded as being deltaic in origin. Typically deltaic sequences show a general upwards coarsening from mudstone at the base to sandstone at the top, over thicknesses from a few yards to many tens of yards. The thickness of the unit gives a rough indication of the depth of water into which the delta advanced. The uppermost sandstones show a variety of features, and geologists may recognize units of mouth bar, beach and distributory channel origin. Many delta-top sands show rootlet beds and coal seams, indicating that the sediment

built up to the point where the surface was above water, or nearly so. Many deltaic sequences end suddenly, and are overlain by the fine unit at the base of a further upwards coarsening unit, suggesting that the earlier delta was suddenly abandoned and subsided rapidly, or that a rise in sea level inundated the delta top.

The sandstone units of deltaic sequences form some of the most important reservoir rocks for the accumulation of oil, while the early movement of masses of such sediments due to instability often creates structures in which the oil may later be trapped.

The sea is a largely unexplored region. Beneath its shimmering surface is a world as hostile as outer space. The sea is a vast resource of power and mineral wealth which we are starting to tap. The ocean-bed imaging and satellite surveillance programmes are breaking down this final frontier. We know that the sea-bed has a surface just as irregular as the land. Mountain ranges rise to great heights, volcanoes pour lava

out across the sea-bed, and submarine 'rivers' full of sediment flow out over the abyssal plains. The level of the sea's surface is ever changing, influenced by the changes in glaciers and movement of the continents. The coastline is where we know the sea best. This zone ranges from one of gently sloping depositional sandy beaches to dramatic, jagged cliffs, as here (*left*) in Dorset, south-west England.

THE OCEAN FRONTIER

*We know the coast well, but the forbidding world of
the deep oceans is largely uncharted.
Sophisticated submersibles and multibeam sonar are two
means by which we are slowly exploring it*

Man's exploration of the frontiers of space are still at the stage of looking and wondering. The first tentative attempts to harvest resources beyond our atmosphere are confined to plans for orbiting photovoltaic solar energy collectors. Meanwhile, back on Earth, the resources of the land are fast running out, and scientists and technologists are turning to the planet's last frontier, the depths of the sea.

Man is now plumbing the depths of the oceans for fuel oils and gas, manganese nodules and other minerals, where once he merely trailed lines and nets for fish. Other future bounties from the sea may include electricity from gigantic underwater turbines powered by the Gulf Stream, and power from the conversion of oceanic thermal energy, for the sea is the world's largest solar collector. To help achieve these aims, today's ocean scientists are developing ever more sophisticated devices to enable them to explore the depths safely and efficiently. The task has been helped along by the enormous strides made in ocean-bed imaging and mapping since the introduction of the Landsat and Seasat satellite programmes.

A dramatic world

With energy and commercially exploitable minerals as the prizes, no expense is being spared on high technology by the new prospectors. The 70 per cent of our planet that is covered by the oceans has a topography as dramatic as any on the continents, with vast plains and soaring mountain ranges, immense ridges and plunging trenches, unguessed-at in previous centuries. Until relatively recently, the most comprehensive ocean maps were Admiralty charts giving a rough idea of sea-bed depths in inshore waters only. The modern sea-explorer has access to ocean-floor information presented in pictorial form by the marvel of geotectonic imaging from satellites. Seasat, launched in 1978, surveyed all the Earth's oceans between latitudes 72°N and 72°S. By

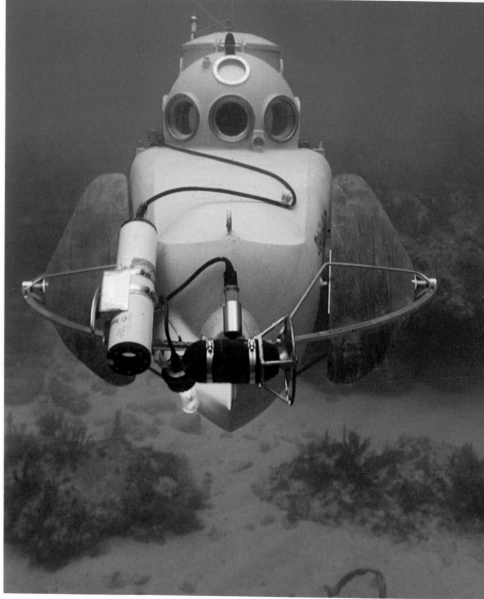

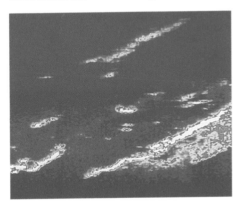

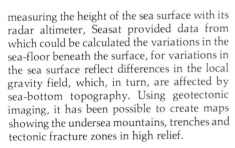

Left The US research submersible *Alvin*.
Below Computer-processed image from the UK sonar device GLORIA shows hills on the Atlantic sea-floor. Warm colours probably represent basalt, cooler colours sediments.

Above London Bridge, in Victoria, Australia, is a dramatic reflection of the sea's ability to select weak strata and carve the coast into strange shapes.
Right Air compressed by powerful waves forces water through a blow-hole.

measuring the height of the sea surface with its radar altimeter, Seasat provided data from which could be calculated the variations in the sea-floor beneath the surface, for variations in the sea surface reflect differences in the local gravity field, which, in turn, are affected by sea-bottom topography. Using geotectonic imaging, it has been possible to create maps showing the undersea mountains, trenches and tectonic fracture zones in high relief.

Multibeam sonar

For more detailed mapping, the ocean surveyors use multibeam sonar, a ship-borne system that works by recording and measuring very-high-frequency acoustic pulses bounced from the ocean floor. Multibeam sonar consists of an array of acoustic transmitters and receivers which can cover a relatively wide area. The SeaBeam system consists of sixteen acoustic beams projected in a fan-shape. The data from the beam readings can be converted into a

high-resolution image. Some multibeam systems can be towed in sled-like, remote-controlled 'fish' close to the ocean bed, and are 'side looking', sending out their acoustic pulses sideways to get a detailed picture of vertical features. GLORIA (Geological Long Range Inclined ASDIC) is one such device, developed by the UK's Institute of Oceanographical Sciences. It can map a swath of the sea-floor about 20 miles (30km) wide. Sea Marc I, developed by International Submarine Technology Ltd, covers a 3-mile (5km) wide section of the sea-bed, and was used to search for the remains of the liner *Titanic* as well as in oceanographic research.

The coastline

Oceanographers divide the ocean floor into several distinct zones, based on water depth, the types of animals and plants found there, and other criteria. The first of these zones — and the most familiar to most of us — is the intertidal zone, loosely equivalent to the popular concep-

tion of 'the coast'. This is the region that feels the full force of ocean waves.

The power released by waves is tremendous. At the height of a full-blooded gale-force storm, compressive forces can reach as much as 60 tons per square inch inside joints in cliff faces. Such impressive hydraulic pressure is caused by the sea compressing air in the fissures in the rock. If these fissures have upward openings a column of water spurts through a 'blow-hole' on the cliff top. Violent waves are able to hurl stones and even boulders at cliff-faces, bringing about the progressive erosion of the rock. The attrition between the clattering boulders makes smaller fragments, which themselves are continually ground together to form sand and ultimately mud.

Where the coastal cliffs are made of limestones an additional agent of erosion is the water itself, supplementing the violent storm forces. These carbonate rocks become dissolved by the sea water. Soft rocks can be cut back at an impressive rate. For example, the easily eroded clay and sand cliffs at Cape Cod, Massachusetts, on the eastern seaboard of the USA, are retreating at a rate of about 3ft (1m) each year.

Rock formations, such as granites, which are naturally well-jointed, are very susceptible to the natural 'quarrying' action of air compressed by wave force. As the joints are enlarged, blocks and columns become detached to form stacks, which ultimately fall into the sea.

The differing resistance of rocks added to their varying angle of dip, and other structural features, leads to the formation of spectacular coastal features. On the south coast of England a hard limestone layer protects softer chalk behind it, and where the limestone has been breached by the sea, the exposed soft chalk has been scooped out behind to make circular bays. Where hard rock layers lie above softer ones, bizarre 'mushroom'-shaped stacks form when the harder layer is removed but small masses of it remain, protecting columns of the softer layer lying beneath them.

Coastlines may advance or retreat, depending on continuing geological processes such as continental drift, erosion and deposition. A coastline experiences submergence whenever the continental crust is pushed downwards or the sea-level rises. Emergence occurs when the crust is uplifted or the general sea-level falls. Advancing coastlines result from a combination of emergence and deposition; coastlines retreat when subsidence and destruction, by erosion or other means, occur together.

Advancing coasts

A gently sloping coastal plain, which is the uplifted former sea-bed, causes larger waves to break well away from the shore, and is a typical feature of emergent shorelines. Small waves advance up the shore to form a low cliff, while the larger waves breaking further out erode the sea-bed and pile up the debris they produce to make an offshore bar. Between the bar and the coast a lagoon may form. The water in the lagoon is linked to that in the open sea by numerous cuts in the bar. Despite these connections, the lagoon is protected from the effects of coastal erosion by wind and waves. Rivers flowing into the lagoon deposit silt and mud from the land, and salt marshes and maybe large deltas will be built up. During this constructional activity at the margin of the land, the sea further out has been pushing the bar landwards and deepening the sea-bed. A so-called 'mature' stage is reached when the bar has been completely eroded away and the sea-bed deepened to such an extent that large waves can now break on the shore.

Retreating coastlines

In contrast to emergent coastlines, those that are submerged develop different features as the sea-level rises and the water floods areas that were only recently dry land. An extremely irregularly shaped coastline, with many small islands and wide estuaries, is typical of a retreating coastline. Wave action on the headlands (previously high areas between now-drowned river valleys) produces cliffs, with features such as caves, natural rock-arches and stacks.

Longshore drift

Progressive development of the coastline makes great heaps of rock debris. Waves rarely hit the coast parallel to it, usually making an oblique angle instead. Material is usually carried along the shore by the process of 'longshore drift'. Cliff-foot debris can be carried along the coast to form a bar, which may extend from the

headland across a bay. Some bars are many miles long, ending in curved 'spits'. Sediment deposited in the bays forms a beach, and rivers entering the sea will add further to the deposition. Ultimately, the bays may become filled with sediment and the headlands completely removed by erosion, to produce a straight coastline.

Disappearing houses

In many of the European countries bordering the North Sea, the land is slowly subsiding by as much as 1ft (30cm) per century, causing the low-lying coastline to be flooded. In south-east England, unprotected coastal rocks are easily washed away by the sea, in some cases causing houses to fall onto the beach below.

Above Depositional and erosive features are linked in this magnificent coastal landscape at Préveza, eastern Greece. Remnants of former cliffs are now joined to the coast by bars and spits, with lagoons behind them.

Left When cliffs retreat due to wave action and other processes, a wave-cut platform, as here in Yorkshire, England, is left in front of the cliff.

Wave-cut platforms

As cliffs are cut back by wave action, a gently sloping 'wave-cut platform' is left at their base. Tidal waters carrying abrasive sand and rock scour this surface. When the cliffs are made of hard igneous and metamorphic rocks, the platform takes a long time to become eroded away, so it may grow very wide. This also helps to reduce the backward erosion of the cliff itself, because the base of the cliff will be in shallow water and the large waves will have broken far out on the smooth wave-cut surface. The cliffs are then predominantly removed from the landward side by processes of weathering and erosion such as freeze-thaw splitting, thermal expansion and the removal of rock by water running over and down the cliff-face. Near Bergen, Norway, a hard-rock wave-cut platform extends from the coast for several miles. In some areas, this 'strandflat', as it is called, extends for more than 30 miles (50km) from the former line of cliffs.

Land from the sea

Material eroded from one part of the coast is deposited elsewhere. Large rivers, such as the Nile and Mississippi, carry millions of tons of sediment to the coast each year, building complex deltas. Volcanic activity, as in Hawaii, Iceland and Tristan da Cunha, adds new land to coastal regions. Allied to volcanism is the growth of land caused by the activities of marine organisms, notably corals.

Coral reefs

Coral reefs are built up by small calcium-

Advancing coastline

Only small waves are able to reach the shore; larger waves break further out and begin to form a bar.

As deposition continues the offshore bar develops and a lagoon, as in photo (top of page) forms.

The bar continues to grow and the lagoon is now becoming silted and filled with deposited sediment.

The sea-bed has been deepened throughout the previous stages; now strong waves erode the bar.

Retreating coastline

When the sea-level rises, areas which were dry land are flooded and valleys become deep estuaries.

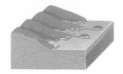

A very irregular coastline develops, with cliffs, stacks, arches and beach development in the estuaries.

The offshore islands, hills before the rise in sea-level, are now eroded and the coast is much straighter.

With much deposition in the estuaries and joining of the coastal beaches, the coast is now straight.

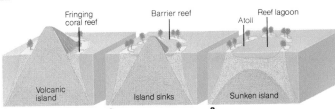

Fringing coral reef   Barrier reef   Atoll   Reef lagoon

Volcanic island   Island sinks   Sunken island

1   2   3

Left Many volcanic islands are in areas which are warm enough for reef-building corals to grow. The gently sloping sides of the volcano are ideal sites for these corals as they need a particular depth of water.

As the coral reef grows, the volcanic cone may subside and the sea-level may rise (perhaps due to melting of ice-sheets), or both may occur. The corals continue to grow at the same depth and a classic atoll develops.

Above Moorea Island, Tahiti, is a volcanic island fringed with coral reefs, which form a shallow coastal apron.
Below At Bora Bora island, French Polynesia, the off-shore reef encloses a tranquil lagoon around the volcano.

secreting animals called polyps, which live together in immense colonies. As the polyps grow, the cups they construct as their living quarters are extended. The polyps extract calcium carbonate from the seawater, secreting it to form their solid, rock-like homes.

In 1837, Charles Darwin suggested that where coral develops around volcanic islands, the growth of the coral keeps pace with the subsidence of the volcano, and a ring-shaped reef, or atoll, is eventually formed. A different theory, first suggested by the US-Canadian geologist Reginald Daly in 1910, suggested that rather than the volcano subsiding, the sea-level rises, as after the melting of the ice-caps some 10,000 years ago, and the corals grow to keep pace with the rise in sea-level. The corals live on submarine platforms, which were the result of wave action when the sea-level was much lower during the Pleistocene period, two million years ago at most, but deep drilling into the reefs has shown that in some areas the animals have existed there for over 50 million years. Even though this evidence seems to invalidate it, Daly's theory may, nevertheless, account for some features not adequately explained by Darwin's theory particularly with regard to the recent growth of reefs.

The continents appear to end at the coast-lines, but if the rocks are traced beneath the waves by echo sounding, it is found that a shallow sloping shelf extends out to sea, often for many tens of miles. This 'continental shelf' ends abruptly where it plunges into the deep ocean at the 'continental slope'. Here, at the 'shelf-break', the depth of water averages 400ft (130m). The average gradient of the continental slope is only a few degrees, though in places it resembles an underwater cliff. The slope of the continental shelf, by contrast, is less than one degree in most parts of the world.

The continental shelves account from some 24 million square miles (62 million sq km), or 12½ per cent of the Earth's surface. They were actively eroded between two million and 10,000 years ago. During the last (Pleistocene) ice age, the sea-level was, on average, some 300ft (90m) lower than it is today. As the ice-caps increased in size, water was drawn from the oceans. During the advance and retreat of the four main Pleistocene glaciations, the coasts were bevelled to make a gently sloping wave-cut platform, which was flooded when the most recent ice retreat occurred. Sediments have been deposited on these shelves, and borehole investigations of the shelf regions show them to be geologically part of the continental crust.

No continental shelf area has been as thoroughly investigated by drilling as that beneath the North Sea between the British Isles and Scandinavia. Since the late 1960s, the search for oil and gas has spurred on this research to such an extent that detailed structural and lithological (rock distribution) maps are now available for the bed of the North Sea. These show continuations of the rock strata from the UK mainland well out from the shore and under the ocean.

Types of continental margin

For many years, oceanographers have recognized two main types of continental margin: the so-called 'Atlantic' margin, which is seismically inactive and often has a broad continental shelf, and the 'Pacific' type, which is seismically active, with a narrower shelf and an offshore ocean trench or trough running parallel to the continental margin. Although they are more common there, each type of margin is by no means restricted to the ocean from which it has taken its name.

Plate tectonics theory helps to explain these two types of continental margin. The 'Atlantic' type tends to occur where a new ocean basin has developed, while the 'Pacific' type is seismically active because of the subduction of ocean-floor material beneath it.

Marine sediments

Marine sediments are of various different types. The most important are the terrigenous, or lithogenous, sediments, which are made of silicate minerals and rock fragments from the land, worn away by erosion and weathering, or ejected from volcanoes; biogenic sediments, which represent the remains of marine animals and plants; and hydrogenous sediments, precipitated from seawater (these include the potentially valuable manganese nodules found on some sea-beds). Other, much rarer, sediments come from meteorites that burn up when they enter the Earth's atmosphere.

Shallow-water sediments

When terrigenous sediments arrive at the end of their journey downriver to the sea, they are usually first deposited near the mouth of the river. Unless they are on sheltered coastlines, however, the action of the waves and tides will carry the sediment deposits along the continental shelf, eventually dumping them in areas where there are only weak currents or waves on the sea-bed. Shallow-water sediments account for as much as 85 per cent by volume of all sediment deposits in the oceans, though, compared with the biogenic oozes covering the vast abyssal plains, they occupy only 25 per cent or so of the total sea-bed area of the world.

The distribution pattern of terrigenous sediments is by no means even: it depends on a number of features, including the water depth, the profile of the ocean floor, the amount of drainage from the adjacent land, and so on. For

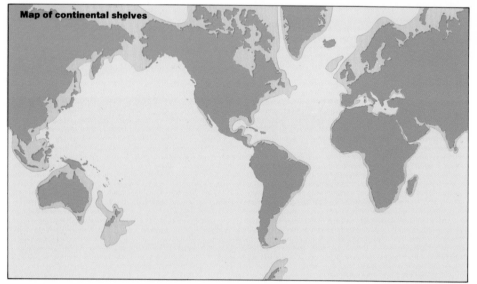

Map of continental shelves

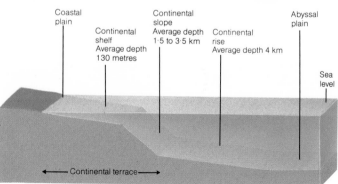

Coastal plain

Continental shelf Average depth 130 metres

Continental slope Average depth 1·5 to 3·5 km

Continental rise Average depth 4 km

Abyssal plain

Sea level

← Continental terrace →

Above The continental shelves (orange) show the real extent of the continents. The links (below sea-level) between North America and Asia and between the countries of northern Europe can be seen. Some shelves are extensive, as in the Northern Hemisphere, but that around Africa is very narrow.
Left Position of the shelf relative to other submarine features.

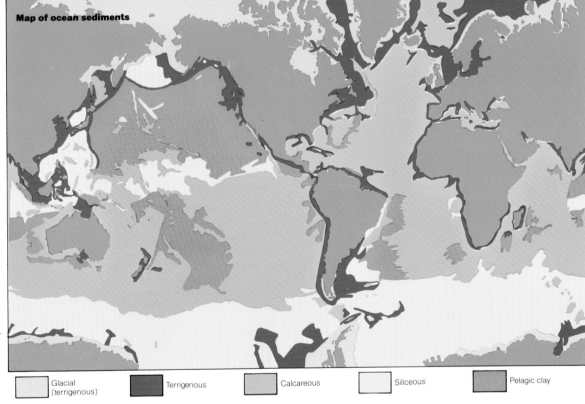

Map of ocean sediments

Glacial (terrigenous)   Terrigenous   Calcareous   Siliceous   Pelagic clay

Above left Co-ordinated teamwork is essential on a North Sea oil rig when the bit has to be changed and all the drill pipe must be pulled up and unscrewed by the man on the right, using power tongs. Each section of drill pipe is 30ft long and weighs almost 1½ tons. As well as oil, natural gas is obtained from the continental shelf of the North Sea.

Above The Ganges, India. Most of the land-derived sediment is carried to the sea by great river systems like this. They often build huge deltas out onto the continental shelf. Millions of tons of sediment are transported, each day, into these delta systems and distributed by channels wandering over the delta top.

Right The map shows the distribution of sediment types on the present-day sea-bed. Land-derived (terrigenous) deposits are concentrated on the shelf area, glaciated ones at high latitudes. The deep ocean contains siliceous or calcareous oozes and clay.

instance, large areas of sediment deposits occur in the northern part of the Indian Ocean, brought down to the sea by the huge river systems of the Brahmaputra, Ganges and others. By contrast, there is relatively little sediment off the Atlantic coast of the United States. Here, as in the rest of the northern continents, giant ice-sheets covered much of the land during the last (Pleistocene) glaciations. The glaciers scoured out large lakes, such as the Great Lakes system, and these trapped sediment which might otherwise have been carried down to the ocean. Also, when the ice finally melted, the sea-level rose, flooding the mouths of many rivers and forming large estuaries, which prevented yet more sediment from reaching the sea.

Deep sediment layers

The granitic crust that forms the continents thins at the edges of the land-masses, and slight depressions in it become filled with terrigenous sediments. The crust may continue to sag downwards under its burden of sediments, allowing yet more to fill the depression. Seismic surveys have told geologists a great deal about the thickness of sediments in various areas of the sea-floor. Typical values for the open ocean basins, overlying oceanic crust, are 1,000-1,600ft (300-500m), while the layer over the mid-ocean ridges is, relatively speaking, a thin veneer. By contrast, the depressions along the edges of the continents collect prodigious depths of sediment. Off the coast of Newfoundland, one such depression has collected nearly 8 miles (13km) of sediment!

The study of marine sediments has taught geologists much about past climates, patterns of circulation and movements of the ocean crust.

A major feature of the continental shelves is the enormous tonnage of mud, sand and silt brought down by river systems. When it reaches the sea, the river water loses its speed and dumps its load. Fine sediment which is not deposited increases the density of the river water, and it travels out over the continental shelf and may continue down the slope. The sudden deposition of large masses of river sediment during periods of flooding may make the earlier formed layers very unstable. Violent ocean storms and earth tremors can cause the muddy sediments to cascade down the continental slope, forming what oceanographers call 'turbidity flows'. These flows are highly charged with rock debris, and may be powerful agents in the erosion and excavation of deep canyons beneath the sea. (Turbidity currents are not, however, confined to the sea; they also occur in lakes and rivers, and are one of the main causes of the silting up of many reservoirs.)

Exploring submarine canyons

Various submarine canyons have been investigated with the aid of remote cameras and other devices. Off the east coast of the USA, there are vertical-walled canyons 3,000ft (900m) deep. Similar canyons are known to exist off the mouth of the River Congo, in West Africa, off the Hudson River in North America, and off the Ganges in north-east India.

The Hudson Canyon has been particularly well studied, from where it starts at the southern edge of the Georges Bank right down onto the deep sea-bed. It carves its way deeply into the sediments of the continental slope. Beyond the mouth of the canyon, at a depth below sea-level of nearly 14,000ft (4,300m) is a vast expanse of debris, made of sediment eroded from the canyon and carried through it from the shelf above.

Graded turbidites

These deposits, which are fan-shaped in plan view, reveal a number of interesting features. The grains of sediment which they contain are graded. In each layer, there are coarse grains at the base and fine mud at the top. In the top surface of older layers are grooves and scratches, made by rock fragments dragged along in later flows. Each layer is called a turbidite, and represents the deposit of one turbidity current.

The neat grading is the result of the gradual lessening in the velocity of the flow as it reaches the deeper sea-bed away from the confines of the canyon, which allows the coarser sediment to be deposited first.

Graded turbidites have been recognized from many parts of the geological record, far back into Palaeozoic and even pre-Cambrian times. By analogy with the deposits formed in modern seas, they are interpreted as deep-sea sediments.

Moving sediments

Possibly the greatest geological significance of turbidity currents is that they provide a means whereby coarse land-derived sediment can be taken out into the deepest sea areas. Investigations of the ocean depths by submersibles have revealed turbidity currents slowly but

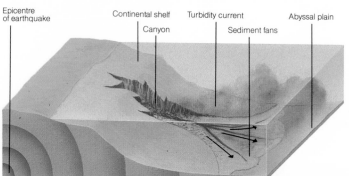

Epicentre of earthquake — Continental shelf — Turbidity current — Canyon — Sediment fans — Abyssal plain

Left Earthquakes often set in motion the slurry of sediment called a turbidity current. Moving down a continental shelf, it is channelled by a submarine canyon, a deep valley cutting through the shelf and steeper continental slope. When the current, heavily charged with sediment, reaches the abyssal plain, it speeds on with erosive power, finally depositing its load.

surely carrying silt right out into the abyssal depths. Such sediments can be transported from the coast for hundreds or even thousands of miles across the sea-bed. Some turbidity currents have been followed from the edge of the North American sub-continent to the Mid-Atlantic Ridge; there are large deposits of sediment on the Atlantic abyssal plain.

A fortunate accident

Because turbidity currents are notoriously difficult to study in the oceans, oceanographers have learnt much of what they know about them from simulated flows in laboratory tanks, as well as from examination of turbidites. However, a fortuitous, though costly, incident at sea over fifty years ago provided scientists with one of the best opportunities of analysing the speed and direction of a major turbidity current. In 1929, the submarine telephone cables lying on the Grand Banks, to the south of Newfoundland, were mysteriously broken. This region was covered with a thick veneer of Pleistocene sediment from the St Lawrence River, and an earth tremor had set this unstable waterlogged mass into motion. The time of the earth tremor was recorded, and its epicentre (the point where the shock waves reach the surface) measured by seismographs. A massive, immensely powerful turbidity flow developed, 1,200ft (370m) thick and 62 miles (100km) wide, cutting southwards through the underlying sediments of the St Lawrence Straits and out

onto a vast area of the Atlantic abyssal plain.

Thirteen submarine telegraph cables were broken, one after the other in a regular sequence out from the coast, and the exact times of breakage of seven of these cables were recorded. The breakage times gave the speed of the current at over 50 knots (56mph). Calculations showed that a massive 24½ cubic miles (100cu km) of sediment had been released.

Turbidites and fossils

The rock formed by ancient turbidity flows can be made of all sorts of sedimentary

materials, depending very much on the nature of the original deposits spread on top of the continental shelf.

Because of their rapid formation, turbidites contain few unbroken fossil remains, but the fragments that are trapped within them are a mixture, from deep-water organisms and shallow-water creatures. The shallow-water organisms were swept out from the area where the turbidity current started, while those from deep water were sucked into the current as it travelled across the sea-bed or buried when it eventually deposited its huge load of sediment.

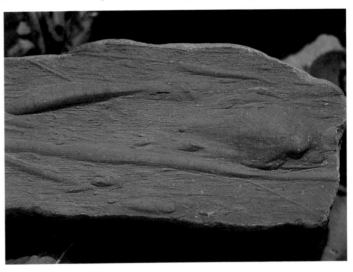

Right Ancient turbidites can be recognized by strange 'sole marks' found on the underside of rock strata. The marks, made by objects in the base of the turbidity flow, are preserved by the mud in the current. Split rock layers show the grooves on one surface, and the casts, as in this example from North Wales, on the other.
Below Today, undersea telephone cables are laid by vessels such as this one, seen here on the continental shelf.
Below left The Johnson Sea Link is typical of the modern exploratory craft used on the deep sea-bed.

Beyond the base of the continental slopes, far beyond the continental shelves, lie the vast submerged regions of the ocean floor. These areas have their own mountain ranges, plains and basins. At times, the submarine mountains rise to form chains of volcanic islands, as in Hawaii and Iceland. On either side of the mountain chain called the Mid-Atlantic Ridge (running from Spitzbergen south almost to Antarctica) lie extensive plains at depths of over 16,000ft (4,900m). The Argentine Plain is the largest, occupying about the same area as the USA. The North American basin is similar in area, as are the Vatteras Plain off Florida and the Sohm Plain south of Newfoundland. In the Pacific the situation is rather more complex, as there is no central ridge with plains on either side. The mountains of the East Pacific Rise run south of Australia and swing northwards parallel to South America, as far north as Mexico, enclosing the basins of the Southeast Pacific, Chile and Peru. To the west of the East Pacific Rise are a series of wide basins, containing mountain-like Christmas Island and the Hawaiian chain. The ocean floor becomes increasingly complex towards Japan, where huge island arcs caused by subduction of the ocean floor form volcanic islands and deep trenches. The ocean floor of the Marianas, Fiji and Kermadec-Tonga groups is far more complex than the Rockies and Himalayas combined.

The great plains and basins

Exciting and important though these mountain chains are, the abyssal plains and basins make up the greatest area of the sea-floor. In the plains of the Pacific Ocean (and to a lesser extent elsewhere) are strange flat-topped truncated volcanoes called guyots. Over 2,000 are known from the Pacific alone, and many more

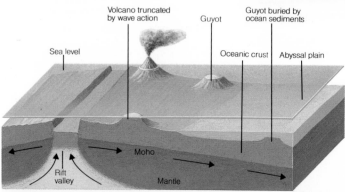

Left The distant ocean bed is a dynamic restless part of the Earth's surface. At the ocean ridges, active spreading of the crust occurs along rift systems. Hot magma reaches the surface here, forming pillow lavas and volcanic seamounts, which may rise as islands. Older volcanoes with eroded peaks are called guyots. On the floor of the ocean, away from the submarine mountains, a veneer of sediment accumulates largely from organic debris.

Bottom left The deep ocean bed seen from *Alvin* shows muddy sediment with brittle stars and (centre) a sea cucumber.

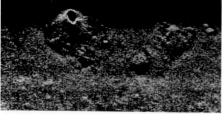

Above A volcano on the floor of the Pacific Ocean, detected by the UK sonar side-looking vehicle GLORIA.

probably exist. They were probably planed off during sea-floor movement as the volcanic cones were carried into deeper water. The majority of the submarine plains are at depths of more than 12,000ft (3,700m) where wave pressure may be more than 6,800 lbs per sq in (46,850kPa). This pressure is exceeded only in the deepest trenches.

Abyssal sediments

Very little sediment accumulates in these regions, which are often far from land and river systems' influence. Into these icy depths settles material which is so fine that it can be carried in suspension, and atmospheric and cosmic dust, together with the dust flung high into the atmosphere by volcanoes.

About 75 per cent of the deep ocean floor is covered by what are termed pelagic sediments. In contrast to the continental shelf sediments,

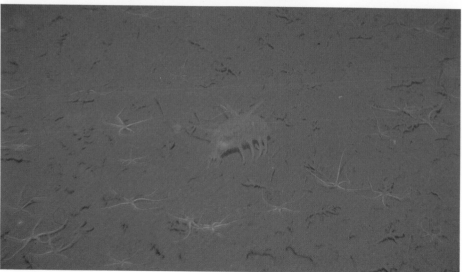

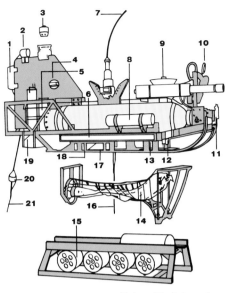

**Scripps Institution
Deep Tow Vehicle**
1 Transponder
   interrogator
2 Emergency
   transponder
   hydrophone
3 Transponder repeater
4 Sound velocimeter
5 TV camera
6 Side-looking sonar
7 Towing cable
8 Photo battery case
9 Upward-looking sonar
10 Suspended
   particle filter
11 Obstacle avoidance
   sonar
12 Differential
   pressure gauge
13 Precision depth gauge
14 Biological sampling net
15 Water samplers
16 Strobe light cable
17 Downward-looking
   sonar
18 Temperature gauge
19 Wide-angle 35mm
   camera (stereo pair)
20 Transducer
21 Magnetometer cable

Left and **above** This device, towed by a ship, is used for mapping the ocean floor.

Below Giant abyssal sediment waves on the Bahama Ridge, east of Florida, imaged by GLORIA.

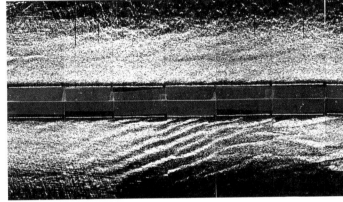

they contain relatively little terrigenous material (from the land), but they do include large amounts of biogenic material, formed from the skeletons of countless millions of marine organisms, ranging down slowly and incessantly from the sunlit waters above. These carpet the sea-bed of the abyssal depths with a soft 'ooze', forming one of the smoothest and most featureless areas on Earth.

If the biogenic material is greater than 30 per cent by volume, the sediments are classified according to the type of organisms they contain. For instance, an ooze containing more than 30 per cent by volume of the skeletons of *Globigerina*, a single-celled marine animal, is called a *Globigerina* ooze. *Globigerina* is just one type of a group of animals called foraminiferans; if the sediment contains various types of foraminiferans, it is termed a foraminiferal ooze. Other organisms that produce such deep-sea oozes are the single-celled animals called radiolarians, and the coccolithophorids and diatoms, which are single-celled plants. The slow rate of accumulation of these oozes has been estimated to be only a few tens of feet every million years.

Calcite oozes

Some of these tiny marine creatures, notably the foraminiferans, have shells made of calcite (calcium carbonate). Long ago, oceanographers discovered that calcite oozes, the most abundant of the biologically produced oozes formed from the skeletal remains of organisms, were more or less restricted to depths less than about 13,000ft (4,000m). They are extremely rare on

the deepest ocean floors. This was puzzling, because foraminiferans are widespread over the oceans, and there should be no reason why their shells did not eventually penetrate the deeper waters. The plot thickened when the scientists examined the deep-ocean sediments more closely: they found small numbers of shells, mostly larger and thicker types.

Oceanographers investigating the chemistry of the oceans had found that the deep ocean waters are considerably colder, under higher pressure and contain more dissolved carbon dioxide gas than do the shallower waters. The end result of all these factors is that calcium carbonate is more soluble in the deep oceans than in the surface or shallow waters, where the foraminiferans live. Drawing on this knowledge, the researchers put forward the theory that although the foraminiferans are very common in the surface waters of the ocean, as their shells slowly fall into the depths, the calcium carbonate of which they are made dissolves away in the water. The first proof of this theory came when an inventive oceanographer at the US Scripps Institution of Oceanography lowered meticulously shaped and precisely weighed spheres of calcium carbonate into the ocean waters for known periods of time. When he hauled them up again and reweighed them, he found that the spheres that had been lowered only to shallow depths showed no change in weight, but those that had gone down to greater depths were lighter, and bore clearly etched pits and other marks, confirming the theory that calcite was being

dissolved. Many other experiments helped tell the same story. The depth of water below which calcium carbonate begins to dissolve is called the calcium carbonate compensation depth. Over most of the oceans this is at about 3 miles (5,000m) deep, though it may be as deep as 3¾ miles (6km) in parts of the Atlantic Ocean, and above 2¼ miles (3½km) in areas of the Atlantic Ocean where there are relatively few marine animals and plants.

Examination of cores obtained by deep drilling into areas of the ocean bed that are today well below the carbonate compensation depth have revealed that the ancient sediments were rich in calcium carbonate. An explanation of this is that plate tectonics movements have carried such areas, formerly parts of spreading ridges, beneath the carbonate compensation depth. Oceanographic research has also indicated that the compensation depth in various parts of the oceans has shifted with changing currents and patterns of circulation, brought about by continental drift and ancient glaciations.

Silica oozes

The other important groups of biogenic oozes are the silica-rich oozes, produced from the shells of diatoms and radiolarians. These are most common today in the Pacific and Antarctic Oceans, in areas of the ocean floor where little of the oozes from the land is able to penetrate.

Sediments from the land

The land-derived, or terrigenous, sediments include brown muds and red clays which together cover 40 million square miles (over 100 million sq km) of the abyssal sea-floor. The red colour of these deposits is due mainly to iron oxides from volcanic sources, both from the atmospheric dust thrown out by volcanoes on land and from submarine eruptions, which form the pillow lavas at the ocean ridges.

Metal-rich sediments

The last types of sediment are the metal-rich deposits flanking the ocean ridges and the fields of manganese nodules. The nodules, first encountered by the British *Challenger* oceanographical expedition in the 1870s, are discrete black concentrically-layered lumps ranging in diameter from less than 1in (2.5cm) to over 1ft (30cm). Though their main content is manganese (between 8 and 40 per cent), they also contain iron (between 9 and 27 per cent) and smaller amounts of copper, nickel and cobalt. Their shape varies from rounded to flat, and in some areas, notably the deep Pacific Ocean floor, they cover over 50 per cent of the area of the sea-bed. Attempts to dredge this rich metal harvest from the sea-bed are fraught with many difficulties. The origin of the nodules is unknown. Their concentric banded structure, often around a nucleus of rock, such as basalt, may be a clue, suggesting that they formed by the process of accretion. This involves the gradual accumulation of a mineral in layers, rather like the way a pearl grows around an oyster. However they form, they are slow developers. Estimates have put their average growth rate at only one twenty-fifth of an inch (1mm) per million years!

The metal-rich sediments contain similar metals to the nodules, and may be formed where thick brines underly young ocean-floor basins. The metals are precipitated from hot brines, at places where seawater is heated at spreading ridges.

Plunging to three times the depth of the abyssal plains are the deep ocean trenches. Some trenches are thousands of miles long and up to 600 miles (1,000km) wide, and lie 1-2 miles (2-4km) below the rest of the deep-ocean floor. Most of them occur around the edges of the Pacific Ocean basin, but there are also some in the Atlantic and Indian Oceans. They usually have an asymmetrical V-shape, with a steeper slope landwards and a gentler slope towards the ocean basin. These are the most active regions on Earth, associated with island arcs and overlooked by often active volcanoes.

Deep ocean trenches can be traced from the west coast of South America, where the southern part of the Chile Trench has become filled with a thick layer of sediment, through the Peru and Central America Trenches, before petering out south of Baja California. The pattern reappears south of Alaska in the form of the Aleutian Trench, the eastern part of which is filled with sediment, like the Chile Trench. On the northwest edge of the Pacific, the Kamchatka Trench is continuous with those of the Kurile Islands and Japan, from where it can be traced in a broad curve via the Marianas and West Caroline Trenches. The deep ocean trenches of South-east Asia form a complex pattern, where a number of small crustal plates are being subducted. Lying between the Marianas Trench and the Chinese mainland are the Nonsei-Shato and Mindanao Trenches, while the Indonesia Trench runs the whole length of the archipelago of islands from which it takes its name, and extends some way southwards. The New Britain Trench and the Tonga-Kermadec Trench lie either side of the Melanesian Rise, a northerly branch of the Pacific-Antarctic Spreading Ridge.

Seamounts and guyots

As well as the trenches, other features of the deep oceans include seamounts, mountains rising abruptly at least 3,300 feet (1,000m) from the ocean floor. These are drowned submarine volcanoes. Over 2,000 have been discovered, mainly in the Pacific Ocean, though a total of well over 20,000 is suspected to exist. Some form islands, such as those of the Hawaiian chain, but many others are completely submerged. Flat-topped 'guyots' (named after Arnold Guyot, a 19th century Swiss-American geologist) also occur, especially in the central North Pacific. One of the largest clusters of guyots is that of the Mid-Pacific Mountains, extending from west of Hawaii to Wake Island. Geologists believe that these guyots are volcanic cones whose tops were planed off by wave erosion as they were carried into deeper and deeper water by sea-floor spreading.

The hadal zone

The deep ocean trenches are among the most extreme environments on Earth. They form what is known as the 'hadal' zone, a minimum of 21,000ft (6,400m) below sea-level. It is named from the Greek *Hades*, meaning 'hell' or 'the underworld'.

In this inhospitable world, there is perpetual darkness and the temperature is near freezing point. The water pressure at such depths is extremely high, and the fact that any living things exist here is amazing. Over 20 years ago, in 1960, Jacques Picard and Don Walsh, in the US bathyscaphe *Trieste*, explored the deepest part of the ocean, the bottom of the Challenger Deep in the Marianas Trench, to a depth of

35,600ft (10,850m). They reported having seen fish living under water pressures of over one ton per square inch!

Hydrothermal vents

In 1978 in the Galapagos Spreading Ridge, 8,200ft (2,500m) below the surface of the Pacific Ocean, near the Galapagos Islands to the west of Ecuador, South America, a team of three geophysicists in the US Navy submersible *Alvin* investigated 'hydrothermal vents' in the ocean floor. They were astonished to find that, far from being around freezing-point, as it usually is at such great depths, the water near the vents was warm, at temperatures of about 68°F (20°C). Over the vents themselves, the water was astonishingly hot—as high as 660°F (350°C)! Despite its high temperature, the water cannot boil because it is under great pressure.

The scientists believe that as cold water seeps through the oceanic crust, it encounters molten rock (magma), is superheated, and gushes out through the open vents at great speed, creating a current that warms the sea around it. The cold water gains more from the magma than heat alone: it also picks up and dissolves sulphur in the rock. The dark sulphide-rich columns of water that shoot out of the vents are aptly named 'black smokers'.

Strange communities of bacteria and animals have been able to develop here. They are unique in that they do not seem to depend on sunlight energy and plant photosynthesis, which sustain life everywhere else on the planet. The animals, including giant worms, sea anemones, clams, crabs and fish, live in the warm waters around the vents, and, while some eat one

another, they all ultimately depend for survival on the bacteria, which are found in the hottest parts of the vent walls, in clumps. These periodically break free and are carried up out of the vent by the hot water shooting through it. The clumps are large enough to be eaten by the filter-feeding worms, anemones and clams, which trap the bacterial clumps in fine sieve-like structures.

As well as the vents and their black smokers with the associated animal communities, the researchers found large deposits of metallic sulphides, including zinc, iron and copper sulphides in high concentrations. These take the form of roughly cylindrical towers about 10-30ft (3-10m) high and about 15ft (5m) in diameter. The different metals give the deposits their variegated colours—shades of red, brown, ochre, grey and white.

Since the discovery of the Galapagos Spreading Ridge hydrothermal vents and mineral sulphide deposits, others have been found, for example in the East Pacific Rise west of Mexico and the Juan de Fuca Ridge off the coast of Oregon, USA.

Submersibles

None of these or the many other discoveries about conditions in the deep oceans would have been possible without the development of submersibles. Most of these have been built either for the purpose of studying marine biology or servicing man-made structures, such as offshore oil-rigs. Underwater television cameras, operated by remote-control and housed in a self-propelled unmanned submersible, have enabled scientists to explore the abyssal depths from the safety and comfort of surface-

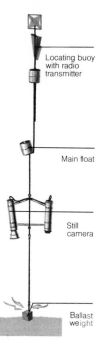

Left A 'black smoker' on the East Pacific Rise contains sulphides dissolved by water heated to 660°F (350°C) at hydrothermal vents in the ocean crust.
Bottom left Giant worms cluster in a Galapagos hydrothermal vent.
Below Developed by the US Scripps Institution of Oceanography, this automatic camera operates on the seabed unattached to ship or submersible.

Locating buoy with radio transmitter

Main float

Still camera

Ballast weight

Left The US research submersible *Alvin*, operated by the Woods Hole Oceanographic Institution, Massachusetts, has been used for a number of studies of the deep sea-bed, including the investigation of hydro-thermal vents. Carrying a crew of two or three, it enables geologists to make a wide range of observations and measure-ments, and to take samples. Its pressurized spherical compartment measures only 6½ft (2m) in diameter.

Right The British WASP submersible is, essentially, a one-man mini-submersible with arms, but equipped with mechanical thrusters instead of legs.

Below left The astonishing dexterity possible with WASP's remote-controlled 'hands' is amply demonstrated as its operator attempts to solve the Rubik's cube puzzle. The arms incorporate ball-and-socket joints which include a fluid cushioning device somewhat similar to that in a human joint. The 'hands' are universal jaws, to which can be fitted a variety of tools, such as cable cutters, wrenches and grinders for carrying out underwater repair work on oil rigs and other situations.

going oceanographic research ships. Even so, only a tiny proportion of the deep-sea environ-ment has been explored, compared with the large areas of the land surface of the globe which have been studied in detail.

Such feats as the record-breaking descent by Picard and Walsh into the Challenger Deep were made possible by rapid advances in the design and construction of submersibles. Because air is easily compressed at depth, it is quite useless as a buoyancy aid. To overcome this problem, a low-density hydrocarbon, such as petroleum spirit, is used. Modern plastics, light alloys and titanium have all been used in attempts to construct craft that are both strong and light. The US research submersible *Alvin*, used for many deep-ocean explorations, has a titanium-alloy hull capable of withstanding

pressure down to a depth of 13,500ft (4,000m), and carries a two- or three-man crew. Powered by electric batteries, it is operated by Woods Hole Oceanographic Institution, Massachusetts.

Deep-sea diving
Before the pioneer French oceanographer Jacques Cousteau invented the aqualung, deep-sea divers wore cumbersome suits with weighted boots and screw-on spherical helmets made of copper. They depended for their air supply on fragile pipes connecting them to a pump on the deck of their parent ship. Today's deep-sea diver uses a diving suit that can weigh up to 1,100lb (500kg) on dry land, and yet gives the diver greater freedom and range than ever before. The atmospheric diving suit (ADS) is large enough to contain its own sealed-in atmosphere, like a manned submersible. As a result, the diver no longer needs to spend long hours of decompression to avoid the 'bends', and need not fear the hypothermia, bone necrosis and nitrogen poisoning that threaten the scuba diver operating at advanced depths.

JIM (named after the diver, Jim Jaratt, who first tested it), the first ADS, needs no connection with the surface once lowered to the sea-floor, carries a 72-hour air supply, and filters carbon dioxide as it accumulates. Cast from lightweight magnesium alloy, JIM's limbs have segmented joints fitted with waterproof ring-seals. Manipu-lators at the end of the arms allow the diver to perform astonishingly delicate tasks, and a four-windowed dome at head level makes for good vision. SAM is a development of JIM, with an aluminium instead of a magnesium alloy body. JAM, the next development, has a glass-fibre body and a double-layered clear

acrylic dome for improved vision. In a JAM suit, a diver can work for days if necessary at a depth of up to 2,300ft (700m). From the 'waist' up, WASP resembles JAM with its dome and jointed arms, but WASP has no legs, and is in fact a powered submersible with arms, though it depends on a cable connection with its parent vessel for the power supply to its thrusters, which replace the legs.

Unmanned submersibles
For really deep-level work, such as oil- and gas-line repair and maintenance, it is too dangerous to use human divers. Pressures of over 3,000lb per sq in (20,685kPa) are encoun-tered at depths of about 7,000ft (2,130m). At such pressures, a 16 in (41cm) diameter steel pipe with a one-inch (2.5cm) thick wall could be flattened as if it were made of paper. To cope with these conditions, remote-controlled vehicles (RCVs) have been developed. These are electronically controlled via an umbilical cable from the surface ship. Robot RCVs equipped with video cameras can swiftly locate problem spots and transmit accurate co-ordinates for the repair RCVs that follow them.

The last frontier but one
The ocean deeps are the last frontier but one—with outer space as the ultimate challenge. Our knowledge of the deep sea multiplies as fast as the development of new technology—satellite and sonar mapping, computer imaging and submarine engineering of every kind. Yet the deep oceans, with their plunging canyons, vast featureless plains and strange animal inhabitants, is still mostly very much a mystery. We are just beginning to dip our feet in it.

To most human beings, with their strongly developed visual and tactile senses, the ocean and the atmosphere are separate regions. Their nature, substances, and inhabitants are widely different, and we imagine a clear boundary between them. Yet the ocean and the atmosphere are in many senses parts of a single system, and share a relationship that is amply demonstrated by the mechanics of ocean circulation.

Both oceanic and atmospheric circulations are controlled by the rotation of the Earth and by the varying effects of solar radiation. In the long polar winters large masses of water are cooled. As the temperature decreases, the water density increases, and is additionally weighted with salt draining from sea ice. The cooled water sinks to fill the deep ocean basins. The Weddell Sea in Antarctica and the Norwegian, Greenland and Labrador Seas in the Arctic are the major sources of this cold, dense water. The spread of this water means that, even at the Equator, sea-bed water temperatures are close to 32°F (0°C), while at the surface, the water temperature can be as high as 86°F (30°C). Antarctic bottom water circles around the Pacific in a clockwise direction, and reaches up north of the Equator on both sides of the Indian Ocean. The Atlantic bottom water originates partly in the Arctic, circulating anticlockwise around the northern Atlantic, and reaching far down the eastern seaboard of the Americas to meet water of Antarctic origin spreading from the south.

Not all deep-water masses originate in polar regions. In the western Mediterranean, surface waters originating in the Atlantic are cooled in winter by the dry mistral wind, sinking to form a water mass that returns to the Atlantic at the bottom of the Straits of Gibraltar. Here, at a depth of 1,600ft (490m), the flow creates high velocity ripples in the coarse sand of the sea-bed. This highly saline water flows out into the central part of the North Atlantic. Here, it sinks below the lighter, less salty waters of that ocean. Some of the lighter ocean water flows into the Mediterranean, while the salty current settles to a depth of about 3,300ft (1,000m) before it spreads out.

The Ekman spiral

While huge masses of water move regularly and, for the most part, relatively slowly in cold bottom-water currents, the most obvious ocean currents are those occurring in the surface water layer, driven primarily by prevailing winds. The direction of the surface currents does not follow exactly that of the governing winds, since the effect of the Earth's rotation is to deflect the surface water flows, to the right of the wind in the Northern Hemisphere, and to the left of the wind in the Southern Hemisphere. The angle of deflection at the sea

surface is small, but increases with depth as the strength of the wind-driven current decreases. The total effect is confined to the upper hundred feet or so, and is known as the Ekman spiral. The total effect of the Ekman spiral when integrated with depth is to make the direction of water transport 90° to left or right of the wind direction.

El Niño

Where winds blow parallel to coastlines the consequence of the Ekman spiral effect is to create onshore or offshore water movements. Where it is offshore, the surface water displaced by the wind must be replaced by subsurface waters rich in nutrients which well up to the surface layers. Abundant plant and animal life supported by the upwelling, nutrient-rich water creates some of the most important fishing areas off continental coasts.

The Peru Current is part of the strongest upwelling system in the world, supporting a prolific fishing industry that is the mainstay of the Peruvian economy. However, periodic incursions of abnormally warm water from the Central Pacific sometimes destroy the familiar pattern. This phenomenon, known as El Niño, inhibits the usual upwelling of cold, rich water, with disastrous effects on the food chain that begins with plankton and ends with human food supplies. An El Niño in 1972 resulted in an abnormal concentration of the anchovy stocks close to the coast where they were fished almost to extinction. A decade later, El Niño was heralded by high sea temperatures and low atmospheric pressure in the central Pacific, causing unusual easterly winds. Surface waters of extremely high temperature surged eastward,

Below Devastating drought and bushfires in Australia in 1983 were among the worldwide climatic effects of the last El Niño, a periodic invasion of the Peru Current by abnormally warm water from the middle of the Pacific Ocean. Drought affected many other places, from India to Africa, and cyclones and floods also resulted.

Above right In this computerized image from a US weather satellite, the warm current (dark red) at the heart of the Gulf Stream shrinks as it meets the cold Labrador Current (blue) coming in from the North.
Right The Benguela Current, off the west coast of Africa, reveals broadly similar patterns.

Right Wind drives water at the ocean surface 45° to the right of the wind in the Northern Hemisphere, and 45° to the left in the Southern Hemisphere. The energy of the surface water is transmitted to successively deeper layers, which move more slowly with increasing depth. The net movement of water is at right angles to the direction of the wind. This phenomenon is known as the 'Ekman effect'.

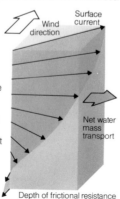

Wind direction
Surface current
Net water mass transport
Depth of frictional resistance

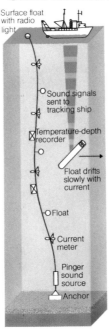

Left Depth probes like this are used to measure ocean temperature and salinity. Thousands of readings are made almost simultaneously at many different locations.
Right Long cables bearing an array of devices such as these are lowered from ships to measure deep ocean currents. The cable is moored by an anchor on the sea-bed. Sound signals help to locate it. Floats are also released, their density adjusted to that of the depth of water at which the oceanographers wish to track the current (the density of sea-water varies according to its temperature and salinity). The float drifts with the current, sending back sound signals to the research vessel.

Surface float with radio light
Sound signals sent to tracking ship
Temperature-depth recorder
Float drifts slowly with current
Float
Current meter
Pinger sound source
Anchor

reversing the surface current for many months. Upwelling still occurred, eventually, off the Peruvian coast, but it was confined to warm water layers, resulting in greatly reduced plankton and fish stocks. From Japan to Panama coral was killed off on a huge scale. Seabirds, starved of their normal fish diet, died in thousands. A long season of droughts, storms and floods circled the globe, continuing in a chain reaction long after El Niño had passed in late 1983, and the west-flowing currents of the eastern Pacific had returned to normal.

The Gulf Stream
The most intense surface-water flows move towards the poles in the western side of each ocean basin. The Gulf Stream in the Atlantic is the best known and most closely studied of these western boundary currents. Satellite tracking of free-floating buoys has shown how the Gulf Stream, travelling at up to 135 miles (220km) per day, leaves the Florida Straits and moving up the eastern coast of the USA,

meanders about its north-eastward course to form large independent rings or gyres that are separate from the main current. Infrared images from the NOAA-5 satellite have shown that these ring formations are often related to subsurface features such as seamounts.

Other western boundary currents
In the Pacific Ocean the equivalent of the Gulf Stream is the Kuroshio, curving north and then east off the islands of Japan. In the Indian Ocean the western boundary current is the Somali Current, which differs from the others in changing its direction seasonally in response to the monsoon winds. The Northern Hemisphere western boundary currents carry large volumes of water towards the North Pole. The Southern Hemisphere western boundary currents are weaker and less well defined. All eventually recirculate their water via weaker currents through the interior and eastern boundaries of the ocean basins, joining with westward-flowing equatorial currents to form large irregular gyres.

Circling the world, the great Southern Ocean Current joins all the major oceans, driven eastward around Antarctica by the westerly winds of the Forties and Fifties.

Measuring currents
Oceanographers originally obtained their knowledge of the surface circulation from reports of ship drift and through these the major features were defined. It is only over the past two decades that subsurface currents have been measured directly. Before the 1960s the subsurface distribution of currents could only be derived from their density fields, calculated from observations of temperature and salinity. Such 'geostrophic' current calculations are still used, but are subject to uncertainties which make them of limited usefulness in some situations.

Direct measurements of currents fall into two groups, Lagrangian, in which a tracer, drifting buoy or drogue (a floating device equipped with a small parachute) is tracked as it moves with the water, and Eulerian, where the current vectors are measured at a fixed position by means of a current meter. Strings of current meters, recording their data internally on magnetic tape, can be placed in the ocean for periods of months and their data later decoded and analysed. The instruments use either a propeller and vane to measure speed and direction or may measure the horizontal velocity components directly using acoustic or electromagnetic sensors.

Lagrangian drifters take two forms. One is a drogue, tracked at the sea surface by means of a satellite or some other electronic navigation device. The other type, used for subsurface observations, is a neutrally buoyant float. The float, less compressible than sea water, is ballasted to remain at a preset equilibrium depth and is then tracked acoustically by an attendant ship or over long distances and periods of time by receiving and analysing their sound signals at moored listening stations. Ocean currents also produce changes in sea surface temperature and sea-level, and satellite-borne radiometers and altimeters have been used to map the strength and geographical positions of currents over much of the globe.

Right The map shows the world's major ocean currents. There is a general drift of warm tropical water towards the poles, and a return flow of cool polar water towards the Equator. Although the polar currents begin life as surface flows, they gradually sink to the ocean bottom.

Key to Map
1 Gulf Stream
2 Labrador
3 East Greenland
4 North Atlantic Drift
5 Canary
6 North Equatorial
7 Brazil
8 Benguela
9 Antarctic Circumpolar
10 Peru
11 South Equatorial
12 West Australian
13 Agulhas
14 Kuroshio
15 California
16 Oyashio
17 North Pacific
18 Antarctic Subpolar

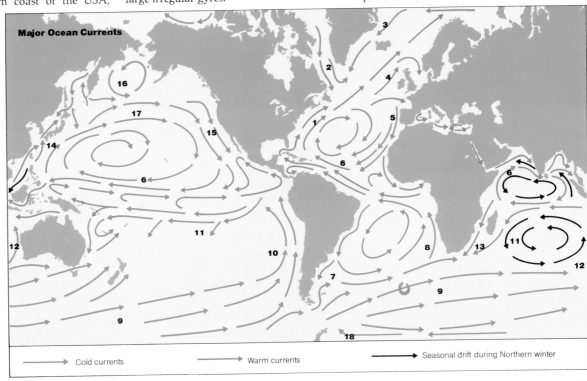

Major Ocean Currents

Cold currents → Warm currents → Seasonal drift during Northern winter →

As the wind blows over the sea, surface waves are produced. The greater the distance, or 'fetch', over which the wind blows, the larger are the waves. As waves approach gently sloping coastlines the friction between the base of the circular wave-motion and the sea-bed causes the wavelength to shorten, resulting in crowding of the wave-crests. The transmission of wave energy needs enough water to allow the circular wave motion to operate. When this cannot happen, as in shallow water, the wave breaks, releasing energy. Attempts have been made to harness this wave power for the production of electricity. The 'Salter duck' is a device with an oscillating vane inside a rocking float that can be used to drive a generator. Another system employs oscillating water columns in inverted 'cans' similar to those used to light buoys. Long rows of these energy converters would be needed, and they would have to be sited away from shipping lanes, in areas where plenty of wave motion of sufficient amplitude was always available (amplitude is the degree of elevation of a wave crest above the base of the adjacent wave trough).

Breaking waves

On steeply shelving beaches waves rise up and curve over as the water abruptly ceases to fill the wave orbit. This produces a cylinder-like hollow of air. The wave will finally roll and break, compressing the air, which bursts out as white foam. During storms such breaking of waves produces explosive jets of spray. When the beach slopes gently, the orbit of the wave motion is not suddenly broken, and the gradually diminishing supply of water causes turbulence at the top of the orbital paths and the formation of a slope of broken water or a sheet of surf. Where the sea-bed is uneven there may be two zones with different wave types in each one.

Wave refraction

On average, the depth of a wave is half its wavelength (the distance from crest to crest). If the sea-floor is below the wave-base it has no

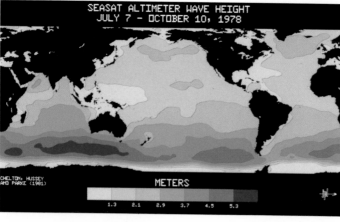

SEASAT ALTIMETER WAVE HEIGHT
JULY 7 – OCTOBER 10, 1978

CHELTON, HUSSEY AND PARKE (1981)

METERS

1.3   2.1   2.9   3.7   4.5   5.3

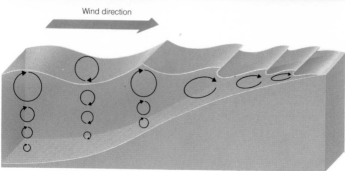

Wind direction

Left This computer-generated map, drawn from information gathered by the US Seasat satellite, shows wave height over the world's oceans. This is determined by a number of factors.
Right FLIP in action: operated by the Scripps Institution of Oceanography, California, USA, this extraordinary Floating Instrument Platform gives scientists a rock-steady base from which to carry out oceanographic research when it is upended by flooding its ballast tanks.

Left Each water particle in a wave moves in a circular orbit, whose diameter decreases with depth. As waves approach a shelving coastline, the orbital motion of the water particles becomes flattened to form an ellipse, and the wave slows down as it loses energy. Succeeding crests pile up on top of each other, eventually breaking as surf.

Above Waves strike coastal rocks on the Canary Isles with tremendous force. As they roll over, air is trapped inside them, and when they break, this compressed air is released in a spray of white foam.
Right A wave in Hawaii curves over suddenly as it hits an abruptly shelving beach.
Left Waves wash majestically against a New Zealand coast. The cliffs show the effects of continuing erosion by the relentless action of the waves, and bays have been formed.

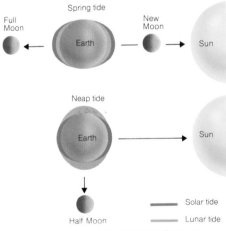

effect on the waves, but if the wave-base makes contact with the sea-bed then friction retards the wave and the crests crowd together. 'Wave refraction' (where waves breaking against a coastline bend inwards) can be explained in this way: where waves enter a bay or inlet, friction at the wave-base retards the waves to varying degrees. The incoming parallel waves become curved around the headland on either side of the bay. If waves meet a coastline in deep water they will be reflected back out to sea and meet incoming waves to produce complex patterns.

Destructive power

Wave formation by the wind is a subtle and rather poorly understood aspect of fluid dynamics, but at times the combination of weather and water can devastate shipping and homes built on clifftops or other coastal sites.

The most destructive oceanic events are the enormous waves called tsunamis, which are triggered off by underwater earthquakes. These giant waves may have wavelengths of up to 90 miles (150km), and they can travel at the amazing speed of 500 miles per hour (800 km/h)! A tsunami is particularly menacing because its amplitude may be as little as 3ft (1m) and so remain undetected in open water.

In the shallow regions, however, tsunamis can rapidly build up to over 100ft (30m), breaking with tremendous force over the shore zone. In the Pacific the earthquakes generated by subduction-zones make tsunamis a frequent event. The Hawaiian Islands receive severe waves on average once every 25 years.

The rhythm of the tides

Superimposed on the wind-generated waves are the tides. These rhythmical rises and falls in the sea surface vary in height for a number of reasons, and are accompanied by horizontal currents. They occur roughly every 12½ hours, and are a result of the gravitational attraction of the Moon and, at times, the Sun. The centrifugal force produced by the Earth's rotation on its axis causes an equatorial 'bulge' in the mobile water of the oceans. In oceans which face the Moon this bulge is pronounced as water is drawn away from the polar regions. If the Sun and Moon are in a straight line then the tidal bulge will develop more to give a high 'spring tide'. When these two bodies are opposed at right angles to each other a low 'neap' tide results. In the open sea the bulge of tidal water may only be 3ft (1m) high, but when the tide approaches the shore and is confined in a bay or river estuary then the water can reach many

Spring tide

Full Moon — Earth — New Moon — Sun

Neap tide

Earth — Sun

Half Moon

—— Solar tide
—— Lunar tide

Above A spring tide (top) occurs when the Moon and Sun are in a straight line and their gravitational pulls are in the same direction. Tides are strong with a great range. Neap tides (weak, with a small range) occur when Sun and Moon are at 90°.

tens of feet high. Such daily tides are well known in the Bay of Fundy and the Severn Estuary in England. In the Bay of Fundy, off Nova Scotia, the tidal bore can be 50ft (15m) high. When combined with certain storm conditions the tidal surges may be increased with devastating results.

We still live in one of the great Ice Ages that have gripped our planet over the past 1,000 million years, albeit in a warmer glacial period. To gain new understanding of the world of ice and the pattern of future ice cycles, scientists are studying the relentless march of glaciers, changing sea-levels and ice-borne sediments. They are analysing cores drilled from deep within ice sheets.

Ice cores, which may be many thousands of years old, reveal past climatic trends. Icebergs, too, are being studied, since they can be a hazard to shipping. Icebergs may be used in the future as a source of fresh water for drought-stricken areas. In the Arctic, major shipping lanes have to be kept open by icebreakers. *Left* Two Soviet icebreakers cut a route through pack ice in the Baltic.

THE WORLD OF ICE

From monitoring the slow but steady advance and retreat of glaciers to drilling deep into the Antarctic ice sheet for samples, scientists seek to understand how ice ages come and go

Ice exists in many forms. It occurs on planets and their moons, and in comets; it is present in the Earth's atmosphere as tiny crystals in high-altitude clouds or as hailstones, which may reach the size of a chicken's egg. Frosts produce a brilliant glistening of fragile ice feathers, while snowfalls slowly accumulate to form huge glaciers. At temperatures below 28.4°F (−2°C) the sea starts to freeze, and in high latitudes frozen ground never thaws. In this chapter the world of snow and ice is considered in the context of glaciers and their effects.

How snowflakes form

In the atmosphere, supercooled water droplets (liquid water at temperatures below 32°F/0°C) gather around dust particles and freeze, forming the basis of a snowflake. Under its

Below The building blocks of glacier ice are snow flakes, with their crystalline perfection and myriad different shapes. These delicate plates of ice are compacted and enlarged to form dense ice.

own weight the new flake falls earthwards, freezing onto more supercooled water on its outside edges. Snowflakes frequently collide during their descent, either coalescing to form larger flakes or breaking into irregularly shaped or even rounded snow grains. The physical conditions under which snow forms vary greatly, and this accounts for the large number of different snow types, from large wet flat flakes to small compact dry snow pellets.

Ice formation

Newly fallen dry snow is extremely light, with a density of about 0.005 Megagrams (million grams) per cubic metre (water has a density of 1 Mg per cu m). The snow crystals are loosely packed at first, but as they are compressed by overlying snow, the crystals change shape by rearrangement of the position of their constituent water molecules, either within the snow crystal or around its edges, so reducing its surface area. This is why fresh snowflakes, with their myriad shapes, gradually become rounded ice grains. At first these settle, slowly increasing the overall density of the snow to about 0.55 Mg per cu m, when the now coarse-grained snow is referred to as firn. Under continuing compression further densification occurs by a process called sintering. Water molecules are transferred by sublimation (the sequence of change from solid to vapour to solid without passing through the liquid phase) to the areas of contact between the grains. This has the effect of reducing the air gaps and increasing the density. Firn becomes glacier ice at a density of 0.83 Mg per cu m, at which point the air spaces between grains close off to form bubbles, and the ice becomes impermeable to water. The only way for ice to densify further is for the bubbles to become compressed, and under great pressures, typically associated with depths greater than 2,600ft (800m) in an ice-sheet, the gas in the bubbles is absorbed into the ice lattice and the bubbles disappear. Now the ice is at its maximum density of

0.92 Mg per cu m. The entire transformation from fresh dry snow to glacier ice can take tens of years, but when melt-water is present maximum ice density can be achieved very much more quickly, even in as short a time as one summer. In such a case the refreezing of melt-water is the prime method of densification.

Ice lattices

A water molecule can be considered to form an isosceles triangle, with hydrogen nuclei (protons) at two corners and the oxygen nucleus at the apex. In the ice lattice, the oxygen atoms form layers of hexagonal rings which are linked to neighbouring layers by weak hydrogen bonds. The plane of these layers is called the basal plane. This structure is fundamental in understanding the behaviour of ice in glaciers. In essence, an ice crystal is like a deck of playing cards. It is easy to shear ice along the basal plane — layers can easily slide over each other, but it is much harder to shear ice across the basal plane (try tearing a pack of cards in two!). Under an applied force, an ice crystal rearranges its lattice by recrystallizing, until the basal plane is aligned with the force, when the ice then deforms easily.

When a foreign (non-water) molecule enters the lattice, it changes the physical properties of the ice crystal. Much research is being done to establish the effects of different contaminants. For example, Scandinavia is being affected detrimentally by acid rain and snow which, if incorporated into glaciers, could affect the ice flow. Similarly the electrical properties of ice differ greatly between glaciers in Europe and those in Greenland and Antarctica, the latter being between 100 and 1,000 times more conductive than the former. Impurities from volcanic eruptions amongst other sources become incorporated in snow and are preserved in the polar ice sheets. Because such impurities affect the electrical properties of ice, these contaminated horizons can be detected electrically. Such methods, still under development, offer exciting possibilities of analysing ice cores to obtain more information on the climatic conditions under which the original snow fell.

How glaciers form

A glacier normally forms when more snow falls than melts over a period of years, building up a body of snow which changes to glacier ice. This flows downslope under its own weight. The upper part of a glacier is called the accumulation zone for it is here that the glacier accumulates snow. The lower part is called the ablation zone as here all the year's snowfall is lost through melting, draining away (run-off) and evaporation, exposing the underlying glacier ice. The boundary between the two zones is called the equilibrium line. It is a misconception to believe that for a glacier to form, a large amount of snow must accumulate. Indeed, the largest ice sheet in the world is virtually the largest desert, for the Antarctic Ice Sheet has a net snow accumulation of less than 1½ft (0.5m) per year over 80 per cent of its area. In some areas the converse is true — very large annual snowfalls melt completely because of very warm summers and hence no glaciers can be sustained — for example, in present-day Scotland or New York.

Glaciers and climate

The relationship between glaciers and climate is extremely complex. Once formed, a glacier

 Chief present-day
areas of glacier ice

Chief areas of glacier ice
during Quaternary

 Present-day maximum
limit of pack ice

▲ Small areas with
Quaternary glaciers

Below These two maps
show the present and
former extent of the
polar ice caps.

Above The Rhône
Glacier, Switzerland,
is a typical valley
glacier with crevasses.

develops its own climate, and this is especially
true with the polar ice sheets. Today glaciers
exist in the high latitudes of Greenland, the
Canadian Archipelago, Alaska, Spitsbergen,
Scandinavia and Iceland, which all experience
very cold winters and short cool summers.
Glaciers also exist at high altitudes, for example,
on Mount Kilimanjaro in Kenya and in many
high mountain chains, such as the Alps, the
Andes, the Rockies and the Himalayas. Contemporary research is seeking to determine the
inter-relationships between glaciers and climate
by developing computer programs to model
global and local climates. Attempts are being
made to determine how climates vary and how
our present climate may change in the future.
Information, from field glaciologists patiently
measuring glaciers, from meterologists monitoring weather stations worldwide, and from
satellites orbiting high overhead, is being co-
ordinated in a concerted effort to understand
the world's climate.

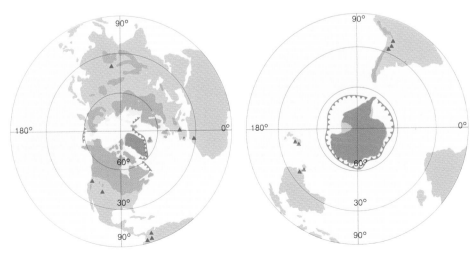

Glaciers come in many different shapes and sizes; surprisingly, and, perhaps, most importantly, their temperatures vary, too. However, they can all be divided according to two main schemes of classification. The first is based on the shape, and to some extent the size, of the ice mass. An ice-sheet, which is the largest of all ice masses, covers a significant proportion of a whole continent, such as that in Antarctica. On a smaller, more local scale, is an ice-cap, such as the one in Greenland, Vatnajökull in Iceland, or Barnes Ice Cap on Baffin Island, Canada. Both ice-sheets and ice-caps are generally domed in cross section. At the crest the rate of ice flow is negligible, but it increases with the distance from the centre to many tens of yards per year at the edges. Near the coast, some ice is funnelled into ice-streams, which can be several hundred miles long, several tens of miles wide and up to 1¼ miles (2km) thick, and which can move at speeds of about half a mile (1km) per year.

Self-contained glaciers confined by the steep flanks of a mountain are called valley glaciers. Typically they are only a few miles long, several hundred yards wide and less than 330ft (100m) thick, and the speed of movement of the surface is commonly only a few tens of yards per year. Similarly slow-moving are cirque glaciers, saucer-shaped icefields measured only in hundreds of yards rather than miles. On reaching flat, comparatively level ground, a glacier may spread out into a lobe, when it is then referred to as a piedmont glacier.

Ice shelves

If a glacier reaches the sea, floats away and spreads out, coalescing with neighbouring floating glaciers, an ice shelf is formed. Currently, the largest ice shelves are found in the Antarctic, and have areas measured in thousands of square miles. Notable examples are the Ross Ice Shelf, the largest, at over 200,000 square miles (535,000sq km) in area, and the Ronne-Filchner and Amery ice shelves. Ice thicknesses vary enormously, from 6,000ft (2,000m) to a more typical 650-1,000ft (2-300m). Ice velocities are of the order of several hundred yards per year.

Avalanche hazards

Remnant glaciers are literally the last fragments of formerly more extensive ice masses. They are found perched high up on the steep flanks of mountains and their snouts are normally steep overhanging ice cliffs from which ice avalanches frequently occur in summer.

Temperature differences

The second glacier classification is based on ice temperature. A temperate glacier is at its pressure melting point throughout, normally 32°F (0°C), and water can occur anywhere within, on and beneath the glacier. Temperate glaciers occur mostly in mid-low latitudes such as throughout Europe, Scandinavia and Africa — essentially areas where the winters are cold but the summers are warm. In complete contrast, polar glaciers are well below the pressure melting point and are not affected by melt-water at all. Ice temperatures within the glacier are normally well below zero. Polar glaciers are found in high latitudes and occur where both winter and summer temperatures remain sub-zero. Sub-polar glaciers are below the pressure melting point except at the surface during summer, when melt-water can form. Such glaciers exist in high latitudes and in high-

Above Here, Le Conte Glacier in SE Alaska has broken up and been weathered by the elements into pinnacles.

Above right Below Mount Robson, in Alberta, Canada, the snout of the Berg Glacier breaks up as it enters Berg Lake.

altitude mountain chains where winters are very cold but summer temperatures can exceed zero. This thermal classification is an oversimplification, because few glaciers fit neatly into one category, but as a broad scheme it can be useful in understanding glaciers.

How glaciers move

A temperate valley or cirque glacier which receives as much snow as it loses per year remains in a steady state. As snow piles up in the accumulation area, the net movement of an ice crystal is *into* the glacier as well as downhill. As ice melts off from the ablation zone at the

front of the glacier, exposing the preceding years' ice, the net movement is still downhill but *out* of the glacier. This submergence and emergence accounts in part for the 'time-lag' of a glacier with respect to changes in climate. If during a particular year much more snow remains than is usual, extra weight, and hence driving force, is added to the glacier system, but it may take many years for such an input to be reflected (if at all) by the position of the snout — between ten and a hundred years for a temperate valley glacier, and up to several thousand years for the Greenland ice cap or the Antarctic Ice Sheet.

Ice can be thought of as a plastic material which, under an applied stress, will flow or creep by movement of layers within the ice lattice and by whole ice grains gliding over each other. Creep is the only means by which a

Above The current ice age, which extended much further south some 8,000 years ago, is still in evidence in the mountains of Europe. Here, in Austria, jagged mountain peaks, crevassed glacier ice and dark heaps of moraine are evidence of active glaciation.

Right The Aletschgletscher in the Swiss Alps is a gracefully curving valley glacier that has formed a U-shaped valley with steep sides rising above the ice surface. Debris falling onto the ice lies dark on the ice as lateral and medial moraines.

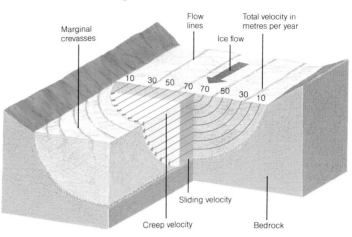

Right In an idealized temperate climate glacier, ice velocities vary both with depth and across the glacier. The slowest-moving ice is at the base and sides, where the ice slides over the bedrock, producing friction which slows down its movement. Within the body of the glacier, the ice 'creeps' by deformation, with the greatest speeds at the surface in the middle of the glacier. The total velocity of the glacier is the sum of the sliding and deformation speeds, as shown by the contours.

glacier frozen to its bed can move. The rate at which ice deforms (its 'strain rate') is related to temperature, increasing as temperature approaches the melting point. Ice fractures if it is stretched too far or too quickly, so forming crevasses. A glacier whose basal ice is at its pressure melting point moves by sliding over its bed, as well as by ice creep. So the ice velocity measured at the glacier surface is the sum of the sliding and creep velocities. The deformation of a glacier and its rate of sliding are governed by frictional forces associated with the valley floor and sides. Velocities increase from the sides and base of a glacier to maximum values at or near the surface of the ice.

Measuring ice-flow

Total glacier ice velocities are traditionally measured by monitoring the movement of a network of stakes implanted into the ice surface. This, however, gives no information about *internal* velocities. These can be measured, using instruments called inclinometers fitted into holes drilled into the ice. As the glacier flows downhill, the once vertical borehole tilts down the glacier, and so the rate of such movement can be determined. Direct measurement of basal sliding velocities can be obtained by setting up instruments in the sole of a glacier, where access permits (although this can be a hazardous task!) Where a borehole does reach bedrock, a remote down-hole camera can be used to monitor movement past bedrock features.

But how does a glacier actually slide over its rough bed? There are thought to be two basic mechanisms. First, ice moves past bumps in the bedrock by melting on the upstream side of the obstacle (because of increased pressure) and then refreezing on the lee side by the process known as regelation (because of reduced pressure), and also by plastic flow. Second, water at the base of a glacier, in addition to that produced by regelation, appears to act as a lubricant and so affects the rate of sliding. The more water there is, as in summer, the faster the sliding. If the ice at the base of a glacier is heavily charged with gravel and rock debris, friction is increased and the sliding velocity is reduced. The varied processes which occur at the base of a glacier are reflected by the diversity of erosional and depositional landforms exposed after the ice has melted. Modern-day researchers, by applying aspects of physics, mathematics, geology and glaciology, are trying to understand these processes which have shaped and still continue to shape much of the world's land surface.

Glaciers have shaped much of the Earth's surface through geological time. They are impressive phenomena, capable of grinding rock to powder, of plucking boulders from the sides of mountains and of transporting millions of tons of debris over great distances, like a giant conveyor belt. The sole of a glacier can act like a powerful sanding block, scratching and polishing the underlying bedrock. Along its path a glacier leaves a trail of tell-tale sculpted shapes, gouge marks and extensive deposits. But not all glaciers are active erosive agents all of the time. Careful studies of the traces of former ice masses have revealed that an individual glacier can have particular phases of erosion and deposition.

The erosive processes of a wholly temperate glacier can be very different from those of a glacier frozen to its bed. Once they know which features are associated with which glacier type, geologists can 'work backwards' on ancient glacial remains to identify whether the glacier was temperate or otherwise. In this way, they can build up a picture of the prevalent climate and environment over many millions of years of geological time.

Agents of glacial erosion

What are the principle types of erosion associated with glaciers? There are two main agents of erosion, sapping and corrasion. Sapping is the process whereby water freezes in cracks in the head and sidewalls of the valley containing the glacier and fragments the rocks, which become incorporated into the glacier's base. Sapping causes the headwall to retreat horizontally. Corrasion is a result of the physical movement of the glacier, and includes abrasion and plucking.

Abrasion occurs when boulders caught up in the sliding basal ice grind against the bedrock, inexorably gouging striations into it or, if the substrate is harder than the boulder, crushing the latter into fragments. The amount of abrasion is directly related to the size of the rock debris contained in the glacier sole: the larger the boulder, the more efficient it is at abrasion. The size of the incorporated rock material ranges from huge blocks as large as a two-storey house down to minute clay particles and rock powder ('rock-flour'), which discolours glacial melt-water streams, turning them a distinctive milky-blue-white colour. The speed of sliding has little short-term effect on the rate

Above This glaciated valley in Switzerland shows many typical features of ice erosion, such as overdeepening and a U-shaped profile.

Below A former glacier eroded the head and side walls of this corrie in N Wales by freeze-thaw action. The corrie floor is filled by a tarn.

of abrasion but it is significant in the long term, as it dictates the number of boulders passing a given point in a unit time.

Plucking occurs when jointed or weathered rock becomes frozen to basal ice and is pulled out of place by the moving glacier. Although they have not been able to observe this process directly, glaciologists have inferred that it happens by examining projecting mounds in the bedrock. These mounds of rock are streamlined on the up-glacier side but jagged on the lee side, where blocks have been plucked out by the passing ice. Such bedrock mounds are called roches

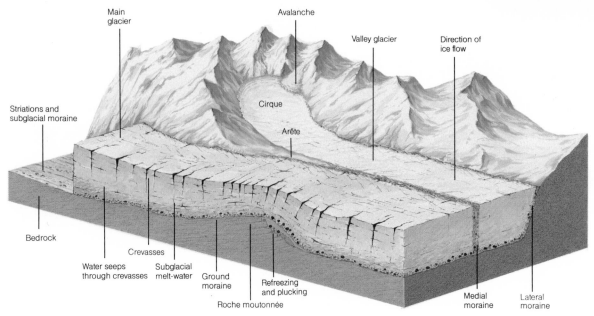

Main glacier

Avalanche

Valley glacier

Direction of ice flow

Striations and subglacial moraine

Cirque

Arête

Bedrock

Crevasses

Water seeps through crevasses

Subglacial melt-water

Ground moraine

Refreezing and plucking

Roche moutonnée

Medial moraine

Lateral moraine

Left Glacial movement and erosion are shown in this diagram. Armed with rock fragments, the ice scrapes grooves in the underlying rock. Large rock obstructions are smoothed as the ice flows over them and the down-stream face is 'plucked' to form a roche moutonnée. Crevasses in the glacier ice allow rock debris to reach the bed of the glacier. When two glaciers merge, their lateral moraines join and become a medial moraine.
Right Milford Sound in South Island, New Zealand, is a glaciated valley now flooded by a rise in sea-level to become a fiord. The steep valley sides tower above the valley floor which, in characteristic glaciated fashion, is relatively flat.

greatest. This results in a powerful sliding of the temperate basal ice, heavily charged with coarse rock material. This is why erosion tends to be more marked at the glacier head than at its terminus, and a saucer-shaped depression called a cirque in the mountain flank is formed and subsequently deepened; the resident glacier is therefore called a cirque glacier. The continuing processes of sapping cause the headwall to retreat and if two cirques lie back to back or even side to side, eventually all that remains of the intervening mountain is a sharp-crested ridge called an arête. A well-known example is Striding Edge on Helvellyn in the English Lake District. If several cirques surround an individual peak, a pyramidal summit results, such as the Matterhorn in the Swiss Alps. Estimates of the rate of erosion associated with cirque glaciers range from 2in (5cm) per 1,000 years in polar regions to about 16in (40cm) per 1,000 years for an area such as western Scotland. After a cirque glacier has disappeared, a small lake, or tarn, forms in the base of the depression. This is dammed by a rock bar or threshold at the cirque's lower edge.

Glacial fiords

A prominent threshold is also a characteristic of a glacially-formed fiord and marks the seaward boundary between the over-deepened fiord basin and the continental shelf. The deepest fiords in the world are those in Antarctica, where depths of over 1¼ miles (2km) below sea-level have been recorded. Fiords are also characteristically flanked by very steep mountainsides, and are found in such situations in Norway, Greenland, Chile and New Zealand, for example. During the last ice age, the Scandinavian ice-sheet existed in one form or another for about a million years. Sognefjord in Norway was glacially deepened by at least 3,600ft (1,100m) during this time, representing an erosion rate of about 3¼ft (1m) every 1,000 years. Similar rates have been deduced for other ice masses, for example, 5¼-10¼ft (1·6-3·1m) per 1,000 years for that known as Hoffelsjökull in Iceland.

It is possible that the ice streams currently draining the Greenland and Antarctic ice sheets are equally erosive. Where small tributary glaciers once fed a massive ice stream responsible for the formation of a fiord, minor U-shaped valleys, called hanging valleys, remain perched high on the sidewalls. From these, waterfalls cascade to the valley floor below, creating alluvial fans at the base. These together with rockfalls and landslides from the sidewalls, gradually infill the base of the main valley. Small rivers and streams then cut channels through this material, gradually turning the U-shaped valley into a V-shaped one. These streams and rivers are far too small to have eroded the whole valley by themselves so they are called 'misfits'.

Glaciated terrain of this type occurs in Wales, the Lake District and Scotland, for instance, having been created during the last ice age. It is characteristic of glaciation by alpine valley glaciers, which are found today in, for example, Austria and Switzerland. Apart from the major ice-streams, ice-sheets are evidently more responsible for the general removal of loose material, exposing and abrading the underlying bedrock. This happened over a vast area of North America during the last ice age, when the Canadian Shield was scoured by the Laurentide Ice Sheet.

Left Rock fragments in the base of the glacier make grooves in the bedrock, as here in South Georgia.

Above This classical U-shaped ice-cut valley was flooded by the sea to make a fiord in Norway.

moutonnées. Glaciologists think that, in some instances at least, plucking occurs more actively during the onset of glaciation, and abrasion assumes a dominant role at a later stage. Rock material also becomes incorporated onto and into glaciers by avalanches, land-slips and rock-falls. Some of this material is trapped within the glacier, either by being washed by melt-water or by falling into crevasses, and

may reach the glacier base, adding to the erosive power of the glacier. Corrasion acts primarily to lower the land surface. The efficiency of a particular glacier in erosion is in part controlled not by the glacier, but by the extent to which the bedrock on which the ice is situated has been weathered and fractured before glaciation.

Cirques

At the head of a glacier, where sapping is most pronounced, the ice is normally at its thickest and the submergence velocity at the base is

A glacier constantly deposits rock material at its margins and at its base. Just what type of deposits are formed, and how and where, are the subject of much modern-day research. The reasons for this are twofold. Glaciers and their associated products (rock material and melt-water) can be viewed either as natural hazards or as resources to be commercially exploited.

As a hazard, for example, a moraine may gradually dam a melt-water river, forming a lake. If this is not carefully monitored and controlled, it may breach through the moraine, unleashing a catastrophic torrent of flood water, which may cause widespread death and destruction. In 1962, for instance, at Huascaràn, Peru, an ice and rock avalanche cascaded into a glacial lake, breached a moraine bar and formed a devastating mixture of mud, rock, ice and water which destroyed six villages, damaged three more and killed about 4,000 people and thousands of livestock. A similar catastrophe occurred in the same place in 1970 after an earthquake and resulted in the deaths of between 15,000 and 20,000 people. Thankfully, such incidents on so large a scale are uncommon, but numerous smaller disasters have occurred in Europe and Scandinavia.

Making use of glaciers

As a resource, glacial sediments provide a good supply of gravels and sand, and melt-water contributes to hydro-electricity generation. In the latter case, careful monitoring of the glaciers in the catchment area is essential, as too large an output of glacial rock material may clog up the reservoir, reducing the useful life of the plant. Alternatively, the glaciers themselves may advance into the reservoir and threaten the survival of the dam itself, a situation which could occur at Mattmarksee in Switzerland, where many workmen engaged in building the Mattmark dam were killed in 1965 by a one-million-ton avalanche of ice from the Allalin glacier.

Engineers are paying increasing attention to the technical properties of glacial sediments, in order to improve the design and construction of foundations for dams, roads, bridges, and so on in areas covered by extensive glacial material or affected by present-day glaciers.

Three distinct glacial landforms

For geologists to gain a better understanding of glacial deposits, they need to determine the processes by which they are formed. As a result of such work in recent years, the landforms and surface sedimentological processes associated with modern-day glaciers have been classified as three distinct landsystems. Each of these has its own characteristic topography, sediments and subsurface conditions.

In essence there are two 'subglacial' land-systems which are associated with geographically distinct areas. These are the 'shield' areas, which are related to continental scale ice sheets (such as the Canadian and Scandinavian shields), and the non-'shield' lowlands. Shields are moderately hilly, with individual areas of rock at heights of up to 1,000ft (300m), and are underlain by hard igneous and metamorphic rocks, typically Pre-Cambrian in age. The bed-rock is scoured over its whole area, rather than linearly eroded, and the resultant topography has a knobbly, or 'mamillated', form. Thick glacial sediments do not occur because the ice sheet is not very effective at depositing them,

especially at its margins, and because of the action of the melt-water streams and relatively fast-flowing ice around knobs of bedrock. This land-system can be distinguished from the supraglacial by examining the underlying soil types. Non-shield areas are characterized by a lower relief in conjunction with soft, deformable sedimentary bedrock which, combined with the effects of repeated glaciations, produces a thick complex soil sequence.

Glacial till

Of the sediments associated with subglacial environments the deposition of 'till' is the most important. Till makes up a significant proportion of the glacial materials which cover some 75 per cent of the mid-latitudes. 'Till' is a generic term describing aggregates whose constituents have been brought together by the direct action of glacier ice. There are six types of till, of which three are associated with subglacial deposition. Massive poorly sorted debris melting out of a glacier base is deposited over extensive areas as 'lodgement till', particularly in non-shield regions. 'Melt-out till' is crudely stratified and is formed by the alternate melting-out of layers of debris-rich and debris-poor basal ice. 'Deformation till' consists of sheared masses of fragmented bedrock (usually sedimentary) and is often found in intimate association with lodgement and melt-out tills.

Drumlins

Of all the glacial landforms, drumlins have attracted the greatest amount of research. A drumlin is shaped like half a boiled egg which

has been cut lengthways; the broad steep end is nearest the glacier and the narrower gently-sloping end faces away. The long axis of the drumlin is oriented parallel to the ice flow. In size, drumlins vary enormously, from 10-230ft (3-70m) in height, 330ft (100m) to several miles in length and 10-1,600ft (3-500m) wide. They can occur in 'clusters', 'fields' or 'swarms', which in some cases comprise several thousand individual drumlins, as in central-western New York State (up to 10,000) and in western Nova Scotia (around 2,400). More commonly, drumlins occur in small groups of 10 or less. For an as yet unknown reason, there appears to be a constant relationship between the size and shape of drumlins and their separation in any particular cluster. There are many hypotheses as to their formation, one of which suggests that drumlins are formed by the build-up of basal rock debris around a rock or boulder obstacle. Another suggests that lodgement till deforms beneath moving ice and is moulded into drumlins. For example, a drumlinized lodgement till plain has become exposed by the retreat of Breida-merkurjökull in Iceland.

Eskers and kames

Eskers are another type of major subglacial deposits, consisting of a gravel core in a sand ridge which can be many tens of yards high and several miles long. These well-defined sinuous features are principally formed by deposition in melt-water tunnels under the ice. They commonly fork, and may end in an alluvial fan. This is taken to mark the furthest extent of the mouth of the under-the-ice tunnel,

Left Hamburg Glacier in South Georgia once filled its valley. Now, after many years of retreat, it has shrunk so much that it has split in two. Rock debris from the base of the upper portion falls onto the surface of the lower part, covering it in a veneer of moraine. A white avalanche cone of a recent icefall can be seen on the debris-covered lower glacier. The lake is fed by melt-water, but is dammed by a terminal moraine. Sediments borne by the melt-water are deposited on the lake floor in layers of sand (summer deposit) and mud (winter).

Top right Unsorted till is being dumped from beneath the snout of the Rettenbachferner Glacier in the Austrian Alps. The till consists of large boulders, pebbles and fine sand and clay.

Right Long, sinuous ridges of sand and gravel, called eskers, were laid down in streams which flowed under glacier ice. When the ice melted, the ridges were exposed, like this one in Scotland.

Below Drumlins are small rounded hillocks made of till, often round a solid rock core. They usually occur in 'swarms' of many hundreds. Their long axes point in the direction of ice flow. The size of this drumlin, Northumberland, UK, is apparent from the person standing on top.

as it is there that the subglacial melt-water stream with its sediment load is released from the constraints of the tunnel sides.

The supraglacial land system consists of sediments which were deposited from the surface of the ice during its retreat, often obscuring the products of subglacial deposition. The margins of continental ice-sheets and ice-caps thin to a wedge where the ice is decelerating. Here, it is slow-moving, and thus under compression. This causes basal debris to become exposed at the ice surface, forming a dirty margin. As the ice retreats, this supraglacial material runs off as 'flowed till' which, through sorting during flow, may produce crudely stratified deposits. Alternatively, as the underlying ice melts, the sediment is lowered onto pre-existing sediments as 'melt-out till'. In addition, a 'kame' may form where supraglacial material has been dumped against a steep ice-front to form isolated hummocks. Where melt-water streams fill a trench between a glacier and an adjacent moraine ridge, flat but thick sequences of sands and gravels are deposited against the ice edge. When the ice has retreated, the stranded gravels form kame terraces.

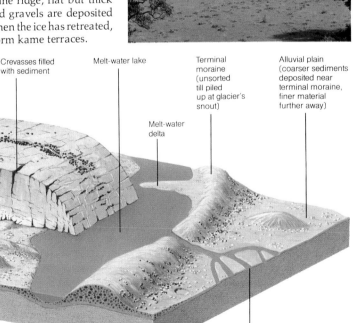

Right Depositional land-forms associated with ice and glaciers are shown here. The terminal moraine in front of the glacier's snout marks the extent of ice movement. Beyond it, an outwash plain develops, with a veneer of water-borne sediment and braided-stream systems. A melt-water lake, typically milky-looking from the fine suspended sediment, is dammed between glacier and moraine. Stratified sediments are formed in the lake, in contrast to the unstratified till of the moraine. Some sediment falls through crevasses which penetrate the glacier ice and becomes incorporated into sub-glacial landforms. Drumlins, kames and eskers are typical examples of these subglacial landforms.

Esker (gravel ridge deposited by sub-glacial stream)

Medial moraine

Crevasses filled with sediment

Melt-water lake

Terminal moraine (unsorted till piled up at glacier's snout)

Alluvial plain (coarser sediments deposited near terminal moraine, finer material further away)

Drumlin (till deposited and shaped beneath moving ice)

Melt-water delta

Bedrock

Drumlin (exposed)

Glacier melts from the bottom

Kame

Braided stream

117

The third glacial land-system is that formed in high-relief mountainous areas where glaciers are commonly discrete units in their own valleys, such as those found today in Scandinavia and other parts of Europe. Supra-glacial debris is produced from rockfalls onto the ice from adjacent steep mountain flanks. Surface debris is commonly confined to the glacier margins, but many glaciers are almost entirely covered, such as those in the Karakorum Mountains in Pakistan. Debris on the surface of a mobile glacier can be transported for many tens of miles before being dumped at the end of the glacier, but it may slide or be washed off the sides along the way. The debris is characterized by a high proportion of large boulders. If these are deposited on geologically dissimilar rocks (for example, a granite boulder situated on purely sedimentary rocks), the boulder is called an 'erratic'. These can be useful to geologists in indicating the direction of flow of an ancient glacier, because some erratics can be traced back to the rock outcrop from which they were plucked by the ice.

Moraines

A glacier may deposit material in sharp-crested ridges along its sides as 'lateral moraines', and at its terminus as a variety of moraine types, depending on the method of formation. Some thin retreating valley glaciers form a low moraine ridge, 3-10ft (1-3m) high, each winter, when the speed of the moving ice is at its greatest due to the extra weight of winter snowfall. These 'annual' moraines can give indirect evidence of the climate, with the separation between successive ridges being related to the mean annual temperature. If the moraines are close together, this suggests a cool intervening summer; if they are far apart, then the summer was hot. A 'push moraine' results from a glacier bulldozing sediments at its terminus, with the moraine ridge being formed during an episodic advance. Push moraines are often stacked on top of each other as the glacier has retreated and advanced repeatedly over the same ground. Where two adjacent glaciers coalesce, their common lateral moraines merge to form a 'medial moraine'. Retreating piedmont glaciers leave an arc-shaped pattern of terminal moraines, and the intervening troughs may become flooded,

Above The Norber Boulders, UK, are glacial erratics from the Silurian Period which have been carried by a glacier and dumped onto a rock 'pavement' of Carboniferous limestone.

Right Winds blowing out from glaciated areas carry much very fine-grained dust, called loess, many miles from the ege of the ice sheet to where it is deposited, as here in China.

forming crescent-shaped ribbon lakes. The nearly flat expanse of apparently barren glacial sediments immediately downslope of a glacier is called an 'outwash plain', or alternatively a 'sandur' (plural: sandar), from the Icelandic word for this feature, as it is particularly characteristic of many glaciers in Iceland. A sandur consists of deposits laid down by braided rivers. Recently the economic potential of sandar has been realized. Metal-rich minerals may occur within them as placer deposits, which can be developed commercially. When stranded blocks of glacier ice have been buried within a sandur and have subsequently melted, round depressions, often water-filled, result. These are called 'kettle holes'.

Varved clays

In freshwater lakes associated with temperate glaciers, finely layered sediments called 'varved

clays' are formed. Each 'varve' represents one year of deposition and comprises a couplet of silt (from increased activity of melt-water streams during summer) and of clay (gradually deposited during the quieter conditions of winter). Coarse silt (the summer deposit) forms the base of the annual varve, passing transitionally into fine silty clay (the winter deposit) at the top. This arrangement allows geologists to count them like tree rings, providing them with a method of dating glacial activity.

Periglacial landforms

As well as glacially-derived landforms, there are many relict landscapes and materials which have developed as a result of 'periglacial' processes. ('Relict' landscapes are those formed by processes which no longer occur, as in areas from which glaciers have long ago disappeared.) Periglacial processes are non-glacial processes

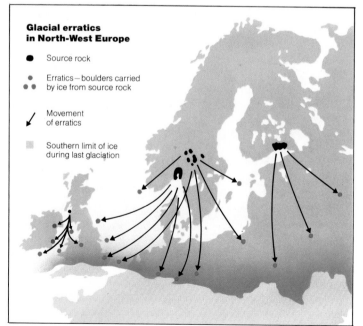

Glacial erratics in North-West Europe

● Source rock

• Erratics—boulders carried by ice from source rock
••

↙ Movement of erratics

▨ Southern limit of ice during last glaciation

Left Certain glacial erratics can be traced to the rock formation from which the ice eroded them. By tracing erratics back to their sources, the direction of ice movement can be deduced. This map shows some erratics, their origins, present positions and the movement of the ice. In the west of Britain igneous rock from Ailsa Craig (an island off SW Scotland) is found on the bed of the Irish Sea and in Ireland, Wales and England. Igneous rocks from Scandinavia occur on the east coast of England and in northern Europe, indicating ice movement from the north.

Right Here, a glacially transported boulder is perched on a slim column of ice at the mouth of a crevasse.

and features which result from intense frost action associated with cold climates. Confusingly, the term 'periglacial' does not imply nearness (at any stage) to a glacier. For example, vast tracts of northern Russia exhibit periglacial landforms remote from any significant glacier. Many fossil periglacial features can be found throughout the UK and Eire. The most common of these features is a pattern of stone circles, where frost action has sorted material into a network of polygons. The raised rims of the polygons are made up of larger stones, with smaller stones and gravel in the centre as, for example, on Dartmoor in south-west England. In East Anglia, England, there are particularly well preserved fossil ice-wedges in sands and silts. In southern Eire and Wales geologists have found evidence for the former presence of massive amounts of ice in the form of 'pingos' (named from an Eskimo word for these features). These are pronounced conical mounds cored by buried (non-glacial) ice and can be up to 130ft (40m) high and 1,970ft (600m) in diameter. They exist today in arctic Canada and Russia.

Relict pingos have also been identified in central London.

Loess

In arid areas where wind scours unvegetated periglacial surfaces and inactive sandar, 'cover sands' and wind-blown silt, or loess, form a veneer and constitute the most widespread of periglacial sediments. Loess occurs extensively in dry continental interiors. The most important loess deposits are found in huge belts, such as those covering the Great Plains region of the United States (193,000 square miles or 500,000 sq km), the Ukraine in the USSR and large areas of northwest China (243,000 square miles, or 630,000sq km). In Lanzhou Province, western China, there are loess deposits thicker than 650ft (200m). In Great Britain loess is much less well-developed. It occurs in north Norfolk, where it is 10-30ft (3-10m) thick, in thinner deposits throughout southern England, and in isolated areas in the Midlands and the northern counties. In Kent loess (known locally as 'brickearth') was used in brickmaking. Cover sands are locally important in north-west England in manufacturing glass and ceramics, and generally for use as building aggregates and as an aquifer for local groundwater supplies.

Frozen fossil evidence

The glacial and periglacial environments are continually changing as the climate cools and warms, and glaciers advance and retreat. These variations are reflected in soil development and by the amount and type of local flora and fauna. The well-preserved remains of animals such as marmot, wolverine and arctic fox, which currently inhabit the cold arctic wastes, have been found in areas which now enjoy a warmer climate. In Siberia perfectly preserved bodies have been found of many creatures, from huge woolly mammoths to fish. In excavations on the Kolyma River in Russia, for example, fish were found frozen in an ice lens which was about 10,000 years old or more. Once thawed they were still edible!

The discovery of such fossils is exciting, and so too is the gleaning of information that dates such finds. The fossil flora and fauna themselves can indicate relative ages, but palaeontologists also try to ascribe an absolute date to their find. Today, they can draw on many areas of research to help them do this. Dendrochronology (the study of tree rings), lichenometry (measuring the growth-rate of lichens) and palynology (analysing pollen and spores) are three dating methods which use ancient plant material. Radiocarbon (carbon-14) dating is also very useful here. For example, if an organic soil horizon has been buried under a push moraine, the radiocarbon date obtained for the soil will indicate when the local glacier advanced to form the moraine.

This powerful combination of dating methods can be a valuable tool for establishing chronologies. These form a time framework, in which glaciologists can place the waxing and waning of the great ice sheets and the formation of their associated landsystems. By painstaking attention to detail, the researchers are obtaining a better picture of the world, both in the past as well as today. Such knowledge will hopefully help lead to a wiser use of natural resources and a greater sensitivity to changes which might take place in our environment, and especially to those over which Man has some degree of control.

Silently, a vast blue-green form looms from the shrouding mist, its bulk passive yet menacing, slow yet apparently unstoppable. Such is the description of many an iceberg seen by a ship-borne observer. But what exactly is an iceberg and from where does it come?

An iceberg is defined as a large mass of floating or stranded ice which has broken away from a glacier. Fragments of icebergs less than 16ft (5m) high are called 'bergy bits' and smaller pieces, typically the size of a family saloon car, are known as 'growlers', because of the noise they make when jostling with adjacent chunks of ice in the sea.

Two types of iceberg

There are two principal types of icebergs, depending on their source. Tabular icebergs, in which five-sixths (83 per cent) of the ice is submerged, come from large ice-shelves. In contrast, glacier bergs, in which as much as nine-tenths (90 per cent) of the ice is submerged, calve from glaciers which end in the sea (tidewater glaciers). Small, short-lived icebergs originate from glaciers in southern Alaska, islands in the Arctic Ocean and in the Canadian Archipelago. The major producer of icebergs in the Northern Hemisphere is the Greenland ice-sheet, which produces between 10,000 and 50,000 icebergs annually, with a total volume of about 60 cu miles (245 cu km) of ice. Typical Greenland icebergs are relatively small, with a mass of between 1 and 3 million tons and approximate dimensions of between 1,200ft by 200ft by 150ft (360m by 60m by 45m) to 1,800ft by 300ft by 180ft (550m by 100m by 55m). Several huge tidewater glaciers of west Greenland regularly produce bergs over half a mile (1km) long and almost 1,000ft (300m) thick. The largest Arctic tabular icebergs are known as ice islands, and can have areas of over a hundred square miles and ice thicknesses of over 150ft (50m). For example, during the winter of 1961-62, Ward Hunt Ice Shelf calved off 230 sq miles (600sq km) of ice in five huge islands.

Antarctic ice shelves are the primary source of tabular icebergs in the Southern Hemisphere. Between 145 and 480 cu miles (600-2,000 cu km) of ice are estimated to calve off each year, although up to several times the total annual volume of ice have been contained within a single giant tabular iceberg, the largest of which had an area of 3,200sq miles (8,400sq km). In 1976, Larsen Ice Shelf was struck by a very large iceberg, causing a berg of some 1,200sq miles (3,100sq km) to calve off. Such large bergs occur with a frequency of about one per decade. Off East Antarctica, an average berg is about 2,600ft long by 1,300ft wide, (800m by 400m) with a freeboard (height of the proverbial tip of the iceberg above the sea) of 100-160ft (30-50m). In the Weddell Sea, the bergs are much squatter in shape, 330ft by 160ft (100m by 50m), with a 65ft (20m) freeboard. An initial ice thickness of 650ft (200m) is typical of Antarctic icebergs, which are in general 20 times larger than in the Arctic.

Iceberg shapes

The visible portion of an iceberg can have one of a great variety of shapes, from a smooth table-top to a highly sculptured, towered pyramid or cathedral-like structure. It is a common sight to see a berg with a platform near the water-line. This ice foot or ice ram is formed by wave action undercutting ice cliffs. Such an ice foot unbalances the berg causing it to tilt. For a

Map of Northern Iceberg Movement

USSR
USSR
Severnaya Zemlya
Finland
Franz Josef Land
Sweden
Transpolar Drift Stream
Spitsbergen
Norway
North Pole
T-3
T-3
East Greenland Drift Stream
Beaufort Gyral Stream
Oct 1952
40°
Iceland
T-3
Ellesmere Island
Greenland
USA
Apr 1947
Baffin Bay
50°
North Atlantic Ocean
Baffin Island
Major drift pattern of Arctic ice
Labrador Sea
Minor drift
60°
Drift track of ice island 'T-3'
SS Titanic sunk 1912
70°
Normal limit of icebergs
USA
80°

long iceberg with rams at opposite ends the buoyancy forces of the submerged ice feet, which are trying to regain hydrostatic equilibrium, cause the berg slowly to bend producing a convex top surface. Ultimately the iceberg splits in two, each part having its own ram.

A flat tabular berg is stable irrespective of how rough the sea becomes. In contrast, a squat blocky berg whose total ice thickness is roughly equal to or even greater than its width is inherently unstable. In a prolonged sea storm the berg could easily capsize. If through the natural processes of deterioration (which affect all bergs) an iceberg develops a square vertical cross-section, it can flip over even in a calm. An analogy is that it is easier for a log floating in a pond to roll over than a plank.

Drifting giants

In the Antarctic, there is a net east-to-west drift within 60 miles (100km) of the coast, caused by the prevailing geostrophic winds. Icebergs can remain in this coastal zone for over a decade. On the eastern side of the Antarctic Peninsula, there is a northward drift associated with the western part of the current called the Weddell Gyre. Icebergs move away from land under the influence of winds and currents until they reach the circumpolar current with the prevailing westerly winds. The northerly extent of the drift of Antarctic bergs is the Antarctic Convergence. A few icebergs have been sighted as far north as 30°S.

In the Northern Hemisphere, there are two principal areas of iceberg drift. One is in the Arctic Ocean and the other is around southern Greenland and Labrador. Icebergs which originate from the ice shelves of Ellesmere Island tend to remain in the Beaufort Sea Gyre and take about 10-12 years to complete one circuit, drifting in a zig-zag and averaging just over a mile (2km) a day. One Arctic ice island

Left Three major ocean currents (broad arrows) affect the movement of sea-ice and icebergs around the North Pole and East Greenland. Large ice islands such as 'T-3' take about 10-12 years to circulate within the Beaufort Gyral Stream. Many icebergs from West Greenland travel from Baffin Bay into the busy shipping lanes and oil-fields in the Labrador Sea, and some eventually reach the North Atlantic. One such iceberg sunk the passenger ship SS *Titanic* on 14 April 1912.
Right An Antarctic glacier berg shows signs of extensive deterioration where wave action has cut into old crevasses to form caves and arches. The ice-cliff is about 50ft (15m) high.
Below A wave-cut ice platform on the right and far sides of this blocky Antarctic iceberg causes the berg to tilt (towards the camera). The nearside face is 65ft (20m) high.
Lower right Extra-buoyant ice-rams at opposite ends of this long Antarctic iceberg have caused the berg to bend in the middle, eventually splitting it in two.

known as 'T-3' was first observed west of Ellesmere Island in April 1947 and was monitored during the following five years or so. 'T-3' circulated around the Beaufort Sea and almost reached the North Pole in July 1952, after which time it drifted southwards to return almost full circle to Ellesmere Island.

A danger to shipping

The greatest concentration of Greenland icebergs occurs off western Greenland north of Disko Island and around Cape York. From north Baffin Bay icebergs travel in the Baffin Island Current and then into the Labrador Current and the busy shipping lanes off the Grand Banks of Newfoundland. It was most likely one of these icebergs which struck the ill-fated SS *Titanic* on 14 April 1912 with such devastating consequences. Extremely rarely, some icebergs have reached the Azores and a few have even travelled as far south as Bermuda.

Today it is not just shipping which is at risk in iceberg-infested waters. For just off the Labrador coast are many hydrocarbon production platforms and drilling rigs. If one of these was involved in a collision with even a relatively small iceberg the consequences could be very serious, both financially and environmentally. Similarly, fixed submarine cables and pipelines are vulnerable to being severed by a deep-drafted iceberg whose bottom can plough through the sea floor sediment leaving a prominent furrow in its wake. It is therefore of great importance to know the whereabouts of any icebergs in either the busy shipping lanes or in the neighbourhood of industrial marine fixtures. Evasive action can be taken by moving the target out of the iceberg's path which can be done easily if a ship is involved, but far less so if it is a drilling platform. In extreme cases, especially if the target is immobile, the iceberg itself may be manoeuvred out of harm's way.

Netting and towing of small icebergs is becoming a common practice in the increasingly busy Arctic Ocean shipping lanes. Vital to the whole operation of successfully avoiding iceberg damage is a regular, accurate advance warning system, using a range of modern technology.

Early warning and monitoring

Such detection systems serve to locate icebergs and to monitor their movement as accurately as possible. Radar is used extensively to this end, from ships, prominent land points, aircraft and increasingly from satellites. However, icebergs smaller than 33ft (10m) across become indistinguishable on radar images from 'sea clutter' (the radar returns produced from large waves) and because of instrument resolution. But the technology is improving all the time, making the sea safer for shipping and for the overall protection of valuable industrial marine installations, such as oil rigs.

Still firmly in the grip of an ice age, Antarctica provides a unique laboratory for Earth scientists. Ninety-eight per cent of the continent is covered by a huge ice sheet up to 3 miles (5km) thick. Fluctuations in the volume of ice are an important factor in controlling both world climate and sea-level; glaciologists have calculated that complete melting of the Antarctic ice sheet would raise the mean world sea-level by as much as 180ft (55m). At the same time, the Antarctic ice sheet is itself sensitive to worldwide climatic changes. Is it possible that increasing levels of carbon dioxide gas in the atmosphere resulting from burning coal and oil and other human activities could, through the 'greenhouse effect', cause a temperature increase large enough to destroy a significant portion of the Antarctic ice sheet?

Before Earth scientists can answer this question, they need extremely accurate maps of the surface elevation and thickness of the ice. More than 50 per cent of the Antarctic continent has now been surveyed by airborne radar sounding, and current estimates of the total volume of ice are probably accurate to 10 per cent. However, to detect *changes* in the ice sheet within periods as short as ten years, very much more precise methods must be used, giving accuracies of about 0·01 per cent. Also, a large proportion of the ice sheet must be monitored to give a representative result, for over short time scales it is possible that two neighbouring glacier drainage basins may behave in opposite ways.

Such problems, combined with difficulties in understanding the complex feedback between climate and the behaviour of the glaciers, have ensured that up to now, glaciologists cannot agree about the direction, let alone the magnitude, of changes in the ice sheet that might correspond to a given change in climate.

Satellite altimetry

The recently developed technique of satellite altimetry may prove ultimately to be the most effective way of monitoring changes in the ice sheets. Extremely sensitive altimeters—instruments for measuring height—are carried in various satellites. In 1978, the US satellite Seasat made altimeter measurements to an accuracy of better than 7ft (2m) either way, up to latitude 72°S. Glaciologists hope that by using an instrument specifically designed for sounding over ice, they will be able to measure changes in average elevations as small as 8in (20cm) and thus detect significant changes in the height of the ice-sheet summit areas within the space of a decade.

Evidence from ice cores

The glaciologists could be much more confident in predicting the future behaviour of the ice sheets if they could establish a firm theory to account for the changes that have occurred already. Luckily, preserved within the ice sheet, there is an unrivalled record of past global changes, including vital evidence for both past climates and ice-sheet thickness.

Antarctica is so cold that, except in the coastal regions, the snow hardly melts at all, even in summer, and each year, a new layer of snow is added. As the snow falls, it picks up fine particles, or aerosols, from the atmosphere. These may include clay and other dusts, sea salts, volcanic particles, cosmic dust from outer space and ash particles and other industrial pollutants. Together with entrapped bubbles of atmospheric gases, the aerosols become

Above The ice-patrol ship HMS *Endurance* calls in at Faraday, the British Antarctic Survey's geophysical observatory on the Argentine Islands off the west coast of the Antarctic peninsula.

Right A climber negotiates a crevasse 130ft (40m) deep in Nye Glacier in the Antarctic. Scientists living in this harsh environment work as part of a team that includes mountaineers, doctors and electricians.

incorporated into the ice in an undisturbed sequence, preserved indefinitely without further chemical or biological changes. The ice is squashed by the enormous pressure of the layers of ice above; consequently, when scientists drill deep into the ice down to the bedrock, they may, if they have chosen the spot well, be rewarded with cores of ice containing a sequence of hundreds of thousands of annual layers. In places, cores only 330ft (100m) deep can sample snow as old as that which fell while the Romans were invading Britain.

A whole range of important environmental variables is currently being investigated by examination of ice cores. These include oxygen isotope ratios in the ice, which relate to air temperature at the time the ice was formed; the concentration and composition of continental dusts, which reflect the turbidity of the polar atmosphere and also tell the scientists a lot about the areas from which they came; the concentration of strong acids and sulphates, which help to identify volcanic activity; the concentration of carbon dioxide and methane, the two chief gases involved in the 'greenhouse effect'; and the concentration of sea salts, which gives information on past storms and the extent of sea ice.

Below left A scientist uses a particle counter in a Cambridge clean-air laboratory to count micro-particles from the air found in Antarctic snow samples. Such research helps establish the extent of global air pollution.

Above A glaciologist collects samples of snow inland from the British Halley geophysical observatory, sited on a floating ice-shelf in the Weddell Sea. Samples are returned, frozen, to Cambridge, UK, for study.

Some of these variables change seasonally, and can also be used to date a core by counting annual layers downwards from the surface. Where annual layers are finally lost by thinning and diffusion in deeper parts of the core, these methods must be supplemented either directly, by radiometric dating, using long-lived radio-nucleides of carbon (^{14}C) and beryllium (^{10}Be), or indirectly, using physical models showing how the ice sheet has been deformed.

Three deep cores have been drilled in Antarctica, including the only borehole yet to reach bedrock in thick ice (a depth of 7,099ft/ 2,164m), which was drilled by the US Army at Byrd Station in 1968. These cores have reached back into the last glaciation some 75,000 to 100,000 years ago. Each shows clearly a large shift in the oxygen isotope ratio between 13,000 and 11,000 years ago, providing powerful evidence for the temperature increase (about 13-14°F (7-8°C) in Antarctica) as the Earth recovered from the last ice age. At the same time, the cores show evidence for massive increases—up to a factor of eight—in the load of atmospheric dusts during the height of the last glaciation, and recent data show that carbon dioxide levels in the atmosphere were some 30 per cent lower than they were before the industrial revolution came about.

Studies such as these highlight the potential value of ice-core research, which makes it possible to study the problem of cause and effect in climatic change. For example, while scientists currently believe that the major changes in the chemistry of the atmosphere which accompanied the final stages of the last

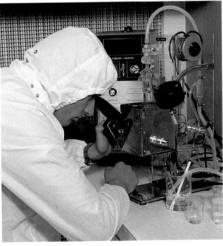

glaciation were probably a direct *result* of ice-age conditions, it also seems likely that their combined *effect* was to reinforce the cooling at the height of the glaciation.

Monitoring pollution

Unlike carbon dioxide and the greenhouse effect, other products of human activity may not be increasing the atmospheric burden enough to influence climate, but they are potentially harmful to man in very small concentrations. When DDT, lead, radioactive fallout and hundreds of other organic and inorganic compounds are released into the atmosphere, they persist for a while before finally returning to the land and to the oceans. Caught up in the general atmospheric circulation, they

may be transported many thousands of miles.

Antarctica is so remote from any industrial centre that it is ideally placed for obtaining evidence for the exact extent of global-scale pollution. By drilling relatively shallow cores, scientists have—in principle—a very simple method for obtaining samples of very old ice. In this way, they can determine the true natural background levels of key pollutants against which the significance of modern trends can be assessed.

Antarctic ice is exceptionally clean, normally as clean as the highest grade of laboratory purified water, so glaciologists have been forced to go to extraordinary lengths to avoid spurious data due to contamination. The heavy metals, including lead, have attracted most attention, but only as recently as 1983 have reliable data been obtained. These suggest that lead concentrations may have increased up to fivefold in Antarctica since AD 500. In Greenland, by contrast, some 300-fold increases seem to have occurred over a similar period. This wide discrepancy between Northern and Southern Hemisphere probably reflects both the geographical pattern of pollutant emissions (90 per cent of which occur in the Northern Hemisphere), and the fact that the atmospheric circulation at the Equator is an effective barrier to the transport of aerosols between the hemispheres. Similarly, while acid rain is a serious intercontinental problem in the Northern Hemisphere, studies on Antarctic ice cores have detected no change in the pattern of natural fluctuations of sulphuric acid concentrations since before the industrial period.

No-one really knows exactly how ice ages are triggered. It is only in the last 10 years that research into palaeoclimatology has started to produce leads which may in the next 15 years or so go someway to solving the problem.

Ice ages evidently occur as a result of climatic cooling, brought on by a drop in the incoming heat from the sun, provided that there is enough water vapour. Such conditions enable a significant ice mass to develop and to be sustained. Such straightforward statements, however, belie the complexity of the factors involved which include astronomical as well as terrestrial processes too numerous to detail.

Ancient glacial features

Modern-day glaciers produce loose rock debris called till. Evidence for ancient glaciations commonly depends on the identification of tillite which is hard consolidated till, and on glacial erosional features such as striations. The earliest known glaciation for which evidence exists has been dated at 2,288 million years (give or take 87 million years) in the Lower Pre-Cambrian and occurred over the Canadian Shield. Tillites from similarly old glaciations have been found in Witwatersrand in South Africa and also in India. Little evidence exists for any glaciations between 1,000 and 2,000 million years ago, but since then many ice ages have occurred, leaving conspicuous deposits and erosive marks on virtually all the continents.

An ancient predecessor of the Pleistocene ice sheet in north-west Europe existed around 670 million years ago. Glaciologists call it the Varangian Ice Age. It is named after Varanger Fjord in north Sweden, where the relevant tillite was first identified. The deposits associated with this ice sheet, which existed before the North Atlantic Ocean was formed, are widespread. They can be found in Spitsbergen, Norway, Sweden, east Greenland, Scotland, Northern Ireland and Eire.

A younger but equally sizeable ice-sheet formed in West Africa during the Ordovician. In the region of the Hoggar Massif in the central Sahara is a complex sequence of undoubted glacial and proglacial sediments. The latter include striations, stone polygons, dropstones (ice-rafted debris) and eskers, and reveal at least three ice advances and retreats. At this time the Sahara was over the South Pole, and thus was the Ordovician 'Antarctica'. Evidence from this ice-sheet has also been found in Brazil, as South America was still juxtaposed with Africa at this time.

During the Permo-Carboniferous period, South Africa was extensively affected by ice in what is known as the Dwyka glaciation. An equivalent to the Dwyka Tillites occurs in Bluff Cove on East Falkland. Simultaneously South America underwent several periods of glaciation, leaving tell-tale sediments in Brazil, Uruguay, Bolivia and Argentina. India too, was extensively covered by ice, but in the form of smaller ice caps rather than as a major ice sheet covering a huge area.

During the Quaternary, four major ice masses formed and advanced and retreated several times. These were the Cordilleran and Laurentide ice sheets of North America, the Greenland Ice Cap, which still exists today, and the Scandinavian ice sheet, which covered most of north-west Europe and northern Russia. Iceland and Spitsbergen were totally icebound too. Over most of the British Isles there is evidence of either where the thick ice sheet once lay

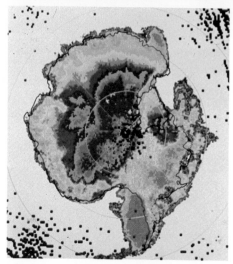

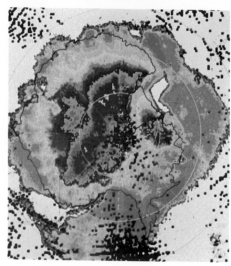

Above The Hoggar Massif in the Sahara Desert. About 500 million years ago, the Central Sahara was covered by glaciers and was where Antarctica is now. Hard sandstones made up of glacial sands, till, debris dropped from ice floes, and erratics form the Hoggar Massif. Some rocks are striated and grooved, having been scoured by passing ice. All the features found are typical of those associated with a polar ice sheet at sea level.

Left These two images of Antarctica obtained by the US Nimbus-5 satellite on 15 Dec 1972 (top) and on 30 Jan 1973 (bottom) show the difference in amount of sea ice (blue/purple) between early (Dec) and late (Jan) summer. Ice in the Ross and Weddell Seas disperses during the southern summer. Each colour relates to a temperature scale, and indicates open sea-water (white/grey); thick glaciers (green/yellow); main ice sheet (light/dark blue). Gaps in the spacecraft data appear as black patches.

Right Drifting snow whistles past sunshine recorders at Halley, a manned British research station on Coats Land, some 1,000 miles (1,600km) from the South Pole. Such instruments provide meteorologists with data about Earth's present climate.

(glacial landforms) or where the periglacial zone was (periglacial landforms). Such relic features are found from Cornwall across to East Anglia where much recent research has illuminated the climatic record over the last 120,000 years or so.

Fossil beetles as clues to climate

This research has included careful and painstaking analysis of fossil beetles in East Anglia and of pollen from the Netherlands. The species of fossil beetles found are identical to those of today. Many species of beetle are fastidious in their environmental requirements and are quite capable of changing their geographical location as local conditions alter. If it is too cold they move south, but if too warm then they travel north. Consequently by applying knowledge of contemporary habitats of particular species of beetles to those found in the sediments, the beetles can then be used as a sensitive environmental index, and a detailed record of changes in climate can be deduced. For example, in the last glacial/interglacial cycle, a succession of insect faunas has inhabited north-western Europe that have included species now confined to the high Arctic, to southern Europe, to the western edges of Eurasia or to the east of Siberia. This migration reflects the drastic changes in climate that have happened in Europe in the recent past. Independent information supports the interpretations. For instance, the beetle record indicates a short-lived cold period around 10,000 years before the present in Britain and this is borne out by the fact that the Loch Lomond Ice Cap reformed in Scotland at approximately this time.

Pollen analysis

Similarly, fossil pollen analysis discloses vegetational changes in the distant past. Pollen and spores, which can be preserved for millions of years, reflect the composition of the vegetation of an area. The careful scrutiny of pollen diagrams (percentages of pollen types per sample) can yield information about climate indirectly. As a crude example, if pollen from an Arctic tundra plant were found in sediments in an area currently vegetated by more temperate plants, it could be surmised that the climate was once much cooler. A comparison between the pollen analysis results and those from the fossil beetles produces a consistent pattern of climatic variation. These techniques are being continually developed, providing improved resolution of events in time. In addition, they are being applied to older and older material, thereby extending the record of climatic change. This also means that the results can be checked against those from other independent analyses for dating samples.

Future ice ages

Research such as this is attempting to construct an accurate measure of climatic change so that it may be understood and that its cause may be explained. One fact which does emerge from the climatic studies is that the interval between successive ice ages is becoming shorter. It is not yet possible to predict the onset of the next ice age, but if the current trends continue then perhaps the ice will return. Luckily for us, it is unlikely, however, that such a situation will begin to develop for many hundreds, if not many thousands, of years to come.

The inhospitable, arid deserts are among the most amazing landscapes on Earth. Vast expanses of ever-shifting sands form gigantic dune systems which can vary from long whalebacks to exquisite crescents in shape. Other deserts are rock wastes with weird pinnacles sculptured by wind-borne sand. The wind is the major former of landscape in arid regions, carrying and depositing millions of tons of sand and dust.

Charged with this natural abrasive, the wind can strip the paint from cars in seconds, and erodes rock surfaces with similar effectiveness. Water, too, can play a very important role in creating desert landscapes. Flash-floods carry debris across the desert surface to deposit it as great alluvial fans below the higher upland regions. Wadis (dry valleys) are a typical feature of many desert landscapes.

THE ARID LANDS

The arid expanses of the Earth's deserts, inhospitable and often remote, are regions where beautiful landscapes are formed in an ever-changing environment of barren rock, shifting sand and sporadic violent floods

The dry sandy wastes and the cold inhospitable continental interiors, which on average receive less than 2in (5cm) of rain annually, are the Earth's desert regions. The form of the desert surface, because of a lack of sediment-binding vegetation, depends on erosion and deposition, mainly by the wind, but also by occasional, devastatingly powerful, turbulent flash-floods. Where great extremes of temperature persist for much of the year, rocks literally crumble through repeated expansion and contraction, baked at over 100°F (38°C) in the afternoon and cooled to below freezing point at night. The resulting rock debris is easily blown away, or swept along by flash-floods. The end-product of this erosional system is a rocky desert, with vast expanses of bare rock surface, scraped and marked by the movement of sand and rock. In the Sahara this is known as the *hamada*. When the rock surface is

covered with the gravel that is not removed by the wind a stony desert, called *reg* in the Algerian Sahara, is formed. When the fine desert sand accumulates in areas where the wind is of lower velocity, an *erg*, or sandy desert, with very large expanses of shifting dune systems, is generally formed.

Hot and cold deserts

Geologists make further distinctions between one desert and another by using criteria such as the moisture index, which is based on understanding how any moisture the desert may receive is evaporated. In the hot deserts such as those of northern Libya, where maximum temperatures approach 140°F (60°C) and minimums are a few degrees below freezing, and in the interior of the Sahara, relative humidity levels may fall to zero per cent (common levels in temperate climates such as

that of western Europe are 80 to 100 per cent). The Sahara is as big as all the other hot deserts added together, but in south-western USA the Gila Desert, of insignificant size in comparison, contains one of the most inhospitable regions in the world, Death Valley. Here the temperature soars to nearly 135°F (57°C) and the hot dry air scorches any exposed moist plant or animal material.

In contrast to the hot deserts are the 'cold' deserts such as the Mongolian wastes. These do not experience very high summer temperatures (about 70°F/21°C) but in winter the thermometer plummets to nearly minus 30°F (−34°C). Here precipitation, in the form of rain, snow, mist or other forms of moisture, may be as much as 10in (25cm) per year, and these higher latitude deserts are characterized by frequent winter frosts. In the Kasgar region in the Takla-Makan desert of Central Asia frost

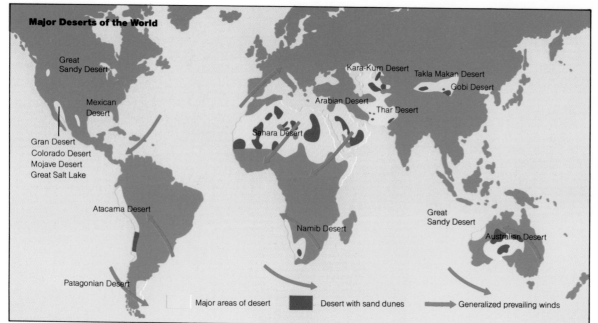

Major Deserts of the World

Great Sandy Desert

Mexican Desert

Gran Desert
Colorado Desert
Mojave Desert
Great Salt Lake

Atacama Desert

Patagonian Desert

Kara-Kum Desert

Takla Makan Desert

Gobi Desert

Arabian Desert

Thar Desert

Sahara Desert

Namib Desert

Great Sandy Desert

Australian Desert

Major areas of desert — Desert with sand dunes — Generalized prevailing winds

Left The position of the main desert regions in relation to a simplified pattern of prevailing winds. Interior continental deserts, such as the Sahara and Gobi deserts, are so far from the sea that the wind has lost almost all its moisture before it reaches them, so that no rain falls. Rain-shadow deserts, such as the Mojave Desert, lie in the lee of high mountain ranges. The winds lose all their moisture as rain when they rise over the mountains, leaving none for the desert region. Cool coastal deserts, such as the Atacama or Namib, are dry because the air passes over nearby cool ocean currents, forming chilling fog instead of rain.
Right The Algerian Grand Erg, a vast 'sand sea'.
Far right The Atacama Desert, Peru.

Above Sand deserts often give way to stone and gravel, as here in Iran. Such areas are called 'reg' in the Sahara. They are largely the end-product of the erosional system by which sand is blown or swept away by floods.

occurs for over half the year and snow is frequently recorded, but in the short summer the average temperature soars to 70°F (21°C). The great distance of deserts like this from the sea means that they are free from cloud. The Takla-Makan desert receives over 3,000 hours of sunshine in a typical year, while places at similar latitudes in Western Europe receive only about 1,800 hours each year.

Desert distribution

Two broad bands of desert girdle the Earth, lying at latitudes between 10° and 40°. The hot deserts lie at about 25° from the Equator, while the cold deserts are restricted to very high latitudes or to the continental interiors. The Southern Hemisphere, because it lacks large land masses, contains only one continental desert, that in central Australia, but two other deserts stretch along the west coasts of Southern Africa and South America. These are not extensive and are very small in comparison with the intensely cold coastal desert in Queen Maud Land, Antarctica.

Coastal deserts

The coastal deserts cross the Equator, one running along the Somalian coast in East Africa, while the Sonora-Arizona desert along the coast of Mexico and USA lies astride the Gulf of California. In contrast to these equatorial sandy wastes, the most northerly deserts are those of northern China and southern USSR which contain the largest salt flats, or playas, that have been found on Earth.

The shifting deserts

Deserts occupy nearly a quarter of the Earth's surface and their extent changes with the world's climatic pattern. The exact area is difficult to define exactly since there are vast regions of semi-arid land in which the annual precipitation is about 5in (12½cm) and where in some years very little rain falls, when they become desert-like areas. There is much recent evidence from satellite mapping and photography to suggest that the Sahara has increased in area over the last 7,000 years and is expanding rapidly in some places. This expansion is probably due to the continued shift of climatic belts since the last ice age and the climatic fluctuations over the last 2 million years. Large river systems can be traced across the Sahara and other now hot arid regions, which in the recent past—geologically speaking—were wet humid areas clothed with vegetation.

The largest deserts on the Earth's surface are the result of a combination of geographical position and geological structure. These arid and semi-arid regions tend to be in the interiors of large continental masses, where the rain from cyclonic depressions rarely falls. The effect of this distance from the sea may become emphasized by the basin-like structure of some interior deserts. Any cyclonic rain which reaches these regions tend to fall on the windward slopes of surrounding mountains and the drying winds which prevail over these basins increase the aridity. In the 'winter', high atmospheric pressure with typically clear skies causes heat loss through radiation, leading to very low temperatures.

Misty coastal deserts

In the two west coast deserts of the Southern Hemisphere, the Atacama (along the Pacific coast of South America) and the Namib (in South-west Africa) frequent cloud cover and high humidity are typical weather conditions. Both these deserts are maintained by the northward movement of a cold near-coast sea current. In South America the Humboldt current brings icy waters up from the Antarctic region, and the Benguela current follows the African coast. The waters of these currents are some 4°F (7°C) below the prevailing environment temperatures. Such cold water creates a stable air-mass in which humidity is high and fog and mist are frequent. Cloud and precipitation are, however, very rare as the cool air-masses are drawn in over the land when it is heated by the sun. In these areas a cool 'oceanic' climate, with a temperature range of some 3-4°F (1·6-2°C)

and a high relative humidity, combines strangely with extreme aridity. Arica on the Atacama coast receives only ½sin (1mm) of rain per year, while Swakopmund in South-west Africa has as much as ½in (12mm) of precipitation, mainly from the clammy mists.

Hot dry deserts

At the low latitudes where the main hot deserts lie, mean annual temperatures are around 72°F (24°C). Cloud tends to be absent because the moist air rising through convection at the

tropics sucks 'trade winds' in beneath it and as the damp tropical air cools at high altitudes tropical rainstorms are generated. As this cool denser air falls outside the tropics it warms and dries, producing clear sun-drenched skies in the desert regions. Though the day-time temperatures may be very high—almost 140°F (60°C) is not uncommon—the lack of cloud cover can produce very cold nights, with temperatures below freezing. The tilt of the Earth on its axis causes the dry destertifying air masses to shift seasonally, and this may allow

rain to be brought in to the desert margins, as in the 'winter' showers over North Africa.

A moister history

There is a good deal of evidence from today's desert regions that in the past they have received much more rain and have even been fertile, well vegetated areas. Recent studies in the Lake Chad area of the Sahara have shown that the present lake is merely a shrunken remnant of a much larger body of water, surrounded by fixed, fossilized dunes. This suggests that the Sahara was previously much more extensive to the south. In the central Sahara the rock paintings of the Tassili Plateau have long been known. These were made by a now vanished society about 7,000 years ago. They represent antelopes, giraffes, elephants and other creatures, which presumably lived in this area where the people herded cattle across rolling acres of grassland.

Salty soils

Over large expanses of the modern deserts, erosion outstrips weathering, and soils develop only on the thin alluvium around the ephemeral streams and on fixed dune-systems in the semi-arid areas. The soils are influenced by the way in which plants and evaporation draw up and concentrate salts and carbonates near the surface, to produce 'saline soils'. These are often stained bright yellow and red by iron oxides. It happens in some regions (as in the Atacama nitrate fields in South America) that the salts so produced are of commercial quantity. These soils are notable for their low organic content, in Central Asia, as low as 2 per cent.

Above left Banks of fog roll in from the ocean across the Namib Desert on the Atlantic coast of South West Africa. Frequent cloud cover and high humidity are typical weather conditions in both the Namib and the Atacama Desert in Chile and Peru, which also hugs the coast.
Left A desert landscape in the Peruvian Atacama Desert features huge sand-dune systems. The sand forms characteristic bedding patterns.
Above right In the American Californian Desert, ancient lake systems have evaporated to leave large deposits of salt, which was previously held in solution in the water. Here, salt 'pinnacles' rise in weird shapes from the desert floor. Salt deposits such as these, but millions of years old, are found in desert rocks in many parts of the world: some, such as the Atacama nitrate fields, are of great economic importance.
Right Many desert areas have expanded in the very recent geological past. The Tassili Plateau, in the central Sahara, is famous for its beautiful cave paintings, made by a long-vanished people who lived there about 5,000 BC. These paintings depict lush grasslands with herds of grazing animals, where now there is only desert.

As the climate grows drier and the soil becomes dessicated, plants die, and the soil, no longer bound by roots, is then open to attack from weathering and erosion. Desert landscapes consist of mountainous regions with intervening 'pediments' and plains, but erosion is constantly reducing the mountainous areas and sediment is deposited in the lower basins. The pediment regions are, because of the erosional processes involved, transitional, and eventually become low-angled slopes leading to sediment-filled basins. Pediments with slopes of up to 10 degrees away from the higher regions are natural surfaces for erosion. The sediment transported over and piled up on these zones is moved by wind and sheet-wash floods. Drainage network 'rills' (narrow, steep-sided streams) are common as a result of this relentless pattern of erosion.

Weathering processes

The development of the highland areas depends very much on their geological structure. The stark volcanic cliffs of the Tibesti mountains in the central Sahara contrasts with the low limestone hills and ledges in the Libyan desert. Weathering processes in deserts may be either 'mechanical' (involving the physical breakdown of the rock) or 'chemical' (the result of chemical reactions which break down the rock structure). Although geologists used to think that the dramatic change between the fierce heat of the desert day and the often cold nights produced stresses that were responsible for mechanical weathering, recent research (in which the desert temperature conditions were carefully simulated in the laboratory) indicates that this is unlikely to be important.

Frost action, too, is of only limited importance in arid regions, because there is not enough water available in the first place for rock-splitting frosts to develop.

On the other hand, salt weathering, for a long time regarded as a minor process, has recently been shown to have a considerable influence in many desert areas. Geologists have found that the growth of salt crystals in rock joints and fractures can generate distruptive stresses capable of shattering rocks. The reinforced concrete structures built in the Suez Canal zone have suffered badly from salt weathering. It is moisture penetrating the rocks that makes the salt crystals grow. Layers are often peeled off from the outer surface of the rock as a result of salt weathering, in a process called 'exfoliation' (also known as 'onion-skin weathering' or 'spalling'). It results in the appearance of increasingly rounded boulders and pebbles. When the rock is coarsely crystalline, the expansion and contraction of the different crystals causes granular disintegration, producing a grit, made up of small fragments, around the weathered rock masses.

Moisture, often the result of the heavy desert dew-falls, is also instrumental in producing features such as the extraordinary ramifying 'tafonis'. These are caves, ranging in size from only a few inches to several feet, and are found along the damp, foggy coastal Atacama Desert of Peru and Chile.

Singing rocks

When wind or water from flash-floods has exposed bare rock surfaces to the searing heat of the desert day and the chilling cold of the night, strange noises may be produced, which have alarmed many a desert explorer. Rocks

Above Sandstone pinnacles at Bryce Canyon, USA, tinted by mineral oxides. Originally formed from huge sand dunes piled up by the wind about 200 million years ago, the softer sandstone layers have been eroded by water percolating down through them.

Right Water, falling in occasional rainstorms, traces hairline cracks in soft desert rock, opening it up like a knife cutting through butter. Chemicals dissolved in the water hasten the erosion. The effects of water erosion may be on a huge scale, as in the Grand Canyon.

Rain water

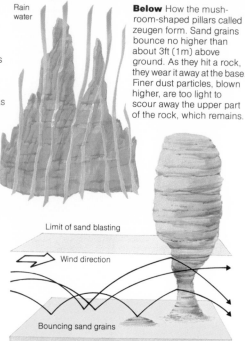

Below How the mushroom-shaped pillars called zeugen form. Sand grains bounce no higher than about 3ft (1m) above ground. As they hit a rock, they wear it away at the base. Finer dust particles, blown higher, are too light to scour away the upper part of the rock, which remains.

Limit of sand blasting

Wind direction

Bouncing sand grains

under stress are heard to crack loudly, or even make weird hissing and humming sounds.

Wind, the great sculptor

The wind is a great natural sculptor of landforms, a polisher and a grinder, scouring at earth and rock with sand as its abrasive. Hard sands with a high quartz content can carve away fences, trees and telegraph poles, blast glass with an opaque frosting, and even scoop out the foundations of buildings. This huge natural sandblasting machine is concentrated near ground-level, and acts in just the same way as do industrial sandblasting processes for cleaning metals or etching glass. Indeed, so powerful an agent of erosion is the sand-laden wind that it

Above Elephant Rock, in the Valley of Fire State Park, Nevada, USA, was created by a combination of wind and water erosion. **Right** In this Sahara rock formation, the softer rock strata have been eroded by the wind. Wind power is amazing: once, a group of people crossing the Libyan desert by car met a sandstorm. The sand stripped the paintwork down to bare metal in 48 hours, and made the windscreens so opaque they had to be knocked out before the convoy could proceed. **Below left** A barely supported zeugen in the Sahara. The name zeugen comes from the German for 'witness' as they stand witness to the former extent of the rock formation, though they too will eventually disappear, as they are transformed by sand into sand.

can strip the paint from the bodies of trucks in a matter of a few hours.

The effect is just as dramatic on the desert rocks. Weak or soft rock strata are selectively eroded and picked out by the wind-borne sand to produce a variety of distinctive and often grotesque shapes. These include the bizarre pinnacles of the Painted Desert, in Arizona, USA, and the great rock arches of Utah. In the Western Desert of the Egyptian Sahara, thousands of years of sand-laden winds have exposed rocks, shredding out their softer layers, and in some cases creating aerodynamically shaped ridges called 'yardangs'. These tail away downwind, all facing, sphinx-like, into the eroding blast. Each yardang is separated from its neighbour by a wind-scoured groove.

Elsewhere, prominent rock masses can be undercut and whittled into table-rocks, pedestals and mushroom shapes, known collectively by the German name of 'zeugen'.

Rock fragments which are too big to be moved by the wind are etched and faceted into 'dreikanter', three-sided pebbles, found in both modern deserts and those from the distant geological past.

The sand-grains involved in the sandblasting process are themselves affected by constantly hitting one another, and become frosted and rounded to form 'millet-seed' sand. Millet-seed sand deposits are found in sandstone formations millions of years old, and by analogy with modern deposits, geologists interpret them as wind-blown deposits, as with the 270-million-year-old rocks from Durham, England, for instance. Other features of such deposits may help to determine whether they were formed in deserts or in a different wind-eroded environment, such as the outwash plains of glaciers or areas near sea-coasts.

Deserts without sand

Where ancient seas once covered the land, the eroding wind reveals limestone banks and hard nodules of silica. Elsewhere, the desert floor is swept and polished. Most desert areas, contrary to popular belief, are devoid of sand: for instance, the dunes occupy a mere 500,000 square miles (1,300,00sq km) of the total 3,500,000 square miles (9,000,000sq km) of the Sahara Desert. The wind has cleared most of it down to the bedrock.

Sand and dust particles are moved across the desert surface by the wind. Their long journey begins when they are hit by another moving grain, or swept up by a strong enough blast of wind. The smallest particles are carried in suspension, the medium-sized ones are bounced over the surface, and the larger ones may be rolled along. During a period of high wind the air over a desert region becomes a choking, searing, thickly-laden mass, in which it is impossible to breathe, and in which vast quantities of sand are carried over many hundreds of miles. Significant falls of wind-borne dust have often been reported by ships west of the Canaries. This dust originates in the Sahara and is carried by strong easterly winds. Each year, an estimated 40 million tons of dust are carried out over the Atlantic in this way to sink to the murky ocean depths, forming deep-water clays. When the finer dust is removed in this way, the heavier particles are left behind to form a 'lag' deposit, typical of the rocky wastes known as the 'hammada' in the Sahara and as 'gibber plains' in Australia.

Fertile oases

The long-term effects of wind erosion are well illustrated on a vast scale to the west of Cairo, Egypt, where a series of basins have been scoured out by the abrasive wind until their floors have become deep enough to intercept the ground water. Wind has little effect on sediment which is wet, and the base level for

wind erosion here is the zone of permanent saturation—the water table. The largest of these basins, the Quattara Depression, lies nearly 450ft (140m) below sea-level, and this and other similar basins have become oases, green islands of fertility and water in the dry sand-swept wastes. Such oases have been used for hundreds of years by nomadic tribes.

Sand seas

The sand-laden wind produces a variety of ripples, mounds, ridges and dunes as it releases and moves its burden. These contribute to the 'sand seas'—large areas of shifting sand, often surrounded by higher mountainous areas. The sand-sea is a highly unstable region, where the individual dunes and ripples are themselves constantly moving down-wind. Among the smaller sand deposits are ripples. These are less than an inch high and form in straight rows or in a sinuous pattern, with their crests some 6in (15cm) or so apart. Like many other deposition features of desert regions, they probably arise when slight obstructions (in this case unevenness of the desert surface) lie in the path of the moving sand current.

Dune types

Dune systems are the most familiar and among the most beautiful features of deserts. When the wind blows in a constant direction, sand is deposited around obstructions in a number of ways. It may heap up against rock cliffs, or in

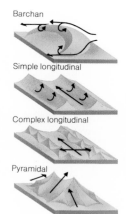

Left Dunes can be divided into four main types, though these do combine in many deserts. A barchan is a crescentic dune with sand spilling over the curved horns. Simple longitudinal dunes lie parallel to a consistent prevailing wind direction and are regularly spaced. They may extend for 30 miles (50km). Complex longitudinal dunes result from variable wind directions, while pyramidal dunes develop when winds below from all points of the compass.

the lee of low cliffs or vegetation, or even behind boulders. Whenever large dune systems develop, the dunes will take on forms determined by the wind and the amount of sand available. The best-known dunes are the curving crescentic 'barchans' (from the Arabic). These vary in height from 6ft (2m) to 120ft (40m), and may measure as much as a quarter of a mile (400m) from one 'horn' to the other. Sand blows over the gently sloping up-wind slope, then spills down the steep lee-slope and around the horns. The most perfectly formed barchans occur as isolated dunes on rocky surfaces. As more sand is blown into the area, however, many barchans may form close together with their horns linking up.

Left In desert regions life is concentrated around the oasis. Here in Tunisia, the Tamerza river bed provides water to sustain life.

Below In this view of Death Valley, California, one of the world's most inhospitable places, sand shifts over the dune tops, blown by the wind.

Longitudinal 'seif' dunes may develop when two wind directions, a gentle persistent one supplying sand, and a stronger occasional one from a different direction, remove the less stable sand areas to form ridges. Such ridges can be traced for tens of miles, and may reach heights of 300ft (90m) in the Sahara and Saudi Arabian deserts. In Australian deserts, longitudinal dunes are smaller, averaging about 40ft (12m) high and 650ft (200m) apart.

In some desert regions, the shifting sands may take on the shape of transverse dunes, with sinuous crests at right angles to the wind. Sometimes, because of the turbulence created by rock masses, the wind stirs the sand up into strange twisting ridges which converge into high peaks, called 'stellate' (star-shaped) dunes.

Very large dunes can form almost permanent hills, or 'draa', as in the eastern Sahara, where they have existed for 4,000 years. Smaller dunes can become superimposed on these stationary forms. These shifting dunes may move across the desert at rates of up to 200ft (60m per year.

Identifying ancient winds

Dunes have characteristic internal structures, such as cross-bedding, which are related to the spilling of sand over the lee slope as the dunes migrate. Geologists can sometimes discover the direction of prevailing winds many millions of years ago by analysing these internal structures in ancient wind-formed sediments.

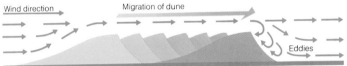

Above Sand blown across the desert surface accumulates as crescent-shaped barchan dunes with curved 'horns', as here in the South Namib Desert.

Wind direction   Migration of dune   Eddies

Left Constant wind direction both deposits and moves dunes. Each dune grows with a forward and upward movement, causing the wind current to rise and eddy over the steeper slip-face. Sand is carried off the top of the dune, and the slip-face thus advances in a downwind direction.

Although deserts are generally very dry, occasionally—often as infrequently as once in 50 years—they experience short periods of torrential rainfall. These rare rainstorms produce dramatic and profound effects. The angle of slope of the desert surface is often very low, and the run-off of water is greatly restricted, allowing several inches of water to collect and flow. The water in such 'sheet floods' collects in hollows, producing temporary pools, or encounters ancient water channels, forming temporary, turbulent, sediment-darkened rivers. These rivers draw their water from over a tremendous area, and, once established, rapidly become swollen torrents of great ferocity. The term 'flash-floods' is an apt description. The 'wadis', or valleys, through which they run are one moment dry dust-channels, and the next filled with a boulder-laden, highly erosive torrent.

Drowning in the desert

Although some desert dwellers or travellers may be warned of the approach of a flash-flood by the noise of the rushing water over the horizon, others are not so fortunate, and may even be drowned by the sudden raging torrent. Desert communities and scientific expeditions alike have been lulled into a false sense of security by the rare and sporadic occurrence of flash-floods. Early hominids may have been the first of us to meet this fate—one group of fossil remains found in 3-million-year-old flash-flood deposits in Ethiopia seems to be of a family of man-like apes.

Modern disasters on a much larger scale include those caused by flash-floods in the Atlas Mountains of the Sahara, in Algeria in 1959 and Tunisia 10 years later. Here, the water claimed many victims and destroyed homes and crops in settlements which had grown up in areas where the last flash-floods occurred fifty or more years ago.

Record levels of erosion

The desert highlands are the regions from which weathered rock debris is slowly carried down slopes onto the lower regions. Most rain falls in the higher parts of the desert, and the flash-floods remove huge quantities of loose debris in the space of a few hours. The combination of this rapid run-off from the slopes and the fact that the desert soil generally lacks plant-cover or humus which would help to bind its particles together means that more soil may be lost from desert drainage basins than from any other environment on Earth. These world record levels of soil and sand loss include a recent estimate that the Paria River, one of the tributaries of the great Colorado River in Arizona, USA, may contain as much as 40 per cent of soil and other material in suspension, turning the water a dense muddy brown colour. This state of affairs is wittily and concisely summed up by a local saying that these rivers are "too thin to plough but too thick to drink"!

Natural highways

As these sudden rivers flow through the desert, they rapidly dry up. The water filters down through the porous bed of the wadi and evaporates in the intense heat. The river soon vanishes completely, leaving its poorly sorted load of debris scattered along the wadi. Wadis, known as 'arroyos' in Spain and America, often provide convenient, if somewhat hazardous, routes for desert travellers.

Playa lakes

When the temporary river flows out through a highland wadi onto the desert plain, it will lose speed rapidly and deposit sediment in the form of a low angled fan-shaped mound, often a few miles broad. If, as occasionally happens, the river flows far out onto the plain, water may accumulate in depressions to form 'playa' (or 'shott') lakes.

Evaporites

Playas and their accumulations of sediment are a store of valuable evidence of past climatic change. Many of the present desert drainage

Left When rain falls in arid regions, it can form powerfully erosive streams, which cut deeply into the bedrock. This 'slot canyon' in Utah, USA, is deeply cut by such a stream.

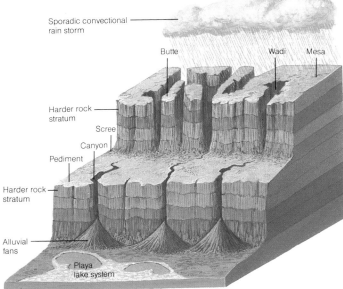

Sporadic convectional rain storm

Butte

Wadi

Mesa

Harder rock stratum

Scree

Canyon

Pediment

Harder rock stratum

Alluvial fans

Playa lake system

Left The Valley of the Colorado River is deeply cut into the arid wastes of the North American desert, providing some of the most impressive stratified cliffs to be found anywhere on the Earth's surface.

Above This idealized diagram shows some of the characteristic features of an arid landscape. Infrequent but heavy rain cuts deep wadis, which isolate buttes and larger mesas. The streams that occasionally pour down the wadis carry sediment, which is dumped onto the plain, building up into alluvial fans. Alternatively, where the water flow is sufficient to carry away all the weathered material, a gently-sloping deeply cut pediment may be formed.

Above Water often fills depressions in the desert landscape to form 'playa lakes'. Here, in Western Australia, a salt lake has developed by the continual evaporation of water laden with salts.

Above right The delta of the Kuiseb River which runs through the Namib Desert. A roaring torrent after an occasional rainstorm, this river carries huge amounts of sediment down to the sea.

basins are shrunken playas which were much more extensive during the Pleistocene period. In North America, 300 playas have been mapped, and 120 of these are small survivors of wetter Pleistocene climates. Many playas are rich in mineral salts, including chlorides, sulphides, nitrates and borates. These salts, or 'evaporites', are produced in playas and in sea lagoons and bays surrounded by desert conditions, by high evaporation rates and low levels of rainfall. The otherwise soluble salts crystallize around the margins of the shrinking lake. In Kara Bogaz Bay, on the eastern margin of the Caspian Sea, there is a fine large-scale evaporite system. This bay is about 100 miles (160km) in diameter but has a depth of only 33ft (10m). It is surrounded by the Kra Kum Desert, and is, in effect, a large evaporating pan. Each day some 310,000 tons of dissolved salt is brought into the bay over a narrow, shallow channel from the Caspian Sea. Halite (common salt) and gypsum (calcium sulphate) are precipitated around the margins, and Glauber's salt (sodium sulphate) on the floor of the bay.

Spectacular landforms

Where deserts are made of soft easily eroded silts, spectacular landforms are produced. In the upper reaches of the Hwang Ho in China there are great thicknesses of wind-blown dust and soil. River action has cut deep, steep-sided valleys through this material.

Rivers of the past

Geologists can often identify the past action of water in arid regions by examining 'fossil' landscapes carved into the solid rock by ancient rivers. Wadis, extinct waterfalls, alluvial fans and even traces of ancient civilizations are all preserved in many regions of the world. Between Tibesti and the Mauritanian mountains of the Sahara is a vast gravel desert, beneath the surface of which lies a well-preserved fossil soil, nearly 1,000 years old—amazing evidence that the area was at an earlier time much wetter than it is today, with lush green vegetation which probably provided rich grazing for wandering herds of browsing animals.

The presence of extensive areas of sand in the Arabian desert known as 'draas', which are not aligned with the present wind direction, and the existence of fossil river systems around the Ahaggar mountains in the central Sahara, or the immobile, vegetated dunes around Lake Chad all show that deserts grow and shrink as climatic conditions change. Over the vast geological time-scale of millions of years, the movement of the continents brought areas which today are far from being arid to regions where they became deserts.

Identifying ancient continental rocks

Continental sedimentary rocks, formed long ago in arid regions, or in rivers and lakes, can be identified by features such as cross-bedding (with dune-type patterns where the wind has carried the sand); ripple-marks on bedding planes; the lack of marine fossils; and the inclusion of such rocks as sandstone, breccia and conglomerate. Rocks from windswept arid areas may contain sand-grains rounded into 'millet seeds', or pebbles faceted to form dreikanter. Red-coloured sediment (in which the grains are coated with red oxidized iron) may not necessarily be from an arid landscape, as many ancient lake and river deposits are also this colour. For instance, North European Triassic rocks were formed in a desert, but Devonian ones are river or lake deposits.

The Devonian continent

The Devonian rocks of northern Britain are one of the most thoroughly researched ancient land deposits. In the Caithness and Orkney regions of Scotland they are over 15,000ft (5,000m) thick. Basically they consist of a top layer of yellow and red sandstones and conglomerates, below which is a strange sequence of sandstones, dark silts, muddy limestones and dark muds. These rocks are rhythmically bedded and were formed over a very long time. Beneath these are breccias and grits. They contain few fossils, apart from the remains of primitive fish. Geologists believe that they are evidence of a large basin of desert type, surrounded by high mountains, which existed about 380 million years ago. The conglomerates and grits are the products of the weathering of the mountains, accumulating at the mountain base. Outwash fans at times spread out away from the mountain slopes, and the finer sands of the basin were carried by turbulent flash-floods after heavy rainstorms. Silt and mud were carried out by winds into playa lakes in the deepest parts of the basin. Ripples are preserved on many rock surfaces, suggesting that the prevailing wind blew from the south-west and the south-east.

The rhythmic sequence of silts, limestones and muds accumulated in a large body of fresh water which fluctuated, possibly seasonally, just as playas do today. Desiccation cracks on the sediment surfaces (which are indicative of a muddy sediment drying out above water-level) are common, and further from the shoreline, mudflats and fine sand deposits are common. In the deeper parts of the lake conditions suited primitive fish. These resemble modern lungfish, which are well adapted to arid conditions and can slither across the land from one pool to the next. Some species can cocoon themselves in mud and slime to survive drought for extended periods. The area of Lake Chad and the Tibesti mountains is a comparable modern area to this ancient Scottish lake.

Left Duncansby Stacks, Caithness, Scotland, contain one of the best exposures of Devonian continental strata in the world. During the Devonian period, much of what is now Northern Europe and Greenland was a large continent situated about 20°S of the Equator. This ancient continent was partly a hot desert with sand-dunes, sporadic flash floods and temporary lakes. Evidence for these conditions is found in rocks in various places in Northern Europe. They contain desert sands and river-bed sandstones from flash-floods, as well as shales and limestones from lake floors. Some of the lakes existed for long periods, and the shales and limestones contain many fossil fishes. These have attracted invasions of collectors, sometimes with devastating results; even power tools have been used, destroying classic rock strata.

Right Similar evidence for Devonian strata is found in coastal rocks of the Orkney Islands, Scotland, as here at the spectacular Old Man of Hoy, a stack 450ft (137m) high which rises from a wave-cut platform and is made of red-coloured sandstone.

Below Lake Chad in Africa may today be a similar environment to that which existed over parts of the Devonian continent, where land-locked basins filled with water became large lakes.

Right The Torridonian sandstones of Northern Scotland were formed over 800 million years ago in a semi-arid environment where rivers and flash-floods carried pebbles and sand to form rock strata such as these.
Below Ancient deserts covered much of Europe during the Permian period, and a land-locked gulf of highly saline water extended from Germany to Britain. This sea gradually dried up, causing much salt to be precipitated. Potash from this sea-bed is mined here in North Yorkshire, England amidst rolling farmland.

Ancient deserts in America

In the Colorado Plateau region of the USA, a desert basin existed for much of the upper Palaeozoic and Mesozoic eras. Dune sandstones formed here are well sorted and contain dreikanter. Wind ripples, footprints of vertebrates and the small pits made in sediments by raindrops ('rain-pits') are found here. The Colorado Plateau area was a desert basin, bounded by mountains, open to rivers and the sea only to the north.

European deserts

By the Permian period the Eurasian continent had drifted to a position some 20 to 30 degrees north of the Equator. Glaciation affected much of Africa and South America at this time and when ice-caps and glaciers melted, sea level rose to cause a shallow sea to invade northern Europe. In north-east England, a land-locked gulf developed, reaching as far south as Poland. Around this sea were muddy salt flats ('sabkhas') and sand-seas, preserved as masses of millet-seed sandstone and pediments. The sea-water continued to evaporate, and salts were precipitated is a series of cycles, producing minerals such as potash, gypsum and halite. After five influxes of water from the north, the sea finally dried up, and became smothered by the relentless wind-blown red sands of the Triassic period. In Germany the salt deposits are extensive and of considerable economic significance, being 3,000ft (100m) thick in places. Valuable deposits are also found in north-east England.

Our atmosphere is of vital importance, providing life-giving oxygen and water vapour and shielding us from harmful short-wavelength ultraviolet radiation from the Sun. It also acts as a giant heat engine, which drives the atmospheric circulation and its major winds. Manned space travel and satellite technology have added immensely to the meteorologists' understanding of this vital layer where our

weather is born. A whole range of modern technological aids, including the most sophisticated computers, Doppler radar, cloud chambers and high-speed photography, are also used to study aspects of our atmosphere, ranging from how to predict, track and even try to tame cyclonic storms, to understanding how clouds form and rain falls, or to the exact nature of a thunderstorm.

THE ATMOSPHERE

Invisible, but having a profound effect on our planet and our lives, Earth's atmosphere is being thoroughly explored, from long-term weather changes to split-second lightning bolts

The envelope of gases surrounding the Earth, which we call the atmosphere, reaches into space some 500 miles (800km), but becomes greatly rarefied above about 50 miles (80km). It is in the lower 50 miles that our wind and weather patterns are determined.

The atmosphere consists of relatively discrete layers, but slowly the light gases, such as hydrogen (0.00005 per cent by volume) and helium (0.0005 per cent), are lost to space. Gases such as nitrogen (75·5 per cent) and oxygen (23·15 per cent), together with some other rarer gases, form the fixed components of the lower atmosphere. Carbon dioxide (0·03 per cent), water vapour (3 per cent) and ozone (0·00006 per cent) are the variable gases. Below 50 miles (80km), the atmosphere is made up of three main layers. The highest of these is called the mesosphere. Here, temperatures increase from $-148°F$ ($-100°C$) at 50 miles above the Earth's surface to $32°F$ ($0°C$) at 6 miles (10km). Below the mesosphere is the stratosphere, where ozone reaches its highest concentrations, at a height of 19 miles (30km), and below this lies the troposphere, where much of the Earth's weather is generated.

The thermosphere

At the highest levels in the atmosphere, above 50 miles (80km), the thermosphere stretches away into space. This zone can be very hot (hence its name): temperatures in the thermosphere can reach $1,700°F$ ($927°C$) at a height of about 220 miles (350km). At these levels, a mere two-millionths of the total atmosphere remains, though this is still sufficient to exert an appreciable drag on spacecraft. It is here that chemical effects are produced by short-wave radiation when oxygen molecules are split to recombine as ozone. Above 60 miles (100km) other gases, such as nitrogen, are ionized when electrons split off, creating an atmosphere which contains free positively-charged atoms and negatively-charged electrons. This electrically-charged 'ionosphere' has im-

portant effects on radio-communication, as radio waves are reflected at its lower levels.

A variable layer

The division between the troposphere and the stratosphere is called the tropopause. It is a world-wide feature, but occurs at different heights in different areas and at different times. Over Northern Europe, for example, the tropopause oscillates between 20,000ft (6,000m) and 40,000ft (12,000m), being lower in winter and during periods of low pressures and temperatures. It is about twice this height over the Equator, where its average temperature is $-112°F$ ($-80°C$).

Auroras

Above about 125 miles (200km), the auroras, which light the skies with shimmering curtains of spectacular colour, form as sudden increases in solar radiation produce streams of charged particles. These are attracted to the Earth's magnetic poles, where they collide with the ionized gases in the ionosphere, releasing energy in the form of light. This is called the Aurora Borealis in the Northern Hemisphere, and the Aurora Australis in the Southern Hemisphere.

Energy in the atmosphere

Energy in the atmosphere comes from two different sources. Heat from the Earth is produced by the radioactive decay of various elements; it slowly seeps to the surface and then into the sky. This source of heat energy is, however, negligible compared with that received from the Sun in the form of solar radiation. A mere two-thousand-millionths part of the energy sent out by the Sun into space is received by the Earth. The temperature of the Sun's surface is about $6,000°K$ (degrees Kelvin, commonly used for scientific measurements of temperature, in which the freezing point of water is $273°K$), or $10,300°F$ ($5,727°C$), but the average for the Earth's atmosphere is only about $250°K$ ($-9·4°F/-23°C$), and for the Earth's surface

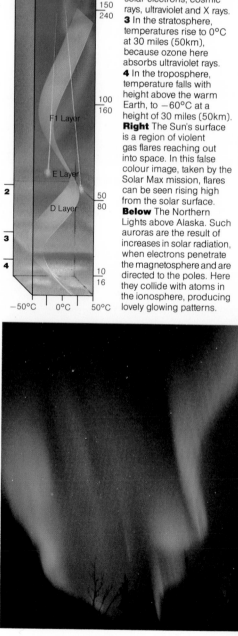

Left This diagram shows the layers into which the atmosphere can be divided. Variations in temperature with height are the basis for separating the different layers.
1 In the thermosphere, the temperature increases steadily until it reaches a maximum of between $225°C$ and $1,500°C$, depending on solar activity. Above the thermosphere are the exosphere and the magnetosphere, which is influenced by the Earth's magnetic field. The upper limit of the atmosphere lies about 21,750 miles (35,000km) above Earth.
2 The mesosphere is characterized by a rapid decrease in temperature to a minimum of $-100°C$. The ionosphere, extending through both layers **1** and **2**, consists chiefly of ionized atoms and free electrons, which reflect long-wavelength radio waves back to Earth. It contains different layers: D, E, F1 and F2. The upper atmosphere acts as a shield protecting us from meteors, solar electrons, cosmic rays, ultraviolet and X rays.
3 In the stratosphere, temperatures rise to $0°C$ at 30 miles (50km), because ozone here absorbs ultraviolet rays.
4 In the troposphere, temperature falls with height above the warm Earth, to $-60°C$ at a height of 30 miles (50km).
Right The Sun's surface is a region of violent gas flares reaching out into space. In this false colour image, taken by the Solar Max mission, flares can be seen rising high from the solar surface.
Below The Northern Lights above Alaska. Such auroras are the result of increases in solar radiation, when electrons penetrate the magnetosphere and are directed to the poles. Here they collide with atoms in the ionosphere, producing lovely glowing patterns.

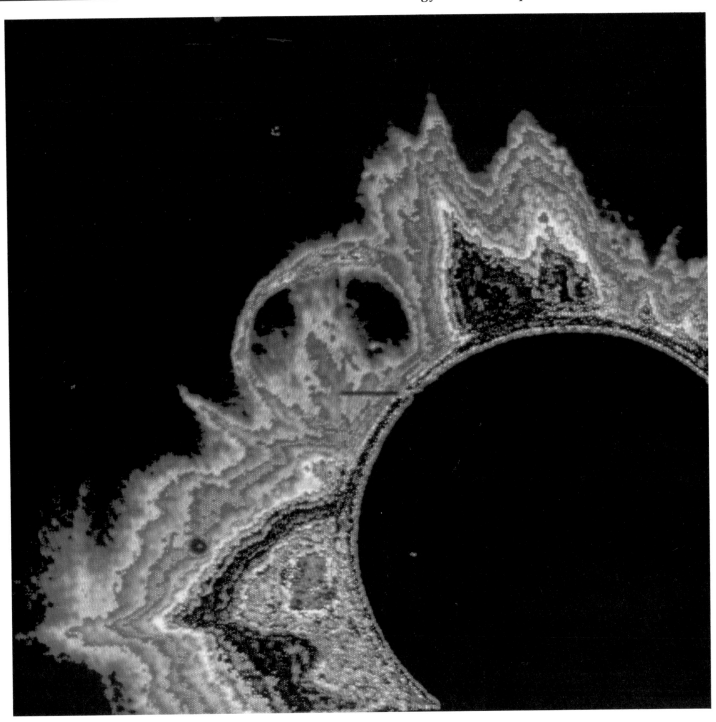

only 283°K (50°F/10°C). Solar radiation is mainly shortwave radiation, and astronomers think that the Sun's output varies. For example, up to twenty times more ultraviolet radiation may be given out by the Sun during a period of maximum sunspot activity.

The amount of energy in the atmosphere changes with the ever-varying distance between the Sun and the Earth. The Earth's orbit around the Sun is not constant: it has changed through geological time (these cyclic variations may partly account for ice ages), and it is slightly eccentric (that is, not perfectly circular). The eccentricity of the Earth's orbit is, however, too small to cause much variation in the amount of energy reaching us from the Sun. The seasonal variations in weather are a result not of the Earth's orbital eccentricity, but of the way in which the planet's axis is tilted in relation to its orbit around the Sun—this tilt is called the 'ecliptic', and varies from 22°-23·5°. This tilt causes the seasonal changes in the amount of solar radiation reaching the Earth,

and hence the weather patterns and differences in the amount of daylight at different times of the year. The height of the Sun in the sky varies with latitude, and at lower latitudes (near the Equator) the heat is more concentrated. Also, the Sun's rays have less atmosphere to pass through here because of the steeper angle at which they fall. At high latitudes, where the Sun's rays strike the Earth at a lower angle than at the Equator, less heat is received. Some energy is absorbed in the complex atmospheric layers, while some is reflected. The degree of reflectivity is called the 'albedo'. Ice and snow, for example, have high albedos (about 90 per cent) while dark rocks, such as dolerite and basalt, and black chernozem soils have an albedo as low as seven per cent. Also, in polar regions, the Sun's rays have to penetrate a greater distance because they strike the Earth at such an oblique angle; combined with their high albedo, this means that the poles receive considerably less solar energy than the rest of the planet, so they remain bound by ice.

The greenhouse effect

Water vapour and carbon dioxide prevent heat escaping from the Earth. They effectively block the loss of heat from within the earth, and of that absorbed by solar radiation. This 'greenhouse' effect is particularly pronounced in some cities. Here, atmospheric pollution creates an excess of carbon dioxide and water vapour which blanket the land. Mexico City, for example, has a particularly dense pollution blanket, because the waste gases produced from thousands of car exhausts and major industrial sites are easily trapped in the bowl-like valley in which the city is situated. Solar heat is easily sandwiched beneath this layer of pollution. Many weather researchers consider the growing impact of the greenhouse effect on the warming of the Earth's climate to be a key issue facing our future.

The greenhouse effect reaches its ultimate limits on the planet Venus, which has an atmosphere ideally suited to capturing heat and not releasing it quickly.

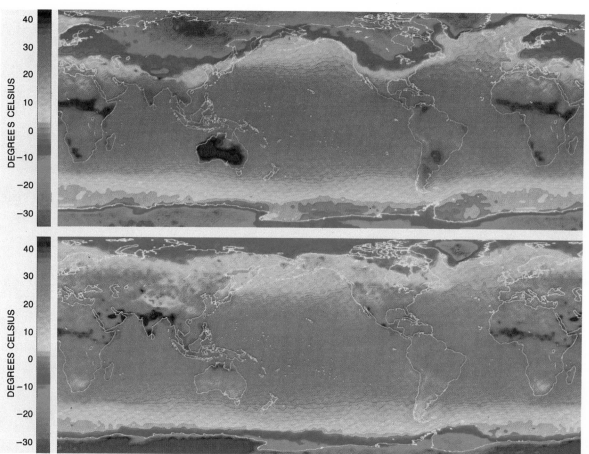

Left These maps of the mean surface temperature of the Earth in January (top) and May (bottom) 1979 were produced from data collected by US weather satellites. They show the temperature gradients between the Equator and poles and between the oceans and continents, which drive the large-scale motion of the Earth's atmosphere.
Right The crew of the US spacecraft Gemini 7 took this photo of the jet stream high above the Middle East. The Red Sea is at the top of the picture, and the Nile left of centre.
Below right A view from the flight-deck window of the US Space Shuttle Columbia of the cloud systems over the Pacific Ocean. A cyclonic cloud system is visible in the centre of the photo.
Below A towering thunder-cloud system, produced by convection cells near the ground, is seen here from above, photographed from the US spacecraft Apollo 9. Such pictures show the complexity of these clouds. This one is over the Amazon Basin, in South America.

The fluid atmosphere is responsible for maintaining the heat energy balance around the surface of the Earth, and the distribution of heat is achieved by the flow of gases which we call wind. It is this constant adjustment of the heat balance that governs day-to-day, and long-term, weather patterns and which determines the zones of the tropics, deserts, temperate and polar regions. The surface of the Earth heats up unequally, causing large masses of air to develop unequal densities. Warm air expands and so has a lower density than cooler air. It will therefore tend to rise relative to the cooler mass, which sinks and spreads out beneath the rising warm air. Since the equatorial regions receive 200 per cent more heat than the poles there is an imbalance, and the excess heat enters into a climatic circulation system which causes equatorial air to move to the poles. As it does so, the irregularities on the surface, such as land-masses and mountain chains, cause friction and produce local variations in what would otherwise be a perfect system.

The intertropical convergence zone
The heat equator, which does not coincide exactly with the geographical Equator, is where the hot, moist, low-density air of the equatorial tropics upsurges in a narrow corridor known as the intertropical convergence zone. As these air-masses encounter cooler air, the water vapour condenses to form towering cumulonimbus thunderclouds which produce the exceptionally heavy tropical rainstorms. Now depleted of much of their moisture, the rising air masses flatten out of the tropical tropopause, at a height of about 12½ miles (20km), and diverge from the Equator and towards the poles, losing heat by radiation to space as they do so. At sea-level the place of the rising warm, moist air is taken by cooler and denser air masses moving in from polar regions.

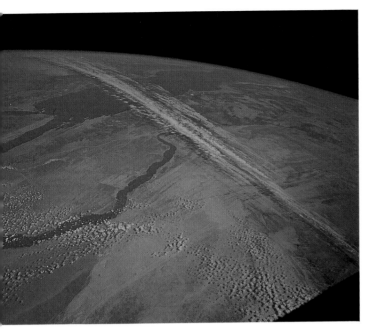

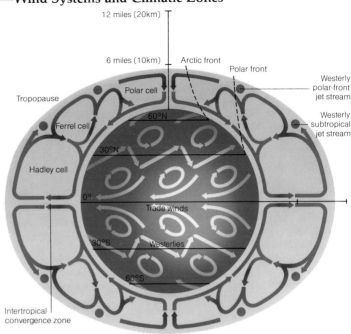

12 miles (20km)

6 miles (10km) Arctic front Polar front

Westerly polar-front jet stream

Westerly subtropical jet stream

Tropopause

Polar cell

60°N

Ferrel cell

30°N

Hadley cell

0°

Trade winds

30°S Westerlies

60°S

Intertropical convergence zone

Below The world's major wind systems result from variations in air pressure caused by the differential heating of the Earth's surface by the Sun, and are influenced by the pattern of the continents and oceans and the rotation of the Earth. Near the surface, winds are usually horizontal, though vertical air movement may occur during periods of turbulence.
☐ Doldrums (calm areas
   Hurricanes/typhoons
   Rain-shadow deserts
→ Westerlies
→ Trade winds
➡ Polar winds
➡ Local winds

Above This model of the global circulation of the atmosphere shows its major components, including the three different types of circulation cell. In the Hadley cells (or trade wind cells) north and south of the Equator, warm air rises, giving up latent heat as its water vapour condenses, and cold air sinks. The middle-latitude Ferrel cells, where cold air rises and warm air sinks, are driven by frictional coupling between the Hadley cells and the weak polar cells. The main mixing of polar and tropical air is at the polar front.

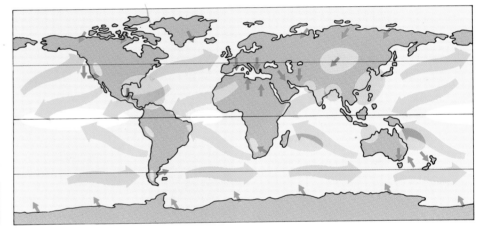

Coriolis force

As the Earth rotates, the Coriolis force causes air-streams moving towards the Equator to be deflected. In the Northern Hemisphere the deflection is clockwise for high-pressure systems and anticlockwise for low-pressure systems. (The converse applies to the Southern Hemisphere). So the cold air-masses streaming towards the Equator are bent westwards, to produce the North-east trade winds north of the Equator, and the South-east trade winds south of the Equator

Circulation cells

At the tropical tropopause the warm air-masses cool as they move polewards and lose energy to space by radiation. At about 30° latitude N and S, air masses have undergone considerable cooling and now sink towards the surface, producing a stable zone of high pressure in the sub-tropical high-pressure zone. Outflow of air to the north produces the westerlies and that to the south the trade winds. The entire circuit, from the Equator to the sub-tropical high pressure zone and back to the Equator is

called the Hadley circulation cell after its discoverer. It is one of a pair which encircle the globe both north and south of the Equator.

In addition to the Hadley cells, there are a pair of Ferrel cells and a pair of polar cells. The Ferrel cells stretch polewards from 30°N and S, where they meet the Hadley cells. Together with the latter, they form a wedge of warm air that moves polewards along the inclined polar front. Two additional fronts, the Arctic and Antarctic fronts, form a division with the polar cells and isolate the disturbed westerlies of the polar front from the large masses of cold air spiralling out from the poles after sinking from the polar tropopause 5½ miles (9km) high.

Jet streams

The polar and subtropical jet streams are narrow bands of wind at high level, moving at up to 300 mph (480 km/hr). They are related to the circulating high- and low-pressure systems that are so common in the temperate zones, whose weather patterns are dominated by the disturbed westerlies. The succession of low-pressure systems across the Northern Hemi-

sphere, associated with unfavourable weather, is controlled by the positions of the polar jet streams.

Doldrums and monsoons

The hot equatorial zone is controlled by the intertropical convergence zone, where heavy precipitation occurs all year round. Associated with this zone are the doldrums of the Atlantic and east Pacific Oceans, and the monsoons of the Indian Ocean. The sub-tropical high pressure zone is marked by aridity, encompassing the desert regions of the world, from where the trade winds originate. The meeting of the Ferrel and polar cells is where the temperate zones occur, characterized by warm summers and cold winters with variable rainfall.

The Antarctic weather system

The vast ocean surrounding Antarctica, uninterrupted by land for over 850 miles (1,370km), constitutes a very stable system, with both strong air and ocean-current circulations. It is virtually independent of atmospheric events that occur elsewhere on Earth.

The rapid collection and organization of data about the weather, which began with the invention of telegraphy, in the mid-1800s, made modern weather forecasting possible. Today, this is increasingly sophisticated, and computers and satellites help to give both long- and short-term forecasts of considerable accuracy. This accuracy depends on the amount of data fed into the system. Details of temperature, humidity and atmospheric pressure are gathered by radiosondes, instruments attached to a large balloon; these send back the information to the ground station. Weather satellites provide scans of the planet which give information on conditions such as cloud cover, and the growth of weather systems.

Two main types of satellites are used. One circles the Earth from pole to pole in an orbit that is fixed relative to a 25° longitude rotation of the Earth for each orbit. This gives a series of scans of successive strips of the rotating planet. The other type of satellite circles the planet over the Equator in the same direction and at the same speed as the Earth. This orbit holds it stationary relative to the ground, giving transmissions of the same place at different times, showing how weather develops. Snow and cloud cover are monitored by infra-red and radar scanners. Radar scans the cloud layer at frequent intervals and produces a time-lapse sequence of cloud movement and the growth and decay of weather systems.

Long-range forecasting

The long-range forecasts which the Weather Bureaux in the USA have issued twice-monthly since the late 1940s as 30-day forecasts are based on statistical methods. A map of the predicted average atmospheric pressure for the coming month is prepared, using current trends and the possible changes in large-scale circulation and the effects of current phenomena such as snow cover. The statistical records for the given locality at that time of year are also considered. The most probable changes in rainfall and temperature are predicted from the map area.

In Britain, the so-called 'analogue method' of long-range forecasting is based on the idea that weather sequences may follow a similar course to earlier ones if the starting conditions are identical. One of the fundamental difficulties of this method is finding a time when conditions were the same as those under investigation. This is the downfall of the method, since no two weather patterns are alike or start in the same way, especially in the medium latitude depression-cursed regions such as north-west Europe. It is common to find, say, six possible analogues for a given month, but the weather sequences which follow them may consist of four cool cloudy periods and two dry warmer months. Many other factors, like sea temperature, need to be taken into account. When all the variables affecting the long-term weather prospect are computed, a reasonable forecast for as long as a month ahead can be made with a high degree of confidence.

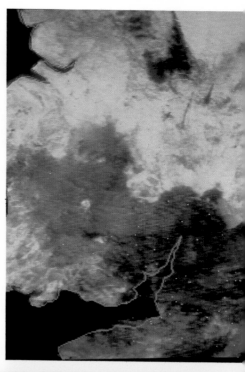

Above Much useful information about daily changes in the weather can be obtained from instruments attached to helium balloons, like this one being made ready for release. Radiosondes are automatic recording devices linked to a radio transmitter; they measure humidity, pressure, temperature and wind patterns when carried aloft by the weather balloon, which is tracked by radar.

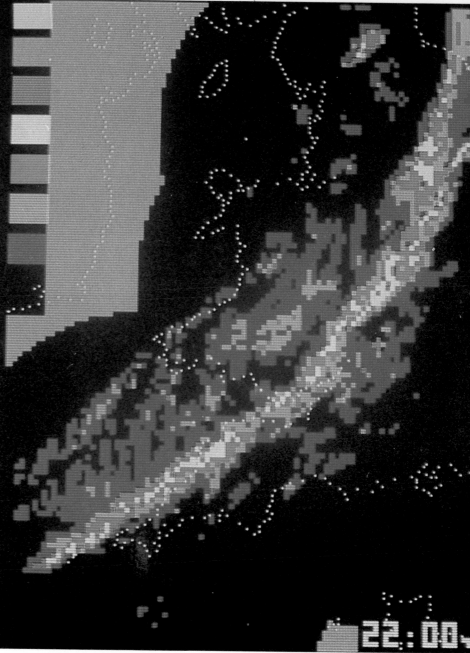

Left This computer-generated map of central Britain was made using infra-red data from the US weather satellite NOAA7. It shows areas of low cloud and fog (red). Such images help forecasters predict future weather more accurately.

Below The satellite reception room at the UK Meteorological Office headquarters at Bracknell, Berkshire.

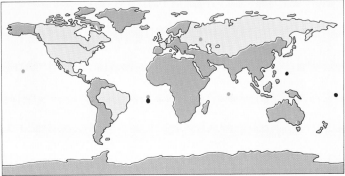

Short-term forecasting

Short-term forecasts giving a daily prediction have for a long while been based on so-called 'synoptic' methods, using maps of pressure and air-mass patterns. Data from many weather stations are used to build up the maps, which, at best, can predict the movement of frontal systems within a few hours. These maps are more successful with some types of weather. For example, the sluggish high-pressure air-masses which may remain over a given region for many days are not difficult to forecast,

once they are established, but the path and velocity of a frontal depression can be very difficult to predict with accuracy.

Numerical methods

Synoptic forecasting was revolutionized by the advent of numerical forecasting methods during the last 15 years. Numerical methods are based on the observation that the rise and fall in surface pressure is affected by convergence or divergence in the higher parts of the atmosphere. Huge amounts of mathematical matter are digested and analysed in order to forecast by this method. A new generation of computers has been developed to handle the data.

International co-operation

The British Meteorological Office collects data from 1,200 land stations, 600 radiosondes and 300 ships. These are spread over the greater part of the Northern Hemisphere. Both the Meteorological Office and the National Weather Service of the USA tend to concentrate on forecasting for their own countries, but their ranges do extend elsewhere, especially through the use of satellite surveillance of cloud systems. The World Weather Service is a unique co-operative venture between over 100 nations of the world. Its meteorological reports are co-ordinated in Geneva, Switzerland. Observers at sites such as airports and coastguard stations, together with those at universities and other scientific institutions, report continuously to a central analysis unit. Time barriers are removed by a standardized data format, and the main analysis centres in Melbourne, Moscow and Washington DC issue regional maps to many minor stations. This information is then used for daily forecasts in the media. More specialized forecasts are also prepared, for aviation, shipping, agriculture and industry.

Above The map shows details of two major projects by the Global Atmospheric Research Programme (GARP): GATE (GARP Atlantic Tropical Experiment, 1974) used 13 specially equipped air-craft, 39 ships and weather satellites to collect data over one-third of the tropical belt. In FGGE (First GARP Global Experiment, 1979) packages of instruments were parachuted from aircraft or sent up in balloons to collect data. Such experiments are designed to improve numerical weather forecasting.

Key to map
Nations involved
● Drop-sonde system
● Balloon bases
● World meteorological centres

Left At 22.00 hours on 2 May 1982, a cold front lay across the UK. This radar image shows the exact position of the front.

Right Using average values of such atmospheric variables as pressure, temperature and wind speed measured worldwide, the European Centre for Medium Range Weather Forecasts generated this computer image of predicted global cloud cover.

Clouds are formed when condensation takes place on a large scale in the atmosphere. Warm air is able to hold within it more moisture than cool air. This means that clouds develop when the air is chilled below the temperature at which the relative humidity (a measure of the degree of saturation of the air with water vapour) is 100 per cent. This is referred to as the 'dew point'. Cooling is usually produced by the lifting of the air which may result from the presence of mountains, which force it to ascend; by the collision of two air masses—one colder and thus denser than the other—at a front; or by local heating. Local heating occurs when a patch of ground becomes hotter than the surrounding terrain because of differences of colour or nature, warms the air next to it by conduction, and then this less dense air rises, often as a plume or a set of discrete bubbles, a few hundred yards in extent.

Condensation nuclei

As soon as the relative humidity reaches 100 per cent, water vapour condenses onto tiny particles (condensation nuclei) suspended in the air. These are about one-thousandth of a millimetre (one micrometre) in size, or even smaller. Most of them are produced by wind-erosion over the land (clays, silicates), industrial processes (acid droplets), or the bursting of air bubbles at the ocean surface (sea-salt). The concentrations of these particles which are activated to become cloud droplets range from about 50 per cu cm in very pure air to 5,000 per cu cm in heavily polluted air.

Lapse rates

In order for a tall cloud to form, the air, once it has started rising, must continue to do so. This can happen only if the rising air remains warmer (less dense) than its surroundings as it moves upwards. Thus the relative values of the lapse rates (decrease in temperature with altitude) in the rising air and the environment through which it is moving become crucial in determining whether or not it continues to ascend for a long way. The environment lapse-rate depends upon the location, the season and the general meteorological situation. The lapse rate within the rising air can be calculated from thermodynamical theory and in the absence of cloud is close to 2°F (1°C) for every 330ft (100m) of ascent; once clouds have formed in the air the lapse rate is reduced because the cooling effect is opposed by the release of latent heat during condensation. So the atmosphere is unstable—conducive to the formation of deep clouds—when the environmental lapse-rate exceeds that of rising cloud-free air.

Cloud formation

As the cloudy air ascends, the droplets grow rapidly by condensation until they achieve sizes of about ten micrometres. Airborne sampling of the cloud shows that at this stage the droplets are of a wide range of sizes, due mainly to the differing sizes of the soluble nuclei upon which they condensed, and the dilution of the cloud by outside air. This mixing process—entrainment—occurs most efficiently at the vigorously growing summit of the cloud. The fall velocity of the nuclei is roughly proportional to the square of their size, and thus the larger ones overtake the smaller. Although the airflow around the larger drops tends to carry the smaller ones with it, prohibiting contact, some collisions do

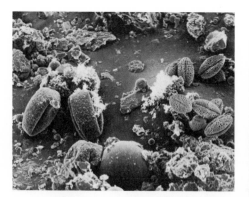

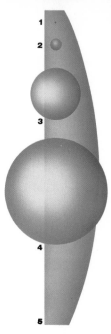

Above Atmospheric dust magnified 400 times by a scanning electron microscope. It includes pollen grains (rounded objects; the smooth sphere, centre, is grass pollen), soot and 'dirt' particles.
Left The diagram shows the comparative sizes of the particles involved in raindrop formation.
1 A typical condensation nucleus (e.g. sea salt): 1/1,000mm (1μ) diameter.
2 A typical cloud droplet; it falls about 10,000 times as fast as a condensation nucleus.
3 A large cloud droplet; this falls about 25 times as fast as the typical droplet.
4 This particle is on the borderline between cloud droplet and raindrop.
5 A typical raindrop; it falls about 650 times as fast as a typical cloud droplet.

occur, resulting in the production of an even larger drop, falling faster through the smaller ones, and therefore sweeping them out more rapidly. This process of growth by collision and coalescence is weak compared with condensation for droplet sizes less than about 20 micrometres, but rapidly becomes dominant for larger sizes. These two processes acting together, in tropical clouds or other clouds which do not contain ice, are able to produce raindrops—several millimetres in size—within 20 or 40 minutes of cloud formation. This corresponds to a size increase of about ten thousand, or a mass increase of a million million! If, as often happens, the cloudy air rises above the 32°F (0°C) isotherm, the cloud droplets remain in the liquid state—supercooled—until much lower temperatures have been reached. (An isotherm is an imaginary line joining all points at the same temperature). Freezing is difficult to initiate in small volumes of water because it involves the creation, within a drop, of an embryonic ice crystal, of unique configuration, which is delicate and highly susceptible to bombardment and destruction by adjacent water molecules. Freezing of cloud droplets is thus a statistical process not governed by a unique temperature, and the freezing of cloud droplets occurs steadily throughout the temperature range 5°F to −31°F (−15°C to −35°C). The release of latent heat of freezing provides a 'buoyancy boost' to the upward-moving air which is less than that occurring at the cloud-base as a result of condensation, in part because it is intrinsically smaller, and also because it is spread out over a vertical distance of several miles.

Left Clouds and fog over the Alps. Fog is common in the morning in valleys as moist air cools by radiation near the cold ground at night. The air is cooled below its dew point, so some of the invisible water vapour it contains condenses to form water droplets, which make up the fog. Clouds are formed in a similar way when rising air cools.
Right Mammae (from the Latin for 'breasts') are sometimes seen hanging down from storm clouds.
Below This is not a flying saucer, but an odd-shaped altocumulus cloud in North Wales.

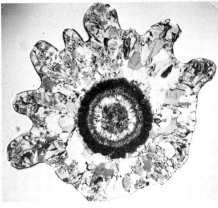

Left Cumulus (on the horizon) and altocumulus clouds off Dinas Island, Pembrokeshire, Wales.
Right This cross-section of a hailstone shows its alternate layers of clear, and opaque ice. The clear layers are formed as the falling hailstone collects water so quickly that it cannot be frozen straight away, but forms a 'skin' of water which later forms transparent ice.
Below Hail formation is associated with the towering clouds of a thunderstorm like this one.

Hail, rain and snow

When an ice crystal is formed inside the rising cloud it grows by condensation substantially faster than the neighbouring droplets. The ice crystals 'feed' on the supercooled droplets and grow in regular crystalline form—assuming shapes which depend upon their temperature—until they are large enough to fall rapidly relative to the droplets, which freeze onto the ice crystal as soon as they are overtaken and captured. This is the initial stage in the growth of hailstones. As the embryonic hailstone collects more and more supercooled drops, it loses its crystalline form and falls faster. In tall clouds with vigorous vertical convection currents, the hailstones are tossed up and down for several minutes, until they are heavy enough to fall to the ground. They may collect water so rapidly that it cannot be frozen immediately. When this 'water skin' does freeze, it forms a transparent shell of ice, contrasting with the opaque ones produced when the collection rate is lower. Alternation of these two regimes of growth gives rise to the characteristic 'onion structure' of hail. One of the largest hailstones known is one recorded in China that weighed 10lb (4·6kg); another that fell in the USA was 17in (43cm) in diameter!

Of the various forms of precipitation involving particles large enough to fall out of the cloud and survive the journey to ground, rain is formed by condensation, by coalescence, or by the melting of snowflakes; hail by the vapour growth of ice-crystals followed by the accumulation, or 'accretion', of supercooled droplets; and snow by the agglomeration of ice crystals. The delicate, classically elegant shapes of snowflakes are a consequence of their journey through a range of temperatures within the cloud where they were born.

Cloud types

The deepest, most vigorous convective clouds produce heavy precipitation and lightning. Shallower clouds undergo only some of the processes involved in the storm clouds. The high-level cirrus clouds are composed entirely of small ice crystals, while medium-level, non-precipitating cumulus clouds are made up of water droplets. Stratus clouds, which cover great distances horizontally, generally contain ice and water. They have low updraught speeds and sometimes do not release precipitation, though on other occasions they may produce rain steadily for many hours, bringing to the ground an enormous quantity of water. There are many permutations and hybrids of these various basic types of cloud.

Two forms of lightning are commonly recognized. Forked lightning passes between the cloud and the ground, while sheet lightning occurs completely within the cloud. If we could see the flash responsible for 'sheet lightning, it would look exactly the same as forked lightning, except that it passes between two regions of a thundercloud instead of to the ground. The different appearance of sheet lightning is entirely due to the flash itself being obscured by the intervening cloud. Both forms are due to a thundercloud being charged with positive electricity at the top and negative electricity at the bottom. On the ground, a moving carpet of positive electric charge is induced, which follows beneath the drifting cloud. Over high points, such as buildings, aerials or trees, its effects are greatly intensified, and point-discharge may release positive ions. Although the proportion of flashes within clouds varies seasonally and in different places, over the Earth as a whole three-quarters of all flashes are internal.

Anatomy of a lightning flash
A discharge to ground is initiated by the enormous difference in electrical potential between the Earth and the cloud, which is of the order of 100 million volts. A total discharge, called a flash, lasts about one-fifth of a second, and consists of one or more intermittent discharges, called strokes, producing a faintly luminous phase lasting for several milliseconds, at intervals of some tens of milliseconds (one millisecond = one thousandth of a second). It is because the eye can just perceive the individual strokes that lightning appears to flicker.

Physicists believe that each lightning stroke to ground begins in the cloud as a local discharge between the negatively charged region and a small positive charge near its base. This frees electrons and forms a conductive channel along which they travel, neutralizing the small positive charge and continuing towards the ground as a stepped 'leader' stroke. This moves from cloud to ground in a succession of steps, each lasting less than a microsecond (one millionth of a second), at intervals of about 50 microseconds. It is these which give lightning its zig-zag appearance. In this way, the negative charge from the cloud moves continuously towards the ground, rapidly extending an electrically conductive path through the non-conductive air along which the return stroke can flow. This is a discharge which leaps upwards from the earth, usually from a high point, for the stepped leader rapidly enhances the positive charge on the surface as it approaches the ground. When the two discharges meet, a conducting channel to earth is established. The conducting channel becomes brilliantly luminous as the result of the return stroke, and it is this which we see as lightning as it moves upwards at one-tenth to half the speed of light. This is so fast that the entire channel appears to become bright instantaneously, obscuring the relatively weak luminosity of the stepped leader.

The sound of thunder
Thunder results from the passage of a return stroke, since the enormous surge of current through a channel, of which the conducting core is only a few inches wide, heats the air to incredible temperatures, estimated at about 30,000° Kelvin. This increases the pressure in the channel so that the air expands with supersonic speed, and produces a shock wave that becomes the thunder we hear.

Below A typical thunderstorm cloud is tall and top-heavy, white above but with an ominous grey base. Thunderstorms occur during periods of instability, usually when a cold front moves in after a long hot spell. In some tropical areas, thunderstorms occur on over 200 days a year.

Right A high-speed photograph shows how an apparently single lightning flash is in fact made up of a series of separate strokes. The time scale involved is measured in thousandths of a second. Lightning appears to flicker because the eye can just see the separate strokes.

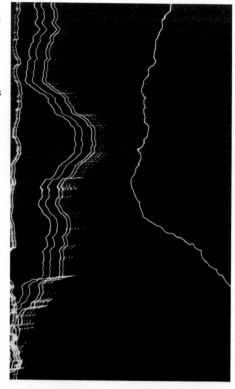

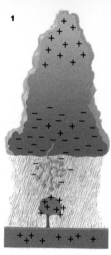 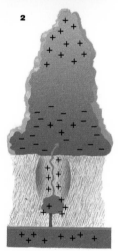 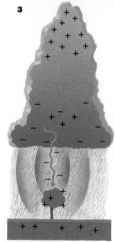

Left Diagram shows how lightning strikes.
1 Positive and negative electrical charges become separated at top and bottom of a thundercloud. The mainly negative charge at the base induces a positive charge on the ground and a huge voltage builds up. Next, a weak stepped leader stroke passes from the cloud, seeking the path of least resistance to earth.
2 A much more powerful return stroke leaps up, following the same path, creating shock waves we hear as thunder.
3 The process is repeated until the difference in charge is neutralized.

How lightning starts
In recent years, scientists have made considerable efforts to try and discover the mechanism responsible for triggering of a lightning discharge. They know that to cause an electrical breakdown of dry air at ground-level pressure and temperature, an electrical field of about 3,000 volts per millimetre is necessary. The largest fields observed in a thundercloud have been a mere 400 volts or so per millimetre, suggesting that the breakdown must be due to particles present in the cloud. The most likely sources of electrical discharge, or 'corona', leading to lightning appears to be the surface of a large ice particle or a pair of colliding raindrops. Experiments have shown that with hailstones or snow crystals, the onset of a corona is particularly dependent upon pressure, temperature, the shape of the particle and the presence of small-scale surface features upon it. In the case of melting hailstones, the skin of water provides a stretchable surface which the electric field can draw out into points and so produce a corona, even if the field is as low as 400 volts per millimetre. In the case of colliding raindrops, a long liquid filament may be drawn out between them as they separate, which may measure several times the diameter of the larger drop.

Since this filament is approximately parallel to the electric field, the shape of the pair of raindrops is particularly likely to produce a corona. Researchers have found that the lowest electrical field in which a corona occurs is 250 volts per millimetre. Lightning may be triggered by coronas from ice particles or colliding raindrops, processes which should probably be regarded as complementary rather than exclusive to each other. In some clouds one or other of these mechanisms may predominate, and this will depend upon the height of the cloud base, the nature and concentration of precipitation present, and other factors.

Difficulties of interpretation
Despite their intensive efforts over the past 25 years, scientists have still not been able to identify the exact mechanism or mechanisms responsible for thundercloud electrification. Aircraft and other means of exploring thunderstorms are unsatisfactory for a number of reasons, the most important being the difficulty of obtaining truly representative data. A thundercloud has a volume of perhaps a hundred cubic kilometres and a lifetime of about an hour. Its properties vary enormously in space and time, yet an aeroplane can pass

Below Spectacular displays of lightning can occur during volcanic eruptions, as here when the new island of Surtsey arose from beneath the waves off Iceland in 1963. The lightning is caused by the build-up of electrostatic charges resulting from friction between dust particles.

Right The intricate pattern of the many forks of a stepped leader stroke is beautifully captured in this photograph, taken with a long exposure. Analysis of photographs, spectroscopic data and acoustic energy spectra help meteorologists understand lightning better.

only five or six times through the cloud during the latter's brief life, and then only along a single line at a particular altitude. For this reason, cloud scientists cannot be confident that the limited information they obtain tells the full story. Nevertheless, a pattern is beginning to emerge, and there is increasing evidence in favour of the theory that the transfer of electrical charge leading to the growth of strong fields—culminating in lightning—results from differences in electrical potential between the surfaces of hailstones and the much smaller ice crystals with which they collect. The crystals become positively charged and the hailstones negatively charged, and as they separate under the influence of gravity, the cloud acquires the observed positive/negative polarity.

Ghostly glows and fiery balls

A luminous glow is often seen at night from the tops of ships' masts, the horns of cattle and even the upper extremities of people when electrified clouds are overhead. This ghostly apparition is commonly known as 'St Elmo's fire', and has sometimes been wrongly reported as a form of lightning. It is, in fact, a corona discharge. The 'flames' may be many inches long and are often accompanied by audible crackling noises.

Although accounts vary widely, most reports about so-called 'ball lightning' mention one or more of the following characteristics: a spherical 'fireball' of a diameter between about ½in (1cm) and 6½ft (2m) descending from, or in the region of, a thunderstorm, occurring simultaneously with or following immediately after a lightning stroke to ground; a white, red, yellow or blue colour; a persistence time of several seconds, during which it may pulsate or be quiescent; a sudden extinction, sometimes accompanied by an explosion or a popping noise and a sulphurous smell; a tendency to follow electrically conducting paths, such as telegraph wires; and a great propensity to enter rooms through chimneys and leave under doors or vice-versa. There is no generally accepted explanation for ball lightning.

Enormous spiral atmospheric vortices, each with a diameter of some 20,000 miles (32,000km), swing outwards from the poles. Embedded in these are smaller cyclonic and anti-cyclonic weather systems, with diameters of about 6,000 miles (9,650km). These smaller spirals produce the mid-latitude storms, winter rains and snow of the temperate regions. The cyclonic spirals swirl in an anti-clockwise direction in the Northern Hemisphere (clockwise south of the Equator) as a result of the Coriolis force. The air in these spirals is a mixture of different temperatures and humidities, as it is sucked in from different areas. A very sharp transition exists between the parts of the cyclone which are cold dry air and those made of warmer moist air. The cold air pushes below the warmer air along a cold front. A warm front develops where the warm air is pushed against the cold air on its leading edge. During its development the cold front overtakes the warm one, in a process known as 'occlusion'. Weather associated with cold fronts is characterized by torrential rainfall in short bursts from towering cumulo-nimbus clouds. Warm fronts produce a series of clouds of increasing thickness, from thin, high, wispy cirrus to the eventual prolonged, rain-bringing nimbostratus. The occlusion stage is characterized by continuous rain falling from thick banks of nimbostratus, which form in the warm air above the cold, ground-hugging layer.

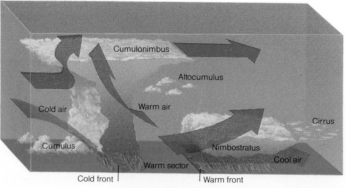

Above Cross-section through a depression. A cold front occurs at the leading edge of a mass of cold air as it undercuts and replaces a slower-moving mass of warm air, forcing the latter to rise, in the process known as occlusion. This is associated with periods of heavy rainfall and sometimes thunderstorms.
Right The rapidly rotating vortex of air and water droplets that form a tornado is seen as a column rising to the clouds. This tornado hit Osnabrook, N Dakota, USA, in 1978.

Right Colour Doppler radar is used to help monitor tornadoes in the USA, producing images such as this one. The different colours relate to the movements of hailstones and raindrops within a thunderstorm. Meteorologists can use the radar images to help identify conditions that are capable of producing a tornado almost half an hour before it forms, providing a valuable early-warning system.

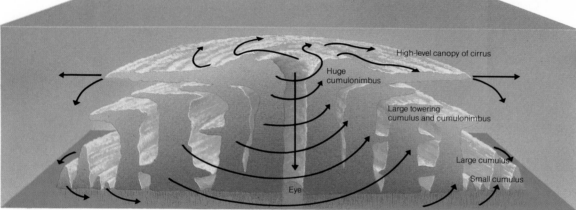

Hurricanes

Tropical cyclones or hurricanes are amazingly energetic. This power is derived from hot moisture-laden air of the tropical oceans when the moisture is released as condensation. The unstable air, which reaches as far up as the subtropical jet-stream, is a major factor in their formation. Here, convection lifts damp air, producing clouds and generating heat. The air spirals inwards towards the 'eye' of the hurricane to replace the rising air and rapidly the spiral increases in speed as it narrows. The whirlpool of air is topped by thin cirrus clouds wisping out in the opposite direction to the main direction of the storm.

Recent research suggests that rather than convection cells, pre-existing disturbances may be the main cause of hurricane development. Few of these disturbances actually reach hurricane proportions. A high-level outflow of air in the upper troposphere may be the most important factor involved. This allows the formation of a very low pressure cell with high winds near the surface. Hurricanes move at about 20 mph (32km/hr), their movement being controlled by the speed of the warm core. After the initial disturbance, the low-pressure tropical depression

may develop into a tropical storm, with wind speeds of up to 70mph (113km/hr), and eventually into a full-blooded hurricane.

At latitudes of about 30° N and S, hurricanes become trapped in the prevailing westerlies and are swept landwards. Their erratic and unpredictable paths add to the danger of these storms, which is greatest in coastal regions before they die over the land, from where they are unable to gain moisture and energy.

Tornadoes

Tornadoes are rapidly rotating vortices of air extending from the cloud-base to the land. They develop in regions of unstable air and high humidity when heat is released due to condensation. Low-level air is dragged inwards to fill the base of the violent updraft and storm conditions produced. The low-pressure system thus formed contains air which is cooled to its dew point and a low-level wall of cloud is formed. A whirlwind funnel of water droplets carries dust and debris from the ground with terrifying force.

The USA experiences over 100 detected tornadoes each year. Radar finds the great majority of these. Most last only a few minutes,

Above This cross section through a hurricane shows the directions of wind motion and development of different cloud types. A strong updraught around the central calm, cloud-free 'eye' produces huge towering thunderclouds, from which issue forth lightning and a deluge of rain. The hurricane increases in speed and energy as air spirals in and rushes down the eye to replace the rising air. The wind speed at ground level increases towards the centre of the hurricane until it reaches over 100mph (160km/hr) near the core. The entire system ranges from 60 miles (100km) to 1,000 miles (1,600km) in diameter.
Right This photo of Hurricane Ellen was taken by the second Skylab mission over the Atlantic Ocean on 20 September 1973. The calm 'eye' is at the centre of the swirling, turbulent spiral of clouds.

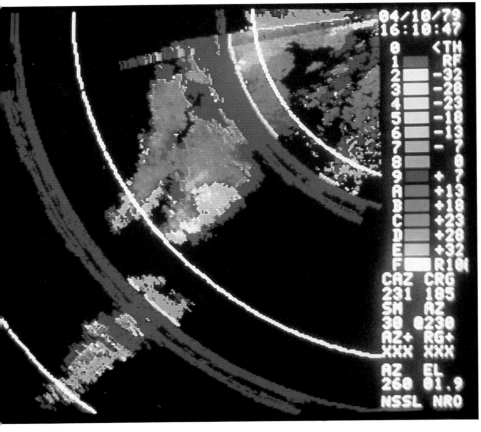

Above Passers-by in the Costa Brava, Spain, seem unperturbed by a water-spout which appeared on 2 September 1965. Water-spouts can capsize a small boat, especially when they suddenly collapse.

Below When hot, rising air, swirling over dry, barren surfaces, is able to pick loose sand and dust off the ground, a dust devil may form, as here, at Amboseli, in Kenya, East Africa.

though some may have a long life-cycle and travel great distances, creating much havoc. The wind speed in the centre may be as much as 370 mph (600km per hr) and the updraft can exceed 150 mph (240km per hr), sufficient to toss cars into the air.

Tornadoes occur in Japan, Australia and Europe as well as in North America.

Waterspouts and dust devils

Waterspouts and dust devils are allied to tornadoes. They are both structurally similar to tornadoes but their velocity is much lower and they do not generally create such widespread damage. Waterspouts are freaky columns of water dragged from the sea surface where strong vertical air movements within large cumulus clouds create a vortex. Smooth sea conditions are associated with the most spectacular waterspouts, which have been known to smash ships apart, simply through the tonnage of water which they contain and suddenly release. Dust devils are formed when hot rapidly rising air collects loose material from the ground. Dust can be picked up to a height of several tens of yards to swirl menacingly over the land surface.

There is a store of geological evidence which proves that places on the Earth which now have, for example, hot dry climates have been covered with ice in the distant past. In Africa and South America, geologists have found great thicknesses of glacial deposits. Other evidence includes marks made by glaciers on rock surfaces, and glacial erratics—boulders carried along by the moving ice. All these features are evidence that these areas, now at much lower latitudes, lay near the South Pole during the Permian and Carboniferous periods. At this time, areas such as North America and Western Europe, now at cool-temperate latitudes, were partly covered by tropical rain-forests. Climatic changes of this nature are the result of the continuing drifting of the continents around the Earth's surface rather than changes in the amount of heat or precipitation at any one place over a relatively short time.

The output of radiation from the Sun is far from constant. Only recently, with observations from spacecraft, such as Solar Max, has it been possible to show accurately how the Sun's output varies in detail. Daily variations of 0.2 per cent have been measured, and there is evidence to suggest that the Sun's output is about 0.5 per cent less when sunspot activity is at a minimum. Though these effects are not really large enough to affect the weather directly, the cycle of solar activity does seem to correlate with theories suggesting that climate is influenced by sunspot activity.

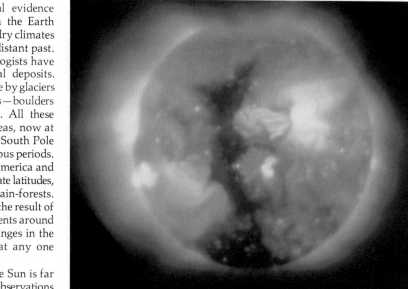

Sunspots and climate

Sunspot activity has been monitored from Earth for many years, but recently spacecraft such as Skylab and Solar Max have studied this phenomenon in more detail, unhindered by the Earth's atmosphere. As they evolve, sunspots may give rise to violent flares. As gaps develop in the Sun's heat envelope, possibly influenced by reversals in the Suns' magnetic field, sunspots and flares appear. This happens with remarkable regularity, every 11 years. Flares up to 5 million miles (8 million km) high burst out, releasing energized particles with short ultra-violet radiation wavelengths. Compared with the Sun's surface, which has a temperature of about 6,000°K, sunspots, with temperatures of about 4,200°K, are relatively cool, and

appear almost black. Events such as these solar flares can change the Sun's output enough to influence the Earth's climate, over thousands, if not hundreds, of years—in other words over very short periods in terms of geological time. The orbit of the Solar System around our great spiral galaxy takes the Earth and Sun through vast clouds of interstellar dust and gas. When absorbed by the Sun, the particles in these clouds promote dramatic bursts in output of solar energy; at the same time the dust may screen the Earth from radiation. The Earth's axis has varied in its tilt from its current 23·5° by up to 2° during the last 25,000 years. High angles may be responsible for severe winter conditions and ice ages. The eccentricity of the Earth's orbit around the Sun undergoes changes every 85,000 years or so. When the Earth is nearest to the Sun, the radiation it receives can be seven per cent greater than at the most distant point. When this is combined with the varying angle of the axis, the incoming radiation may vary by up to 20 per cent.

Short-term climatic changes

Apart from influences due directly to the radiation received by the Earth, the composition of the atmosphere, which is changing, may

have a short-term influence on climate. The heat budget of the troposphere is influential here, and in the last 80 years the proportion of carbon dioxide in the upper air has increased by up to 12 per cent, resulting in the 'greenhouse effect'. This has led to an increase in heat absorption by the atmosphere, warming the lower regions by as much as ½°F. The sea, acting as a gigantic heat-sink, also influences climate. For example, the extreme period of cold experienced in north-west Europe in the 17th century may have been produced by instability in the atmosphere caused, in turn, by changing ocean-atmosphere relationships.

Ice ages

The most fascinating climatic changes, and possibly the most important in terms of their effect on life on Earth in the near future, are those concerned with glaciation. Countless millions of people live today where only a few thousand years ago the land was burdened with thick ice sheets and glaciers. Since their last major retreat, fluctuations have occurred in the weather which lead some glaciologists and climatologists to predict a future ice advance of such proportions that much of the area covered by the last glaciation would again be buried

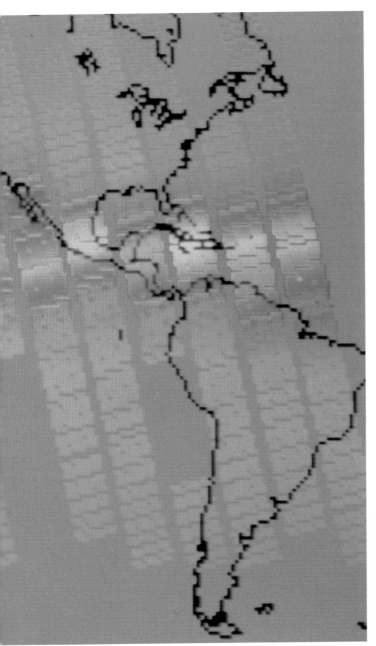

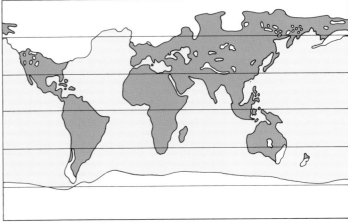

Above The map shows the extent of ice (white) over the continents 18,000 years ago, at the height of the last ice age, when the northern regions of North America, Europe and Asia lay under a thick layer of ice.

There have been several major ice ages during the history of the Earth. An ice age occurs as continents slowly drift to high latitudes where snow can build up into ice sheets. It could also result from overall cooling.

Below Huge fires lift dust and water vapour high into the atmosphere, often affecting climate. Sunlight is cut out and the land cools. Forest fires in Australia are seen here from Apollo 7, some 150 miles (240km) above ground.

beneath the ice. As well as solid geological evidence in the form of glacially deposited sediments and other effects on the landscape, there is a wealth of biological evidence to show how climate has fluctuated over the last few thousand years. Assemblages of plant fossils, including pollen, give good clues as to climates in the past.

Different plants are characteristic of the increasingly temperate conditions that follow a glacial retreat. Study of insects, such as beetles, gives similar clues to the post-glacial climatic details. In the oceans live tiny one-celled animals called foraminiferans which secrete shells of calcium carbonate. The abundance of the two isotopes of oxygen O^{16} and O^{18} in the calcite of these shells is related to the temperature of that sea water. The study of deep-sea cores containing fossil foraminiferans throws much light on the climatic fluctuations during the last ice age. For example, researchers have shown that the surface water of the Atlantic fluctuated by 10°F (6°C). During the glacial stages, the bottom waters of the eastern equatorial Atlantic grew colder by up to 4°F (2°C). Climatologists have observed a fair measure of correlation between these cores and the glacial deposits found on land.

Recent climatic changes

In Northern Europe details of climatic changes over the last 3,000 years are well documented, and some of the causes are also known. About 7,000 to 5,000 years ago, the so-called Flandrian optimum, with a mean temperature 4°F (2°C) above present, occurred. Between 1,000 and 700 years ago, another climatic optimum existed, separated from the earlier one by a 'sub-boreal' cold phase. The Little Ice Age occurred between 450 to 150 years ago (AD 1550-1850) and has been attributed to reduced solar activity. Between 1650 and 1715 practically no sunspots were visible, and astronomers believe that the sunspot cycle virtually stopped at this time. This was first pointed out by an astronomer called Maunder during the 19th Century. Called the 'Maunder minimum' after him, this lack of sunspot activity has been associated with periods of colder than average climate, and is often put forward as the reason for the Little Ice Age. Also, 22-year recurrent droughts in the high plains of western USA have been shown to coincide with even-numbered solar cycles. Since the cold of the Little Ice Age, we have enjoyed a climatic optimum up to about 1950, but since then there has been a deterioration in our overall climate.

Predicting future ice ages

The possibility that an overall astronomical control is exerted on the Earth's climate has fascinated many scientists. In 1911, the Yugoslav geophysicist Milutin Milankovitch began to work out a mathematical model which he hoped would explain the climate not only of the Earth, but also of Venus and Mars for the past and future. Explaining the ice ages was his prime concern. After 30 years of climatic calculations during which he considered the axial tilt and orbital eccentricity of the planets, he was able to give his account of the way in which he thought ice-sheets responded to changes in the output of solar radiation. Milankovitch's theories were met mainly with scepticism by geologists until, in 1976, deep-sea-drilling in the Indian Ocean proved that they were essentially correct, on the evidence of a study of the isotopes of oxygen in fossil shells. This oxygen analysis shows that the ice advanced in a cycle, starting 100,000 years ago, then 43,000, 24,000 and 19,000 years ago. This matches closely the astronomical cycles proposed by Milankovitch: orbital eccentricity 100,000 yrs, axial tilt 41,000 yrs, precession 24,000 yrs and 19,000 yrs. From research such as this, future ice ages may be predicted.

We know of the life forms of the past because a handful of the former inhabitants of our planet have been preserved, usually as fragments of bone or shell, in the rock layers of the Earth's crust. The so-called 'fossil record' is a sparse reminder of the multitude of beautiful plants and animals which have swum in the oceans or lived on the land. Far back in the mists of Pre-Cambrian time, primitive organisms

such as *Medusina mawsoni* (left), from the famous Ediacara Hills of Australia, lived in the seas. All that is left is this flattened disc. To appreciate fossils fully it is necessary always to think of them as the remains of organisms which were once alive, and not just as strange shapes in the rocks. Palaeontologists are the naturalists of the past, reconstructing the ecologies and habitats of the Earth as it was millions of years ago.

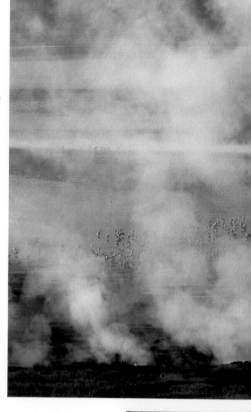

FOSSILS AND EVOLUTION

From traces of primaeval bacteria to remains of the first humans, fossils are studied by palaeontologists as they help to unravel the complex story of life's evolution

There is great biological uniformity among the amazing variety of organisms which live on the Earth. Two main types of macro-molecules, the nucleic acids and the proteins, exist in cells which are bounded by membranes. Living organisms have a highly ordered structure, respond to and take energy from the environment, and can reproduce, giving their offspring the information they need to survive. Some of these characteristics are not unique to living organisms, but most non-living systems are without them. Characteristics such as these are difficult, if not impossible, to detect in fossil material from the distant Pre-Cambrian Era, and it is not easy to suggest when life first stirred in freshwater pools or primitive seas. The petrified remains and impressions of unmistakably living organisms, very like some present-day algae and microbes, are present in remarkably old rocks.

When life appeared on the Earth, conditions were very different from those of today. The early atmosphere was 'anoxic', containing nitrogen, hydrogen sulphide, ammonia, methane and carbon dioxide, but lacking oxygen. The gases it contained were probably produced by volcanic activity in the turbulent early crust. Oxygen, abundant in our life-support system today, has become abundant through the photosynthesis of green plants. This gas, needed for the survival of most of the Earth's present inhabitants, is the last thing that pre-biological chemical systems required in order to grow molecules big enough to form living cells. Molecular oxygen would combine with any proto-organic molecules and quickly destroy them before they could interact and produce complex living cells. Other early requirements, besides the lack of oxygen, were the appropriate chemicals (likely to have occurred in volcanic rocks and gases) and water. The first rains had fallen on Earth very soon after the crust consolidated, if not during that process. Given enough time, the chemistry of life could develop in these conditions, and time, of the unimaginable

proportions which Earth scientists have to deal with, allows for the inevitable happening of seemingly improbable events. In these terms, it did not take too long from the formation of the Earth until the first living cells—possibly, about 1,000 million years.

Primeval soup

Even though organic monomers (simple molecules) have been found in meteorites, and some scientists have argued in favour of an extra-terrestrial origin of life, a more plausible theory is that they formed from inorganic chemicals on the primitive Earth. To prove that this could have happened, a now-famous and beautifully simple experiment (which has been repeated many times, even in schools) was set up by the American Stanley Miller in 1953. He simulated the Earth's early atmosphere and through this pre-biotic gas a spark was discharged, representing electrical storms. The products were collected in water. After only a week, not millions of years, a 'soup' containing many organic compounds had been produced. These included amino acids, the building-blocks of life from which proteins are made. Though by no means alive, these are the notes of the music of life. Variations on this original theme have been played by other scientists; using, instead of sparks, heat, ultra-violet light, and the particles from radio-active decay, all manner of organic compounds have been made. Volcanic craters bring to the surface hot metallic carbides which, like the meteorites, contain organic monomers. Life may even have begun underground! Research by S.W. Fox, subjecting amino acids to the kind of dry heat of volcanic eruptions, caused them to link up to form 'proteinoids', which, when put in water, enveloped themselves in a boundary layer, like a cell wall. No-one has yet put chemicals into a test-tube and seen something crawl out of the end, but, given time, inorganic chemists may yet manage to discover the way to produce life.

Above Life on Earth probably first stirred in the chemically-rich pools produced by volcanic upheavals on the primitive planet's surface. Similar places exist today, but the air is now rich in oxygen. When living cells first drifted through the volcanic springs, sulphurous and ammonia-rich mixes filled the air. Here hot springs in Kenya mimic life's first home.
Right In Hamelin Pool, Shark Bay, north-west Australia, stromatolites flourish today.

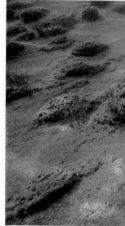

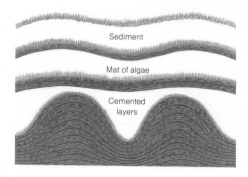

Sediment

Mat of algae

Cemented layers

Above Stages in the growth of a stromatolite: the algae trap sediment; as it accumulates, it becomes cemented into a solid mass.

Right The layered form of a stromatolite, built by blue-green algae secreting a cushion of lime, is well seen in this Ordovician fossil.

The earliest signs of life

By looking at the scanty Pre-Cambrian fossil record, it seems that living cells first developed about 3,800 million to 4,000 million years ago, in the anoxic fluids warmed by the cool young Sun. Two main types of fossil material give palaeontologists the clues. 'Stromatolites', mounds of layered calcite deposited by blue-

green algae, still exist in some areas today, notably Western Australia, while 'cherts', hard flinty siliceous rocks, may contain slender filaments and globular structures.

The Warrawoona group of rocks in Western Australia contains the remains of 3,500 million-year-old stromatolite-like structures. Similar fossils are recorded from the Bulawayan formation which, at 2,900 million years, is much younger. Cherts of the Onverwacht formation contain filament structures suggesting early life 3,300 million years ago. Near Lake Superior, the cherts of the Gunflint Series suggest a possible great step forward by living things because, here, 2,000 million years old, is evidence in fossils comparable to modern microscopic plants, of two types of cell. These are budding bacterial matter and filamentous structures resembling modern blue-green algae. The filaments of *Gunflintia minuta* suggest that oxygen was beginning to accumulate in the atmosphere because their cells are thick-walled like those of the present-day blue-green alga *Nostoc*. The thick cell wall shields *Nostoc's* nitrogen-fixing enzymes from destructive oxygen. Geological evidence indicating that early conditions on Earth were very different from the oxygen-rich ones of more recent times includes the banded ironstone rocks of Greenland and other regions, which may have accumulated in oxygen 'sinks', and kept this gas from being released into the atmosphere. It is impossible to interpret the formation of these ancient rocks by using modern analogies; rather, they seem to point to conditions which have never been repeated. Oxygen and the development of the blue-green algae increased together. Eventually, as larger, more complex plants developed, a continuous supply of the vital gas was ensured.

The origin of sex

Before about 1,500 million years ago, the fossil record shows evidence of only very very small cells, less than 50 micrometres long. Such cells were the parts of microbes which stored their genetic material in strands of DNA not encased in a cell membrane, as more advanced organisms do. They are called 'prokaryotic' cells and multiply simply, by splitting. A different type of cell rules today's world. This type, the eukaryotic, developed around 1,500 million years ago. Eukaryotic cells multiply by 'mitotic' division, in which one cell nucleus divides into two nuclei, each of which are identical to the original one. Such cells introduced sex to the Earth. 'Meiosis', a process in which genetic material is split in half during cell division, is also possible with these eukaryotes. These 'split' cells can then join with others from different individuals. The great value of this sexual joining of cells is that information can be shared between individuals. More competent forms will survive and become better suited to their environment. This eukaryotic revolution could not have happened any sooner because mitosis depends on the contractile ability of a protein called actomyosin, which cannot form without oxygen. The fossil record suggests a date of about 1,500 million years for the advent of the eukaryotes, because around this time, fossil cells become significantly larger. The fossil record also becomes much richer from this time on. Eukaryotic organisms (which include many single-celled organisms as well as more complex multi-celled creatures such as ourselves), are able to secrete silica and other chemicals which help their fossilization. Evolution proceeded apace.

By 700 million years ago this evolution had produced the so-called 'Ediacaran assemblage' of fossils. These fossils are found in a number of now widespread places including Russia, England, Sweden, Namibia and the Ediacara Hills of South Australia, where they were first discovered. Most of them are preserved as impressions and casts in the fine-grained sediments. Metazoans, such as jellyfishes, are common, as are sea pens (colonial creatures fixed to the sea-bed) and worm-like animals. *Dickinsonia* resembles the modern sea mouse, and *Praecambridium* may well be an early arthropod, a group including insects, spiders and crabs. From these organisms it is a much smaller step to the Burgess Shale invertebrates and the trilobites than the leap from the pools of pre-biotic chemicals and anoxic lightning-rent sky which surrounded the Earth some 4,000 million years before Man's arrival.

The rocks which make up much of the Earth's crust contain evidence, ranging from the shells of molluscs, the trails of trilobites and the wings of dragonflies to the bones of dinosaurs, of the life forms which used to inhabit the sea, the land and the air. Palaeontologists call this evidence the fossil record. From it, they can trace the story of evolution and the changing environments of the past.

Unfortunately, this fossil record is far from complete, preserving evidence of only a handful of the wonderful variety of animals and plants that have inhabited our planet. Sedimentary rocks, such as sandstones, shales and limestones, are the ones which preserve fossils best. When the grains that make the rock are very small, great detail can be preserved, as with the amazingly delicate feathers of the primitive bird *Archaeopteryx*. If the particles are coarse and pebbly, then delicate organisms, such as plants and thin-shelled invertebrates, are crushed and destroyed.

Fossils are occasionally found in rocks of igneous origin. Volcanic dust and ash which settle down through sea-water form layers that can entomb organisms on the sea-bed. Similar choking dust fossilized the inhabitants of Pompeii when Vesuvius erupted in AD 79. More often, however, the heating effect of igneous activity burns and destroys organic material.

Metamorphism, either by heat or extreme pressure, recrystallizes rocks containing fossils, thus obliterating them.

A matter of chance

Whether or not an animal or plant ends up as a fossil is very much a matter of chance. Creatures with hard shells and bones stand a good chance, whereas one composed of softer tissues is either eaten by scavengers or rots when it dies. A creature living in the sea, where considerable thicknesses of sediment pile up rapidly, can be covered and preserved more easily than one living on land, where erosion will fragment its skeleton and sedimentation is slow. Rapid burial and removal from air and bacteria is crucial if an organism is to become a fossil.

The minerals secreted by an organism may have considerable influence on how it is fossilized. Many shellfish (molluscs and brachiopods) have calcium carbonate in their skeletons, as do some arthropods (insects, crabs, spiders and relatives) and vertebrates. Calcium carbonate is a substance that is stable in a number of geological environments and is easily preserved, as is silica in the structures of marine sponges and radiolarians. Chitin, a horny, fibrous, nitrogen-rich carbohydrate, is common in the defensive outer armour, or exoskeleton, of many arthropods. This material can withstand many geological processes, and survives in fossils hundreds of million of years old.

Replacement by minerals

It is common to find fossils in which the original organic minerals have been converted to a substance which is in equilibrium with the alien environment deep within the rocks. This change may be slight or complete. Petrification involves the impregnation of the skeleton with minerals brought in by water seeping through the strata. These solutions can carry calcite, quartz and iron pyrites to replace the original organic material and thus preserve the fossil. The beautiful golden ammonites from the Jurassic clays of Europe are now made of pyrites, which gives them their opulent colour.

In Australia, fossil trees have been replaced by opal, which shimmers with blue and green. It is possible for the original coloured pattern of the fossil to be preserved, but usually in new colours resulting from replacement minerals. When the honeycombed structure of the interior of bone is impregnated by mineral-rich waters, its outward appearance remains, but internal features may be lost and the weight increased.

Carbon is the basis of living chemistry. Organisms such as plants, graptolites and some fish are preserved as a thin film of this black element. The volatile material in the organic structure of the organism is removed, producing a relative increase in carbon. The delicate tree- and seed-ferns from the coal-bearing strata of Carboniferous age are preserved in this way. Large marine vertebrates, such as the ichthyosaurs, have been found in which a film of carbon outlines the body, surrounding a bony skeleton.

As well as introducing new minerals, ground water can remove shells to leave a hollow cavity in the rocks. Later, this may become filled with sediment or with another mineral, and so takes on the shape of the original shell. This replica may have sufficient detail to show muscle scars and other markings.

Trace fossils

When they are alive, organisms leave many traces of their existence. Fossil excrement, called coprolite, is usually mineralized with phosphates. Such fossils can give valuable clues to ancient diets. Dinosaurs, worms and trilobites, among others, leave tracks, burrows and trails which, when gently filled by sediment, become preserved.

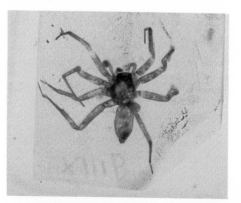

Preservation of soft tissues

It is rare enough for the hard parts of organisms to become fossilized: the odds against soft tissue and whole organisms becoming preserved are millions to one. This can happen, however, if the conditions are just right. Along the south Baltic coast in Northern Europe, pine forests grew during the Tertiary era. Insects creeping and flying through these forests easily became stuck on the fragrant resin seeping from the trees. In time, this resin hardened to form amber, which today can often be found with the insects embedded in it as complete fossils.

In southern USA, natural tar and pitch forms pools on the surface. Million of years ago, large mammals, caught by surprise, floundered in the sticky morass and were dragged down to their fossilizing fate. Protected from decay by air and bacteria, they were entirely preserved. Among the sloths, mammoths and bison are sabre-toothed tigers, which, seeing the helpless herbivores, leapt in to feed on them, little realizing that this would be their last meal.

Peat bogs preserve organisms in the same way. Giant deer are found in Irish peat, and in Denmark, human bodies have been perfectly preserved for thousands of years in peat bogs. The 10,000-year-old deep-frozen Siberian mammoths are well documented, their meat even being fit for dogs to eat today! All these examples are of complete preservation which is of no great geological age. Mummification by the drying out of tissues in hot, dry environments can preserve the skin and flesh of dinosaurs for millions of years.

Much farther back in the geological past, the entire organism, or at least an imprint of its soft

Left The preservation of even part of an organism is a chance event, but the fossilization of a whole creature, such as this spider in amber from the Pleistocene rocks of the Baltic, is exceptional.
Below Sometimes no part of an organism is preserved, but we still know of its existence because of its tracks or, as here, by borings in wood made by *Teredina*, a mollusc of Eocene age.

Above right The hollow shells of creatures such as these gastropod molluscs *Viviparus sussexiensis*, from the Cretaceous rocks of Kent, England, are filled with either sediment or minerals, and are so preserved.
Right The delicate soft-bodied organisms found fossilized in the Burgess Shales of British Columbia are reconstructed here as they may have lived 550 m.y. ago.

the rock layers and the wealth of fossils they contain, the probable environment of this ancient sea-bed has been worked out. All manner of organisms are found in the shales. There are arthropods which crawled over the sea-bed, worms which burrowed into it, and sponges which would have lived attached to the rocks. Other organisms, such as polychaete worms and early chordates, swam above the sea-bed. This rich variety of organisms is preserved in the same layers of sediment, flattened in various positions by the compressed mud. Near to the shale layers is a limestone reef some 500ft (150m) high, and the muddy sediment is piled up against its base. There are no traces of the animals' burrows or trails.

From all this evidence it is suggested that the Burgess Shales were deposited by avalanches of muddy sediment which periodically swept down the underwater cliff, carrying with them organisms which lived on the ledges to become trapped and entombed in the fine, soft muds accumulating on the sea-bed below. This would account for the jumbled and squashed nature of the fossils. Because the mud was so fine-grained, even the most delicate details of the organisms are preserved, and the Burgess Shale fauna gives us a privileged insight into the kinds of creatures which lived on the Cambrian sea-bed along with the shelled ones, which are usually the only ones preserved. The Burgess Shale is unique, but the organisms it contains are almost certainly not. They probably lived in many parts of the world, but are only preserved there. Many of them provide a link between the shelled arthropods and other invertebrates and the more primitive non-shelled earlier forms.

tissues, may be preserved when the sediment is very fine-grained and covers the creatures rapidly. One of the most important examples of this is the remarkable Burgess Shale deposit discovered accidentally by the American geologist Charles Doolittle Walcott in 1909, high in the Rocky Mountains of British Columbia, Canada. The significance of this deposit is that it has preserved in its soft fine muds the impressions of entire soft-bodied organisms when other rocks of this age (550 million years) contain only the remains of shelled creatures such as trilobites and brachiopods.

The Burgess Shales

The unique Burgess Shales are one of the greatest palaeontological flukes. A combination of chance events formed them, and their discovery was another piece of luck. During the Cambrian period, this region, which is today thousands of feet above sea-level, was deep in the ocean. By careful interpretation of

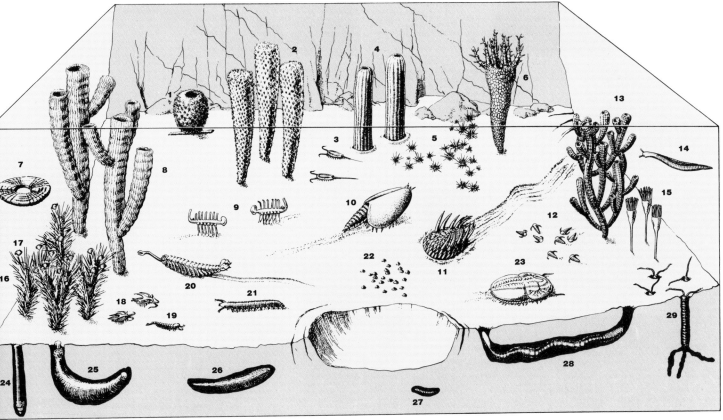

Key
1 The sponge *Eiffelia*.
2 The sponge *Chancelloria*.
3 An arthropod, *Burgessia*, armed with a tail spine.
4 *Mackenzia*, an immobile coelenterate.
5 The highly gregarious sponge *Choia*.

6 The primitive crinoid *Echmatocrinus*, attached to an empty worm tube.
7 The free-swimming coelenterate *Peytoia*.
8 The sponge *Vauxia*.
9 *Hallucigenia*, a bizarre creature with no known relatives.

10 *Canadaspis*, a crustacean.
11 The mollusc *Wiwaxia*, which was protected by scales and spines.
12 The mollusc *Hyolithes*.
13 A more delicate, many-branched species of the sponge *Vauxia* (compare **8**).
14 *Pikaia*, a member of the

chordates (which include fish, reptiles and mammals).
15 The unique creature *Dinomischus*.
16 The sponge *Pirania*.
17 Small brachiopods living attached to *Pirania*.
18 The arthropod *Marella*.
19 Another arthropod, with

the amusing name *Yohoia*.
20 Another unique creature, *Opabinia* had a single forked appendage for grasping prey.
21 The arthropod *Aysheaia*.
22 The molluscs *Scenella*.
23 The trilobite *Naraoia* was an atypical species which retained larval characters.

24 The priapulid worm *Selkirkia*.
25 Another priapulid *Ottoia*.
26 The priapulid *Ancalagon*.
27 The polychaete worm *Peronochaeta*.
28 The priapulid *Louisella*.
29 The polychaete worm *Burgessochaeta*.

Two of the many techniques used in economic geological prospecting are rock drilling and coring. The first simply features a rotating drill-head equipped with many teeth to grind a hole through solid rock, whilst the second employs a cylindrical drill, usually equipped with diamond teeth, to obtain a long rod-shaped core of rock for examination. In the case of drilling, the rock material reaches the surface as fine fragments in the drilling muds. While coring can yield perfectly unbroken cores, many sediments tend to break up in the core tube.

Because much of the material from below the surface is available only in fragmentary form, the palaeontologist has to use the tiny microfossils within the fragments in order to tell from which geological time-period or rock layer the fragments have come. The micro-palaeontologist (a scientist who studies micro-fossils) uses these tiny 'index fossils' to help locate oil- or coal-bearing rocks. It is mainly fossils of tiny animals called Protozoa that are the most useful, although conodonts and plant microfossils are also valuable.

Introducing the Protozoans

The Protozoa, or protozoans, are structurally the simplest members of the animal kingdom whose bodies consist of a single cell. A typical protozoan is microscopic in size and has only a single nucleus, although similar individuals may group together to form a colony and some protozoans may have several nucleii. The body of protozoans consists of a nucleus and two types of cytoplasm, the outer, jelly-like layer being known as the ectoplasm and the inner, more fluid layer the endoplasm. The protozoans of interest to micropalaeontologists are those that were able to secrete a shell-like external cover, or 'test', which could be preserved. The two protozoan orders of importance are the Foraminifera and the Radiolaria.

The Foraminifera

The test of a foraminiferan (often abbreviated to 'foram') has one chamber or interconnected chambers and is made of calcite or silica. The forams span the entire range of time from the Cambrian period to the present day—a duration of over 500 million years! They are valuable 'index' (or 'zone') fossils for dating rocks from the Mesozoic and Cenozoic eras. During the early part of this century their significance in dating rocks was quickly recognized when their value to the oil industry was demonstrated. Today it is a routine procedure to use these fossils for determining the age of rocks, particularly those from the Cretaceous and Tertiary periods, in which most of the petroleum reserves are found. Most fossil and recent species are marine, but a few can also tolerate freshwater.

The forams are very widespread, and live in practically all marine environments, where they may number from 2 million per sq yd (2½ million per sq m) of ocean floor. They are vegetarian, feeding on algae and organic debris by means of foot-like projections of the cytoplasm

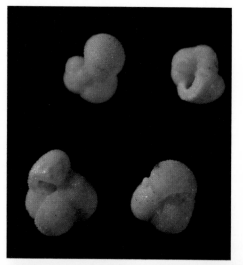

Left The tiny 'shells' of *Globigerina* are made of calcite, and contain many small pores. They are common foraminiferans in rocks of Tertiary to Recent age.
Right *Nummulites* is another foram shell which is coiled in a flat spiral and divided into many small chambers. This creature is fossilized in rocks of Tertiary age.
Below The high power magnification of the electron microscope is of great value to the mirco-palaeontologist. Here are radiolarians, diatoms and foraminiferans of Miocene age from the USA.

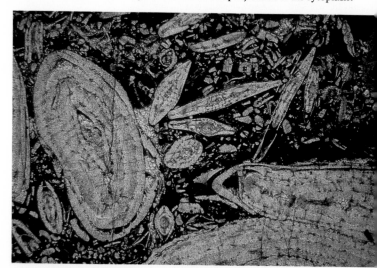

called pseudopodia. The distribution of modern species is controlled by water-temperature, salinity, oxygen and food availability. So their fossils are not only valuable in dating rocks, but also, by analysing their distribution, they can reveal valuable information about their environment. Their form is so infinitely variable that it is impossible to describe a general structure for these tiny creatures.

The spiky Radiolarians
The radiolarians include marine organisms that have a complex test made of silica. The protoplasm of radiolarians consists of several parts: a horny central capsule, surrounded by a dark ectoplasm where food is digested and a layer called the 'calymna', containing fat globules and pigment molecules. The beautiful, intricate test is variable in shape, but does show some degree of symmetry. It is secreted by more than one body layer, and thus it can form as a series of perforated and lace-like spheres, one inside the other and supported by a number of radial spiky growths. Modern radiolarians are important contributors to the bottom sediments which carpet the abyssal plains of the Pacific and Indian Oceans.

Fossil radiolarians are common in all silica-rich sediments, such as cherts. But they are also found in a variety of other rocks, including limestones, clays, tuffs and sandstones. Although the radiolarians make an important contribution to deep-ocean deposits, their presence alone does not indicate deep-sea conditions; many radiolaria formed rich deposits in the shallow partially enclosed continental-shelf seas.

Since most radiolarians have long stratigraphic ranges, their use as index fossils is generally limited to those species of Tertiary age with a short vertical distribution in the rocks.

The enigmatic conodonts
The conodonts form a large group of highly enigmatic extinct marine organisms. They appeared in the Cambrian and seem to have vanished by the Cretaceous. They consist of skeletal parts 1/25in (1mm) in size, which resemble single teeth, or groups and rows of even tinier teeth. These are the only parts of the organisms that remain preserved, any soft body having been broken down. Some conodonts resemble tiny fish teeth, some are similar to the radular teeth of gastropods (sea-snails), and others look like the jaws of annelid worms. Many palaeontologists believe them to be of vertebrate origin.

Since conodonts have a wide geographical and a narrow stratigraphic distribution, they are one of the important index fossil groups of the Palaeozoic era, allowing the zonation of rocks from some periods, such as the Silurian and Ordovician, to be more detailed and refined than that based on other fossils.

Fossil pollen analysis
The study of plant spores and pollen grains is called palynology. Because of the wide distribution of spores and pollen, and the ease with which they are preserved in peat and other sediments, they reveal the conditions of both the vegetation and climate over wide areas far back in time. By analysing the distribution of fossil spores and pollen, palynologists have been able to draw maps of ancient forests. The economic value of plant microfossils is closely linked to the formation of oil and certain types of coal. Plant spores feature in all varieties of

coal, but principally in cannel coal, which is dull greyish-coloured and fine-grained. Boghead coal is similar, but is composed mainly of the remains of various types of marine algae.

Electron microscopes
Among the most useful of the tools available to the micropalaeontologist is the electron microscope, of which there are two basic types.

The source of radiation in all electron microscopes is a stream of electrons emitted in vacuum from a hot metal filament. The electrons can be accelerated by an electric potential and focused by magnetic coils. In the transmission electron microscope (TEM) a condenser coil focuses the electron beam onto the object, an objective coil deflects the beam to magnify the image, and an ocular coil magnifies the objective image onto a fluorescent screen or photographic emulsion. Image formation in the TEM is due to electron scattering, whereas in the light microscope it depends upon light absorption

Below The phosphatic conodont *Spathognathodus stabilus* is typical of this strange tooth-like group of micro-fossils.

These well-preserved fossils are an enigmatic group with debatable affinities, but are valuable for dating rocks.

by the object. The image on the TEM screen actually results from the absence of those electrons which collide against atomic nuclei in the object and are deflected out of the aperture of the microscope column.

The TEM is used to look through specimens. These have to be less than 500nm thick, otherwise the beam cannot penetrate and the specimen appears opaque (one nanometre, or nm, is one ten-millionth of a centimetre). Thin sections of many materials are increased in contrast by 'staining' with salts of heavy metals. Thin fragments of material can be highlighted by casting shadows with directionally vapourized heavy metals, such as gold or palladium. Alternatively, thin plastic or carbon replicas can be made and studied instead of the specimen itself.

The scanning electron microscope (SEM) uses the secondary electron emission that is ejected after the primary beam has hit the surface of a solid object. A thin beam of high intensity is moved back and forth across the specimen, the secondary electrons are collected by a photomultiplier, and a magnified image of the surface of the specimen is displayed on a television screen.

The resolving power of any microscope depends upon its numerical aperture and the wavelength of radiation used. The light microscope uses visible light of wavelength 400-800nm, and can resolve points not less than 250nm apart; the total useful magnification by light microscopy is approximately 1000 times. The wavelength of the electron beam under an accelerating voltage of 40-120kV in the TEM is 0·003-0·006nm, and the limit of resolution is 0·2 to 0·5nm; total useful magnification in the TEM is 1,000,000 times. The SEM is used with accelerating voltages of 1-50kV, and effective resolution ranges from 3nm at best to 15-20nm in standard instruments; total useful magnification in the SEM is about 50,000 times.

Right Placing a specimen into the specimen chamber of a scanning electron microscope.
Below Adjusting the picture: in this model, the vacuum column, in which the stream of electrons is focused onto the specimen to produce the image, is horizontal and is housed with the specimen chamber in a unit separate from the TV screen and the electronic controls.

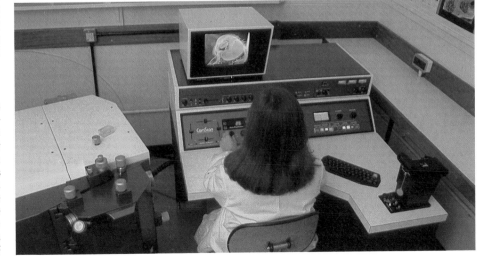

Some of the earliest fossils, from the Pre-Cambrian rocks of Australia and Canada, are the structures called stromatolites, which were built by blue-green algae. During the late Pre-Cambrian, the forerunners of the rich and varied flora of the Lower Palaeozoic must have developed, but the fossil record is poor. The main groups of algae had developed during the Pre-Cambrian, and the blue-green algae produced a change in the atmosphere (to be continued by the later plants) which has never been reversed and which altered the course of all evolution since that time. These primitive plants made oxygen and began to enrich the air with this vital gas. The algae were the only plants on Earth for hundreds of millions of years in the distant past. The land at this time must have been a colourless sand and rock-strewn waste, without the green mantle that we take for granted today. Some of the water-dwelling algae are able to reproduce sexually. These simple plants need a moist environment to allow the male sex cells to swim and reach the female ones. The earliest land plants were probably similar to modern mosses and liverworts, and lived in damp places.

Rigid stems

In the Lower Palaeozoic rocks microscopic plant spores are fossilized. These were probably carried by the wind. In Wales, rocks of Silurian age contain filaments of carbon representing branches and stems. When they examined these carefully through microscopes, botanists found that they consist of water-transporting 'xylem' cells. Such rigid stems could stand upright. These are the remains of the oldest vascular plants. *Cooksonia*, the genus of plant to which these remains belong, had no leaves but carried spores, and so was restricted to damp environments, the reproductive system relying on moist conditions.

The evolution of seeds

By the Devonian period the fossil record becomes well endowed with plant remains. In Aberdeenshire, Scotland, well preserved plant material is fossilized in siliceous cherts. The 'flora' (plant community) found here is a bog-

Above This painting takes us back to the luxuriant tropical swamp forests which flourished during the Carboniferous period. Tall ferns and clubmosses form a jungle, while amphibians wallow on the stream banks. A dragonfly hunts over the water.

flora which represents a possible link between water and land plants. The genus *Rhynia* has slender leafless stems with sporangia (spore-bearing structures) at the ends of the branches. The stems are woody and have a protective, waxy cuticle over the outer skin, a feature in keeping with plant life on land. The spores are fern-like. *Asteroxylon* is generally like a modern club-moss. It has a smooth underground stem, with spirally arranged leaves on the branched aerial axis. If we could see them, the early Devonian 'forests' would seem strange miniature jungles to us, the green carpet of fern- and moss-like plants being less than knee-high.

Though these plants were small, they made an important step onto the land, and by late Devonian times true ferns and seed-bearing plants appeared. *Archaeosperma*, an upper Devonian fossil, represents an early stage in the development of the gymnosperms, a group including the pines, firs, junipers and cycads. Seeds develop into new plants similar to their parents, whereas spores, typical of the more primitive plants, give rise to an intermediate stage, the prothallus, bearing male and female reproductive organs. A new plant only forms after fusion of the reproductive cells.

Plant diseases first appear in the Devonian period; *Rhynia*, for example, carries traces of a parasitic fungus.

Plants that become coal

The vast layers of coal formed during the Carboniferous period are evidence of the luxuriant vegetation that abounded some 300

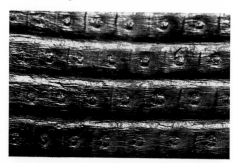

Left The delicate fronds of the fern *Mariopteris* are preserved as carbon films. **Right** This close-up of a lycopod (clubmoss) trunk shows the leaf scars as small rounded marks lying between the longitudinal ribs. **Below** Another lycopod is seen in this specimen. These clubmosses grew to gigantic size, often reaching over 100 feet (33m).

million years ago. Between the coal seams, in the sedimentary strata of rocks such as shales and sandstones, plant fossils, often of great beauty, are common. The dominant group at this time were lycopods (clubmosses) which often grew to great size, reaching 100ft (30m) in height and over 3ft (1m) in diameter. They grew in dense swamp forests where amphibians wallowed and large dragonflies drifted overhead. Species of *Lepidodendron* and *Sigillaria* were many-branched tall plants with long narrow leaves up to 3ft (1m) long. They reproduced by means of spores. So abundant were these giant lycopods that in some regions entire coal seams are made of their carbonized spores. Another group of plants which today is represented only by relatively small plants is that of the horsetails (Equisetales). The Carboniferous horsetail *Calamites* had a number of characteristics typical of modern horsetails such as leaves in whorls, but it was treesized. By this time a layered vegetation was developing with lower shrubby plants growing near the ground. True ferns existed in the Carboniferous jungles and 'seed-ferns' grew to tree proportions. Many of the fern-like fossil leaves found in Carboniferous rocks are the remains of these seed-ferns, such as *Neuropteris* and *Alethopteris*, and not those of true ferns. These extinct plants were abundant in the coal-swamps of North America and Britain and another group reproducing by seed, the Gymnosperms, was also widespread. *Cordaites* is a tall gymnosperm with long narrow leaves.

Permian and Triassic plants

During the Permian and Triassic periods many parts of the land masses in the Northern Hemisphere were dry arid deserts, and floras were thus diminished. The pteridophytes (ferns, clubmosses, horsetails and allies) were reduced in numbers and variety, but the woody coniferous trees flourished in favourable climates, and during the Triassic period palm-like cycads and ginkgos developed. At the end of the Permian period the giant Lepidodendrons and *Calamites* became extinct. One of the Permian seed-ferns, *Glossopteris*, is well known because the meteorologist Alfred Wegener used the

distribution of this fossil plant in South America, Southern Africa, India, Australia and Antarctica as strong evidence that these land masses were once joined and have since drifted apart.

The age of Cycads

The Jurassic period has been called the age of cycads. Two groups are well-known as fossils; the Bennettitales are extinct, the cycads still survive today. The Bennettitales lived worldwide during the Jurassic and Cretaceous periods and are well preserved in the Yorkshire Jurassic deltaic series of rocks. Also found in these same deposits are leaves and other remains of ginkgos. The conifers, which first appeared in the late Palaeozoic, became dominant land plants in the Jurassic and Cretaceous. They are able to protect their trunks with sticky resin and some species live for extraordinary lengths of time, annual growth rings having been counted for ages of over 5,000 years.

The rise of flowering plants

Today's world is coloured by those species of plants which bear flowers. These plants, the Angiosperms, have colonized a great variety of habitats. The flowers carry male and female organs, most commonly on the same plant.

Such plants developed during the Jurassic period and very recently fossil material from Sweden, of a complete flower of Cretaceous age, has been found. Flowers are a means of sexual reproduction, many flowers being designed to encourage cross-pollination, which enables a new gene combination to occur, giving the species more adaptability. Pollination can be achieved by water, wind or by insects. Flowers which attract insects to carry out this vital function are usually large and brightly coloured or perfumed, or supplied with a lure of nectar.

By the end of the Jurassic period and into the Cretaceous, when the colours of flowers began to transform the Earth's vegetation, insects had also begun to evolve with speed and diversity. Feeding both on pollen and nectar, the insects evolved hand in hand with the flowering plants. Some plants, notably the orchids, have gone to great lengths to mimic and attract insects which pollinate them. By the end of the Cretaceous period the angiosperms had displaced the gymnosperms as the dominant land plants, and many of the early genera have survived to this day. The Tertiary flora shows a gradual development to that which we know today. The fossils from the Eocene clay deposits around London have been thoroughly investigated, and because they include many genera known today, accurate accounts of ancient climatic fluctuations can be made. Many of the fossils are of fruit, leaves and seeds of flowering plants, especially those such as the nipa palm which today lives in tropical regions. During the Quaternary ice age the flora was very similar to that found in the modern world. The same species living in the same communities are found in glacial and periglacial sediments as fossils. These are of great value to the stratigrapher and palaeoclimatologist. The gradual changes from temperate to glacial climates and back can be accurately plotted using fossil plant remains (frequently pollen). In Northern Europe fossil glacial floras usually contain few shrub or tree species, having more sedge and grass pollen. Alpine and arctic species such as Mountain Avens and Purple Saxifrage are also found.

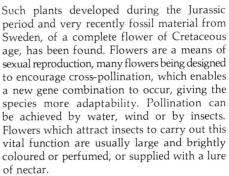

Above A fossil horsetail.
Left In the Triassic rocks of the Arizona National Park, the 'petrified forest' has trunks of *Araucarioxylon* in volcanic ash and sand.
Below An Eocene leaf is very modern in structure.
Right With the development of flowering plants came the rise of insects, such as this bee, which acted as pollinators.

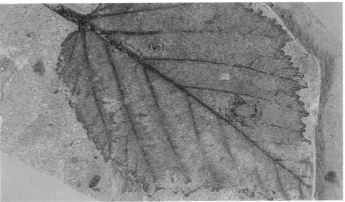

During the late Pre-Cambrian Era, a variety of invertebrate organisms evolved which were to develop and flourish, dominating the seas for hundreds of millions of years. Much of the fossil record of these ancestral invertebrates is lacking because they had no shells. The development of shells about 600 million years ago suddenly provides a wealth of fossil material. With hard shells, and the obvious advantages of protection and adaptability to a variety of environments, marine invertebrates took a great step forward.

Introducing the trilobites

Among the best known Palaeozoic organisms are the trilobites. These highly developed creatures are found fossilized in rocks ranging in age from Cambrian to Permian. A class within the phylum Arthropoda (which today contains over 80 per cent of all known species of animals), the trilobites are ancient relatives of crabs, insects and woodlice. The name 'trilobite' is derived from the threefold structure of the segmented body, which had a head shield (cephalon), body (thorax) and tail (pygidium). The trilobites were able to secrete a hard dorsal external skeleton, or exoskeleton, made of chitin, usually strengthened with calcite. The skeleton was flexible, allowing the organism to roll up (like a woodlouse) for protection. Sometimes large numbers of rolled-up fossils are found together. These presumably tried to defend themselves against a threat, but to no avail. Organisms with exoskeletons, such as the trilobites, could not grow very large, because movement and articulating mechanisms become awkward above a certain size. Also, it is difficult to obtain enough energy to move efficiently with a large exoskeleton.

The segmented nature of the carapace suggests evolution from a flexible worm-like organism. By the start of the Cambrian period, when the trilobites are first found, they are highly developed creatures. Their Pre-Cambrian evolutionary history must be a long one.

Beneath and within the exoskeleton are the soft parts of the body. In certain ideal conditions these have been fossilized, and from such fossils palaeontologists have discovered that the organism had gills, walking and swimming appendages and jaws. The 'feathery' appendages are in pairs, as are the antennae protruding from the front of the cephalon. To grow, a trilobite must moult its exoskeleton, in common with many other arthropods, such as crabs, scorpions and insects. Trilobites have left many broken moulted shells behind them, which have become fossilized. As well as the exoskeleton possibly splitting between its main divisions, the cephalon broke along suture lines and the articulating segments of the thorax also broke individually. Fossils are very often of these parts only.

Trilobite eyes

Trilobites had one great advantage over their contemporaries. They possessed sophisticated eyes. Modern arthropods have compound eyes, which are highly developed in many insects, such as dragonflies which have superb wide-ranging vision—necessary for catching fast-moving prey on the wing. The problems of underwater vision are different, but no doubt the trilobites had a distinct advantage over other invertebrates.

Trilobite eyes, placed high on the front of the cephalon, sometimes on extended stalks, are

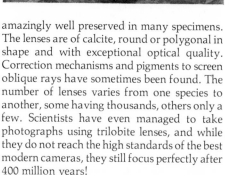

amazingly well preserved in many specimens. The lenses are of calcite, round or polygonal in shape and with exceptional optical quality. Correction mechanisms and pigments to screen oblique rays have sometimes been found. The number of lenses varies from one species to another, some having thousands, others only a few. Scientists have even managed to take photographs using trilobite lenses, and while they do not reach the high standards of the best modern cameras, they still focus perfectly after 400 million years!

For what purpose was this advanced sight developed? Some trilobite groups lacked eyes and still managed to survive for considerable lengths of time. Trilobites lived on the sea-bed, or swam slightly above the soft sediment. Different species were adapted to various precise habitats and lifestyles. Many are found fossilized in rocks formed in the shallow areas of the continental shelf, but others are sometimes found in extremely deep ocean sediments. Some species burrowed into the mud, sifting it for food; others were active hunters, even cannibals; some preyed on other marine invertebrates. Such active organisms would benefit greatly from a good sense of vision. Some

palaeontologists have suggested that those with the best eyes were nocturnal.

The delicate graptolites

While the trilobites scurried and crawled over the Palaeozoic sea-bed, a group of strange colonial organisms drifted among the plankton high above in the sunlight, where tides and currents carried them around the world. These were the fragile graptolites. With no near modern relatives, our interpretation of these fossil organisms is at times difficult. Their systematic classification has for long been open to debate, but their similarity to the pterobranchs, an obscure group of animals showing affinities with both invertebrates and vertebrates, leads most zoologists to classify them in the phylum Hemichordata.

The basic graptolite body-plan is a small, delicate skeleton, often less than 1in (2·5cm) long, called a stipe, along which grow numerous cups or thecae. The stipes were often joined together to produce 'tuning-fork' shapes and even dendroid forms resembling miniature flattened trees. These dendroids are the most ancient of the graptolites, appearing first in rocks of Cambrian age. Later forms are less

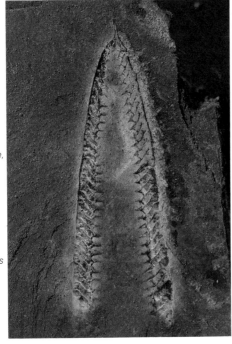

Right The delicate branched graptolite, *Didymograptus*, from the Ordovician period, shows the structure of these planktonic organisms. Such creatures are only rarely fossilized as they are very fragile.

Left The segmented exo-skeleton of a trilobite is sometimes fossilized in a defensive, rolled-up posture, as in this specimen of *Flexicalymene*, from the Ordovician rocks of the United States. From the onset of Cambrian times, trilobites teemed on the sea bed. It is rare to find unbroken specimens of the exo-skeleton. These three complete specimens are:
Below far left *Dalmanites* from the Silurian rocks of Shropshire, central England.
Below left *Lloydolithus* of Ordovician age.
Below *Biceratops* from rocks of Cambrian age.

Below The Silurian brachiopod shell of *Conchidium knighti* shows the larger pedicle valve curving up behind the smaller brachial valve.

Above The Silurian Wenlock limestone contains many fossils of marine, shallow-water creatures, like this brachiopod, *Leptaena depressa*.

complex, consisting of only a few stipes or a single one. Their evolution into a great variety of forms was rapid and, mainly for this reason, stratigraphers find graptolites very useful for putting the rocks in which they are found into a relative sequence through time.

A tiny organism, called a zooid, with a slender body and small tentacles, lived in each theca, so that the whole stipe was rather like an ancient tiny underwater towerblock. Their way of life is difficult to assess, since the animals have no modern counterparts, but their widespread distribution suggests that they were planktonic. Some graptolites, however, probably lived anchored to the seabed. Their delicate protein-containing structures are not easily fossilized in many rocks. They are relatively common in the fine muddy sediments of the deeper areas of the Lower Palaeozoic seas. In these rocks flattened impressions or films of pyrite (iron sulphide) are all that represent the original creature. Fortunately, three-dimensional fossils have been found in some limestones. When these are carefully freed from the rock matrix by dissolving it away with acids, microscopic analysis provides much detail about their structure. Their relations with the pterobranchs

is based on such analysis, which shows that the thecae are built up of sections of horny material arranged like bricks in a wall.

From their first appearance in the Cambrian period to their extinction during the Permian, the graptolites must have graced the seas in great numbers. Rock surfaces can be found smothered in their remains. It is probable that they drifted through the surface waters of the deep oceans and also were stranded on beaches. Here, however, they were broken and fragmented by the coarse grains of sediment.

The ancient brachiopods

Another group of organisms which developed hard external shells at the beginning of the Palaeozoic Era were the shell-fish called brachiopods. These sea-bed dwellers are protected by unequal-sized shells of calcite, or, in more primitive forms, of chitin. The shell is secreted by a fleshy mantle, which itself envelops the soft body. It is shaped like a Roman oil-lamp, a similarity that has given the animals their common name 'lamp shells'.

Brachiopods are not as numerous today as they have been at many times during the past They formed large parts of the sea-bed fauna

from the Lower Palaeozoic to the end of the Mesozoic, but today there are only about 260 species. Modern brachiopods live in shallow temperate and cool waters, mostly on the continental shelf, but occasionally down to 12,000ft (4,000m).

Modern and fossil brachiopods can be divided into two main types. The inarticulate brachiopods are unable to open and close their two valves as they lack a hinge mechanism. Developing early in the Cambrian period, most of them had chitinous shells and were burrowers. Modern forms of this 600 million-year-old genus work their way down about a foot (30cm) into the mud and, anchored by a fleshy pedicle stuck to the base of the burrow, feed from the sea-bed. If disturbed or threatened, a brachiopod contracts its pedicle and withdraws to the bottom of its burrow. Modern species of the genus *Lingula*, typical of the burrowing forms, live in brackish and salt-water, especially around Japan.

The articulate brachiopods, which have a detailed muscle and hinge mechanism for opening and closing the two dissimilar valves, are a very numerous fossil group. During their long evolution, they became adapted to all manner of sea-bed environments. Some were covered with spines, to help them move across muddy sediments, while one extreme group, the rhictofenids, had one tube-shaped valve and a small flattened lid for the other valve, resembling solitary corals. Other types developed strong ribbing for life in rocky or turbulent regions. In all forms the pedicle, a tough horny stalk, projected through a hole on the beak-shaped end of the shell to anchor the organism to the sea-bed. Unlike molluscs, the brachiopods feed by means of a feathery, coiled lophophore, consisting of arms and numerous tentacles. This is supported inside the shell by a loop-shaped calcareous structure unique to this phylum. Brachiopods, stuck permanently to the sea-bed, cannot actively hunt, but must attract their food—tiny floating plankton and organic debris—to them. This they do by moving cilia (tiny hairs) on the lophophore tentacles, causing a current of water to circulate through the open front end of the shell, from which food (and oxygen) can be filtered out by the cilia and used by the animal.

A major group of animals which first appear in a shell form during the Cambrian period is the Mollusca. Today molluscs inhabit environments as different as the deepest oceans and highest mountains. Their success is truly amazing, and is due to their impressive diversity and beautiful adaptations. Their ancestors in the Pre-Cambrian may have been segmented worm-like creatures. The fossil record contains excellent evidence of the various classes of molluscs, from the burrowing, swimming and creeping bivalves to the swimming and floating cephalopods or the crawling gastropods. Less important classes are the tube-like 'tusk shells' (Scaphopoda) and the chitons (Amphineura).

A 'living fossil'

The Lower Palaeozoic rocks contain the remains of another group of molluscs, the primitive Monoplacophorans, which superficially resemble flattened limpets. These are unknown from rocks younger than 500 million years old. In the 1950's the international biological community was stunned by the discovery of a living monoplacophoran (named *Neopilina*) in deep sea-water off the Pacific coast of Mexico. This segmented, flattened shell of *Neopilina* may be a link between the early molluscs and the segmented worms, or annelids.

Oysters and other bivalves

The bivalve molluscs can be distinguished from the other classes found as fossils by their two similar, mirror-image shells. In most species the shells can be articulated by a strong hinge and adductor muscles. Oysters, such as the Jurassic *Gryphaea*, have dissimilar shells, an adaptation to life on the sediment of the sea-bed. In this genus, one shell is much heavier and thicker than the other to keep the animal in the same position. The soft body is held inside the shell-secreting mantle, within the hard shell. A muscular foot projects through the opened ventral margin and is used for movement or burrowing. The gills, which move currents of water through the mantle, collect oxygen and food. The margins of the mantle are formed into two siphons, one inhalant, to take in food and oxygen, the other exhalant, to remove waste matter. Because the shell is hard and mainly calcareous, thickened with layers of aragonite, chitin and mother-of-pearl, bivalves are commonly found as fossils in various sedimentary rocks.

The way of life of fossil forms can be worked out not only by their geological situation but also by reference to similar modern species. The environment will have great influence on the shape and thickness of the shell. Those that live in shallow turbulent waters, such as rock pools, have thick, strong-ribbed shells. Freshwater forms have thin shells, as do marine species which live deeper, where currents and waves are absent. Some, with elongated shells, protect themselves in burrows. These have long siphons to reach up out of the burrow to feed. Genera such as *Teredo* bore into wood or rock, while mussels stick fast to various surfaces with a fibrous byssus. *Pecten*, a common Mesozoic and modern genus, including the tasty scallops, swims in short bursts by flapping its two large

Above Oysters, such as this species, *Lopha marshi*, were common in the warm shallow seas of the Jurassic period.

Below A mass of small bivalve shells is preserved in sandstone. The random orientation may indicate sudden deposition.

saucer-shaped valves together, using a single large muscle. Even in fossils where no soft tissue is left, much can be learnt about the muscles by studying the impressions in the shell where they and other soft parts of the animal are attached.

The bivalves became numerous during the Mesozoic and reached a zenith during the Tertiary Era. They can be important to stratigraphers dating rocks, and in the river sediments of the coal-bearing strata 'mussel bands' help to locate the relative coal seams. Because of their susceptibility to climatic change, some species help glaciologists work out the changing conditions during ice ages.

Jet-propelled molluscs

The cephalopods are the only group of molluscs which are entirely free-swimming. They moved gracefully by jet propulsion through the seas from the early Palaeozoic onwards. The nautiloids are the earliest shelled members of the class to be found as fossils. The large straight-shelled species, some over 10ft (3m) long, were without rival as active carnivores. During the Mesozoic Era the ammonoids became dominant. Today, only the *Nautilus*, squids, cuttlefish, octopus and *Argonauta* remain.

The internal structure of the cephalopod shell is an architectural masterpiece. The shell is divided into many chambers, separated by partitions called septa. The largest chamber at the opening of the shell housed the animal. The other, smaller, chambers, which are connected by a thin tube (the siphuncle), are buoyancy chambers filled by a changeable gas and fluid mixture. The animal can control its buoyancy by regulating the density of this mixture, enabling it either to swim to deeper water or float near the surface at will. In the nautiloids the siphuncle is near the centre of the shell and the septa are simple. The ammonoids have a marginal siphuncle and the septa form

Below Early cephalopods were active carnivores, hunting on the Palaeozoic sea-bed. The straight chambered shell, seen here in *Orthoceras*, from the Ordovician period, was buoyant and stood up from the sea-bed, with the body reaching out below.

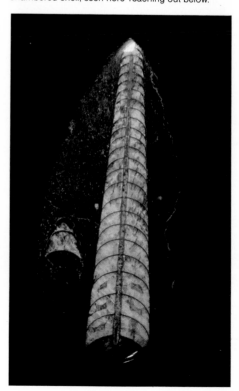

very complex and ornate suture lines where they join the inner surface of the shell. The early straight nautiloids lived on the sea-bed, with their buoyant shell upwards and their tentacled bodies resting on the sediment surface. In order to rest at an angle to the sea-bed they secreted calcareous thickenings to bring the long shell down to a horizontal position.

The Mesozoic ammonoids, unlike the smooth-shelled *Nautilus*, evolved rapidly into a series of varied coiled and uncoiled species, ranging in size from about an inch (2·5cm) to 3ft (1m) in diameter. The soft, squid-like body with eight hooked tentacles, a head and a funnel, would protrude from the aperture, with the coiled shell vertically above. The remains of fossil ink-sacs have been found and even used for writing and drawing! As with modern cephalopods, the ink was used by the animals as a defensive screen. The great variety of species, from smooth to coarsely ribbed, and flat to bulbous, suggests that the ammonites enjoyed many different environments. Some were

relatively competent free-swimmers and hunters; others floated near the surface; less active forms browsed on the sea bed. That they had their own enemies is known by the impressions of large teeth on the outside of some fossil shells and from the masses of hooks from ammonite tentacles found in the stomachs of fossil ichthyosaurs. Ink is no defence against a sea monster!

The rapid evolution of the ammonoids makes them invaluable for dating strata (goniatites in the upper Palaeozoic, ammonites in the Mesozoic). We also know from the two size frequencies of shells of many species that the sexes looked different. During the late Cretaceous, the ammonites suffered a massive extinction. The high levels of platinum-group metals in sediments of this age has been put down to a large meteorite impact. This catastrophe may have led to the extinction of many groups. Not only the ammonites died out at this time. The dinosaurs and 90 per cent of the marine plankton also perished then. Juvenile

ammonites were planktonic for some months after birth. Young nautiloids were not planktonic, and they survived the late Cretaceous crisis. Their juvenile planktonic stage may have proved the ammonites' downfall. Even though at many times during their evolution they expanded rapidly into many varied forms, these expansions were followed by the extinctions of many species. The Cretaceous crisis was their last. The days of the beautifully constructed chambered shell would seem to be numbered, today, with only *Nautilus* and a few other forms remaining.

The squid-like belemnites were contemporaries of the ammonites. Their fossil remains are cigar-shaped calcareous shells, which were the animal's internal skeleton. These fast-moving predators had a similar lifestyle to that of the modern decapods—the cuttlefish and squids.

Snails and slugs

One of the most adaptable classes of molluscs, living in the oceans, in freshwater, on land and even in trees, are the gastropods. The snails and shell-less slugs are not commonly found as fossils, unlike the bivalves and cephalopods. Those with shells could withdraw their body into the shell but when active the head and slimy foot were extended—just as in a modern snail. Tentacles above the head carry the eyes and a rasping, food-gathering radula lies beneath. The body organs are different from other molluscs in that they undergo a twisting process when very young. This torsion has no bearing on the spiral coiling of the shell which is a feature of some species. Most gastropods are vegetarians, but some bivalve fossils have been found in which a sea-snail has made a neat hole in the bivalve shell to eat the soft tissue inside. The fossil record has become increasingly rich in gastropods through time from their first appearance in the Cambrian, and today they are more numerous than ever.

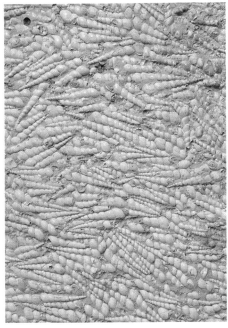

Above A specimen of the ammonite *Asteroceras stellare*, eroded by the sea, shows the shell's internal chambers.

Below The white shell of *Liparoceras cheltiense*, a Jurassic ammonite, is a massive bulbous structure.

Left Slender shells of the snail *Potamaclis* are fossilized as a mass, indicating orientation by water currents.

Below These gastropods, *Galba longiscata*, are more snail-like and are preserved both as whole and broken shells.

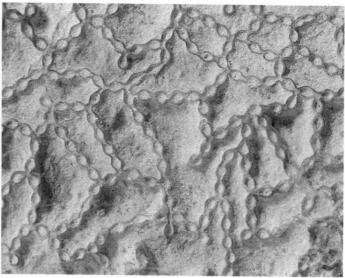

Left This scleractinian coral skeleton is typical of the complex, beautiful structures built on the bed of the sea which covered Mesozoic Europe.

Above The 'chain coral' *Halysites catenularius*, from the Silurian limestone of Britain, is a tabulate coral which graced the Palaeozoic sea bed.

Below The echinoid, or sea urchin, *Micraster coranguinum* from the Cretaceous period is used as a zone fossil in dating the European chalk.

The beautiful many-coloured corals are the supreme architects of modern seas, building huge reefs and other underwater structures. These provide a home for a great range of other organisms. Algae which secrete lime also help to build up the reef structures and the cavities in the underwater mazes provide homes for fish and for invertebrates such as brachiopods, molluscs and echinoderms. The reef-building corals live only in rather special regions where the sea is warm (averaging 77°F, 25°C), free from mud and shallow—usually less than 70ft (20m). Calcite, from which corals and other invertebrates build their shells, is less soluble in warm water and is therefore easily obtained by the creatures. Corals which do not build reef structures are less particular and can live in deeper water, where sunlight is virtually absent and the temperature much lower.

The modern corals are descended from primitive coelenterates, a group which includes jellyfishes, sea anemones and other colourful invertebrates. The class which builds the familiar coral structures is the Anthozoa. The animal is a small polyp, ranging in size from a tenth of an inch to up to a few inches in diameter, with tentacles extending above the central mouth. These soft bodies are practically unknown from the fossil record, but as the polyp grows it builds a calcareous coral tube, commonly found as fossils. After the polyp has anchored itself to the substrate it grows and lifts itself off the sea-bed, living on the top storey of the coral tube. Here the food-grasping tentacles are better positioned.

The first corals
The corals first appeared early in the Palaeozoic. These were not reef builders. Ancient lime-mounds which form the reef limestones of the Devonian and Carboniferous periods contain coral fossils, but are built and bound by algae and stromatoporoids, mat- and net-like organisms related to the corals.

Tabulate corals
The tabulate corals flourished on the sea-bed from the Ordovician well into the upper Palaeozoic. Descended from Pre-Cambrian metazoans, these corals built a simple hollow tube of calcite divided horizontally by flat 'tabulae', like the floors in a minature building. These tubes are always colonial and are fossilized in great numbers in limestones. They are often rounded, but can be angular and polygonal (as in the Silurian *Favosites*) or oval and linked together like a chain, as in *Halysites*. As these masses of tubes develop, lime-rich mud fills in the gaps between them, producing ready-made limestone.

Rugose corals
After enjoying a colonial life-style for some time, many corals took to a solitary existence. The rugose corals (so called because of the ridges along their outer walls) may be either solitary or colonial. From their first appearance as fossils in the upper Ordovician they proliferated and were common throughout the upper Palaeozoic. Not being as particular in their requirements as modern reef corals, the rugose corals inhabited a variety of environments from shallow continental shelf seas to deeper off-shore regions. *Lithostrotion* and *Lonsdalia* lived with brachiopods and other organisms on the shallow sea-bed over what is now Northern Europe during the Carboniferous period. *Zaphrentis*, meanwhile, lived in the deeper off-shore waters.

There are some important structural differences between the tabulate and rugose types. The rugose corals are more complex with radiating inner partitions, or 'septa', and thickenings of their walls, called 'dissepiments', as well as curved tabulae cutting their calcite tubes horizontally. The septa are grouped in fours, and as the rugose coral grows upwards, it builds more septa to increase its strength and preserve its original narrow base, now below an ever-widening structure. Some rugose corals may be 6in (15cm) or more high.

The scleractinian corals, or hexacorals, are the modern representatives, building the colourful, shallow reefs. Their history begins in the Mesozoic, when they began to take over from the tabulate and rugose forms. Their polyps may be solitary or may reach over and join with the soft body in the next theca (the cup at

the top of the coral), becoming linked by soft tissue. The sea-anemone-like polyps are bag-shaped with rings of tentacles around the central mouth. They differ from the rugose corals in having their septa grouped in sixes. Palaeontologists usually consider that these fossils in limestones indicate warm, shallow conditions at the time when the animals were alive.

Living clocks
Modern corals secrete daily growth-bands onto their calcareous skeletons. These increments seem to be controlled by the rise and fall of the tide. Seasonal variations are superimposed on this pattern, and it is possible to interpret an annual growth pattern for an individual coral. Ancient corals, too, were influenced by the moon and the seasons: evidence for this lies in the same type of pattern and banding in fossil corals. Coral banding in Devonian limestones suggests that 400 million years ago the year was 400 hundred days long!

Echinoids
Among the many invertebrate organisms which inhabit similar marine areas to the corals are the echinoids, or sea urchins. These are solitary

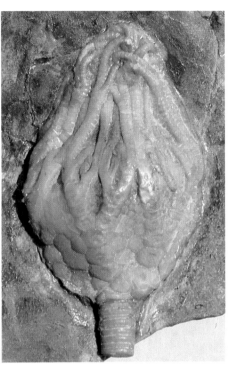

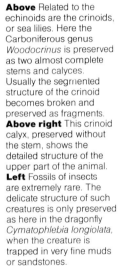

Above Related to the echinoids are the crinoids, or sea lilies. Here the Carboniferous genus *Woodocrinus* is preserved as two almost complete stems and calyces. Usually the segmented structure of the crinoid becomes broken and preserved as fragments.
Above right This crinoid calyx, preserved without the stem, shows the detailed structure of the upper part of the animal.
Left Fossils of insects are extremely rare. The delicate structure of such creatures is only preserved as here in the dragonfly *Cymatophlebia longiolata*, when the creature is trapped in very fine muds or sandstones.

complex organisms with highly organized structures. Their name describes their spiny outer layer, which can be a hazard to bare feet! Ranging down to the abyssal depths, they may be free-moving, fixed by their spines among rocks, or may burrow into the soft sea bed. Echinoids have separate sexes and a plank-tonic larval stage. The shell, which is usually all that becomes fossilized, is typically a globular structure of calcite which contains the soft body. It is marked by thousands of pin-holes, called pores, through which project the tube feet, flexible appendages with flattened disc-shaped suckers at their ends. These are used for moving and clinging to the sea-bed and for gas exchange. On the outside of the shell are numerous thin spines, or in some forms, fewer large club-shaped spines which are used for locomotion or burrowing. These articulate by a ball-and-socket joint on the shell. Inside the shell the few major organs are suspended in a watery fluid which can be pumped into the tube feet to extend them. The shell is composed of many delicate calcite plates, joined along zigzag sutures.

A five-fold symmetry is given to many groups of 'regular' echinoids by the rows of encircling plates called 'ambulacra'. When alive,

the animal's shell is covered by membranous skin; this is lost in fossils. The 'irregular' forms have lost the five-fold symmetry, in many cases by atrophy of the ambulacra into shortened petal-shaped structures. Also, rather than having the round outlines of their regular relatives, the irregular echinoids, in response to different habitats, become flattened, dome-shaped or heart-shaped. Also the anus and mouth, central on top and underneath respectively in the regular echinoids, are posterior and anterior in the irregular forms, sometimes both appearing on the same side of the shell quite close together. The powerful mouth of sea-urchins is armed with triangular rasping teeth, enabling them to feed on a great variety of other marine creatures.

From the Ordovician, when echinoids first appear as fossils, to the present day, they have flourished all over the oceans. Their numbers were greatly reduced at the end of the Palaeozoic, but increased again during the Mesozoic, when the irregular forms flourished. Fossils occasionally abound, as in some of the Jurassic limestones which contain groups such as the sand dollars *Clypeus*, and in the Cretaceous chalk in Europe where the common, burrowing, heart-shaped *Micraster* is used as a zone fossil.

The delicate sea lilies

A strangely beautiful group of organisms, the crinoids, is classified with the echinoids in the phylum Echinodermata because of biological similarities, including five-fold symmetry. These plant-like animals, some of which are even called sea lilies, could well have served as the models for some of the strange creatures beloved of science-fiction writers! Their skeleton is a delicate waving stem of calcareous plates (called 'ossicles'), usually circular in outline but sometimes star-shaped as in the Jurassic form *Pentacrinus*. Above the stem (which may be a few inches high) is a cup (the 'calyx') of larger plates from which extend articulating arms. The soft body is within the calyx, and bears tube feet equipped with thousands of tiny hairs, or 'cilia', which reach up to gather food. A mucous web may envelop these extended organs to help trap their minute prey. The base of the structure is rooted into the soft sediment. Modern crinoids live in colonies, ranging from very shallow waters to the deep ocean-bed. From their first appearance in the Ordovician period, crinoids have been important as builders of limestone. Great masses of limestone are formed from the easily broken stems and ossicles of these creatures. The majority of the crinoids remained rooted to the sea-bed through-out their existence, but the modern *Pentacrinites* picks up its anchor and swims through the sea with its stem trailing below, when it reaches adulthood.

Brittle stars and starfishes

Other groups of echinoderms are the wonderfully fragile Ophiuroids or brittle stars, common today and ranging back to the Ordovician, and the starfishes, which have left only a poor fossil record, but are well known in modern seas.

Insects

The remains of insects first grace the fossil record in Devonian rocks, such as the Rhynie Chert in Scotland, which contains fossil spring-tails. Dragonflies and cockroaches are found in the overlying Carboniferous rocks. Beetles, with their hard outer carapaces, appear in the Upper Palaeozoic, and butterflies in the Tertiary.

With their complex, mostly bony skeletons, the vertebrates have left a good fossil record, enabling palaeontologists to sketch a general outline of their evolutionary history. The origin of the group is obscure, because they probably evolved from some soft-bodied, non-fossilized invertebrate group, and because the earliest known vertebrate fossils are actually only fragments of bone. These date from the late Cambrian of Wyoming, USA, some 500 million years ago.

Jawless fishes

These early vertebrates were peculiar fish, called the Agnatha (meaning 'no jaws'). They are represented today only by their remote descendants the lampreys and hagfishes. However, during the Silurian and early Devonian periods, they were a dominant group of fishes. The Osteostraci are one of the best-known groups. They had greatly flattened heads, covered by a continuous bony shield, broken only by the sockets for the small pair of eyes on top, a single dorsal nostril, and a pineal or third eye. One peculiarity is the presence of areas of small plates, which are believed to indicate some kind of special sense organs. Perhaps these are related to the lateral-line sensory system, found in most fish, which detects pressure changes in the water. On the underside of the head region, there is a series of small gill openings. Behind the head, the body is triangular in section and covered by rows of large scales, and it ends in a well developed, asymmetrical tail fin. Judging by the flattened, heavy body, the osteostracans were bottom-dwelling fishes, incapable of particularly active or well-coordinated movement, and feeding by taking in organic debris and mud from the bottom, in a more or less unselective way through the simple, hole-like mouth.

The Heterostraci were a second important group of fossil agnathans, which differ from the osteostracans in having paired nostrils. The head was supported by a number of bony plates and the eyes were placed well to the side. The mouth lay on the underside and, although true jaws had not evolved, there was a series of small bony plates along the hind margin, indicating that, at least to some extent, particular items of food could be dealt with. The Heterostraci were a particularly diverse group; for example, some forms had enormously elongated snouts, while others were completely flattened from top to bottom, like modern flatfish.

In general, the Agnatha dominated the freshwater habitats until the start of the Devonian Period, living on or close to the bottom, protected from their only serious predators, the large, scorpion-like eurypterids by their heavy, bony armour, and feeding by taking in and sifting mud and detritus.

The development of jaws

During the Devonian, the Agnatha declined and became extinct, having been replaced by the second great group of vertebrates, the gnathostomes or jawed fishes. In fact, the first record of jawed fishes is somewhat earlier, during the Silurian Period, after which time they gradually spread throughout the world.

None of the known agnathans were ancestral to the jawed fish, although it is possible that the heterostracans, with their paired nostrils, could have been distantly related. The characteristics shared by all the jawed fishes include the presence of true jaws evolved from the front

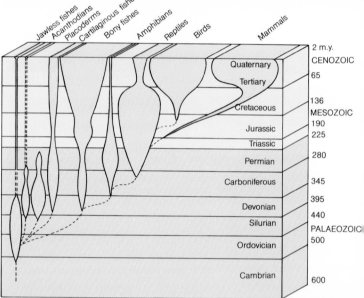

Above The Jurassic fish *Leptolepis* is beautifully preserved as a flat impression with the hard scales in position.
Right The evolution of the main vertebrate groups is shown in this diagram, from the primitive jawless fishes to modern mammals.
Below The Devonian lakes which existed in northern Britain contained many freshwater fish, some of which are now preserved in the Caithness Flagstones. Here, *Thursius pholidotus* is fossilized as a mass of black scales. There are many 'fish beds' in these rocks, containing numerous such fossils. They were formed when water levels in the lakes fluctuated, causing wide areas to dry out, killing the fish.

gill arch, which enabled them to feed selectively, and two sets of paired fins that must have greatly improved their swimming ability. Four distinct groups of jawed fish are known by the start of the Devonian Period, although the relationships between them are not at all certain, as they are surprisingly different from one another. The earliest group of all, the Acanthodii, appeared in the Upper Silurian. They were shaped like typical modern fishes, but bore spines in front of the fins, and had a number of very primitive features such as the absence of dermal bones along the margins of the jaw. The acanthodians were a very long-lived group of fishes, surviving throughout the Carboniferous and into the Lower Permian. The Placodermi formed a more important part of the Devonian fauna, both marine and freshwater, and were characterized by a heavy head-shield composed of several plates, and a similar bony covering protecting the front part of the trunk. Clearly they spent most of their

Above The Devonian fish *Cheirolepis*, preserved in Old Red Sandstone rocks from northern Scotland.

Below The bony fish *Dapedius*, of Mesozoic age, has a bony skeleton covered with scales.

time living on the bottom, and several of them actually became flattened.

The remaining two groups of jawed fishes were the ones that are still represented today. The Chondrichthyes, or cartilaginous fish, are known from isolated teeth in the Lower Devonian. Although cartilage does not usually

fossilize, many of the early members of this group laid down calcium salts within the cartilage, and have therefore left fossils. The Upper Devonian *Cladoselache* was remarkably shark-like, but was primitive in possessing such features as a terminal rather than a ventral mouth, and spines in front of the dorsal fins. Sharks of an essentially modern type, such as *Hybodus*, appeared within the Permian.

A success story

The most successful of all the jawed fish groups were the bony fish, or Osteichthyes, at least in terms of the number of species and the width of their adaptive radiation. Biologists use the term 'adaptive radiation' to describe evolution from a common 'basic' type of ancestor, leading to the appearance of several different species, each adapted to different lifestyles and habitats.) From a modest beginning in the Lower Devonian, there arose a radiation that is still with us today. The Actinopterygii or ray-finned fish are characterized by their fins, which are supported only by fine bony rays. The group gradually evolved, through the Palaeozoic and succeeding Triassic Period, becoming progressively more agile and able to exploit new sources of food. The earliest teleosts, the most advanced of the actinopterygians, made their appearance in Lower Jurassic rocks, from which time a vast radiation of teleosts occurred, coming to occupy the majority of the aquatic habitats available to fishes, and resulting in the 24,000 or so species alive today.

Lobefins, lungfishes and coelacanth

A rather less spectacular group of bony fishes are the Sarcopterygii, or lobe-finned fishes. They are characterized by the fins which have bones and muscles extending into them to make organs suitable for use in shallow water, and during the Devonian and Carboniferous they were a widespread and important group. The lungfishes, or Dipnoi, occurred throughout the world in marine as well as freshwater habitats. They gradually declined, but there are still three species left in tropical freshwaters today. The Crossopterygii were similarly important in the Mesozoic, but today are represented only by the very untypical coelacanth *Latimeria*. Crossopterygians were rapacious carnivores, feeding on the other fish and invertebrates of the time. To palaeontologists, their interest is, as we shall see, that they are the group from which the land-living amphibians evolved.

Evolutionary Tree of the Fishes

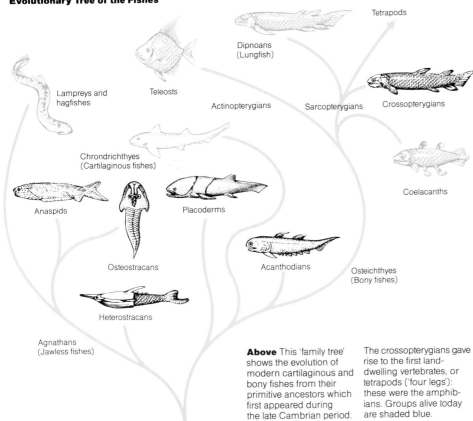

Above This 'family tree' shows the evolution of modern cartilaginous and bony fishes from their primitive ancestors which first appeared during the late Cambrian period.

The crossopterygians gave rise to the first land-dwelling vertebrates, or tetrapods ('four legs'): these were the amphibians. Groups alive today are shaded blue.

Sometime during the later part of the Devonian Period, perhaps 350 million years ago, the next great leap forward in vertebrate evolution took place. This was the origin of the tetrapods ('four-legs'), vertebrates adapted for life on land. The earliest known tetrapod is called *Ichthyostega*, and has been found in the Upper Devonian rocks of Greenland; traces of what are probably rather similar forms have been discovered recently in Australia. *Ichthyostega* was 3ft (1m) or so in length, and had well-developed front and hind limbs, a strong rib cage, and no sign of fish-like gills. There is therefore no doubt that it was a true tetrapod, although it did still retain several characteristics of the fishes. For example, the tail was supported by fin rays, and there was a well developed lateral line canal system running over the head.

Ancestors of the tetrapods

Of all the groups of fish living in the Devonian, those closest to the ancestry of the tetrapods were the crossopterygians, in particular those called the rhipidistians, such as *Osteolepis* from the Old Red Sandstones of Scotland, and *Eusthenopteron* from Canada. There are several reasons for believing this, particularly the structure of the fins. The paired fins of rhipidistians were supported by a series of bones and associated muscles that extended into the body of the fin. These bones, although much smaller, are closely comparable with the bones of the tetrapod leg. Of course, the outer part of the fish fin was still supported by fin-rays, and there is no sign of the evolution of the characteristic tetrapod foot at this stage. Rhipidistians also resemble tetrapods in possessing internal nostrils, and no doubt they were already capable of breathing air to a limited degree, with their incipient, lungfish-like lungs. The pattern of the bones of the skull of this particular group of fishes also shows a basic resemblance to that of *Ichthyostega* and other early tetrapods, although the actual proportions of the skull differ. The fishes have much shorter snouts than the tetrapods. There has been a great deal of discussion and argument among palaeontologists about the exact conditions that permitted the rhipidistian fishes to invade the land. Certainly the Devonian Period saw a great burst of evolution of land

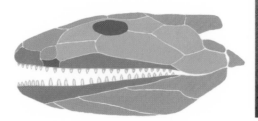

■	Tooth-bearing bones
■	Circumorbital bones
■	Temporal bones
■	Opercular bones

Above left The early amphibian skull is flatter and has a much more complete series of teeth than that of its fish ancestor *Osteolepis* (**below**).

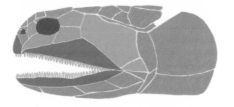

plants, with the appearance of new, larger ferns and horsetails. Accompanying these plants, there must also have been an increasingly important fauna of terrestrial invertebrates, such as primitive insects, and no doubt earthworms, snails and spiders. The potential for terrestrial vertebrate life was clearly established.

One commonly held idea is that the invasion of land actually occurred because of increasingly seasonal, arid conditions. Perhaps natural selection favoured those rhipidistian fishes that were most capable of crawling out onto land and migrating in search of more permanent bodies of water during the dry season. Thus, as time passed, there would be evolution of

increasingly effective limbs, air-breathing ability and so on.

An alternative theory, and in many ways a more attractive one, is that the origin of the tetrapods occurred during a period of warm, moist, tropical conditions. Here a new, terrestrial food source, and perhaps an area free of predators were available. There would be a high selective advantage bestowed upon any fish which could move up the muddy bank, however little at first, to colonize these new niches. As time passed, the evolution of the ability to remain out of water for a longer and longer period would follow, marked by the ever improving limbs, lungs, behaviour

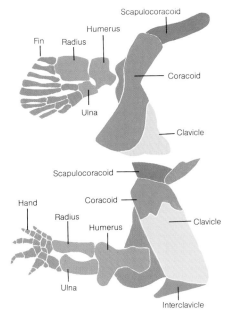

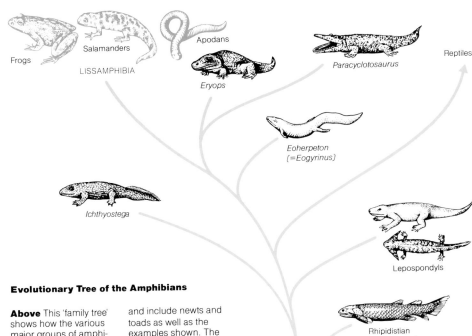

Evolutionary Tree of the Amphibians

Above These two draw-ings compare the shoulder girdles and fore-limbs of a rhipidistian fish (top) and an early tetrapod (bottom), such as the amphibian *Ichthyostega*. Both have the same basic layout, and the skeleton did not have to change very much to equip the tetrapod for a life spent (at least partly) on land. The elbow joint had to be formed, and the bones that made up the fish's fins became smaller and altered in shape so that they formed a hand with five separate fingers.

Above This 'family tree' shows how the various major groups of amphi-bians evolved from crossopterygian fishes such as *Osteolepis* (see also skulls on opposite page). The surviving groups are often referred to as the lissamphibians, and include newts and toads as well as the examples shown. The size of fossil amphibians ranged from the diminu-tive lepospondyls to the 6½ft (2m)-long *Eryops*, a labyrinthodont from the Lower Permian, which was a fish-eater.

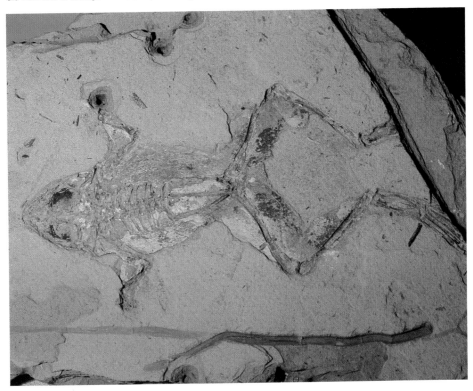

Above left The fossil skull of a labyrinthodont shows the heavy bony armour which typify these amphibians.

Above A well-preserved fossil frog. Frogs first appeared in the early Mesozoic period, but their fossil record is poor.

patterns and other features suiting the animals to life on land.

The heyday of the amphibians

Whatever may have been the initial selective pressures for the invasion of land, they were certainly followed by an explosive radiation of terrestrial tetrapods. The ensuing Carboniferous Period was a time of extensive lush, tropical and semi-tropical swamps, associated with the formation of the Coal Measure deposits. Potential invertebrate animal prey was abundant in the dense forests, creating conditions that were ideal for the early amphibians. These still depended on water to some extent, particularly for their reproduction, since they still had gill-breathing, tadpole-like larvae, which are occasionally found as fossils.

The most prominent group of fossil amphi-bians were the labyrinthodonts, mostly large animals up to 6ft (2m) in length, which were still quite well adapted for a partially aquatic life. They tended to have relatively small limbs, and long powerful tails, as in *Eoherpeton* from the Coal Measures of Britain. Their many

sharp teeth suggest that they lived mainly on a diet of fish. In fact, the labyrinthodonts were a very long-lived group, finally becoming extinct as late as the Upper Triassic, some 150 million years after their origin. Permian labyrinthodonts, such as the squat *Eryops* from the Lower Permian redbeds of North America, were often very much better adapted for life on dry land, with their relatively large, powerful limbs and reduced lateral line systems. Triassic labyrinthodonts, such as the African *Para-cyclotasaurus*, tended to return to the water, equippped with reduced limbs, flattened bodies and huge, fish-trapping mouths.

A second group of fossil amphibians which made their entrance in the Carboniferous were the lepospondyls, all small creatures, but of a great variety of types. Some, the aistopods, were actually without any trace of legs, although the rest of their structure shows that they were descended from normal tetrapods. Others were newt-like, with well-developed limbs indicating that they were adapted to drier conditions than other members of the group.

Modern amphibians

The modern amphibians—frogs, salamanders and the limbless apodans—did not appear in the fossil record until relatively much later. Indeed, the earliest undoubted member of the group is *Triadobatrachus*, a very primitive frog from the Upper Triassic of Madagascar. Otherwise, fossils of the modern groups do not occur until the Jurassic and succeeding periods. The origin of the modern Amphibia, (often termed the Lissamphibia) is by no means certainly established, but the most likely theory is that they descended from one of the labyrin-thodonts sometime during the Permian or early Triassic. *Doleserpeton* from Lower Permian rocks of North America has at least a number of lissamphibian characteristics. These include the structure of its teeth and the vertebrae forming its backbone.

Amongst the early Carboniferous tetrapods one particular group was destined to become extraordinarily successful as land vertebrates. These were the reptiles, which had evolved a new type of egg, the amniote egg, within which the embryo could develop directly, without the need for hatching as a larva in water. This enabled the reptiles to break free from a limited range of habitats close to water, in contrast to the amphibians, so that they could invade a much wider range of the land surface.

The first reptiles

The earliest reptiles are from the Middle Carboniferous, about 300 million years ago, and were small, superficially lizard-like animals, such as *Hylonomus* from North America. This creature had well-developed limbs, and no trace of a lateral-line canal system. It had many small, sharp teeth, indicating that insects formed its main diet. The actual origin of these primitive reptiles is not certain, for they differed from all the other early tetrapod groups in such features as the pattern of their skull bones. They are probably most closely related to some small labyrinthodont amphibian, although they may have evolved from some as yet undiscovered early 'prototetrapod'.

During the Upper Carboniferous, the reptiles remained less common than the amphibians that lived alongside them. Nevertheless, they were about to embark on a period of dramatic adaptive radiation. Two particularly important groups made their first appearances at this time. *Archaeothyris* was a synapsid reptile, distinguished by the presence of a pair of fenestrae, or 'windows', in the cheek region of the skull, behind the eyes. *Petrolacosaurus* is recognized as the earliest diapsid reptile, in this case distinguishable by the presence of two pairs of such fenestrae in the skull roof, one above the other. These two reptiles represent, respectively, the beginning of the two great phases of the reptilian adaptive radiation, which were to succeed one another during the next 215 million years of vertebrate history, throughout the whole of the Permian period and the succeeding Mesozoic Era. The first group contained the synapsids, or mammal-like reptiles; these were followed by the diapsid reptiles, such as the dinosaurs and their allies.

The mammal-like reptiles

The Synapsida are called the mammal-like reptiles because they are the group from which the mammals eventually arose. During the early part of the Permian, however, they were still very primitive, sprawling limbed animals called pelycosaurs, living within the tropics: by far the best-known come from the extensive redbeds of the Lower Permian of North America. During this time, the pelycosaurs came to occupy a range of niches, and many had evolved into quite large animals, often 6½-10ft (2-3m) in overall length. *Ophiacodon* was adapted for a crocodile-like mode of life, with long, fairly slender jaws and a formidable array of sharp teeth suitable for catching fish. Others, of which *Dimetrodon* is the best known example, adopted the role of large carnivore by developing enlarged canine teeth and a powerfully built skull. The sail on the back of *Dimetrodon* is believed to have helped it to maintain a suitable body temperature, by increasing the animal's surface area exposed to the sun. Yet other pelycosaurs, notably

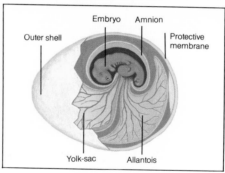

Above The development of the amniote egg enabled vertebrates to break free from a watery habitat. The amphibians needed water for their larval stages, but the closed amniote egg, retained within the mother, allowed reptiles to inhabit a variety of habitats.

Top The mammal-like reptile *Dimetrodon* in its Permian landscape. **Above** Palaeontologists extracting a plesiosaur from Jurassic clay. **Below** Fossil bones being channelled before extraction from rock. **Bottom** Preparation of an *Antrodemus* reptile skull in the laboratory.

Edaphosaurus (which also had a sail on its back), evolved short, powerful jaws with batteries of blunt teeth suitable for dealing with a plant diet.

Thus the pelycosaurs dominated the land, although they seem to have been restricted mainly to low-lying regions. They probably still depended on a freshwater habitat, with fish as an important part of the delicate natural balance, and labyrinthodont amphibians such as *Eryops* and *Cacops* very much in evidence. Other kinds of reptiles, such as the primitive *Captorhinus*, were also present during the early Permian, but not in any abundance.

Mass extinction of the pelycosaurs

Sometime during the Middle Permian, about 250 million years ago, the pelycosaurs disappeared from the fossil record. What actually caused their extinction is not clear, but certainly they were almost immediately replaced by their descendants, the therapsids, or advanced mammal-like reptiles. These had evolved more powerful jaws and jaw muscles, and more

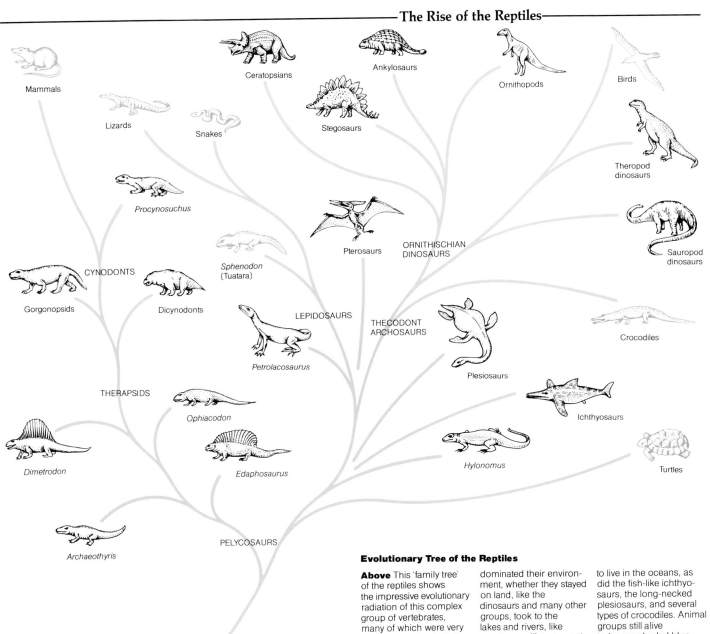

Mammals

Lizards

Snakes

Procynosuchus

CYNODONTS

Gorgonopsids

Dicynodonts

THERAPSIDS

Ophiacodon

Dimetrodon

Edaphosaurus

Archaeothyris

PELYCOSAURS

Ceratopsians

Ankylosaurs

Stegosaurs

Sphenodon
(Tuatara)

Petrolacosaurus

LEPIDOSAURS

Pterosaurs

ORNITHISCHIAN
DINOSAURS

THECODONT
ARCHOSAURS

Plesiosaurs

Hylonomus

Ornithopods

Birds

Theropod
dinosaurs

Sauropod
dinosaurs

Crocodiles

Ichthyosaurs

Turtles

Evolutionary Tree of the Reptiles

Above This 'family tree' of the reptiles shows the impressive evolutionary radiation of this complex group of vertebrates, many of which were very successful animals that dominated their environment, whether they stayed on land, like the dinosaurs and many other groups, took to the lakes and rivers, like most crocodiles, or went to live in the oceans, as did the fish-like ichthyosaurs, the long-necked plesiosaurs, and several types of crocodiles. Animal groups still alive today are shaded blue.

efficient walking and running. Like the pelycosaurs before them, the therapsids radiated widely to occupy the majority of the terrestrial niches, evolving into carnivores and herbivores of great variety. The dicynodonts, for example, lost their teeth early on, except for a pair of upper tusks. Instead, they had a horny, turtle-like beak adapted for plant-eating. Both in terms of numbers of individuals and of species, this group was the most successful therapsid group of all, forming great herds which roamed over the landscape. The main predators were the gorgonopsids, which had long, powerful canine teeth for killing their prey, and strong, interlocking incisors for dismembering it. Most gorgonopsids were moderate in size, but some reached a length of over 6½ft (2m).

On the road to true mammals

At the end of the Permian, another mass extinction affected the mammal-like reptiles, as indeed it affected virtually all the world's animals. Most of the therapsid groups disappeared, but one group which survived into the Triassic was the Cynodontia. These had actually appeared right at the end of the Permian in the form of *Procynosuchus*, for example, which had advanced over other therapsids by evolving extra little points on the teeth, and more elaborate, powerful jaw muscles. During the

ensuing Triassic, the cynodonts showed a progressive evolution towards mammalian characters. The teeth and associated jaw muscles became increasingly complex and capable of chewing food, while the limbs and vertebral column show that the animals were tending to move more like mammals with the knees and elbows turned under the body.

Sometime near the close of the Triassic period, true mammals finally appeared. However, during this period of cynodont evolution, the actual numbers of therapsids had been declining as the diapsid reptiles increased. Eventually, the diapsids completely replaced the synapsid reptiles, leading to the next great phase of reptilian evolution.

The diapsid reptiles, which had been represented in the Upper Carboniferous by *Petrolacosaurus*, remained as a very insignificant group throughout the Permian and early Triassic, even though members of the two major diapsid groups had in fact evolved during the Permian. The lepidosauromorphs, which were to include the later lizards and snakes, were represented by the primitive Upper Permian *Youngina*, a small, superficially very lizard-like animal. The Archosauromorpha, which later included crocodiles and dinosaurs, were represented at this time only by another rather lizard-like form called *Proterosaurus*.

Rise of the diapsids

During the Lower Triassic, while the synapsids were still important, neither of these diapsid groups radiated extensively. However, as the synapsids declined, so diapsids increased, particularly the archosauromorphs. In the Lower Triassic, the semi-aquatic, rather crocodile-like *Proterosuchus*, and more terrestrially adapted forms such as *Euparkeria* appeared as members of a group called the Thecodontia. By the Middle Triassic, the thecondonts were beginning to flourish, with quite a variety of forms, particularly well known from South America. However, they all still walked on all fours, with only a partial improvement on the primitive sprawling gait of their ancestors. It was from these later Triassic, more advanced thecodonts that the crocodiles and the dinosaurs evolved.

The strange rhynchosaurs

Before the appearance of the dinosaurs, there was a brief flourishing of a strange group of archosauromorphs called the rhynchosaurs. These were herbivores with horny beaks at the front of the mouth and multiple rows of blunt teeth at the back, and they achieved a size of some 6½ft (2m). Their origin is not clear, and they disappeared without trace before the end of the Triassic, but in between these creatures became very common.

From their origin in the second half of the Triassic period, the dinosaurs radiated with increasing pace until, by the Lower Jurassic, they had completely replaced the synapsids and become far and away the most important group of terrestrial vertebrates. Palaeontologists still do not know exactly which thecodont group they are most closely related to, or understand the detailed interrelationships amongst the various dinosaurs. There are three main groups of dinosaurs, and it is possible that they evolved independently of one another from a thecodont grade of ancestor. Whatever the truth, all dinosaurs do share one characteristic, which is an advanced, erect mode of locomotion. The knees and, at least in the case of the quadrupedal forms (those that walked on all fours), the elbows, have turned inwards below the body and the legs are held more or less vertically. Although most of the dinosaurs were very large, even gigantic, quite a number of rather smaller forms also occurred.

Vegetarian giants

The Sauropodomorpha included the large herbivorous prosauropods of the Upper Triassic, which were probably quadrupedal, and also their descendants the gigantic sauropods, or 'brontosaurs', of the Jurassic and Cretaceous. Sauropods too were quadrupedal and herbivorous, and grew to as much as 50 tons in weight. A well-known example is *Brachiosaurus* from the Upper Jurassic of North America and Africa. Sauropods have often been thought of as inhabitants of shallow lakes, but it seems much more likely that they actually lived on dry land, and used their enormously long necks and leaf-shaped, serrated teeth for browsing upon trees.

Carnivorous dinosaurs

The Theropoda were the carnivorous bipedal dinosaurs of the Jurassic and Cretaceous. Carnosaurs, such as the infamous *Tyrannosaurus*, were large and heavily built, usually with reduced forelimbs. However, there were smaller and more lightly built theropods too — the coelurosaurs, such as the ostrich-like dinosaur *Struthiomimus*, and the chicken-sized *Compsognathus* from Upper Jurassic rocks in Germany.

Duckbills, plated dinosaurs and their relatives

The sauropods and theropods have usually been grouped together as the Saurischia, defined by the particular structure of their pelvic bones. However, it is unlikely that they are actually closely related, and indeed it is possible that the sauropods are related to the third great dinosaur group, the Ornithischia, consisting of both bipedal and quadrupedal dinosaurs. The bipedal forms were the ornithopods, such as the large Lower Cretaceous *Iguanodon*, the duckbilled hadrosaurs with strange crests on their heads, and the 3ft (1m) high, possibly tree-dwelling *Hypsilophodon*, from the Isle of Wight, UK. Several groups of quadrupedal dinosaurs occurred, apparently living in great herds, much as do the larger mammalian herbivores of today. The earliest group were the stegosaurs, which are characterized by the row of large bony plates along the back. Possibly these plates were for protection, but maybe they also played a part in the animal's temperature regulation. Stegosaurs are one of the few groups to appear as early as the Upper Triassic, and they survived into the Lower Cretaceous. The ankylosaurs, or plated dinosaurs,

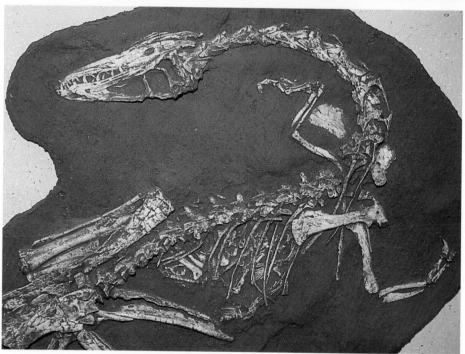

and the horned ceratopsians are both essentially Cretaceous dinosaur groups, both of which survived until the general extinction of the dinosaurs at the end of the Cretaceous.

Death of the dinosaurs

For 120 million years, the dinosaurs were the dominant land animals, occupying a wide range of habitats. Individual species of dinosaurs appeared, flourished and disappeared but the group as a whole persisted. Then, at the close of the Cretaceous period, about 65 million years ago, the dinosaurs disappeared completely. Many theories have been proposed to explain this mysterious event, but none is completely satisfactory. For a start, no-one

knows whether the dinosaurs died out abruptly, or whether they declined more gradually over some tens, or even hundreds, of thousands of years, because the techniques for dating fossils are not very accurate. Also, other groups of animals became extinct at the same time, such as the flying pterosaurs, the marine reptiles, and many marine invertebrates, such as the ammonites. On the other hand, several groups survived, such as the crocodiles, the birds and the mammals. At one extreme, there is the idea that a giant meteorite hit the Earth, causing a temporary, but, for many animals, intolerable alteration to the environment. At the other, there are suggestions that there was a slow but sure change in conditions associated with the

crocodiles took to the seas during the Jurassic and Cretaceous. Inexplicably, unlike the rest of the archosauromorphs, crocodiles survived the Cretaceous extinction, going on to give rise to the modern forms during the Tertiary.

The other main group of diapsid reptiles were the lepidosauromorphs, which had a much more modest, though more persistent, radiation. During the Triassic period, while the dinosaurs were replacing the mammal-like reptiles, lepidosauromorphs were a rare group. Only the sphenodontids (represented today by a single species, the tuatara of New Zealand) were of much significance. These were fairly small, lizard-like animals with specialized teeth forming cutting edges, which they may have used for feeding on soft invertebrates and perhaps also plants.

The first true lizards, the lacertilians, have been found in Lower Jurassic deposits, and they gradually increased in diversity throughout the rest of the Mesozoic and into the Tertiary. During the days of the dinosaurs, lizards were important small carnivores or insectivores, and no doubt they formed a significant part of the food of the smaller carnivorous dinosaurs. The mosasaurs of the Cretaceous were giant lizards which lived exclusively in the sea. They reached extraordinary lengths, of as much as 33ft (10m), and had a long powerful tail for swimming. The paired limbs were modified to form short steering organs. The last important group of lepidosauromorphs to appear were the snakes, the Ophidia. They are believed to have evolved from burrowing lizards during the Cretaceous period, although the details are not known. *Dinilysia*, for example, is a 6½ft (2m) long snake from Late Cretaceous rocks of Patagonia, in South America.

Major marine reptiles
Two other groups of reptiles were also prominent during the Jurassic and Cretaceous periods, only to become extinct at the end of the Mesozoic. These were, respectively, the completely marine plesiosaurs and ichthyosaurs. They are not at all closely related to one another, and the origin of neither is yet known. The ichthyosaurs were the more completely adapted for aquatic life, having a fish-like shape and limbs reduced to little more than fins. There was even a tail-fin at the end of the body, which was discovered preserved in some remarkably complete specimens from Holzmaden in Germany. Plesiosaurs were much less streamlined in outline, and the limbs were rather better developed, forming paddles which the animals used for swimming. The head was carried on a definite neck, which in many cases was long and flexible. Both these reptiles were adapted for catching fish, and occupied the kind of role in the Mesozoic seas that the dolphins and whales occupy nowadays.

Among the most remarkable reptiles are the turtles, terrapins and tortoises placed in the order Chelonia. These interesting animals seem to have descended directly from the very primitive reptiles, although they do not actually appear in the fossil record until *Proganochelys*, from Upper Triassic rocks of Germany. While turtles never became a particularly important part of the fauna, they were nevertheless extraordinarily persistent, being virtually unaffected by the Cretaceous extinction that befell many reptiles, and occurring little changed throughout the fossil record to the present day.

Above left Large sauropods like *Apatosaurus* are often depicted, as here, as swamp-dwellers, but probably lived on dry land instead.
Left The fossilized bones of *Coelophysis*. This small bipedal dinosaur walked upright, balancing its slender body with a long tail. A flesh-eater, it lived during the late Triassic.

Above *Tyrannosaurus*, a 50 ft (15m) carnivorous dinosaur, towers above the armoured *Ankylosaurus*, while *Anatosaurus*, a duck-billed dinosaur, wanders behind. The large *Pteranodon* flies above the luxuriant late Cretaceous landscape.
Right and **below** Fossil ichthyosaurs, Jurassic marine reptiles.

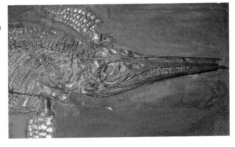

shifting of the continents, which led to a gradual deterioration of the climatic conditions required by the dinosaurs.

Flying reptiles
The pterosaurs were the flying reptiles of the Jurassic and Cretaceous. They are usually classified as archosauromorphs, although they are so highly modified that their exact relationships are not clear. The fourth finger was enormously elongated, and supported a membranous wing, while the hind limbs were small and weak. Like that of a bird, the entire skeleton of a pterosaur was lightly built and fragile. In size, pterosaurs varied from a few inches long to *Pteranodon* with a span of

nearly 33ft (10m), while even larger forms have been discovered recently in North America. Many species lived on the seashore, probably using the cliffs to launch themselves, and catching fish by gliding along just above the water. Others, however, lived inland. Like the dinosaurs, the pterosaurs died out completely at the end of the Cretaceous.

Crocodiles and others
Crocodiles are also archosauromorphs, descended from thecodont ancestors. Their earliest record is from the Middle Triassic, when they had already evolved the characteristic long snout, and from the start fish probably formed the main part of their diet. Several species of

Perhaps the most famous vertebrate fossils of all are those of *Archaeopteryx*, the primitive bird from the 150 million-year-old Solnhofen Limestones of Bavaria. These rocks were laid down in a large, very calm lake, and are so fine-grained that incredibly detailed fossils are preserved. That *Archaeopteryx* was a bird is attested by the clear impressions of large flight feathers on the forelimbs and tail. However, it was very primitive, for it retained many reptile characteristics such as teeth, a long tail, and the absence of a keel on the sternum bone for the attachment of the flight muscles. Altogether, five specimens have been discovered, and one feather impression.

The origin of birds

Palaeontologists have debated the relationships of *Archaeopteryx*, and therefore of the birds as a whole, for many years. The most favoured view is that it was descended from a group of very small, carnivorous bipedal dinosaurs, the coelurosaurs, such as the chicken-sized *Compsognathus* which also occurs at Solnhofen. They share with *Archaeopteryx* a long, flexible neck, well-developed forelimbs, and a very similar hind limb and pelvic girdle. Feathers probably evolved originally for insulation in a warm-blooded animal, rather than for flight, and may even have been present in dinosaurs.

Probably, some such small, bipedal dinosaur took to living in trees and at first it would have used its forelimbs to balance with, as it jumped from branch to branch. Gradually, evolution by natural selection would favour increasingly large feathers on the forelimbs and tail, to improve the bird's balance, and eventually the feathers became sufficiently well-developed to allow the creature to glide through the air. The ability to use these new wings for flapping flight would follow, which is the likely stage reached by *Archaeopteryx*.

Birds with teeth

All other birds evolved from some *Archaeopteryx*-like form. They next appear in the fossil record during the Cretaceous period, about 100 million years ago, in offshore marine deposits. These were the so-called 'toothed birds' for, like *Archaeopteryx*, they still had reptilian teeth in their jaws. *Ichthyornis* was the size and general shape of a tern, and probably a powerful flier. In contrast, *Hesperornis* had greatly reduced wings and large, presumably webbed feet. It seems to have been a kind of diving bird, floating on the sea and swimming by paddling its feet.

Evolution of modern birds

After the extinction of the dinosaurs and pterosaurs at the end of the Cretaceous, the birds commenced their major adaptive radiation. Unfortunately, bird skeletons are very fragile, so they are only rarely preserved as fossils. For this reason, palaeontologists know little in any detail of the evolution of the group. A number of large, flightless birds appear during the early part of the Tertiary. *Diatryma*, for example, was about 6½ft (2m) high and had a massive skull and beak, and powerful claws on its feet. This seems to have been a group of birds which took over the large, rapacious carnivore role that was left vacant with the disappearance of the carnivorous dinosaurs.

For the rest, most of the groups of modern birds appear sporadically in the fossil record of the Tertiary, usually as rare fragments.

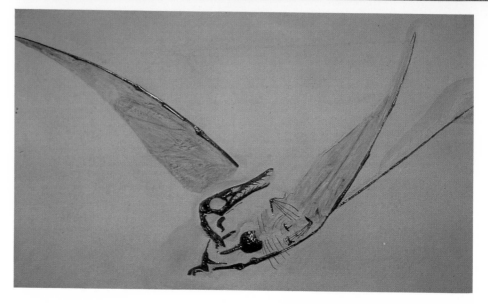

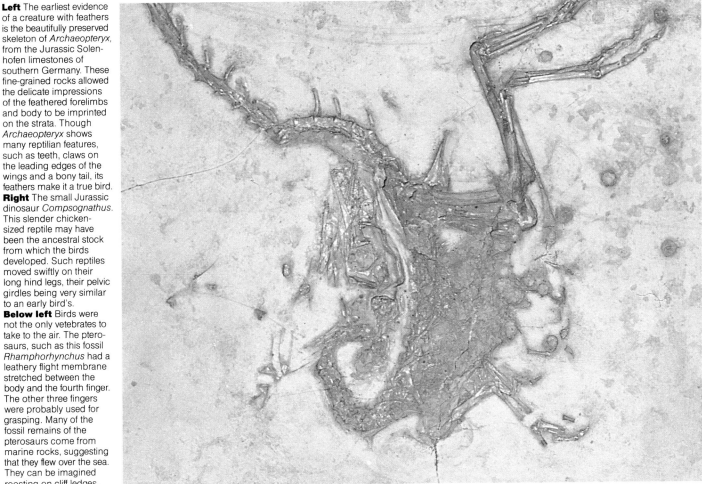

Left The earliest evidence of a creature with feathers is the beautifully preserved skeleton of *Archaeopteryx*, from the Jurassic Solenhofen limestones of southern Germany. These fine-grained rocks allowed the delicate impressions of the feathered forelimbs and body to be imprinted on the strata. Though *Archaeopteryx* shows many reptilian features, such as teeth, claws on the leading edges of the wings and a bony tail, its feathers make it a true bird.

Right The small Jurassic dinosaur *Compsognathus*. This slender chicken-sized reptile may have been the ancestral stock from which the birds developed. Such reptiles moved swiftly on their long hind legs, their pelvic girdles being very similar to an early bird's.

Below left Birds were not the only vetebrates to take to the air. The pterosaurs, such as this fossil *Rhamphorhynchus* had a leathery flight membrane stretched between the body and the fourth finger. The other three fingers were probably used for grasping. Many of the fossil remains of the pterosaurs come from marine rocks, suggesting that they flew over the sea. They can be imagined roosting on cliff ledges.

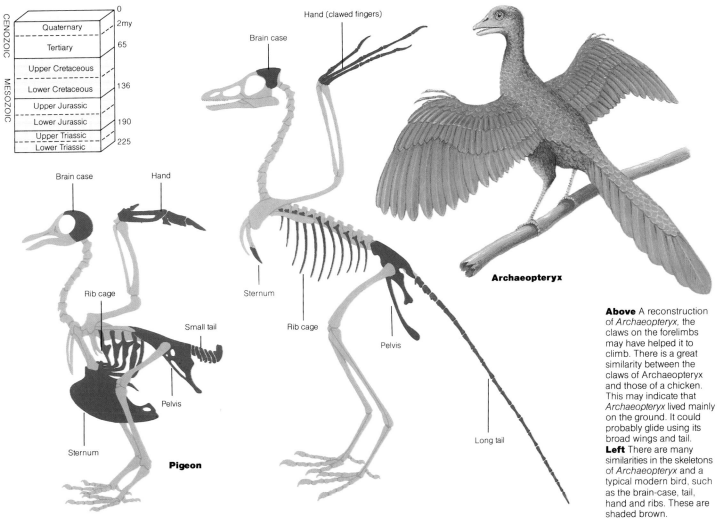

CENOZOIC	Quaternary	0 / 2my
	Tertiary	65
MESOZOIC	Upper Cretaceous	136
	Lower Cretaceous	
	Upper Jurassic	
	Lower Jurassic	190
	Upper Triassic	225
	Lower Triassic	

Hand (clawed fingers)

Brain case

Brain case

Hand

Sternum

Rib cage

Sternum

Rib cage

Small tail

Pelvis

Pelvis

Pigeon

Archaeopteryx

Long tail

Above A reconstruction of *Archaeopteryx*, the claws on the forelimbs may have helped it to climb. There is a great similarity between the claws of Archaeopteryx and those of a chicken. This may indicate that *Archaeopteryx* lived mainly on the ground. It could probably glide using its broad wings and tail.

Left There are many similarities in the skeletons of *Archaeopteryx* and a typical modern bird, such as the brain-case, tail, hand and ribs. These are shaded brown.

175

After the extinction of the great reptiles at the close of the Cretaceous period, some 65 million years ago, the mammals began to replace them as the most successful and diverse of terrestrial vertebrates. However, they had waited some 120 million years for this, since the first mammals occurred at the end of the Triassic. The mammals form the only vertebrate class whose origins are known in any detail from the fossil record, for they evolved from advanced cynodont mammal-like reptiles. They represent the culmination of the evolutionary trends seen within the Triassic cynodonts towards complex teeth and jaw musculature, more agile movements, with the knees and elbows turned under the body, and so on.

The first mammals

The first mammals are best represented by the morganucodontids, which had a world-wide distribution. They were very small animals, no larger than the smallest of living shrews, and are believed to have been nocturnal, like most of the primitive living mammals. The molar teeth had become very complex; each was equipped with several projections, or cusps, and there was a precise match between the upper and the lower teeth to give a strong but accurately cutting bite. Such teeth could cope with an insect diet. Apart from the skull, the skeleton was completely mammalian in form, with relatively long, slender limbs and the feet placed underneath the body. Certainly, the morganucodontids were very agile, and perhaps some of them were tree-dwellers.

Throughout the Jurassic and the Cretaceous periods, mammals remained small and mostly insectivorous. The only exception was a group called the multituberculates, which possessed broad, rodent-like teeth and must have fed at least in part on vegetation. Indeed, they seem to have occupied the niches later taken over by the rodents themselves. Why the mammals remained so small for all this time is not certain, but it may have been because of competition from the dinosaurs for the niches available to large animals.

Mesozoic mammals are quite rare in the fossil record, but this is probably because of their small size and woodland habitats. Occasionally, they do occur in considerable numbers, as in the fissure-fill deposits within Carboniferous limestones, for example in South Wales. Quite a number of different groups evolved, known mostly from isolated teeth and jaw fragments. The most important were the first true advanced 'therian' mammals, with their specially complex molar teeth, for these were the ancestors of the later radiation that led to the mammals of today.

The appearance of large mammals

The situation changed dramatically at the start of the Tertiary, for within only a few million years, a wide range of new kinds of therian mammals had appeared. During the Palaeocene, the first epoch of the Tertiary, relatively large mammals suddenly appeared. The creodonts were primitive carnivores, rather like large dogs in size and appearance, and possessing specialized shearing, or carnassial, molar teeth. The condylarths were corresponding herbivores, again primitive forms but with their molar teeth flattened and broadened for grinding tough plants. The feet carried little hoofs rather than claws on the ends of each of the five toes. There was also a considerable number of more specialized herbivores which had evolved from the condylarths, some of which were rather larger. For example,

Uintatherium occurred in North America and was as large as a rhinoceros, with peculiar horn-like protuberances on the skull. The litopterns of South America were very like horses; for example, they shared a tendency towards reduction of the number of toes to one, and enlargement of the crowns of the molar teeth—both features of modern horses.

Modern mammals evolve

Environmental conditions seemed to have been particularly favourable for mammals during the Eocene, when the numbers increased. This was the time of appearance of most of the modern mammalian orders, which existed alongside the archaic mammal groups. The miacids were the first members of the true Carnivora, although they were quite small and cat-like at first. The horses, or Perissodactyla, were represented by *Hyracotherium*, often called 'Eohippus', which was only about 1½ft (0·5m) in height and had three hind toes and four front ones. The other great placental herbivore group, the Artiodactyla, appeared in the form of the palaeodonts, which were ancestral to the deer, antelopes and cattle. Many other mammalian groups also appeared. These included the elephants, the bats, which evolved from insectivores, and the whales, whose ancestry is a mystery. Primitive primates were also quite common.

The next epoch, the Oligocene, suffered a deterioration of environmental conditions, and the number of mammal groups declined. It was the archaic groups that suffered most, the new, modern groups surviving. Thus the Oligocene was the time at which the essentially modern mammalian fauna began to take shape. A radiation of these groups occurred during the Miocene epoch, often however producing

Left Fossil bats are very rare in the geological record. This well-preserved specimen from the Eocene is an early example.
Right An artist's impression of various fossil mammals. **1** is the diminutive *Morganucodon* from the Triassic rocks of South Wales. This early mammal has features, like its jaw-joint, which have both reptile and mammal characteristics.
2 is a creodont, an early carnivore from the Tertiary. These creatures were parallels to the modern weasels, dogs and lions. The condylarth, **3**, is the ancestor of the ungulates, plant-eaters which have hooves. *Uintatherium*, **4**, a large rhinoceros-sized herbivore from the Eocene, had strange protuberances on its skull. One of the largest of mammals was *Baluchitherium*, **5**, which stood some 16ft (5m) at the shoulder. Giant elks, **6**, flourished in the Pleistocene, while the ancestral horse *Hyracotherium*, **7**, was widespread in Europe and North America early in the Tertiary. *Megatherium*, **8**, a giant ground sloth, lived during the Pliocene and Pleistocene, at the same time as the Sabre-tooth, **9**.

Left *Didelphis azarae*, one of the 76 species of opossum that live today in South America. Marsupials such as this evolved in South America and Australia when the two land-masses were joined, developing in isolation after they became separated in the early Tertiary period.
Right As Australia drifted northwards, the grasslands developed, and fast-moving marsupials with a new jumping method of locomotion, such as this red kangaroo, evolved to exploit the new source of food. Australia contains many such creatures which are unique to that continent.

quite unfamiliar forms, such as the giant rhinoceros *Baluchitherium*, standing about 16ft (5m) at the shoulder. This burst of evolutionary activity corresponded to an event of great importance for mammals, the spreading of the grasses. Suddenly, there was a vast new food resource available for those herbivores with teeth sufficiently well developed to be able to grind it up. Thus great numbers of artiodactyls and perissodactyls evolved, and following them a range of carnivores, which preyed on the herds of plant-eaters.

A puzzling extinction
The Pliocene and Pleistocene epochs saw a general consolidation of the radiation of modern mammals until, about 20,000 years ago, the last dramatic event took place. Simultaneously, throughout the world, many of the large mammal species disappeared. These included such diverse forms as the mammoths, the sabre-toothed tigers, the giant Irish elk, the giant sloth *Megatherium* and so on. The cause of this extinction is unknown; possibly it was a result of predation by early Man. At any event, it resulted in the mammal fauna that occurs on Earth today.

The marsupials
The mammals mentioned so far have all been members of the dominant group known as the placentals (in which the young remain within the mother's womb for a long time and are born at a relatively developed stage). A similar radiation of marsupial mammals (in which the young are born in a very undeveloped state and usually sheltered in a pouch) must also have been occurring, although at the moment very little is known about it. Soon after the start of the Tertiary period, South America and Australia had become isolated as island continents, and mammal evolution occurred on them independently of the rest of the world. Marsupials appear for some reason to have been isolated in these two areas. In South America, they coexisted with the unique placentals of that continent, and evolved into a range of carnivores, both large and small. When North and South America eventually became rejoined during the Pliocene, these marsupials declined in the face of a placental invasion from the north. In Australia, with no natural placentals, the marsupials were free to radiate into all the main niches, evolving into herbivores, such as the kangaroos and wombats, and carnivores, such as the thylacine 'wolf' *Thylacinus* and the native cat *Dasyurus*.

1 Morganucodon *Triassic*
2 Creodont *Early Tertiary*
3 Condylarth *Tertiary*
4 Uintatherium *Eocene* (*Early Tertiary*)
5 Baluchitherium *Oligocene* (*Tertiary*)
6 Giant Irish Elk *Quaternary*
7 Hyracotherium *Eocene* (*Early Tertiary*)
8 Megatherium *Pliocene* (*Late Tertiary*)
9 Sabre-Tooth Tiger *Pliocene* (*Late Tertiary*)

Man falls within the scientific definition of a mammal, so biologists presume humans to be the product of an evolutionary process similar to that which is known to have occurred with other groups of animals. In modern systems of classification Man is placed in the order of primates (from the Latin *primus*, meaning 'first'), the group of mammals that includes lemurs, monkeys, apes and Man. This classification is based upon studies of skeletal structures, muscles, organs, embryological development, vestigial organs, blood tests and the fossil record. Accordingly, any search for fossil primate remains is a search for potential ancestors of Man. In common with other primates, humans and their ancestors have binocular, stereoscopic vision, which helps in judging distances accurately, a shortish nose, which suggests that smell is less important than vision, a largish brain to coordinate body movement and the senses, and an opposable thumb allowing manipulation of objects with the hand.

Man is a member of the family Hominidae, which is a distinct family from that of the apes, the Pongidae. Included in the family Hominidae are both modern Man and the fossil ancestors. All human beings today belong to the same genus and species, *Homo sapiens*. It was once believed that Man had evolved from apes, not unlike those of today; however, the current view is that both man and the other living primates evolved from a common ancestor many millions of years ago and have developed separately since that time.

Fossil remains of man and his ancestors

Anthropologists can learn about our hominid ancestors from two sources: firstly, actual fossil remains, and, secondly, evidence of various implements used by early humans in their gradual progress towards culture and civilization, which tend to reflect intellectual development. The actual classification of the fossil remains depends very largely in some instances upon the definition of what constitutes 'Man'. Important criteria are the capacity to use tools, the size of the brain, the nature of jaws and teeth, and the ability to stand erect. In Man's erect posture, the skull is carried on the top of the backbone, rather than being hooked on the end as in apes.

Brain size

All primates have a relatively large, well-developed brain. The average cranial capacity of modern man is 1,350cc, which is about two-and-a-half times that of a much-bulkier adult gorilla, with a cranial capacity (on average) of 550cc. Although there is no simple direct relationship between skull capacity and mental ability, it does seem likely that there is a general relationship between the size of certain parts of the brain and mental development, and it is not unreasonable to assume that as the brain grew larger through time the intelligence of Man's ancestors also increased. When the skull

of a modern human is compared with that of a gorilla certain similarities are apparent, but also several important differences: the thicker skull of the gorilla features a protruding mouth with projecting canine teeth, no chin and a low sloping forehead with a prominent eyebrow ridge. Certain of these features appear in fossils of both early Man and others best described as near-men. Problems are, however, involved in the classification of these remains, as the skulls of juveniles are more Man-like than those of mature adult specimens.

Rare finds

Until recently, scientists were rather sweeping in the generalizations they made from hominid fossil remains. Every specimen of a fossil hominid was subjected to close study, and differences which would be regarded as minor in other animals were accorded great importance. Although an increasing number of fossil finds of early Man have been made in recent years, they are still rarities compared with the remains of other animals. Even the hard skeletal parts which do remain may have become distorted during the fossilization process, making accurate analysis rather difficult. There may be several reasons why relatively few of Man's ancestors have left a permanent record of their existence. For bones to be preserved, a body must be buried quickly or naturally covered by sediments. Early hominids were highly intelligent compared with other animals, and generally succeeded in avoiding being caught by floods and having their bodies covered by water-laid deposits. Until formal burial became widely practised, many remains would be scattered by scavengers and broken down by weathering processes. It is likely, too, that early hominids inhabited forested areas where organic acids in the soil would have tended to destroy their remains before they could become fossilized.

The distribution of fossil Man

Study of the distribution of early hominids is full of controversy. Human fossil discoveries and many archaeological excavations have

Above left Many of the most important fossil remains of early humans have come from the Olduvai Gorge in Tanzania, in East Africa.
Left Richard Leakey and Kamoya Kimeio examine a fossil hominid skull at Lake Turkana, Kenya.

Below The Leakey family have for many years worked at Olduvai Gorge extracting hominid fossils from the beds of volcanic ash. Richard Leakey has also worked in Kenya and is seen here excavating a skull at the Lake Turkana site.

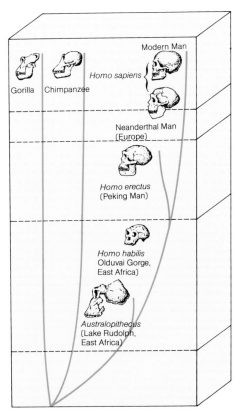

Hominid Evolutionary Tree

LATE PLEISTOCENE

250,000 years

MIDDLE PLEISTOCENE

800,000 years

EARLY PLEISTOCENE

1,500,000 years

PLIOCENE

5,000,000 years

LATE MIOCENE

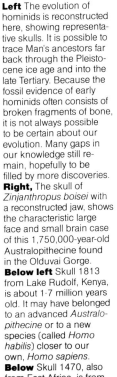

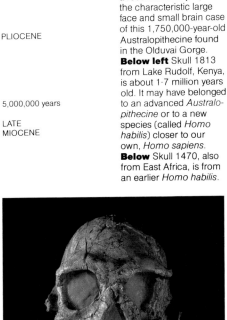

Left The evolution of hominids is reconstructed here, showing representative skulls. It is possible to trace Man's ancestors far back through the Pleistocene ice age and into the late Tertiary. Because the fossil evidence of early hominids often consists of broken fragments of bone, it is not always possible to be certain about our evolution. Many gaps in our knowledge still remain, hopefully to be filled by more discoveries.
Right, The skull of *Zinjanthropus boisei* with a reconstructed jaw, shows the characteristic large face and small brain case of this 1,750,000-year-old Australopithecine found in the Olduvai Gorge.
Below left Skull 1813 from Lake Rudolf, Kenya, is about 1·7 million years old. It may have belonged to an advanced *Australopithecine* or to a new species (called *Homo habilis*) closer to our own, *Homo sapiens*.
Below Skull 1470, also from East Africa, is from an earlier *Homo habilis*.

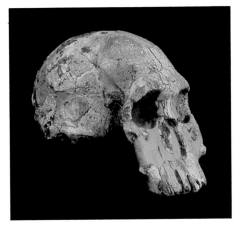

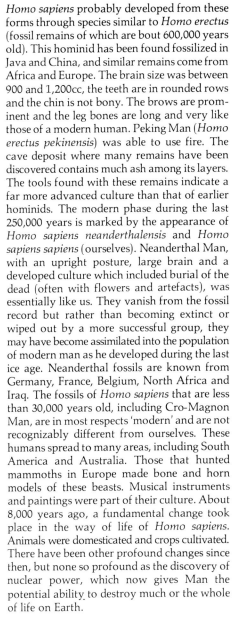

tended to be located in areas which are easily accessible, both politically and geographically. Once a find is made in an area, attention is focused there, giving a distorted overall view of the distribution of the species during its lifetime on the planet.

A number of fossil men, near-men and hominid ancestors have been identified, including *Australopithecus africanus, Homo habilis, Homo erectus, Homo sapiens neanderthalens and* early *Homo sapiens sapiens.* The creatures represented by such finds have usually been named after the localities in which the remains were found. Many of these discoveries have been very fragmentary: part of a jaw, a limb bone, a few teeth or a few pieces of shattered skull are all that have been found. The reconstruction and interpretations which have been made of such limited finds are always tentative. The evolutionary picture has been complicated by the classification of many finds as different genera and species, and maybe there was really a wider range of variation and geographic distribution within a particular genus or species.

Stages in hominid evolution
In sketching out the broad outlines of hominid evolution, we can trace the following development. From the late Miocene period there is

evidence of several hominids differentiated from the apes. As recently as 3 to 4 million years ago, the fossil record, particularly in South and East Africa, is relatively rich in the remains of the Australopithecines. These are true hominids. They were agile creatures with an average height of about 4½ft (1·35m). The fossil limb-bones suggest a bipedal stance and gait, and the teeth are those of animal which included meat in the diet. Australopithecines probably hunted their prey with the aid of stone weapons. They had a small brain, about the size of a chimpanzee's, but its structure resembled that of humans. Very striking evidence of the upright gait of these 'ape-men' is in the form not of bones but as a series of fossil footprints belonging to two adults and a child. Dated at 3·6 million years, these were found by Dr. Mary Leakey, a member of the famous Leakey family, who have devoted a lifetime of research to homininid evolution. The footprints are in a layer of hardened volcanic mud in Tanzania. *Homo habilis,* found by Dr. Leakey, and dated at 1·75 million years, is though to be nearer to a modern man than were the Australopithecines, having a larger brain (at 670cc, about half the size of a modern human's) and the ability to use tools. Some researchers regard *Homo habilis* as an advanced Australopithecine.

Homo sapiens probably developed from these forms through species similar to *Homo erectus* (fossil remains of which are bout 600,000 years old). This hominid has been found fossilized in Java and China, and similar remains come from Africa and Europe. The brain size was between 900 and 1,200cc, the teeth are in rounded rows and the chin is not bony. The brows are prominent and the leg bones are long and very like those of a modern human. Peking Man (*Homo erectus pekinensis*) was able to use fire. The cave deposit where many remains have been discovered contains much ash among its layers. The tools found with these remains indicate a far more advanced culture than that of earlier hominids. The modern phase during the last 250,000 years is marked by the appearance of *Homo sapiens neanderthalensis* and *Homo sapiens sapiens* (ourselves). Neanderthal Man, with an upright posture, large brain and a developed culture which included burial of the dead (often with flowers and artefacts), was essentially like us. They vanish from the fossil record but rather than becoming extinct or wiped out by a more successful group, they may have become assimilated into the population of modern man as he developed during the last ice age. Neanderthal fossils are known from Germany, France, Belgium, North Africa and Iraq. The fossils of *Homo sapiens* that are less than 30,000 years old, including Cro-Magnon Man, are in most respects 'modern' and are not recognizably different from ourselves. These humans spread to many areas, including South America and Australia. Those that hunted mammoths in Europe made bone and horn models of these beasts. Musical instruments and paintings were part of their culture. About 8,000 years ago, a fundamental change took place in the way of life of *Homo sapiens.* Animals were domesticated and crops cultivated. There have been other profound changes since then, but none so profound as the discovery of nuclear power, which now gives Man the potential ability to destroy much or the whole of life on Earth.

The Earth contains many resources and treasures exploited by Man from metals, minerals, oil, gas and coal to water and rock. The land is used for crops and stock rearing, rivers and lakes are dammed and canals, even in the sandy wastes of the Middle East (*right*), provide shipping routes for large ships. This exploitation of the Earth has usually been without thought of consequences.

Man's mark is rarely to improve the Earth for anything but himself. We test devastating nuclear weapons by blowing up beautiful coral islands; we flood fertile valleys, often producing earthquakes. The raw materials and fuels we plunder are finite. Coal and oil have a short life. Nuclear fuels, which so easily become weapons, could, if harnessed with the as yet lacking safety and confidence, be a fuel to last forever.

THE MARK OF MAN

Man has the power to exploit the Earth's riches. Modern technology helps us to gain metals and fuels, often with no respect for the land. With sensible and efficient use of our power, both Man and the Earth could benefit

The world's greatest waterfall system, measured by volume, is the Guairá Falls on the Paraná River that divides Paraguay from Brazil. Sometime before the end of the 1980s the Guairá Falls will disappear, inundated by the rising waters of a 100-mile (60km) long reservoir piling up behind the Itaipú Dam. The commercial benefits will be immediate and large. Long-term environmental and ecological effects have escaped official calculations. This is typical of Man's earth-shaping activities through the ages.

Man is a latecomer to the planet. If Earth's history could be condensed into a feature-length film, the story of mankind would occupy no more than a couple of frames at the end. Yet, in his brief history, Man has affected his physical environment more than any other creature, with the possible exception of the corals in the oceans.

For millennia, Man was no great earth-shaper. Aerial photographs reveal the dim outlines and shapes of early forts and earthworks, field systems and enclosures. But the Earth's own steady cycles, the weather and the growth of plants, and the slow accretion of soil, have taken back most of the early advances made with plough, dam and dyke. Man's early shapings have been blurred and overtaken by the natural forms and lines of the planet. We see them now as vague shadows of what they once must have been.

Increasing demands

As Man has become more sophisticated, his needs and relationships more complicated, so have his demands on the land grown, along with his ability to implement them. The desire for territory became insatiable, particularly in crowded communities, and Man was inspired to struggle to wrest arable land from marshes, sea-flats and other wetlands.

The constant fight of the modern Netherlander against the encroachments of the wild North Sea has a history at least as old as Christianity.

Above The Guairá Falls on the Paraná river, Brazil, will disappear before the end of 1980s when the water level rises after the river has been dammed.

Above right The Itaipú Dam in Brazil and Paraguay shows the scale of Man-made water diversion projects. Here are the main dam and a diversion canal.

Below A massive dam in the Dutch Delta Project. This scheme uses huge steel and concrete dams to seal off the mouths of the Schelde, Maas and Rhine.

Right American cities like Los Angeles are the epitome of the 'concrete jungle', with highways and buildings obliterating millions of acres of land.

The Friesian settlers of the lowland bogs, lakes and estuaries survived by means of artificial mounds, or 'terps', connected by embankments that were the first dykes, enclosing the protected 'polders' typical of modern Holland. A see-saw struggle with the sea culminated in 1953 in a disastrous tidal breakthrough, with 1,800 dead and almost half a million dispossessed. As a direct result, the Dutch commenced the awesome Delta Project, to seal off the mouths of the Schelde, Maas and Rhine rivers with giant steel and concrete dams controlled by huge sluices. With constant wind and tide monitoring, and computer regulation of flows, Delta is earth-shaping on an ambitious scale, transforming the great tidal estuaries into freshwater lakes, with the enclosed islands linked by a network of highways on top of the dams.

Concrete landscapes

Man's conscious earth-shaping takes many forms. After the invention of the mass-produced automobile he proceeded to concrete and asphalt over ever-increasing acres of land in the form of roads, highways, freeways, motor-ways and all the other burgeoning tributes to the internal combustion engine. With the growth of the roads came a further growth of the cities,

with suburbs spreading outwards like ripples in a pond, and ribbon developments making the roads themselves into elongated cities, so that it has become difficult to know where one metropolis ends and the next begins. In some places, the land itself seems to have disappeared for countless miles beneath the seemingly endless acres of concrete and the brick.

Building canals and taming rivers

The first irrigators dug trenches, and their descendants in the 20th century have continued to divert, block, and rearrange the natural disposition of water courses, as well as introducing canals and canal systems to act as highways, to lift cargo vessels over high terrain, to carve thousands of nautical miles off sea routes, and to link seas and oceans by means of daring short cuts. Many canals were cut and lost again over the centuries across the Isthmus of Suez to provide direct access from the Mediterranean to the Red Sea, before the current Suez Canal was completed in 1869, and Port Said built up on its excavated mud from a handful of huts to a major world port. The Panama Canal, opened in 1914, links the Pacific and Atlantic oceans, using a system of locks to lift ships to Lake Gatun, 100ft (30m) above sea level. A second Panama Canal will have almost three times the depth of the first, to take larger vessels. The St Lawrence Seaway, opened in 1959, allows shipping to penetrate over 2,000 nautical miles into the American continent from the Atlantic by providing a deep passage into the Great Lakes.

In the USSR ambitious irrigation schemes include the diversion of north-flowing rivers into south-flowing ones in an attempt to cultivate arid desert land. The Soviets also plan to use canals to bring south water which would normally flow out northwards into the Barents Sea off north-west Russia.

Living in the sea

Our ability—and willingness—to change the world grow along with our technological expertise. The Japanese, one of the most technologically advanced nations in the world, use their engineering know-how to extend the physical limitations of their crowded, mountainous islands. Instead of taking up precious land, new coastal highways are cantilevered out over the ocean. In Tokyo Bay, large areas of land reclaimed from the sea around river estuaries have been converted into modern industrial port facilities. Artificial islands are already being used as sites for industrial units such as steelworks, and Japanese architects and engineers have produced a host of schemes for water-sited cities and commercial centres. As land throughout the world becomes scarcer, Man is turning increasingly to the expanses of the oceans. In the Caribbean, scientists are building experimental artificial reefs, using electrical charges to stimulate organic growth on large submerged steel-net structures. Elsewhere, advanced concrete technology has led to designs for schemes such as Sea City, a concrete and steel 'island' built on piles in the North Sea, to house a self-contained population of 30,000, complete with its own climate.

We have come from digging-sticks to nuclear physics in a relatively short time. We move mountains and flood valleys with the same assurance with which we once hoed crude rows for planting. But we may have to pay a high price for our godlike behaviour.

Man's greatest effect on the physical world has been involuntary. As he changed from a hunter and gatherer into a crop-grower and farmer, he assumed, unwittingly, a responsibility for the fragile layer that is the planet's fertile soil. Man's wisdom and practice have often fallen short of that responsibility, and the results can be seen in ruined land.

At some of the earliest farming community sites to be examined, in the hills to the east of the Tigris and Euphrates Plain in present-day Iraq, 10,000 years of continuous human habitation have denuded the land, depleted the soil, and led to its erosion through exposure to weathering. Archaeological evidence indicates that the earliest inhabitants farmed more fruitfully, and enjoyed a more nutritious diet than their modern descendants. The Neolithic farmers who lived there grew subsistence crops. Modern farmers grow to sell, and the steady increase in monoculture farming—the concentration upon a single marketable crop—has been responsible for large-scale erosion.

Reaping the results of monoculture
Cotton was king until well into the 20th century, and throughout the Southern States of the USA plantation after plantation grew little else. The chief cotton-growing area, Piedmont region, lies between the East Coast and the long ridge of the Appalachian mountains, crossing several states, including Virginia, Georgia, and North and South Carolina. The planting, tending and cropping of the cotton required continuous, scrupulous weeding, and at the end of each season the land was completely cleaned for the next planting. The soil was laid wide open to the weather, and became vulnerable to sheet erosion.

Bare earth is swiftly broken up by heavy rains. One heavy downpour can strip away a layer of soil that has taken a thousand years to develop. As the rain runs off, seeking the lines of least resistance, it carries the soil with it, and begins to dig escape channels in the bare earth. This process is progressive. As the channels become deeper, and the substrata less porous, the water runs faster, digging deeper still. In parts of Georgia some of the gullies excavated by rains in vulnerable ground have reached depths of up to 150ft (45m).

In Natal, South Africa, deep gullying has resulted from the overgrazing flocks of sheep on steep hills. The stripped hillsides allow a very heavy run-off of rain into the valley below, where the gullies have been carved.

Above Terracing steep hillsides has for thousands of years been a way of countering erosion, as here in Bali, Indonesia.

Below Tropical rain-forests are being destroyed at an alarming rate. Here in Malaysia the jungle is scarred by a new road.

Interfering with nature

In the natural order and rhythm of things there is a constant production of soil, of which some is washed away to be deposited by water courses on their banks, flood-plains and deltas. Man's intervention has speeded up the process to the point where delicate and complex balances are lost. Soil production can never keep up with the soil-loss caused by ignorant land-use. In some societies the land has been sculpted into careful terraces to prevent rain erosion.

Man also causes unplanned physical changes through his interference in the functions of rivers. The increase of eroded material, and mechanical innovations, such as dams and levees, shake 'mature' rivers out of their repose. Dams creating artificial lakes in the river's course can disrupt alluvium deposition patterns, as can the building of substantial flood barriers. Lake Mead, on the Colorado River in the USA, is held in place by the massive Hoover Dam, and is one of the world's largest artificial lakes. Ranking second only to the Mississippi in the USA as an alluvium-bearing river, the Colorado lays down heavy deposits where it enters the lake, creating a delta which will have entirely filled the lake with silt within 400 years. The Mississippi carries over 500 million tons of suspended material every year, to be distributed between flood-lands and delta. However, since extensive levees and flood barriers have been built by communities living near to the river, all the alluvium is carried straight down to the expanding delta. Silt that once annually replenished Mississippi wetlands now pours along with the river between high banks, ultimately to fall over the leading edge of the delta, which is expanding seawards at a rapid 200ft (60m) per year. The wetlands, deprived of their annual silt replenishment, are sinking permanently below water level.

Problems on the beach

Man has always been attracted to coastal areas both to live and to take recreation. A house on the beach sounds idyllic, but when we start to build sea-walls, breakwaters and groins to 'protect' our house and stretch of beach from the sea's ravages, we as often as not end up destroying the very beach that attracted us in the first place. The effect of such mechanical 'stabilization' of a beach is often to increase the steepness of the shore-face, which in turn increases the localized power of the waves. The man-made structures greatly enhance the tide's ability to remove beach material, until nothing is left except bedrock or clay, and the structures themselves.

Miami Beach, crammed tight, shoulder to shoulder, with hotels as well as holiday-makers, lost most of its beach for twenty years until, in the 1970s, a limited section was replenished artificially—at a cost of $64 million. This replenishment will have to be repeated regularly every ten years. Geologists at Duke University claim that the best way to look after a beach is to leave it alone. Mechanical intervention upsets the balance which exists almost everywhere between sea and beach. So many beaches were lost in this way along the New Jersey coast, that the process is sometimes called 'New Jerseyization'.

In the Soviet Union, where harbour and shore installations have resulted in the loss of many miles of beach on the Baltic, Caspian and Black Seas, the sea's own power is being utilized to replenish depleted areas. Thousands of tons of material are strategically dumped at the sea's edge so that tide, storm and wind can combine to carry large loads of sand and pebbles to areas needing restitution, sometimes situated many hundreds of miles away from the dumping site.

Above left This Syrian shepherd tends his flock on a stony desert, the end result of overgrazing.
Left In Natal, S Africa, the original grassland can be seen behind the over-grazed eroded wastes.

Above and **below** Two views of the Hoover Dam which holds the water of the man-made Lake Mead, on the Colorado River in Nevada, USA. This huge artificial lake will silt up within 400 years.

Above In Winter Park, Florida, a sink hole 400ft (120m) wide and 125ft (40m) deep has led to the collapse of houses and roads.
Left Water can suddenly build up to devastate the land as here, near Punta Cormorante, in the Galapagos Islands, off the coast of Ecuador.
Below The area near Gilgit, on the fringes of the Hindu Kush Mountains, N India, shows the great erosive power of running water.

Man's ingenuity is matched all too often by his talent for disaster. Some of his proudest engineering achievements have produced unforeseen side effects comparable in scale to natural calamities, and including landslides, floods and even earthquakes.

In his enthusiasm to change the Earth's face, man excavates material in one place and heaps it up in another, sometimes unaware that excavation destroys complex soil structures, while piling can produce stresses and forces which the unstructured spoil is not equipped to withstand. Flow slides occur when a mass suddenly loses cohesive strength and flows like a liquid. Sudden shocks, such as explosions, can trigger flow slides in waste tips in the same way that they can set off avalanches in snow.

Accumulated stresses can also initiate the flow once a critical point is reached. On the morning of October 22, 1966, in the Welsh mining village of Aberfan, the waste dump above the village suddenly flowed down to bury the local school, killing 144 people, 116 of them schoolchildren. Natural slopes usually have an optimum profile geared to their internal strength. The artificial cutting of banks and slopes can create landslide conditions where the ground was firm before. The 45° slopes of the Gaillard Cut on the Panama Canal have several times collapsed into landslides of over 35 million cubic feet (1 million cubic metres) of soil thundering down the slopes.

When the earth falls in
Subsidence, the vertical collapse of the earth, is most obviously caused by roof failure in mine tunnels, but can also result from pumping operations which have altered local soil pressures and geological structures. The Long Beach region of California, USA, has been sinking

Left The Kariba Dam in Zimbabwe is one of the large dams on the Earth which has caused many earth tremors by putting great pressure on the crust.

Above Nuclear tests, as here at Bikini Atoll in 1954, make shock waves capable of triggering earthquakes. Other Pacific atolls have been vapourized.

steadily at a rate of up to 10in (25cm) a year since the 1940s, because oil pumping has reduced the 'neutral' stresses which give the oil-bearing rock its structural strength. As the oil is pumped away, the oil-bearing rock consolidates, and the earth above it subsides. Water pumping can have the same effect. Significant subsidence in Houston, Texas and in Mexico City is attributable to the removal of water from layers of sand and soft clay which depend on their water content for stability.

Degraded mountain-sides
We have seen how the thoughtless stripping of vegetation can cause soil erosion. Where this is done on steep terrain, the results can be faster and more dramatic. The main culprit in mountainous country is more often the timber company than the farmer. Loggers cut tree cover, which serves a vital purpose both in protecting the soil from direct rain erosion with its foliage, and in holding the soil firm with its roots.

The steeper the country, the more immediate the effect of logging. The valleys of Nepal are often thousands of feet deep, with rivers in the valley bottom carrying upland water all the way south into the plains of India. Intensive logging in Nepalese valleys has resulted in complete deforestation in many cases. The harsh winter storms and spring snow-melts swiftly strip from the bedrock earth that has taken millennia to be deposited.

The loss is not just water-borne, but sometimes, as in the 3,300ft (1,000m) deep Trisuli valley in Nepal, takes the form of gigantic landslides, which sweep away whole farming communities. The damage does not stop there. The steep mountain-sides, radically eroded, become 'degraded'. Without a soil and plant repository

for seasonal snows and rains, the naked hillsides become instant cataracts instead of serving to regulate a steady and delayed water run-off. Seasonal snows and rains are shed instantly from the valley walls, pouring directly down into the river far below. The rapid increase in water burden causes disastrous floods hundreds of miles downstream where the land flattens out into the Indian plains.

Triggering earthquakes
Perhaps the most feared of natural disasters is the earthquake. Throughout history Man has ascribed earthquake activity to angry gods, but for all his arrogance has never considered himself capable of affecting such awesomely powerful events. However, a growing body of evidence seems to suggest that seismic patterns can be directly influenced by Man and his works. On December 10th, 1967, a major earthquake shook Konya in India, a region with no history of seismic activity until five years previously. In 1962 the Konya dam and reservoir had been completed, and from that time on, there began a series of seismic indications that appear related to the water level in the reservoir. The powerful 1967 earthquake occurred after four months of high water, and it seems most likely that the weight of the water triggered the event.

The filling of both the Hoover Dam on the Colorado River in the USA, and the Kariba Dam in what is now Zimbabwe, were followed by earthquake patterns. The Hoover Dam created the largest artificial lake in the world, Lake Mead, and in a ten year period after filling, over 600 tremors were recorded locally.

Liquid pressure, too, seems capable of affecting seismic behaviour. For instance the US Geological Survey studied and recorded the effects of

waste fluids disposed of in an artificial well over 3,600ft (1,100m) deep near Denver, Colorado. The deep bore-hole penetrated crystalline rocks of the Precambrian Era, and the geologists found that the waste fluid levels were closely related to the number of shocks. This example, and those from oilfields, where water injection under pressure during secondary oil extraction was also observed to cause tremors, have led some scientists to speculate that it might be possible to relieve the major stresses leading to large earthquakes. They propose using fluid injection to bring about a series of smaller, safer shocks.

Nuclear weapon testing
There is no doubt that Man's greatest potential for triggering earthquakes lies in the enormous energies and pressures released by nuclear explosions. Underground weapons tests in Nevada, USA, have released tectonic energies as well as energy emanating from the bomb explosions, and the 'strain field' of local tectonic plate formations has been moved permanently many miles from the pre-test position.

There is a considerable difference in the shock-wave patterns emitted by underground nuclear explosions and earthquakes. While there have, to date, been no major earthquakes as a result of nuclear explosions, this may just be because the size of many tests has been limited. Seismic activity is erratic, unpredictable, and comes in a vast range of intensities. Nuclear weapons are already capable of 'earth-changing' on a massive scale—Pacific atolls used for H-bomb tests have been virtually vapourized. To that threatening power must now be added the possibility of inadvertently unleashing seismic energy as a result of underground nuclear weapons tests.

No other creature fouls its own nest with quite the same thoroughness as Man. Since he considers the whole planet to be his nest, the effects of this fouling are felt by the whole community of living creatures. Up until relatively modern times the Earth's own efficient cleaning systems took care of Man's bad housekeeping. Rivers and tides disposed of sewage, and the scars left upon the landscape were easily healed in a few short years by plant growth. Smoke and fumes from hearths and kilns were quickly dissipated by breezes into the purifying atmosphere. However, for the last two hundred years industrial Man has been producing increasing quantities of pollutants, which at first challenged and eventually overcame the planet's ability to neutralize them. Not only the quantity of these pollutants, but also their toxicity and destructive power, have grown alarmingly over the years.

Industrial production, energy generation, and the day-to-day processes of modern life all produce wastes. It is a peculiar modern schizophrenia that we create and employ ever-updated technologies with the contemporary and progressive side of our natures, yet when it comes to disposing of the inevitable waste products we revert to the unscientific, unenquiring attitudes of a previous age. Anything not needed is thrown away: into the river, into the sea, into the atmosphere, into the nearest ditch. Only very recently have we begun to devise, often reluctantly, the necessary technologies to deal with the Pandora's box full of exotic wastes perpetually upturned by industrial society.

Chimneys of death

The chimney of the copper and nickel smelter at Sudbury, Ontario, Canada, reaches a quarter of a mile (0·4km) into the sky. The 1,300ft (400m) stack emits one per cent of all artificial sulphur emissions on the planet, equalling from this one site the average annual amount of all the natural sulphur emissions from the world's volcanoes. The Sudbury chimney, and others like it in other countries, is a prime example of how not to deal with harmful wastes. The chimney was built tall so that the sulphur dioxide it belches forth in giant clouds is blown by winds away from Sudbury, away from Ontario, and eventually away from Canada, travelling far south into the USA. Some would call it a fair exchange, as it is estimated that eastern Canada receives an annual three million tons of sulphur dioxide from the USA's fossil-fuel-burning plants.

Acid rain

Sulphur dioxide and nitrogen oxide released into the atmosphere return as acidic gases and particles, or mix with rain to form solutions of sulphuric and nitric acid, falling to earth as the now infamous 'acid rain'. Often as acidic as vinegar, the acid rain kills plant and animal life alike, wipes out fish stocks in lakes and rivers, and destroys forests. Britain uses the 'tall-chimney solution' to send a large proportion of its sulphur emissions across the North Sea to Scandinavia, where in some areas 50 per cent of mature pine trees are visibly suffering from acid rain damage. Many of the chief offenders in this type of industrial pollution have actively resisted the idea of emission reductions. With pH levels of 4·5 and lower being recorded in streams and lakes, great numbers of fish die. The eggs are killed by the acid, which also upsets the mature fishes' delicate chemical

Above After a severe oil spillage in the Channel, this English beach at Folkestone became seriously polluted. A bulldozer tackles the thick black oil.

Below This coal-burning power station in the UK is like many which make acid rain. This may lead, **right** to the rapid destruction of stonework.

balance. The acid rain also leaches metals such as aluminium out of bedrocks, and this clogs the fishes' gills. The leaching effect is also passed on to humans, adding heavy metals from rock and water pipes to their domestic supplies. Scientists have calculated that before the end of the century 50,000 lakes in the USA and Canada will be biologically dead. Damage to plants, animals, and humans is incalculable. The solution could be expensive filtration and scrubbing of emissions, or a change away from fossil-fuel burning. Both alternatives are strongly resisted by the polluters. One thing is certain, taller smoke stacks are nothing but a selfish evasion of the problem, merely carrying the damaging emissions further from the culprit.

Toxic time-bombs

The disposal of hazardous wastes is itself a growth industry. Years of irresponsible or ignorant dumping of toxic and other dangerous by-products created 'time-bomb' situations where, as containers leaked and became corroded, it was only a matter of time before chemical reactions caused explosions and fires, and local communities suffered horrific contamination effects. The most notorious example was that of Love Canal in upstate New York, USA, where miscarriages, infant deformities, and cancer deaths were linked by health workers to an old industrial dump, causing 800 families to abandon their houses. The Love Canal episode triggered political reactions, leading to expensive

Above The King river in Tasmania shows serious effects of copper pollution.
Right The dumping of waste from nuclear industries has been carried out by many governments with sheer irresponsibility. Here members of Greenpeace environmental pressure group are sprayed with high pressure water jets as they try to prevent a ship dumping nuclear waste.
Below Simulation of nuclear waste dumping in France.

penalties and surcharges on major polluters such as the chemical industry. These penalties, plus an abundance of million-dollar lawsuits by victims against large corporations, have forced polluters to reassess the economics of proper scientific disposal. Professional disposal concerns manage dumping sites where incoming wastes are analysed and treated accordingly. Some industrial sludges are washed and filtered in series of tanks, and the end-products buried along with other wastes under regulated minimum depths of overfill. Some of the most toxic chemicals need to be incinerated at high temperatures in special incinerators in order to destroy the particular molecular structure which constitues the hazard. Incineration usually reduces the waste to gases and ash. Pyrolysis, where wastes are heated in the absence of oxygen, causes a thermal decomposition producing a solid residue as well as gases. Both heating methods can cost hundreds of dollars per cubic yard of waste treated: leaving a strong incentive to cheat by 'pirate' dumping on unauthorized sites.

Nuclear waste

Of all Man's scientific endeavours, the development of nuclear technology is the most contentious, not least because of its association with weapons of terrible destruction. The wastes resulting from nuclear reactor activity are equally controversial. Governments and state nuclear organizations are secretive and defensive on the subject of nuclear waste disposal. The ideas considered and used are often bizarre, and no-one has confidently come forward with a foolproof method of dealing with potentially disastrously dangerous substances, often with an active life of thousands of years. Nuclear wastes include reactor cooling

waters, exhausted fuel elements, contaminated tools and clothing, the spent fuel itself, and, ultimately, the entire reactor after it has finished its 30- to 40-year lifespan. Plans for decommissioning redundant reactors include entombing the foundations, along with some contaminated material, under a thick concrete slab; flooding the reactor and containment vessls prior to cutting them up into small pieces by remote-controlled robots; removing all contaminated soil; and burying all sludges and demolition equipment.

Plans for disposing of radioactive fuels and wastes from the core include sealing it in glass before burying it in remote and 'geologically suitable' regions, and sending it off to the heart

of the Sun in carefully designed spaceships. For thirty and more years the British Sellafield (formerly Windscale) nuclear complex has pumped its radioactive effluent along a pipeline into the Irish Sea. As its Chief Health Physicist explained, "Not the least of the attractions of the sea as a dumping ground has been the lack of administrative controls." Increasing discharges over the years through the two-mile pipeline have distributed Sellafield's wastes as far afield as Greenland, where Caesium 137 has been identified and measured. Plutonium 239, one of the most toxic substances known, with a radioactive half-life of 24,400 years, has contaminated silts which migrate on tides and currents all around the Cumbrian coast and into estuaries as far away as the Solway Firth. Some researchers have estimated that cancer and leukaemia figures are several times the national average, and while others disagree, the British government's nuclear authority has consistently denied responsibility.

We live in a world where hundreds of new automobile models appear each year, while traffic police in some city areas have to take regular doses of oxygen in order to survive the fumes; where huge amounts of hydrocarbon fuel are used to produce agricultural chemicals; while acidic fallout from fossil fuel combustion destroys the land; where we attempt to overcome an energy 'crisis' by evolving a nuclear industry with waste products that could provide us with another sort of crisis for the foreseeable future. The irony of the situation is that the polluters themselves, the large corporations and the governments that support them and are supported by them, are the ones most able to halt the headlong process of global pollution, for they control both the technologies involved and the funds necessary to rectify the damage.

In the aptly-named Dismal Swamp that stretches along the border between Virginia and Carolina in the southern US, an infant coalfield is in the making. This great peat bog, 1,500sq miles (3,900sq km) in area, is no more than 20ft (6m) above sea-level at its highest, and 5ft (1.5m) above sea-level at its lowest. The peat layer is 6½ft (2m) thick, on average, increasing beneath the overlying swamp water at a rate of up to 12in (30cm) every ten years. The peat is formed from the accumulated detritus of the trees—cypresses, gums, junipers and pines—that grow in the swamp. Here are clearly demonstrated the sort of conditions which created most of the world's coalfields. A relatively small drop in land level or rise in sea level would be sufficient to inundate the Dismal Swamp peat bog in exactly the way that set off the coalification processes which produced today's established coalfields.

Stored sunlight energy

Like oil and gas, coal is a form of stored ancient solar energy. Of all the fossil fuels, coal is the most accessible and the most abundant. Over periods of millions of years successive combinations of compaction through burial, heat, and pressure turn vegetable matter into peat, and thence into the stages of lignite, sub-bituminous coal, bituminous coal, and finally anthracite. Anthracite, with a fixed carbon level of between 92 and 98 per cent, burns with a smokeless blue flame, and is the top 'rank' of coal, the furthest along the coalification process.

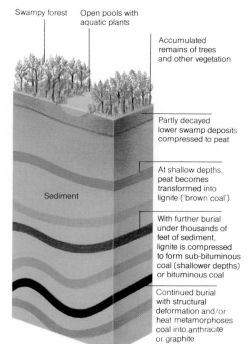

Above Coal is the end-product of various processes of which the main one is increase in heat which accompanies depth of burial. Structural changes like folding further increase the carbon content of coal.

Below The central control room at the Betws drift mine, Wales, indicates the advanced technology now applied to the mining industry. The room is filled with VDUs and other modern technological aids.

It is very hard, and shines with an almost metallic black lustre. Semi-anthracite is very similar, and has a fixed carbon content of between 86 and 92 per cent. Bituminous coal is the most common of the world's coal grades. It ranges in colour from brown to black, and burns with a smokey flame, containing up to 20 per cent volatile material. It is commonly known as 'soft' coal, and nearly all the huge bituminous reserves were laid down in the warm-temperate to subtropical coal forests of the Carboniferous period between 345 million and 280 million years ago, mainly in what is now northern Europe and the USA. Sub-bituminous coal, which is black, and lignite (or brown coal), have higher levels of volatile material than bituminous coal, and lower calorific values. There are extensive deposits in central Europe, the USSR, and parts of the USA. As the youngest rank of coal after the initial peat stage, lignite usually has an obvious layered structure, and may even contain recognizable wood fragments. Lignite's fixed carbon content can be as low as 38 per cent.

The abundance of coal

Coal is found in most parts of the world, though the great majority of known reserves are in the Northern Hemisphere. According to the World Energy Conference Survey of Energy Resources in 1976, the four largest deposits of potentially recoverable coal are in North America, the USSR and Eastern Europe, Western Europe and China.

Left Modern mining technology provides efficient transport of the coal from the face to the surface, as here at Betws drift mine.

Below At the Wath colliery, Yorkshire, UK, automatic steering of this coalface power-loading machine doubled output.

Technological advances in both prospecting and mining have greatly increased the amounts of potentially recoverable coal. Most coal exploration is carried out by means of diamond-core drilling, and electric geologging, as used in the gas and oil industries, is now being employed in coal prospecting as well. Geologging uses sensors which are lowered down drill holes, transmitting information via the hoist cable to instruments at the surface.

Coal is found on the surface and deep under-ground, in narrow, barely workable seams, and in massive layers hundreds of feet thick. While most coal mined in the eastern USA is found in beds between 3 and 8ft (0.9-2.4m) thick, surface mines in Wyoming contain several 50-100ft (15-30m) seams. One drill hole in the same State revealed a sub-bituminous bed 223ft (68m) thick. Some German brown coal seams have been measured at 300ft (90m).

The automated coalface

Advanced technology is bringing the age of the completely automated coalface rapidly closer. Increasingly, subterranean coal is cut by a shearer, a conveyor-mounted rotating drum with attached picks, that cuts, loads and transports out the coal all in one coordinated operation, spraying the coalface with water at the same time to reduce the coaldust which has crippled generations of coalminers with lung diseases. Most mines use the longwall system, in which two parallel tunnels are joined at right angles by a third, which becomes the progressing

coalface. As the coal is cut away and the third tunnel is widened, the roof is kept safe by the steady advance of powered roof-supports. Continuous tunnelling machinery, with boom-mounted spiral cutting heads, and fast conveyor systems have speeded coalmining up beyond all recognition from the days of the pick and shovel.

Below Brown coal, or lignite, contains less carbon than bituminous coal, but is still worth mining, as here by giant bucket-wheel excavators at the Rheinbraun open-cast mine, W Germany, for use as an industrial fuel.

Above This close-up view of one of the Rheinbraun bucket-wheel excavators, which rip the brown coal from the ground, gives an idea of the immense scale of this method of winning fuel from the Earth.

Open cast mining

Surface mining, either by removing earth and rock overburdens to get at the seams in the opencast method, or by cutting a succession of trenches to form a strip mine, has advanced more in terms of the scale of the machinery than in any other way. In an opencast operation, huge bucket-wheel excavators on crawler tracks remove both overburden and coal. In strip mining the strata are drilled and blasted before being scraped out by giant dragline shovels. Both methods of surface mining can drastically damage the land unless great care is taken to restore it as work progresses.

A long-lasting resource

Coal will long outlive oil and gas as a fossil-fuel resource. While many oil and gas deposits will run out well within the next fifty years, even at current rates of use, the resource life of coal can be measured in centuries. In the search for higher levels of productivity even the automated coalface, with its minimal use of human labour, may eventually be phased out. New cutting techniques are being tried, including the use of lasers and high-pressure water jets. Studies and experiments have been carried out on the viability of converting coal while it is still in the mine into a fluid or gas which can then be used for electricity generation. Coalmines of the future could well incorporate automated generating units, where coal is cut, processed and converted according to computerized programmes, with a small maintenance crew.

To all intents and purposes, Man has become addicted to petroleum. Every nation on Earth needs oil and its products to run its cars, boats, planes and transport systems, and, often, to fuel its electricity-generating plants, too. A whole range of industries also depends to a great degree on oil-based raw materials. The further up the industrial ladder a nation is, the more dependent it is on oil and oil products. Whoever controls oil supplies and prices controls the destinies of a large proportion of the world's population.

The substance that can create such wealth and power and has hooked our industrial culture like a narcotic in the process is, like coal, a fossil fuel, the transformed remains of organic material that died millions of years ago. Crude oil is a mixture of carbon and hydrogen compounds, varying greatly in the proportions of the hydrocarbons that make up between 97% and 99.7% of its weight. Some of the hydrocarbons are solids and some are gases, and all are held in liquid hydrocarbon solution. Despite the varying proportions, the basic structure of crude or rock oils varies little, with between 11 and 14% hydrogen, and between 83 and 87% carbon.

How oil is formed

Nearly all petroleum deposits have been formed from marine sediments, and occur in marine sedimentary rocks. They originated in coastal waters containing rich populations of organisms, where the sedimentary layers of the sea-floor lack sufficient oxygen to oxidize all deposited organic debris. As with coal, the transformation process takes place during millions of years of burial, but unlike coal, the low-density liquids and gases resulting from chemical reaction migrate upwards through permeable strata.

An 'oil-trap' occurs where there is an impermeable barrier to further upward migration. The oil and gas float on top of water in the permeable layer beneath the impermeable barrier, or 'cap-rock'. Typical cap-rocks include the denser limestones, shale, salt and gypsum. Structural traps are arch-like folds caused by geological movements, or by such intrusions as salt domes. The migrating oil and gas is trapped beneath the highest part of the arch.

Stratigraphic traps result from the original stratification of a formation, laid down by sedimentation, rather than from deformations which have occurred after the oil has been deposited. The Middle Eastern oilfields typically consist of structural traps in folded limestones and sandstones. The deposits of the southern USA and also of the southern North Sea are associated often with salt-controlled formations. Stratum faulting can also create traps. Oilfields in the North Sea, East Africa and Angola occur along rifts and fracture coastlines.

Occasionally, where there are no cap-rock barriers present, gas and oil reach the surface to be evaporated and oxidised, or to accumulate like the bitumen lakes of Trinidad. Oil-sands, such as those at Athabasca in Canada, lie above Devonian limestones containing oil. The oil seeps upwards into the sands, but is too heavy to be pumped. Huge stocks, estimated at over 500 billion barrels, might profitably be 'mined' along with the sand.

Above left In Trinidad, pitch and asphalt occur on the surface in bitumen lakes such as this one.
Left Oil prospecting: the 'bell wire' on the left of the picture carries the bell for seismic surveys, while to the right is the umbilical cable containing gas, electricity and communication links.
Below The North Sea has provided much oil for Western Europe. Here, Piper, a fixed platform in the North Sea, flares with excess gas, while cooling water from the gas turbines flushes into the sea.

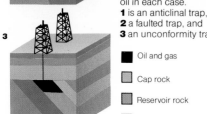

Left Oil can be trapped in a variety of geological situations. Its fluid nature allows it to rise through pore spaces in many rocks, such as sandstones and limestones, and migrate under pressure towards the surface. For the oil to be trapped, there must be an impermeable barrier to prevent its upward movement. If this is not present, the oil may seep out naturally onto the surface. Three typical oil traps are shown in this diagram: an impermeable cap rock traps the oil in each case.
1 is an anticlinal trap, **2** a faulted trap, and **3** an unconformity trap.

- Oil and gas
- Cap rock
- Reservoir rock
- Source rock

Oil prospecting

Geological recognition is the basis of most petroleum prospecting, followed by test drilling to discover whether promising formations actually contain releasable deposits plentiful enough to justify the considerable expense of production drilling. Initial surveying can now employ a wide range of techniques, including seismic surveying, in which sounds produced artificially by means of explosions or mechanical devices are bounced through formations, picked up on the rebound by sensitive geophones, and measured for characteristic differences between differing rock types. Gravimeters are used to establish rock densities by measuring gravity anomalies. Electrical apparatus for resistivity surveying is passed down drill-holes to identify the porous strata which could be associated with oil deposits.

Drilling for oil

The passage of the drill-bit is lubricated with water or mud. Drilling mud is specially concocted, and its density, viscosity and weight adjusted according to the conditions. Clays such as bentonite are added to help the drilling mud to gel when rotation stops, so as not to lose fluid. Salinity and filtration of the mud are also carefully controlled.

When the drilled well reaches a deposit, oil and gas are often forced to the surface, along with the brine on which they float, by the pressures already existing in the trap. As these pressures subside, pumping is used to keep the oil flowing. Oil viscosity and rock permeability determine the rate of recovery. Light oils, and those contained in fissured formations rather than in pored systems, give a higher flow rate. This primary production can recover between 20 and 40 per cent of the oil present. Secondary recovery techniques are increasingly used as primary oil production levels fall. These usually involve the pumping of substances into the well in order either to displace more oil upwards, or else to increase the fluidity of viscous deposits and flush out the finer capillary deposits. Steam is sometimes used to help fluidize viscous oil. Surfactant, or detergent, injection also helps to release oils from water, and will probably be used in North Sea sites as their oil supplies begin to dwindle. Other chemical methods include the use of polymers and alkalines to budge stubborn secondary deposits after the first pressurized recovery.

Natural gas

Petroleum gas is found in association with the oil, usually floating above the oil in the trap, and the two are pumped up together as a mixture, to be separated in separation tanks. The gas is further 'dried', and can then be used in a variety of ways. Some is pumped back down into the well to maintain the pressure. It can be used as domestic gas, and also as a chemical feedstock.

Natural gas is also found in separate deposits. North Sea gas was being produced a decade before North Sea oil began to flow. Much of continental Europe is serviced by a huge pipelined grid built to transport gas from the Dutch Groningen field. The trans-Mediterranean pipeline connects with North Africa, and the vast gas reserves of Algeria and Libya. The Siberian gas pipeline comes in from the east, and to the north are the large gas fields of Norway, Holland and the UK. The world's biggest natural gas customer is Japan and the biggest supplier, in the form of liquefied natural gas (LNG) is Indonesia. Japan also buys LNG from Abu Dhabi, Brunei, Malaysia, and may in the future buy it from Australia. Crude oil is three times as profitable as gas, partly because of the very high cost of gathering systems, pipelines, LNG conversion plants, and shipping. However a far higher proportion of deposited gas is recoverable.

The bottom of the barrel

Our consumption of petroleum has been so profligate that the end of the reserves is in sight in many fields. The USA's stocks are the most depleted. OPEC, the Organisation of Petroleum Exporting Countries, was specifically set up in the 1970s so that the producer countries could have more control over the fast dwindling reserves of what is, in many cases, their main asset. New fields are still being discovered, but the rate of exhaustion is greater than ever. Every two hours the Prudhoe Bay oilfield on the far North Slope of Alaska produces as much oil as was produced in the entire two centuries of Alaska's recorded history (just over 150,000 barrels). Despite this, and despite the use of secondary recovery to squeeze the last drops of oil out of flagging wells, or new schemes to release its huge sand and shale-locked oil deposits, the USA has long since lost her petroleum self-sufficiency, and has become a net importer of oil. Arab supplies are being far more strictly regulated than in the careless days when the US oil companies completely controlled production at give-away prices. The new interest in alternative energy sources, such as solar and tidal energy, has been sparked partly by environmental considerations, but also partly because with consumption rates always rising, the great oil bonanza is over.

Left In the Libyan desert, gas burns at a small refinery. The flares in the distance are natural gas fires, with thick black fumes rising into the air.
Right Aerial view of a large oil refinery in Port-of-Spain, Trinidad, with storage tanks and other industrial plant. Oil seeps naturally to the surface in this region, and prospecting is not fraught with the same problems as in the North Sea.
Below The 800-mile (1,290km) long Trans-Alaskan pipeline carries over a million barrelfuls of oil a day.

Alone of the world's creatures, Man consumes non-renewable resources. While plant cycles generally take a year to complete, the processes that form the minerals of the Earth's crust are often measured in many millions of years. To all intents and purposes, these minerals are non-renewable. The industrial development of a country can be measured in terms of the quantities of minerals it uses.

Right up until the 20th century, Man's demands on mineral stocks, although escalating rapidly through the preceding century, did not threaten any particular resource with imminent extinction. The most commonly exploited industrial minerals, such as coal and iron, were also among the most plentiful. Even today coal stocks are likely to last hundreds of years, and alternative energy programmes could cause a drastic drop in coal usage, so that the reserves last even longer. Iron, the foundation mineral of the industrial revolution, constitutes some five per cent of the Earth's crust, and is available in large concentrations near the surface, where it can be mined by means of opencast operations. Between 800 and 900 million tons of iron ore are mined annually, yet iron stocks, too, should last hundreds of years. The banded iron formations which are today's major sources are hundreds of yards thick, extend in strata sometimes over 100 miles (160km) long, and contain very high proportions of iron oxides—often as high as 60 per cent.

Runaway exploitation

In the second decade of the 20th century, boosted by the mass production techniques originating in its automobile industry, and facilitated by the lines of communication opened up by and for the products of that industry, the USA became the world's first advanced consumer society. It has been estimated that by 1948 the US had, in a thirty year period of expansion, consumed more minerals than had been used up by the rest of the world in its entire history. This alarming calculation underlines the exponential nature of increasing mineral use. The amounts swallowed up by modern industrial production double in relatively short periods of time. The doubling time decreases as more and more sectors of the world's population become advanced consumers. Everything conspires to accelerate the rate.

The family of consuming nations increases, particularly as each advanced consumer society has satellite states, which both provide it with raw materials and other services, and are also client states, market-places for the original state's products. In either case the satellites are themselves encouraged to consume. Population increases further swell demand, as do improved production techniques, and the proliferation of new products as the competition becomes more intense. Some calculated doubling times for mineral demand include: iron, 35 years; manganese, 26 years; nickel, 20 years; molybdenum, 16 years; tungsten, 20 years; copper 15 years; lead, 24 years; zinc, 26 years; tin, 63 years; aluminium, 11 years; gold, 38 years; silver, 26 years; and uranium, 6 years.

Moving mountains

Iron and coal are still abundant, as is aluminium, constituting about eight per cent of the Earth's crust. Many minerals, however, are present in much smaller quantities than these, and are usually also found in much smaller proportions relative to their lode-bearing ores. As minerals

Above Vast quantities of metal are taken from the Earth to make the 'essentials' of Western life. The limited existence of such manufactured items as automobiles leads to massive dumps, as at this European scrap yard.
Left In Brazil, a huge iron mine scars the land.
Below The industrial military machine of the space age demands the strong, light metal titanium. In Australia rutile (titanium dioxide) is extracted from placer sand deposits.

Right Diamonds are found in pipe-like seams in South Africa and are mined using cheap labour and up-to-the minute technology. The swirling spiral of the Koffiefontein Mine dwarfs the large vehicles on the perimeter roadway.
Below right At the Orangemund diamond mine, this 'space-age' control room bristles with electronics.
Below far right In the depths of a South African gold mine, black workers labour among pit props.

become rarer, the efforts to recover as large a slice as possible of the dwindling cake become more extreme. In 1972, a study initiated by the Club of Rome published figures indicating the probable diminishment times to non-economic levels of a range of minerals. The figures for copper showed it to have a short 'life', with known reserves becoming exhausted after 21 years at an exponential growth rate in consumption of 4·6 per cent per annum. Even if known reserves were to be increased five times, the life of copper was reckoned to be no more than 48 years.

In an effort to recover ever lower grades of copper ore (down to 0·25 per cent copper content), mining companies have literally moved mountains. In Bougainville in the Solomon Islands local villagers were forced off their lands by bulldozers and police using gas grenades and truncheons. Villages were 're-located', while the jungle cover was eradicated

with herbicides and chainsaws prior to the removal of 40 million tons of overburden. Copper silts were poured into local rivers and bays. *Mining Magazine* reported that by the end of the mine's estimated 30-year life an entire mountain would have been removed, and a pit dug 1,900ft (580m) deep, 7,000ft (2,100m) long, and 5,000ft (1,500m) wide. This prodigious feat was achieved with the aid of modern technology in the form of 25-ton capacity shovels and dozens of giant 100-ton-capacity ore-trucks.

Precious metals

The Club of Rome's study (titled *The Limits to Growth*) showed gold as having an exponential life of only nine years, though since that forecast production has been cut back, and grades have dropped to below 5 grams of gold per tonne of ore. To recover this tiny proportion, men work literally miles underground in some

of the deepest mines in the world in extremely hot, wet and dangerous conditions. The same sites that contain the gold also contain uranium in the South African fields, and uranium residues are often stockpiled after gold extraction for later processing. Gold demand figures are distorted by the fact that large amounts of gold are hoarded by governments and banks, and further amounts are recycled as jewelry and other artefacts are scrapped and melted down.

Gold is in many ways an artificial market. However, there are genuine industrial uses for the metal. Gemstone diamonds, however, represent a completely artificial market, as the monopoly grouping which controls diamond sales can and does create shortages or gluts according to financial expediency, having vast stocks of stones with which to operate. Industrial diamonds are a different matter, with far lower market values, less of a producer's monopoly, and a growing synthetic industry in competition

with mined stones. To mine the best deposits of gemstone diamonds, one operation in Namibia, South-west Africa, uses enormous rotary bucket-wheel excavators along a 60-mile (100km) stretch of coast, literally pushing back the sea with a series of sand-ramps in order to get at deposits in the inshore shallows.

The pressure of consumerism

The USA currently consumes some 50 per cent of the world's principal minerals, though it has only six per cent of the world's population. As other nations achieve higher technological development, consumerism increases, and with it the pressure on fast diminishing resources. Developing countries with two-thirds of the world's population use only six per cent of the mineral resource production, but countries such as Japan and South Korea have large manufacturing industries, and even the poorest Third World countries are being caught up in

the consumer whirlwind, though they fall deep into debt in order to do so. The immediate glitter of the transistor radio or cheap motorbike effectively blinds new and old consumers alike to the inescapable reality of mineral stocks which will be exhausted in one generation. Allowing for growth rates, and deducting 12 years from the Club of Rome's 1972 figures, further resource lives include: lead, 9 years; mercury, 1 year; tin, 3 years; tungsten, 16 years; and zinc, 6 years. New deposits such as those present in manganese nodules may extend the lives of such minerals as nickel, manganese, cobalt, and possibly copper, although the economics of recovery together with the political problems attending ocean-floor-mining agreements could delay recovery operations until well beyond the end of the century, by which time several of our most important minerals may have ceased to exist in quantities that are worth attempting to extract.

The planet's landmasses were long ago patchworked by the man-made borders that claim dominion over particular areas for individual sovereign states. Antarctica may be the last to go, and much of it is already divisioned, cake-like, with claim and counter-claim. Airspace and coastal waters have likewise received the stamp, often contested, of proprietorial control. The last regions to escape Man's lust for ownership are the outer reaches of the Earth's atmosphere, and the enormous tracts of the deep-sea-bed. Attempts to reach international agreements on a Law of the Sea Treaty, which would give rights of access to the sea-bed to all nations, have foundered, partly due to the realization that lumps of mineral accretion known as manganese nodules, first discovered over a century ago by the British *HMS Challenger* expedition, could constitute a major marine treasure trove.

Manganese nodules

Although the *Challenger* survey of the Atlantic and Pacific Oceans in the 1870's first discovered manganese nodules, it was not until 1962, when a vast deposit was located in the equatorial North Pacific, that commercial interests began to do their arithmetic, and the following decade witnessed a flurry of commercially backed exploration and research projects. Analysis has shown that the nodules, which are found thickly clustered in their deposit fields, mainly at depths of around 16,500ft (5,000m) on the abyssal plain, contain relatively high proportions of economically desirable metals. The manganese content of the nodules can be as high as 35 per cent, but it is the smaller proportions of nickel, copper and cobalt which could make nodule mining a commercially attractive proposition. With copper contents of up to 1.2 per cent, nickel up to 1.6 per cent and cobalt up to 1 per cent, the potato-sized nodules could be a rich source of strategic metals. Both manganese and cobalt are ingredients of the special alloys needed for catalytic equipment in oil refineries, and for the engines of jet aircraft. The United States is particularly keen to find an alternative source for these metals, for which it currently depends on foreign countries, including South Africa and the USSR.

Layered like an onion, a manganese nodule is usually built up around a 'seed' nucleus such as a grain of sand, a volcanic pumice fragment, or a shark's tooth. Various theories exist as to how they are formed, growing slowly over millions of years. According to the 'hydrothermal theory', a hot volcanic percolation of water releases metallic ions from beneath the ocean bottom, which then cluster and condense around natural nuclei. More generally accepted is the 'hydrogenous theory', according to which metals already present in solution in seawater are deposited on seed nuclei. Radioactive dating has been used to establish that it takes about 40 million years for a 4in (10cm) nodule to grow. The most puzzling aspect of the nodule phenomenon is the fact that they are found on the surface of the ocean floor, rather than buried under many yards of sediment. Although found in areas of low sedimentation, their extremely slow growth rates are a thousand times slower than the rate at which the surrounding sediments accumulate.

Nodule distribution

The Pacific is the richest ocean in terms of manganese nodule deposits so far discovered, with large fields both north and south of the Equator. The Atlantic concentrations are mainly in the southern part of that ocean, with some

Above R/V *Deepsea Miner*, a US vessel designed to collect manganese nodules by ocean-floor dredging.

Below A group of nodules on the sea bed. They contain nickel, copper and cobalt as well as manganese.

Below right Nodules dredged up by *Deepsea Miner* pass onto conveyor belts which carry them into the ship's hold.

Right The gimballed pipe handling system on *Deepsea Miner*. After dredging, the nodules are sucked up a pipe by air pump.

rich patches in the Caribbean area. Indian Ocean deposits are nearly all south of the Equator. The richest area so far evaluated lies between California and Hawaii, and is estimated to hold 15 billion tons of high-grade nodules, according to surveys made jointly by the US National Oceanographic and Atmospheric Administration (NOAA) and private industry, as part of the Deep Ocean Mining Environmental Study. NOAA estimated in 1981 that a commercially viable operation would need to mine and process at least 2 million tons of nodules per annum, with each mining ship raising 5,500 tons of nodules every working day.

Black smoker deposits
Another potential ocean floor harvest of great commercial value, discovered more recently than the manganese nodule deposits, is the product of the oceanic fracture zones, where a constant relentless upwelling of material fuels the movement of tectonic plates, and fissure-heated seawater is vented upwards from 'black smokers', in the form of hot plumes dark with particles of sulphides from the crustal rock. These sulphides solidify and are deposited as they come in contact with the colder water,

forming mounds along the fracture zones that are often exceptionally rich in metal content. Iron, copper and zinc are all deposited in sulphide bodies, and concentrations assayed have revealed up to 50 per cent zinc and 10 per cent copper. The Red Sea may contain up to 2.5 million tons of zinc in its Atlantis II Deep, in the bottom sediments of basins filled with hot brines. Large sulphide deposits have also been found in the Pacific Ocean, along the Juan de Fuca Ridge, and also near the Galapagos Islands, 600 miles (1,000km) west of Ecuador.

Problems of exploitation
The future development of deep-sea mining programmes depends on the success or failure of international agreements to control exploitation. International agreements in turn are jeopardized by the simple fact that the technology of ocean-bed exploration and mining is vastly expensive, and very few countries have the resources to undertake such investment.

The technology of deep-sea mining
For exploration of mining sites deep-tow systems using sled units equipped with lights, television and photographic cameras and side-scanning

sonar give the best resolution pictures, being towed a few feet above the ocean floor.

Early mining rigs consisted of continuous line bucket loops running between the sea-floor and two mining ships. Most research programmes are now carried out using hydraulic apparatus for recovery. The Ocean Minerals Company (OMCO) of California has experimented with a prototype mining vehicle that crawls along the seafloor by means of archimedean screws, scooping nodules out of the bottom sludge and feeding them to an intermediate 'buffer' pumping station through a flexible pipe. From the buffer, which is tens of yards above the miner, the nodules are pumped hydraulically up 3 miles (5km) of 1²⁄₃ft (0·5m) diameter pipe to the control ship, in slurry form. Eventually, shipboard processing could save transportation costs, and mining ships could be equipped with apparatus for grinding the nodules, also facilities for copper-iron-reduction, chemical ore reduction using electricity (electrolysis) and cobalt-precipitation by means of hydrogen sulphide. Smelting might also be used in order to recover the manganese.

The Law of the Sea Convention
At the end of the third United Nations conference on the Law of the Sea in December 1982, the United States, the UK, and West Germany all refused to sign the Sea Law Convention, although an unprecedented 118 nations did sign. In April 1983 a preparatory commission, opened to all those who had signed, met to set up the International Seabed Authority which would license and regulate seabed exploitation. The UK and West Germany participated as observers, though the USA refused to do even this. Instead, in March 1983, the USA unilaterally declared its own 200-mile (320-km) Exclusive Economic Zone.

Left The dredge control centre aboard *Deepsea Miner*. Monitoring and control by computer is essential for success.

Below This offshore dredge not only mines tin from the sea bed, but also partially refines it before shipping it ashore.

To date, there has been no commercial exploitation of the mineral resources of Antarctica. Such a development is, however, becoming increasingly likely, and this is provoking a good deal of discussion about its relation to sovereignty and jurisdiction over the coldest continent. Even if these matters are satisfactorily resolved, there will remain enormous physical difficulties in extracting minerals under the most rigorous and isolated conditions in the world. Nevertheless, technological development of mining and drilling in Arctic locations such as Spitsbergen, Greenland, Yukon, Alaska and Siberia have already laid substantial foundations for Antarctic operations. Also, the stimulus of declining reserves of minerals elsewhere coupled with increasing demand by industrialized nations is becoming more important every year.

The only significant commercial activities in Antarctic regions this century have been whaling, fishing, and krill harvesting; all involve renewable resources and are conducted principally on the high seas, thus presenting few political difficulties. The whaling industry has declined enormously in the last decade, while the other two are now rapidly becoming far more important. Commercial exploitation of the land containing the mineral resources has occupied the attention of the signatory nations of the Antarctic Treaty increasingly over the last few years. When the Treaty was drafted, such exploitation was not covered as, at that time, mineral extraction was impracticable and the enormous political problems apparent today were foreseen as a serious difficulty in establishing the Treaty.

International recognition
With the exception of the Falkland Islands (Malvinas) and Dependencies, where Argentina disputes British sovereignty, all the Antarctic islands north of the Treaty limits have an internationally recognized status. None of these are known to have economic deposits of minerals, but some may become important for communications facilities for future developments on the Antarctic continent and as sites for airports and harbours suitable for use throughout the year. On the Antarctic continent, six countries claim mutually recognized territories: Australia, France, New Zealand, Norway, the UK and the USA. Two, Argentina and Chile, have made later claims which partly overlap the British claim and each other's. Other claims have been made but not ratified by Belgium, Japan, Norway, and the United States, while one-sixth of the continent remains either unclaimed or is covered by unratified claims. Several nations active in Antarctica, notably Japan, Poland, the Soviet Union and the USA at present neither make claims nor recognize those made by other states.

A co-operative effort
Since the International Geophysical Year, 1957-58, when the enormous benefits of international co-operation in scientific research were abundantly demonstrated, a rational co-operative attitude to Antarctic development, almost all of which has a scientific basis, has prevailed. At present, there are stations from Argentina, Australia, Chile, France, Japan, West Germany, New Zealand, Poland, the Soviet Union, South Africa, the UK and the USA operating in Antarctic regions, while Brazil, India and Spain may soon join them. Only one state—Argentina—has yet resorted to initiating armed

conflict to defend her Antarctic claims (but has done so three times), and it is to be hoped that this will not prove to be a further complication. The exploitation of minerals is an entirely new matter for the Antarctic Treaty, which presently limits activity to scientific research, and negotiations are complex. Although the Treaty is intended to last indefinitely, an initial agreed period of 30 years, after which it will be reviewed, will expire in 1991—an important date for the resolution of the problems of mineral exploitation. The United Nations Law of the Sea Convention may provide some guidance for a protocol covering Antarctic minerals, and the complex legal aspects remain a strong disincentive for investment of money in the region which would be the most expensive part of the world for mineral exploitation.

Protecting the environment
As well as the problems of sovereignty, there are also the important matters of protection of the environment and ensuring that exploitation is subject to appropriate controls. This involves detailed scientific research on the environment and the likely impact of future developments. Properly controlled, this need present no insuperable difficulties—the Antarctic environment has shown a substantial degree of resilience in places where exploitation has already occurred (sealing and land-based whaling). The potential effects of Antarctic meteorology and the stability of the ice-cover on the world as a whole are also important matters attracting research.

A wealth of minerals
The minerals which are known to occur in the Antarctic continent include coal, chromium, copper, cobalt, gold, iron, lead, manganese, molybdenum, nickel, silver, tin, titanium, uranium, and zinc. Such an assessment is, however, preliminary, and estimates of reserves are possible in only a few instances. Nevertheless, those of iron and copper are known to be large. Owing to the ice which covers 98 per cent of the land to an average depth of 7,200ft (2,200m), very little is known directly about mineral deposits. Antarctica was originally part of the ancient southern supercontinent of Gondwana, which has proved to be rich in minerals in its other modern fragments (Australasia, southern Africa, India, and South America). It has been estimated statistically that, from analogy with these other remnants of Gondwana, perhaps 900 economic mineral deposits occur in Antarctica—but only 21 are likely to be in ice-free areas. Similar computations suggest there should also be substantial petroleum fields in the region. At the present state of scientific knowledge, however, these remain only theoretical. Two types of mineral may be detected through the ice-cap, depending on their concentrations and the depth of ice; radioactive elements (by their radiation emissions) and iron deposits (by their magnetic effects); little has yet been found of the former, but some interesting magnetic anomalies may indicate the whereabouts of some large deposits of iron lying buried beneath the ice.

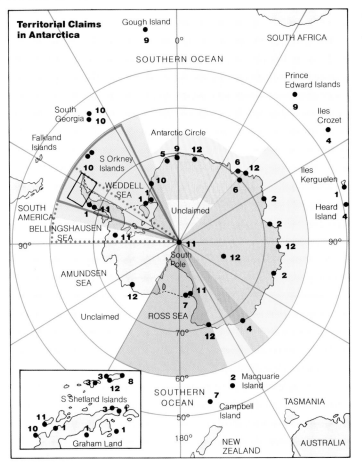

Territorial Claims in Antarctica

Left This map shows the current state of the various nations' territorial claims in the Antarctic continent and associated islands. The USA, Japan, USSR and several other nations so far neither make claims nor recognize those made by other countries. Also shown are the research stations operated by twelve nations (for key, see below).

Key
1 Argentina
2 Australia
3 Chile
4 France
5 Japan
6 Federal Republic of Germany
7 New Zealand
8 Poland
9 South Africa
10 United Kingdom
11 USA
12 USSR

Dates of claims to Antarctic sectors

United Kingdom 1908
New Zealand 1923
France 1924 (enlarged in 1938)
Australia 1933
Norway 1939
••• Chile 1940
— Argentina 1943 (enlarged 1945, 1948)

Left Antarctica is rich in mineral wealth, as yet unexploited. There has been little agreement so far between the Antarctic Treaty nations in establishing controls on possible future extraction of the minerals.

Key
● Coal
▼ Chromium
● Copper
◆ Gold
■ Iron
▼ Lead
● Manganese
◆ Molybdenum
■ Nickel
■ Silver
● Tin
◆ Titanium
■ Uranium
▼ Zinc
● Cobalt

Oil and gas extraction

As well as looking for minerals, geologists can prospect for petroleum—oil and gas—by geophysical methods, notably in offshore regions. Geophysical maps of parts of the continent, the continental shelf regions off Antarctica, and many of the outlying islands have been prepared, and these indicate some geological basins which might contain petroleum. Again, however, this supposition remains unproven. The technology of petroleum extraction in the North Sea and off Alaska might, in the future, find application in Antarctic waters, but there are additional problems. One is that the icebergs of Antarctica are far larger than Arctic ones, and frequently plough great furrows, as much as 650ft (200m) deep, across the shallower areas of the continental shelf. Such giant moving islands of ice could play havoc with submarine well-heads and other sophisticated and expensive components essential for oil or gas recovery.

Towing icebergs to the tropics

Exploitation of the enormous reserves of freshwater in the form of ice in Antarctica has been proposed several times over the last decade. This has been suggested as a source of high-quality water for the arid parts of the Southern Hemisphere, notably Australia, and for the Arabian countries. The icebergs would be towed across the ocean to the areas where the water was needed. Much theoretical calculation of the efficiency of such operations has been done and between 1980 and 1981 some experiments on the dynamics of Antarctic icebergs were performed. The results of these indicated that there are many tough practical problems to overcome before such operations become economically feasible.

Although the continent and islands of Antarctica have potentially great but unproven reserves of valuable minerals, there are many matters to consider prior to their exploitation. The political ones are presently under discussion, while scientific knowledge of the region and its minerals is increasing yearly, technology is constantly improving and extending to more rigorous regions, reserves are declining elsewhere and demand increasing; hence, although exploitation in the region is minimal, the future will be strikingly different. Typically, some of the most accessible minerals, notably copper, occur near Graham Land—at the tip of Lesser Antarctica—the politically most complex part of the continent.

Known Mineral Deposits in Antarctica 1983

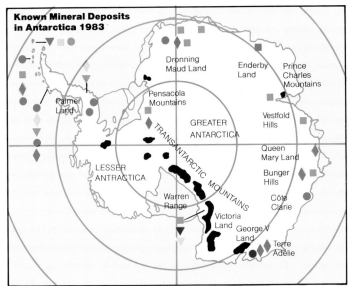

Left Flexible plywood tubes protect new buildings at Halley, one of the British Antarctic Survey's geophysical observatories.

Below A chemical glaciologist collects filters used for analysis of air pollution in Palmer Land, Antarctica.

Right Collecting clean ice samples for analysis of trace metals. The gown and gloves are worn to avoid contamination.

In one of the worst dust storms of 1934, some three million tons of Nebraska topsoil was lifted miles into the sky. Travelling eastwards on the wind the dust was carried over a thousand miles (1,600km), passing the coast and continuing out to sea. In Washington and New York, both in the wind's path, the daytime sky turned as black as night. The great mid-Western dustbowls of the United States were reaching the point of no return. The wind finished the job, but it was Man who had done the spadework.

Man is only just beginning to understand the gravity of the mistakes which have created deserts ever since he first began to farm. The American dustbowls of Nebraska, Oklahoma, Kansas and other mid-Western areas are the result of generations of one-sided farming. Crops were taken repeatedly from the soil without replenishing lost nutrients and humus. Grasslands, with close, soil-hugging root systems, established over centuries, were changed over to nutrient-hungry annual crops requiring regular ploughing. Worked to death, the topsoil became a barren dust, vulnerable to winds. The road from prairie to desert had been a depressingly short one.

The dangers of irrigation

Through ignorance, greed or both, Man has developed a number of farming techniques guaranteed to denude and destabilize the topsoil. Simple irrigation is a major offender. Although newly introduced irrigation schemes can be seen to make deserts bloom dramatically in the short term, constant irrigation combined with evaporation from direct sun heat and loss of water through plant leaves eventually saturates the soil with deposited mineral salts. The saline earth becomes bare of vegetation, while fierce heat and strong winds do the rest.

In an attempt to reverse this process, farmers have tried sluicing away the salts, using far more water than the plants need for growth. This leaches the salts away from the plants' roots, carrying them down to the permanent water table at a deeper level. However, without close regulation, this can cause the water table to rise, waterlogging the land, reintroducing a disastrously high saline concentration, and leading even more swiftly to barren soil and the relentless effects of desertification.

Such induced salinity is a problem from the Indus Plains of Pakistan to California's Imperial Valley, the largest irrigated area in the Western Hemisphere. In the Soviet Union, hundreds of thousands of square miles of once fertile land had become eroded and salinated in the desperate rush to match Western production levels. The rescue of salinated ground is a long and expensive business. One method is to lay perforated pipes below root level, leading to sumps from which the brackish water can be pumped to removal channels. Sometimes the 'brine lines' carry the pumped brine long distances to salt sinks or the ocean.

Overgrazing

Stock rearing can affect topsoils as drastically as arable farming. In Colorado and Oregon, USA, overgrazing destroyed ground cover sufficiently for desertification to begin. In many parts of Africa the animals of nomadic and semi-nomadic peoples have to compete for ever smaller amounts of scrub bush and sand grass. Natural and man-made desertifi-

Right Desert irrigation in the Middle East. Here, huge wheeled water-carrying devices cross the desert surface. Desert irrigation often leads to problems, by making the land highly saline.
Below Here, in Morocco, the semi-desert has been teraced and planted to combat the erosive action of strong winds and to allow soil development to progress. In this view, rows of trees growing on terraces replace the bare desert, which can be seen in the background.

cation complement one another as the southern boundary of the African Sahel desert works its way remorselessly south. Dryness creates dryness.

The same overgrazing that reduces the plant cover, also increases the albedo—the ratio of solar radiation reflected to that received by denuding the hard ground. As the ground absorbs less heat, the air becomes more stable. The effect is accentuated by atmospheric dust from parched soil. In the still air, convection currents, essential for rain, are reduced. Rainy seasons shrink, or disappear for years. Occasional downpours do nothing but flood thousands of acres briefly, carrying away villages and camps as well as topsoil. Dispossessed populations, newly immobilized nomads, and other casualties of 20th century political upheavals have turned increasingly to the large-scale use of living wood for their camps and their fires. The escalating search for firewood has added new

wildernesses to the old, from the Gulf of Aden to the Atlantic Ocean. Researches in West Africa show a measurably drier climate due directly to the destruction for firewood of green forest trees.

Land clearance for new crops is one of Man's most efficient, if unwitting methods of creating deserts. In the Kajiado Plains of Kenya the use of fire to clear land for new grass planting has been carried out too often and too thoroughly. Combined with regular overgrazing this has destroyed the plains as pastures.

Death of the forests

The biggest misunderstanding of all occurs when ancient forests are cleared to create farmland. In the tropics, luxurious and exotic forest growth is supported on thin topsoils. Plant growth is often fast and extensive, yet much of it is parasitic, and deep root systems have little place in rainforests, despite the towering height and bulk of some trees. Nutrients and moisture are held in the plants and leaves themselves rather than in the earth. Throughout the tropics, huge areas of rainforest have been levelled by saw, fire and bulldozer. But replacement crops and grazing lands rarely last beyond a couple of seasons. The thin, poor soil is soon exhausted, leaving a barren layer which, without the protection of forest shade, is soon baked into dust and sluiced away by heavy rains.

Some soils, particularly in the tropics, are lateritic—rich in minerals such as aluminium and iron. On exposure to air by clearing and ploughing, lateritic soils are chemically transformed, turning literally brick-hard. Laterite is widely used as a building and road-making material, but is impossible for agricultural use.

Redressing the balance

Man is beginning to apply his imagination and technical skills to reversing the desertification process. The first step is to recognize the factors which create deserts, and to alert agriculturalists to the dangers. In Israel, good results have been achieved by careful soil studies, followed by stabilizing techniques and careful irrigation. Dunes have been planted with tough, stabilizing grasses; contour ploughing and cultivation minimize gradient erosion; flash floods are channelled and stored; crop rotations include vegetables, such as sugar beet, which can absorb a certain amount of mineral salts and help desalinate the earth. Regulated sprinkler irrigation has been widely introduced, combined with a careful monitoring of mineral levels, and efficient brine drainage. Generations of sheep, goats and camels have grazed the Near and Middle East down to bare rock. The Israeli government banned goats, a measure which prompted a fast return of grass and other vegetation that had been in abeyance for many years previously.

Re-establishing desert lands is a reversal of the processes that created them in the first place. What soil remains has to be anchored with selected plants, cleaned of excessive salts, protected from overgrazing, and replenished with humus and nutrients. New approaches to soil chemistry are providing granular plastic bulking mediums and a new generation of soil conditioners which can break down unyielding clays or bond sand particles into a viable growing tilth. The process of re-establishment takes time, patience and money. Meanwhile, Man continues to create deserts at an alarming speed. It is a race against time.

Top The effects of irrigation can be dramatic, as here in the Indus Valley, North Pakistan. The lush vegetation provides a striking contrast to the bare mountains beyond.
Above Irrigation channels in the Saudi Arabian desert.
Left The rape of the tropical rainforest is one of Man's greatest crimes. Here, the forest is devastated in Malaysia.
Below In Bahia State, Brazil, the rainforest is cut and burned, destroying the soil and all the organisms living there.

In May 1977 the foreign ministers of the USA and the USSR, together with other participants in the Geneva Arms Limitation Conference, signed a treaty proposal forbidding environmental warfare, defined as 'the deliberate manipulation of natural processes', and including weather, climate, and ecological balances, as well as earthquakes, tidal waves and the course of ocean currents.

Man has always harboured a desire to influence the weather, to bring rain for parched crops and a breeze for becalmed ships. In the twentieth century scientists have joined the ranks of the shamans and rain dancers in claiming that they can affect weather and climate. Yet despite specialized governmental departments and the growth of a flourishing weather modification industry, there are no proofs that the results achieved by many modern techniques such as cloud seeding would not have occurred naturally had there been no human intervention.

Rainmaking

Rain and snow are formed naturally within clouds as ice crystals which develop around condensation nuclei—microscopic airborne particles of dust, salt, or organic material. In November 1946, Vincent Schaefer, a scientist working for the General Electric Corporation in the USA sprinkled finely ground dry ice (frozen carbon dioxide) from an aircraft onto a stratus cloud, producing snowflakes which fell 3,000ft (1,000m) before evaporating. Repeated tests proved that dry-ice seeding causes ice crystal formation. Another General Electric scientist, Bernard Vonnegut, discovered that silver iodide is also a good seeding material, since its atomic configuration closely resembles that of ice crystals.

Ambitious claims and official programmes in many countries notwithstanding, the only firmly established evidence is that seeding can cause precipitation, of snow or rain, in certain specific conditions, such as when the cloud top temperature is within the range -55 to $-77\,°F$ (-13 to $-25\,°C$). Nevertheless, seeding is carried out optimistically in order to increase water supplies in given watersheds, and also to extinguish forest fires. Cumulus or frontal cloud approaching the fire region is seeded. The upcurrents of warm air lift the clouds and create conditions favourable to precipitation. Soviet authorities claim that between 1971 and 1975, 121 out of 308 forest fires tackled were extinguished by induced rainfall.

Taming hailstorms

Seeding has also been used to control hailstorms, the aim being to create large numbers of small hailstones in preference to the large ones which flatten crops. In the absence of control experiments, it is impossible to verify results, though high success rates have been claimed by commercial companies and official bodies. The Soviets claim to have lowered hail damage by up to 90 per cent by using large rockets to carry lead iodide and silver iodide into hail-formation zones. As many as 5,000 Soviet citizens are employed by the state agency responsible for dealing with hail.

Tackling hurricanes and lightning

In the USA seeding experiments on hurricanes appear to have succeeded in bringing down internal wind-speeds significantly, using rockets specially developed by the Navy to deliver the

Above Cloud seeding has been used in attempts to control the devastating effects of hail from clouds such as this one. **Left** A field of corn lies broken and battered, ruined by a severe hailstorm in Indiana, USA. Large areas of agricultural land are regularly threatened by severe hailstorms. **Right** Colour Doppler radar, like this US unit with its antenna housed inside a geodesic dome, has helped meteorologists predict embryonic tornadoes by measuring wind speeds in thunderclouds. Despite such advanced technology, however, there is no immediate prospect of taming these damaging phenomena.

silver iodide to the outer edge of the hurricane's vortex. Experiments in both the USA and the USSR have also shown that cloud-seeding can reduce lightning flashes by up to 50 per cent.

Another way of dealing with lightning is to drop metallic or carbon strips known as chaff from aircraft. Air conductivity is increased, and the resulting constant low level discharge between thundercloud and ground prevents a build up of dangerously powerful charges. On the same basis small rockets are used to trigger electrical field discharges, keeping electrical tension low and reducing the risk of damaging lightning strikes.

Unintentional weather changes

While weather modification experiments continue, other theories, and worries, are concerned with the possibly disastrous effects on climate which some human activities may be having.

Activities as apparently disparate as driving a car and cutting down a tree are related, for both affect the levels of carbon dioxide (CO_2) gas present in the atmosphere. The burning of fossil fuels—coal, peat, oil and natural gas—releases CO_2 into the atmosphere as the carbon in the fuel combines with oxygen. Carbon dioxide levels are also increased by industrial processes such as cement production, which release mineral carbonates by chemical reaction. Carbon dioxide molecules are the main absorbers of reflected infra-red solar radiation in the atmosphere. Acting as an insulator, they hold heat inside the atmosphere envelope. The more CO_2, the greater the heat. This is the infamous greenhouse effect.

Right Aircraft such as this WP-3D Orion are used by the US National Oceanic and Atmospheric Administration to monitor the atmosphere during research into weather modification.
Below Lightning over Tucson, Arizona, USA. Severe thunderstorms over large cities can cause damage and even endanger life. Research on lightning control has used cloud seeding and other methods.

Below Increased levels of carbon dioxide in the atmosphere result in a rise in global temperatures as a result of the infamous 'greenhouse effect'.

Sun

Visible radiation from Sun penetrates the atmosphere

Visible rays partly converted to infra-red (heat) waves

Infra-red rays absorbed by carbon dioxide and heat reflected back to Earth

It seems a far cry from the belching chimneys and vehicle exhausts of the industrialized countries to the tropical rainforests, located mainly in developing countries, but the link is there. The felling and burning of the forest trees not only causes the release of carbon dioxide, but also removes a major link in the cyclical breakdown of atmospheric CO_2 through photosynthesis. The CO_2 released by burning the trees is not recycled, as plant substitutes for the felled trees rarely survive a second season on depleted soils. There is both a CO_2 gain and an oxygen loss.

Many scientists believe that the climatic effects of the CO_2 build-up are inevitable, as fossil-fuel consumption increases and rainforest destruction goes ahead. Fifty million acres (20 million hectares) of rainforest are demolished

each year. It has been calculated that for every doubling of atmospheric CO_2 levels over pre-industrial levels, there will be an overall global temperature increase of 2-3°C.

At the beginning of the Industrial Revolution, before the fuel-hungry age of steam, CO_2 levels in the atmosphere were about 280 parts per million (ppm). Current levels stand at an average of 335 ppm. Half of this increase has occurred in the last thirty years. In August 1980 scientists at the NASA Institute for Space Studies published hard evidence of a 0·4°C increase in global temperature since 1900. Extrapolating from this figure, worried experts estimate that if fossil fuels continue to be burned at current rates, the inevitable increase in world temperature could total at least 2-3°C. Changed rainfall patterns resulting

from this would turn prairie-land into dust bowls, and cold northern regions into newly productive farming areas. As the increase in temperature would be greater nearer the poles, (7°C if the global average is 2°C), glacial ice would melt, leading to major flooding of coastal regions. In the last advance of the Ice Age, global temperatures were only 2½ per cent lower than they are now.

These climatic changes would not be stable. Ice-cap melting would greatly increase the surface area of the Earth's oceans. As water is an effective absorber of carbon dioxide, atmospheric CO_2 would suffer a major decrease in the longer term. That could result in an Ice Age from which there might be no return. The only certainty is that we live in an ever-changing — and eternally fascinating — world.

GLOSSARY

Ablation The loss of ice and snow from the surface of a glacier or snow field by melting and evaporation.

Abrasion The wearing away of rock fragments by mechanical rubbing.

Absolute zero temperature scale A scale with the theoretical absolute zero ($-273°C$, $-459.4°F$), that at which heat emission ceases, as the base of the scale. The degree intervals are the same as on the Celsius (°C) scale.

Abyssal Refers to the extreme depths of the oceans, at least 12,000 ft (3,700m) below sea level.

Acid rock An igneous rock, such as granite or rhyolite, which contains more than 10% quartz and more than 65% total silica. Commonly such rocks are made of quartz, mica and felspars, are low in density and pale in colour.

Adaptive radiation (or simply 'radiation') The evolution from a common ancestor of several divergent forms of animal or plant, each adapted to a distinct mode of life or occupying a distinct 'niche' within a habitat.

Agate A form of quartz with a banded structure, often in concentric layers and prized as a semi-precious stone.

Albedo The reflectiveness of a surface expressed as the ratio of light reflected to the total light received. Snow has a high albedo, dark soils have a low albedo.

Alluvial Refers to deposits formed by rivers. These include sands which may contain concentrations of heavy minerals called placer deposits.

Amphibian A class of cold-blooded vertebrates which resemble reptiles, but which have softer skin and need water in which to breed. The young pass through a gill-breathing tadpole stage.

Amphibole A group of silicate ferromagnesian minerals which are important igneous rock formers. They include hornblende and cummingtonite.

Anticyclone A circular weather system with high atmospheric pressure. Such air masses are sluggish, and once established, their weather conditions are easy to forecast. In middle and high latitudes, anticyclones produce dry settled weather, hot in summer and very cold in winter.

Apollo A three-manned spacecraft developed by the USA for lunar investigation.

Arthropod An invertebrate animal characterized by a segmented exoskeleton. The extinct trilobites belong to this phylum, as do insects, crabs and scorpions.

Asphalt A very sticky, naturally occurring hydrocarbon, often containing tar and pitch.

Bar A deposit of sand or gravel, usually of linear form, resulting from marine or river deposition. Marine examples often lie parallel to the coastline.

Basic rock An igneous rock, such as gabbro, which contains less than 10% quartz and a total silica content of between 45% and 55%. Such rocks contain much plagioclase felspar and pyroxene, often with olivine. They have a higher density than acid rocks and are dark in colour.

Batholith An enormous mass of igneous rock which is intruded deep in the Earth's crust. Such structures are usually many miles in extent, and have a far-reaching metamorphic effect on the country rock. The vast majority of batholiths are made of granite. Their actual mode of emplacement is open to debate. Some may be forcefully intruded, others may melt their way in, consuming country rock by assimilation.

Bedding plane A surface of deposition. A bed of rock (stratum) lies between two bedding planes. Bedding planes may have been originally almost horizontal, but sediment deposited by a moving current of wind or water will have cross-bedding, where the bedding planes are not horizontal.

Big Bang A theoretical explosion, for which there is much evidence, from which the universe may have developed.

Bivalve An invertebrate, shelled animal belonging to the phylum Mollusca. The term is also used to describe the two-shelled nature of other creatures.

Bone bed A conglomerate layer containing many fragments of bone, teeth and scales. Such layers are usually thin but may persist over wide areas.

Brachiopod A phylum of small two-shelled marine creatures which are common in the fossil record but relatively rare today. Some of the earliest Cambrian fossils are of brachiopods.

Braided stream A network of constantly changing interwoven channels in a broad valley, where the valley sides are made of soft, easily eroded material.

Breccia A sedimentary rock consisting of coarse angular fragments, formed either by deposition, e.g. as on a scree slope, or by the fragmentation of rock along a fault plane. Agglomerate is a volcanic breccia.

Butte The prolonged erosion of a mesa will lead to the development of a small flat-topped hill called a butte. The landscapes of many cowboy films are full of such landforms.

Calcite A very common mineral composed of calcium carbonate which occurs both inorganically in veins and rocks such as limestone and marble, and in the shells and bones of many organisms.

Caldera A large volcanic crater, with a diameter many times that of the original volcanic vent: often the result of the collapse of a volcano.

Canyon A very deep, steep-sided valley cut by a rejuvenated river.

Carapace The exoskeleton of an organism such as a trilobite, which is carried above and around the animal's soft body.

Chernozem A black soil, rich in humus, often formed in areas of only moderate rainfall.

Chert A type of silica made of such small crystals that they can be studied only under great magnification. Chert forms discrete masses and nodules in limestones, and in the chalk formation of Europe it is called flint. The origin of the silica may be organic.

Chitin A horny material made of nitrogen-rich carbohydrate of fibrous structure, which forms the exoskeletons of many arthropods and parts of a wide variety of organisms.

Coccolith Minute plates of calcium carbonate which are a major constituent of the chalk. They are probably secreted by algae.

Concordant The term used in igneous geology to describe the way certain intrusions follow existing structures in the Earth's crust. Sills typically are concordant intrusions.

Condensation In meteorological usage this term is applied to the production of water vapour by the cooling of saturated air. This may occur when warm air rises to higher, colder levels (by rising over mountains, for example) or when the warm air in a room touches a cold window and water droplets form.

Conodont Very small tooth- and jaw-shaped phosphatic structures of uncertain, but probably organic, origin.

Coprolite Fossil excrement.

Country rock The pre-existing rock into which an igneous mass is intruded. The country rock is often sedimentary and is metamorphosed by the igneous intrusion. Blocks of country rock may become engulfed by the magma of the intrusion to form xenoliths.

Cyclonic An adjective describing circular, fast moving low-pressure air masses. These are characterized by unsettled stormy wet weather, and are notoriously difficult to predict.

Daughter element The element formed by the radioactive decay of another element. The parent element decays into the daughter element at a constant rate, the half-life period being the time taken for half of the parent element atoms to decay.

Depression A fast-moving cyclonic weather system with high winds and much rain, common in middle and high latitudes.

DNA Deoxyribonucleic acid, a large coiled biological molecule which contains genetic material.

Doppler effect The change in the frequency of sound or electro-magnetic waves which results from the relative movement of observer and source.

Drainage pattern The shapes which a river network cuts on the landscape. This will depend on a variety of influences, such as rock structure, slope and climate.

Earthquake Disturbances in the Earth's crust and upper mantle centred around a definite point or focus. These usually are of natural origin but nuclear explosions can cause similar far-reaching effects.

Eclogite A rock of metamorphic (or possibly igneous) origin, coarse-grained and of basic or ultra-basic composition, containing much garnet and pyroxene.

Eukaryote A cell with a nuclear membrane surrounding the genetic material and with other membrane-bound organelles (structures with distinct functions) in the cytoplasm.

Evaporation The transition from liquid to gas. When water containing salts in solution evaporates, the salts are precipitated as solid crystals.

Evaporite Rocks or minerals formed by the evaporation of saline water. Typical evaporites are gypsum, rock salt and potash. These are frequently found in a definite sequence, the least soluble salts being deposited first.

Exoskeleton The external skeleton which covers the soft bodies of animals such as the arthropods. This is usually a flexible covering of chitin.

Facies The total of all the characteristics of a rock type. This includes chemistry, grain size, structure, fossil content, colour, bedding and other features. The term is generally used for sedimentary rocks, but is also used of metamorphic rocks. The facies is a result of the mode of formation of the rock and is therefore of great use in determining how an ancient rock formed.

Fault A fracture in the rocks of the crust with displacement on one side relative to the other.

Flash flood A sudden, often short-lived flood, characteristic of arid regions which only rarely receive rain. When rain comes to such regions it usually occurs as torrential convectional storms producing much water in a short time. This rapidly fills dry water-courses and produces sheet floods over the land surface.

Front A boundary surface that separates two air-masses. These are regions of great conflict and it is here that the unsettled weather typical of higher latitudes is generated.

Gangue The material in a mineral vein or ore deposit which is not of economic value. With changing economic circumstances a mineral which in the past was a 'gangue' mineral may become valuable.

Geomorphology The interpretation and study of landforms, which in turn make up the landscape. In recent years this has become a discipline in its own right, rather than being a subject area on the boundary of geology and geography.

Geostationary orbit An orbit some 22,300 miles (35,880km) above the Equator. In this position a satellite revolves around the Earth at the same rate as the rotation of the Earth, and so it seems to be stationary in longitude.

Geosyncline A major depression in the Earth's crust, usually of linear shape, in which a vast thickness of sediment accumulates. Eventually an orogeny may take place on this site.

Granitization Granite, an igneous rock, is formed by the freezing of magma, but rock of similar chemistry and feature to granite can be produced in other ways. Granitization includes all the processes by which granitic rocks can arise other than by freezing of magma. These include the alteration of pre-existing rocks by metamorphism or by hot fluids in the Earth's crust.

Greenhouse effect Because the Earth's atmosphere is transparent to much solar radiation, this heats up the Earth's surface and infra-red radiation is emitted. This cannot escape from the planet because it is trapped by carbon dioxide and water vapour in the atmosphere. On Venus the effect is far more pronounced.

Guyot A flat-topped submarine mountain, probably of volcanic origin.

Heat sink A naturally occurring store of heat.

Hydrocarbon The naturally occurring varieties of hydrogen and carbon compounds, including oil, tar, pitch and bitumens, coal and natural gas.

Hydrothermal Very-high-temperature water is very active and capable of dissolving all manner of minerals and rocks. Such waters may be the residual fluids from the cooling of magma, or may come partly from waters trapped in deep sediments. Many minerals, often of great economic value, are formed by deposition from these solutions; these include lead, zinc, copper and iron minerals.

Hypabyssal Igneous rocks which have cooled at relatively shallow depths, and which are usually in small bodies. Such rocks are generally medium-grained.

Igneous rock That formed by consolidation of molten magma (underground) or lava (on the surface). This is one of the three main groups of rocks, the others being metamorphic and sedimentary.

Ionosphere The upper layers of the Earth's atmosphere, where atoms have become ionized by the Sun's radiation.

Island arc A chain of volcanic mountains forming a string of islands, usually on the margin of an ocean.

Joint A fracture in any rock which has no displacement. Joints may arise in igneous rocks as a result of the cooling and shrinkage of the magma or lava. Often spectacular hexagonal columns of lava result in this way. Jointing can also arise during folding when rocks are under stress. Joints are often enlarged by weathering and erosion.

Laccolith A mass of igneous rock which is intruded in a dome-shaped body, usually with a flat base. Such bodies of rock are generally of moderate size.

Lagoon An area of salt or brackish water practically cut off from the sea by a bar or sandbank.

Landform An element in the landscape. Landforms vary in size, shape and origins from small hills to huge valleys. Many landforms are associated with each other through their origin due to certain, often climatically controlled, systems such as glaciation.

Laser Light amplification by stimulated emission of radiation. A coherent monochromatic beam of light which has a multitude of uses from measuring the movements of the continents to monitoring earthquakes.

Latent heat The heat needed to produce the change from solid to liquid or liquid to gas without a change in temperature.

Laterite A deposit formed in climates which have a definite dry and wet season. Laterites are residual deposits often containing hydrated iron and aluminium oxides. During the wet season leaching of elements occurs and during the dry season upward movement, by capillary action, draws some salts to the surface where they can be washed away. By repetition of these two processes the most easily dissolved mineral salts are removed and iron and aluminium oxides tend to become concentrated.

Lava Molten rock extruded from a volcano.

Levée A bank of sediment (usually silt and sand) deposited on the edge of a river channel by the flooding of the river water out onto the flood-plain. Such banks rise above the flood plain and allow the level of the river to stand high above this flat surface.

GLOSSARY

Lignite Brown, impure coal. Lignite is usually considered to be one step away from peat in the increasing rank (carbon content) towards anthracite (the highest-ranking coal). In many areas lignite is used as an industrial fuel.

Limestone A rock of sedimentary origin which contains a high proportion of calcium and/or magnesium carbonate. The calcareous matter in such rocks may be organic in origin or may result from inorganic chemical activity.

Lithology A term usually used of sedimentary rocks, meaning 'rock type'.

Loess Wind-carried dust which is derived either from deserts or from the tundra and vegetation-free areas around major ice sheets.

Lopolith An igneous intrusion, shaped like a saucer with its concave side upwards.

Magma Molten rock material, in the crust and upper mantle of the Earth, which may solidify at depth to form intrusions or emerge onto the surface, when it is called lava. It is essentially a silicate melt, and can form a variety of different crystalline igneous rocks, depending on its cooling history.

Magnetometer An instrument used for measuring a magnetic field.

Mammal Vertebrate animals which usually suckle their young. The young are born live, and mammals often have a covering of hair or fur and are warm-blooded.

Mariner A type of spacecraft developed by the USA for investigation of the planets.

Meiosis A process of nuclear divisions that reduces the amount of genetic material in each resulting 'daughter' nucleus to half that in the original nucleus.

Mesa An isolated flat-topped, steep-sided area which, with continued active erosion and weathering, may become a butte.

Metamorphic rock Any rock which has been so altered by heat and pressure that it has lost much of its original character and changed into a definable new rock. Rocks in contact with hot magma and lava will be altered by contact heating. Rocks buried to great depth in the crust will be altered by heat and pressure.

Meteorite A meteor which has survived passage through the Earth's atmosphere to hit the planet.

Milky Way The part of our galaxy that is easily seen from the Earth.

Mobile belt An elongated, linear part of the Earth's crust where rocks become altered through metamorphism and folding.

Molluscs An invertebrate phylum of animals which often have shells. It includes the cephalopods (including the extinct ammonites), bivalves and gastropods.

Mountain building The formation of mountains by a series of processes including folding, metamorphism and igneous activity. The term is synonomous with orogeny.

Mylonite A fine-grained, crushed rock produced by the movement of large faults, especially thrusts.

Nebula A dust and gas cloud in deep space.

Orogeny A period of mountain building. All the various processes which lead to the formation of a mountain range may take many tens of millions of years.

Outcrop The total area over which a rock formation occurs at the surface, even if for some part of that area the rock is not exposed and visible.

Paramammal A group of mammal-like reptiles. The mammals probably evolved from these creatures during the Triassic period.

Peat A layer of partially decomposed vegetable matter. It is dark brown in colour and even though recent peat contains much water and other impurities, it is used as a fuel. Ancient forest peats, by undergoing metamorphism, turn into coal.

Pediment A plain made of eroded rock, usually in an arid region.

Pegmatite A very coarse-grained igneous rock, usually of granitic composition. The term is also used to describe a band of coarser rock in a generally finer-grained mass.

Phanerozoic The part of the geological record which contains abundant evidence, in the form of fossils, of life. This is the time from the base of the Cambrian period to the present.

Photosynthesis The process by which green plants make carbohydrates from water and carbon dioxide, using the Sun's energy.

Phylum One of the major kinds of groups used in classifying animals, consisting of one or more similar classes, further divided in turn into orders, families, genera and species.

Pillow lava When basaltic lavas are erupted on the sea-bed an outer skin cools immediately but still contains mobile lava which moves to form large pillow-shaped masses. Such rocks are common on the ocean floor and when found in the geological record are taken to be indicative of a deep-sea environment.

Pioneer A spacecraft developed by the USA for planetary investigation.

Placer deposit A concentration of heavy minerals in alluvial sand.

Plate tectonics A theory of the Earth which brings together many phenomena to explain continental drift and most geological processes.

Plutonic A term used in igneous geology to describe deep igneous activity. Batholiths are plutonic intrusions.

Pre-Cambrian The earliest stages of the Earth's development, from the initial consolidation of the planet (4,500 million years ago) until the start of Cambrian times, 600 million years ago. We know very little about this enormous part of time (some ⅞th of the geological record) compared with our knowledge of the Phanerozoic.

Precession An extremely slow, gradual change in the direction of the Earth's axis, resulting from the gravitational pull of the Moon.

Precipitation A term used in meteorology for all forms of atmospheric moisture such as rain, hail, snow, sleet and dew.

Pyrites The commonest sulphide of iron (FeS_2), found in the upper parts of the Earth's crust. Occurs in many situations, including the replacement of organic matter in fossilization. Chalcopyrite ($CuFeS_2$) is a sulphide of copper and iron.

Pyroclastic rocks Fragmentary volcanic material such as dust, ash, pumice and bombs.

Pyroxene A group of silicate minerals, including augite and diopside, which are common constituents of igneous rocks.

Red beds Sedimentary layers which are reddened, usually because of oxidized iron coating the grains. Typically, red beds are sandstones and conglomerates, and lack fossils. They may be indicative of an arid environment of deposition, but can also be formed in other situations.

Red shift The movement of spectral lines towards longer wavelengths resulting from the recession of galaxies.

Relative humidity A way of expressing the extent to which the air is saturated, usually expressed as a percentage. It is important to realize that because warm air can hold more water than cold air, a relative humidity of 80% in winter will represent a moisture content of only 5 g/cu m, but on a hot day a relative humidity of 80% represents at least 12 g/cu m.

Reptile A vertebrate animal, usually cold-blooded, egg-laying and scaly-skinned.

Rock An aggregate of mineral particles.

Sea mount A mountain which rises abruptly from the sea bed, often over 3,300ft (1,000m). Seamounts are volcanic in origin.

Sediment Particles derived from pre-existing rocks by weathering and erosion, dust particles from volcanic and other sources and organic debris can all be classed as sediment. These and other materials can be transported and deposited by a variety of means, such as water, to form sedimentary rocks. Sediment particles can vary greatly in size from boulders to fine silt and mud.

Sedimentary rock A rock which is usually deposited in layers and formed at low temperatures and pressures at the Earth's surface. It commonly contains eroded and weathered fragments of pre-formed rocks. Fossils are common in sedimentary rocks and many limestones are composed of a high proportion of organic material. Some sedimentary rocks are the result of low-temperature chemical activity, such as precipitation of salts from water.

Seismic Tomography A new technique, currently being refined, which in the last few years has, by using the velocities of seismic waves rather than their absorption (as with more long-standing methods), been able to map the three-dimensional nature of the Earth's interior, especially the mantle. By using methods similar to medical computer aided tomography (CAT), seismic tomography uses the information from many crisscrossing seismic waves to construct a 3-D image. (A CAT scan uses X-rays to scan the human body.) The long-standing seismic techniques have provided a radial model of the Earth's interior; tomography adds a third dimension.

Seismometer An instrument used for measuring the shock waves from an earthquake or a nuclear explosion.

Stoping A process whereby large igneous intrusions invade the country rock. The process involves the subtle permeation of the country rock by the magmatic fluids, surrounding large blocks of country rock which are then assimilated as they sink into the magma. The igneous rock thus takes the space of the country rock without having to push it aside.

Stromatolite Large mounds of calcareous matter built by algae. Such structures are known from the geological record from the Pre-Cambrian rocks, and are among the oldest fossils. They are still being formed today in Australia.

Supercooling Lowering the temperature of a substance below its normal freezing point without it freezing.

Superheating Raising the temperature of a substance above its normal boiling point without it boiling.

Tectonic Anything to do with movement and structure in the Earth, especially in the crust.

Tephra The collective term for all the fragmentary particles that come out of a volcano, including ash, dust, pumice and scoria.

Trace fossil Evidence of past life which is not actually a fossil of part of the organism, but the fossil of its burrow, droppings, footprints or trails.

Unconformity A time gap. Part of the geological record which is missing at a certain locality, either by erosion and then later by deposition, or by original non-deposition. Unconformities are often old land surfaces.

Viscosity Stickiness. A molten rock with a high viscosity is less runny than one with a low viscosity.

Voyager An advanced US spacecraft developed from the Mariner class to reach the outer planets.

Wadi A dry valley or water course in an arid region which at times of heavy rainfall may become a turbulent river.

Xenolith A fragment of country rock, which retains most of its original characteristics, included in solidified magma or lava.

FURTHER READING

Attenborough, D. Life on Earth Collins/BBC 1979
Booth, B. & Fitch, F. Earthshock Dent 1979
Brace, C.L. & Montagu. M.F.A. Human Evolution Macmillan 1977
Charig, A. A New Look at the Dinosaurs Heinemann 1979
Clarkson, E.N.K. Invertebrate Palaeontology & Evolution Allen & Unwin 1979
Collinson, J.D. & Thompson, D.B. Sedimentary Structures Allen & Unwin 1982
Cox, C.B., Healey, I.N. & Moore, P.D. Biogeography: An Ecological and Evolutionary Approach Blackwell Scientific Publications 1980
Eyles, N., Ed. Glacial Geology Pergamon 1983
Francis, P. Volcanoes Penguin 1976
Gass, I.G., Smith, P.J. & Wilson, R.C.L. Eds. Understanding the Earth Artemis Press 1971
Geological Museum, London: The Story of the Earth (2nd ed. 1981); The Age of the Earth (1980); Volcanoes (2nd imp. 1977); Earthquakes (1983) All titles published by HMSO
Gribbin, J. Future Weather: Carbon Dioxide, Climate & The Greenhouse Effect Penguin 1982

Halstead, L.B. Hunting the Past Hamish Hamilton 1982
Halstead, L.B. Patterns of Vertebrate Evolution Oliver & Boyd 1969
Hamilton, W.R., Wooley, A.R. & Bishop, A.C. The Hamlyn Guide to Minerals, Rocks & Fossils Hamlyn 1974
Hardy, R., Wright, P., Griggin, J. & Kington, J. The Weather Book Michael Joseph 1982
Heezen, B.C. & Hollister, C.D. The Face of the Deep Oxford University Press 1971
John, B.S., Ed. The Winters of the World: Earth Under the Ice Ages David & Charles 1979
Kemp, T.S. Mammal-like Reptiles & The Origin of Mammals Academic Press 1982
Leakey, R. & Lewin, R. Origins E.P. Dutton 1977
Lewis, R.L. The Illustrated Encyclopedia of Space Exploration Salamander 1983
Mabbutt, J.A. Desert Landforms MIT Press 1977
Press, F. & Siever, R. Earth W.H. Freeman 3rd ed. 1982
Read, H.H. & Watson, J. Introduction to Geology, Vols. 1 & 2 Macmillan 1974

Scientific American authors: The Dynamic Earth Freeman 1984
Sheffield, C. Earthwatch Sidgwick & Jackson 1981
Skinner, B.J. & Turekian, K.K. Man and the Oceans Prentice Hall 1976
Smith, D.G. The Cambridge Encyclopedia of Earth Sciences Cambridge University Press 1982
Tarling, D.H. Palaeomagnetism: Principles & Applications in Geology, Geophysics & Archaeology Chapman & Hall 1984
Tarling, D.H. & M.P. Continental Drift: A Study of the Earth's Moving Surfaces Penguin 2nd ed. 1977
Thomas, B. Evolution of Plants & Flowers Peter Lowe 1981
Thurman, H.V. Essentials of Oceanography Merrill 1983
The Times Atlas of the Oceans Times Books Ltd 1983
Watson, J. Geology & Man: An Introduction to Applied Earth Science Allen & Unwin 1983
Whitten, D.G.A., with Brooks, J.R.V. The Penguin Dictionary of Geology Penguin 1972
Whittow, J. The Penguin Dictionary of Physical Geography Penguin 1984

INDEX

INDEX

INDEX

PICTURE CREDITS

Photographs are credited by page number and by their position on the page, as follows: (T) Top; (C) Centre; (B) Bottom; BL (Bottom Left); FL (Far Left), etc.

Bryan & Cherry Alexander: P.Drummond Front jkt (Inset FL), Preface pages.
Heather Angel: 17(TR), 24, 28(T), 118(T), 127(BR), 130/131(T), 133(TR), 158(CR,BR), 165(BL,G), 173(B), 184(C).
Ardea: I.Beames 18, 149(CR); G.Behrens 135(CR); J.P.Ferraro 94/94(TR), 134/135(C); F.Gohier 112(T); P.J.Green 163(CR, BR), 170(CL); J.M.Labat 25(C); E.Mickleburgh 26/27(B); P.Morris 159(TR), 163(CL); 165(TL,C), 167(C), 168, 169, 172(C), 173(C), 174(B); V.Taylor 192(C); W.Weisser 28(C), 132/133(B).
L.Beckel, Austria, aerial photos: Back jkt (Main inset), 68/69, 96(T), 99(T), 124/125(T), 129(B), 135(T), 182(B), 184(B), 198(B).
Biofotos: B.Rogers 115(B); S.Summerhayes Title pages, 21(C), 76/77(T); M.Watson 77(CR), 89.
Biophoto Associates: 144(T), 156(B), 157(CR,BR); C.Pellant 17(BL,BC), 19, 25(CL), 26(CR), 27(TL,TC,BC), 30, 31, 85(B), 86/87(T), 87(CR), 137(TR,CR), 162(BL), 163(BL); P.Tye 74(BR).
British Antarctic Survey: D.G.Allen 196(B); S.J.R.Fraser 197(BL); C.J.Gilbert 123(C); A.B.Moyes 122(B); J.G.Paren 197(BR); J.R.Rouse 124/125(B); M.Vallance 123(TR).
Camerapix Hutchinson Library: 136/137(B), 181(B), 182(T), 193(BR); R.Constable 183(CL); R.House 192(TC).
Centre National d'Études Spatiales: 35(C).
John Cleare/Mountain Camera: 87(B), 88(T), 112/113(T), 137(TL).
Bruce Coleman Ltd: P.Baker 152/153(C); J. & D.Bartlett 177(TR); R.Boardman 193(BR); R.I.M.Campbell 178(BL,BR), 179(TR,CL,CR); G.Cubitt 183(BL); A.Davies 146(CR); A.J.Deane 199(T); N.Devore Front jkt (Inset R), 96/97(TR), 97(B); F.Erize 177(TL); C.B.Frith 195(T); T.O'Keefe 184(TL); L.C.Marigo 199(B); C.Molyneux 188(CL,CR); G.Ziesler 152/153(T).
Colorado University: 150/151.
Colorific: P.Boulat 131(CR,BL).
Crown Copyright/HMSO: 142/143(T,B), 143(T).
Deepsea Ventures Inc: 194(CL,CR,BR), 195(C).
ESA: 35(B), 44(B), 49(CR).
ESA/DFVLR: 54, 54/55(B).
European Centre for Medium Range Weather Forecasts: 193(T).
Explorer: 193(T).
Gamma/Frank Spooner Pictures: 185(T).
GeoScience Features: Front Jkt (Inset FL), Half-title, 27(CR), 59(T), 62/63(T), 70, 71, 72/73(T), 73(BL,BR), 74(TL,BL),

74/75(TR), 77(TR), 78(T,TC), 78/79(B,T), 79(BR), 80(T,B), 81(BR), 84(T,C), 85(T), 86(BL,BR), 90(T), 94(TL), 111, 112(B), 113(B), 114(T,C), 117(T), 126/127(T), 138(T), 155, 160(T), 162(BR), 164(T,C), 165(TR), 170(B,BR), 186/187(T).
Geoslides Photo Library: 114/115.
Sally & Richard Greenhill: 119(T).
Greenpeace: 187(C).
Robert Harding Picture Library: 183(CR,BR); D.Holden 199(CL).
Hasselblad: Front & back jkts (main picture), 10, 141(TL).
Dr R.Haydn, University of Munich: Contributing Authors' pages, 32/33.
Hughes Aircraft Co: 45, 46(C), 46/47(TC), 47(TR).
Institute of Geological Sciences: Endpapers, 117(C,B), 158(BL), 160(CL,CR), 161(CL), 166(B), 167(C).
Institute of Oceanographic Sciences: 65(TC); R.B.Kidd 56(TR,CR), 65(TC); R.Searle 95(CL), 102(CR), 103(C).
Jet Propulsion Laboratory: 140(T).
King & Reid: R.Fletcher 136(T).
Frank Lane Picture Agency: 145(B); J.C.Allen & Son 200(B); D.Hoadley 145(T); S.McCutcheon 14(BL), 14/15(BR), 138(B); R.Maranges 149(TR); Mrs R.Otto 148(T); B.Stone 144/145(B), 200/201(T); R.Thompson 145(C).
J.Latham: 110(B), 146(TR), 147(TL).
Messerschmitt-Bolkow-Blöhm: 55(BR).
P.Morrow: 134(BL).
NASA: 11, 32(TL), 34(BL), 34/35, 36(TL,TR), 36/37(B), 37(TL), 38(TR), 40(T,C), 40/41, 41(B), 42(TL,CL), 42/43(B), 44(CR,BR), 46(TL), 48(B), 48/49(T,BC), 50(C,BL), 50/51(B), 51, 52(B), 52/53(T), 69(CR), 139, 140(B), 141(CL), 148/149(B), 150(T,C), 151(CR).
National Coal Board: 188(BL).
National Environment Satellite Service: 43(CR).
National Severe Storms Lab/NOAA: 149(TL), 201(B).
Netherlands Board of Tourism: 180(B).
NHPA: P.Fagot 187(T); P.Johnson 128(T).
NOAA: 43(CR), 201(TR).
Oceaneering Intnl. Services Ltd: 105(TR).
Oxford Scientific Films: M.Fogden 106(B).
Picturepoint: 62(C).
RAE, Farnborough: 46(CR).
RCA Astro-Electronics: 38(TL,C), 39(TL,TR).
J.M.Reynolds: 114(CR), 116/117, 118/119, 120, 121(T,C), 122/123.
RIDA Photo Library: D.Bayliss 64/65(T), 65(T), 152(T), 153(B), 154(C,B), 156(CL,CR), 157(C), 159(BR), 161(TL,TR,CR), 162(CR), 164(TR), 166(T); R.J.Moody 101(T); P.Wellenhoffer 174(T), 175(T); B.Wood 178(C).
G.A.Robinson: 142(T).
Science Photo Library: 14(C); Aerospace Corporation

92(T); ESA 16/17(TC), 23; R.Folwell 190(C,B); Gull, Fielden & Smith 64/65; M.Kobrick/NASA 13 (TR); R.Legeckis 106(T,C); NASA 63(T); R.Royer 12/13(T); S.Stammers 27(CL).
Scripps Institution of Oceanography, Univ. of California, San Diego: 102/103(T), 108(T).
Seaphot/Planet Earth Pictures: D.Clarke Back jkt (Inset R), 100; P.David 107(T); L.F.Grannis 109(CR); R.Hessler 56(TL), 194(BL); R.Matthews 199(CL); F.Schulke 101(B); P.Scoones 105(BL); G.Wilson 102(B).
Shell Photo Library: 98(T).
South American Pictures: M.Morrison Back jkt (Inset FL), 28/29, 181(BL); T.Morrison Contents page, 88(C), 180/181(T).
Space Frontiers/Daily Telegraph Colour Library: 66/67(TC), 67(T,TC).
Spectrum Colour Library: 21(T), 59(C), 60/61(T), 184/185(T).
Frank Spooner Pictures: R.Masson 187(B).
Spot Image: 49(BR).
TASS: 53(C), 110(T).
US Geological Survey: 82(B); J.D.Griggs 82/83; J.Judd Front jkt (main inset), 82(C); D.W.Peterson 82(C); R.E.Wallace 57(T).
Westinghouse: 60/61(T).
J.B.Wilson: 144/145(C).
Woods Hole Oceanographic Institution: 94/95(B); R.Catanach 105(TL); J.Donnelly 104(B); D.Foster 104(C).
Yale Peabody Museum: 158(T), 170(T), 172(T), 173(T).
ZEFA: Front jkt (inset FR), Back jkt (insets L,FR), 20/21(T), 80/81(TC), 81(TR), 90/91(TC), 91(T), 92(C), 93, 108/109(T), 109(TR), 126(TL), 128(B), 129(T), 132(BL), 144/145(T), 146(TC), 147(TR), 176, 180(T), 186(C), 188/189(B), 189(T), 190(T), 191(BL,CR,BR), 192(TR), 198(CR), 201(CR).

ARTISTS

Copyright of the artwork on the pages following the artists' names is the property of Salamander Books Ltd.

Mike Badrocke: 35, 36, 37, 39, 41, 44, 47, 49, 50, 52, 55.
Bob Chapman: 16, 18(T), 22, 22/23, 28, 31, 56(B), 58, 60/61, 72, 73, 75, 76, 77, 83, 85, 86, 88, 89, 90, 91, 92, 93, 96, 97, 98(B), 100, 102, 108, 113, 114, 117, 135, 146, 148, 152, 168, 169(TL), 170, 175, 179, 188, 190.
Alan Hollingbery: 12/13, 14, 15, 18/19(B), 19, 56(T), 63, 65, 66, 69, 70, 78, 98(T), 99, 103, 106, 107, 109, 111, 118, 120, 126, 133, 138, 166, 197, 201.
Janos Marffy: 167, 169(TR), 171.
Tom Macarthur: 26.
Cathleen McDougal: 24/25, 155.
Graham Rosewarne: 158.
Tudor Art Studios: 104, 130.
Tim Widdel: 141, 143, 144, 151.

190 million-year-old Jurassic ammonites from Yeovil, Somerset, England.

HAMLYN
ALL COLOUR
QUICK & EASY

FAST SIMPLE DELICIOUS

HAMLYN
ALL COLOUR
QUICK & EASY

OVER 250 MOUTHWATERING RECIPES

Bounty
Books

- Both metric and imperial measurements are given for the recipes. Use one set of measures only, not a mixture of both.

- Ovens should be preheated to the specified temperature. If using a fan-assisted oven, follow the manufacturer's instructions for adjusting the time and temperature. Grills should also be preheated.

- This book includes dishes made with nuts and nut derivatives. It is advisable for those with known allergic reactions to nuts and nut derivatives and those who may be potentially vulnerable to these allergies, such as pregnant women and nursing mothers, invalids, the elderly, babies and children, to avoid dishes made with nuts and nut oils. It is also prudent to check the labels of pre-prepared ingredients for the possible inclusion of nut derivatives.

- The Department of Health advises that eggs should not be consumed raw. This book contains some dishes made with raw or lightly-cooked eggs. It is prudent for more vulnerable people, such as pregnant women and nursing mothers, invalids, the elderly, babies and young children, to avoid uncooked or lightly-cooked dishes made with eggs.

- Meat and poultry should be cooked thoroughly. To test if poultry is cooked, pierce the flesh through the thickest part with a skewer or fork – the juices should run clear, never pink or red.

- Where pepper is listed in the recipe ingredients, always use freshly ground black pepper.

First published in Great Britain in 2007 by Hamlyn,
a division of Octopus Publishing Group Ltd

This edition published in 2011 by Bounty Books,
a division of Octopus Publishing Group Ltd
Endeavour House
189 Shaftesbury Avenue
London WC2H 8JY

www.octopusbooks.co.uk

An Hachette UK Company
www.hachette.co.uk

Copyright © Octopus Publishing Group Ltd 2007

ISBN: 978-0753720-95-0

A CIP catalogue record for this book is available from the British Library

Printed and bound in China

Contents

Introduction

We all appreciate and enjoy home-cooked meals, and we are also all aware of how important eating good, wholesome food rather than junk fast food is to our physical, and mental, well-being. But finding enough time and energy in our pressured lives to cook a proper meal is a constant challenge. Help is here at hand with this bumper collection of more than 250 quick and easy recipes, each taking a maximum of just 30 minutes, and some considerably less, to prepare and cook. Choose from speedy yet satisfying soups, snacks and starters; vegetable dishes and salads, made in moments and mouthwatering; pasta, pizza, noodle and rice dishes, both quick and comforting; effortless yet delicious fish and seafood, poultry and game, meat and vegetarian mains; and desserts that are as sumptuous as they are simple.

After-work solutions

At the end of a long, hard day, what we crave and deserve is to fast-forward to an enticing, tasty and nutritious meal, and there are lots of ideas on offer here that will deliver just that. In less time than it takes to heat up a supermarket ready meal, you can rustle up Maple and Mustard Glazed Salmon (see recipe 159), quickly cooked under the grill while you steam some vegetables, or Marinated Tofu with Pak Choi (see recipe 140), simply and speedily stir-fried. If you are in need of something really hearty, Venison Sausages with Spicy Bean Sauce (see recipe 190) or Chorizo and Chickpea Stew (see recipe 210), both using convenient canned pulses, are sure to hit the spot. And for dessert there are some ultra-quick no-cook options, such as Raspberry and Shortcake Mess (see recipe 228) or Pink Grapefruit Parfait (see recipe 227).

Easy entertaining

It's not just everyday meals that can be quick and easy. In under 15 minutes you can serve up a stylish dinner party dish of Angel Hair Pasta with Prawns (see recipe 99), or really impress your guests with the alluringly crispy Duck with Honey and Lime Sauce (see recipe 183) or Grilled Snapper with Salmoriglio (see recipe 155) with its classy Italian garlic, lemon and fresh herb sauce. To round off your dinner on a high note, invite your guests to dip into the luxurious Strawberries with Chocolate Spread (see recipe 260) or wow them with a platter of pastries in the form of Orange Palmiers with Plums (see recipe 235).

Storecupboard staples

The key to producing successful home-cooked dishes with the minimum of fuss is to build up and maintain a storecupboard of good-quality ingredients that can form the basis of a wide variety of meals, with the addition of a few fresh ingredients, or provide that all-important flavouring for fresh ingredients on any given day. These are the most useful items to keep in store:

• **Dried goods** – strand, ribbon and shaped pasta; rice and egg noodles; basmati, quick-cooking white long-grain rice and risotto rice; quick-cooking polenta, cornflour and plain and self-raising flour; couscous and bulgar wheat; ground and whole almonds, walnut halves, cashew nuts and pine nuts; sesame seeds; ready-to-eat dried apricots and figs, sultanas and raisins; brown, caster and icing sugar

• **Canned and bottled foods** – canned pulses, including chickpeas, lentils and beans; canned tomatoes, anchovy fillets, tuna, crabmeat, coconut milk and black cherries; bottled roasted red peppers and artichoke hearts; olives and capers; passata (sieved tomatoes), sun-blush tomatoes, tomato purée and sun-dried tomato paste

• **Flavourings** – dried herbs and spices; wholegrain, Dijon and dry English mustard; red and white wine, balsamic vinegar and rice vinegar; Thai and Indian curry pastes; Worcestershire, Tabasco, soy, Thai fish and hoisin sauces; rice wine, dry sherry, cider, brandy and liqueurs; honey, maple syrup and jam; stock cubes and/or bouillon powder

• **Oils** – sunflower, olive, groundnut and sesame oils

Freezer standbys

A well-stocked freezer can be used to great effect in helping you to cook quick and easy meals. The following are the essentials:

• **Frozen vegetables** – peas, sweetcorn, leaf spinach, broad beans

• **Cooked peeled prawns**

• **Bread** – partly baked baguettes; ciabatta; ready-made pizza dough bases and/or Italian flatbreads; soft flour tortillas; pitta breads

• **Pastry** – filo pastry; ready-rolled puff pastry

• **Berries** – mixed berry fruits and/or raspberries and blueberries

• **Vanilla ice cream**

Time-saving tips

• Cut down on preparation time by opting for pre-prepared ingredients, such as pitted olives, ready-washed mixed salads, fish fillets and ready trimmed and cubed meat.

• Invest in a food processor, which can be used to speed up a variety of tasks, such as chopping ingredients, blending soups and sauces, whipping up batter and making breadcrumbs.

• A heavy-based griddle pan will prove a worthwhile addition to your kitchen, enabling you quickly to cook meat, poultry and game cuts, as well as seafood and vegetables, and all with a delicious chargrilled flavour and appearance.

• Use ready-made sauces and flavourings to add an instant boost to all manner of dishes, such as miso paste for enhancing oriental soups and marinades, pesto and tapenade for pepping up poultry or fish, black bean sauce for jazzing up stir-fries, and cranberry, mint and horseradish sauces as well as redcurrant jelly for giving a lift to meat dishes.

• For preparing desserts in a hurry have some meringue nests and sweet biscuits like amaretti and shortcake fingers in store to crumble up and swirl with cream and fruit, as well as plain dark chocolate for melting.

1 Soups

1 Tomato and almond soup

2 Beetroot gazpacho

Preparation time:
5 minutes

Cooking time:
20 minutes

Serves: **4**

1 kg (2 lb) vine-ripened tomatoes, roughly chopped
2 garlic cloves, crushed
300 ml (½ pint) vegetable stock
2 tablespoons extra virgin olive oil
1 teaspoon caster sugar
100 g (3½ oz) ground almonds, toasted
salt and pepper

BASIL OIL
150 ml (¼ pint) extra virgin olive oil
15 g (½ oz) basil leaves

Preparation time:
15 minutes

Cooking time:
No cooking

Serves: **4**

500 g (1 lb) cooked beetroot in natural juices, drained and chopped
1 small onion, roughly chopped
2 garlic cloves, roughly chopped
2 tomatoes, roughly chopped
2 tablespoons capers, drained and rinsed
4 baby cornichons, drained, rinsed and chopped
25 g (1 oz) dried white breadcrumbs
600 ml (1 pint) vegetable stock
150 ml (¼ pint) extra virgin olive oil
2 tablespoons white wine vinegar
salt and pepper

TO SERVE
crème fraîche
dill sprigs

Put the tomatoes in a saucepan with the garlic, stock, oil, sugar and salt and pepper to taste. Bring to the boil, then reduce the heat and simmer gently for 15 minutes.

Meanwhile, to make the basil oil, put the oil, basil leaves and a pinch of salt in a blender or food processor and blend until really smooth. Set aside.

Stir the almonds into the soup, heat through and then serve in warmed bowls, drizzled with the basil oil.

Put the beetroot, onion, garlic, tomatoes, capers and cornichons in a food processor and process until smooth. Add the breadcrumbs and pulse. With the machine running, gradually add the stock, oil and vinegar until completely incorporated and smooth. Season to taste with salt and pepper.

Serve in bowls, topped with a spoonful of crème fraîche and some dill sprigs and sprinkled with pepper.

COOK'S NOTES This makes a perfect no-fuss appetizer for entertaining because you can prepare it in advance, leave it in the refrigerator to chill and simply garnish it and serve when you and your guests are ready to eat.

3 Potato soup with parsley

4 Minestrone

Preparation time:
10 minutes

Cooking time:
20 minutes

Serves: **4**

1.5 litres (2½ pints) beef stock
4 potatoes, peeled and coarsely grated
1 egg yolk
1 hard-boiled egg yolk, mashed
50 ml (2 fl oz) single cream
50 g (2 oz) Parmesan cheese, freshly grated
1 tablespoon finely chopped parsley
salt and pepper
125 g (4 oz) croûtons, to serve

Preparation time:
5 minutes

Cooking time:
25 minutes

Serves: **4**

2 tablespoons olive oil
1 onion, chopped
1 garlic clove, crushed
2 celery sticks, chopped
1 leek, finely sliced
1 carrot, chopped
400 g (13 oz) can chopped tomatoes
600 ml (1 pint) chicken stock or vegetable stock
1 courgette, diced
½ small cabbage, shredded
1 bay leaf
75 g (3 oz) canned haricot beans, drained
75 g (3 oz) dried spaghetti, broken into small pieces, or small pasta shapes
1 tablespoon chopped flat leaf parsley
salt and pepper
50 g (2 oz) Parmesan cheese, freshly grated, to serve

Pour the stock into a saucepan and bring to the boil. Sprinkle the potatoes with salt and pepper to taste, then drop them into the boiling stock. Cook for about 15 minutes, stirring occasionally.

Meanwhile, beat the egg yolk in a soup tureen and add the mashed hard-boiled egg yolk. Blend the cream, Parmesan and parsley into the egg mixture and whisk together.

Carefully pour 250 ml (8 fl oz) of the stock into the egg mixture. Reheat the remaining stock and potatoes and gradually add to the soup tureen. Sprinkle with croûtons and serve in warmed bowls.

Heat the oil in a large saucepan. Add the onion, garlic, celery, leek and carrot and cook over a medium heat, stirring occasionally, for about 3 minutes.

Add the tomatoes, stock, courgette, cabbage, bay leaf and haricot beans. Bring to the boil, lower the heat and simmer for 10 minutes.

Add the pasta and season to taste with salt and pepper. Stir well and cook for a further 8 minutes. Keep stirring because the soup may stick to the base of the pan. Just before serving, add the parsley and stir well. Ladle the soup into warmed bowls and serve with grated Parmesan.

COOK'S NOTES To make croûtons, remove the crusts from 2 slices of white bread, then cut the bread into 1 cm (½ inch) dice. Heat about 2 tablespoons vegetable oil in a heavy-based frying pan, add the bread cubes and cook, turning and stirring frequently, for 5 minutes or until golden and crisp all over. Remove with a slotted spoon and drain on kitchen paper.

5 Pea, lettuce and lemon soup

6 Chilli bean soup

Preparation time:
10 minutes

Cooking time:
20 minutes

Serves: **4**

Oven temperature:
200°C (400°F) Gas Mark 6

25 g (1 oz) butter
1 large onion, finely chopped
425 g (14 oz) frozen peas
2 Little Gem lettuces, roughly chopped
1 litre (1¾ pints) vegetable or chicken stock
finely grated rind and juice of ½ lemon
salt and pepper

SESAME CROÛTONS
2 thick slices of bread, crusts removed, cubed
1 tablespoon olive oil
1 tablespoon sesame seeds

Preparation time:
5 minutes

Cooking time:
25 minutes

Serves: **3–4**

2 tablespoons olive oil
1 onion, chopped
1 garlic clove, crushed
1 teaspoon hot chilli powder
1 teaspoon ground coriander
½ teaspoon ground cumin
400 g (13 oz) can red kidney beans, drained and rinsed
400 g (13 oz) can chopped tomatoes
600 ml (1 pint) vegetable stock
12 tortilla chips
50 g (2 oz) Cheddar cheese, grated
salt and pepper
soured cream, to serve

To make the sesame croûtons, brush the bread cubes with the oil and put in a roasting tin. Sprinkle with the sesame seeds and bake in a preheated oven, 200°C (400°F), Gas Mark 6, for 10–15 minutes until golden.

Meanwhile, heat the butter in a large saucepan, add the onion and cook for 5 minutes until softened. Add the peas, lettuce, stock, lemon rind and juice and salt and pepper to taste. Bring to the boil, then reduce the heat, cover and simmer for 10–15 minutes.

Leave the soup to cool slightly, then transfer to a blender or food processor and blend until smooth. Return the soup to the pan, adjust the seasoning, if necessary, and heat through. Spoon into warmed bowls and sprinkle with the sesame croûtons.

Heat the oil in a saucepan, add the onion, garlic, chilli powder, coriander and cumin and cook, stirring frequently, for 5 minutes or until the onion has softened. Add the beans, tomatoes, stock and salt and pepper to taste.

Bring the soup to the boil, then reduce the heat, cover and simmer for 15 minutes. Transfer to a blender or food processor and blend until fairly smooth. Return the soup to the pan and heat through.

Pour the soup into heatproof bowls. Top with the tortilla chips, scatter over the Cheddar and put under a preheated high grill for 1–2 minutes until the cheese has melted. Serve immediately with soured cream.

COOK'S NOTES To save time, you can prepare the croûtons in advance. Simply store them in an airtight container until you make the soup later on.

Preparation time:
10 minutes

Cooking time:
20 minutes

Serves: **4**

1 teaspoon olive oil
1 leek, thinly sliced
1 large potato, peeled and chopped
450 g (14½ oz) prepared mixed summer vegetables, such as peas, asparagus spears, broad beans and courgettes
2 tablespoons chopped mint
900 ml (1½ pints) vegetable stock
2 tablespoons crème fraîche
salt (optional) and pepper

Heat the oil in a medium saucepan, add the leek and potato and cook for 3–4 minutes until softened.

Add the mixed vegetables to the pan with the mint and the stock and bring to the boil. Reduce the heat and simmer for 10 minutes.

Transfer the soup to a blender or food processor and blend until smooth. Return the soup to the pan with the crème fraîche and season to taste with salt, if you like, and pepper. Heat through and serve in warmed bowls.

Preparation time:
10 minutes

Cooking time:
20 minutes

Serves: **4**

4 tablespoons olive oil
12 thick slices of baguette
5 garlic cloves, sliced
1 onion, finely chopped
1 tablespoon paprika
1 teaspoon ground cumin
good pinch of saffron threads
1.2 litres (2 pints) vegetable stock
25 g (1 oz) dried soup pasta
4 eggs
salt and pepper

Heat the oil in a heavy-based saucepan, add the bread and cook gently, turning once, until golden. Remove with a slotted spoon and drain on kitchen paper.

Add the garlic, onion, paprika and cumin to the pan and cook gently, stirring, for 3 minutes. Add the saffron threads and stock and bring to the boil. Stir in the pasta. Reduce the heat, cover and simmer for 8 minutes or until the pasta is tender but still firm to the bite. Season to taste with salt and pepper.

Break the eggs on to a saucer and slide them into the pan one at a time. Cook for 2 minutes or until just set.

Stack 3 fried bread slices in each of 4 warmed bowls. Ladle the soup over the bread, making sure that each serving contains an egg. Serve immediately.

COOK'S NOTES Frozen vegetables make a quick and easy alternative to fresh, as they are prepared and ready to cook. Freshly frozen vegetables retain all their nutrients and goodness.

9 Cauliflower and cumin soup

10 Spinach and broccoli soup

Preparation time:
10 minutes

Cooking time:
20 minutes

Serves: **4**

1 teaspoon vegetable oil
1 onion, chopped
1 garlic clove, crushed
1 teaspoon cumin seeds
1 cauliflower, cut into florets
1 large potato, peeled and chopped
450 ml (¾ pint) vegetable stock
450 ml (¾ pint) milk
2 tablespoons crème fraîche
2 tablespoons chopped fresh coriander
salt (optional) and pepper

Heat the oil in a medium saucepan, add the onion, garlic and cumin seeds and cook, stirring, for 3–4 minutes until the onion is softened. Add the cauliflower, potato, stock and milk and bring to the boil. Reduce the heat and simmer for 15 minutes.

Transfer the soup to a blender or food processor and blend until smooth. Return it to the pan with the crème fraîche and coriander and season to taste with salt, if you like, and pepper. Heat through and serve in warmed bowls.

Preparation time:
10 minutes

Cooking time:
20 minutes

Serves: **4**

2 tablespoons olive oil
50 g (2 oz) butter
1 onion, diced
1 garlic clove, finely chopped
2 potatoes, peeled and diced
250 g (8 oz) broccoli, chopped
300 g (10 oz) spinach, chopped
900 ml (1½ pints) vegetable or chicken stock
125 g (4 oz) Gorgonzola cheese, crumbled
2 tablespoons lemon juice
½ teaspoon freshly grated nutmeg
salt and pepper
75 g (3 oz) toasted pine nuts, to garnish
warm crusty bread, to serve

Heat the oil and butter in a saucepan, add the onion and garlic and cook for 3 minutes. Add the potatoes, broccoli, spinach and stock and bring to the boil, then reduce the heat and simmer for 15 minutes.

If you like, transfer the soup to a blender or food processor and blend until smooth. Return it to the pan and heat through. Add the Gorgonzola with the lemon juice, nutmeg and salt and pepper to taste and stir well. Spoon into warmed soup bowls, garnish with toasted pine nuts and serve with warm crusty bread.

COOK'S NOTES This soup is especially delicious served with multigrain bread topped with melted Gruyère cheese.

11 Butter bean soup

12 Tuscan bean soup

Preparation time:
5 minutes

Cooking time:
20 minutes

Serves: **4**

3 tablespoons olive oil
1 onion, finely chopped
2 celery sticks, thinly sliced
2 garlic cloves, thinly sliced
2 x 400 g (13 oz) cans butter beans,
  drained and rinsed
4 tablespoons sun-dried tomato paste
900 ml (1½ pints) vegetable stock
1 tablespoon chopped rosemary or thyme
salt and pepper
fresh Parmesan cheese shavings, to
  serve

Heat the oil in a saucepan, add the onion and cook for 3 minutes. Add the celery and garlic and cook for 2 minutes.

Add the beans, sun-dried tomato paste, stock, rosemary or thyme and a little salt and pepper. Bring to the boil, then reduce the heat, cover and simmer gently for 15 minutes. Serve the soup in warmed bowls, sprinkled with Parmesan shavings.

Preparation time:
10 minutes

Cooking time:
20 minutes

Serves: **4**

2 tablespoons olive oil
4 shallots, chopped
2 garlic cloves, crushed
150 g (5 oz) piece of green bacon, diced
1 carrot, diced
2 celery sticks, diced
½ red pepper, cored, deseeded and diced
400 g (13 oz) can borlotti beans, drained
  and rinsed
1 litre (1¾ pints) chicken stock
1 bay leaf
1 teaspoon chopped oregano
1 teaspoon chopped marjoram
handful of flat leaf parsley, chopped
salt and pepper
extra virgin olive oil, for drizzling

Heat the olive oil in a saucepan, add the shallots, garlic, bacon, carrot, celery and red pepper and cook for 5 minutes.

Add the beans, stock, bay leaf, oregano and marjoram and bring to the boil. Reduce the heat and simmer for 15 minutes. Skim off any scum that rises to the surface from the beans. Taste and season well.

Just before serving, add the chopped parsley. Ladle the soup into warmed bowls and drizzle each one with a little extra virgin olive oil.

COOK'S NOTES This nutritious soup is perfect for speedy lunches or dinners. Serve with crusty bread for a more substantial meal.

13 Gazpacho

14 Quick and easy miso soup

Preparation time:
15 minutes, plus chilling

Cooking time:
No cooking

Serves: **6**

2 garlic cloves, roughly chopped
¼ teaspoon salt
3 thick slices of white bread, crusts removed
1 kg (2 lb) tomatoes, skinned and roughly chopped
2 onions, roughly chopped
½ large cucumber, peeled, deseeded and roughly chopped
2 large green peppers, cored, deseeded and roughly chopped
5 tablespoons olive oil
4 tablespoons white wine vinegar
1 litre (1¾ pints) iced water
pepper
small ice cubes, to serve

Combine the garlic and salt in a mortar and pound with a pestle until smooth. Put the bread into a bowl, cover with cold water and leave to soak for 5 seconds. Drain the bread, then squeeze out the moisture.

Set aside a quarter of the tomatoes, onions, cucumber and green peppers for garnishing. Put the remaining vegetables in a food processor. Add the garlic paste, bread and oil and process until smooth.

Pour the mixture into a bowl and stir in the vinegar and measured iced water with pepper to taste. Cover and chill in the freezer for 15 minutes.

Meanwhile, chop the reserved vegetables finely. Serve the soup in chilled bowls, adding 2–3 ice cubes to each bowl and topping the soup with the chopped vegetables.

Preparation time:
5 minutes

Cooking time:
8 minutes

Serves: **4**

1 litre (1¾ pints) vegetable stock
2 tablespoons miso paste
125 g (4 oz) shiitake mushrooms, sliced
200 g (7 oz) firm tofu, cubed
fresh bread, to serve

Pour the stock into a saucepan and bring to a simmer.

Add the miso paste, mushrooms and tofu to the stock and simmer gently for 5 minutes. Serve in warmed bowls with bread.

COOK'S NOTES Just a few ingredients produce a soup that is packed full of flavour. Serve as a starter to a Japanese meal or on its own for a light lunch.

15 Beef and noodle broth

16 Black bean soup with soba

Preparation time:
15 minutes

Cooking time:
10 minutes

Serves: **2**

300 g (10 oz) rump or sirloin steak
15 g (½ oz) fresh root ginger, peeled and grated
2 teaspoons soy sauce
600 ml (1 pint) beef or chicken stock
1 red chilli, deseeded and finely chopped
1 garlic clove, thinly sliced
2 teaspoons caster sugar
50 g (2 oz) dried vermicelli rice noodles
2 teaspoons vegetable oil
75 g (3 oz) sugar snap peas, halved lengthways
small handful of Thai basil, torn into pieces

Preparation time:
10 minutes

Cooking time:
8 minutes

Serves: **4**

200 g (7 oz) dried soba (Japanese noodles)
2 tablespoons groundnut or vegetable oil
1 bunch of spring onions, sliced
2 garlic cloves, roughly chopped
1 red chilli, deseeded and sliced
3.5 cm (1½ inch) piece of fresh root ginger, peeled and grated
125 ml (4 fl oz) black bean sauce or black bean stir-fry sauce
750 ml (1¼ pints) vegetable stock
200 g (7 oz) pak choi or spring greens, shredded
2 teaspoons soy sauce
1 teaspoon caster sugar
50 g (2 oz) unsalted raw peanuts

Trim any fat from the steak. Mix the ginger with half the soy sauce and spread over both sides of the steak.

Pour the stock into a saucepan and add the chilli, garlic and sugar. Bring to a gentle simmer and cook for 5 minutes.

Meanwhile, soak the noodles in a saucepan of boiling water according to the packet instructions. Drain and rinse thoroughly under cold running water.

Heat the oil in a small, heavy-based frying pan, add the beef and cook for 2 minutes on each side. Transfer the meat to a board, cut it in half lengthways and then cut it across into thin strips.

Add the noodles, sugar snap peas, basil and remaining soy sauce to the soup and heat gently for 1 minute. Stir in the beef and serve immediately in warmed bowls.

Bring a large saucepan of water to the boil, add the noodles and cook for 5 minutes, or according to the packet instructions, until just tender.

Meanwhile, heat the oil in a saucepan, add the spring onions and garlic and cook gently for 1 minute.

Add the chilli, ginger, black bean sauce and stock and bring to the boil. Stir in the pak choi or spring greens, soy sauce, sugar and peanuts, then reduce the heat and simmer gently for 4 minutes.

Drain the noodles, rinse with fresh hot water and spoon into the base of 4 warmed bowls. Ladle the soup over the top and serve immediately.

COOK'S NOTES When slicing the beef, use a sharp knife and cut it across the grain so that it falls into tender, succulent slices.

17 Thai prawn broth

18 Fragrant tofu and noodle soup

Preparation time:
15 minutes

Cooking time:
10 minutes

Serves: **4**

1.2 litres (2 pints) vegetable stock
2 teaspoons red Thai curry paste
4 kaffir lime leaves, torn into pieces
4 teaspoons Thai fish sauce
2 spring onions, sliced
150 g (5 oz) shiitake mushrooms, sliced
125 g (4 oz) dried soba (Japanese noodles)
½ red pepper, cored, deseeded and diced
125 g (4 oz) pak choi, thinly sliced
250 g (8 oz) frozen prawns, defrosted and rinsed
small bunch of fresh coriander leaves, torn into pieces

Pour the stock into a saucepan and add the curry paste, lime leaves, fish sauce, onions and mushrooms. Bring to the boil, then reduce the heat and simmer for 5 minutes.

Meanwhile, bring a separate saucepan of water to the boil, add the noodles and cook for 5 minutes, or according to the packet instructions, until just tender.

Add the remaining ingredients to the soup and cook for 2 minutes until piping hot.

Drain the noodles, rinse with fresh hot water and spoon into the base of 4 warmed bowls. Ladle the hot prawn broth over the top and serve immediately.

Preparation time:
10 minutes

Cooking time:
10 minutes

Serves: **2**

125 g (4 oz) firm tofu, diced
1 tablespoon sesame oil
75 g (3 oz) dried thin rice noodles
600 ml (1 pint) vegetable stock
2.5 cm (1 inch) piece of fresh root ginger, peeled and thickly sliced
1 large garlic clove, thickly sliced
3 kaffir lime leaves, torn into pieces
2 lemon grass stalks, halved
handful of spinach or pak choi
50 g (2 oz) bean sprouts
1–2 red chillies, to taste, deseeded and thinly sliced
2 tablespoons chopped fresh coriander
1 tablespoon Thai fish sauce

TO SERVE
lime wedges
chilli sauce

Put the tofu on a plate covered with kitchen paper and leave to stand for 5 minutes to drain.

Heat the oil in a wok or large frying pan, add the tofu and stir-fry for 2–3 minutes or until golden brown all over. Remove with a slotted spoon and drain on kitchen paper.

Meanwhile, soak the noodles in a saucepan of boiling water according to the packet instructions. Drain, rinse thoroughly under cold running water and drain again.

Put the stock in a large saucepan, add the ginger, garlic, lime leaves and lemon grass and bring to the boil. Reduce the heat, add the tofu, noodles, spinach or pak choi, bean sprouts and chillies and heat through for 2 minutes. Stir in the coriander and fish sauce, then pour into warmed deep bowls to serve. Serve with lime wedges and chilli sauce.

COOK'S NOTES If you are serving this soup to vegetarians, leave out the prawns and fish sauce.

19 Prawn and noodle soup

20 Hot and sour soup

Preparation time:
5 minutes

Cooking time:
15 minutes

Serves: **4**

900 ml (1½ pints) vegetable or chicken stock
2 kaffir lime leaves, torn into pieces
1 lemon grass stalk, lightly bruised
150 g (5 oz) dried egg noodles
50 g (2 oz) frozen peas
50 g (2 oz) frozen sweetcorn
100 g (3½ oz) large cooked peeled prawns
4 spring onions, sliced
2 teaspoons soy sauce

Pour the stock into a large saucepan and add the lime leaves and lemon grass. Bring to the boil, then reduce the heat and simmer for 10 minutes.

Add the noodles to the pan and cook according to the packet instructions, adding the remaining ingredients after 2 minutes of cooking. Serve in warmed bowls.

Preparation time:
10 minutes

Cooking time:
10 minutes

Serves: **4**

1 litre (1¾ pints) fish stock
4 kaffir lime leaves, torn into pieces
4 slices of peeled fresh root ginger
1 red chilli, deseeded and sliced
1 lemon grass stalk
125 g (4 oz) mushrooms, sliced
100 g (3½ oz) dried rice noodles
75 g (3 oz) baby spinach leaves
125 g (4 oz) cooked peeled tiger prawns
2 tablespoons lemon juice
pepper

Pour the stock into a large saucepan and add the lime leaves, ginger, chilli and lemon grass. Cover and bring to the boil. Add the mushrooms, reduce the heat and simmer for 2 minutes.

Break the noodles into short lengths, drop them into the soup and simmer for 3 minutes.

Add the spinach and prawns and simmer for 2 minutes until the prawns are heated through. Add the lemon juice. Remove and discard the lemon grass stalk and season the soup with pepper then serve in warmed bowls.

COOK'S NOTES The addition of kaffir lime leaves and lemon grass results in a fresh, zingy soup that is a meal in a bowl.

2 Snacks and Starters

21 Fennel and anchovy crostini

22 Tomato bruschetta

Preparation time:	**12 slices of baguette**
10 minutes	**1 fennel bulb, trimmed**
	1 small garlic clove, crushed
Cooking time:	**2 tablespoons chopped parsley**
8–10 minutes	**6 tablespoons extra virgin olive oil**
	2 tablespoons lemon juice
Serves: **4**	**24 bottled marinated anchovy fillets, drained**
Oven temperature:	**salt and pepper**
220°C (425°F) Gas Mark 7	

Arrange the bread slices on a baking sheet and cook in a preheated oven, 220°C (425°F), Gas Mark 7, for 8–10 minutes until crisp and golden, turning halfway through. Transfer to a serving platter.

Remove the tough outer layer of fennel and discard. Cut the bulb in half lengthways and then cut it crossways into wafer-thin slices (you will need about 100 g (3½ oz) of prepared fennel). Put in a bowl with the garlic and parsley. Add the oil, lemon juice and salt and pepper to taste and toss together until well coated.

Spoon the fennel mixture on to the crostini and top each with 2 anchovy fillets. Drizzle over any remaining dressing from the bowl.

Preparation time:	**12 cherry tomatoes**
10 minutes	**50 g (2 oz) mozzarella cheese**
	3 thick slices of ciabatta
Cooking time:	**olive oil, for brushing**
5 minutes	**a few basil leaves**
Serves: **1**	

Chop the tomatoes into small pieces and thinly slice the mozzarella.

Lightly toast the ciabatta on both sides under a preheated high grill. Brush with a little oil, then arrange the mozzarella and tomatoes on the toast. Tear the basil leaves into small pieces and scatter them over the bruschetta.

Cook the bruschetta under the grill until the cheese has melted slightly. Serve immediately.

COOK'S NOTES These bruschetta are an ideal starter as you can prepare the mozzarella and tomatoes in advance and the whole dish is ready in a matter of minutes.

23 Mediterranean bruschetta

Preparation time:
10 minutes

Cooking time:
10 minutes

Serves: **4**

1 yellow pepper, cored, deseeded and cut lengthways into 8 strips
1 red pepper, cored, deseeded and cut lengthways into 8 strips
2 courgettes, diagonally sliced
1 red onion, sliced and separated into rings
4 tablespoons olive oil
2 garlic cloves, peeled but left whole
1 ciabatta loaf or baguette
1 small tomato, halved
salt and pepper
8–12 basil leaves, to garnish

Arrange the peppers, courgettes and onion in a single layer on a grill rack. Brush with a little of the oil and rub with the garlic. Put under a preheated grill on its highest setting and cook the vegetables on one side only for 5 minutes or until lightly browned but still firm. Set aside and keep warm.

Cut the bread diagonally into medium-thick slices and toast on both sides under the grill. Rub the top of each slice with the garlic and tomato, then pile the grilled vegetables on top.

Drizzle the remaining oil over the vegetables and season well with salt and pepper. Garnish with basil leaves and serve immediately.

24 Butterbean, anchovy and coriander pâté

Preparation time:
10 minutes

Cooing time:
No cooking

Serves: **2–3**

400 g (13 oz) can butter beans, drained and rinsed
50 g (2 oz) drained anchovy fillets in oil
2 spring onions, finely chopped
2 tablespoons lemon juice
1 tablespoon olive oil
4 tablespoons chopped fresh coriander
salt and pepper

TO SERVE
lemon wedges
toasted rye bread

Put all the ingredients, except the coriander, in a blender or food processor and blend until well mixed but not smooth. Alternatively, mash the beans with a fork, finely chop the anchovies and mix the ingredients together by hand.

Stir in the coriander and season well with salt and pepper. Transfer to a serving dish. Serve with lemon wedges and toasted rye bread.

COOK'S NOTES You can use other canned beans in place of the butter beans, such as cannellini or red kidney beans.

25 Warm turkey focaccia

26 Oven-roasted mushrooms on toast

Preparation time:
10 minutes

Cooking time:
10 minutes

Serves: **4**

1 tablespoon olive oil
250 g (8 oz) boneless, skinless turkey breast, cut into thin strips
1 onion, thinly sliced
2 focaccia loaves, thickly sliced
2 tablespoons black olive tapenade
100 g (3½ oz) sun-dried tomatoes in oil, drained (oil reserved) and sliced
4 tomatoes, roughly chopped
handful of basil leaves (optional)
salt and pepper
rocket leaves, to serve

Preparation time:
10 minutes

Cooking time:
20 minutes

Serves: **4**

Oven temperature:
220°C (425°F) Gas Mark 7

8 large flat mushrooms, trimmed
2 garlic cloves, crushed
125 ml (4 fl oz) extra virgin olive oil
2 teaspoons chopped thyme
finely grated rind and juice of 1 lemon
2 tablespoons chopped parsley
salt and pepper

TO SERVE
4 slices of buttered toast
rocket leaves
fresh Parmesan cheese shavings

Heat the oil in a large frying pan, add the turkey and onion and cook for 5 minutes until the turkey is lightly browned all over and cooked through.

Meanwhile, lightly toast the focaccia slices on both sides. Spread thinly with the olive tapenade and drizzle with a little of the reserved oil from the sun-dried tomatoes.

Add the fresh and sun-dried tomatoes to the turkey with the basil, if using, and season to taste with salt and pepper. Cook for 3 minutes or until heated through, then spoon on to the toasted focaccia and top with rocket leaves. Serve immediately.

Put the mushrooms, stalk sides up, in a large roasting tin and season to taste with salt and pepper. Put the garlic, oil and thyme in a small bowl. Add the lemon rind, reserving a little for garnishing, then mix together. Spoon half the oil mixture over the mushrooms.

Roast the mushrooms in a preheated oven, 220°C (425°F), Gas Mark 7, for 20 minutes or until tender. Sprinkle with the parsley and drizzle over the lemon juice.

Arrange the mushrooms on the buttered toast, drizzle over the remaining oil mixture and serve topped with rocket leaves and Parmesan shavings and garnish with the reserved lemon rind.

COOK'S NOTES The olive tapenade, made from crushed black olives, gives an instant boost to the flavour of these open sandwiches.

COOK'S NOTES Use mushrooms that are of an equal size so that they cook evenly.

27 Smoky hummus with warm flatbread

28 Broad bean, pear and pecorino crostini

Preparation time:
10 minutes

Cooking time:
20 minutes

Serves: **4**

Oven temperature:
160°C (325°F) Gas Mark 3

400 g (13 oz) can chickpeas, drained and rinsed
3 tablespoons lemon juice
1 large garlic clove, crushed
2 tablespoons tahini paste
1 teaspoon hot smoked paprika, plus extra for sprinkling
½ teaspoon ground cumin
150 ml (¼ pint) extra virgin olive oil, plus extra for drizzling
2 tablespoons sesame seeds
salt and pepper

TO SERVE
4 sheets of Lebanese or Turkish flatbread
crunchy raw vegetables (optional)

Put all the ingredients, except the oil and sesame seeds, in a blender or food processor and blend until smooth. With the machine running, very slowly drizzle in the oil until it is completely incorporated. Season to taste with salt and pepper and scrape into a serving dish.

Wrap the flatbread in foil and heat in a preheated oven, 160°C (325°F), Gas Mark 3, for 20 minutes until warmed through.

Meanwhile, heat a nonstick frying pan, add the sesame seeds and cook, stirring constantly, for 2–3 minutes until lightly browned. Stir most of the toasted sesame seeds into the hummus and sprinkle the remainder over the top. Drizzle the hummus with oil, sprinkle with paprika and serve with the flatbread and raw vegetables, if you like.

Preparation time:
10 minutes

Cooking time:
15 minutes

Serves: **6**

Oven temperature:
190°C (375°F) Gas Mark 5

1 thin French baguette
extra virgin olive oil, for brushing and mixing
250 g (8 oz) fresh broad beans, shelled
1 small ripe pear, peeled, cored and finely chopped
drop of balsamic or sherry vinegar
125 g (4 oz) pecorino, salted ricotta or feta cheese, cut into small cubes
salt and pepper

Slice the bread into thin rounds, brush them with olive oil and arrange on a baking sheet. Bake in a preheated oven, 190°C (375°F), Gas Mark 5, for about 10 minutes or until golden and crisp.

Meanwhile, blanch the beans for 3 minutes in a saucepan of boiling water. Drain and refresh in cold water. Pop the beans out of their skins. Mash them roughly using a fork, moisten with a little olive oil and season well with salt and pepper.

Mix the chopped pear with a drop of balsamic or sherry vinegar. Stir in the cubes of cheese. Spread each crostini with a mound of bean purée and top with a spoonful of the pear and cheese mixture. Serve immediately.

COOK'S NOTES If you can't get hold of Lebanese or Turkish flatbread, pitta breads or even soft flour tortillas would make a good substitute.

29 Haloumi with lemon and paprika

30 Thai fishcakes with sweet chilli sauce

Preparation time:
5 minutes

Cooking time:
5 minutes

Serves: **4**

6 tablespoons extra virgin olive oil
4 tablespoons lemon juice
½ teaspoon smoked paprika
250 g (8 oz) haloumi cheese, cut into chunks
salt and pepper

Mix the oil, lemon juice and paprika together in a small bowl and season to taste with salt and pepper.

Heat a heavy-based frying pan until hot, add the haloumi and toss over a medium heat until golden.

Immediately transfer to a serving plate, drizzle over the oil mixture and serve with cocktail sticks to spike the haloumi chunks.

Preparation time:
15 minutes

Cooking time:
15 minutes

Serves: **4**

250 g (8 oz) raw tiger prawns, peeled and deveined
250 g (8 oz) firm white fish, such as haddock, cod or ling, diced
4 kaffir lime leaves, very finely chopped
4 spring onions, finely chopped
2 tablespoons chopped fresh coriander
1 small egg, beaten
2 tablespoons Thai fish sauce
65 g (2½ oz) rice flour
sunflower oil, for shallow-frying
lime wedges, to garnish
sweet chilli sauce, to serve

Put all the ingredients, except the oil, in a food processor and pulse briefly until blended. Use wet hands to shape the mixture into 12 flat cakes about 5 cm (2 inches) across.

Heat 1 cm (½ inch) oil in a frying pan, add the fishcakes, in batches, and cook for 2 minutes on each side until golden. Remove with a slotted spoon and drain on kitchen paper. Keep the cooked fishcakes warm in a low oven while cooking the remainder.

Garnish with lime wedges and serve with sweet chilli sauce for dipping.

COOK'S NOTES Haloumi is a semi-hard ewes' milk cheese from Cyprus with a wonderfully salty, sharp flavour, which really comes into its own with this quick and easy treatment – the outside becomes deliciously crisp and the inside meltingly soft.

Preparation time:
20 minutes

Cooking time:
about 10 minutes

Serves: 4

DIPPING SAUCE
2.5 cm (1 inch) piece of fresh root ginger, peeled and grated
½ red chilli, deseeded and finely chopped
4 tablespoons soy sauce
2 tablespoons dry sherry
4 tablespoons vegetable stock
1 garlic clove, finely chopped

VEGETABLES
500 g (1 lb) broccoli florets, sliced
150 g (5 oz) cup mushrooms, thinly sliced
150 g (5 oz) baby sweetcorn
150 g (5 oz) mangetout
75 g (3 oz) baby red Swiss chard leaves

TEMPURA BATTER
1 egg
100 ml (3½ fl oz) iced water
50 g (2 oz) plain flour
40 g (1½ oz) cornflour
½ teaspoon baking powder
¼ teaspoon salt
sunflower oil, for deep-frying

Mix all the dipping sauce ingredients together in a small bowl and divide among 4 small dishes. Arrange the vegetables in individual groups. To make the batter, mix the egg and water together in a bowl. Gradually whisk in the dry ingredients until smooth.

Half-fill a large saucepan with oil and heat to 180–190°C (350–375°F), or until a cube of bread browns in 30 seconds. Drop a small handful of the vegetables into the batter. Lift them out one at a time, draining the excess, add to the oil, in small batches, and cook for 2–3 minutes until crisp. Remove with a slotted spoon and drain on kitchen paper. Keep warm in a low oven while cooking the remainder. Divide the vegetables among serving plates and add the bowls of dipping sauce.

Preparation time:
10 minutes

Cooking time:
4–5 minutes

Serves: 4

500 g (1 lb) skinless haddock fillets, chopped
1 tablespoon chopped mint
2 tablespoons chopped fresh coriander
2 teaspoons red Thai curry paste
2 kaffir lime leaves, finely chopped, or finely grated rind of 1 lime
2 lemon grass stalks, quartered lengthways
olive oil, for brushing

TO SERVE
sweet chilli sauce
lime wedges

Put the fish, mint, coriander, curry paste and lime leaves or rind in a food processor and process for 30 seconds until well combined.

Divide the mixture into 8 portions, then mould each portion around a lemon grass stalk 'skewer', forming it into a sausage shape.

Brush with a little oil, then cook under a preheated high grill, turning occasionally, for 4–5 minutes until cooked through. Serve with a little sweet chilli sauce and lime wedges.

COOK'S NOTES If you have time, soak the lemon grass stalks in cold water for 30 minutes to prevent them from burning under the grill.

33 Thai chicken shells with coconut rice

34 Melon trio with green tea

Preparation time:
10 minutes

Cooking time:
15 minutes

Serves: **4**

1 teaspoon vegetable oil
2 chicken breasts, about 150 g (5 oz) each, sliced
1 tablespoon red or green Thai curry paste
400 ml (14 fl oz) can coconut milk

RICE
250 g (8 oz) basmati rice
100 ml (3½ fl oz) water
3 tablespoons chopped fresh coriander

TO SERVE
3 spring onions, sliced
4 Little Gem lettuces, separated into individual leaves
2 limes, cut into wedges

Heat the oil in a nonstick frying pan, add the chicken and cook for 2 minutes.

Add the curry paste and stir-fry for 1 minute. Add half the coconut milk and bring to the boil, then reduce the heat and simmer gently for 10 minutes.

Meanwhile, put the rice in a saucepan with the remaining coconut milk and measured water. Bring to the boil, then reduce the heat, cover and simmer for 10–12 minutes until all the liquid has been absorbed, adding a little extra water if necessary. Stir through the coriander.

To serve, spoon a little of the chicken mixture, spring onion and rice on to the individual lettuce leaves. Serve with the lime wedges.

Preparation time:
15 minutes, plus cooling/chilling

Cooking time:
No cooking

Serves: **6**

2 orange-flavoured green teabags
300 ml (½ pint) boiling water
1 orange-fleshed cantaloupe melon, such as charentais
½ green-fleshed melon, such as galia or ogen
½ honeydew melon
2 tablespoons light cane sugar
finely grated rind and juice of 1 lime

TO GARNISH
lime wedges
6 fresh lychees

Put the teabags in a heatproof jug and pour over the measured boiling water. Leave to infuse for 2 minutes. Lift out the bags, draining well. Break open one of the bags, remove a few tea leaves and add to the tea infusion. Leave to cool for 15 minutes.

Meanwhile, halve the whole melon, scoop out the seeds and discard. Deseed the other melons. Cut away the skin with a small knife. Cut the orange- and green-fleshed melons into long, thin slices and dice the honeydew melon. Put all the melon into a large, shallow dish, cover and chill in the freezer while the tea is cooling.

Sprinkle the sugar and lime rind and juice over the melon and pour over the tea. Arrange the long melon slices in fan shapes on individual serving plates. Spoon the diced melon alongside and serve each one with lime wedges and a partially peeled lychee.

COOK'S NOTES These impressive chicken shells would also be great for buffets or drinks parties, as they can be eaten by hand.

COOK'S NOTES Don't be tempted to leave the tea to infuse for longer than 2 minutes, or it will taste bitter.

35 Figs with ricotta and Parma ham

Preparation time:
10 minutes

Cooking time:
No cooking

Serves: **4**

8 ripe figs
1 teaspoon Dijon mustard
125 g (4 oz) ricotta cheese
85 g (3¼ oz) Parma ham
2 tablespoons balsamic vinegar
salt and pepper

Cut a cross down through each fig, but not completely through the base. Open out slightly.

Stir the mustard into the ricotta in a bowl and season to taste with salt and pepper.

Divide the ricotta mixture among the figs, spooning it over the top. Put 2 figs on each serving plate and top with an equal quantity of the Parma ham. Serve drizzled with the vinegar.

36 Smoked salmon Thai rolls

Preparation time:
15 minutes

Cooking time:
No cooking

Makes: **12**

12 slices of smoked salmon
1 cucumber, peeled, deseeded and cut into matchsticks
1 long red chilli, deseeded and thinly sliced
handful each of fresh coriander, mint and Thai basil leaves

DRESSING
2 tablespoons sweet chilli sauce
2 tablespoons clear honey
2 tablespoons lime juice
1 tablespoon Thai fish sauce

Separate the smoked salmon slices and lay out flat on a work surface. Divide the cucumber, chilli and herbs among the smoked salmon slices, arranging them in a mound on each slice.

Mix all the dressing ingredients together in a small bowl and drizzle over the filling. Roll up the salmon slices to enclose the filling and serve on a large platter.

COOK'S NOTES Thai basil, which has purplish stems, has a slight aniseed flavour.

37 Red pepper, olive and feta rolls

Preparation time:
10 minutes, plus standing

Cooking time:
7–8 minutes

Serves: **4**

**2 red peppers, cored, deseeded and
    quartered lengthways**
**100 g (3½ oz) feta cheese, thinly sliced or
    crumbled**
16 basil leaves
16 pitted black olives, halved
15 g (½ oz) pine nuts, toasted
1 tablespoon pesto
1 tablespoon French dressing

TO SERVE
rocket leaves
crusty bread

Put the red pepper quarters, skin side up, on a baking sheet and
cook under a preheated high grill for 7–8 minutes until the skins are
blackened.

Transfer the pepper quarters to a polythene bag. Fold over the top to
seal and leave for 10 minutes, then peel away the skins.

Lay the skinned pepper quarters on a board and layer some feta, basil,
olives and pine nuts on each one. Carefully roll up each pepper quarter
and secure with a cocktail stick. Put 2 pepper rolls on each serving plate.

Whisk the pesto and French dressing together in a small bowl and
drizzle over the pepper rolls. Serve with rocket leaves and some crusty
bread to mop up the juices.

38 Prawn, mango and avocado wrap

Preparation time:
10 minutes

Cooking time:
No cooking

Serves: **4**

2 tablespoons crème fraîche
2 teaspoons tomato ketchup
a few drops of Tabasco sauce, to taste
300 g (10 oz) cooked peeled prawns
1 mango, peeled, stoned and thinly sliced
1 avocado, peeled, stoned and sliced
100 g (3½ oz) watercress
4 soft flour tortillas

Mix together the crème fraîche, ketchup and Tabasco in a bowl.
Add the prawns, mango and avocado and toss gently to mix.

Divide the prawn mixture and the watercress among the tortillas,
roll up and serve immediately.

COOK'S NOTES Although this quick and easy starter is simple to
prepare, it looks and tastes delicious. Serve the wraps in small bowls or
cups for a variation.

39 Asparagus with lemon and anchovy butter

40 Sesame steamed prawns

Preparation time:
10 minutes, plus chilling

Cooking time:
5 minutes

Serves: 4

50 g (2 oz) drained anchovy fillets in oil
150 g (5 oz) butter, softened
a pinch of chilli powder
juice of 1 lemon, or to taste
1 kg (2 lb) asparagus spears, trimmed
pepper

Put the anchovies, butter, chilli powder and pepper to taste in a blender or food processor and blend until smooth. Add lemon juice to taste. Roll the butter into a log, wrap in foil and chill in the freezer for 15 minutes.

Steam the asparagus in a steamer for 4–5 minutes or until just tender. Meanwhile, remove the butter from the freezer, unwrap it and cut into 1 cm (½ inch) slices.

Serve the asparagus immediately, topped with the slices of butter.

Preparation time:
15 minutes

Cooking time:
5 minutes

Serves: 4

16 raw tiger prawns, peeled and
    deveined but tails left intact
2 garlic cloves, sliced
1 red chilli, deseeded and chopped
finely grated rind and juice of 1 lime
2.5 cm (1 inch) piece of fresh root ginger,
    peeled and chopped
2 tablespoons rice wine
2 tablespoons Thai fish sauce
4 Savoy cabbage leaves
1 tablespoon sesame oil
salt
a few fresh coriander, mint and basil
    leaves, to garnish

To butterfly the prawns, cut down the deveining slit on the back of each prawn so that it opens up and lies flat, leaving the tail intact. Rinse and pat dry with kitchen paper.

Mix together the garlic, chilli, lime rind and juice, ginger, rice wine and fish sauce in a bowl. Add the prawns and toss well.

Blanch the cabbage leaves in a saucepan of lightly salted boiling water for 30 seconds. Drain, refresh under cold running water, drain again and pat dry with kitchen paper.

Arrange the cabbage leaves in a bamboo steamer and carefully spoon the prawns and marinade on top of the leaves. Cover and steam for 2–3 minutes until the prawns have turned pink.

Meanwhile, heat the oil in a small saucepan. Arrange the cabbage leaves and prawns in a serving dish. Pour the hot oil over them, garnish with the herbs and serve immediately.

COOK'S NOTES You could use 1 tablespoon dried shrimp or
2 tablespoons Thai fish sauce instead of the anchovies if you prefer.

41 Chicken satay

42 Aromatic chicken pancakes

Preparation time:
15 minutes

Cooking time:
about 15 minutes

Serves: **4**

**500 g (1 lb) boneless, skinless chicken
   breasts, cut into 2.5 cm (1 inch) pieces**

MARINADE
**1 tablespoon ground cinnamon
1 tablespoon ground cumin
1 teaspoon pepper
150 ml (¼ pint) groundnut oil
100 ml (3½ fl oz) soy sauce
2 tablespoons light muscovado sugar**

SATAY SAUCE
**1 heaped teaspoon red Thai curry paste
1 tablespoon groundnut oil
250 ml (8 fl oz) coconut milk
50 g (2 oz) light muscovado sugar
2 tablespoons Thai fish sauce
juice of 1 lime
65 g (2½ oz) crushed unsalted roasted
   peanuts
1 teaspoon crushed dried red chillies**

TO GARNISH
**roughly chopped onion
cucumber chunks**

Preparation time:
15 minutes

Cooking time:
7 minutes

Serves: **4**

**4 boneless, skinless chicken breasts,
   about 150 g (5 oz) each
6 tablespoons hoisin sauce**

TO SERVE
**12 Chinese pancakes
½ cucumber, cut into matchsticks
12 spring onions, thinly sliced
handful of fresh coriander
4 tablespoons hoisin sauce mixed with
   3 tablespoons water**

Lay the chicken breasts between 2 sheets of clingfilm or nonstick
baking paper and flatten with a rolling pin or meat mallet until they
are 2.5 cm (1 inch) thick. Transfer to a baking sheet and brush with
some of the hoisin sauce.

Cook the chicken breasts under a preheated high grill for 4 minutes. Turn
them over, brush with the remaining hoisin sauce and cook for a further
3 minutes or until the chicken is cooked through. Meanwhile, warm the
pancakes in a bamboo steamer for 3 minutes or until heated through.

Thinly slice the chicken and arrange it on a serving plate. Serve with
the pancakes, accompanied by the cucumber, spring onions, coriander
and diluted hoisin sauce in separate bowls, for everyone to assemble
their own pancakes.

Mix all the marinade ingredients together in a bowl. Add the chicken
and turn to coat. Cover and leave to marinate in a cool place while you
make the sauce.

Put the curry paste in a pan with the oil and stir over a low heat for
1 minute. Add the remaining sauce ingredients and cook over a medium
heat until thickened. Turn into a serving bowl and leave to cool.

Thread the chicken on to skewers. Cook under a preheated high grill, in
batches, for 2 minutes or until cooked through, turning once. Keep the
cooked chicken warm in a low oven while you cook the remainder.
Garnish with chopped onion and cucumber and serve with the sauce.

COOK'S NOTES Often served as part of a Chinese meal, this is a
time-saving starter as you don't need to put the pancakes together.

43 Haloumi with sun-dried tomatoes

44 Spiced pumpkin with coconut pesto

Preparation time:
10 minutes

Cooking time:
8–10 minutes

Serves: **4**

200 g (7 oz) haloumi cheese, sliced
2 teaspoons onion seeds
1 tablespoon finely chopped fresh
  coriander leaves
a few saffron threads

TO SERVE
20 g (¾ oz) sun-dried tomatoes in oil,
  drained and sliced
½ orange, peeled and pith removed,
  separated into segments
2 tablespoons lemon juice
rocket leaves, to garnish

Lay the cheese slices on a foil-lined grill pan and sprinkle over the onion seeds, coriander leaves and saffron threads.

Cook the cheese under a preheated medium grill for 4–5 minutes on each side until soft and slightly browned.

Serve the cheese immediately on a bed of the sun-dried tomato slices and orange segments. Drizzle the lemon juice over the cheese just before serving and garnish with a few rocket leaves.

Preparation time:
10 minutes

Cooking time:
15–20 minutes

Serves: **4**

1 teaspoon cumin seeds
1 teaspoon coriander seeds
2 green cardamom pods
1 kg (2 lb) pumpkin, cut into 1 cm (½ inch)
  thick wedges
3 tablespoons sunflower oil
1 teaspoon caster sugar

COCONUT PESTO
25 g (1 oz) fresh coriander leaves
1 garlic clove, crushed
1 green chilli, deseeded and chopped
pinch of sugar
1 tablespoon shelled pistachio nuts,
  roughly chopped
6 tablespoons coconut cream
1 tablespoon lime juice
salt and pepper

Heat a nonstick frying pan until hot, add the whole spices and cook over a medium heat, stirring constantly, until lightly browned. Grind to a powder in a spice grinder or in a mortar with a pestle.

Put the pumpkin wedges in a dish. Toss well with the oil, sugar and spice mix to coat evenly. Cook the wedges on a preheated barbecue or under a high grill for 6–8 minutes on each side until charred and tender.

Meanwhile, to make the pesto, put the coriander, garlic, chilli, sugar, pistachio nuts and salt and pepper to taste in a food processor and process until fairly smooth. Add the coconut cream and lime juice and process again. Transfer to a bowl and serve with the pumpkin.

COOK'S NOTES Haloumi makes a good substitute for meat as it has a wonderful coarse texture when grilled. Serve this starter if you have a mixture of vegetarian and meat-eating guests.

45 Tortillas with aubergine and yogurt

46 Provolone cheese and steak panini

Preparation time:
10 minutes

Cooking time:
10 minutes

Serves: **2**

4 tablespoons olive oil
1 aubergine, thinly sliced
small handful of mint, chopped
small handful of parsley, chopped
2 tablespoons chopped chives
1 green chilli, deseeded and thinly sliced
200 ml (7 fl oz) Greek yogurt
2 tablespoons mayonnaise
2 large soft flour tortillas
7 cm (3 inch) length of cucumber, thinly sliced
salt and pepper
paprika, to garnish

Heat the oil in a frying pan, add the aubergine and cook for 10 minutes or until golden. Remove with a slotted spoon, drain on kitchen paper and leave to cool slightly.

Meanwhile, mix the herbs with the chilli, yogurt and mayonnaise in a bowl and season to taste with salt and pepper.

Arrange the warm aubergine slices over the tortillas and spread with the yogurt mixture. Arrange the cucumber slices on top. Roll up each tortilla, sprinkle with paprika to garnish and serve.

Preparation time:
15 minutes

Cooking time:
about 15 minutes

Serves: **2**

4 tablespoons olive oil
½ red pepper, cored, deseeded and thinly sliced
½ green pepper, cored deseeded and thinly sliced
1 small onion, halved and thinly sliced
300 g (10 oz) rib-eye steak, thinly sliced
75 g (3 oz) mushrooms, trimmed and sliced
1 garlic clove, chopped
75 g (3 oz) provolone cheese, thinly sliced
2 tablespoons Worcestershire or steak sauce
4 long slices of French country bread
1 dill pickle, thinly sliced (optional)
salt and pepper
cherry tomatoes, to serve

Heat the oil in a frying pan, add the peppers and onion and cook for 3–4 minutes. Add the steak and cook for 2–3 minutes, then add the mushrooms and garlic and cook for 3–4 minutes.

Reduce the heat to low, season well with salt and pepper and then use 2 wooden spatulas to form the steak mixture into 2 piles, about the size of the bread slices. Lay half the cheese slices on top of each pile and leave to melt for 2 minutes.

Spread a little of the sauce over 2 slices of bread and then very carefully lift the cheese-steak mixture on to the bread, again using 2 spatulas. Splash over the remaining sauce and arrange the pickle slices on top, if using.

Top with the remaining bread slices and toast in a sandwich grill for 2–3 minutes, or according to the manufacturer's instructions, until the bread is crisp and the cheese is completely melted. Serve immediately with a bowl of cherry tomatoes.

COOK'S NOTES Prepare the yogurt mixture in advance and keep it in the refrigerator until you are ready to assemble the tortillas.

47 Ricotta and red onion tortillas

48 Roasted rosemary chicken sandwich

Preparation time:
10 minutes

Cooking time:
5 minutes

Serves: **1**

25 g (1 oz) ricotta cheese
½ red onion, thinly sliced
1 tomato, finely chopped
¼ green chilli, finely chopped
1 tablespoon chopped fresh coriander
2 small soft flour tortillas
olive oil, for brushing
green salad, to serve

Mix together the ricotta, onion, tomato, chilli and coriander in a bowl.

Heat a griddle pan until hot. Brush the tortillas with a little oil, add to the pan and cook very briefly on each side.

Spread half the ricotta mixture over one half of each tortilla and fold over the other half to cover. Serve immediately with a green salad.

Preparation time:
8 minutes

Cooking time:
22 minutes

Serves: **2**

Oven temperature:
180°C (350°F) Gas Mark 4

2 boneless, skinless chicken breasts, about 150 g (5 oz) each
2 teaspoons black olive tapenade
4 sun-dried tomatoes in oil, drained
1 garlic clove, cut into slivers
3–4 rosemary sprigs
2 tablespoons olive oil
2 large wholegrain rolls, halved horizontally
50 g (2 oz pecorino) cheese, freshly shaved
salt and pepper
rocket leaves, to garnish

Using a sharp knife, make a horizontal slit in each chicken breast. Do not cut all the way through but just deep enough to create a pocket in the flesh. Divide the tapenade, sun-dried tomatoes and garlic slivers between the pockets and close up.

Lay the chicken breasts on top of the rosemary sprigs in a roasting tin and drizzle with the oil. Season with a little salt and pepper and cook in a preheated oven, 180°C (350°F), Gas Mark 4, for 18 minutes or until the chicken is cooked through.

When the chicken is cool enough to handle, cut it into slices. Arrange the chicken on the wholegrain roll bases, sprinkle with the pecorino shavings and top with the lids. Toast in a sandwich grill for 3–4 minutes, or according to the manufacturer's instructions, until the bread is golden and the chicken is hot. Serve immediately, garnished with rocket leaves.

COOK'S NOTES The ideal snack or lunch dish that is as quick to prepare as a sandwich. If you don't have a griddle pan wrap the tortillas in foil and heat them through in the oven.

49 Goats' cheese and herb soufflés

50 Caesar salad

Preparation time: **10 minutes**	**25 g (1 oz) margarine** **50 g (2 oz) plain flour** **300 ml (½ pint) semi-skimmed milk**
Cooking time: **15 minutes**	**4 eggs, separated** **100 g (3½ oz) goats' cheese, crumbled** **1 tablespoon chopped mixed herbs, such** **as parsley, chives and thyme**
Serves: **4**	**vegetable oil, for oiling** **1 tablespoon freshly grated Parmesan**
Oven temperature: **190°C (375°F) Gas Mark 5**	**cheese** **salt and pepper**

TO SERVE
75 g (3 oz) rocket leaves
2 tablespoons French dressing

Preparation time: **20 minutes**	**1 garlic clove, crushed** **4 anchovy fillets in oil, drained and** **chopped**
Cooking time: **5 minutes**	**3 tablespoons lemon juice** **2 teaspoons English mustard powder** **1 egg yolk**
Serves: **4**	**200 ml (7 fl oz) extra virgin olive oil** **3–4 tablespoons vegetable oil** **3 slices of country bread, crusts** **removed, cut into 1 cm (½ inch) dice** **1 cos lettuce, torn into pieces** **3 tablespoons freshly grated Parmesan** **cheese** **pepper**

Melt the margarine in a medium saucepan, add the flour and cook, stirring constantly, for 1 minute. Gradually add the milk, whisking constantly, and cook for 2 minutes until thickened.

Remove the pan from the heat. Beat in the egg yolks, one at a time, then stir in the goats' cheese. Season well with salt and pepper.

Whisk the eggs whites in a large bowl until stiff peaks form, then gradually fold them into the cheese mixture with the herbs. Transfer the soufflé mixture to 4 lightly oiled ramekins, sprinkle over the Parmesan and bake in a preheated oven, 190°C (375°F), Gas Mark 5, for 10–12 minutes until risen and golden.

Meanwhile, toss the rocket leaves and dressing together in a bowl. Serve with the soufflés hot from the oven.

Put the garlic, anchovies, lemon juice, mustard and egg yolk in a small bowl and season to taste with pepper. Using a hand-held blender or small electric whisk, blend or beat until well combined. Slowly drizzle in the olive oil, mixing constantly, to form a thick, creamy sauce. If the sauce becomes too thick, add a little water.

Heat the vegetable oil in a heavy-based frying pan, add the bread cubes and cook, turning and stirring frequently, for 5 minutes or until they are golden and crisp all over. Remove them with a slotted spoon and drain on kitchen paper.

Put the lettuce in a large bowl, add the dressing and 2 tablespoons of the Parmesan and mix well.

Serve the salad in a large bowl or on individual plates, sprinkled with the croûtons and the remaining Parmesan.

COOK'S NOTES For a more substantial meal you could add some chicken to the salad. Grill or bake 2 chicken breasts, cut them into long strips and arrange over the other ingredients before serving.

51 Peppered beef with green salad

52 Griddled aubergines with chilli toasts

Preparation time:
20 minutes

Cooking time:
4–7 minutes

Serves: **6**

2 thick-cut sirloin steaks, about 500 g (1 lb) in total
3 teaspoons mixed peppercorns, coarsely crushed
2 teaspoons coarse salt flakes
200 ml (7 fl oz) natural yogurt
1–1½ teaspoons horseradish sauce, to taste
1 garlic clove, crushed
150 g (5 oz) mixed green salad leaves
100 g (3½ oz) button mushrooms, sliced
1 red onion, thinly sliced
1 tablespoon olive oil
salt and pepper

Trim any fat from the steak and rub the meat with the crushed peppercorns and salt flakes.

Mix together the yogurt, horseradish sauce and garlic in a large bowl and season to taste with salt and pepper. Add the salad leaves, mushrooms and most of the onion and toss gently.

Heat the oil in a frying pan, add the steaks and cook over a high heat for 2 minutes until browned. Turn them over and cook for 2 minutes for medium rare, 3–4 minutes for medium or 5 minutes for well done.

Spoon an equal quantity of the salad leaves into the centre of 6 serving plates. Thinly slice the steaks and arrange the slices on top of the leaves, then garnish with the remaining onion.

Preparation time:
15 minutes

Cooking time:
10 minutes

Serves: **4**

Oven temperature:
220°C (425°F) Gas Mark 7

2 aubergines, about 550 g (1lb 2 oz) in total
2 teaspoons olive oil
50 g (2 oz) sun-blush tomatoes
2 garlic cloves, crushed
4 tablespoons lemon juice
pepper
4 basil leaves, to garnish

CHILLI TOASTS
4 slices of multigrain bread
1 tablespoon chilli oil

To make the chilli toasts, cut the crusts from the bread slices and cut each slice into 2 neat triangles. Brush each side with the chilli oil and arrange on a baking sheet. Bake the chilli toasts in a preheated oven, 220°C (425°F), Gas Mark 7, for 8–10 minutes until crisp and golden.

Meanwhile, cut the aubergines lengthways into 5 mm (¼ inch) slices and season to taste with pepper. Brush a ridged griddle pan with the olive oil and heat until hot. Add the aubergine slices and tomatoes with the garlic and cook for 4 minutes or until starting to soften. Turn the aubergines over and cook for a further 4 minutes. Sprinkle over the lemon juice.

Serve the chilli toasts with the aubergines and tomatoes piled high in the centre of individual serving plates, garnished with basil leaves and pepper.

COOK'S NOTES The quantities given here would also make a main course for two.

53 Parmesan polenta with salsa

54 Tomato and green bean salad

Preparation time:
10 minutes, plus standing

Cooking time:
about 15 minutes

Serves: **4**

75 g (3 oz) quick-cooking polenta
500 ml (17 fl oz) simmering water
75 g (3 oz) butter, plus extra for greasing
40 g (1½ oz) Parmesan cheese, freshly grated
6 tablespoons chopped mixed herbs, such as chervil, chives and parsley
salt and pepper

SALSA
300 g (10 oz) cherry tomatoes, quartered
2 red chillies, deseeded and finely chopped
1 small red onion, finely chopped
2 tablespoons chilli oil
2 tablespoons olive oil
2 tablespoons lime juice
2 tablespoons shredded mint

Preparation time:
10 minutes

Cooking time:
5 minutes

Serves: **4**

250 g (8 oz) mixed red and yellow baby tomatoes, plum if possible
250 g (8 oz) thin green beans, trimmed
handful of mint leaves, chopped
1 garlic clove, crushed and chopped
4 tablespoons extra virgin olive oil
1 tablespoon balsamic vinegar
salt and pepper

Cut the tomatoes in half and put them in a large bowl.

Blanch the beans in a large saucepan of boiling water for 2 minutes. Drain well and add to the tomatoes.

Add the mint, garlic, oil and vinegar. Season to taste with salt and pepper and mix well. Serve warm or cold.

Pour the polenta into a saucepan of the simmering measured water and beat well with a wooden spoon until thick and smooth. Reduce the heat and cook, stirring constantly, for 6–8 minutes, or according to the packet instructions.

Remove the pan from the heat and stir in the butter, Parmesan, herbs and salt and pepper to taste. Turn the polenta into a greased 25 cm (10 inch) pizza or cake tin at least 2.5 cm (1 inch) deep. Smooth the top and leave to stand for 5 minutes or until set.

Meanwhile, mix all the salsa ingredients together in a bowl. Season to taste with salt and pepper.

Carefully transfer the polenta to a chopping board and cut it into 8 wedges. Heat a griddle pan until hot, add the polenta wedges and cook for 2–3 minutes on each side until heated through and golden. Serve immediately with the salsa.

COOK'S NOTES This simple salad is very easy to prepare but the wonderful combination of flavours and colours makes it an attractive and delicious starter. If serving cold, it can be prepared a little in advance.

55 Griddled artichokes and fennel

Preparation time: **15 minutes**	**3 tablespoons olive oil** **3 teaspoons finely chopped rosemary leaves**
Cooking time: **7–8 minutes**	**200 g (7 oz) fennel, trimmed and cut into small wedges** **400 g (13 oz) can artichoke hearts, drained and halved**
Serves: **6**	**100 g (3½ oz) feta cheese, crumbled** **rosemary sprigs, to garnish**

DRESSING
finely grated rind and juice of 1 lemon
2 teaspoons capers, drained and rinsed
4 teaspoons balsamic vinegar
salt and pepper

Put the oil, chopped rosemary and a little salt and pepper into a polythene bag. Add the fennel and artichoke hearts and shake gently in the bag to coat.

Heat a ridged griddle pan until smoking. Add the dressed vegetables and cook for 3–4 minutes until the undersides are browned. Turn them over and cook for 2 minutes. Crumble the feta over the top, put the pan under a preheated high grill and cook for 2 minutes until the cheese is hot but not melted.

Meanwhile, mix all the dressing ingredients together with any remaining oil in the polythene bag.

Spoon the vegetables on to serving plates and drizzle the dressing over the top. Garnish with extra rosemary leaves torn from the sprigs.

56 Mixed leaf and pomegranate salad

Preparation time: **10 minutes**	**3 tablespoons raspberry vinegar** **2 tablespoons light olive oil** **1 pomegranate**
Cooking time: **No cooking**	**125 g (4 oz) mixed salad leaves, including baby spinach leaves, red mustard and mizuna**
Serves: **6**	**salt and pepper** **raspberries, to garnish (optional)**

Put the raspberry vinegar, oil and a little salt and pepper in a salad bowl and mix together lightly.

Cut the pomegranate in half, then cut it into large pieces and flex the skin so that the small red seeds fall out. Pick out any stubborn ones with a small knife and discard, then add the remainder to the salad bowl, discarding the skin and pith.

Tear any large salad leaves into bite-sized pieces and toss in the dressing. Sprinkle with raspberries, if you like, and serve immediately.

COOK'S NOTES To save time, squeeze the pomegranate on a lemon juicer to release the seeds.

3 Vegetables and Salads

57 Orange and avocado salad

58 Watermelon and feta salad

Preparation time:
15 minutes

Cooking time:
No cooking

Serves: **4**

4 large juicy oranges
2 small ripe avocados, peeled and stoned
2 teaspoons green cardamom pods
3 tablespoons light olive oil
1 tablespoon clear honey
pinch of ground allspice
2 teaspoons lemon juice
salt and pepper
watercress sprigs, to garnish

Remove the peel and pith from the oranges. Working over a bowl to catch the juice, cut between the membranes to remove the segments. Slice the avocados and toss gently with the orange segments. Pile on to serving plates.

Reserve a few whole cardamom pods for garnishing. Put the remainder in a bowl and crush with the end of a rolling pin or put in a mortar and crush with a pestle to extract the seeds. Pick out and discard the pods.

Mix the cardamom seeds with the oil, honey, allspice, lemon juice, salt and pepper to taste and the reserved orange juice.

Garnish the salads with the watercress sprigs and reserved cardamom pods, and serve with the dressing spooned over the top.

Preparation time:
10 minutes

Cooking time:
5 minutes

Serves: **4**

1 tablespoon black sesame seeds
500 g (1 lb) watermelon, peeled, deseeded and diced
175 g (6 oz) feta cheese, diced
75 g (3 oz) rocket leaves
handful of mint, parsley and fresh coriander sprigs
6 tablespoons extra virgin olive oil
1 tablespoon orange flower water
1½ tablespoons lemon juice
1 teaspoon pomegranate syrup (optional)
½ teaspoon sugar
salt and pepper
toasted pitta bread, to serve

Heat a nonstick frying pan, add the sesame seeds and cook, stirring constantly, for 2–3 minutes until lightly browned. Set aside.

Arrange the watermelon and feta on a large plate with the rocket leaves and herbs.

Whisk together the oil, orange flower water, lemon juice, pomegranate syrup, if using, and sugar in a small bowl and season to taste with salt and pepper. Drizzle the dressing over the salad, scatter over the toasted sesame seeds and serve with toasted pitta bread.

COOK'S NOTES The avocados need to be completely ripe for this recipe. If they are a little hard, put them in the airing cupboard for a couple of hours and they should soften.

COOK'S NOTES Orange flower water is used in a lot of Middle Eastern recipes, both sweet and savoury. You will find it in specialist grocers or larger supermarkets.

59 Papaya and lime salad

60 Asparagus salad

Preparation time:
15 minutes, plus cooling

Cooking time:
5 minutes

Serves: **4**

3 firm ripe papayas
finely grated rind and juice of 2 limes
2 teaspoons soft light brown sugar
50 g (2 oz) blanched almonds, toasted
lime wedges, to decorate

Cut the papayas in half lengthways, scoop out the seeds and discard. Peel the halves, roughly dice the flesh and put it in a bowl.

Finely grate the rind of both limes, then squeeze the juice from one of the limes and reserve. Remove the pith from the other lime. Working over the bowl of papaya to catch the juice, cut between the membranes to remove the segments. Add the lime segments and grated rind to the papaya.

Pour the reserved lime juice into a small saucepan, add the sugar and heat gently until the sugar has dissolved. Remove from the heat and leave to cool for 10 minutes.

Pour the sweetened lime juice over the fruit and toss thoroughly. Add the toasted almonds to the fruit salad, decorate with lime wedges and serve immediately.

Preparation time:
15 minutes

Cooking time:
5–10 minutes

Serves: **4**

3 tablespoons olive oil (optional)
500 g (1 lb) asparagus spears, trimmed
50 g (2 oz) rocket or other salad leaves
2 spring onions, thinly sliced
4 radishes, thinly sliced
salt and pepper
roughly chopped herbs, such as tarragon,
**   parsley, chervil and dill, to garnish**

DRESSING
finely grated rind of 1 lemon, plus extra
**   thin strips to garnish**
2 tablespoons tarragon vinegar
1 tablespoon chopped tarragon
¼ teaspoon Dijon mustard
pinch of sugar
5 tablespoons olive oil

To make the dressing, put all the ingredients in a screw-top jar and shake until well blended.

Heat the oil, if using, in a griddle pan. Arrange as many asparagus spears as will fit in a single layer over the base of the pan and cook, turning occasionally, for 5 minutes or until just tender and slightly charred. Transfer to a shallow dish, season to taste with salt and pepper and set aside while you cook the remainder. Pour over the dressing, toss gently to coat evenly and leave to stand for 5 minutes.

Arrange the rocket or other leaves on a platter, scatter the spring onions and radishes over the top and arrange the asparagus in a pile in the centre. Garnish with the chopped herbs and thin strips of lemon rind.

COOK'S NOTES Papaya and lime complement each other beautifully. This simple but utterly delicious fruit salad can be served for brunch or breakfast with muesli and yogurt, or on its own.

61 Spring vegetable salad with garlic bread

62 Smoked chicken and avocado salad

Preparation time:
10 minutes

Cooking time:
10 minutes

Serves: **4**

200 g (7 oz) fresh or frozen peas
200 g (7 oz) asparagus spears, trimmed
200 g (7 oz) sugar snap peas
2 courgettes, cut into long thin ribbons
with a vegetable peeler
1 fennel bulb, trimmed and very thinly
sliced
finely grated rind and juice of 1 lemon
1 teaspoon Dijon mustard
1 teaspoon clear honey
1 tablespoon chopped parsley
2 tablespoons olive oil

GARLIC BREAD
4 ciabatta rolls, halved horizontally
1 garlic clove, peeled but left whole

Blanch the peas, asparagus and sugar snap peas in a large saucepan of boiling water for 3 minutes. Drain, refresh under cold running water and drain again.

Transfer the vegetables to a large bowl with the courgette ribbons and fennel and mix together.

Whisk together the lemon rind and juice, mustard, honey, parsley and half the oil in a small bowl. Toss the dressing through the vegetables.

Rub the cut sides of the rolls with the garlic, drizzle over the remaining oil, then place the rolls on a baking sheet and toast on both sides under a preheated high grill. Serve with the vegetables.

Preparation time:
15 minutes

Cooking time:
5 minutes

Serves: **4**

5 tablespoons extra virgin olive oil
4 slices of day-old bread, crusts
removed, cut into 1 cm (½ inch) dice
500 g (1 lb) cold cooked smoked chicken
breast, sliced
3 Little Gem or baby cos lettuce hearts
1 large ripe avocado, peeled, stoned and
diced
25 g (1 oz) Parmesan cheese, freshly
grated

DRESSING
125 ml (4 fl oz) extra virgin olive oil
2 tablespoons tarragon vinegar
1 tablespoon wholegrain mustard
1 tablespoon chopped tarragon
1 teaspoon caster sugar
salt and pepper

To make the croûtons, heat the oil in a heavy-based frying pan, add the bread cubes and cook, turning and stirring frequently, for 5 minutes or until golden and crisp all over. Remove with a slotted spoon and drain on kitchen paper.

Cut the chicken breast slices into bite-sized pieces and put in a large bowl. Separate the lettuce leaves and add to the chicken with the avocado, croûtons and Parmesan.

Whisk together all the dressing ingredients in a small bowl and season to taste with salt and pepper. Pour the dressing over the salad and toss well to coat evenly. Serve immediately.

COOK'S NOTES Because smoked chicken is hot-smoked, it is already cooked and ready to eat. If you are especially short of time, you can buy ready-made croûtons, but it is easy to make your own.

63 Italian broccoli and egg salad

Preparation time:
10 minutes

Cooking time:
10 minutes

Serves: **4**

4 eggs
300 g (10 oz) broccoli
2 small leeks, about 300 g (10 oz)
4 tablespoons lemon juice
2 tablespoons olive oil
2 teaspoons clear honey
1 tablespoon capers, drained and rinsed
2 tablespoons chopped tarragon, plus
  extra sprigs to garnish (optional)
salt and pepper
wholemeal bread, to serve

Half-fill the base of a steamer with water, add the eggs and bring to the boil. Cover with the steamer top and simmer for 8 minutes until hard-boiled.

Meanwhile, cut the broccoli into florets and thickly slice the broccoli stems and the leeks. Add the broccoli to the top of the steamer and steam for 3 minutes. Add the leeks and steam for a further 2 minutes.

Mix together the oil, honey, capers and tarragon in a salad bowl to make the dressing.

Crack the hard-boiled eggs, cool quickly under cold running water, then shell and roughly chop the eggs.

Add the broccoli and leeks to the dressing, toss together and sprinkle with the chopped eggs. Garnish with tarragon sprigs, if you like, and serve warm with thickly sliced wholemeal bread.

64 Spinach, Gorgonzola and walnut salad

Preparation time:
10 minutes, plus cooling

Cooking time:
5 minutes

Serves: **4**

1 tablespoon clear honey
125 g (4 oz) walnut halves
250 g (8 oz) green beans, trimmed
200 g (7 oz) baby spinach leaves
150 g (5 oz) Gorgonzola, crumbled

DRESSING
4 tablespoons walnut oil
2 tablespoons extra virgin olive oil
1–2 tablespoons sherry vinegar
salt and pepper

Heat the honey in a small frying pan, add the walnuts and cook over a medium heat, stirring, for 2–3 minutes until the nuts are glazed. Tip on to a plate and leave to cool until required.

Meanwhile, blanch the beans in a saucepan of lightly salted boiling water for 3 minutes. Drain, refresh under cold running water, drain again and shake dry. Put in a large bowl with the spinach leaves.

Whisk together all the dressing ingredients in a small bowl and season to taste with salt and pepper. Pour over the salad and toss well to coat evenly. Arrange the salad in bowls, scatter over the Gorgonzola and honeyed walnuts and serve immediately.

COOK'S NOTES Gorgonzola has a strong, piquant taste and creamy texture. If you prefer a milder blue cheese flavour, use dolcelatte instead.

65 Chickpea and olive salad

66 Bulgar wheat salad

Preparation time:
10 minutes

Cooking time:
No cooking

Serves: **4**

**200 g (7 oz) can chickpeas, drained and
    rinsed**
50 g (2 oz) pitted black olives, halved
½ red onion, finely chopped
150 g (5 oz) cherry tomatoes, halved
**3 tablespoons chopped flat leaf parsley,
    plus extra to garnish**
50 g (2 oz) watercress, to serve

DRESSING
1 garlic clove, crushed
100 ml (3½ fl oz) Greek yogurt
juice of ½ lime
pepper

To make the dressing, mix together the garlic, yogurt and lime juice in
a small bowl. Season to taste with pepper.

Mix together the chickpeas, olives, onion, tomatoes and parsley in a
large bowl.

Add the dressing to the chickpea mixture and toss well to coat evenly.
Serve the salad on a bed of watercress, garnished with chopped parsley.

Preparation:
15 minutes, plus soaking

Cooking time:
about 10 minutes

Serves: **4**

150 g (5 oz) bulgar wheat
2 tablespoons olive oil
2 fennel bulbs, trimmed and thinly sliced
175 g (6 oz) baby spinach leaves
**3 oranges, peel and pith removed,
    separated into segments**
2 tablespoons pumpkin seeds, toasted

DRESSING
4 tablespoons natural yogurt
2 tablespoons chopped fresh coriander
½ small cucumber, finely chopped
salt (optional) and pepper

Put the bulgar wheat in a heatproof bowl, cover with plenty of boiling
water and leave to soak for 15 minutes.

Meanwhile, heat half the oil in a frying pan, add the fennel and cook
for 8–10 minutes until tender and browned. Add the spinach and cook,
stirring, until just wilted. Remove from the heat.

Drain the bulgar wheat thoroughly in a sieve, pressing out as much
moisture as possible with the back of a spoon. Add to the pan and toss
well to mix, then add the orange segments and pumpkin seeds.

Mix together all the dressing ingredients with the remaining oil in a
small bowl, stir through the salad and serve.

COOK'S NOTES This is a very simple salad that uses mainly storecupboard ingredients. You can substitute regular tomatoes for cherry and,
if you don't have watercress, other salad leaves, such as rocket, will
work equally well.

67 Spiced couscous salad

68 Tabbouleh with fruit and nuts

Preparation time:
10 minutes, plus standing

Cooking time:
3 minutes

Serves: **4**

200 ml (7 fl oz) vegetable stock
200 ml (7 fl oz) orange juice
1 teaspoon ground cinnamon
½ teaspoon ground coriander
250 g (8 oz) couscous
75 g (3 oz) raisins
2 tomatoes, chopped
¼ preserved lemon, chopped (optional)
½ bunch of parsley, roughly chopped
½ bunch of mint, roughly chopped
1 garlic clove, crushed
4 tablespoons extra virgin olive oil
salt and pepper

Preparation time:
15 minutes, plus soaking

Cooking time:
No cooking

Serves: **4**

150 g (5 oz) bulgar wheat
75 g (3 oz) unsalted shelled pistachio nuts
1 small red onion, finely chopped
3 garlic cloves, crushed
25 g (1 oz) flat leaf parsley, chopped
15 g (½ oz) mint, chopped
finely grated rind and juice of 1 lemon or lime
150 g (5 oz) ready-to-eat prunes, sliced
4 tablespoons olive oil
salt and pepper

Mix together the stock, orange juice, spices and ½ teaspoon salt in a saucepan. Bring to the boil and stir in the couscous. Remove from the heat, cover and leave to stand for 10 minutes until all the liquid has been absorbed.

Mix together the raisins, tomatoes, preserved lemon, if using, herbs, garlic and oil in a large bowl, stir in the soaked couscous and season to taste with salt and pepper.

Serve warm or leave to cool and serve at room temperature.

Put the bulgar wheat in a heatproof bowl, cover with plenty of boiling water and leave to soak for 15 minutes.

Meanwhile, put the pistachio nuts in a separate heatproof bowl and cover with boiling water. Leave to stand for 1 minute, then drain. Rub the nuts between several thicknesses of kitchen paper to remove most of the skins, then peel away any remaining skins with your fingers.

Mix the nuts with the onion, garlic, parsley, mint, lemon or lime rind and juice and prunes in a large bowl.

Drain the bulgar wheat thoroughly in a sieve, pressing out as much moisture as possible with the back of a spoon. Add to the bowl with the oil and toss together. Season to taste with salt and pepper and serve.

COOK'S NOTES Couscous has a light, fluffy texture and makes a perfect base for salads. The varieties readily available in supermarkets are generally pre-prepared and need only to be soaked in boiling water, but double check the packet instructions, because some types need longer cooking times.

69 Chicken, grape and chicory salad

70 Thai beef salad

Preparation time:
10 minutes

Cooking time:
No cooking

Serves: **1**

**100 g (3½ oz) cold cooked chicken breast,
   sliced**
**75 g (3 oz) mixed black and green grapes,
   halved**
1 head of chicory
handful of watercress
bread, to serve

DRESSING
1 teaspoon clear honey
½ teaspoon Dijon mustard
1 tablespoon crème fraîche
pepper

Preparation time:
10 minutes, plus resting

Cooking time:
about 10 minutes

Serves: **4**

**2 lean rump or sirloin steaks, about 150 g
   (5 oz) each, trimmed of fat**
150 g (5 oz) baby corn cobs
1 large cucumber
1 small red onion, finely chopped
3 tablespoons chopped fresh coriander
4 tablespoons rice vinegar
4 tablespoons sweet chilli sauce
**2 tablespoons sesame seeds, lightly
   toasted**

Put the chicken and grapes in a salad bowl. Separate the chicory into leaves and break the watercress into small sprigs. Add the chicory and watercress to the bowl and toss the ingredients together.

To make the dressing, put all the ingredients in a small bowl, season to taste with pepper and whisk well.

Pour the dressing over the salad and toss well to coat evenly. Serve with a slice of bread.

Heat a griddle pan until smoking, add the steaks and cook for 3–4 minutes on each side. Remove the steaks from the pan and leave to rest for 10 minutes, then thinly slice.

Meanwhile, blanch the baby corn in a saucepan of boiling water for 3–4 minutes. Drain, refresh under cold running water and drain again thoroughly.

Slice the cucumber in half lengthways, then scoop out and discard the seeds with a teaspoon. Cut the cucumber into 5 mm (¼ inch) slices.

Put the beef, baby corn, cucumber, onion and coriander in a large bowl. Stir in the vinegar and sweet chilli sauce and mix together well. Garnish the salad with the sesame seeds and serve immediately.

COOK'S NOTES This is a great way of using up leftover chicken from a Sunday roast. The sweetness of the grapes combines well with the crisp, fresh flavour of the chicory.

71 Spiced chicken and mango salad

72 Turkey and avocado salad

Preparation time: **15 minutes**	**4 boneless, skinless chicken breasts, about 150 g (5 oz) each** **6 teaspoons mild curry paste**
Cooking time: **5 minutes**	**juice of 1 lemon** **150 ml (¼ pint) natural yogurt** **1 mango**
Serves: **4**	**50 g (2 oz) watercress, torn into bite-sized pieces** **½ cucumber, diced** **½ red onion, chopped** **½ iceberg lettuce**

Cut the chicken breasts into long, thin slices. Put 4 teaspoons of the curry paste in a polythene bag with the lemon juice and mix together by squeezing the bag. Add the chicken and shake gently in the bag to coat.

Half-fill the base of a steamer with water and bring to the boil. Put the chicken in the top of the steamer in a single layer, cover and steam for 5 minutes until thoroughly cooked – the juices should run clear when pierced with a knife.

Meanwhile, mix the remaining curry paste with the yogurt in a bowl. Cut a thick slice off either side of the mango to reveal the large, flat stone. Trim the flesh away from the stone, then remove the skin and cut the flesh into bite-sized chunks. Add the mango to the yogurt mixture with the watercress, cucumber and onion and toss together gently.

Tear the lettuce into pieces and divide among 4 plates. Spoon the mango mixture on top and add the warm chicken strips.

Preparation time: **10 minutes**	**350 g (12 oz) cold cooked turkey, sliced** **1 large avocado, peeled, stoned and sliced**
Cooking time: **No cooking**	**1 punnet of mustard and cress** **150 g (5 oz) mixed salad leaves** **50 g (2 oz) mixed seeds, such as pumpkin and sunflower, toasted**
Serves: **4**	**wholegrain rye bread, toasted, or flatbreads, to serve**

DRESSING
2 tablespoons apple juice
2 tablespoons natural yogurt
1 teaspoon clear honey
1 teaspoon wholegrain mustard

Toss together all the salad ingredients and seeds in a large bowl.

Whisk together all the dressing ingredients in a small bowl. Pour over the salad and toss well to coat evenly.

Serve the salad with toasted wholegrain rye bread or rolled up in flatbreads.

COOK'S NOTES To remove the stone from an avocado, slice around the circumference with a sharp knife. Twist the halves until they separate and hold the half with the stone. Very carefully tap the middle of the stone with the blade of the knife and then lift it out – the stone should come too.

73 Panzanella

74 Fig, mozzarella and prosciutto salad

Preparation time:
10 minutes, plus standing

Cooking time:
7–8 minutes

Serves: **4**

**3 red peppers, cored, deseeded and
  quartered lengthways**
375 g (12 oz) plum tomatoes, skinned
6 tablespoons extra virgin olive oil
3 tablespoons white wine vinegar
2 garlic cloves, crushed
125 g (4 oz) stale ciabatta bread
50 g (2 oz) pitted black olives
small handful of basil leaves, shredded
salt and pepper

Put the red peppers, skin side up, on a baking sheet and cook under a preheated high grill for 7–8 minutes until the skins are blackened.

Transfer the pepper quarters to a polythene bag. Fold over the top to seal and leave for 10 minutes.

Meanwhile, quarter the tomatoes, scoop out the pulp and put it in a sieve over a bowl to catch the juice. Set the tomato quarters aside. Press the pulp with the back of a spoon to extract as much juice as possible. Whisk the oil, vinegar, garlic and salt and pepper to taste into the tomato juice.

Peel away the skins from the peppers. Roughly slice the flesh and put it in a bowl with the tomato quarters. Break the bread into small chunks and add to the bowl with the olives and basil.

Add the dressing and toss the ingredients together before serving.

Preparation time:
10 minutes

Cooking time:
No cooking

Serves: **4**

8–12 ripe figs
250 g (8 oz) buffalo mozzarella
8 slices of prosciutto
a few basil leaves

DRESSING
3 tablespoons extra virgin olive oil
1 tablespoon verjuice
salt and pepper

Cut the figs into quarters, tear the mozzarella and prosciutto into bite-sized pieces and arrange on a large platter with the basil leaves.

Whisk together the oil and verjuice in a small bowl and season to taste with salt and pepper. Drizzle over the salad and serve immediately.

COOK'S NOTES Verjuice, made from unripe grapes, has a strong, acidic flavour and is used in cooking as an alternative to lemon juice or vinegar. It gives the dressing a lovely flavour, but if you cannot find it, use a good quality white wine vinegar sweetened with a pinch of sugar.

75 Avocado and smoked salmon salad

76 Hot chicken liver salad

Preparation time:
10 minutes

Cooking time:
No cooking

Serves: **2**

2 slices of smoked salmon, about 100 g (3½ oz) each
1 small firm avocado, peeled, stoned and cut into wedges
juice of ½ lime
2 teaspoons mayonnaise
1 teaspoon wholegrain mustard
2 tablespoons chopped dill

TO SERVE
25 g (1 oz) rocket leaves
2 teaspoons sunflower seeds

Preparation time:
10 minutes

Cooking time:
5 minutes

Serves: **4**

2 teaspoons chopped thyme leaves
400 g (13 oz) chicken livers, trimmed and halved
1 tablespoon olive oil
2 garlic cloves, crushed
1 red chilli, deseeded and thinly sliced (optional)
200 g (7 oz) can water chestnuts, drained and halved

TO SERVE
200 g (7 oz) chicory, leaves separated
1½–2 tablespoons balsamic vinegar

Wrap the smoked salmon slices around the avocado wedges and sprinkle with the lime juice.

Mix together the mayonnaise, mustard and dill in a small bowl.

Serve the wrapped avocado on a bed of rocket leaves with the mustard mayonnaise and sprinkled with the sunflower seeds.

Sprinkle the thyme over both sides of the chicken livers.

Heat the oil in a large frying pan, add the garlic and chilli, if using, and cook, stirring, for 30 seconds, then add the chicken livers and water chestnuts. Cook over a medium heat for 3–4 minutes until the livers are browned on the outside but still slightly pink inside.

Serve the chicken livers on a bed of chicory leaves, drizzled with the vinegar and the pan juices.

COOK'S NOTES This is a speedy salad that would work well as a starter as there is hardly any preparation. It is also a healthy option, with the smoked salmon, avocado and sunflower seeds, which are packed full of vitamins and minerals.

77 Chorizo with broad beans

78 Cavolo nero with pancetta

Preparation time:
10 minutes

Cooking time:
10 minutes

Serves: **4–6**

250 g (8 oz) shelled young broad beans
1 tablespoon extra virgin olive oil
2 garlic cloves, roughly chopped
125 g (4 oz) chorizo sausage, cut into
 5 mm (¼ inch) thick slices
1 tablespoon chopped dill
1 tablespoon chopped mint
2 tablespoons lemon juice
salt and pepper
crusty bread, to serve

Preparation time:
10 minutes

Cooking time:
10 minutes

Serves: **4**

1 tablespoon olive oil
1 onion, sliced
1 garlic clove, crushed
1 red chilli, deseeded and diced
125 g (4 oz) pancetta, diced
1 head of cavolo nero
75 ml (3 fl oz) chicken stock
75 g (3 oz) Parmesan cheese, freshly
 coarsely grated
salt and pepper

Blanch the beans in a saucepan of lightly salted boiling water for 1 minute. Drain, rinse under cold running water and drain again. Pat dry with kitchen paper.

Heat the oil in a frying pan, add the garlic and cook gently for 2–3 minutes until softened, then discard. Increase the heat, add the chorizo and cook, stirring, for 2–3 minutes until golden and some of its oil has been released.

Stir in the beans and cook for a further 2–3 minutes, then add the herbs and lemon juice and season to taste with salt and pepper. Mix well. Serve warm with crusty bread.

Heat the oil in a large saucepan, add the onion, garlic, chilli and pancetta and cook for 5 minutes or until the onion is softened.

Meanwhile, trim any wilting leaves from the cavolo nero, then cut the head in half lengthways. Remove and discard the hard central stem and roughly chop the leaves.

Add the cavolo nero to the onion mixture and stir well. Pour in the stock and season to taste with salt and pepper. Cook over a medium heat, stirring constantly, for 4 minutes.

Stir in the Parmesan and serve immediately.

COOK'S NOTES If you want to save time and avoid shelling beans you can use frozen broad beans. They work really well in this recipe as they cut through the rich flavour of the chorizo.

79 Aubergine salad

80 Bean, kabanos and red pepper salad

Preparation time:
10 minutes, plus cooling

Cooking time:
15 minutes

Serves: **4**

4 tablespoons olive oil
1 onion, chopped
2 garlic cloves, crushed
2 aubergines, cubed
4 tomatoes, skinned and roughly chopped
4 anchovy fillets in oil, drained and
chopped
2 tablespoons pitted black olives
75 g (3 oz) pine nuts, toasted
2 tablespoons chopped capers
handful of flat leaf parsley, chopped
salt and pepper

DRESSING
1 tablespoon white wine vinegar
3 tablespoons olive oil
2 tablespoons lemon juice
1 teaspoon Dijon mustard

Heat the oil in a saucepan, add the onion, garlic and aubergines and cook for 15 minutes.

Meanwhile, to make the dressing, put all the ingredients in a screw-top jar, season to taste with salt and pepper and shake until well blended.

Add the tomatoes, anchovies, olives, pine nuts, capers and parsley to the aubergine mixture and season to taste with salt and pepper. Pour over the dressing, mix well, then leave the salad to cool for 5 minutes before serving.

Preparation time:
10 minutes, plus standing

Cooking time:
about 15 minutes

Serves: **4**

3 red peppers, cored, deseeded and
quartered lengthways
1 red chilli, halved and deseeded
1 tablespoon olive oil
1 onion, sliced
75 g (3 oz) kabanos sausage, thinly sliced
2 x 400 g (13 oz) cans butter or flageolet
beans, drained and rinsed
1 tablespoon balsamic vinegar
2 tablespoons chopped fresh coriander
walnut bread, to serve

Put the red pepper quarters and chilli halves, skin-side up, on a baking sheet and cook under a preheated high grill for 7–8 minutes until the skins are blackened.

Transfer the pepper quarters and chilli halves to a polythene bag. Fold over the top to seal and leave for 10 minutes, then peel away the skins and slice the flesh.

Meanwhile, heat the oil in a nonstick frying pan, add the onion and cook for 5–6 minutes until softened. Add the kabanos sausage and cook for 1–2 minutes until crisp.

Add the beans, vinegar and coriander with the peppers and chilli and mix well. Serve the salad warm with walnut bread.

COOK'S NOTES Aubergines contain a lot of moisture and you can remove this by placing the chopped aubergines on a large plate and sprinkling them with salt. Leave for about 30 minutes then rinse, or drain on kitchen paper, before using.

81 Celeriac remoulade with asparagus

82 Potato wedges and peppers with yogurt dip

Preparation time:
15 minutes

Cooking time:
10 minutes

Serves: **4**

500 g (1 lb) celeriac, peeled
375 g (12 oz) potatoes, peeled
1 tablespoon extra virgin olive oil, plus
**   extra for drizzling (optional)**
500 g (1 lb) asparagus spears, trimmed

SAUCE
150 ml (¼ pint) mayonnaise
150 ml (¼ pint) Greek yogurt
1 teaspoon Dijon mustard
6 cocktail gherkins, finely chopped
2 tablespoons capers, chopped
2 tablespoons chopped tarragon
salt and pepper

Preparation time:
15 minutes

Cooking time:
about 15 minutes

Serves: **2**

1 potato, about 175 g (6 oz), scrubbed
1 red pepper, cored, deseeded and sliced
1 teaspoon olive oil
paprika
rock salt

YOGURT DIP
3 tablespoons Greek yogurt
1 tablespoon chopped parsley
2 spring onions, chopped
1 garlic clove, crushed (optional)
salt and pepper

Cut the celeriac and potato into matchstick-sized pieces, but keep the 2 vegetables separate.

Bring a saucepan of lightly salted water to the boil, add the celeriac and cook for 2 minutes until softened. Add the potatoes and cook for 2 minutes until just tender. Drain the vegetables, refresh under cold running water and drain again.

Meanwhile, thoroughly mix together all the ingredients for the sauce in a bowl and set aside.

Heat the oil in a frying pan or griddle pan, add the asparagus spears and cook for 2–3 minutes until just beginning to colour.

Mix the celeriac and potato with the sauce and spoon on to 4 serving plates. Top with the asparagus and serve immediately, drizzled with a little extra oil, if you like.

Cut the potato into 8 wedges. Bring a saucepan of lightly salted water to the boil, add the potato wedges and cook for 5 minutes. Drain the wedges thoroughly, then put them in a bowl with the red pepper slices and oil. Toss well to mix. Sprinkle with paprika and rock salt to taste.

Put the potato wedges and pepper slices on a baking sheet and cook under a preheated high grill, turning occasionally, for 6–8 minutes until lightly browned and tender.

Meanwhile, to make the yogurt dip, put all the ingredients in a bowl, season to taste with salt and pepper and mix together well.

Serve the potato wedges and pepper slices hot with the yogurt dip.

COOK'S NOTES This piquant sauce can be used to accompany other salads. It could also be used as a sauce for fish or even as a dip to serve with vegetable crudités.

COOK'S NOTES For a buffet party dish double the quantities and serve the wedges on a platter for guests to help themselves. You could also try using sweet potatoes for a variation.

83 Charred leek salad with hazelnuts

84 Spiced beetroot

Preparation time:
10 minutes

Cooking time:
15 minutes

Serves: **4**

500 g (1 lb) baby leeks
1–2 tablespoons hazelnut oil
dash of lemon juice
40 g (1½ oz) blanched hazelnuts
2 Little Gem or baby cos lettuce hearts
a few mint sprigs
15 g (½ oz) pecorino cheese
20 black olives, to garnish

DRESSING
4 tablespoons hazelnut oil
2 tablespoons extra virgin olive oil
2 teaspoons sherry vinegar
salt and pepper

Preparation time:
10 minutes

Cooking time:
4–6 minutes

Serves: **4**

1 tablespoon vegetable oil
2 garlic cloves, finely chopped
1 teaspoon grated fresh root ginger
1 teaspoon cumin seeds
1 teaspoon coriander seeds, coarsely crushed
½ teaspoon dried red chilli flakes
625 g (1¼ lb) cooked beetroot in natural juices, drained and cut into wedges
150 ml (¼ pint) canned coconut milk
¼ teaspoon ground cardamom
finely grated rind and juice of 1 lime
handful of chopped fresh coriander leaves
salt and pepper

Brush the leeks with the hazelnut oil to taste and cook in a preheated griddle pan or under a preheated high grill, turning frequently, for 6–8 minutes until evenly browned and cooked through. Transfer the leeks to a bowl, toss with the lemon juice and season to taste with salt and pepper. Leave to cool.

Meanwhile, heat a nonstick frying pan, add the hazelnuts and cook, stirring constantly, for 4–5 minutes until lightly browned. Remove the nuts from the pan and leave to cool slightly, then roughly chop. Separate the lettuce leaves and pull the mint leaves from their stalks.

Arrange the leeks in bowls or on plates and top with the lettuce leaves, mint and nuts.

Whisk together all the dressing ingredients in a small bowl and pour over the salad. Shave the pecorino over the salad and serve immediately, garnished with the olives.

Heat the oil in a wok or large frying pan, add the garlic, ginger, cumin and coriander seeds and chilli flakes and stir-fry for 1–2 minutes. Add the beetroot and cook, stirring gently, for 1 minute. Add the coconut milk, cardamom and lime rind and juice and cook over a medium heat for 2–3 minutes.

Stir in the fresh coriander, season to taste with salt and pepper and serve hot, warm or at room temperature.

COOK'S NOTES Cooked fresh beetroot is now available everywhere; do not use beetroot that has been preserved or cooked in vinegar.

85 Ginger broccoli with fennel seeds

86 Pumpkin with walnut and rocket pesto

Preparation time:
5 minutes

Cooking time:
5 minutes

Serves: **4**

2 teaspoons olive oil
1 teaspoon crushed fresh root ginger
½ teaspoon fennel seeds
500 g (1 lb) broccoli florets
3 tablespoons soy sauce
pepper

Heat the oil in a nonstick wok or large frying pan, add the ginger and fennel seeds and stir-fry over a medium heat for a few seconds.

Add the broccoli, soy sauce and pepper to taste and stir-fry until the broccoli is just tender. Serve immediately.

Preparation time:
10 minutes

Cooking time:
20 minutes

Serves: **4**

Oven temperature:
220°C (425°F) Gas Mark 7

1 kg (2 lb) pumpkin
extra virgin olive oil, for brushing
salt and pepper
rocket leaves, to serve

PESTO
50 g (2 oz) walnuts, toasted
2 spring onions, chopped
1 large garlic clove, crushed
50 g (2 oz) rocket leaves
3 tablespoons walnut oil
3 tablespoons extra virgin olive oil

Cut the pumpkin into 8 wedges and remove and discard the seeds, but leave the skin on. Brush the pumpkin with oil, season to taste with salt and pepper and arrange on a large baking sheet. Roast in a preheated oven, 220°C (425°F), Gas Mark 7, for 20 minutes or until tender, turning it over halfway through.

Meanwhile, to make the pesto, put the walnuts, spring onions, garlic and rocket leaves in a food processor and process until finely chopped. With the machine running, very slowly drizzle in the oils until completely incorporated. Season to taste with salt and pepper.

Serve the roasted pumpkin with the pesto and rocket leaves.

COOK'S NOTES Choose a small, round pumpkin to make cutting easier. Any leftover pesto can be stored in an airtight container in the refrigerator for up to 5 days and tossed with spaghetti for a quick and simple supper dish.

87 Potatoes wrapped in Parma ham

88 Sesame greens with black bean sauce

Preparation time:
10 minutes

Cooking time:
20 minutes

Serves: **4**

Oven temperature:
200°C (400°F) Gas Mark 6

**12 small new potatoes, cooked until just
   tender
12 very thin slices of Parma ham
2 tablespoons olive oil
sea salt**

Roll each potato in a slice of Parma ham, patting with your hands to mould the ham to the shape of the potato.

Brush a roasting tin with the oil, add the potatoes and roast in a preheated oven, 200°C (400°F), Gas Mark 6, for 20 minutes. Keep an eye on the potatoes while they are cooking as they may need turning or moving around; often the ones on the edge become browner than the ones in the centre.

Serve immediately, sprinkled with sea salt to taste.

Preparation time:
10 minutes

Cooking time:
about 10 minutes

Serves: **6**

**5 teaspoons sunflower oil
2 tablespoons sesame seeds
1 tablespoon soy sauce
400 g (13 oz) spring greens or a mix
   of spring greens and Brussels
   sprouts tops
1–2 garlic cloves, finely chopped
3 tablespoons black bean sauce**

Heat 1 teaspoon of the oil in a large frying pan, add the sesame seeds and cook, stirring, for 2–3 minutes, until lightly browned. Remove the pan from the heat, add the soy sauce and quickly cover. When the seeds have stopped popping, stir, recover and leave to cool while you prepare the greens.

Trim the spring greens and discard the stems. Thickly slice the leaves and rinse in cold water. Drain well and pat dry with kitchen paper.

Tip the seeds out of the pan, wash and dry the pan, then add the remaining oil and heat. Add the greens and garlic and stir-fry for 2–3 minutes until just tender. Stir in the black bean sauce and cook for 1 minute. Sprinkle with the toasted sesame seeds, transfer to a serving dish and serve immediately.

COOK'S NOTES You can toss the cooked greens with 1 tablespoon soy sauce instead of the black bean sauce.

89 Asparagus with toasted sesame seeds

90 Tomato and aubergine parmigiana

Preparation time:
10 minutes

Cooking time:
about 15 minutes

Serves: **6**

500 g (1 lb) asparagus spears
1 tablespoon olive oil
25 g (1 oz) butter
4 teaspoons sesame seeds
1 teaspoon wholegrain mustard

Preparation time:
10 minutes

Cooking time:
20 minutes

Serves: **4**

Oven temperature:
190°C (375°F) Gas Mark 5

olive oil, for frying
1 large aubergine, thinly sliced
500 g (1 lb) ripe plum tomatoes, cut into
** wedges**
50 g (2 oz) Parmesan cheese, freshly
** grated**
salt and pepper
sprigs of flat leaf parsley, to garnish

Snap off any woody parts of the asparagus stems by bending the ends of the spears.

Heat the oil and butter in a flat, heavy-based frying pan. Arrange as many asparagus spears as will fit in a single layer over the base of the pan and cook, turning occasionally, for 5 minutes or until just tender and slightly charred. Transfer to a warmed serving dish and keep warm in a low oven while you cook the remainder.

Meanwhile, heat a nonstick frying pan, add the sesame seeds and cook, stirring constantly, for 2–3 minutes until lightly browned.

Stir the mustard into the asparagus and serve immediately, topped with the toasted sesame seeds.

Heat the olive oil in a large, heavy-based frying pan and fry the aubergine slices in batches until golden brown. Drain on kitchen paper.

Arrange the tomato wedges and the fried aubergine slices in alternate layers in a shallow ovenproof dish, with a sprinkling of grated Parmesan between each layer. Season with salt and pepper. Bake in a preheated oven, 190°C (375°F), Gas Mark 5, for 15 minutes, until lightly browned and bubbling.

Allow the vegetables to cool slightly and serve garnished with parsley.

COOK'S NOTES If you're not sure how much of the asparagus stalks to remove, simply hold each spear with one hand at either end, then gently bend: the stalk will give way and break at the right place.

91 Balsamic braised leeks and peppers

92 Warm courgette and lime salad

Preparation time:
5 minutes

Cooking time:
20 minutes

Serves: **4**

2 tablespoons olive oil
2 leeks, cut into 1 cm (½ inch) pieces
1 orange pepper, cored, deseeded and cut into 1 cm (½ inch) chunks
1 red pepper, cored, deseeded and cut into 1 cm (½ inch) chunks
3 tablespoons balsamic vinegar
handful of flat leaf parsley, chopped
salt and pepper

Preparation time:
10 minutes

Cooking time:
8 minutes

Serves: **4**

1 tablespoon olive oil
finely grated rind and juice of 1 lime
1 garlic clove, finely chopped
2 tablespoons roughly chopped fresh coriander leaves, plus extra to garnish
2 courgettes, about 325 g (11 oz) in total, cut into thin diagonal slices
salt and pepper

Heat the oil in a saucepan, add the leeks and peppers and stir well. Cover and cook very gently for 10 minutes.

Add the vinegar and cook, uncovered, for a further 10 minutes. The vegetables should be brown from the vinegar and all the liquid should have evaporated.

Season well with salt and pepper, then stir in the parsley and serve immediately.

Put the oil, lime rind and juice, garlic, coriander and a little salt and pepper in a polythene bag. Add the courgettes and shake gently in the bag to coat. Seal and set aside until ready to cook.

Heat a ridged frying pan until smoking. Arrange as many courgette slices as will fit in a single layer over the base of the pan and cook for 2–3 minutes until the undersides are browned. Turn the courgettes over and brown on the other side, then transfer them to a warmed serving dish while you cook the remainder.

Pour any remaining dressing over the courgettes, sprinkle with chopped coriander to garnish and serve immediately.

COOK'S NOTES As an alternative, you can cook thin slices of aubergine in the same way.

4 Pizza, Pasta, Rice and Noodles

93 Tomato, artichoke and mozzarella pizza

94 Asparagus and taleggio pizzas

Preparation time:
10 minutes

Cooking time:
15–20 minutes

Serves: **4**

Oven temperature:
230°C (450°F) Gas Mark 8

250 g (8 oz) self-raising flour, plus extra for dusting
3 tablespoons olive oil, plus extra for oiling
1 teaspoon salt
2 tablespoons sun-dried tomato paste
100 ml (3½ fl oz) water

TOPPING
1 tablespoon sun-dried tomato paste
2 large, mild red or green chillies, halved and deseeded
3 tablespoons chopped mixed herbs, such as parsley, oregano, rosemary and chives
50 g (2 oz) sun-dried tomatoes in oil, drained and sliced
2 plum tomatoes, quartered
150 g (5 oz) baby artichokes in oil, drained
150 g (5 oz) mozzarella cheese, sliced
50 g (2 oz) black olives
salt and pepper

Put the flour, oil, salt and sun-dried tomato paste in a large bowl. Add the measured water and mix to a soft dough, adding a little more water if necessary.

Roll out the dough on a lightly floured surface to a 28 cm (11 inch) round. Put the round on a large, oiled baking sheet and bake in a preheated oven, 230°C (450°F), Gas Mark 8, for 5 minutes.

Spread the pizza base to within 1 cm (½ inch) of the edge with the sun-dried tomato paste. Cut the chillies in half lengthways again and scatter over the pizza with half the herbs, the tomatoes, artichokes, mozzarella and olives. Scatter the remaining herbs on top and season lightly with salt and pepper. Bake for a further 10–15 minutes until the cheese has melted and the vegetables are beginning to colour.

Preparation time:
5 minutes

Cooking time:
10 minutes

Serves: **4**

Oven temperature:
200°C (400°F) Gas Mark 6

5 tablespoons passata (sieved tomatoes)
1 tablespoon red pesto
pinch of salt
4 x 25 cm (10 inch) ready-made pizza dough bases
250 g (8 oz) taleggio cheese, derinded and sliced
175 g (6 oz) fine asparagus spears, trimmed
2 tablespoons olive oil
pepper

Mix together the passata, pesto and salt in a small bowl and spread the mixture over the pizza dough bases. Top with the taleggio and asparagus spears and drizzle with the oil.

Bake the pizzas directly on the shelves at the top of a preheated oven, 200°C (400°F), Gas Mark 6, for 10 minutes or until the asparagus is tender and the pizza bases crisp. Grind over some pepper over the tops before serving.

COOK'S NOTES Look out for fine asparagus spears that will roast quickly. If you can only find large spears, halve them lengthways before scattering over the pizza.

95 Flatbread pizzas with blue cheese

96 Fresh vegetable pizza

Preparation time:
5 minutes

Cooking time:
7–8 minutes

Serves: **4**

Oven temperature:
200°C (400°F) Gas Mark 6

4 x 20 cm (8 inch) Mediterranean flatbreads
200 g (7 oz) Gorgonzola or dolcelatte cheese, crumbled
8 slices of prosciutto
50 g (2 oz) rocket leaves
extra virgin olive oil, for drizzling
pepper

Put the flatbreads on 2 baking sheets and scatter the centres with the blue cheese.

Bake the flatbreads in a preheated oven, 200°C (400°F), Gas Mark 6, for 7–8 minutes until the bases are crisp and the cheese has melted.

Top the pizzas with the prosciutto and rocket leaves, grind over some pepper and drizzle with oil. Serve immediately.

Preparation time:
15 minutes

Cooking time:
10 minutes

Serves: **4**

Oven temperature:
230°C (450°F) Gas Mark 8

4 x 25 cm (10 inch) ready-made pizza dough bases
5 tablespoons olive oil
2 garlic cloves, crushed
1 red onion, thinly sliced
2 courgettes, thinly sliced lengthways
1 red pepper, cored, deseeded and cut into thin strips
1 yellow pepper, cored, deseeded and cut into thin strips
4 plum tomatoes, skinned, cored and cut into small wedges
500 g (1 lb) fine asparagus tips
4 thyme sprigs, leaves stripped
handful of basil leaves, roughly torn
salt and pepper
75 g (3 oz) Parmesan cheese, freshly shaved (optional), to serve

Put the pizza dough bases on to warmed baking sheets, brush with a little of the oil, then arrange the vegetables on the bases. Sprinkle with the thyme and basil.

Season the pizzas well with salt and pepper, drizzle with the remaining oil and bake at the top of a preheated oven, 230°C (450°F), Gas Mark 8, for 10 minutes. The vegetables should be slightly charred around the edges as this adds to the flavour.

Serve immediately, with Parmesan shavings, if you like.

COOK'S NOTES Flatbread is very versatile and, as well making the perfect speedy pizza, it can be used for sandwiches and for dipping. You'll find it in delicatessens, specialist Mediterranean grocers and in some supermarkets.

97 Flatbread pizzas with goats' cheese

98 Warm pasta salad

Preparation time:
10 minutes

Cooking time:
7–8 minutes

Serves: **4**

Oven temperature:
200°C (400°F) Gas Mark 6

4 x 20 cm (8 inch) Mediterranean
flatbreads
2 tablespoons sun-dried tomato paste
300 g (10 oz) mozzarella cheese, sliced
6 plum tomatoes, roughly chopped
4 tablespoons olive oil
1 garlic clove, crushed
small handful of basil leaves, roughly
torn
100 g (3½ oz) goats' cheese
salt and pepper

Put the flatbreads on 2 baking sheets and spread with the sun-dried tomato paste. Top with the mozzarella and bake in a preheated oven, 200°C (400°F), Gas Mark 6, for 7–8 minutes until the bases are crisp and the cheese has melted.

Meanwhile, put the tomatoes in a bowl, add the oil, garlic and basil and season well with salt and pepper. Toss well to mix. Top the cooked pizza bases with the tomato mixture and crumble over the goats' cheese. Serve immediately.

Preparation time:
10 minutes, plus standing

Cooking time:
about 10 minutes

Serves: **4**

250 g (8 oz) dried malloreddus or orzo
pasta
250 g (8 oz) frozen peas, defrosted
6 tablespoons extra virgin olive oil
6 spring onions, roughly chopped
2 garlic cloves, crushed
8 bottled marinated artichoke hearts,
drained and thickly sliced
4 tablespoons chopped mint
2 tablespoons lemon juice
salt and pepper
lemon rind, to garnish

Bring a large saucepan of lightly salted water to the boil. Add the pasta, return to the boil and cook for 6 minutes. Add the peas and cook for a further 2–3 minutes until the peas and pasta are tender. Drain well.

Meanwhile, heat 2 tablespoons of the oil in a frying pan, add the spring onions and garlic and cook for 1–2 minutes until softened. Stir in the pasta and peas with the artichokes, mint and the remaining oil.

Toss the ingredients gently until combined, season to taste with salt and pepper, then leave to stand for 10 minutes. Stir in the lemon juice and serve the salad warm, garnished with lemon rind.

COOK'S NOTES Mediterranean flatbreads crisp up beautifully in the oven or under the grill, making them a perfect, time-saving alternative to the classic bread dough pizza base.

COOK'S NOTES Malloreddus is a rice-shaped pasta, traditionally flavoured with saffron, and is available from larger supermarkets and specialist Italian food stores. It is often added to soups.

99 Angel hair pasta with prawns

Preparation time:
5 minutes

Cooking time:
8 minutes

Serves: **4**

375 g (12 oz) dried angel hair pasta
25 g (1 oz) butter
4 plum tomatoes, chopped
2 tablespoons brandy
200 g (7 oz) cooked peeled prawns,
  defrosted if frozen
3 tablespoons double cream
1 tablespoon chopped tarragon
salt and pepper

Bring a large saucepan of lightly salted water to the boil. Add the pasta, return to the boil and cook for 5 minutes, or according to the packet instructions, until tender but still firm to the bite. Drain well.

Meanwhile, heat the butter in a frying pan, add the tomatoes and cook for 2–3 minutes until softened. Pour in the brandy, increase the heat to high and cook for 2 minutes.

Add the prawns, cream and tarragon and heat through. Season well with salt and pepper.

Toss the sauce with the hot pasta and serve immediately.

COOK'S NOTES Small prawns, often sweeter than tiger prawns, are ideal for this dish, and convenient frozen ones, defrosted, are fine to use. Make sure you boil off the brandy properly to remove its slightly 'raw' taste before adding the prawns and herbs.

100 Black pasta with monkfish and spinach

Preparation time:
10 minutes

Cooking time:
about 15 minutes

Serves: **4**

Oven temperature:
200°C (400°F) Gas Mark 6

375 g (12 oz) dried black (squid ink) pasta
25 g (1 oz) butter
200 g (7 oz) monkfish tail, cut into 2.5 cm
  (1 inch) cubes
2 large red chillies, deseeded and finely
  chopped
2 garlic cloves, chopped
2 tablespoons Thai fish sauce
150 g (5 oz) baby spinach leaves
juice of 2 limes or to taste
salt
lime wedges, to serve

Bring a large saucepan of lightly salted water to the boil. Add the pasta, return to the boil and cook for 8–12 minutes, or according to the packet instructions, until tender but still firm to the bite. Drain well, add the butter and toss well to coat evenly.

Meanwhile, cut out a large rectangle of foil. Put the monkfish cubes in the centre and pull the edges of the foil up around the fish. Top the fish with the chillies, garlic and fish sauce. Bring the edges of the foil up to meet and fold over tightly to seal the parcel. Transfer to a baking sheet and cook in a preheated oven, 200°C (400°F), Gas Mark 6, for 8–10 minutes until cooked through.

Carefully open the parcel and toss the contents with the hot pasta. Add the spinach and stir until it has wilted. Add lime juice and salt to taste and serve immediately with lime wedges.

COOK'S NOTES Black pasta, coloured and flavoured with squid ink, has a very subtle taste of fish and looks stunning, making it the perfect choice when entertaining friends or family.

101 Spaghetti with asparagus

102 Ravioli with burnt sage butter

Preparation time: **10 minutes**	**375 g (12 oz) dried spaghetti**
	375 g (12 oz) asparagus spears, trimmed and cut into 8 cm (3 inch) lengths
Cooking time: **10 minutes**	**5 tablespoons olive oil**
	50 g (2 oz) butter
	½ teaspoon crushed dried red chilli flakes
Serves: **4**	**2 garlic cloves, sliced**
	50 g (2 oz) anchovy fillets in oil, drained and chopped
Oven temperature: **200°C (400°F) Gas Mark 6**	**2 tablespoons lemon juice**
	75 g (3 oz) Parmesan cheese, freshly shaved
	salt

Bring a large saucepan of lightly salted water to the boil. Add the pasta, return to the boil and cook for 9 minutes, or according to the packet instructions, until tender but still firm to the bite. Drain well.

Meanwhile, arrange the asparagus spears in a roasting tin, drizzle with the oil and dot with the butter. Scatter with the chilli flakes, garlic and anchovies and roast in a preheated oven, 200°C (400°F), Gas Mark 6, for 8 minutes until tender.

Toss the asparagus with the hot pasta and sprinkle over the lemon juice. Scatter the Parmesan shavings over the top, season to taste with salt and serve immediately.

COOK'S NOTES Make this simple, flavoursome dish when asparagus is in season and at its best. You can use other types of long pasta if you prefer, such as linguine or bucatini.

Preparation time: **5 minutes**	**500 g (1 lb) good quality fresh ravioli**
	50 g (2 oz) butter
	50 g (2 oz) pine nuts
Cooking time: **about 10 minutes**	**15 sage leaves, sliced**
	2 tablespoons lemon juice
	salt
Serves: **4**	**fresh Parmesan cheese shavings, to serve**

Bring a large saucepan of lightly salted water to the boil. Add the pasta, return to the boil and cook for 6–8 minutes, or according to the packet instructions, until tender but still firm to the bite. Drain well and divide among 4 warmed plates.

Meanwhile, heat the butter in a frying pan, add the pine nuts and sage and cook, stirring, until the pine nuts are lightly browned and the butter is pale golden. Have the lemon juice to hand and, once the butter is the right colour, turn off the heat and quickly pour in the lemon juice.

Season the butter to taste with salt and pour over the hot ravioli. Scatter with Parmesan shavings and serve immediately.

COOK'S NOTES Burnt butter tastes fantastic and is one of the simplest things to make, but the timing is absolutely crucial. You need only to brown the butter a little, so once you see it turning, throw in the lemon juice to prevent it from cooking any further.

103 Roasted tomato and ricotta pasta

104 Pasta with aubergines and pine nuts

Preparation time:
10 minutes

Cooking time:
15–20 minutes

Serves: **4**

Oven temperature:
200°C (400°F) Gas Mark 6

500 g (1 lb) cherry tomatoes, halved
4 tablespoons extra virgin olive oil
2 teaspoons chopped thyme
4 garlic cloves, sliced
pinch of dried red chilli flakes
400 g (13 oz) dried pasta
1 bunch of basil leaves, torn
125 g (4 oz) ricotta cheese, crumbled
salt and pepper

Preparation time:
10 minutes

Cooking time:
15 minutes

Serves: **4**

125 ml (4 fl oz) olive oil
2 aubergines, diced
2 red onions, sliced
75 g (3 oz) pine nuts
3 garlic cloves, crushed
5 tablespoons sun-dried tomato paste
150 ml (¼ pint) vegetable stock
300 g (10 oz) cracked pepper-, tomato- or
**   mushroom-flavoured fresh ribbon pasta**
100 g (3½ oz) pitted black olives
salt and pepper
3 tablespoons roughly chopped flat leaf
**   parsley, to garnish**

Put the tomatoes in a roasting tin with the oil, thyme, garlic and chilli flakes and season to taste with salt and pepper. Roast in a preheated oven, 200°C (400°F), Gas Mark 6, for 15–20 minutes until the tomatoes have softened and released their juices.

Meanwhile, bring a large saucepan of lightly salted water to the boil. Add the pasta, return to the boil and cook for 8–12 minutes, or according to the packet instructions, until tender but still firm to the bite. Drain the pasta and return it to the pan.

Stir the tomatoes with their pan juices and most of the basil leaves into the pasta and toss gently until combined. Season to taste with salt and pepper and spoon into warmed bowls. Chop the remaining basil, mix into the ricotta and season to taste with salt and pepper. Spoon into a serving dish for people to spoon on to the pasta.

Heat the oil in a large frying pan, add the aubergines and onions and cook for 8–10 minutes until golden and tender. Add the pine nuts and garlic and cook for 2 minutes. Stir in the sun-dried tomato paste and stock and cook for 2 minutes.

Meanwhile, bring a large saucepan of lightly salted water to the boil. Add the pasta, return to the boil and cook for 2 minutes, or according to the packet instructions, until tender but still firm to the bite.

Drain the pasta and return to the pan. Add the sauce and olives, season to taste with salt and pepper and toss together over a medium heat for 1 minute until combined. Serve garnished with the parsley.

COOK'S NOTES This piquant, herb-scented dish can be made with just about any shape or variety of pasta you like. Always check the packet instructions because cooking times will vary.

105 Pasta with radicchio and cheese crumbs

Preparation time:
5 minutes

Cooking time:
15 minutes

Serves: **2**

175 g (6 oz) dried spaghetti
65 g (2½ oz) butter
25 g (1 oz) fresh white breadcrumbs
15 g (½ oz) Parmesan cheese, freshly grated
2 shallots, finely chopped
1 garlic clove, sliced
1 head of radicchio, shredded
dash of lemon juice
salt and pepper

Bring a large saucepan of lightly salted water to the boil. Add the pasta, return to the boil and cook for 9 minutes, or according to the packet instructions, until tender but still firm to the bite. Drain well, reserving 2 tablespoons of the cooking water.

Meanwhile, heat half the butter in a frying pan, add the breadcrumbs and cook for 5 minutes or until evenly golden and crisp. Transfer to a bowl, leave to cool slightly, then stir in the Parmesan.

Heat the remaining butter in a wok or large saucepan, add the shallots and garlic and cook for 5 minutes until softened. Add the radicchio and lemon juice and season to taste with salt and pepper. Cook over a low heat, stirring, for 2 minutes until the radicchio has wilted. Add the pasta, toss until heated through and serve topped with the cheese crumbs.

106 Pasta with spinach and goats' cheese

Preparation time:
10 minutes

Cooking time:
8 minutes

Serves: **4**

500 g (1 lb) baby spinach leaves
pinch of grated nutmeg, plus extra to serve
125 g (4 oz) goats' cheese, roughly chopped
150 ml (¼ pint) low-fat crème fraîche
2 teaspoons Dijon mustard
500 g (1 lb) fresh wholewheat pasta
75 g (3 oz) pine kernels, toasted
1 tablespoon chopped parsley
2 tablespoons grated Parmesan cheese
salt and pepper

Blanch the spinach leaves in boiling water for 1 minute. Drain the leaves, squeezing out any excess water, and roughly chop. Mix the spinach with the grated nutmeg, goats' cheese, crème fraîche and mustard.

Bring a pan of water to the boil, add the pasta, return to the boil and cook for 4–5 minutes, or according to the packet instructions, until tender. Drain well.

Return the hot pasta immediately to the pan and add the spinach mixture, salt, pepper and pine kernels and toss together. Add the parsley and Parmesan and a touch more grated nutmeg and serve while still piping hot.

107 Pasta salad with crab   108 Lemon and basil orzo

Preparation time:	150 g (5 oz) dried rigatoni or other pasta
5 minutes, plus cooling	**shape**
	finely grated rind and juice of ½ lime
Cooking time:	**2 tablespoons crème fraîche**
10 minutes	**85 g (3½ oz) can crabmeat, drained**
	8 cherry tomatoes, halved
Serves: **1**	**handful of rocket leaves**

Bring a large saucepan of lightly salted water to the boil. Add the pasta, return to the boil and cook for 8–10 minutes, or according to the packet instructions, until tender but still firm to the bite. Drain well and leave to cool for 15 minutes.

Meanwhile, mix together the lime rind and juice, crème fraîche and crabmeat in a large bowl.

Add the cooled pasta to the sauce mixture and mix again. Add the tomatoes and rocket leaves, toss together and serve.

Preparation time:	**2 garlic cloves, crushed**
10 minutes	**large handful of basil leaves**
	5 tablespoons olive oil
Cooking time:	**finely grated rind and juice of 2 lemons**
10 minutes	**150 g (5 oz) Parmesan cheese, freshly**
	grated
Serves: **4**	**300 g (10 oz) dried orzo**
	salt and pepper

Put the garlic, basil, oil and lemon rind and juice in a food processor and process until smooth, then add the Parmesan, process again briefly and season to taste with salt and pepper. Alternatively, pound the garlic, basil, oil and lemon rind and juice in a mortar with a pestle, then add the Parmesan, blend well and season to taste with salt and pepper.

Meanwhile, bring a large saucepan of lightly salted water to the boil. Add the pasta, return to the boil and cook for 6–8 minutes, or according to the packet instructions, until tender but still firm to the bite.

Drain the pasta well and return to the pan. Add the basil mixture and toss well to coat evenly. Serve immediately.

COOK'S NOTES Orzo pasta is small and shaped like large grains of rice. This recipe uses flavoursome and simple ingredients – make sure you buy good quality Parmesan as this really makes the dish special.

109 Lemon and chilli prawn linguine

Preparation time:
15 minutes

Cooking time:
10 minutes

Serves: **4**

375 g (12 oz) dried linguine or spaghetti
1 tablespoon olive oil
1 tablespoon butter
1 garlic clove, finely chopped
2 spring onions, thinly sliced
2 red chillies, deseeded and thinly sliced
425 g (14 oz) raw tiger prawns, peeled and deveined but tails left intact
2 tablespoons lemon juice
2 tablespoons finely chopped fresh coriander leaves, plus extra whole leaves to garnish
salt and pepper

Bring a large saucepan of lightly salted water to the boil. Add the pasta, return to the boil and cook for 9 minutes, or according to the packet instructions, until tender but still firm to the bite. Drain well.

Meanwhile, heat the oil and butter in a large frying pan, add the garlic, spring onions and chillies and cook for 2–3 minutes. Add the prawns and cook for 3–4 minutes or until they turn pink and are just cooked through.

Stir in the lemon juice and coriander, then remove from the heat. Add the pasta, season well with salt and pepper and toss together. Serve immediately, garnished with coriander leaves.

110 Tuna lasagne with rocket

Preparation time:
10 minutes

Cooking time:
5–10 minutes

Serves: **4**

8 sheets of fresh lasagne
1 teaspoon olive oil
1 bunch of spring onions, sliced
2 courgettes, diced
500 g (1 lb) cherry tomatoes, quartered
2 x 200 g (7 oz) cans tuna in spring water, drained
65 g (2½ oz) rocket leaves
4 teaspoons pesto
pepper
basil leaves, to garnish

Bring a large saucepan of salted water to the boil. Add the lasagne, a few sheets at a time, checking that it does not stick together, return to the boil and cook for 3 minutes, or according to the packet instructions, until tender but still firm to the bite. Drain and return to the pan to keep warm.

Meanwhile, heat the oil in a frying pan, add the spring onions and courgettes and cook for 3 minutes. Remove from the heat, add the tomatoes, tuna and rocket leaves and gently toss together.

Put a little of the tuna mixture on 4 serving plates and top with a sheet of the cooked lasagne. Spoon the remaining tuna mixture over the lasagne, then top with the remaining sheets of lasagne. Season well with pepper, top with a spoonful of pesto and garnish with basil leaves. Serve immediately.

COOK'S NOTES This is a quick version of the classic lasagne. It doesn't require oven cooking so it can be ready in a fraction of the time. Have fun with the presentation and serve as a quick dinner party dish.

111 Mushroom and mozzarella stacks

Preparation time: **10 minutes**

Cooking time: **20 minutes**

Serves: **4**

2 tablespoons olive oil, plus extra for oiling
50 g (2 oz) butter
2 onions, chopped
2 garlic cloves, crushed
500 g (1 lb) mushrooms, sliced
4 tablespoons double cream
4 tablespoons dry white wine
1 teaspoon chopped thyme
8 sheets of fresh lasagne
2 canned pimientos, drained and thickly sliced
125 g (4 oz) baby spinach leaves, chopped
125 g (4 oz) packet of buffalo mozzarella cheese, drained and sliced
50 g (2 oz) Parmesan cheese, freshly shaved
salt and pepper

Heat the oil and butter in a saucepan, add the onions and cook over a medium heat for 3 minutes. Add the garlic and cook, stirring, for 1 minute. Add the mushrooms, increase the heat and cook for 5 minutes. Add the cream, wine and thyme, season to taste with salt and pepper and simmer for 4 minutes.

Meanwhile, bring a large saucepan of lightly salted water to the boil. Add the lasagne, a few sheets at a time, checking that it does not stick together, return to the boil and cook for 3 minutes, or according to the packet instructions, until tender but still firm to the bite. Drain and transfer 4 pieces to a well-oiled, large ovenproof dish.

Put a generous spoonful of mushroom mixture on each piece of lasagne in the dish, add some pimiento slices and half the spinach and top with another piece of lasagne. Add the remaining spinach, the mozzarella and top with the remaining mushroom mixture. Finish with some Parmesan shavings. Put the lasagne stacks under a very hot preheated grill and cook for 5 minutes or until the mushroom mixture is bubbling and the Parmesan is golden.

112 Pasta bake with spinach and ham

Preparation time: **10 minutes**

Cooking time: **20 minutes**

Serves: **4**

Oven temperature: **200°C (400°F) Gas Mark 6**

2 tablespoons olive oil, plus extra for oiling
1 onion, chopped
1 garlic clove, crushed
750 g (1½ lb) baby spinach leaves, chopped
pinch of freshly grated nutmeg
8 sheets of no-precook lasagne
250 g (8 oz) ham, chopped into large chunks
125 g (4 oz) packet of buffalo mozzarella cheese, drained and thinly sliced
125 g (4 oz) fontina cheese, grated
salt and pepper

Heat the oil in a saucepan, add the onion and garlic and cook for 3 minutes. Add the spinach and mix well. Cook for 2 minutes until the spinach starts to wilt. Add the nutmeg and season to taste with salt and pepper.

Put a layer of lasagne in the base of a lightly oiled, large, shallow baking dish, followed by a layer of the spinach mixture, a layer of ham, then a layer of mozzarella. Repeat until all the ingredients are used up, finishing with a layer of lasagne and the fontina.

Bake the pasta at the top of a preheated oven, 200°C (400°F), Gas Mark 6, for 15 minutes until golden brown and bubbling.

COOK'S NOTES Buffalo mozzarella has the richest flavour and creamiest texture so it's important to buy this variety. It will melt and combine with the other ingredients, while the fontina will create a lovely golden topping.

113 Courgettes with linguine and gremolata

Preparation time:
10 minutes

Cooking time:
12 minutes

Serves: **4**

450 g (14½ oz) dried linguine
2 tablespoons olive oil
6 large courgettes, thickly sliced
8 spring onions, thinly sliced
fresh Parmesan cheese shavings,
  to serve

GREMOLATA
finely grated rind of 2 lemons
1 tablespoon oil
10 tablespoons chopped flat leaf parsley
2 garlic cloves, crushed

Bring a large saucepan of lightly salted water to the boil. Add the pasta, return to the boil and cook for 9 minutes, or according to the packet instructions, until tender but still firm to the bite.

Meanwhile, heat the oil in a nonstick frying pan, add the courgettes and cook over a high heat for 10 minutes or until browned. Add the spring onions and cook for 1–2 minutes.

To make the gremolata, mix together all the ingredients in a bowl.

Drain the pasta well and return to the pan. Stir in the courgette mixture and gremolata. Serve immediately, topped with Parmesan shavings.

COOK'S NOTES Prepare the gremola in advance to make this pasta dish even quicker. Linguine is similar to spaghetti but the strands are thinner so it has a more delicate texture.

114 Risotto with wild mushrooms and sage

Preparation time:
10 minutes

Cooking time:
20 minutes

Serves: **4**

1 litre (1¾ pints) vegetable stock
125 g (4 oz) butter
1 tablespoon olive oil
1 garlic clove, crushed
1 onion, finely diced
250 g (8 oz) wild mushrooms, such as
  morels, porcini, chanterelles or
  cultivated open cap mushrooms,
  halved or quartered
300 g (10 oz) risotto rice
75 ml (3 fl oz) dry white wine
1 tablespoon chopped sage
salt and pepper
125 g (4 oz) Parmesan cheese, freshly
  grated, to serve
truffle oil, to drizzle (optional)

Pour the stock into a saucepan and bring to a gentle simmer.

Heat half the butter and all the oil in a heavy-based saucepan, add the garlic and onion and cook gently for 3 minutes. Add the mushrooms and cook gently for 2 minutes. Add the rice and cook, stirring, for 1 minute. Add enough stock to just cover the rice and stir well. Simmer gently, stirring frequently.

When most of the liquid has been absorbed, add more stock. Continue adding the stock in stages and stirring until it has all been absorbed. Add the wine with the final amount of stock, mix well and cook for 2 minutes.

Remove te risotto from the heat and add the remaining butter, sage and salt and pepper to taste. Mix well and serve immediately with Parmesan, drizzled with truffle oil, if you like.

115 Green risotto

Preparation time:
10 minutes

Cooking time:
20 minutes

Serves: **4**

1 litre (1¾ pints) vegetable stock
125 g (4 oz) butter
1 tablespoon olive oil
1 garlic clove, crushed
1 onion, finely diced
300 g (10 oz) risotto rice
125 g (4 oz) green beans, trimmed and cut
  into short lengths
125 g (4 oz) frozen peas
125 g (4 oz) frozen broad beans
125 g (4 oz) asparagus tips
125 g (4 oz) baby spinach leaves,
  chopped
75 ml (3 fl oz) dry vermouth or white wine
2 tablespoons chopped parsley
125 g (4 oz) Parmesan cheese, freshly
  grated
salt and pepper

Pour the stock into a saucepan and bring to a gentle simmer.

Heat half the butter and the oil in a heavy-based saucepan, add the garlic and onion and cook gently for 5 minutes. Add the rice and cook, stirring, for 1 minute. Add enough stock to just cover the rice and stir well. Simmer gently, stirring frequently.

When most of the liquid has been absorbed, add more stock and stir well. Continue adding the stock in stages and stirring until it has all been absorbed. Add the vegetables and vermouth or wine with the final amount of stock, mix well and cook for 2 minutes.

Remove the risotto from the heat and add the remaining butter, the parsley, Parmesan and salt and pepper to taste. Mix well and serve immediately.

COOK'S NOTES You need to use special risotto rice such as carnaroli or arborio, as the grains are short and plump and can soak up a lot of liquid.

116 Asparagus and dolcelatte risotto

Preparation time:
5 minutes

Cooking time:
25 minutes

Serves: **4**

1.2 litres (2 pints) vegetable stock
1 teaspoon olive oil
1 small onion, finely chopped
300 g (10 oz) asparagus spears, halved
  and the stem ends finely sliced
375 g (12 oz) risotto rice
2 tablespoons dry white wine
75 g (3 oz) dolcelatte cheese, chopped
2 tablespoons chopped parsley
rocket and tomato salad, to serve

Pour the stock into a saucepan and bring to a gentle simmer.

Heat the oil in a large, nonstick frying pan, add the onion and sliced asparagus and cook for 2–3 minutes until beginning to soften. Add the rice and cook, stirring, for 1 minute, then add the wine and cook until it has been absorbed. Add enough stock to just cover the rice and stir well. Simmer gently, stirring frequently.

When most of the liquid has been absorbed, add more stock. Continue adding the stock in stages and stirring until it has all been absorbed. Add the asparagus tips with the final amount of stock and mix well.

Remove the risotto from the heat and gently stir through the dolcelatte and parsley. Serve immediately with a rocket and tomato salad.

117 Nasi goreng

Preparation time:
10 minutes

Cooking time:
10 minutes

Serves: **4**

2 tablespoons vegetable oil
150 g (5 oz) boneless, skinless chicken
breast, finely chopped
50 g (2 oz) cooked peeled prawns,
defrosted if frozen
1 garlic clove, crushed
1 carrot, grated
¼ white cabbage, thinly sliced
1 egg, beaten
300 g (10 oz) cold cooked basmati rice
2 tablespoons ketchup manis (sweet soy
sauce)
½ teaspoon sesame oil
1 tablespoon chilli sauce
1 red chilli, deseeded and cut into strips,
to garnish

Heat the oil in a wok or large frying pan, add the chicken and stir-fry for 1 minute. Add the prawns, garlic, carrot and cabbage and stir-fry for 3–4 minutes.

Pour in the egg and spread it out using a wooden spoon. Cook until set, then add the rice and break up the egg, stirring it in.

Add the ketchup manis, sesame oil and chilli sauce and heat through. Serve immediately, garnished with the chilli strips.

118 Chicken, pea and mint risotto

Preparation time:
5 minutes

Cooking time:
25 minutes

Serves: **4**

Oven temperature:
200°C (400°F) Gas Mark 6

25 g (1 oz) butter
1 onion, finely chopped
150 g (5 oz) boneless, skinless chicken
breast, cut into strips
200 g (7 oz) risotto rice
1 teaspoon fennel seeds
900 ml (1½ pints) hot chicken stock
75 g (3 oz) frozen peas, defrosted
finely grated rind and juice of 1 lemon
2 tablespoons double cream
100 g (3½ oz) Parmesan cheese, freshly
grated
2 tablespoons chopped mint
salt and pepper

Heat the butter in a flameproof casserole, add the onion and chicken and cook for 3 minutes. Add the rice and fennel seeds and cook, stirring, for 30 seconds, then add the stock and peas.

Cover the casserole tightly and cook in a preheated oven, 200°C (400°F), Gas Mark 6, for 20 minutes until the rice is tender and all the liquid has been absorbed.

Stir in the lemon rind and juice, cream and Parmesan and season to taste with salt and pepper. Cover and leave to stand for 2 minutes, then stir in the mint. Serve immediately.

COOK'S NOTES Risotto cooked in the oven is incredibly simple. The final result is not usually as creamy as a risotto stirred over the hob, but this recipe includes a little cream to add at the end to make up for it. Be sure to use arborio or another risotto rice because you cannot achieve the taste and texture of an authentic risotto using any other rice.

119 Jambalaya

Preparation time:
10 minutes

Cooking time:
15 minutes

Serves: **4**

2 tablespoons olive oil
1 onion, finely chopped
100 g (3½ oz) frankfurters or smoked
  sausages, sliced
100 g (3½ oz) cooked chicken, cubed
125 g (4 oz) quick-cooking rice
400 g (13 oz) can chopped tomatoes
200 g (7 oz) bottled roasted peppers in oil,
  drained and chopped
600 ml (1 pint) chicken stock
2 bay leaves
pinch of ground allspice
salt and pepper
chopped oregano, to garnish
soured cream, to serve (optional)

Heat the oil in a large frying pan, add the onion and cook for 3 minutes. Add the sausages and chicken and cook for 2 minutes.

Add the rice, tomatoes, peppers, stock, bay leaves and allspice. Cover the pan and simmer very gently for 10 minutes or until the rice is tender and all the liquid has been absorbed.

Season to taste with salt and pepper and scatter with oregano. Serve with soured cream, if you like.

COOK'S NOTES This Creole dish is a great way of making a quick, delicious meal from the leftovers of a roast chicken. Oregano, which is sprinkled over just before serving, is one of the few herbs that retains its flavour when dried, so if you can't find the fresh herb, use a little of the dried version instead.

120 Beetroot risotto with blue cheese

Preparation time:
5 minutes

Cooking time:
25 minutes

Serves: **4**

Oven temperature:
200°C (400°F) Gas Mark 6

3 tablespoons olive oil
1 red onion, finely chopped
250 g (8 oz) cooked beetroot in natural
  juices, chopped
200 g (7 oz) risotto rice
600 ml (1 pint) vegetable stock
150 ml (¼ pint) fruity red wine, such as
  Merlot
150 g (5 oz) dolcelatte or other blue
  cheese, crumbled
salt and pepper

TO SERVE
50 g (2 oz) rocket leaves
25 g (1 oz) pecan nuts, chopped and
  toasted

Heat the oil in a flameproof casserole, add the onion and cook for 2 minutes. Add the beetroot and rice and cook, stirring, for 1 minute, then pour in the stock and wine.

Cover the casserole tightly and cook in a preheated oven, 200°C (400°F), Gas Mark 6, for 20 minutes until the rice is tender and all the liquid has been absorbed. Stir in the blue cheese and season to taste with salt and pepper. Divide the risotto among 4 warmed serving bowls, scatter with the rocket leaves and pecan nuts and serve immediately.

COOK'S NOTES Vacuum-packed beetroot is best for this dish – it is quick, convenient and gives a wonderful jewel-like colour to the risotto. However, be sure to choose beetroot in natural juice, not vinegar, otherwise the flavour of the dish will be spoilt.

121 Noodle pancakes with stir-fried vegetables

122 Vegetable noodles in coconut milk

Preparation time:
15 minutes

Cooking time:
10 minutes

Serves: **4**

175 g (6 oz) dried wide rice noodles
1 green chilli, deseeded and sliced
2.5 cm (1 inch) piece of fresh root ginger, peeled and grated
3 tablespoons chopped fresh coriander
2 teaspoons plain flour
2 teaspoons groundnut oil, plus extra for shallow-frying

STIR-FRIED VEGETABLES
125 g (4 oz) broccoli
2 tablespoons groundnut oil
1 small onion, sliced
1 red pepper, cored, deseeded and sliced
1 yellow or orange pepper, cored, deseeded and sliced
125 g (4 oz) sugar snap peas
6 tablespoons hoisin sauce
1 tablespoon lime juice
salt and pepper

Preparation time:
10 minutes

Cooking time:
12 minutes

Serves: **4**

125 g (4 oz) dried medium egg noodles
2 tablespoons groundnut or vegetable oil
1 onion, chopped
1 red bird's eye chilli, deseeded and sliced
3 garlic cloves, sliced
5 cm (2 inch) piece of fresh root ginger, peeled and grated
2 teaspoons ground coriander
½ teaspoon ground turmeric
1 lemon grass stalk, thinly sliced
400 ml (14 fl oz) can coconut milk
300 ml (½ pint) vegetable stock
125 g (4 oz) spring greens or cabbage, finely shredded
275 g (9 oz) runner beans or green beans, trimmed and diagonally sliced
150 g (5 oz) shiitake mushrooms, sliced
75 g (3 oz) unsalted peanuts
salt and pepper

Bring a large saucepan of lightly salted water to the boil. Add the noodles, return to the boil and cook for 3 minutes. Drain well. Transfer to a bowl, add the chilli, ginger, coriander, flour and 2 teaspoons oil and mix well.

Meanwhile, thinly slice the broccoli stalks and cut the florets into small pieces. Blanch the stalks in boiling water for 30 seconds, add the florets and blanch for 30 seconds. Drain well.

Heat 1 cm (½ inch) oil in a frying pan. Add 4 large separate spoonfuls of the noodles (half the mixture) and shallow-fry for 5 minutes until crisp. Drain on kitchen paper. Keep warm while cooking the remainder.

Meanwhile, heat the 2 tablespoons oil in a wok or large frying pan, add the onion and stir-fry for 2 minutes. Add the peppers and stir-fry for 3 minutes. Add the broccoli, sugar snap peas, hoisin sauce, lime juice and salt and pepper to taste and heat through. To serve, put 2 pancakes on each of 4 serving plates and pile the vegetables on top.

Soak the noodles in a saucepan of boiling water for 4 minutes, or according to the packet instructions, until just tender.

Meanwhile, heat the oil in a large saucepan, add the onion, chilli, garlic, ginger, coriander, turmeric and lemon grass and cook gently for 5 minutes.

Drain the noodles. Add the coconut milk and stock to the onion mixture and bring just to the boil. Reduce the heat and stir in the spring greens or cabbage, beans, mushrooms and drained noodles. Cover and simmer for 5 minutes. Stir in the peanuts and season to taste with salt and pepper. Serve in deep bowls.

123 Thai fried noodles

124 Stir-fried noodles with mushrooms

Preparation time:
10 minutes, plus soaking

Cooking time:
about 7 minutes

Serves: **4**

250 g (8 oz) flat rice noodles
2 tablespoons vegetable oil
150 g (5 oz) raw tiger prawns, peeled and
    deveined
2 garlic cloves, crushed
1 egg, beaten
1 carrot, grated
200 g (7 oz) bean sprouts
1 tablespoon brown sugar
3 tablespoons Thai fish sauce
2 tablespoons lime juice

TO SERVE
50 g (2 oz) unsalted raw peanuts, toasted
1 red chilli, thinly sliced
4 spring onions, sliced
fresh coriander sprigs
lime wedges

Soak the noodles in a saucepan of lightly salted boiling water for 10 minutes, or according to the packet instructions, until just tender. Drain and set aside.

Meanwhile, heat the oil in a wok or large frying pan over a high heat, add the prawns and garlic and stir-fry for 1 minute. Push to one side of the wok and add the egg, stir until lightly scrambled and then add all the remaining ingredients, including the noodles.

Toss thoroughly until all the ingredients are well combined and heated through. Transfer to a large serving dish, top with the peanuts, chilli, spring onions and coriander and serve with lime wedges.

COOK'S NOTES Although there are a lot of ingredients in this recipe it is still very quick to prepare – the key is to have everything to hand before you begin.

Preparation time:
10 minutes

Cooking time:
10 minutes

Serves: **4**

225 g (7½ oz) dried thread egg noodles
1 tablespoon corn oil
1 large onion, sliced lengthways
1 cm (½ inch) piece of fresh root ginger,
    peeled and finely chopped
200 g (7 oz) field or portobello mushrooms
125 g (4 oz) bean sprouts
2 large red peppers, cored, deseeded and
    thinly sliced
1 tablespoon plum sauce
2 tablespoons light soy sauce
6 spring onions, diagonally sliced into
    1.5 cm (¾ inch) pieces

Bring a large saucepan of lightly salted water to the boil. Add the noodles, return to the boil and cook for 3–4 minutes, or according to the packet instructions, until just tender. Drain, rinse under cold running water and drain again.

Meanwhile, heat the oil in a wok or large frying pan over a high heat, add the onion and ginger and stir-fry for 2–3 minutes. Add the mushrooms and stir-fry over a medium heat for 1–2 minutes.

Stir in the bean sprouts, red peppers, plum sauce, soy sauce and spring onions and cook, stirring occasionally, for a further few minutes.

Stir in the noodles, taste and adjust the seasoning, if necessary, and heat through before serving.

COOK'S NOTES Try to resist the temptation to stir the noodles too much while they are cooking, or they will get very tangled.

5   Vegetarian

125 Chilli tofu kebabs

Preparation time:
10 minutes, plus soaking

Cooking time:
6–8 minutes

Serves: **4**

150 g (5 oz) bulgar wheat
250 g (8 oz) firm tofu
50 g (2 oz) fresh white breadcrumbs
75 g (3 oz) vegetarian bacon, diced (optional)
2 garlic cloves, crushed
25 g (1 oz) fresh root ginger, peeled and grated
½ teaspoon dried red chilli flakes
1 small red onion, finely chopped
10 large mint leaves, chopped
1 egg
2 tablespoons groundnut or soya oil
½ small ripe mango, peeled, stoned and finely chopped
2 teaspoons lime juice
100 ml (3½ fl oz) natural soya yogurt
salt
crisp salad leaves, to serve

Put the bulgar wheat in a bowl, cover with plenty of boiling water and leave to soak for 15 minutes, then drain thoroughly. Meanwhile, soak 8 bamboo skewers in cold water until required.

Pat the tofu dry with kitchen paper. Put it in a food processor with the bulgar wheat and process to a thick paste. Tip the mixture into a bowl and add the breadcrumbs, bacon, if using, garlic, ginger, chilli flakes, onion, mint and a little salt. Add the egg and beat the mixture well to form a thick paste.

Divide the mixture into 8 evenly sized balls. Thread a ball on to each skewer and flatten into a sausage shape. Brush with the oil.

Cook the skewers under a preheated medium grill, turning once or twice, for 6–8 minutes until golden. Meanwhile, mix together the mango, lime juice and yogurt in a small serving dish. Serve the kebabs with crisp salad leaves and the mango yogurt.

126 Nut koftas with minted yogurt

Preparation time:
15 minutes

Cooking time:
10 minutes

Serves: **4**

5–6 tablespoons groundnut or vegetable oil
1 onion, chopped
½ teaspoon crushed dried red chilli flakes
2 garlic cloves, roughly chopped
1 tablespoon medium curry paste
400 g (13 oz) can borlotti or cannellini beans, drained and rinsed
125 g (4 oz) ground almonds
75 g (3 oz) honey-roast or salted almonds, chopped
1 small egg
200 ml (7 fl oz) Greek yogurt
2 tablespoons chopped mint
1 tablespoon lemon juice
salt and pepper
mint sprigs, to garnish
warm naan bread, to serve

Heat 3 tablespoons of the oil in a frying pan, add the onion and cook for 4 minutes. Add the chilli flakes, garlic and curry paste and cook, stirring constantly, for 1 minute. Transfer to a food processor with the beans, nuts, egg and salt and pepper to taste and process until the mixture starts to bind together.

Using lightly floured hands, divide the mixture into 8 portions, then mould each around a metal skewer, forming it into a sausage shape about 2.5 cm (1 inch) thick. Put them on a foil-lined grill rack and brush with 1 tablespoon of the remaining oil. Cook under a preheated medium grill, turning once, for 5 minutes or until golden.

Meanwhile, mix together the yogurt and mint in a small serving bowl and season to taste with salt and pepper. Mix the remaining oil, lemon juice and a little salt and pepper in a separate bowl.

Brush the koftas with the lemon dressing and serve with the yogurt dressing on warm naan bread, garnished with mint sprigs.

127 Smoked tofu and apricot sausages

128 Tofu burgers with cucumber relish

Preparation time:
15 minutes

Cooking time:
10 minutes

Serves: **4**

225 g (7½ oz) smoked tofu
4 tablespoons olive or soya oil
1 large onion, roughly chopped
2 celery sticks, roughly chopped
100 g (3½ oz) ready-to-eat dried apricots, roughly chopped
50 g (2 oz) fresh white breadcrumbs
1 egg
1 tablespoon chopped sage
plain flour, for dusting
salt and pepper

Pat the tofu dry on kitchen paper and tear into chunks. Heat the half the oil in a frying pan, add the onion and celery and cook for 5 minutes. Tip the onion and celery into a food processor and add the tofu and apricots. Process the ingredients to a chunky paste.

Tip the mixture into a large bowl and add the breadcrumbs, egg and sage. Season to taste with salt and pepper and beat well until evenly combined.

Divide the mixture into 8 portions. Using lightly floured hands, shape each portion into a sausage, pressing the mixture together firmly. Heat the remaining oil in a nonstick frying pan, add the sausages and cook for 5 minutes or until golden all over.

COOK'S NOTES This quantity makes 8 small sausages, so you might want to make double the quantity for people with larger appetites. Serve with chunky chips and a spicy relish.

Preparation time:
15 minutes

Cooking time:
15 minutes

Serves: **4**

4 tablespoons soya or groundnut oil
1 small red onion, finely chopped
1 celery stick, finely chopped
2 garlic cloves, crushed
200 g (7 oz) can red kidney beans, drained and rinsed
75 g (3 oz) salted peanuts
250 g (8 oz) firm tofu
2 teaspoons medium curry paste
50 g (2 oz) fresh white breadcrumbs
1 egg
plain flour, for dusting (optional)
½ small cucumber, peeled, deseeded and chopped
2 tablespoons chopped flat leaf parsley
1 tablespoon white wine vinegar
2 teaspoons caster sugar
burger buns and lettuce, to serve

Heat 1 tablespoon of the oil in a frying pan, add all but 1 tablespoon of the onion and the celery and cook for 5 minutes. Add the garlic and cook for 2 minutes.

Put the beans in a bowl and mash lightly with a fork. Put the peanuts in a food processor and process until finely chopped. Pat the tofu dry with kitchen paper, break it into pieces and add to the food processor. Process until the tofu is crumbly, then add the mixture to the beans together with the fried vegetables, curry paste, breadcrumbs and egg. Mix well to form a thick paste.

Divide the mixture into 4 portions and shape into burgers, dusting your hands with flour if the mixture is sticky. Heat the remaining oil in the pan, add the burgers and cook for 4 minutes on each side or until golden.

Meanwhile, mix the cucumber with the remaining tablespoon of onion, the parsley, vinegar and sugar in a small bowl. Line the burger buns with lettuce, add the burgers and serve with the relish.

Preparation time:
10 minutes

Cooking time:
15–20 minutes

Serves: **4**

4 tablespoons extra virgin olive oil
500 g (1 lb) cherry tomatoes, halved
a little chopped basil
12 eggs
2 tablespoons wholegrain mustard
50 g (2 oz) butter
100 g (3½ oz) soft goats' cheese, diced
salt and pepper
watercress, to garnish

Heat the oil in a large frying pan, add the tomatoes and cook for 2–3 minutes until softened (you may have to do this in 2 batches). Add the basil and salt and pepper to taste, transfer to a bowl and keep warm.

Beat the eggs with the mustard in a bowl and season to taste with salt and pepper. Melt a quarter of the butter in an omelette pan or small frying pan until it stops foaming, then swirl in a quarter of the egg mixture. Fork over the omelette so that it cooks evenly.

As soon as the omelette is set on the bottom but still a little runny in the centre, scatter over a quarter of the goats' cheese and cook for a further 30 seconds. Carefully slide the omelette on to a warmed serving plate, folding it in half as you go. Keep it warm in a low oven while you repeat with the remaining mixture to make 3 more omelettes. Serve with the tomatoes, garnished with watercress.

Preparation time:
10 minutes

Cooking time:
20 minutes

Serves: **4**

200 g (7 oz) sweet potato, peeled and
thinly sliced
100 g (3½ oz) fresh or frozen peas
1 tablespoon olive oil
2 shallots, thinly sliced
1 red pepper, cored, deseeded and thinly
sliced lengthways
6 eggs, beaten
1 tablespoon milk
1 tablespoon freshly grated Parmesan
cheese
4 tablespoons chopped mint
pepper
frisée, to serve

Bring a large saucepan of water to the boil, add the sweet potato slices and peas and cook for 5 minutes or until the sweet potato is just tender. Drain.

Heat the oil in a deep, nonstick, ovenproof frying pan, add the shallots and red pepper and cook for 1–2 minutes. Add the peas and sweet potato slices and warm through for a further 2 minutes.

Mix together the eggs, milk and Parmesan in a bowl and season to taste with pepper. Pour the egg mixture over the vegetables, lifting the vegetables slightly so that the egg runs to the base of the pan. Cook over a low heat until starting to set and lightly stir in the mint.

Put the pan under a preheated medium-high grill and cook for 3–4 minutes until the top of the frittata is brown and fluffy. Remove the frittata from the pan, cut it into wedges and serve with a grind of pepper, accompanied by some frisée.

COOK'S NOTES Use a combination of red and yellow cherry tomatoes for maximum colour impact.

131 Aubergine cannelloni

Preparation time:
15 minutes

Cooking time:
15 minutes

Serves: **4**

**4 aubergines, about 250 g (8 oz) each,
    thinly sliced lengthways
olive oil, for brushing
250 g (8 oz) ricotta cheese
250 g (8 oz) soft goats' cheese
150 g (5 oz) Parmesan cheese, grated,
    plus extra shavings to serve
4 tablespoons chopped basil
4 large pieces of sun-dried tomato in oil,
    drained and sliced
rocket leaves, to garnish**

TOMATO SAUCE
**2 tablespoons olive oil
1 onion, chopped
2 garlic cloves, crushed
1 kg (2 lb) sun-ripened tomatoes,
    skinned, deseeded and chopped
150 ml (¼ pint) vegetable stock
1 tablespoon sun-dried tomato purée
salt and pepper**

To make the tomato sauce, heat the oil in a saucepan, add the onion and cook gently, until soft. Stir in the garlic, tomatoes, stock and tomato purée, then simmer until thickened to a fairly light sauce. Season to taste.

Meanwhile, brush the aubergine slices lightly with oil. Cook under a preheated grill until evenly browned on both sides. Drain on kitchen paper.

Mix together the ricotta and goats' cheeses, 125 g (4 oz) of the Parmesan and the chopped basil. Season to taste. Spoon the cheese mixture along each aubergine slice and add a sun-dried tomato slice. Roll the aubergine slices, from the short end, around the filling. Place the rolls, seam side down, in a single layer in a shallow, ovenproof dish and sprinkle with the remaining Parmesan. Place under a preheated grill for 5 minutes until the filling is hot.

Serve on warmed plates. Scatter over shavings of Parmesan and garnish with rocket leaves. Serve the tomato sauce separately.

132 Sweet potato and goats' cheese frittata

Preparation time:
10 minutes

Cooking time:
20 minutes

Serves: **4**

**500 g (1 lb) sweet potatoes, peeled and
    sliced
1 teaspoon olive oil
5 spring onions, sliced
2 tablespoons chopped fresh coriander
4 large eggs, beaten
100 g (3½ oz) round goats' cheese with
    rind, cut into 4 slices
pepper
crisp green salad, to serve**

Bring a large saucepan of boiling water to the boil, add the sweet potato slices and cook for 7–8 minutes until tender. Drain well.

Heat the oil in a nonstick, ovenproof frying pan, add the spring onions and sweet potato slices and cook for 2 minutes.

Stir the coriander into the eggs, season well with pepper and pour into the pan. Arrange the goats' cheese slices on top and cook for a further 3–4 minutes until almost set.

Put the pan under a preheated medium-high grill and cook for 2–3 minutes until the top of the frittata is golden and bubbling. Serve with a crisp green salad.

COOK'S NOTES Sweet potato and goats' cheese are a wonderful combination; they work particularly well together in this quick and easy lunch or dinner recipe.

133 Leek and lentil filo tarts

134 Goats' cheese and tomato tarts

Preparation time:	**1 teaspoon olive oil**
10 minutes	**3 baby leeks, thinly sliced**
	100 g (3½ oz) can green lentils, drained
Cooking time:	**and rinsed**
20 minutes	**25 g (1 oz) feta cheese, crumbled**
	1 egg
Serves: **2**	**6 tablespoons milk, plus extra for**
	brushing
Oven temperature:	**6 sheets of filo pastry, each 15 cm**
200°C (400°F) Gas Mark 6	**(6 inches) square, defrosted if frozen**
	salad, to serve

Heat the oil in a nonstick frying pan, add the leeks and cook for 3–4 minutes until softened. Stir in the lentils and half the feta.

Whisk the remaining feta, egg and milk in a bowl.

Brush the filo pastry squares with a little milk and use them to line 2 x 10 cm (4 inch) fluted flan tins. Divide the leek mixture between the tins and pour over the egg mixture.

Transfer the tins to a baking sheet and bake in a preheated oven, 200°C (400°F), Gas Mark 6, for 15 minutes or until the filling is set. Serve hot with salad.

Preparation time:	**4 sheets of filo pastry, each 25 cm**
15 minutes	**(10 inches) square, defrosted if frozen**
	1 tablespoon olive oil, plus extra for
Cooking time:	**oiling**
10–12 minutes	**20 cherry tomatoes, halved**
	200 g (7 oz) goats' cheese, cut into 1 cm
Serves: **4**	**(½ inch) cubes**
	20 g (¾ oz) pine nuts
Oven temperature:	**2 teaspoons chopped thyme leaves**
200°C (400°F) Gas Mark 6	**salt and pepper**
	green salad, to serve

Lightly oil 4 x 10 cm (4 inch) individual tartlet tins. Brush a sheet of filo pastry with a little of the oil. Cut in half, then across into 4 equal-sized squares and use these to line one of the tins. Repeat with the remaining pastry. Brush any remaining oil over the pastry cases.

Put 5 tomato halves in the base of each tart. Top with the cheese, then add the remaining tomato halves and pine nuts. Sprinkle with the thyme leaves and season well with salt and pepper.

Bake the tarts in a preheated oven, 200°C (400°F), Gas Mark 6, for 10–12 minutes or until crisp and golden. Serve hot with a green salad.

COOK'S NOTES This would make a lovely dinner party dish for vegetarian guests. Filo pastry is light and delicate but very versatile and can used for any number of sweet and savoury recipes.

COOK'S NOTES You can prepare the tarts in advance and then just cook them when you're ready to serve. Try dry roasting the pine nuts for a minute before adding them to the tarts – this will give a rich, smoky flavour.

135 Wild mushroom filo baskets

Preparation time:
15 minutes

Cooking time:
15 minutes

Serves: **2**

Oven temperature:
180°C (350°F) Gas Mark 4

4 tablespoons avocado oil
1 red onion, chopped
375 g (12 oz) oyster mushrooms, stalks finely chopped and tops trimmed
50 g (2 oz) pine nuts
2 garlic cloves, chopped
25 ml (1 fl oz) brandy or whisky
50 ml (2 fl oz) vegetable stock
1 tablespoon soy sauce
4 sheets of filo pastry, each 30 cm (12 inches) square, defrosted if frozen
125 ml (4 fl oz) soya cream
1 tablespoon sweet chilli sauce, plus extra for drizzling
1 tablespoon maple syrup (optional)

TO SERVE
steamed mangetout
boiled brown basmati rice

Heat 2 tablespoons of oil in a saucepan, add the onion, mushrooms, pine nuts and garlic and cook until golden brown. Stir in the brandy or whisky, stock and soy sauce. Remove from the heat and set aside.

Lay a filo pastry sheet on a work surface and brush lightly with a little of the remaining oil. Put a second sheet on top and brush lightly with oil. Cut the double thickness in half and put one half in a diamond shape over the other half, to make a star shape with 8 points. Drape the prepared pastry over a small baking potato wrapped in foil. Brush the pastry lightly with oil and put on a baking sheet. Repeat with the remaining pastry sheets until you have 4 filo baskets. Bake in a preheated oven, 180°C (350°F), Gas Mark 4, for 10 minutes.

Stir 75 ml (3 fl oz) of the soya cream into the mushroom mixture, followed by the chilli sauce and maple syrup, if using. Return to a simmer. Lift the baskets from their supports, then fill with the mushroom mixture. Add drizzles of the remaining soya cream and chilli sauce to each basket. Serve with steamed mangetout and brown basmati rice.

136 Cherry tomato tarts with pesto

Preparation time:
10 minutes

Cooking time:
20 minutes

Serves: **4**

Oven temperature:
220°C (425°F) Gas Mark 7

2 tablespoons olive oil, plus extra for oiling
1 onion, finely chopped
375 g (12 oz) cherry tomatoes
2 garlic cloves, crushed
3 tablespoons sun-dried tomato paste
325 g (11 oz) ready-made puff pastry, defrosted if frozen
plain flour, for dusting
beaten egg, to glaze
150 g (5 oz) crème fraîche
2 tablespoons pesto
salt and pepper
basil leaves, to garnish

Heat the oil in a frying pan, add the onion and cook for 3 minutes. Halve about 150 g (5 oz) of the tomatoes. Remove the pan from the heat, add the garlic and sun-dried tomato paste, then stir in all the tomatoes.

Roll out the pastry on a lightly floured surface and cut out 4 rounds, each 12 cm (5 inch) across, using a plain cutter or small bowl. Transfer to an oiled baking sheet. Use a sharp knife to make a shallow mark about 1 cm (½ inch) from the edge of each round to form a rim. Brush the rims with beaten egg.

Pile the tomato mixture in the centres of the pastry cases within the rims. Bake in a preheated oven, 220°C (425°F), Gas Mark 7, for 15 minutes or until risen and golden.

Meanwhile, lightly mix the crème fraîche, pesto and salt and pepper to taste in a bowl so that the crème fraîche is streaked with the pesto. Transfer the cooked tarts to serving plates and spoon over the pesto sauce. Garnish with basil leaves and serve.

137 Devilled tofu and mushrooms

138 Gingered tofu and mango salad

Preparation time:
10 minutes

Cooking time:
12 minutes

Serves: **2**

½ teaspoon cornflour
juice of 1 large orange
2 tablespoons mango chutney
2 tablespoons Worcestershire sauce
1 tablespoon wholegrain mustard
125 g (4 oz) firm tofu
40 g (1½ oz) butter
375 g (12 oz) large flat mushrooms
**2 chunky slices of wholegrain bread,
    toasted**
salt
chopped parsley, to serve

Blend the cornflour with a little of the orange juice in a small bowl until smooth. Add the chutney, chopping up any large pieces, together with the Worcestershire sauce, mustard and the remaining orange juice.

Pat the tofu dry with kitchen paper and cut it into 1 cm (½ inch) dice. Melt the butter in a frying pan, add the tofu and cook for 3–5 minutes until golden all over. Remove the tofu with a slotted spoon. Add the mushrooms to the pan and cook for 5 minutes.

Return the tofu to the pan with the orange juice mixture and cook gently, stirring, for 2 minutes until the sauce is slightly thickened and bubbling. Season to taste with salt and pepper and spoon over the hot toast. Garnish with chopped parsley to serve.

Preparation time:
**15 minutes, plus
marinating**

Cooking time:
about 5 minutes

Serves: **2**

125 g (4 oz) firm tofu
**25 g (1 oz) fresh root ginger, peeled and
    grated**
2 tablespoons light soy sauce
1 garlic clove, crushed
1 tablespoon seasoned rice vinegar
2 tablespoons groundnut or soya oil
**1 bunch of spring onions, diagonally
    sliced into 1.5 cm (¾ inch) lengths**
40 g (1½ oz) cashew nuts
1 small mango, halved, stoned and sliced
½ small iceberg lettuce, shredded
2 tablespoons water

Pat the tofu dry with kitchen paper and cut into 1 cm (½ inch) cubes. Mix together the ginger, soy sauce, garlic and vinegar in a small bowl. Add the tofu and toss the ingredients together. Cover and leave to marinate for 10 minutes.

Lift the tofu from the marinade with a fork, drain and reserve the marinade. Heat the oil in a frying pan, add the tofu and cook for 3–5 minutes or until golden all over. Remove with a slotted spoon and keep warm. Add the spring onions and cashew nuts to the pan and cook quickly for 30 seconds. Add the mango slices and cook for 30 seconds until heated through.

Pile the shredded lettuce on to serving plates and scatter the tofu and mango mixture over the top. Heat the reserved marinade in the pan with the measured water, pour over the salad and serve immediately.

COOK'S NOTES Use a really chunky, grainy bread for the toast so that it absorbs all the sweet and spicy devilled sauce.

139 Sizzling tofu with sesame greens

140 Marinated tofu with pak choi

Preparation time:
5 minutes, plus soaking

Cooking time:
10 minutes

Serves: **4**

250 g (8 oz) firm tofu, chilled
4 teaspoons sesame oil
3 tablespoons soy sauce
3 tablespoons sesame seeds
4 teaspoons sunflower oil
3.5 cm (1½ inch) piece of fresh root ginger, peeled and finely chopped
2 garlic cloves, finely chopped
2 shallots, halved and thinly sliced
2 x 250 g (8 oz) packs of exotic baby leaves and sprouts, including peanut sprouts, pak choi, Swiss chard and asparagus tips
1 tablespoon rice vinegar

Cut the tofu into 8 slices and arrange in a single layer in a shallow dish. Make diagonal cuts all over the tofu and sprinkle with half the sesame oil and half the soy sauce. Cover and leave to soak for 15 minutes, then drain, reserving the marinade.

Heat a wok or large, nonstick frying pan until hot, add the sesame seeds and cook, stirring, for 2–3 minutes until lightly browned. Remove from the heat, pour the reserved marinade over the top and quickly cover. When the seeds have stopped popping, stir and tip the seeds into a dish.

Wash and dry the pan, then add the sunflower oil and the remaining sesame oil and heat. Add the ginger, garlic and shallots and stir-fry for 2 minutes. Add the baby leaves and sprouts and stir-fry for 2–3 minutes until just wilted. Stir in the vinegar and remaining soy sauce.

Meanwhile, cook the tofu under a preheated high grill, turning once, for 4–5 minutes or until browned.

Spoon the leaf and sprout mixture on to plates and top with the grilled tofu and toasted sesame seeds and serve.

Preparation time:
10 minutes, plus marinating

Cooking time:
about 7 minutes

Serves: **1**

125 g (4 oz) firm tofu, cubed
1 garlic clove, crushed
1 teaspoon sesame oil
1 tablespoon soy sauce
1 red chilli, sliced
1 tablespoon chopped fresh coriander
2 pak choi, quartered lengthways
3 spring onions, sliced
boiled noodles, to serve

Put the tofu in a non-reactive bowl with the garlic, half the oil, the soy sauce, chilli and coriander. Toss thoroughly, then cover and leave to marinate for 10 minutes.

Heat the remaining oil in a nonstick frying pan. Lift the tofu from the marinade with a fork, drain and reserve the marinade. Add the tofu to the pan and stir-fry for 2 minutes. Add the pak choi and stir-fry for 3–4 minutes until tender. Add the reserved marinade and heat through. Serve immediately with noodles.

COOK'S NOTES Tofu is made from soya, which has many health benefits and so is a good choice for vegetarians. Although it has a rather bland flavour, tofu is delicious when marinated and cooked in a stir-fry.

141 Baked polenta with fontina

Preparation time:
10 minutes

Cooking time:
20 minutes

Serves: **4**

Oven temperature:
200°C (400°F) Gas Mark 6

150 g (5 oz) quick-cooking polenta
600 ml (1 pint) simmering water
125 g (4 oz) butter, plus extra for greasing
handful of marjoram, chopped
200 g (7 oz) fontina cheese, grated
salt and pepper

SAUCE
3 tablespoons olive oil
2 garlic cloves, crushed
1 onion, chopped
400 g (13 oz) can chopped tomatoes
1 thyme sprig
1 teaspoon white wine vinegar
1 teaspoon sugar

To make the sauce, heat the oil in a saucepan, add the garlic and onion and cook for 3 minutes. Add the tomatoes, thyme, vinegar, sugar and salt and pepper to taste and simmer for 10 minutes until reduced.

Meanwhile, pour the polenta into the saucepan of simmering measured water and beat well with a wooden spoon until thick and smooth. Reduce the heat and cook, stirring constantly, for 6–8 minutes, or according to the packet instructions.

Remove from the heat and stir in the butter, marjoram and salt and pepper to taste. Transfer the polenta to a chopping board, roll out to 1.5 cm (¾ inch) thick and leave for 5 minutes until set. Alternatively, shape into a loaf shape and cut into 1.5 cm (¾ inch) thick slices.

Butter a shallow ovenproof dish, cut the polenta into squares and line the bottom of the dish with half the squares. Sprinkle over half the fontina. Spoon over half the sauce and top with the remaining polenta. Add the remaining sauce and the remaining fontina and bake in a preheated oven, 200°C (400°F), Gas Mark 6, for 10 minutes until the cheese is golden and the sauce is bubbling.

142 Aubergine and mozzarella stacks

Preparation time:
10 minutes

Cooking time:
15 minutes

Serves: **4**

Oven temperature:
190°C (375°F) Gas Mark 5

1 aubergine, cut into 8 slices
4 beef tomatoes, skinned and cut into 8 slices
250 g (8 oz) packet of buffalo mozzarella, drained and cut into 8 slices
2 tablespoons olive oil, plus extra for oiling
salt and pepper
mint sprigs, to garnish
pesto, to serve

Heat a ridged griddle pan until smoking. Add the aubergine slices in a single layer and cook for 2–3 minutes until the undersides are browned. Turn them over and brown on the other side. Alternatively, cook under a preheated high grill.

Put 4 of the aubergine slices on a lightly oiled baking sheet. Put a tomato slice and a mozzarella slice on each one, then make a second layer of aubergine, tomato and mozzarella, sprinkling each layer with salt and pepper to taste as you go. Skewer with a cocktail stick through the centre to hold the stacks together.

Bake the stacks in a preheated oven, 190°C (375°F), Gas Mark 5, for 10 minutes.

Transfer the stacks to individual serving plates and carefully remove the cocktail sticks. Drizzle with the oil and top with a spoonful of pesto. Serve warm or at room temperature, garnished with mint sprigs.

143 Gnocchi with spinach and cheese

144 Macaroni cheese

Preparation time:
10 minutes

Cooking time:
about 10 minutes

Serves: **4**

500 g (1 lb) ready-made gnocchi
250 g (8 oz) frozen leaf spinach, defrosted
250 g (8 oz) mascarpone cheese
50 g (2 oz) dolcelatte cheese
pinch of freshly grated nutmeg
2 tablespoons freshly grated Parmesan
 cheese
salt and pepper

Bring a large saucepan of lightly salted water to the boil. Add the gnocchi, return to the boil and cook for 3–4 minutes, or according to the packet instructions. Drain well and return to the pan.

Meanwhile, drain the spinach, using your hands to squeeze out all the excess water, and roughly chop. Stir into the cooked gnocchi with the mascarpone, dolcelatte and nutmeg. Stir gently until creamy and season to taste with salt and pepper.

Spoon the spinach mixture into a shallow, heatproof dish, sprinkle over the Parmesan and cook under a preheated high grill for 5–6 minutes until bubbling and golden.

Preparation time:
10 minutes

Cooking time:
20 minutes

Serves: **4**

Oven temperature:
230°C (450°F) Gas Mark 8

250 g (8 oz) dried macaroni
2 tablespoons extra virgin olive oil
1 onion, finely chopped
2 garlic cloves, crushed
2 teaspoons chopped rosemary
125 g (4 oz) vegetarian bacon, diced
 (optional)
200 ml (7 fl oz) single cream
200 ml (7 fl oz) milk
200 g (7 oz) Cheddar cheese, grated
salt and pepper
green salad, to serve (optional)

Bring a large saucepan of lightly salted water to the boil. Add the pasta, return to the boil and cook for 10 minutes, or according to the packet instructions, until tender but still firm to the bite. Drain well.

Meanwhile, heat the oil in a large saucepan, add the onion, garlic, rosemary and bacon, if using, and cook for 5 minutes. Add the cream and milk and bring to boiling point. Remove the pan from the heat and stir in two-thirds of the cheese. Season to taste with salt and pepper.

Stir in the cooked macaroni and divide it among 4 small ovenproof dishes. Scatter over the remaining cheese and bake in a preheated oven, 230°C (450°F), Gas Mark 8, for 10 minutes or until bubbling and golden. Leave to cool slightly then serve with a crisp green salad, if you like.

COOK'S NOTES Ready-made gnocchi make a great, ultra-quick alternative to pasta. For a special occasion, divide the little potato dumplings and the spinach and cheese sauce among individual gratin dishes and grill for 3–4 minutes until golden and bubbling.

COOK'S NOTES This hearty dish includes vegetarian bacon, which is widely available in health food shops and larger supermarkets. It makes a good substitute for the real thing, but for vegetarians who prefer not to eat meat substitutes, the bacon can be omitted.

145 Polenta chips with saffron mushrooms

146 Rice noodle and vegetable stir-fry

Preparation time:
10 minutes, plus infusing

Cooking time:
20 minutes

Serves: **4**

1 teaspoon saffron threads
1 tablespoon boiling water
500 g (1 lb) ready-cooked polenta
1 tablespoon plain flour
2 teaspoons chilli powder
vegetable oil, for shallow-frying
25 g (1 oz) butter
1 onion, chopped
2 garlic cloves, crushed
400 g (13 oz) mixed wild and cultivated mushrooms, halved if large
250 g (8 oz) mascarpone cheese
2 tablespoons chopped tarragon
finely grated rind and juice of ½ lemon
salt and pepper

Preparation:
10 minutes

Cooking time:
10 minutes

Serves: **2**

50 g (2 oz) dried rice noodles
1 dessertspoon coconut oil
1 red onion, sliced
250 g (8 oz) rehydrated soya chunks or tofu
2 tablespoons soy sauce
1 teaspoon finely chopped fresh root ginger
1 garlic clove, finely chopped
125 g (4 oz) cabbage, finely sliced
125 g (4 oz) bean sprouts
8 lychees, peeled, stoned and quartered
1 dessertspoon blackstrap molasses

TO SERVE
nori flakes
sesame seeds
lime wedges (optional)

Put the saffron threads in a small bowl with the measured water and leave to infuse until required.

Cut the polenta into 1 cm (½ inch) slices, then cut the slices into 1 cm (½ inch) chips. Mix the flour, chilli powder and salt and pepper to taste in a bowl and use to coat the polenta.

Heat 1 cm (½ inch) oil in a frying pan, add the polenta chips, half at a time, and fry for 10 minutes or until golden. Remove with a slotted spoon and drain on kitchen paper. Keep the polenta chips warm in a low oven while you cook the remainder.

Meanwhile, heat the butter in a separate frying pan, add the onion and garlic and cook for 5 minutes. Stir in the mushrooms and cook for 2 minutes. Add the mascarpone, tarragon, lemon rind and juice and the saffron and its soaking liquid and season to taste with salt and pepper. Stir until the mascarpone has melted. Serve with the polenta chips.

Soak the noodles in a saucepan of lightly salted boiling water for 4 minutes, then rinse under cold running water and drain.

Heat a wok or large frying pan until smoking, add the oil and then the onion and soya or tofu and stir-fry until golden all over. Pour in the soy sauce and stir to coat the mixture.

Reduce the heat, add all the remaining ingredients, including the noodles, and toss thoroughly until all the ingredients are well combined and heated through.

Transfer the stir-fry to warmed serving bowls, sprinkle with the nori flakes and sesame seeds and serve with lime wedges, if you like.

COOK'S NOTES Cooked polenta comes in rectangular blocks that can be sliced and then grilled, fried or baked. It is made from cornmeal and is used extensively in Italian cuisine.

147 Thai vegetable curry

Preparation time:
10 minutes

Cooking time:
15 minutes

Serves: **1**

1 teaspoon groundnut or vegetable oil
1 small onion, sliced
1 small green pepper, cored, deseeded and chopped
1 small red pepper, cored, deseeded and chopped
3 baby aubergines, halved, or 125 g (4 oz) large aubergine, chopped
3 baby courgettes, halved lengthways, or 1 medium courgette, chopped
75 g (3 oz) shiitake mushrooms
1 teaspoon green Thai curry paste
150 ml (¼ pint) coconut milk
100 ml (3½ fl oz) vegetable stock
1 tablespoon chopped fresh coriander
boiled rice, to serve

Heat the oil in a nonstick frying pan, add the onion, peppers, aubergines, courgettes and mushrooms and cook for 5–6 minutes until all the vegetables are beginning to soften.

Stir in the curry paste and cook, stirring, for 1 minute. Pour in the coconut milk and stock and bring to the boil. Reduce the heat and simmer for 5 minutes. Stir through the coriander and serve immediately with rice.

COOK'S NOTES Thai curries generally take less time to prepare and cook than Indian ones do, so this recipe is a great choice for a quick meal. It's packed full of fresh vegetables so it's good for you, too.

148 Rice pancakes with ginger sauce

Preparation time:
15 minutes, plus softening

Cooking time:
5 minutes

Serves: **4**

SAUCE
1 garlic clove, roughly chopped
5 cm (2 inch) piece of fresh root ginger, peeled and roughly chopped
3 tablespoons light muscovado sugar
4 teaspoons soy sauce
5 teaspoons wine or rice vinegar
2 tablespoons tomato purée
2 tablespoons sesame seeds, plus extra to garnish

PANCAKES
8 rice pancakes
2 carrots, finely shredded
100 g (3½ oz) bean sprouts or mixed sprouting beans
small handful of mint, roughly chopped
1 celery stick, thinly sliced
4 spring onions, thinly sliced diagonally
1 tablespoon soy sauce

Put all the sauce ingredients, except the sesame seeds, in a blender or food processor and blend to a thin paste. Alternatively, crush the garlic, grate the ginger and whisk with the remaining ingredients. Stir in the sesame seeds and transfer to a serving bowl.

Soften the rice pancakes according to the packet instructions. Meanwhile, mix together the carrots, bean sprouts or sprouting beans, mint, celery, spring onions and soy sauce in a large bowl.

Divide the mixture evenly among the pancakes, spooning some into the centre of each. Fold in the bottom edge of each pancake to the centre, then roll it up from one side to the other to form a pocket.

Steam the pancakes in a vegetable or bamboo steamer for 5 minutes until heated through or put them on a wire rack set over a roasting tin of boiling water and cover with foil. Serve with the sauce, garnished with sesame seeds.

149 Mixed bean ratatouille

150 Red beans with coconut and cashews

Preparation time:
10 minutes

Cooking time:
10 minutes

Serves: **4**

**175 g (6 oz) green beans, trimmed and
  halved**
2 tablespoons vegetable oil
1 onion, finely chopped
2 garlic cloves, crushed
400 g (13 oz) can plum tomatoes
2 tablespoons tomato purée
1 teaspoon dried mixed herbs
¼–½ teaspoon sugar
**400 g (13 oz) can cannellini beans,
  drained and rinsed**
**2 tablespoons chopped basil, plus extra
  to garnish**
salt and pepper

Preparation time:
8 minutes

Cooking time:
22 minutes

Serves: **4**

3 tablespoons groundnut or vegetable oil
2 onions, chopped
2 small carrots, thinly sliced
3 garlic cloves, crushed
**1 red pepper, cored, deseeded and
  chopped**
2 bay leaves
1 tablespoon paprika
3 tablespoons tomato purée
400 ml (14 fl oz) can coconut milk
200 g (7 oz) can chopped tomatoes
150 ml (¼ pint) vegetable stock
**400 g (13 oz) can red kidney beans,
  drained and rinsed**
**100 g (3½ oz) unsalted raw cashew nuts,
  toasted**
**small handful of fresh coriander, roughly
  chopped**
salt and pepper
boiled rice, to serve

Blanch the green beans in a saucepan of lightly salted boiling water
for 2 minutes. Drain, rinse immediately under cold running water and
drain again.

Heat the oil in a saucepan, add the onion and garlic and cook for
2–3 minutes. Add the tomatoes and break them up with a wooden
spoon. Add the tomato purée, herbs, sugar and salt and pepper to
taste. Bring to the boil, stirring constantly.

Add the green and cannellini beans to the pan and toss until they are
heated through and coated in the sauce. Remove the pan from the heat
and stir in the basil. Taste and adjust the seasoning, if necessary. Serve
immediately, garnished with basil.

Heat the oil in a large saucepan, add the onions and carrots and cook
for 3 minutes. Add the garlic, red pepper and bay leaves and cook for
5 minutes until the vegetables are soft and well browned.

Stir in the paprika, tomato purée, coconut milk, tomatoes, stock and
beans and bring to the boil. Reduce the heat and simmer for 12 minutes
until the vegetables are tender.

Stir in the cashew nuts and coriander, season to taste with salt and
pepper and heat through for 2 minutes. Serve with rice.

COOK'S NOTES Ring the changes with the ingredients if you like,
using different kinds of canned beans or substituting another fresh
vegetable, such as mangetout or baby corn cobs, for the green beans.

151 Baby squash with red bean sauce

152 Wild rice with feta and orange

Preparation time:
10 minutes

Cooking time:
about 20 minutes

Serves: **4**

600 ml (1 pint) vegetable stock
1 kg (2 lb) mixed baby squash, such as gem, butternut or acorn
125 g (4 oz) baby spinach leaves

SAUCE
4 tablespoons olive oil
4 garlic cloves, thinly sliced
1 red pepper, cored, deseeded and finely chopped
2 tomatoes, chopped
400 g (13 oz) can red kidney beans, drained and rinsed
1–2 tablespoons hot chilli sauce, to taste
small handful of fresh coriander, chopped
salt

TO SERVE
steamed white rice
soured cream (optional)

Pour the stock into a saucepan and bring to the boil. Meanwhile, quarter and deseed the squash. Add to the stock, then reduce the heat, cover and simmer for 15 minutes or until the squash is just tender.

To make the sauce, heat the oil in a frying pan, add the garlic and red pepper and cook for 5 minutes. Add the tomatoes, beans, chilli sauce and a little salt and simmer for 5 minutes until pulpy.

Drain the squash from the stock, reserving the stock, and return it to the pan. Scatter over the spinach leaves, cover and cook for 1 minute or until the spinach has wilted.

Pile the vegetables on to steamed rice on serving plates. Stir 8 tablespoons of the reserved stock into the sauce with the coriander. Spoon over the vegetables and serve with soured cream, if you like.

Preparation time:
15 minutes

Cooking time:
No cooking

Serves: **1**

150 g (5 oz) cold cooked mixed long-grain and wild rice
25 g (1 oz) feta cheese, crumbled
2 tomatoes, chopped
15 g (½ oz) toasted mixed seeds, such as pumpkin, sesame and sunflower
2 oranges

Put the rice, feta, tomatoes and seeds into a bowl and toss together.

Squeeze the juice from 1 orange into the bowl. Working over the bowl to catch the juice, remove the peel and pith from the remaining orange, then cut between the membranes to remove the segments.

Add the orange segments to the bowl and toss well to mix. Serve immediately.

COOK'S NOTES Wild rice isn't actually rice at all: it's the grain of a grass grown in lakes and marshes. It has a lovely nutty flavour and works well when mixed with regular rice.

6 Fish and Shellfish

153 Mullet with orange and olive salad

Preparation time:	3 large oranges
15 minutes, plus soaking	50 g (2 oz) raisins
	¼ teaspoon ground cinnamon
Cooking time:	5 tablespoons extra virgin olive oil, plus
5 minutes	extra to serve (optional)
	large handful of flat leaf parsley
Serves: 4	100 g (3½ oz) green olives
	4 red mullet fillets, about 150 g (5 oz)
	each
	salt and pepper

Squeeze the juice from 1 orange into a bowl and add the raisins, cinnamon and 4 tablespoons of the oil. Leave to soak for 10 minutes.

Remove the peel and pith from the remaining oranges, then cut between the membranes to remove the segments, cutting them in half if large. Put the segments in a large bowl. Pick the leaves from the parsley and add to the orange segments with the olives. Season to taste with salt and pepper.

Brush the mullet fillets with the remaining oil and season to taste with salt and pepper on both sides. Heat a heavy-based frying pan until hot, add the fillets, skin-side down, and cook for 2 minutes. Turn them over and cook for a further 2 minutes. Transfer the mullet to serving plates and leave to rest briefly.

Add the orange juice mixture to the orange and olive salad, toss well and serve with the mullet. Drizzle with a little extra oil, if you like.

COOK'S NOTES This pretty, refreshing dish is perfect for laid-back summertime entertaining. When cooking small fish fillets, always fry them skin side down first to prevent the fish from curling up in the pan. You could also use other fish fillets such as bream or trout.

154 Spiced swordfish with fennel salad

Preparation time:	2 teaspoons crushed coriander seeds
10 minutes	4 swordfish steaks, about 200 g (7 oz)
	each
Cooking time:	4–6 tablespoons extra virgin olive oil
5 minutes	1 large fennel bulb, trimmed
	1 garlic clove, thinly sliced
Serves: 4	2 tablespoons baby capers in salt, rinsed
	handful of mint leaves
	1–2 tablespoons lemon juice
	salt and pepper
	rocket leaves, to serve

Mix the crushed coriander seeds with some salt and pepper. Brush the swordfish fillets with a little of the oil and rub over the spice mix.

Remove the tough outer layer of fennel and discard. Cut the bulb in half lengthways and then crossways into wafer-thin slices. Put it in a bowl with the garlic, capers, mint leaves, the remaining oil and lemon juice. Season to taste with salt and pepper.

Heat a ridged griddle pan until smoking. Add the swordfish and cook for 1½ minutes on each side. Remove from the pan, wrap loosely in foil and leave to rest for 5 minutes.

Serve the swordfish and any juices from the pan with the fennel salad and rocket leaves.

COOK'S NOTES Swordfish is a wonderfully meaty fish, which requires only a short cooking time; if you overcook this type of fish, it can become dry and tough. It's also a good idea to let your fish rest, like meat, before eating to maximize its moistness and tenderness.

155 Grilled snapper with salmoriglio

Preparation time:
10 minutes

Cooking time:
10–15 minutes

Serves: **4**

4 red snapper, about 375 g (12 oz) each, scaled and gutted, heads and tails removed
150 ml (¼ pint) extra virgin olive oil
4 tablespoons lemon juice
2 garlic cloves, crushed
2 tablespoons chopped parsley
1 teaspoon dried oregano
salt and pepper

TO SERVE
tomato, red onion, olive and basil salad
crusty bread

Using a sharp knife, make 4 slashes in each side of each fish. Season to taste with salt and pepper and brush all over with a little of the oil.

Heat a ridged griddle pan until hot. Add the fish and cook for 5–7 minutes on each side until cooked through. Alternatively, cook under a preheated high grill.

Meanwhile, whisk together the remaining oil, the lemon juice, garlic and herbs in a bowl and season to taste with salt and pepper. Transfer the cooked fish to a large warmed platter and spoon over the dressing. Cover loosely with foil and leave to rest for 5 minutes.

Serve with a tomato, red onion, olive and basil salad and crusty bread.

COOK'S NOTES In spite of its simplicity, this dish of red snapper, served with the classic Italian garlic and lemon sauce, salmoriglio, is sure to impress your dinner party guests. Serve with plenty of crusty bread for mopping up the delicious juices.

156 Lemon sole with caper sauce

Preparation time:
10 minutes

Cooking time:
10 minutes

Serves: **2**

2 lemon sole, about 300 g (10 oz) each, skinned
extra virgin olive oil spray
65 g (2½ oz) butter
4 tablespoons baby capers, drained and rinsed
1 tablespoon chopped parsley
1 tablespoon chopped chives
2 tablespoons lemon juice
salt and pepper
steamed carrot and courgette batons, to serve

Spray the lemon sole with oil and season well with salt and pepper on both sides. Put them in a foil-lined grill pan and cook under a preheated high grill for 3 minutes on each side. Transfer to warmed serving plates, cover with foil and leave to rest for 5 minutes.

Meanwhile, heat the butter in a saucepan, add the capers and cook gently, stirring, for 1 minute. Stir in the herbs, lemon juice and pepper to taste, then remove from the heat.

Pour the sauce over the sole and serve immediately with steamed carrot and courgette batons.

157 Salmon trout and shiitake parcels

158 Swordfish with sage crumb

Preparation time:
10 minutes

Cooking time:
6–7 minutes

Serves: **4**

Oven temperature:
180°C (350°F) Gas Mark 4

**4 salmon trout or salmon fillets, about
  150 g (5 oz) each
100 g (3½ oz) shiitake mushrooms
8 spring onions, sliced
75 g (3 oz) butter, cut into 4 cubes
4 tablespoons sake or dry sherry
4 tablespoons light soy sauce
steamed vegetables, to serve**

Cut 4 pieces of foil about 25 cm (10 inches) square. Put a salmon trout or salmon fillet in the centre of each. Divide the mushrooms and spring onions among the fillets and add a cube of butter to each.

Pull the edges of the foil squares up around the fish and drizzle over the sake or sherry. Bring the edges of each foil square up to meet and fold over tightly to seal the parcels.

Transfer the parcels to a baking sheet and bake in a preheated oven, 180°C (350°F), Gas Mark 4, for 6–7 minutes. Carefully open the parcels and drizzle in the soy sauce. Serve with steamed vegetables, such as pak choi, baby corn cobs, courgettes and carrots.

Preparation time:
10 minutes

Cooking time:
10 minutes

Serves: **4**

**5 tablespoons extra virgin olive oil, plus
  extra to serve
2 garlic cloves, chopped
2 tablespoons chopped sage
125 g (4 oz) fresh white breadcrumbs
finely grated rind and juice of 1 lemon
250 g (8 oz) fine green beans, trimmed
4 swordfish fillets, about 200 g (7 oz) each**

Heat 4 tablespoons of the oil in a frying pan, add the garlic, sage, breadcrumbs and lemon rind and cook for 5 minutes until crisp and golden. Drain thoroughly on kitchen paper.

Bring a saucepan of lightly salted water to the boil, add the beans and cook for 3 minutes until tender. Drain well, season to taste with salt and pepper and toss with a little of the lemon juice. Keep warm.

Meanwhile, brush the swordfish with the remaining oil and season to taste with salt and pepper. Heat a ridged griddle pan until smoking. Add the swordfish and cook for 1½ minutes on each side. Remove the fish from the pan, wrap loosely in foil and leave to rest for 5 minutes.

Transfer the swordfish to individual plates, drizzle with the remaining lemon juice and top with the breadcrumb mixture. Serve with the beans and drizzle with extra oil.

COOK'S NOTES You could use any fish you want for this recipe, but salmon trout goes particularly well with the flavours of sake and soy sauce and the texture of the mushrooms.

159 Maple and mustard glazed salmon

Preparation time:
5 minutes

Cooking time:
8–10 minutes

Serves: **4**

2 tablespoons wholegrain mustard
1 tablespoon maple syrup
4 salmon fillets, skin on, about 125 g
  (4 oz) each
450 g (14½ oz) asparagus spears or
  tender-stem broccoli, trimmed
new potatoes, to serve

Mix the mustard with the maple syrup in a cup to make a glaze for the salmon.

Put the salmon fillets, skin side down, on a baking sheet or foil-lined grill rack and spread the glaze over the top. Place under a preheated medium grill and cook for 4–5 minutes on each side, depending on thickness, until just cooked through.

Meanwhile, steam the asparagus or broccoli until just tender. Transfer to 4 warmed plates, top with the salmon and serve with new potatoes.

160 Five-spice salmon with Asian greens

Preparation time:
10 minutes

Cooking time:
10 minutes

Serves: **4**

2 teaspoons crushed black peppercorns
2 teaspoons Chinese five-spice powder
1 teaspoon salt
¼ teaspoon cayenne pepper
4 salmon fillets, about 200 g (7 oz) each,
  skinned
3 tablespoons sunflower oil
500 g (1 lb) choi sum or pak choi, sliced
3 garlic cloves, sliced
3 tablespoons rice wine or dry sherry
75 ml (3 fl oz) vegetable stock
2 tablespoons light soy sauce
1 teaspoon sesame oil
boiled rice, to serve

Mix together the crushed peppercorns, five-spice powder, salt and cayenne on a plate. Brush the salmon with a little of the sunflower oil and dust with the spice mixture.

Heat a griddle pan over a medium heat. Add the salmon and cook for 4 minutes. Turn it over and cook for a further 2–3 minutes until just cooked through. Transfer to a plate, cover loosely with foil and leave to rest for 5 minutes.

Meanwhile, heat the remaining sunflower oil in a wok or large frying pan, add the greens and stir-fry for 2 minutes. Add the garlic and stir-fry for a further 1 minute. Add the wine or sherry, stock, soy sauce and sesame oil and cook for a further 2 minutes until the greens are tender. Serve the salmon and greens with boiled rice.

COOK'S NOTES Fish is the perfect quick dish and it's a healthy option as well. This tasty salmon recipe is ready to serve in minutes, and the glaze will add a lovely colour and flavour to the fish.

161 Pan-fried halibut with papaya

Preparation time:
10 minutes

Cooking time:
about 15 minutes

Serves: **4**

2 teaspoons olive oil
3 garlic cloves, crushed
4 halibut steaks, about 625 g (1¼ lb)
  in total
salt and pepper

SALSA
1 papaya, peeled, deseeded and cubed
½ red onion, finely chopped
15 g (½ oz) fresh coriander leaves, finely
  chopped
¼–½ teaspoon chilli powder, to taste
1 red pepper, cored, deseeded and finely
  chopped
juice of ½ lime

TO SERVE
watercress
lime wedges

Heat the oil in a large, nonstick frying pan, add the garlic and cook, stirring, for a few seconds. Add the halibut and cook for 10–12 minutes until just cooked, turning it halfway through cooking.

Meanwhile, to make the salsa, mix together all the ingredients in a bowl.

Serve the halibut on a bed of watercress, with the salsa and lime wedges on the side.

162 Halibut parcels

Preparation time:
15 minutes, plus infusing

Cooking time:
10 minutes

Serves: **4**

Oven temperature:
190°C (375°F) Gas Mark 5

4 tablespoons orange juice
pinch of saffron threads
4 halibut fillets, about 200 g (7 oz) each
2 tablespoons extra virgin olive oil
3 tomatoes, diced
2 garlic cloves, finely chopped
4 tablespoons dry sherry
4 basil sprigs
finely grated rind of ½ orange
salt and pepper
mashed potatoes, to serve

Put the orange juice and saffron threads in a bowl and leave to infuse until required.

Cut 4 large rectangles of foil and put a halibut fillet in the centre of each. Pull the edges of the foil up around the fish.

Divide the oil, tomatoes, garlic, sherry, basil, orange rind and saffron-infused orange juice among the fillets and season well with salt and pepper. Bring the edges of each foil rectangle up to meet and fold over tightly to seal the parcels.

Transfer the parcels to a baking sheet and bake in a preheated oven, 190°C (375°F), Gas Mark 5, for 10 minutes. Remove the parcels from the oven and leave to rest for 5 minutes. Carefully open the parcels and tip the contents on to warmed plates. Serve with mashed potatoes.

COOK'S NOTES This is an effortless way to cook fish, with the foil parcels trapping all the wonderful juices. Be careful when opening the parcels because the escaping steam will be hot.

163 Grilled sea bass with tomato sauce

Preparation time:
15 minutes

Cooking time:
about 15 minutes

Serves: **6**

1 tablespoon olive oil
1 onion, finely chopped
300 g (10 oz) cherry tomatoes, halved
2 large pinches of saffron threads
  (optional)
150 ml (¼ pint) dry white wine
125 ml (4 fl oz) fish stock
finely grated rind of 1 lemon
12 small sea bass fillets, about 100 g
  (3½ oz) each
1 teaspoon fennel seeds
salt and pepper
basil or oregano leaves, to garnish
  (optional)

Heat the oil in a frying pan, add the onion and cook for 5 minutes. Add the tomatoes, saffron, if using, wine and stock, then stir in the lemon rind and a little salt and pepper. Bring to the boil and cook for 2 minutes.

Pour the tomato mixture into the base of a foil-lined grill pan, add the lemon slices and set aside. Arrange the fish fillets, skin side up, on top. Spoon some of the tomato mixture over the skin, then sprinkle with salt and pepper to taste and the fennel seeds.

Cook the sea bass under a preheated high grill for 5–6 minutes until the skin is crisp and the fish flakes easily when pressed with a knife. Transfer the fillets to warmed serving plates and garnish with basil or oregano leaves, if you like, before serving.

164 Snapper with carrots and caraway

Preparation time:
10 minutes

Cooking time:
15 minutes

Serves: **4**

500 g (1 lb) carrots, sliced
2 teaspoons caraway seeds
4 red snapper fillets, about 175 g (6 oz)
  each
2 oranges
1 bunch of fresh coriander, roughly
  chopped, plus extra to garnish
4 tablespoons olive oil
salt and pepper

Heat a ridged griddle pan over a medium heat. Add the carrots and cook for 3 minutes on each side, adding the caraway seeds for the last 2 minutes of cooking. Transfer to a bowl and keep warm.

Add the snapper fillets to the pan and cook for 3 minutes on each side. Meanwhile, squeeze the juice from 1 of the oranges into a bowl. Cut the other orange into quarters. Add the orange quarters to the pan for the last 2 minutes of cooking and cook until charred.

Add the coriander to the carrots and mix well. Season to taste with salt and pepper and stir in the oil and orange juice. Serve the snapper with the carrots and griddled orange quarters, garnished with coriander.

COOK'S NOTES This dish is all cooked on a griddle pan, which is a really healthy way of cooking, as no fat is used and all the nutrients stay in the food. The orange juice adds a touch of sweetness.

165 Parmesan-crusted cod burger

Preparation time:
15 minutes

Cooking time:
10 minutes

Serves: **4**

1 egg
1 teaspoon English mustard powder
75 g (3 oz) fresh white breadcrumbs
2 tablespoons finely chopped basil
25 g (1 oz) Parmesan cheese, freshly grated
4 tablespoons plain flour
4 cod fillets, about 175 g (6 oz) each
2 tablespoons light olive oil
salt and pepper

TO SERVE
4 crusty poppy seed rolls
mixed salad leaves
1 beef tomato, sliced
4 tablespoons mayonnaise
lemon wedges

Beat the egg and mustard with a little salt and pepper in a bowl. Mix together the breadcrumbs, basil and Parmesan on a plate. Spread the flour out on a separate plate.

Coat the cod fillets in the flour. Dip them into the egg mixture, then press them into the breadcrumb mixture to coat evenly.

Heat the oil in a shallow saucepan, add the fish and cook for 4 minutes on each side until golden and cooked through. Meanwhile, halve the rolls horizontally and toast under a preheated grill.

Fill the toasted rolls with the salad leaves, tomato slices and crusted cod fillets. Serve with the lids on the side, accompanied by mayonnaise, lemon wedges and extra salad leaves.

COOK'S NOTES You can prepare these burgers in advance and keep them in the refrigerator until you're ready to cook. This makes them a great choice for kids when they come in from school.

166 Griddled salmon with a chilli crust

Preparation time:
10 minutes

Cooking time:
about 10 minutes

Serves: **4**

3 teaspoons crushed dried red chillies
3 tablespoons sesame seeds
1 large bunch of parsley, chopped
4 salmon fillets, about 150 g (5 oz) each, skinned
1 egg white, lightly beaten
salt and pepper

TO SERVE
2 limes, halved
boiled noodles (optional)

Heat a ridged griddle pan over a medium heat. Mix the crushed chillies, sesame seeds, parsley and salt and pepper to taste on a plate. Dip the salmon fillets into the egg white, then press them into the chilli mixture to coat evenly.

Add the salmon fillets to the pan and cook for 4 minutes on each side, turning them carefully with a spatula to keep the crust on the fish. Add the lime halves for the last 2 minutes of cooking and cook until charred.

Serve the salmon with the griddled lime halves, accompanied by noodles, if you like.

COOK'S NOTES This Asian-inspired recipe has a bit of a kick because of the dried chillies. If you are serving noodles with the salmon, drizzle over a little soy sauce for extra flavour.

167 Stuffed monkfish with balsamic dressing

168 Lime and coconut squid

Preparation time:	4 monkfish fillets, about 150 g (5 oz) each
15 minutes	**4 teaspoons black olive tapenade**
	8 basil leaves
Cooking time:	**8 rashers of streaky bacon, stretched**
10 minutes	**with the back of a knife**
	125 ml (4 fl oz) balsamic vinegar
Serves: **4**	**375 g (12 oz) green beans**
	125 g (4 oz) frozen peas
	6 spring onions, finely sliced
	125 g (4 oz) feta cheese, crumbled
	2 tablespoons basil oil
	salt

Preparation time:	10–12 prepared baby squid, about 375 g
15 minutes	**(12 oz) including tentacles**
	4 limes, halved
Cooking time:	**mixed green leaf salad, to serve**
5 minutes	
	DRESSING
Serves: **2**	**2 red chillies, finely chopped**
	finely grated rind and juice of 2 limes
	2.5 cm (1 inch) piece of fresh root ginger,
	peeled and grated
	100 g (3½ oz) dried, creamed or freshly
	grated coconut
	4 tablespoons groundnut oil
	1–2 tablespoons chilli oil
	1 tablespoon white wine vinegar

Lay the monkfish fillets on a chopping board and, using a sharp knife, make a deep incision about 5 cm (2 inches) long in the side of each fillet. Stuff each incision with 1 teaspoon tapenade and 2 basil leaves. Wrap 2 rashers of bacon around each fillet, sealing in the filling. Secure with a cocktail stick.

Heat a ridged griddle pan over a medium heat, add the monkfish fillets and cook for 4–5 minutes on each side or until cooked through. Remove from the pan and leave to rest for 1–2 minutes.

Meanwhile, pour the vinegar into a small saucepan. Bring it to the boil, then reduce the heat and simmer for 8–10 minutes until it is thick and glossy. Leave to cool slightly, but keep warm.

Bring a saucepan of salted water to the boil, add the beans and cook for 3 minutes. Add the peas and cook for a further minute. Drain, then toss the beans and peas with the spring onions, feta and basil oil.

Transfer the vegetable mixture to warmed serving plates. Top each pile with a monkfish fillet and serve immediately, drizzled with the warm balsamic dressing.

Cut down the side of each squid so that they can be laid flat. Using a sharp knife, score the inside flesh lightly in a crisscross pattern.

Mix all the dressing ingredients together in a bowl. Toss the squid in half the dressing until thoroughly coated.

Heat a ridged griddle pan until smoking, add the limes, cut side down, and cook for 2 minutes or until well charred. Remove from the pan and set aside.

Keeping the griddle pan very hot, add the squid and cook for 1 minute. Turn them over and cook for a further minute until charred. Transfer the squid to a chopping board and cut them into strips. Drizzle with the remaining dressing and serve immediately with the charred limes and a mixed green leaf salad.

COOK'S NOTES Be careful not to overcook the squid, because they will quickly go rubbery and taste unpleasant.

169 Grilled sardines with tomato salsa

170 Grilled haddock with lentils and spinach

Preparation time:
10 minutes

Cooking time:
3–4 minutes

Serves: **1**

**2 fresh sardines, about 125 g (4 oz) in
  total, gutted**
4 tablespoons lemon juice
1 tablespoon chopped parsley
salt and pepper
toasted ciabatta, to serve

TOMATO SALSA
8 cherry tomatoes, chopped
1 spring onion, sliced
1 tablespoon chopped basil
**½ red pepper, cored, deseeded and
  chopped**

Preparation time:
10 minutes

Cooking time:
about 15 minutes

Serves: **1**

1 teaspoon olive oil
½ onion, finely chopped
pinch of ground cumin
pinch of ground turmeric
pinch of dried red chilli flakes
**125 g (4 oz) can lentils, drained and
  rinsed**
75 g (3 oz) baby spinach leaves
2 tablespoons crème fraîche
**1 skinless haddock fillet, about 125 g
  (4 oz)**
lemon wedge, to garnish
grilled tomatoes, to serve

To make the tomato salsa, mix all the ingredients together in a bowl.

Put the sardines on a baking sheet and drizzle with the lemon juice. Season to taste with salt and pepper.

Cook the sardines under a preheated high grill, turning once, for 3–4 minutes until cooked through. Sprinkle with the chopped parsley and serve immediately with the tomato salsa and toasted ciabatta.

Heat half the oil in a nonstick frying pan, add the onion and cook for 3–4 minutes until softened. Add the cumin, turmeric and chilli flakes and cook, stirring, for 1 minute. Add the lentils, spinach and crème fraîche and cook gently for 3 minutes until the spinach has wilted.

Meanwhile, brush the haddock on each side with the remaining oil. Put the haddock on a nonstick baking sheet and cook under a preheated high grill for 2–3 minutes on each side until just cooked through.

Arrange the lentils and spinach mixture on a warmed serving plate and top with the haddock. Garnish with a lemon wedge and serve with grilled tomatoes.

COOK'S NOTES Sardines are an oily fish so they're packed full of beneficial omega-3 oils. The tomato salsa provides a crisp, light contrast to the fish and can also be used to accompany other dishes.

171 Baked trout parcel with tartare sauce

172 Griddled red snapper with steamed spinach

Preparation time:
10 minutes

Cooking time:
12–15 minutes

Serves: **1**

Oven temperature:
200°C (400°F) Gas Mark 6

1 rainbow trout fillet, about 150 g (5 oz)
finely grated rind and juice of 1 lime
potatoes and green vegetables, to serve

TARTARE SAUCE
2 cocktail gherkins, finely chopped
1 teaspoon capers, roughly chopped
2 teaspoons crème fraîche
1 spring onion, sliced
1 tablespoon chopped parsley

Cut a piece of foil about 25 cm (10 inches) square. Put the trout fillet in the centre and pull the edges of the foil up around the fish. Sprinkle with half the lime rind and juice. Bring the edges of the foil up to meet and fold over tightly to seal the parcel.

Transfer the parcel to a baking sheet and bake in a preheated oven, 200°C (400°F), Gas Mark 6, for 12–15 minutes.

Meanwhile, to make the tartare sauce, mix all the ingredients together in a small bowl and stir in the remaining lime rind and juice.

Carefully open the parcel and tip the contents on to a warmed plate. Serve the trout with the tartare sauce, accompanied by potatoes, green vegetables and carrots.

Preparation time:
5 minutes

Cooking time:
8 minutes

Serves: **4**

4 red snapper fillets, about 175 g (6 oz)
each
250 g (8 oz) spinach
1 teaspoon pumpkin seeds
1 teaspoon sunflower seeds
2 teaspoons olive oil
1 bunch of spring onions, shredded, to
garnish

Heat a griddle pan over a medium heat. Add the snapper fillets and cook for 4 minutes on each side.

Meanwhile, steam the spinach until just tender. Drain.

Mix the pumpkin seeds, sunflower seeds and oil with the spinach. Serve immediately with the snapper fillets, garnished with the shredded spring onions.

COOK'S NOTES This recipe would also work well on a barbecue as the foil keeps the fish intact and the steam helps to cook it. Make sure the fish is cooked through completely before serving.

173 Mackerel with lemon and olives

Preparation time:
15 minutes

Cooking time:
15 minutes

Serves: **4**

Oven temperature:
220°C (425°F) Gas Mark 7

4 mackerel, about 300 g (10 oz) each, gutted and heads removed
1 small bunch of thyme, bruised
1 teaspoon cumin seeds, bruised
2 tablespoons extra virgin olive oil, plus extra for drizzling
1 lemon, sliced
2 bay leaves
125 g (4 oz) black olives
2 tablespoons lemon juice
salt and pepper
tomato, onion and basil salad, to serve

Using a sharp knife, make 3 slashes in each side of each fish. Mix the thyme, cumin, oil and salt and pepper to taste in a bowl. Rub the mixture all over the fish, making sure that some of the flavourings are pressed into the cuts.

Arrange the mackerel in a roasting tin and scatter over the lemon slices, bay leaves and olives. Drizzle with the lemon juice and a little extra oil and season to taste with salt and pepper. Roast in a preheated oven, 220°C (425°F), Gas Mark 7, for 15 minutes until the fish are cooked through. Serve immediately with a tomato, onion and basil salad.

COOK'S NOTES Bruising the thyme and cumin seeds helps to release their flavour. The easiest way to do this is in a mortar with a pestle or on a chopping board with a rolling pin.

174 Roasted cod with prosciutto

Preparation time:
10 minutes

Cooking time:
15 minutes

Serves: **4**

Oven temperature:
220°C (425°) Gas Mark 7

375 g (12 oz) cherry tomatoes, halved
50 g (2 oz) pitted black olives
2 tablespoons capers, drained and rinsed
finely grated rind and juice of 1 lemon
2 teaspoons chopped thyme
4 tablespoons extra virgin olive oil
4 cod fillets, about 175 g (6 oz) each
4 slices of prosciutto
salt and pepper
basil leaves, to garnish

TO SERVE
new potatoes
green salad

Mix together the tomatoes, olives, capers, lemon rind, thyme and oil in a roasting tin and season to taste with salt and pepper. Arrange the cod fillets in the tin in a single layer, spooning some of the tomato mixture over the fish. Scatter the prosciutto over the top.

Roast in a preheated oven, 220°C (425°), Gas Mark 7, for 15 minutes. Remove from the oven and drizzle over the lemon juice. Cover loosely with foil and leave to rest for 5 minutes.

Serve the cod garnished with basil leaves and accompanied with new potatoes and a green salad.

COOK'S NOTES This attractive all-in-one dish is a great quick and easy solution to mid week entertaining.

175 Tuna and warm bean salad

176 Seared sesame tuna

Preparation time:
10 minutes

Cooking time:
10 minutes

Serves: **4**

**4 tuna steaks, about 200 g (7 oz) each
100 ml (3½ fl oz) extra virgin olive oil,
 plus extra to serve
2 garlic cloves, crushed
2 teaspoons chopped rosemary leaves
 pinch of dried red chilli flakes
2 x 400 g (13 oz) cans cannellini beans,
 drained and rinsed
4 plum tomatoes, deseeded and diced
½ red onion, finely chopped
1½ tablespoons red wine vinegar
2 tablespoons chopped parsley, plus
 extra leaves to garnish
salt and pepper**

Preparation time:
10 minutes

Cooking time:
about 3 minutes

Serves: **4**

**1 tablespoon black sesame seeds
1 tablespoon white sesame seeds
1 tuna steak, about 2.5 cm (1 inch) thick
 and 375 g (12 oz)
1 tablespoon sunflower oil
100 g (3½ oz) mixed herb or baby leaf
 salad
6 radishes, sliced
¼ cucumber, peeled and sliced**

**DRESSING
3 tablespoons light soy sauce
3 tablespoons mirin (Japanese rice wine)
1 tablespoon rice vinegar
½ teaspoon wasabi**

Brush the tuna with a little of the oil and season to taste with salt and pepper. Heat 4 tablespoons of the remaining oil in a frying pan, add the garlic, rosemary and chilli flakes and cook for 1–2 minutes.

Add the beans, tomatoes and onion and season to taste with salt and pepper. Cook gently for 5 minutes until heated through. Remove the pan from the heat and stir in the remaining oil, the vinegar and chopped parsley.

Meanwhile, heat a heavy-based frying pan or ridged griddle pan until smoking. Add the tuna and cook for 45 seconds on each side until seared on the outside but still pink in the centre, or longer for a less-pink centre. Remove the tuna from the pan, wrap it loosely in foil and leave to rest for 5 minutes.

Spoon the bean mixture on to individual plates. Slice the tuna and arrange on top with any juices from the pan. Serve immediately, drizzled with a little extra oil.

Mix together all the dressing ingredients in a small bowl and set aside.

Mix the sesame seeds on a plate. Rub the tuna steak with the oil, then roll it in the sesame seeds to coat.

Heat a heavy-based frying pan or ridged griddle pan until smoking. Add the tuna and cook for 45 seconds on each side until seared on the outside but still pink in the centre, or longer for a less-pink centre. Remove the tuna from the pan, wrap it loosely in foil and leave to rest for 5 minutes, then slice it as thinly as you can.

Arrange the tuna on a serving platter, top with the herb or salad leaves, radishes and cucumber, then drizzle over the dressing.

COOK'S NOTES Tuna is best cooked so that the centre of the steak is still pink and juicy. You can cook it for a little longer if you prefer, but be careful not to overcook because it will become tough and dry.

177 Monkfish and prawn Thai curry

Preparation time:
15 minutes

Cooking time:
about 6 minutes

Serves: **4**

3 tablespoons green Thai curry paste
400 ml (14 fl oz) can coconut milk
1 lemon grass stalk, bruised (optional)
2 kaffir lime leaves, torn into pieces
(optional)
1 tablespoon soft light brown sugar
1 teaspoon salt
300 g (10 oz) monkfish tail, cubed
75 g (3 oz) green beans, trimmed
12 raw tiger prawns, peeled and
deveined
3 tablespoons Thai fish sauce
2 tablespoons lime juice
boiled rice, to serve

TO GARNISH
fresh coriander sprigs
sliced green chillies

Put the curry paste and coconut milk in a saucepan with the lemon grass and lime leaves, if using, sugar and salt. Bring to the boil and add the monkfish.

Reduce the heat and simmer gently for 2 minutes. Add the beans and cook for 2 minutes. Remove the pan from the heat and stir in the prawns, fish sauce and lime juice. The prawns will cook in the residual heat, but you will need to push them under the liquid.

Transfer the curry to a warmed serving dish and garnish with coriander sprigs and chilli slices. Serve with boiled rice.

COOK'S NOTES This recipe includes lemon grass and kaffir lime leaves for a real Thai flavour, but if you find a good-quality, authentic curry paste from Thailand, you can leave them out.

178 Mussel and lemon curry

Preparation time:
15 minutes

Cooking time:
15 minutes

Serves: **4**

1 kg (2 lb) live mussels, scrubbed and
debearded
125 ml (4 fl oz) lager or beer
50 g (2 oz) unsalted butter
1 onion, chopped
1 garlic clove, crushed
2.5 cm (1 inch) piece of fresh root ginger,
peeled and grated
1 tablespoon medium curry powder
150 ml (5 oz) single cream
2 tablespoons lemon juice
salt and pepper
chopped parsley, to garnish
crusty bread, to serve (optional)

Discard any mussels that are broken or do not close immediately when sharply tapped with a knife. Put them in a large saucepan with the beer, cover and cook, shaking the pan frequently, for 4 minutes until all the mussels have opened. Discard any that remain closed. Strain, reserving the cooking liquid. Keep the cooking liquid warm.

Meanwhile, melt the butter in a large saucepan, add the onion, garlic, ginger and curry powder and cook, stirring frequently, for 5 minutes. Strain in the reserved cooking liquid and bring to the boil. Boil until reduced by half. Whisk in the cream and lemon juice and simmer gently.

Stir in the mussels, warm through and season to taste with salt and pepper. Garnish the curry with chopped parsley and serve with crusty bread, if you like.

179 Prawn laksa

Preparation time:
15 minutes

Cooking time:
15 minutes

Serves: **1**

1 teaspoon olive oil
½ red pepper, cored, deseeded and sliced
100 g (3½ oz) mushrooms, sliced
1 teaspoon red or green Thai curry paste
150 ml (¼ pint) fish stock
150 ml (¼ pint) coconut milk
100 g (3½ oz) raw tiger prawns, peeled and deveined
2 spring onions, sliced
100 g (3½ oz) cooked rice noodles
1 tablespoon chopped fresh coriander

Heat the oil in a saucepan, add the red pepper and mushrooms and cook for 3–4 minutes. Add the curry paste and cook, stirring, for 1 minute.

Add the stock and coconut milk and bring to the boil. Reduce the heat and simmer for 5 minutes.

Add the prawns, spring onions, noodles and coriander, stir to mix and cook for 3–4 minutes until the prawns have turned pink and are cooked through.

COOK'S NOTES You can make this recipe with ready-prepared cooked peeled prawns, for added convenience, in which case add them right at the end so that they don't overcook but just heat through.

180 Stir-fried tofu with prawns

Preparation time:
10 minutes, plus marinating

Cooking time:
10 minutes

Serves: **2**

250 g (8 oz) firm tofu
3 tablespoons soy sauce
1 tablespoon clear honey
1 tablespoon soya or groundnut oil
150 g (5 oz) spring greens, shredded
300 g (10 oz) cooked rice noodles
200 g (7 oz) cooked peeled prawns
4 tablespoons hoisin sauce
2 tablespoons chopped fresh coriander

Pat the tofu dry with kitchen paper and cut it into 1.5 cm (¾ inch) dice. Mix the soy sauce and honey in a small bowl, then add the tofu and mix gently. Cover and leave to marinate for 10 minutes.

Lift the tofu from the marinade with a fork; drain and reserve the marinade. Pat the tofu dry with kitchen paper. Heat the oil in a wok or large frying pan, add the tofu and stir-fry for 3–5 minutes or until golden all over. Remove with a slotted spoon, drain on kitchen paper and keep warm.

Add the greens to the pan and quickly stir-fry until wilted. Return the tofu to the pan with the noodles and prawns and heat through, tossing the ingredients together, for 2 minutes.

Mix the hoisin sauce with the reserved marinade. Stir into the pan, scatter over the coriander and serve immediately.

COOK'S NOTES Stir-frying is one of the best, and quickest, ways to cook tofu, particularly when it has been marinated in soy sauce for extra flavour. Pre-packed, ready-cooked noodles make a perfect partner, cutting down on cooking time as well as saucepans.

7 Poultry and Game

181 Chicken thighs with fresh pesto

182 Duck with oranges and cranberries

Preparation time:
5 minutes

Cooking time:
25 minutes

Serves: **4**

1 tablespoon olive oil
8 chicken thighs
steamed vegetables, to serve

PESTO
6 tablespoons olive oil
50 g (2 oz) pine nuts, toasted
50 g (2 oz) Parmesan cheese, freshly grated
50 g (2 oz) basil leaves, plus extra to garnish
15 g (½ oz) parsley, roughly chopped
2 garlic cloves, chopped
salt and pepper

Heat the oil in a nonstick frying pan, add the chicken thighs and cook gently, turning frequently, for 20 minutes or until cooked through.

Meanwhile, to make the pesto, put all the ingredients in a blender or food processor and blend until smooth.

Remove the chicken from the pan and keep it hot. Reduce the heat, add the pesto and heat through for 2–3 minutes.

Pour the warmed pesto over the chicken thighs, garnish with basil and serve with steamed vegetables.

Preparation time:
10 minutes

Cooking time:
10–16 minutes

Serves: **4**

Oven temperature:
200°C (400°F) Gas Mark 6

4 duck breasts, about 200 g (7 oz) each
salt and pepper
mashed potatoes, to serve (optional)

SAUCE
2 oranges
50 g (2 oz) cranberries
4 tablespoons soft light brown sugar
1 tablespoon clear honey

Score the skin of each duck breast through to the flesh 4 times and rub generously with salt and pepper. Heat a heavy-based frying pan or ridged griddle pan until hot. Add the duck breasts, skin side down, and cook for 6–10 minutes, then turn over and cook on the other side for a further 4–6 minutes.

Transfer the duck to a roasting tin, skin side down, and roast in a preheated oven, 200°C (400°F), Gas Mark 6, for 5 minutes. Remove from the oven and leave to rest for 3 minutes.

Meanwhile, remove the peel and pith from the oranges. Working over a bowl to catch the juice, cut between the membranes to remove the segments. Put the segments and juice, cranberries and sugar in a saucepan with salt and pepper to taste and simmer until the cranberries are soft. Stir in the honey.

Remove the duck from the pan, cut it into diagonal slices and arrange them on warmed serving plates. Pour over the sauce. Serve with mashed potatoes, if you like.

COOK'S NOTES This quick, cheap dish is great served with fresh vegetables or a spinach salad. If you want to make it even easier, simply buy a jar of high-quality pesto from your usual supermarket. Use a couple of tablespoons per portion.

183 Duck with honey and lime sauce

Preparation time:
10 minutes

Cooking time:
10 minutes

Serves: **4**

Oven temperature:
200°C (400°F) Gas Mark 6

4 duck breasts, about 200 g (7 oz) each
3 tablespoons clear honey
150 ml (¼ pint) white wine
finely grated rind of 1 lime
75 ml (3 fl oz) lime juice
100 ml (3½ fl oz) chicken stock
1 tablespoon finely chopped fresh root ginger
½ teaspoon arrowroot
1 tablespoon water
salt and pepper
steamed carrots and mangetout, to serve

Score the skin of each duck breast through to the flesh 4 times and rub generously with salt and pepper. Heat a heavy-based frying pan or ridged griddle pan until hot. Add the duck breasts, skin side down, and cook for 3 minutes. Drain off all the fat from the pan.

Transfer the duck to a roasting tin, skin side down, and brush with 1 tablespoon of the honey. Roast in a preheated oven, 200°C (400°F), Gas Mark 6, for 5 minutes. Remove from the oven and leave to rest for 3 minutes, then diagonally slice.

Meanwhile, add the wine, lime rind and juice, stock, ginger and remaining honey to the frying pan, bring to the boil and cook for 5 minutes. Blend the arrowroot with the measured water in a cup and add to the sauce. Return to the boil, stirring constantly, and cook until thickened. Spoon the sauce over the duck. Serve immediately with steamed carrots and mangetout.

COOK'S NOTES This makes a dinner party dish that is guaranteed to impress guests every time, and it's so speedy to prepare. Make sure that the duck skin really crisps up without burning before transferring the meat to the oven to finish cooking. The duck should be slightly pink inside.

184 Grilled poussins with citrus glaze

Preparation time:
10 minutes

Cooking time:
about 20 minutes

Serves: **4**

2 poussins, halved, about 750 g (1½ lb) each
50 g (2 oz) butter, softened
2 tablespoons olive oil
2 garlic cloves, crushed
½ teaspoon dried thyme
¼ teaspoon cayenne pepper
finely grated rind and juice of 1 lemon
finely grated rind and juice of 1 lime
2 tablespoons clear honey
salt and pepper

TO SERVE
grilled tomatoes
green salad

Roll the poussin halves with a rolling pin to flatten them slightly. Put the butter in a small bowl and beat in half the oil, the garlic, thyme, cayenne, salt and pepper to taste, half the lemon and lime rind and 1 tablespoon each of the lemon and lime juice.

Carefully loosen the skin of each poussin breast and, using a round-bladed knife, spread the citrus mixture evenly between the skin and breast meat.

Mix together the remaining oil, lemon and lime juice and rind and honey in a small bowl. Put the poussins, skin-side up, on a grill pan and brush with the mixture. Cook under a preheated medium-high grill on one side for 10–12 minutes, basting once or twice with the juices. Turn over and grill on the other side for 7–10 minutes. The bird is cooked once the thigh juices run clear when pierced with a knife.

Serve with grilled tomatoes and a green salad.

COOK'S NOTES Use this recipe for any small game birds, such as quails, pigeons and partridges.

185 Chicken with apple and Calvados

Preparation time:	**1 tablespoon olive oil**
10 minutes	**4 boneless, skinless chicken breasts, about 150 g (5 oz) each**
Cooking time:	**200 g (7 oz) shallots, halved**
15 minutes	**1 garlic clove, finely chopped**
	1 apple, cored and diced
Serves: **4**	**75 g (3 oz) button mushrooms, sliced**
	4 tablespoons Calvados or brandy
	250 ml (8 fl oz) chicken stock
	1 teaspoon Dijon mustard
	small bunch of thyme, leaves stripped and finely chopped, plus extra to garnish
	salt and pepper

Heat the oil in a ridged frying pan or griddle pan, add the chicken breasts and shallots and cook for 4 minutes until the chicken is browned on the underside.

Turn the chicken over and add the garlic, apple and mushrooms. Cook for 6 minutes until the chicken is cooked through.

Spoon the Calvados or brandy over the chicken and, when bubbling, flame with a match and stand well back. When the flames subside, add the stock, mustard, thyme and salt and pepper to taste and cook for 5 minutes.

Cut each chicken breast into quarters and arrange the slices on a bed of the shallots, apple and mushrooms. Spoon the sauce around and sprinkle with thyme to garnish.

186 Venison with cranberry confit

Preparation time:	**25 g (1 oz) butter**
10 minutes	**1 tablespoon olive oil**
	4 venison fillets, about 175 g (6 oz) each, cut from the saddle, tied at intervals with fine string
Cooking time:	**2 red onions, diced**
15–20 minutes	**150 ml (¼ pint) ruby port**
	2 teaspoons tomato purée
Serves: **4**	**200 g (7 oz) frozen cranberries**
	4 teaspoons clear honey
Oven temperature:	**salt and pepper**
200°C (400°F) Gas Mark 6	
	TO SERVE
	mashed potatoes or swede (optional)
	steamed asparagus tips

Heat the butter and oil in a large frying pan, add the venison fillets and cook over a high heat, turning frequently, for 5 minutes until browned.

Transfer the venison to a small roasting tin and roast in a preheated oven, 200°C (400°F), Gas Mark 6, for 10–12 minutes for rare to medium or 13–15 minutes for medium to well done.

Meanwhile, add the onions to the frying pan and cook for 5 minutes. Add the port, tomato purée and cranberries, cover and cook for 5 minutes until the cranberries have softened. Stir in the honey and salt and pepper to taste.

Using a slotted spoon, transfer the onion mixture to the centre of 4 serving plates. Thinly slice the venison and arrange in an overlapping line on top of mashed potatoes or swede, if you like. Spoon the pan juices around the edge of the plates and serve with steamed asparagus tips.

COOK'S NOTES Full of gamey flavour, venison fillets are the most prized of all cuts and take just a matter of minutes to cook. Instead of venison, you can use pork fillets, which should be roasted for 15 minutes in the oven.

187 Venison with blackberry sauce

Preparation time:
10 minutes

Cooking time:
10–12 minutes

Serves: **2**

125 g (4 oz) blackberries, defrosted if
    frozen
150 ml (¼ pint) game or beef stock
2 venison steaks, about 175 g (6 oz) each
40 g (1½ oz) butter
3 tablespoons crème de cassis
salt and pepper
stir-fried green vegetables, to serve

Reserve a quarter of the blackberries and blend the remainder in a blender or food processor with a splash of the stock. Press the purée through a small sieve, preferably non-metallic, into a bowl.

Pat the venison steaks dry with kitchen paper and season generously with salt and pepper.

Heat half the butter in a frying pan until bubbling, add the venison steaks and cook for 3–4 minutes on each side until well browned. Drain and transfer to warmed serving plates.

Add the blackberry purée to the pan with the remaining stock. Bring to the boil and cook until the sauce is thick enough to coat the back of a spoon. Add the cassis and the remaining butter and reserved berries. Heat through, stirring, until the butter has melted and the sauce is rich and glossy. Spoon it over the venison steaks and serve immediately with stir-fried green vegetables.

COOK'S NOTES Tender, succulent fillet or loin steaks are ideal for this dish, although haunch makes a good, if a little firmer, alternative. Fry the steaks for 6 minutes on each side if you prefer them well done. Serve with some stir-fried green vegetables.

188 Oriental duck with roasted squash

Preparation time:
10 minutes

Cooking time:
20 minutes

Serves: **2**

Oven temperature:
220°C (425°F) Gas Mark 7

250 g (8 oz) butternut squash, peeled,
    deseeded and diced
4 teaspoons olive oil
2 duck breasts, about 200 g (7 oz) each
1 teaspoon Thai seven-spice seasoning
2 star anise
50 g (2 oz) frisée
1 tablespoon chopped chives, plus extra
    whole chives to garnish
salt and pepper

SMOKE MIX
8 tablespoons jasmine tea leaves
8 tablespoons soft light brown sugar
8 tablespoons white long-grain rice

DRESSING
2.5 cm (1 inch) piece of fresh root ginger,
    peeled and grated
1 tablespoon rice vinegar
pinch of dried red chilli flakes
4 tablespoons sunflower oil

Toss the squash with 3 teaspoons of the oil in a roasting tin. Season to taste with salt and pepper. Roast in a preheated oven, 220°C (425°F), Gas Mark 7, for 20 minutes.

Meanwhile, mix all the dressing ingredients in a bowl. Brush the duck with the remaining oil and rub with 1 teaspoon salt and the seven-spice seasoning. Line a wok with 1 or 2 sheets of foil, making sure that it touches the base. Add the smoke mix ingredients and star anise and stir together, then place a trivet over the top. Put the duck on the trivet, cover tightly and smoke over medium heat for 12 minutes. Remove from the heat and leave to stand, covered, for 5 minutes.

Put the frisée and chives in a serving bowl, add the squash and dressing and toss to mix. Slice the duck breasts, garnish with whole chives and serve with the vegetables.

189 Duck salad with roasted peaches

190 Venison sausages with spicy bean sauce

Preparation time:
10 minutes

Cooking time:
15 minutes

Serves: **4**

Oven temperature:
220°C (425°F) Gas Mark 7

4 peaches, stoned and quartered
1 tablespoon caster sugar
½ teaspoon ground cinnamon
4 duck breast fillets, about 250 g (8 oz) each, skinned
4 tablespoons extra virgin olive oil
50 ml (2 fl oz) Marsala
2 tablespoons balsamic vinegar
salt and pepper
salad leaves, to serve

Put the peach quarters, cut side up, in a roasting tin. Mix the sugar and cinnamon in a cup and sprinkle evenly over the peaches. Bake in a preheated oven, 220°C (425°F), Gas Mark 7, for 15 minutes or until softened but not collapsed.

Meanwhile, season the duck breasts to taste with salt and pepper. Heat 1 tablespoon of the oil in a frying pan, add the duck and cook for 3–4 minutes on each side. Remove it from the pan, wrap loosely in foil and leave to rest for 5 minutes.

Stir the Marsala and vinegar into the pan, bring to the boil and cook until reduced by half, then strain into a bowl. Whisk in the remaining oil and any juices from the duck, then season to taste with salt and pepper.

Arrange the peach quarters on serving plates. Thinly slice the duck and add to the plates with some salad leaves. Pour over the dressing and serve immediately.

Preparation time:
10 minutes

Cooking time:
12 minutes

Serves: **4**

8 venison sausages
1 tablespoon sunflower oil
1 onion, chopped
1 red pepper, cored, deseeded and diced
1 courgette, diced
2 flat cap mushrooms, sliced
400 g (13 oz) can red kidney beans, drained and rinsed
400 g (13 oz) can chopped tomatoes
1 teaspoon chopped red chilli
1 teaspoon wholegrain mustard
2 teaspoons brown sugar
salt and pepper
crusty bread, to serve

Cook the sausages under a preheated high grill for 10–12 minutes until browned and cooked through.

Meanwhile, heat the oil in a large frying pan, add the onion and cook for 3 minutes. Add the red pepper, courgette and mushrooms and cook for 3 minutes. Stir in the remaining ingredients and bring to the boil. Reduce the heat, cover and simmer for 5 minutes until thickened.

Spoon the bean mixture into warmed serving bowls and serve with the sausages and crusty bread.

COOK'S NOTES Marsala is a Sicilian fortified wine with an intense, sweet herb flavour. It is available from supermarkets and wine shops, but you could use port instead. To remove the duck skin, simply hold the breast fillet at one end and pull the skin away from the meat. You may need to use a sharp knife to help ease the skin away from the flesh.

191 Blue cheese and chicken wraps

192 Chicken and goats' cheese burger

Preparation time:
10 minutes

Cooking time:
18–20 minutes

Serves: **4**

Oven temperature:
190°C (375°F) Gas Mark 5

4 boneless, skinless chicken breasts, about 150 g (5 oz) each
125 g (4 oz) Gorgonzola cheese, quartered
4 sun-dried tomatoes in oil, drained
4 slices of Serrano ham, about 50 g (2 oz) in total
2 tablespoons olive oil
salt and pepper

TO SERVE
griddled asparagus
griddled tomatoes on the vine

Using a sharp knife, make a horizontal slit in each chicken breast. Do not cut all the way through but just deep enough to create a pocket in the flesh. Tuck a piece of Gorgonzola and a sun-dried tomato into each pocket, season to taste with salt and pepper, then wrap each breast in a slice of ham.

Lay the chicken breasts, the join in the ham downwards, on a foil-lined baking sheet. Drizzle with the oil, then cook in a preheated oven, 190°C (375°F), Gas Mark 5, for 18–20 minutes until the ham has darkened and the chicken is cooked through. Transfer to individual plates and serve with griddled asparagus and tomatoes.

COOK'S NOTES These wraps can be prepared ahead of time and popped in the oven just before you are ready to eat. For a slightly milder tasting dish, use brie, Camembert or Cheddar instead of Gorgonzola.

Preparation time:
10 minutes

Cooking time:
20 minutes

Serves: **4**

Oven temperature:
200°C (400°F) Gas Mark 6

500 g (1 lb) cooked chicken breast, thickly sliced
2 tablespoons chopped thyme
2 garlic cloves, crushed
4 thin slices of Parma ham
150 g (5 oz) goats' cheese, sliced
salt and pepper

HONEY-ROASTED FIGS
6 figs, quartered
2 tablespoons olive oil, plus extra for brushing
2 tablespoons clear orange blossom honey
salt and pepper

TO SERVE
4 crusty rolls
75 g (3 oz) rocket leaves

Put the figs in an ovenproof dish and drizzle with the oil and honey. Season well with salt and pepper and roast in a preheated oven, 200°C (400°F), Gas Mark 6, for 10 minutes until the figs just start to colour.

Meanwhile, lay the chicken breasts between 2 sheets of clingfilm or nonstick baking paper and flatten slightly with a rolling pin or meat mallet. Rub the thyme and garlic into the chicken, season to taste with salt and pepper and wrap with the ham.

Heat a ridged griddle pan until smoking. Brush the chicken with oil, then add to the pan, reduce the heat to medium and cook for 8 minutes on each side or until cooked through. Top each breast with a slice of goats' cheese and melt slightly under a preheated high grill.

Halve the rolls horizontally and toast under the grill. Top each base with rocket leaves and a chicken breast. Spoon the figs over each burger and serve with the lids on the side with extra rocket leaves.

193 Peppered chicken skewers with rosemary

194 Chicken fajitas

Preparation time:
10 minutes, plus marinating

Cooking time:
8–10 minutes

Serves: **4**

4 boneless, skinless chicken breasts, about 150 g (5 oz) each
2 tablespoons finely chopped rosemary
2 garlic cloves, finely chopped
3 tablespoons lemon juice
2 teaspoons prepared English mustard
1 tablespoon clear honey
2 teaspoons pepper
1 tablespoon olive oil
salt
salad, to serve (optional)

Lay the chicken breasts between 2 sheets of clingfilm or nonstick baking paper and flatten slightly with a rolling pin or meat mallet. Cut the chicken into thick strips.

Put the chicken in a large, shallow bowl. Add all the remaining ingredients and mix well. Cover and leave to marinate in a cool place for 5–10 minutes.

Thread the chicken strips on to 8 metal skewers and cook under a preheated grill on its highest setting for 4–5 minutes on each side or until the chicken is cooked through. Serve immediately with a salad, such as baby spinach leaves with red onion, if you like.

Preparation time:
15 minutes

Cooking time:
10 minutes

Serves: **4**

1 tablespoon olive oil
1 large red onion, thinly sliced
1 red pepper, cored, deseeded and thinly sliced
1 yellow pepper, cored, deseeded and thinly sliced
450 g (14½ oz) boneless, skinless chicken breasts, sliced into thin strips
⅛ teaspoon paprika
⅛ teaspoon mild chilli powder
⅛ teaspoon ground cumin
¼ teaspoon dried oregano
4 soft flour tortillas
½ iceberg lettuce, finely shredded
guacamole, to serve (optional)

TOMATO SALSA
1 small red onion, finely chopped
425 g (14 oz) small vine-ripened tomatoes
2 garlic cloves, crushed
large handful of fresh coriander leaves, chopped
pepper

To make the salsa, mix all the ingredients together in a bowl and season to taste with pepper.

Heat the oil in a wok or large, nonstick frying pan, add the onion and peppers and stir-fry for 3–4 minutes. Add the chicken, paprika, chilli powder, cumin and oregano and stir-fry for 5 minutes or until the chicken is cooked through.

Meanwhile, wrap the tortillas in foil and warm in the oven for 5 minutes, or according to the packet instructions

Spoon a quarter of the chicken mixture into the centre of each tortilla, add a couple of tablespoons of the salsa and the lettuce and roll up. Serve immediately, accompanied by guacamole, if you like.

195 Chicken teriyaki

Preparation time: **10 minutes**	**750 g (1½ lb) boneless, skinless chicken breasts, cubed** **12 spring onions, cut into 5 cm (2 inch) lengths**
Cooking time: **10 minutes**	**2 red peppers, cored, deseeded and cut into chunks** **2 tablespoons vegetable oil** **boiled rice, to serve**
Serves: **4**	

SAUCE
3 tablespoons dark soy sauce
3 tablespoons clear honey
3 tablespoons sake or dry sherry
1 garlic clove, crushed
3 slices of peeled fresh root ginger

Put all the sauce ingredients in a small saucepan and simmer for 5 minutes until thickened.

Meanwhile, divide the chicken cubes, spring onions and red peppers among 8 metal skewers and brush with oil.

Heat a ridged griddle pan until hot. Add the chicken skewers and cook for 4 minutes on each side or until cooked through. Alternatively, cook under a preheated high grill.

Brush the skewers with the teriyaki sauce and serve on a bed of boiled rice, drizzled with more sauce.

COOK'S NOTES Sake is widely used in Japanese cooking and adds a really authentic flavour, but if you don't have any to hand, you can use dry sherry instead. Try to use Japanese-brewed soy sauce rather than Chinese soy sauce, which has a saltier, less malty taste. You can use bamboo skewers instead of metal ones, but they need to be presoaked in cold water for 30 minutes.

196 Lemon grass chicken with vegetables

Preparation time: **15 minutes**	**18 lemon grass stalks** **8 boneless, skinless chicken thighs** **1 garlic clove**
Cooking time: **5–10 minutes**	**2 kaffir lime leaves, torn into pieces** **2 tablespoons soy sauce** **1 teaspoon sesame oil**
Serves: **4**	**1 red pepper, cored, deseeded and sliced** **1 green pepper, cored, deseeded and sliced** **350 g (12 oz) sugar snap peas** **2 pak choi, quartered lengthways**

Chop 2 of the lemon grass stalks. Put the chicken, chopped lemon grass, garlic, lime leaves and half the soy sauce in a food processor and process until well combined.

Divide the mixture into 16 portions, then mould each portion around a lemon grass stalk 'skewer', forming it into a sausage shape.

Put on a baking sheet, drizzle with half the oil and cook under a preheated high grill for 4–5 minutes, turning occasionally, until golden and cooked through (you may need to cook the skewers in 2 batches).

Meanwhile, heat the remaining oil in a wok or large frying pan, add the vegetables and stir-fry for 2–3 minutes until just tender, then add the remaining soy sauce. Serve the stir-fried vegetables with the chicken.

COOK'S NOTES If you have time, presoak the lemon grass stalks in cold water for 30 minutes to prevent them from burning under the grill.

197 Chicken with pak choi and ginger

198 Chargrilled chicken with coriander salsa

Preparation time:
10 minutes, plus marinating

Cooking time:
about 20 minutes

Serves: **2**

1 cm (½ inch) piece of fresh root ginger, peeled and grated
1 small garlic clove, crushed
1 tablespoon dark soy sauce
1 tablespoon tangerine syrup
1½ teaspoons mirin (Japanese rice wine)
1 teaspoon sugar
pinch of Chinese five-spice powder
2 boneless, skinless chicken breasts, about 150 g (5 oz) each
2 pak choi, halved
fresh coriander sprigs, to garnish

GINGER SALSA
2.5 cm (1 inch) piece of fresh root ginger, peeled and very finely shredded
1 red chilli, deseeded and finely chopped
a few fresh coriander leaves, chopped
1 teaspoon sesame oil
juice of ½ lime
salt and pepper

Mix together the ginger, garlic, soy sauce, tangerine syrup, mirin, sugar and five-spice powder in a bowl. Put the chicken in a shallow, heatproof dish, pour over the mixture and turn to coat thoroughly. Cover and leave to marinate in a cool place for 5–10 minutes.

Meanwhile, to make the ginger salsa, mix all the ingredients together in a small bowl and season to taste with salt and pepper.

Put the chicken with the marinade in a bamboo steamer and steam for 8 minutes. Remove the chicken and keep warm. Steam the pak choi in the cooking juices for 2–3 minutes. Serve the chicken and pak choi with the salsa, garnished with coriander sprigs.

Preparation time:
10 minutes, plus marinating

Cooking time:
16 minutes

Serves: **4**

2 tablespoons dark soy sauce
2 teaspoons sesame oil
1 tablespoon olive oil
2 teaspoons clear honey
pinch of dried red chilli flakes
4 large boneless, skinless chicken breasts, about 200 g (7 oz) each
diced tomato and steamed couscous, to serve

CORIANDER SALSA
1 red onion, diced
1 small garlic clove, crushed
1 bunch of fresh coriander, roughly chopped
6 tablespoons extra virgin olive oil
finely grated rind and juice of 1 lemon
1 teaspoon ground cumin
salt and pepper

Mix the soy sauce, oils, honey and chilli flakes together in a shallow dish. Add the chicken and turn to coat thoroughly. Cover and leave to marinate in a cool place for 10 minutes.

Heat a ridged griddle pan until smoking. Lift the chicken from the marinade, drain and reserve the marinade. Add the chicken to the pan, reduce the heat to medium and cook for 8 minutes on each side until charred and cooked through. Remove from the pan, wrap loosely in foil and leave to rest for 5 minutes.

Meanwhile, pour the marinade juices into a small saucepan, bring to the boil and boil vigorously for 2 minutes, then remove from the heat but keep warm. Mix all the salsa ingredients together in a bowl and season to taste with salt and pepper.

Serve the chicken with couscous tossed with diced tomato, and top with the salsa and the marinade sauce.

199 Duck with cinnamon and redcurrant sauce

200 Thai chicken with cashews

Preparation time:
10 minutes

Cooking time:
20 minutes

Serves: **2**

Oven temperature:
200°C (400°F) Gas Mark 6

2 duck breasts, about 300 g (10 oz) each
1 tablespoon olive oil
1 small red onion, finely chopped
1 garlic clove, finely chopped
200 ml (7 fl oz) chicken stock
200 ml (7 fl oz) red wine
pinch of ground cinnamon
1 tablespoon redcurrant jelly
salt and pepper
Puy lentils and sugar snap peas, to serve (optional)

Preparation time:
10 minutes

Cooking time:
8 minutes

Serves: **4**

2 tablespoons vegetable oil
750 g (1½ lb) boneless, skinless chicken breasts, thinly sliced
4 garlic cloves, crushed
2 large green chillies, deseeded and chopped
1 onion, cut into chunks
1 green pepper, cored, deseeded and cut into chunks
5 tablespoons Thai fish sauce
2 tablespoons dark soy sauce
2 tablespoons soft light brown sugar

TO SERVE
25 g (1 oz) cashew nuts, toasted
15 g (½ oz) Thai basil or fresh coriander leaves
boiled rice

Score the skin of each duck breast through to the flesh 4 times and rub generously with salt and pepper. Heat a heavy-based frying pan or ridged griddle pan until hot. Add the duck breasts, skin side down, and cook for 2–3 minutes. Turn over and brown the other side.

Transfer the duck to a roasting tin and roast in a preheated oven, 200°C (400°F), Gas Mark 6, for 15 minutes or until cooked through.

Meanwhile, heat the oil in a nonstick frying pan, add the onion and garlic and cook for 2–3 minutes. Add the stock, wine and cinnamon and bring to the boil. Leave the sauce to bubble for 10 minutes or until reduced by half. Strain the sauce and discard the onion. Season to taste with pepper and stir in the redcurrant jelly.

Thickly slice the duck and transfer to 2 warmed plates. Spoon over a little of the sauce and serve with Puy lentils and sugar snap peas, if you like.

Heat the oil in a wok or large frying pan until smoking. Add the chicken, garlic and chillies and stir-fry for 1 minute. Add the onion and green pepper and stir-fry for a further 5 minutes until the chicken is cooked through.

Add the fish sauce, soy sauce and sugar and mix well. Bring to the boil, then transfer to a warmed serving dish. Scatter with the cashew nuts and basil or coriander, and serve with boiled rice.

COOK'S NOTES Duck and redcurrant is a classic combination, with the tart flavour of the berries complementing the rich duck meat. Use real chicken stock for the sauce and a good red wine, as this will make all the difference.

COOK'S NOTES To make this simple Thai stir-fry, look out for Thai sweet, or holy, basil leaves, which have a slightly spicy aniseed flavour. If you can't find them, you can use fresh coriander leaves instead.

8 Meat

201 Lamb cutlets with anchovies

202 Meatballs with fresh tomato sauce

Preparation time:
**10 minutes, plus
marinating**

Cooking time:
10 minutes

Serves: **4**

**finely grated rind and juice of ½ lemon
2 garlic cloves, crushed
2 tablespoons extra virgin olive oil, plus
    extra for brushing
4 rosemary sprigs, finely chopped
4 anchovy fillets in oil, drained and finely
    chopped
2 tablespoons lemon cordial
12 lamb cutlets, about 40 g (1½ oz) each
salt and pepper**

TO SERVE
**rocket leaves
sweet potato skins (optional – see Cook's
    Notes)**

Mix together the lemon rind and juice, garlic, oil, rosemary, anchovies and lemon cordial in a bowl. Add the lamb cutlets, season to taste with salt and pepper and turn to coat thoroughly. Cover and leave to marinate in a cool place for 10 minutes.

Cook the lamb cutlets under a preheated high grill for 3–5 minutes on each side or until charred and cooked through. Remove from the heat, keep warm and leave to rest for 5 minutes. Serve the cutlets with rocket leaves and sweet potato skins, if you like.

Preparation time:
10 minutes

Cooking time:
8–10 minutes

Serves: **1**

**125 g (4 oz) lean minced pork
1 teaspoon pesto
pinch of dried red chilli flakes
a little beaten egg
75 g (3 oz) dried pasta, such as fusilli or
    rigatoni
1 teaspoon olive oil
100 g (3½ oz) cherry tomatoes, halved
handful of basil, torn
salt and pepper**

Mix together the minced pork, pesto, chilli flakes and salt and pepper to taste in a bowl. Mix in enough beaten egg to bind the mixture.

Bring a large saucepan of water to the boil. Add the pasta, return to the boil and cook for 8–10 minutes, or according to the packet instructions, until tender but still firm to the bite.

Meanwhile, heat the oil in a nonstick frying pan. Shape the meat mixture into 8 small, evenly sized balls. Add the meatballs to the pan and cook for 4–5 minutes until browned all over and cooked through.

Drain the pasta thoroughly. Toss with the tomatoes, basil and meatballs and serve immediately.

COOK'S NOTES These lamb cutlets are delicious served with sweet potato skins, which are easy to make. Simply bake 4 sweet potatoes in their skins in a preheated oven, 200°C (400°F), Gas Mark 6, for about 45–60 minutes, depending on size, until soft. Quarter, scoop out some of the flesh and brush the skins with oil. Season to taste with salt and pepper and cook under a preheated high grill until crisp.

203 Cheesy pork with parsnip purée

204 Calves' liver with leeks and beans

Preparation time: **10 minutes**	**4 lean pork steaks, about 125 g (4 oz)** **each** **1 teaspoon olive oil**
Cooking time: **20 minutes**	**50 g (2 oz) crumbly cheese, such as** **Wensleydale or Cheshire, crumbled** **½ tablespoon chopped sage**
Serves: **4**	**75 g (3 oz) fresh granary breadcrumbs** **1 egg yolk, beaten**
Oven temperature: **200°C (400°F) Gas Mark 6**	**steamed green beans or cabbage, to** **serve**

PARSNIP PURÉE
625 g (1¼ lb) parsnips, chopped
2 garlic cloves
3 tablespoons crème fraîche
pepper

Season the pork steaks with plenty of pepper. Heat the oil in a nonstick frying pan, add the pork steaks and cook for 2 minutes on each side until browned, then transfer to an ovenproof dish.

Mix together the cheese, sage, breadcrumbs and egg yolk in a bowl. Divide the mixture into 4 and use it to top each of the pork steaks, pressing down gently. Cook in a preheated oven, 200°C (400°F), Gas Mark 6, for 12–15 minutes until the topping is golden.

Meanwhile, bring a large saucepan of water to the boil, add the parsnips and garlic and cook for 10–12 minutes until tender. Drain and mash with the crème fraîche and plenty of pepper, then serve with the pork steaks and some steamed green beans or cabbage.

COOK'S NOTES This is a quick and nutritious recipe that is ideal for a family meal. The cheesy breadcrumb topping would also work well on cod or salmon steaks – just substitute chopped parsley for the sage.

Preparation time: **10 minutes**	**1 piece of calves' liver, about 125 g (4 oz)** **1 tablespoon seasoned flour** **1 teaspoon olive oil**
Cooking time: **10 minutes**	**4 baby leeks or 1 large leek, sliced** **1 rasher of lean back bacon, chopped** **125 g (4 oz) can cannellini beans, drained** **and rinsed**
Serves: **1**	**1 tablespoon crème fraîche** **pepper** **1 tablespoon chopped parsley or thyme,** **to garnish** **green salad, to serve**

Lightly coat the liver in the seasoned flour. Heat half the oil in a nonstick frying pan, add the liver and cook for 2 minutes on each side or until cooked to your liking. Remove from the pan to a warmed serving plate and keep warm in a low oven.

Heat the remaining oil in the frying pan, add the leeks and bacon and cook for 3–4 minutes.

Stir in the beans and crème fraîche, season to taste with pepper and heat through. Serve with the liver, garnished with the parsley or thyme, accompanied by a green salad.

205 Lamb with hummus and tortillas

206 Minty lamb kebabs

Preparation time:
10 minutes, plus marinating

Cooking time:
5–10 minutes

Serves: **4**

500 g (1 lb) fillet of lamb, cut into 1.5 cm (¾ inch) thick slices
finely grated rind and juice of 1 lemon
1 rosemary sprig, chopped
3 mixed peppers, cored, deseeded and chopped
1 small aubergine, sliced
4 soft flour tortillas
rocket leaves, to serve

HUMMUS
400 g (13 oz) can chickpeas, drained and rinsed
2 tablespoons Greek yogurt
2 tablespoons lemon juice
1 tablespoon chopped parsley

Put the lamb, lemon rind and juice, rosemary and peppers in a non-metallic bowl and stir well. Cover and leave to marinate in a cool place for 10 minutes.

Heat a large, heavy-based frying pan or ridged griddle pan until smoking. Add the lamb and pepper mixture and the aubergine and cook, turning once or twice, for 3–4 minutes until the lamb is cooked through (you may need to do this in 2 batches).

Meanwhile, put all the hummus ingredients in a blender or food processor and blend for 30 seconds, then spoon into a bowl. Wrap the tortillas in foil and warm in the oven for 5 minutes, or according to the packet instructions.

When the lamb and vegetables are cooked, wrap in the tortillas with the hummus and serve with rocket leaves.

Preparation time:
10 minutes, plus marinating

Cooking time:
8–10 minutes

Serves: **4**

1 garlic clove, crushed
2 tablespoons chopped mint
1 tablespoon mint sauce
150 ml (¼ pint) low-fat natural yogurt
350 g (12 oz) lean lamb, cubed
2 small onions, cut into wedges
1 green pepper, cored, deseeded and cut into wedges

TO SERVE
green salad
couscous
lemon wedges (optional)

Mix together the garlic, mint, mint sauce and yogurt in a bowl. Add the lamb and stir well. Cover and leave to marinate in a cool place for 10 minutes.

Thread the lamb and onion and pepper wedges on to 8 metal skewers and cook under a preheated high grill for 8–10 minutes until cooked through.

Serve immediately with green salad, couscous and lemon wedges, if you like.

COOK'S NOTES If you have more time, allow the lamb to marinate for an hour in the fridge to absorb more of the flavours. The kebabs can be cooked on the barbecue in summer. The metal skewers help to cook the meat through, but always check it's thoroughly cooked before serving.

207 Lamb cutlets with herb crust

Preparation time:
10 minutes

Cooking time:
15 minutes

Serves: **4**

Oven temperature:
200°C (400°F) Gas Mark 6

12 lean lamb cutlets, about 40 g (1½ oz) each
2 tablespoons pesto
3 tablespoons fresh granary breadcrumbs
1 tablespoon chopped walnuts, toasted
1 teaspoon olive oil
2 garlic cloves, crushed
625 g (1¼ lb) greens, finely shredded and blanched

TO SERVE
baby carrots
cabbage

Heat a large nonstick frying pan or ridged griddle pan until smoking. Add the lamb cutlets and cook for 1 minute on each side, then transfer them to a baking sheet.

Mix together the pesto, breadcrumbs and walnuts in a small bowl and use to top each of the cutlets, pressing down gently. Cook in a preheated oven, 200°C (400°F), Gas Mark 6, for 10–12 minutes.

Meanwhile, heat the oil in a wok or large frying pan, add the garlic and stir-fry for 1 minute, then add the greens and stir-fry for 3–4 minutes until tender.

Serve the stir-fried greens with the lamb, accompanied by baby carrots and cabbage.

208 Peppered lamb with yogurt dressing

Preparation time:
10 minutes

Cooking time:
6–8 minutes

Serves: **4**

2 teaspoons pepper
2 teaspoons salt
2 teaspoons ground cumin
2 lamb loin fillets, about 250 g (8 oz) each
extra virgin olive oil, for brushing
75 g (3 oz) watercress
250 g (8 oz) cooked beetroot in natural juices, drained and chopped

MINT YOGURT
125 ml (4 fl oz) Greek yogurt
1 tablespoon chopped mint

DRESSING
1 tablespoon walnut oil
1 teaspoon white wine vinegar
salt and pepper

Mix together the pepper, salt and cumin on a plate. Brush the lamb loins with oil, then press into the spice mixture to coat evenly.

Heat a heavy-based frying pan until hot. Add the lamb loins and cook for 3–4 minutes on each side. Remove them from the pan, wrap loosely in foil and leave to rest for 5 minutes.

Meanwhile, mix together the yogurt and mint in a small bowl and season to taste with salt and pepper. Mix together the watercress and beetroot in a large bowl. Whisk together the dressing ingredients in another small bowl and season to taste with salt and pepper, add to the salad ingredients and toss to coat evenly. Slice the lamb and serve with the salad and the yogurt dressing.

COOK'S NOTES The meat used in this dish comes from the eye fillet, or tenderloin, which runs along the back of the lamb and is particularly sweet and tender.

209 Gammon steaks with creamy lentils

Preparation time: **5 minutes**	**125 g (4 oz) Puy lentils** **50 g (2 oz) butter** **2 shallots, peeled but left whole**
Cooking time: **25 minutes**	**1 garlic clove, chopped** **2 thyme sprigs, crushed, plus extra** **leaves to garnish** **1 teaspoon cumin seeds**
Serves: **4**	**4 teaspoons Dijon mustard** **2 teaspoons clear honey** **4 gammon steaks, about 175 g (6 oz) each** **125 ml (4 fl oz) dry cider** **75 ml (3 fl oz) single cream** **salt and pepper**

Put the lentils in a saucepan and cover with cold water. Bring to the boil, then reduce the heat and simmer for 20 minutes.

Meanwhile, heat the butter in a frying pan, add the shallots, garlic, thyme and cumin and cook for 10 minutes until the shallots are soft and golden.

Blend the mustard and honey together in a cup and season to taste with salt and pepper. Brush the mixture over the gammon steaks. Cook under a preheated high grill for 3 minutes on each side until golden and cooked through. Keep warm.

Drain the lentils and add to the shallot mixture. Add the cider, bring to the boil and cook until reduced to about 4 tablespoons. Stir in the cream, heat through briefly and season to taste with salt and pepper. Serve with the gammon steaks, garnished with thyme leaves.

210 Chorizo and chickpea stew

Preparation time: **5 minutes**	**500 g (1 lb) new potatoes** **1 teaspoon olive oil** **2 red onions, chopped**

Cooking time:
25 minutes
	2 red peppers, cored, deseeded and
	   chopped
	100 g (3½ oz) chorizo sausage, thinly
	   sliced

Serves: **4**	**500 g (1 lb) plum tomatoes, chopped, or a**
	   400 g (13 oz) can tomatoes, drained
	400 g (13 oz) can chickpeas, drained and
	   rinsed
	2 tablespoons chopped parsley
	crusty bread, to serve

Bring a saucepan of water to the boil. Add the potatoes and cook for 12–15 minutes until tender. Drain, then slice.

Meanwhile, heat the oil in a large frying pan, add the onions and red peppers and cook for 3–4 minutes. Add the chorizo and cook for 2 minutes.

Add the potato slices, tomatoes and chickpeas and bring to the boil. Reduce the heat and simmer for 10 minutes. Scatter over the parsley and serve with some crusty bread to mop up all the juices.

COOK'S NOTES This chunky stew is based on hearty rustic Italian recipes. The chorizo sausage provides a wonderfully rich flavour, while the chickpeas make it a filling meal. Use fresh crusty bread to mop up the delicious juices.

211 Roast pork with rosemary and fennel

212 Polenta pork with parsnip mash

Preparation time:
5 minutes

Cooking time:
25 minutes

Serves: **4**

Oven temperature:
230°C (450°F) Gas Mark 8

**1 large rosemary sprig, plus extra sprigs
  to garnish
3 garlic cloves, peeled
750 g (1½ lb) pork fillet
4 tablespoons olive oil
2 fennel bulbs, trimmed and cut into
  wedges, central core removed
150 ml (¼ pint) white wine
75 g (3 oz) mascarpone cheese
salt and pepper**

Break the rosemary sprig into short lengths and cut the garlic into slices. Pierce the pork with a sharp knife and insert the pieces of rosemary and garlic evenly all over the fillet. Heat half the oil in a frying pan, add the pork and cook for 5 minutes or until browned all over.

Lightly brush a roasting tin with some of the remaining oil, add the fennel and drizzle with the remaining oil. Put the pork on top and season well with salt and pepper. Roast in a preheated oven, 230°C (450°F), Gas Mark 8, for 20 minutes.

Meanwhile, pour the wine into the frying pan, bring to the boil and cook until reduced by half. Stir in the mascarpone and salt and pepper to taste.

Cut the pork into slices and arrange on a warmed serving dish with the fennel. Pour the sauce into the roasting tin and stir with a wooden spatula to scrape up any sediment from the tin, then spoon over the pork and fennel. Serve immediately, garnished with rosemary sprigs.

Preparation time:
10 minutes

Cooking time:
15 minutes

Serves: **1**

**1 small lean boneless pork chop, about
  125 g (4 oz)
1 teaspoon seasoned flour
a little beaten egg
2 tablespoons quick-cooking polenta
1 tablespoon freshly grated Parmesan
  cheese
1 teaspoon vegetable oil
2 parsnips, chopped
1 garlic clove, peeled but left whole
1 teaspoon chopped thyme
15 g (½ oz) butter or margarine
pepper
lemon wedges, to garnish
Savoy cabbage, to serve**

Lightly coat the pork chop in the seasoned flour, then dip in the beaten egg. Mix the polenta and Parmesan together on a plate, then press the chop into the mixture to evenly coat.

Heat the oil in a nonstick frying pan, add the chop and cook for 5–6 minutes on each side or until cooked through. Remove from the pan to a warmed serving plate and keep warm.

Meanwhile, bring a saucepan of water to the boil, add the parsnips and garlic and cook for 12–15 minutes. Drain and mash with the thyme and butter or margarine, then season well with pepper.

Serve the chop with the parsnip mash and Savoy cabbage, garnished with lemon wedges.

COOK'S NOTES Try preparing this recipe for a quick and delicious Sunday lunch. The meat is infused with the rosemary and garlic and the sauce makes a lovely alternative to the traditional gravy.

213 Lamb with tangy butter beans

214 Lamb noisettes with leeks

Preparation time:
10 minutes

Cooking time:
10 minutes

Serves: **4**

2 tablespoons finely chopped mint
1 tablespoon finely chopped thyme
1 tablespoon finely chopped oregano
½ tablespoon finely chopped rosemary
4 teaspoons wholegrain mustard
4 lamb noisettes, about 125 g (4 oz) each
mixed salad leaves, to serve (optional)

TANGY BUTTER BEANS
2 teaspoons vegetable oil
1 onion, chopped
1 tablespoon tomato purée
50 ml (2 fl oz) pineapple juice
2 tablespoons lemon juice
a few drops of Tabasco sauce
250 g (8 oz) drained canned butter beans
pepper

Mix together all the chopped herbs on a plate. Spread mustard on both sides of each noisette, then press into the herb mixture to coat evenly.

To make the tangy butter beans, heat the oil in a frying pan, add the onion and cook for 5 minutes. Add the remaining ingredients to the pan and cook gently for 5 minutes.

Meanwhile, cook the lamb noisettes under a preheated high grill for 4 minutes on each side or until cooked but still slightly pink in the centre.

Serve the lamb immediately, surrounded by the tangy butter beans and accompanied by mixed salad leaves, if you like.

Preparation time:
10 minutes

Cooking time:
10 minutes

Serves: **4**

8 loin lamb chops
3 tablespoons redcurrant jelly
1 tablespoon olive oil
25 g (1 oz) butter
2 leeks, thinly sliced
1 tablespoon capers, drained and rinsed
small handful of rosemary or mint leaves, chopped, plus extra to garnish
2 teaspoons pink peppercorns in brine, drained and rinsed
salt and pepper

Roll up the lamb chops tightly and secure each with 2 cocktail sticks. Put the chops on a foil-lined grill pan, dot with the redcurrant jelly and season to taste with salt and pepper.

Cook under a preheated high grill for 5 minutes. Turn them over, spoon the redcurrant jelly juices over the lamb and cook for a further 5 minutes.

Meanwhile, heat the oil and butter in a frying pan, add the leeks, capers, herbs and peppercorns and cook for 5 minutes until softened and just beginning to brown. Spoon on to warmed serving plates. Arrange the lamb on top of the leek mixture, remove the cocktail sticks and serve, sprinkled with extra herbs to garnish.

COOK'S NOTES This elegant yet effortless dish is the perfect choice for special-occasion entertaining.

215 Pork medallions with figs

216 Pork fillet with pesto

Preparation time:
10 minutes

Cooking time:
15 minutes

Serves: **4**

2 tablespoons olive oil
8 pork medallions, about 675 g (1 lb 6 oz)
** in total**
2 onions, thinly sliced
2 garlic cloves, crushed
150 g (5 oz) ready-to-eat dried figs,
** thickly sliced**
125 ml (4 fl oz) cream sherry or Marsala
300 ml (½ pint) chicken stock
3 teaspoons thick-set honey
2 tablespoons crème fraîche
salt and pepper
torn flat leaf parsley leaves and paprika,
** to garnish**
buttered soft polenta, to serve

Heat the oil in a large frying pan over a high heat, add the pork medallions and cook until browned on one side. Turn the pork over, add the onions and garlic and cook, turning the pork once or twice and stirring the onions, for 5 minutes until both are browned.

Add the figs, sherry or Marsala, stock, honey and salt and pepper to taste and cook over a medium heat for 5 minutes until the sauce has reduced and the pork is thoroughly cooked. Stir in the crème fraîche.

Garnish with torn parsley leaves and a little paprika, and serve on a bed of soft polenta.

Preparation time:
10 minutes

Cooking time:
20 minutes

Serves: **4**

Oven temperature:
190°C (375°F) Gas Mark 5

2 pork tenderloin fillets, about 400 g
** (13 oz) each**
6 tablespoons extra virgin olive oil
50 g (2 oz) blanched almonds
1 garlic clove, crushed
1 bunch of flat leaf parsley
2 tablespoons freshly grated Parmesan
** cheese**
salt and pepper

TO SERVE
boiled new potatoes
green salad

Trim any gristle from the pork fillets, cut in half crossways and season to taste with salt and pepper. Heat 1 tablespoon of the oil in a frying pan, add the meat and cook for 2–3 minutes until browned all over. Transfer to a roasting dish and cook in a preheated oven, 190°C (375°F), Gas Mark 5, for 15 minutes until cooked through. Remove from the oven, wrap loosely in foil and leave to rest for 5 minutes.

Meanwhile, heat a nonstick frying pan, add the almonds and cook, stirring, until lightly browned. Remove from the pan and leave to cool slightly. Transfer to a food processor with the garlic, parsley, remaining oil and salt and pepper to taste. Process to form a fairly smooth paste. Stir in the Parmesan and taste and adjust the seasoning, if necessary.

Slice the pork, arrange on warmed serving plates with any pan juices and serve with boiled new potatoes and salad, drizzled with spoonfuls of the pesto.

COOK'S NOTES Look out for extra-trimmed, lean pork loin steaks, or medallions, in the supermarket, which are ideal for this wonderfully easy Italian-style dish.

COOK'S NOTES You could use pork chops in place of the pork tenderloin fillets.

217 Lambs' liver with cranberries

218 Red-hot hamburgers

Preparation time:
10 minutes

Cooking time:
15 minutes

Serves: **4**

2 tablespoons olive oil
2 onions, thinly sliced
150 g (5 oz) smoked back bacon, diced
25 g (1 oz) butter
625 g (1¼ lb) lambs' liver, sliced
2 tablespoons cranberry sauce
2 tablespoons red wine vinegar
75 g (3 oz) frozen cranberries
2 tablespoons water
salt and pepper
mashed potatoes, to serve

Heat the oil in a large frying pan, add the onions and bacon and cook over a medium heat, stirring occasionally, for 10 minutes until deep golden brown. Remove from the pan and set aside.

Heat the butter in the pan, add the liver slices and cook over a high heat, turning once or twice, for 3 minutes until browned on the outside and just pink in the centre.

Add the cranberry sauce, vinegar, cranberries and measured water. Season to taste with salt and pepper and cook, stirring, for 2 minutes until the cranberry sauce has melted and the cranberries are heated through and soft. Stir in the fried onions and bacon, then serve with mashed potatoes.

Preparation time:
10 minutes

Cooking time:
8–16 minutes

Serves: **4**

600 g (1 lb 3 oz) minced beef
2 garlic cloves, crushed
1 red onion, finely chopped
1 red chilli, finely chopped
1 bunch of parsley, chopped
1 tablespoon Worcestershire sauce
1 egg, beaten
4 baps or wholegrain hamburger buns, split
spicy salad leaves, such as rocket or mizuna
1 beef tomato, sliced
salt and pepper
relish, to serve

Put the mince in a large bowl, add the garlic, onion, chilli, parsley, Worcestershire sauce, egg and a little salt and pepper and mix well.

Heat a ridged griddle pan until smoking. Divide the meat mixture into 4 and shape into burgers. Add the burgers to the pan and cook for 3 minutes on each side for rare, 5 minutes on each side for medium or 7 minutes on each side for well done. Remove from the pan, keep warm and leave to rest while you griddle the baps or buns.

Wash and dry the pan, then reheat, add the baps or bun halves and cook briefly on each side until lightly charred. Fill each bun with some salad leaves, tomato slices and a burger. Serve immediately with the relish of your choice.

COOK'S NOTES Lambs' liver takes only the briefest time to cook and has a wonderful flavour and succulent texture.

219 Quick-fried veal

220 Lamb with salmoriglio sauce

Preparation time:
10 minutes

Cooking time:
5–8 minutes

Serves: **4**

4 veal escalopes, about 150 g (5 oz) each
3 tablespoons plain flour
½ tablespoon paprika
3 tablespoons extra virgin olive oil
2 lemons
100 g (3½ oz) pitted queen green olives, sliced
3–4 tablespoons chopped chervil, plus extra to garnish
salt and pepper

TO SERVE
thick ribbon pasta
circles of lemon rind, boiled to soften (optional)

Lay the veal escalopes between 2 sheets of clingfilm or nonstick baking paper and beat as thinly as possible with a rolling pin or meat mallet. Mix the flour, paprika and salt and pepper to taste together on a plate, then lightly coat each escalope in the seasoned flour.

Heat 2 tablespoons of the oil in a large frying pan over a medium-high heat. Add the veal escalopes and cook for 1 minute on each side or until golden and crisp (you may have to use 2 pans or cook the veal in 2 batches). Remove with a slotted spoon and keep warm.

Reduce the heat to medium-low. Squeeze the juice of 1 lemon into the pan with the remaining oil and stir with a wooden spatula to scrape up any sediment from the pan. Cut the remaining lemon into slices and add to the pan with the olives. Leave to bubble for a few seconds, then remove from the heat and sprinkle over the chervil.

Put the escalopes on warmed serving plates and pour over the mixture in the pan. Serve immediately, with thick ribbon pasta and the circles of lemon rind, if using, garnished with chervil.

Preparation time:
10 minutes

Cooking time:
15 minutes

Serves: **4**

8 loin lamb chops or 4 large chump chops
1 tablespoon chopped fresh oregano
2 tablespoons chopped flat leaf parsley
1 tablespoon capers, drained, rinsed and chopped
1 teaspoon dried oregano
3 garlic cloves, crushed
finely grated rind and juice of 1 small lemon
150 ml (¼ pint) extra virgin olive oil, plus extra for brushing
salt and pepper

Trim any excess fat from the chops. If using loin chops, tie each chop into a neat shape with fine string.

Mix the fresh oregano, parsley and capers together on a chopping board, then transfer to a bowl with the dried oregano, garlic, lemon rind and juice, oil and salt and pepper to taste. Whisk well until combined.

Lightly brush a ridged griddle pan with oil and heat until smoking. Add the chops and cook for 6–7 minutes on each side, brushing halfway through with a little of the sauce. Alternatively, cook under a preheated high grill. Serve with the remaining sauce.

COOK'S NOTES With their lemony, garlicky, herby sauce, these lamb chops are ideal for alfresco dining and show how an unfussy meal can be really special. The salmoriglio sauce can be made several hours in advance for added convenience.

221 Steak with Roquefort sauce

222 Veal saltimbocca

Preparation time:
10 minutes

Cooking time:
4–5 minutes

Serves: **4**

25 g (1 oz) butter
4 fillet steaks, about 150 g (5 oz) each
cauliflower mash, to serve

SAUCE
1 garlic clove, crushed
25 g (1 oz) parsley leaves, roughly chopped
15 g (½ oz) mint leaves, roughly chopped
1 tablespoon roughly chopped walnuts
75 ml (3 fl oz) extra virgin olive oil
2 tablespoons walnut oil
50 g (2 oz) Roquefort cheese, crumbled
15 g (½ oz) Parmesan cheese, freshly grated
salt and pepper

To make the sauce, put the garlic, parsley, mint, walnuts and oils in a food processor and process until fairly smooth.

Add the Roquefort and Parmesan, process again and season to taste with salt and pepper.

Heat the butter in a heavy-based frying pan. Season the steaks to taste with salt and pepper, add to the pan and cook for 2 minutes each side for rare or a little longer for medium rare.

Transfer the steaks to warmed serving plates, top with the cheese sauce and serve immediately with cauliflower mash.

Preparation time:
10 minutes

Cooking time:
10–15 minutes

Serves: **4**

2 teaspoons plain flour
8 small veal escalopes
50 g (2 oz) butter
8 slices of prosciutto
8 large sage leaves
250 ml (8 fl oz) dry white wine
salt and pepper

Season the flour to taste with salt and pepper. Lay the veal escalopes between 2 layers of clingfilm or nonstick baking paper and beat as thinly as possible with a rolling pin or meat mallet. Lightly coat the escalopes in the seasoned flour.

Heat half the butter in a large, heavy-based frying pan over a medium-high heat. Add the escalopes, in batches, and cook for 1 minute on each side or until golden and crisp. Remove with a slotted spoon to a plate.

Lay a slice of prosciutto and 1 sage leaf on the centre of each escalope, return to the pan and cook for a further 2–3 minutes, carefully turning each escalope once to sear the prosciutto and sage. Remove with a slotted spoon to warmed serving plates.

Pour the wine into the pan and leave to bubble until reduced by about half. Cut the remaining butter into pieces and whisk into the wine. Season to taste with salt and pepper and pour the sauce over the escalopes to serve.

COOK'S NOTES Any remaining sauce can be stored, topped with a layer of oil, in a screw-top jar in the refrigerator for up to 5 days.

COOK'S NOTES Bashed thin, veal escalopes are quick to cook and stay moist and tender. The quantities can be easily halved if you are cooking for only two.

223 Pork patties with soured cream sauce

224 Fillet steak with horseradish cream

Preparation time:
20 minutes

Cooking time:
10 minutes

Serves: **4**

500 g (1 lb) lean minced pork
40 g (1½ oz) breadcrumbs
1 small onion, grated
1 teaspoon paprika
1 egg, beaten
8 slices of pancetta or thin rashers of
  smoked streaky bacon
25 g (1 oz) butter
1 tablespoon vegetable oil
150 ml (¼ pint) soured cream
2 tablespoons chopped dill
2 teaspoons pink or green peppercorns,
  lightly crushed
salt and pepper

Put the pork, breadcrumbs, onion, paprika, egg and a little seasoning in a bowl and mix until evenly combined. This is most easily done with your hands.

Divide the mixture into 8 equal pieces and pat them into burger shapes. Wrap a slice of pancetta or streaky bacon around each one, securing it with a wooden cocktail stick.

Melt the butter with the oil in a large, heavy-based frying pan and gently fry the patties for 5 minutes on each side until golden. Drain and transfer to serving plates. Add the soured cream, dill and peppercorns to the pan and heat gently, stirring, until smooth and creamy. Season to taste and serve with the patties.

Preparation time:
5 minutes

Cooking time:
2–12 minutes

Serves: **4**

1 teaspoon vegetable oil
4 fillet steaks, about 125 g (4 oz) each
shredded lettuce leaves, to serve

HORSERADISH CREAM
175 ml (6 fl oz) Greek yogurt
65 g (2½ oz) walnuts, chopped
40 g (1½ oz) horseradish sauce

To make the horseradish cream, mix all the ingredients together in a small bowl.

Heat a ridged griddle pan until smoking and brush the surface with the oil. Add the steaks and cook, turning once only to achieve a decorative ridged effect. The following timing is a rough guide for steaks that are about 2.5 cm (1 inch) thick – blue: 1–2 minutes on each side (soft with no feel of resistance); rare: 2–3 minutes on each side (soft and spongy; may still ooze some red meat juices when pressed); medium rare: 3–4 minutes on each side (a little firmer); medium: 4–5 minutes on each side (firm to the touch); well done: over 5 minutes on each side (solid).

Serve the steaks accompanied by the horseradish cream and shredded lettuce leaves.

COOK'S NOTES These little patties make a quick and easy supper dish and, once shaped, can be frozen if you don't want to cook them all. Serve with chunky chips and a herb salad.

9 Desserts

225 Summer fruit compote   226 Summer berry sorbet

Preparation time:
5 minutes, plus cooling

Cooking time:
5 minutes

Serves: **2**

250 g (8 oz) mixed summer berries, such as raspberries, blueberries and strawberries, defrosted if frozen
finely grated rind and juice of 1 large orange
1 tablespoon redcurrant jelly
250 ml (8 fl oz) natural yogurt, to serve

Preparation time:
5 minutes, plus freezing

Cooking time:
No cooking

Serves: **2**

250 g (8 oz) frozen mixed summer berries
75 ml (3 fl oz) spiced berry cordial
2 tablespoons Kirsch
1 tablespoon lime juice

Put the berries, orange rind and juice and redcurrant jelly in a large, heavy-based saucepan. Cover and cook gently for 5 minutes or until the juices start to flow and the fruit is softened. Remove from the heat and leave to cool.

Divide the compote between 2 serving dishes and serve with the yogurt.

Put all the ingredients in a blender or food processor and blend to a smooth purée. Be careful not to over-process as this will soften the mixture too much.

Spoon the sorbet into a chilled shallow plastic container and freeze for 25 minutes. Spoon into bowls and serve immediately.

COOK'S NOTES You can use any combination of berries for this compote and it would also make a lovely light breakfast. For an extra touch of sweetness, drizzle a little runny honey on top of the desserts.

227 Pink grapefruit parfait

228 Raspberry and shortcake mess

Preparation time:
15 minutes

Cooking time:
No cooking

Serves: **4**

2 pink grapefruits
5 tablespoons soft dark brown sugar,
**   plus extra for sprinkling**
250 ml (8 fl oz) double cream
150 ml (¼ pint) Greek yogurt
3 tablespoons elderflower cordial
½ teaspoon ground ginger
½ teaspoon ground cinnamon
brandy snaps, to serve (optional)

Finely grate the rind of one grapefruit, avoiding any of the bitter white pith. Remove the peel and pith from both grapefruits, then cut between the membranes to remove the segments. Put in a large dish, sprinkle with 2 tablespoons of the sugar and set aside.

Whisk the cream and yogurt together in a large bowl until thick but not stiff. Fold in the elderflower cordial, spices, grapefruit rind and remaining sugar until smooth. Pour the mixture into attractive glasses, arranging the grapefruit segments between layers of parfait. Sprinkle the top with extra sugar and serve immediately, accompanied with brandy snaps, if you like.

Preparation time:
5 minutes

Cooking time:
No cooking

Serves: **4**

300 g (10 oz) raspberries, defrosted if
**   frozen, roughly crushed**
4 shortbread fingers, roughly crushed
400 g (13 oz) fromage frais
2 tablespoons icing sugar

Reserving a few raspberries for decoration, gently combine all the remaining ingredients in a bowl.

Divide among 4 serving dishes. Decorate with the reserved raspberries and serve immediately.

COOK'S NOTES This recipe is perfect for a lazy summer lunch. It also works really well with orange segments and chocolate shavings in place of the grapefruit and ginger.

229 Chocolate and raspberry soufflés

Preparation time:	100 g (3½ oz) plain dark chocolate
10 minutes	**3 eggs, separated**
	50 g (2 oz) self-raising flour, sifted
Cooking time:	**40 g (1½ oz) caster sugar**
12–15 minutes	**150 g (5 oz) raspberries, plus extra to**
	serve (optional)
Serves: **4**	**unsalted butter, for greasing**
	sifted icing sugar, to decorate
Oven temperature:	
190°C (375°F) Gas Mark 5	

Break the chocolate into squares and put in a heatproof bowl set over a saucepan of simmering water, then leave until melted.

Transfer the melted chocolate to a large bowl and whisk in the egg yolks. Fold in the flour.

Whisk the egg whites and caster sugar in a medium bowl until soft peaks form. Beat a spoonful of the egg whites into the chocolate mixture to loosen, then gently fold in the remainder.

Divide the raspberries among 4 lightly greased ovenproof ramekins, pour over the chocolate mixture, then bake in a preheated oven, 190°C (375°F), Gas Mark 5, for 12–15 minutes until the soufflés have risen.

Dust with sifted icing sugar to decorate and serve with extra raspberries, if you like.

230 Orange, rhubarb and ginger slump

Preparation time:	750 g (1½ lb) rhubarb, chopped into 1.5 cm
10 minutes	**(¾ inch) pieces**
	½ teaspoon ground ginger
Cooking time:	**50 g (2 oz) golden caster sugar**
about 20 minutes	**finely grated rind and juice of 1 orange**
	4 tablespoons mascarpone cheese
Serves: **6**	**175 g (6 oz) self-raising flour**
	50 g (2 oz) unsalted butter, diced
Oven temperature:	**finely grated rind of ½ lemon**
200°C (400°F) Gas Mark 6	**6 tablespoons milk**
	ready-made custard, to serve

Put the rhubarb, ginger, half the sugar and orange rind and juice in a medium saucepan. Bring to the boil, then reduce the heat and simmer gently for 5–6 minutes until the rhubarb is just tender. Transfer to an ovenproof dish and spoon over dollops of the mascarpone.

Sift the flour into a bowl. Add the butter and rub in with the fingertips until the mixture resembles fine breadcrumbs. Quickly stir in the remaining sugar, the lemon rind and milk until combined. Arrange spoonfuls of the mixture over the rhubarb and mascarpone.

Bake in a preheated oven, 200°C (400°F), Gas Mark 6, for 12–15 minutes until golden and bubbling. Serve with custard.

COOK'S NOTES Many people shy away from soufflés as they think it's almost impossible to get them to rise perfectly. In fact, they're not really that difficult. The secret is to get them to the table as soon as possible, before they start to deflate.

231 Vanilla and banana pancakes

232 Drunken orange slices

Preparation time:
15 minutes

Cooking time:
about 15 minutes

Serves: **4**

2 bananas
1 teaspoon vanilla extract
150 g (5 oz) self-raising flour
1 teaspoon baking powder
1 tablespoon caster sugar
1 egg
75 ml (3 fl oz) milk
1 tablespoon unsalted butter, melted
sunflower oil, for frying
maple syrup or maple syrup butter (see Cook's Notes), to serve

Preparation time:
15 minutes

Cooking time:
12 minutes

Serves: **4**

4 large sweet oranges
4 tablespoons cold water
4 tablespoons brown sugar
3 tablespoons Cointreau
2 tablespoons whisky
juice of 1 small orange
1 vanilla pod, split
1 cinnamon stick
4 cloves
2–3 mace blades (optional)
ginger or other ice cream, to serve

Mash the bananas with the vanilla extract in a bowl to make a smooth purée. Sift the flour and baking powder into a separate bowl and stir in the sugar.

Beat the egg, milk and melted butter together in another bowl and beat into the dry ingredients until smooth. Stir in the banana purée.

Heat a little oil in a large frying pan or griddle pan over a medium heat. Using a large metal spoon, drop 4 spoonfuls of the batter, well spaced apart, in the pan and cook for 2 minutes or until bubbles form on the surfaces and the undersides are golden brown. Using a spatula, turn the pancakes over and cook on the other side for 1–2 minutes. Remove from the pan, wrap in a tea towel and keep warm while cooking the remaining batter in the same way.

Transfer the pancakes to a serving plate and serve with maple syrup or maple syrup butter.

Using a small, sharp knife, cut off the base and the top of each orange. Cut down around the curve of the orange to remove all the peel and pith, leaving just the orange flesh. Cut the flesh horizontally into 5 mm (¼ inch) slices and set aside.

Put the measured water, sugar, 2 tablespoons of the Cointreau, the whisky, orange juice, vanilla pod, cinnamon stick, cloves and mace (if used) in a small saucepan and heat very gently until the sugar has dissolved. Increase the heat and boil vigorously for 5 minutes. Leave to cool slightly, but keep warm.

Heat a ridged griddle pan until smoking. Add the orange slices and cook for 1 minute on each side until caramelized. Sprinkle over the remaining Cointreau, flame with a match and stand well back. When the flames subside, transfer the orange slices to serving dishes and drizzle with the flamed syrup. Serve immediately with ginger ice cream or an ice cream of your choice.

COOK'S NOTES To make maple syrup butter, gradually beat 2 tablespoons maple syrup and 1 tablespoon icing sugar into 125 g (4 oz) softened unsalted butter, together with a few drops of vanilla extract, if you like. Cover and chill until required. It can be kept in the refrigerator for up to 1 week.

233 Peach strudel fingers

234 Apple fritters with blackberry sauce

Preparation time:
15 minutes

Cooking time:
10–13 minutes

Serves: **4**

Oven temperature:
180°C (350°F) Gas Mark 4

3 ripe peaches, stoned and thinly sliced
2 tablespoons caster sugar, plus extra to decorate
2 tablespoons ground almonds
½ teaspoon ground cinnamon
2 tablespoons sultanas
6 sheets of filo pastry, each 30 x 18 cm (12 x 7 inches), defrosted if frozen
40 g (1½ oz) unsalted butter, melted
sifted icing sugar, to decorate
whipped cream or crème fraîche, to serve

Preparation time:
10 minutes

Cooking time:
about 15 minutes

Serves: **4**

2 eggs
125 g (4 oz) plain flour
4 tablespoons caster sugar
150 ml (¼ pint) milk
sunflower oil, for deep-frying
4 dessert apples, cored and thickly sliced
150 g (5 oz) frozen blackberries
2 tablespoons water
sifted icing sugar, to decorate

Put the peaches in a bowl with the caster sugar, ground almonds, cinnamon and sultanas and toss gently together. Lay a sheet of filo pastry on a work surface, with the longest edge towards you, and brush with a little of the melted butter. Spoon a quarter of the peach mixture horizontally (or follow the longest edge) in a line down the centre, stopping about 5 cm (2 inches) from either end.

Fold the short sides of the pastry over the filling. Fold one long side over the filling, then roll up to enclose the filling completely. Transfer the strudel to a baking sheet. Repeat to make 3 more strudels.

Cut the remaining pastry sheets in half. Brush the outside edges of the strudels with a little more butter, then roll up in the remaining pastry sheets. Brush with the remaining butter.

Bake in a preheated oven, 180°C (350°F), Gas Mark 4, for 10–13 minutes until golden brown. Dust with a little sifted icing sugar and serve warm with whipped cream or crème fraîche.

Separate one egg and put the white in one bowl and the yolk and the whole egg in a second bowl. Add the flour and half the caster sugar to the second bowl. Whisk the egg white until soft peaks form, then use the same whisk to beat the flour mixture until smooth, gradually whisking in the milk. Fold in the egg white.

Pour the oil into a saucepan until it comes one-third of the way up the side, then heat to 180–190°C (350–375°F) or until a cube of bread browns in 30 seconds. Add a few apple slices to the batter and turn gently to coat. Lift out one slice at a time with a fork and lower carefully into the oil. Cook, in batches, for 2–3 minutes, turning until evenly golden. Remove with a slotted spoon and drain on kitchen paper.

Meanwhile, put the blackberries, remaining sugar and measured water in a small saucepan and heat for 2–3 minutes until hot. Arrange the fritters on serving plates, spoon the blackberry sauce around and dust with a little sifted icing sugar.

COOK'S NOTES Filo pastry is perfect for making a simple, speedy strudel. You can also serve it with ice cream.

COOK'S NOTES For an extra treat, serve with big scoops of vanilla ice cream. Thick slices of banana can be coated in this batter and cooked in the same way if you prefer.

235 Orange palmiers with plums

236 Barbecued fruits with palm sugar

Preparation time:
15 minutes

Cooking time:
10 minutes

Serves: **4**

Oven temperature:
200°C (400°F) Gas Mark 6

1 sheet of ready-rolled frozen puff pastry, about 25 cm (10 inches) square, defrosted
beaten egg, for brushing
3 tablespoons light muscovado sugar
finely grated rind of ½ orange
vegetable oil, for oiling
6 tablespoons orange juice
50 g (2 oz) caster sugar
400 g (13 oz) plums, stoned and sliced
sifted icing sugar, to decorate
crème fraîche, to serve

Brush the pastry with some of the beaten egg, then sprinkle with the muscovado sugar and orange rind. Roll up one edge of the pastry until it reaches the centre. Repeat from the opposite edge until both rolls meet in the centre.

Brush with more beaten egg, then cut into 8 thick slices. Arrange on a lightly oiled baking sheet. Bake in a preheated oven, 200°C (400°F), Gas Mark 6, for 10 minutes until well risen and golden.

Meanwhile, put the orange juice and caster sugar into a saucepan. Add the plums and cook for 5 minutes.

Sandwich the palmiers in pairs with the plums, dust with sifted icing sugar and serve with crème fraîche.

Preparation time:
15 minutes

Cooking time:
6–14 minutes

Serves: **4**

25 g (1 oz) palm sugar
finely grated rind and juice of 1 lime
2 tablespoons water
½ teaspoon cracked black peppercorns
500 g (1 lb) mixed prepared fruit, such as pineapple slices, mango wedges and peaches

TO SERVE
cinnamon or vanilla ice cream
lime slices

Put the sugar, lime rind and juice, measured water and peppercorns in a small saucepan and heat very gently until the sugar has dissolved. Remove from the heat and dip the base of the saucepan in ice-cold water to cool.

Brush the cooled syrup over the prepared fruits and cook over a preheated barbecue for 3–4 minutes on each side or under a preheated high grill for 6–7 minutes on each side until charred and tender.

Serve with scoops of cinnamon or vanilla ice cream and lime slices.

COOK'S NOTES These crisp, delicate pastries look very professional, but they can be made in minutes, using ready-made and -rolled puff pastry. Vary the fruit for sandwiching between the pastries to suit the season – rhubarb, greengages and raspberries also work well.

237 Almond angel cakes with berries

Preparation time: **15 minutes**	**sunflower oil, for oiling** **4 egg whites** **3 tablespoons granulated sugar**
Cooking time: **10–12 minutes**	**50 g (2 oz) ground almonds** **generous pinch of cream of tartar** **15 g (½ oz) flaked almonds**
Serves: **6**	**400 g (13 oz) frozen mixed berry fruits** **200 g (7 oz) fromage frais**
Oven temperature: **180°C (350°F) Gas Mark 4**	**1 tablespoon sifted icing sugar, to** **decorate (optional)**

Lightly oil 6 sections of a deep muffin tin and line the bases with rounds of greaseproof paper.

Whisk the egg whites in a large bowl until stiff, moist peaks form. Whisk in the granulated sugar, a teaspoonful at a time, until it has all been added, then continue to whisk for 1–2 minutes until the mixture is thick and glossy.

Fold in the ground almonds and cream of tartar and spoon the mixture into the sections of the prepared muffin tin. Sprinkle the flaked almonds over the tops.

Bake in a preheated oven, 180°C (350°F), Gas Mark 4, for 10–12 minutes until golden brown and set. Loosen the edges of the cakes with a knife, then lift on to a cooling rack.

Warm the fruits in a saucepan. Arrange the angel cakes on serving plates, add a spoonful of fromage frais to each and spoon the fruits around. Dust with the icing sugar, if you like.

238 Roasted plums with ginger sauce

Preparation time: **15 minutes**	**625 g (1¼ lb) dessert plums** **4 bay leaves** **100 ml (3½ fl oz) white wine**
Cooking time: **10–15 minutes**	**2 tablespoons clear honey** **50 g (2 oz) fresh root ginger, peeled** **1 tablespoon caster sugar**
Serves: **6**	**75 ml (3 fl oz) water** **150 g (5 oz) white chocolate, chopped** **100 g (3½ oz) crème fraîche**
Oven temperature: **220°C (425°F) Gas Mark 7**	

Halve and stone the plums, then arrange in a single layer in a roasting tin or shallow ovenproof dish in which they fit snugly. Tuck the bay leaves around them.

Mix together the wine and honey and pour over the plums. Roast in a preheated oven, 220°C (425°F), Gas Mark 7, for 10–15 minutes or until the plums begin to colour but still retain their shape.

Meanwhile, grate the ginger and put in a small, heavy-based saucepan, scraping the gratings from the board and grater into the pan. Add the sugar and measured water. Heat gently until the sugar has dissolved, then bring to the boil and boil for 1 minute. Strain into a clean pan. Add the chocolate and leave until melted, stirring frequently until smooth. If the chocolate doesn't melt, heat the mixture very gently. Stir in the crème fraîche.

To serve, warm the sauce through gently. Transfer the plums to serving dishes, spoon over the cooking juices and serve with the sauce.

COOK'S NOTES You can make this quick and easy pudding with almost any reasonably decent plums, because roasting in wine softens them and brings out their flavour.

239 Seared pineapple with plum sauce

240 Cranachan with raspberries

Preparation time:
20 minutes

Cooking time:
5–6 minutes

Serves: **6**

500 g (1 lb) ripe red plums, stoned and diced
6 star anise
generous pinch of chilli powder and ground cinnamon, or to taste
8 tablespoons water
1 large pineapple, about 800 g (1 lb 10 oz) prepared weight, cored and sliced
2 tablespoons sifted icing sugar
crème fraîche or ice cream, to serve (optional)

Preparation time:
10 minutes, plus cooling

Cooking time:
5–8 minutes

Serves: **6**

Oven temperature:
180°C (350°F) Gas Mark 4

40 g (1½ oz) medium oatmeal
150 ml (¼ pint) whipping cream
200 g (7 oz) fromage frais
2 tablespoons thick-set honey, preferably lavender or other flower honey
250 g (8 oz) raspberries, just defrosted if frozen

Put the plums, star anise, chilli powder, cinnamon and measured water in a saucepan, cover and simmer for 5 minutes until softened.

Meanwhile, halve the pineapple slices and arrange on a foil-lined grill rack. Dust with half the sugar and cook under a preheated grill for 2–3 minutes on each side until lightly browned.

Arrange the pineapple on serving plates, spoon the hot plum sauce by the side and dust with the remaining sugar. Serve immediately, with crème fraîche or ice cream, if you like.

Put the oatmeal in a shallow baking tin and toast in a preheated oven, 180°C (350°F), Gas Mark 4, stirring once, for 5–8 minutes until evenly browned. Leave to cool.

Whip the cream in a large bowl until it forms soft peaks. Fold in the fromage frais, then the honey and, finally, the cooled oatmeal.

Reserving a few raspberries to top the desserts, divide half the remaining raspberries among 6 small glass dishes. Spoon half the cream mixture on top, then repeat the layering with the other raspberries and the remaining cream mixture. Arrange the reserved raspberries on top and serve.

COOK'S NOTES Sweetened with natural sugars and just a light dusting of icing sugar, this fresh-tasting, eye-catching dessert can be quickly and simply put together when time is short. The riper the plums you use, the sweeter they will be. If you can find only under-ripe fruit, sweeten them with a little light cane sugar.

COOK'S NOTES The oatmeal can be toasted well in advance, but it is best to mix it with the cream only at the last minute because oatmeal swells with standing.

241 Baked pear with almond crumble

Preparation time:
10 minutes

Cooking time:
20 minutes

Serves: **4**

Oven temperature:
220°C (425°F) Gas Mark 7

75 g (3 oz) wholemeal flour
65 g (2½ oz) ground almonds
75 g (3 oz) soft light brown sugar
65 g (2½ oz) unsalted butter, diced
4 pears, quartered, cored and sliced
  lengthways
juice of 1 lime
2 tablespoons flaked almonds
150 g (5 oz) crème fraîche, to serve
  (optional)

Mix together the flour, ground almonds and sugar in a large bowl. Add the butter and rub in with the fingertips until the mixture resembles fine breadcrumbs.

Arrange the pear slices in 4 tall, ovenproof ramekins and drizzle with the lime juice. Cover the pears with the crumble mixture and sprinkle over the flaked almonds.

Bake in a preheated oven, 220°C (425°F), Gas Mark 7, for 20 minutes. Serve warm, topped with the crème fraîche, if you like.

242 Peach and raspberry tartlets

Preparation time:
15 minutes

Cooking time:
8–10 minutes

Serves: **4**

Oven temperature:
190°C (375°F) Gas Mark 5

15 g (½ oz) butter, melted
4 sheets of filo pastry, each about 25 cm
  (10 inches) square, defrosted if frozen
125 ml (4 fl oz) double cream
1 tablespoon soft light brown sugar
2 ripe peaches, skinned, halved, stoned
  and sliced
50 g (2 oz) raspberries
sifted icing sugar, to decorate

Grease 4 deep muffin tins with the melted butter. Cut a sheet of filo pastry in half, then across into 4 equal squares. Use the filo pastry squares to line one muffin tin, arranging them at slightly different angles. Press down well, tucking the pastry into the tin neatly. Repeat with the remaining pastry sheets.

Bake the tartlet cases in a preheated oven, 190°C (375°F), Gas Mark 5, for 8–10 minutes or until golden. Carefully remove the tartlet cases from the tins and leave to cool on a wire rack.

Meanwhile, pour the cream into a bowl and add the sugar. Whip lightly until it holds its shape. Spoon the cream into the tartlet cases and top with the peaches and raspberries. Dust with icing sugar and serve immediately.

COOK'S NOTES The tartlet cases can be baked several hours in advance for added flexibility, but should be filled just before eating to prevent the pastry from going soft.

243 Pears with minted mascarpone

244 Hot berries with orange cream

Preparation time: **10 minutes**	**30 g (1¼ oz) unsalted butter** **2 tablespoons clear honey** **4 ripe dessert pears, such as Red William, cored and sliced lengthways**
Cooking time: **5 minutes**	**lemon juice, for sprinkling**
Serves: **4**	MINTED MASCARPONE **1 tablespoon finely chopped mint** **1 tablespoon granulated sugar** **175 g (6 oz) mascarpone cheese**
	TO DECORATE **mint sprigs** **sifted icing sugar** **ground cinnamon**

Melt the butter in a small saucepan. Remove from the heat and stir in the honey.

Sprinkle the pear slices with a little lemon juice as soon as they are prepared to prevent them from discolouring. Line a baking sheet with foil and lay the pear slices on it. Brush the pears with the butter and honey mixture. Cook the pears under a preheated grill on its highest setting for 5 minutes.

Meanwhile, to make the minted mascarpone, lightly whisk the mint and granulated sugar into the mascarpone in a bowl.

Divide the pear slices among 4 plates and add a dollop of the minted mascarpone. Decorate each portion with a mint sprig, then lightly dust with icing sugar and cinnamon and serve immediately.

Preparation time: **15 minutes**	**150 ml (¼ pint) Greek yogurt** **125 ml (4 fl oz) single cream** **1 egg yolk**
Cooking time: **5–8 minutes**	**1 teaspoon orange flower water** **1 orange, peeled and pith removed, separated into segments**
Serves: **4**	**150 g (5 oz) blueberries** **150 g (5 oz) strawberries, hulled and cut into bite-sized pieces**

Mix together the yogurt, cream, egg yolk and orange flower water in a medium-sized bowl.

Mix together all the fruit in a separate bowl.

Divide the fruit among 4 ovenproof serving dishes, then spoon the yogurt mixture over to cover the fruit.

Cook under a preheated high grill for 5–8 minutes until the cream starts to bubble and turn brown. Serve immediately, being sure to warn your guests about the hot dishes.

COOK'S NOTES **Mascarpone is a soft cheese that is used in many sweet and savoury Italian dishes. It takes well to other flavours, and the mint in this quick dessert gives it a lovely fresh flavour.**

245 Pears with chocolate crumble

Preparation time:
10 minutes

Cooking time:
8 minutes

Serves: **4**

50 g (2 oz) light muscovado sugar
150 ml (¼ pint) water
25 g (1 oz) raisins
½ teaspoon ground cinnamon
**4 ripe dessert pears, peeled, halved and
    cored**
40 g (1½ oz) unsalted butter
50 g (2 oz) porridge oats
25 g (1 oz) hazelnuts, roughly chopped
**50 g (2 oz) plain dark or milk chocolate,
    chopped**
**lightly whipped cream or Greek yogurt,
    to serve (optional)**

Put half the sugar in a frying pan or wide sauté pan with the measured water, raisins and cinnamon. Bring just to the boil and add the pears. Reduce the heat and simmer gently for 5 minutes or until the pears are slightly softened.

Meanwhile, melt the butter in a separate frying pan or saucepan. Add the porridge oats and cook gently for 2 minutes. Stir in the remaining sugar and cook over a low heat until golden.

Spoon the pears on to serving plates. Stir the hazelnuts and chocolate into the oat mixture. Once the chocolate starts to melt, spoon over the pears. Serve topped with whipped cream or Greek yogurt, if you like.

246 Waffles with berry compote

Preparation time:
10 minutes

Cooking time:
20 minutes

Serves: **2**

**65 g (2½ oz) strawberries, hulled and
    quartered**
65 g (2½ oz) raspberries
65 g (2½ oz) blueberries
1 tablespoon elderflower cordial
2 tablespoons Greek yogurt, to serve

WAFFLES
50 ml (2 fl oz) milk
1 egg, separated
**40 g (1½ oz) unsalted butter, melted, plus
    extra for greasing**
50 g (2 oz) self-raising wholemeal flour
1½ tablespoons icing sugar, sifted
finely grated rind of ¼ lemon

To make the waffles, pour the milk into a bowl, add the egg yolk and whisk lightly. Add 2 teaspoons of the melted butter and work in lightly with a fork.

Heat a waffle iron on the hob or preheat an electric one while you sift the flour into a bowl. Make a well in the centre of the flour and gradually beat in the milk mixture and the remaining melted butter. Whisk the egg white in a separate bowl until stiff, moist peaks form, then fold into the batter with 2 teaspoons of the icing sugar and the lemon rind. Grease the waffle iron and pour in about a quarter of the batter. Close and cook for 4–5 minutes, turning once or twice if using a hob-top model. When the waffle is golden brown, cover and keep warm while you cook the remainder.

Meanwhile, put all the berries and the elderflower cordial in a small saucepan and heat gently until the juices just start to flow.

Put 2 waffles on each plate and serve with the berries and a spoonful of Greek yogurt.

247 Strawberry and lavender crush

248 Cherry and cinnamon zabaglione

Preparation time:	400 g (13 oz) strawberries
10 minutes	2 tablespoons icing sugar, plus extra for decorating
Cooking time:	4–5 lavender flowers, plus extra to decorate
No cooking	400 ml (14 fl oz) Greek yogurt
Serves: **4**	4 ready-made meringue nests

Reserving 4 small strawberries for decoration, hull and mash the remainder with the icing sugar using a fork or a blender or food processor. Pick the individual lavender flowers from the stems and crumble into the strawberry mixture to taste.

Put the yogurt in a bowl, crumble in the meringues, then lightly mix together. Add the strawberry mixture, fold together with a spoon until marbled, then spoon into 4 glasses.

Cut the reserved strawberries in half, then decorate the desserts with the strawberry halves and extra lavender flowers. Lightly dust with icing sugar and serve immediately.

Preparation time:	4 egg yolks
10 minutes	125 g (4 oz) caster sugar
	150 ml (¼ pint) cream sherry
Cooking time:	large pinch of ground cinnamon
about 10 minutes	400 g (13 oz) can black cherries in syrup
	2 amaretti biscuits, crumbled, to
Serves: **4**	decorate

Pour 5 cm (2 inches) water into a medium saucepan and bring to the boil. Set a large heatproof bowl over the pan, making sure that the water does not touch the base of the bowl. Reduce the heat so that the water is simmering, then add the egg yolks, sugar, sherry and cinnamon to the bowl. Whisk for 5–8 minutes until very thick and foamy and the custard leaves a trail when the whisk is lifted above the mixture.

Drain off some of the cherry syrup and then tip the cherries and just a little of the syrup into a small saucepan. Warm through, then spoon into 4 glasses. Pour the warm zabaglione over the top and decorate with crumbled amaretti biscuits. Serve immediately.

COOK'S NOTES Capture the essence of summer with this delicately flavoured, light strawberry and meringue dessert in a matter of moments. If you don't have fresh lavender at home, buy a small pot from a garden centre or use a few dried flowers instead.

COOK'S NOTES A classic Italian dessert, zabaglione makes the perfect partner for warmed cherries and a great standby for unexpected guests. Measure out the ingredients before you sit down to your main course so that you can whip up the dessert in a few minutes.

249 Soufflé berry omelette

250 Nectarine and blueberry tartlets

Preparation time:
15 minutes

Cooking time:
5–8 minutes

Serves: **4**

6 eggs, separated
2 teaspoons vanilla extract
4 tablespoons icing sugar
40 g (1½ oz) unsalted butter
4 tablespoons raspberry jam
100 g (3½ oz) raspberries, defrosted if frozen
100 g (3½ oz) blueberries, defrosted if frozen
single cream, to serve

Preparation time:
15 minutes

Cooking time:
6–8 minutes

Makes: **12**

Oven temperature:
180°C 350°F Gas Mark 4

25 g (1 oz) butter
2 teaspoons olive oil
4 sheets of filo pastry, each 30 x 18 cm (12 x 7 inches) or 65 g (2½ oz) in total, defrosted if frozen
2 tablespoons red berry jam
juice of ½ orange
4 ripe nectarines, halved, stoned and sliced
150 g (5 oz) blueberries
sifted icing sugar, to decorate
fromage frais or yogurt ice cream, to serve

Whisk the egg whites in a large bowl until soft peaks form. Put the egg yolks, vanilla extract and 1 tablespoon of the sugar in a separate bowl and use the same whisk to beat together. Fold a spoonful of the egg whites into the yolk mixture to loosen, then add the remainder and fold in gently with a large metal spoon.

Heat half the butter in a 20 cm (8 inch) frying pan. Pour in half the egg mixture and cook for 3–4 minutes until the underside is golden. Quickly flash the omelette under a preheated high grill for 1–2 minutes to brown the top. Slide into a shallow dish and quickly make a second omelette in the same way with the remaining ingredients.

Dot the omelettes with the jam and berries, then fold in half to enclose the filling. Dust the tops with the remaining sugar, cut in half and serve immediately with cream.

Melt the butter with the oil in a small saucepan. Separate the filo pastry sheets and brush lightly with the butter mixture, then cut into 24 pieces, each about 10 x 8 cm (4 x 3 inches).

Arrange a piece of filo in each section of a deep 12-hole muffin tin, then add a second piece at a slight angle to the first to give a jagged edge to each pastry case.

Bake the tartlet cases in a preheated oven, 180°C (350°F), Gas Mark 4, for 6–8 minutes until golden. Meanwhile, warm the jam and orange juice in a saucepan, then add the nectarines and blueberries and warm through.

Carefully remove the tartlet cases from the tin and transfer to a serving dish. Fill with the warm fruit mixture and dust with sifted icing sugar to decorate. Serve with spoonfuls of fromage frais or yogurt ice cream.

COOK'S NOTES These light, fluffy soufflé omelettes can be made in just a few minutes. Frozen berries make a great standby and they can be quickly defrosted in the microwave if you haven't had an opportunity to buy fresh fruit.

251 Banana samosas with stem ginger cream

Preparation time:
20 minutes

Cooking time:
5–10 minutes

Serves: **4**

2 bananas
1 tablespoon soft brown sugar
12 filo pastry sheets, each about
**   30 x 18 cm (12 x 7 inches)**
oil for deep-frying

STEM GINGER CREAM
4 pieces of preserved stem ginger, finely
**   diced**
2 tablespoons syrup from the ginger
100 ml (3½ fl oz) double cream
icing sugar, to dust

Coarsely mash the bananas in a bowl and add the sugar. Mix well and set aside.

Fold a sheet of filo pastry in half lengthways. Place 2 tablespoons of the banana mixture at one end of the filo, then fold the corner of the pastry over the mixture, covering it in a triangle shape. Fold the triangle of pastry and filling over and over along the length of the filo to make a neat triangular samosa. Moisten the edge with water at the end to seal it in place. Repeat with the remaining filling and sheets of filo pastry.

Heat the oil for deep-frying to 180–190°C (350–375°F) or until a cube of bread browns in 30 seconds. Deep-fry the samosas in 2–3 batches, according to the size of pan, for 3–4 minutes until golden brown.

Use a slotted spoon to remove the samosas from the pan and place on kitchen paper to drain.

To make the stem ginger cream, mix the ginger with the syrup. Lightly whip the cream until it is just firm, then fold in the ginger and syrup.

Dust the samosas lightly with icing sugar and serve hot or warm with the ginger cream.

252 Banana and cardamom filo parcels

Preparation time:
15 minutes

Cooking time:
15 minutes

Serves: **4**

Oven temperature:
200°C (400°F) Gas Mark 6

3 large bananas
3 tablespoons demerara sugar
½ teaspoon ground cardamom
4 sheets of filo pastry, each 40 x 28 cm
**   (16 x 11 inches), defrosted if frozen**
15 g (1 oz) unsalted butter, melted, plus
**   extra for greasing**
1 tablespoon sesame seeds
Greek yogurt or fromage frais, to serve

Mash the bananas with the sugar and ground cardamom in a bowl to make a purée.

Lay a filo pastry sheet on a work surface, brush lightly with a little of the melted butter, then fold into thirds lengthways. Spoon a quarter of the banana mixture on to the pastry about 3.5 cm (1½ inches) from the end. Fold the left corner of the pastry diagonally to the right side of the pastry to cover the filling. Continue folding in the same way until you reach the end of the sheet. Repeat the process with the remaining pastry sheets to make 3 more parcels. Transfer the parcels to a lightly greased baking sheet, brush with the remaining melted butter and sprinkle over the sesame seeds.

Bake in a preheated oven, 200°C (400°F), Gas Mark 6, for 15 minutes or until golden. Serve hot with a spoonful of Greek yogurt or fromage frais.

COOK'S NOTES This is an unusual dessert that is easy to prepare but looks very impressive when served. The cardamom adds a warm spicy flavour to the sweet bananas.

253 Spice-infused fruit salad

254 Exotic fruit salad

Preparation time:
15 minutes

Cooking time:
5 minutes

Serves: **6**

1 vanilla pod
175 ml (6 fl oz) water
2½ tablespoons caster sugar
1 small hot red chilli, halved and deseeded
4 clementines
2 peaches
½ cantaloupe melon, deseeded
75 g (3 oz) blueberries

Use the tip of a small, sharp knife to score the vanilla pod lengthways through to the centre. Put the measured water and sugar in a medium pan and heat gently until the sugar has dissolved. Add the vanilla pod and chilli and heat gently for a further 2 minutes. Remove from the heat and leave to cool while you prepare the fruit.

Remove the peel from the clementines and slice the flesh. Stone and slice the peaches. Cut the melon flesh into small chunks, removing and discarding the skin.

Mix the fruit in a dish and pour over the warm syrup, discarding the chilli. Serve immediately or cover and chill until you are ready to serve.

Preparation time:
10 minutes, plus standing

Cooking time:
3 minutes

Serves: **1**

6 tablespoons apple juice
1 green cardamom pod, crushed
1 star anise
150 g (5 oz) pineapple, mango and kiwifruit
1 teaspoon toasted shredded coconut

Put the apple juice in a saucepan with the cardamom and star anise and bring to the boil. Remove from the heat and leave to stand for 10 minutes.

Meanwhile, peel, core and slice the pineapple, peel, stone and slice the mango and peel and slice the kiwifruit.

Put the prepared fruit in a bowl. Pour the juice mixture over the fruit and leave to stand for 5 minutes. Top with the coconut and serve.

COOK'S NOTES The 'hotness' of the syrup will depend on the type of chilli you use. Go for a small, fiery one, but remove it from the syrup before you pour it over the fruit so that it doesn't mask the warmth of the vanilla. Ideally, serve the fruit salad with scoops of vanilla ice cream for an icy-cool contrast.

255 Figs with yogurt and honey

Preparation time:
5 minutes

Cooking time:
10 minutes

Serves: **4**

8 ripe figs
4 tablespoons natural yogurt
2 tablespoons clear honey

Heat a griddle pan over a medium heat. Add the figs and cook for 8 minutes, turning occasionally, until charred on the outside. Remove and cut in half.

Arrange the figs on 4 plates and serve with a spoonful of yogurt and some honey drizzled over the top.

256 Pancake stack with maple syrup

Preparation time:
10 minutes

Cooking time:
about 15 minutes

Serves: **4**

75 g (3 oz) unbleached plain flour
1 egg
125 ml (4 fl oz) milk
2½ tablespoons sunflower oil
1 tablespoon sugar
8 scoops of vanilla ice cream
maple syrup, to serve

Put the flour, egg, milk, oil and sugar in a food processor and process until smooth and creamy.

Heat a large frying pan or ridged griddle pan over a medium heat. Using a large metal spoon, drop 4 tablespoonfuls of the batter, well spaced apart, in the pan and cook for 2 minutes or until bubbles form on the surfaces and the undersides are golden brown. Using a spatula, turn the pancakes over and cook on the other side for 1–2 minutes. Remove from the pan, wrap in a tea towel and keep warm while cooking the remaining batter in the same way, making 12 small pancakes in all.

Bring to the table as a stack, drizzled with maple syrup. Serve 3 pancakes to each person, with 2 scoops of ice cream.

COOK'S NOTES Buy figs when they are in season and full of flavour and juice to make this amazingly easy yet delicious dessert.

257 Chocolate risotto

258 Bananas with toffee sauce

Preparation time: **5 minutes**	**600 ml (1 pint) milk** **25 g (1 oz) granulated sugar** **50 g (2 oz) butter**
Cooking time: **20 minutes**	**125 g (4 oz) risotto rice** **50 g (2 oz) hazelnuts, toasted and chopped**
Serves: **4**	**50 g (2 oz) sultanas** **125 g (4 oz) plain dark chocolate, grated, plus extra to decorate**

Put the milk and sugar in a saucepan and bring to a gentle simmer.

Melt the butter in a separate, heavy-based saucepan. Add the rice and cook, stirring, for 1 minute. Add enough hot milk to just cover the rice and stir well. Simmer gently, stirring frequently.

When most of the liquid has been absorbed, add more milk. Continue adding the milk in stages and stirring until it has all been absorbed. Add the hazelnuts, sultanas and grated chocolate and mix quickly. Try not to overmix the chocolate, as the marbled effect looks attractive. Serve the risotto immediately, decorated with a little grated chocolate.

Preparation time: **5 minutes**	**4 bananas** **125 g (4 oz) unsalted butter** **125 g (4 oz) palm sugar**
Cooking time: **5 minutes**	**125 ml (4 fl oz) double cream** **dash of lime juice, to taste** **vanilla ice cream, to serve**
Serves: **4**	**ground cinnamon or freshly grated nutmeg, to decorate (optional)**

Peel the bananas and cut them into quarters or in half lengthways. Melt the butter in a frying pan, add the bananas and cook for 30 seconds on each side or until lightly golden. Transfer to a warmed dish with a slotted spoon.

Stir the sugar and cream into the pan and heat gently until the sugar has dissolved. Simmer gently for 2–3 minutes until thickened. Add lime juice to taste.

Serve the bananas drizzled with the sauce and with a scoop of vanilla ice cream. Sprinkle with cinnamon or nutmeg to decorate, if you like.

COOK'S NOTE For a special treat, add a splash of brandy just before decorating and serving the risotto.

259 Chocolate lime creams

260 Strawberries with chocolate spread

Preparation time:
5 minutes, plus chilling

Cooking time:
5 minutes

Serves: **4**

100 g (3½ oz) plain dark chocolate
50 g (2 oz) caster sugar
finely grated rind and juice of 2 limes
2 tablespoons water
300 ml (½ pint) double cream

Preparation time:
5 minutes

Cooking time:
No cooking

Serves: **1**

200 g (7 oz) strawberries
2 tablespoons chocolate hazelnut spread

Coarsely grate the chocolate. Heat the sugar in a small, heavy-based saucepan with the lime rind and juice and water until the sugar has dissolved. Leave to cool slightly.

Put the lime syrup into a bowl with the cream and whisk until soft peaks form. Reserve a little of the grated chocolate. Fold the remainder into the cream mixture and spoon the mixture into serving glasses. Cover and chill in the freezer for 15 minutes, then serve sprinkled with the reserved grated chocolate.

Hull, then quarter or halve the strawberries.

Serve with the chocolate hazelnut spread for dipping.

COOK'S NOTES You can use milk chocolate instead of plain dark chocolate. Always buy good-quality chocolate with a high proportion of cocoa solids.

Index

Acknowledgements

Executive Editor Nicky Hill
Senior Editor Jessica Cowie
Executive Art Editor Penny Stock
Designer Ginny Zeal
Senior Production Controller Martin Croshaw
Picture Researcher Taura Riley

PICTURE ACKNOWLEDGEMENTS
Octopus Publishing Group Limited 90 right, 102 left, 117 right; /**Clive Bozzard-Hill** 85 left; /**Stephen Conroy** 17 left, 28 right, 37 left, 39 left, 39 right, 57 right, 59 right, 85 right, 87 left, 101 left, 114 left, 114 right, 115 left, 115 right, 133 right, 134 left, 134 right, 135 left, 144 left, 144 right, 145 left, 145 right, 146 right, 147 left; /**Gus Filgate** 25 left, 133 left; /**Sandra Lane** 32 left; /**William Lingwood** 10 left, 10 right, 12 left, 18 left, 18 right, 19 right, 22 left, 23 right, 24 left, 24 right, 29 right, 32 right, 44 right, 45 left, 45 right, 47 left, 49 left, 50 right, 54 left, 56 right, 62 right, 63 left, 64 left, 64 right, 65 left, 65 right, 66 left, 66 right, 67 left, 72 left, 74 left, 74 right, 75 left, 75 right, 77 left, 82 left, 89 left, 89 Right, 96 left, 96 right, 97 left, 97 right, 98 left, 98 right, 99 left, 99 right, 100 right, 106 left, 106 right, 107 left, 107 right, 108 left, 113 left, 116 left, 116 right, 117 right, 118 right, 119 left, 120 right, 121 left, 121 right, 127 right, 130 right, 131 left, 131 right, 132 left, 138 left,

142 left, 142 right, 143 left, 148 right, 149 left, 149 right, 150 left, 150 right, 151 right; /**David Loftus** 14 right, 15 right, 36 right, 38 right, 52 right, 53 left, 57 left, 59 left, 63 right, 69 right, 71 left, 71 right, 72 right, 73 left, 88 left, 88 right, 129 left, 154 left; /**Neil Mersh** 23 left, 84 right, 118 left, 151 left; /**Diana Miller** 16 left; /**Sean Myers** 105 right; /**Lis Parsons** 16 right, 28 left, 30 left, 30 right, 33 left, 34 right, 35 right, 36 right, 37 right, 42 left, 42 right, 43, 44 left, 46 left,49 right, 51 left, 51 right, 56 left, 58 left, 70 left, 70 right, 73 right, 77 right, 80 left, 81 left, 81 right, 82 right, 83 right, 86 left, 86 right, 100 left, 108 right, 109 right, 124 left, 125 left, 126 left, 126 right, 127 left, 128 right, 130 left, 135 right, 136 top left, 139 left, 139 right, 140 left, 140 right, 146 left, 147 right; /**William Reavell** 13 right, 15 left, 17 right, 19 left, 29 left, 34 right, 47 right, 48 right, 50 left, 52 left, 55 right, 62 left, 67 right, 68 right, 76 left, 76 right, 80 right, 90 left, 91 right, 92 left, 92 right, 93 left, 148 left; /**Gareth Sambidge** 13 left, 14 left, 22 right, 31 left, 35 left, 38 left, 43 right, 46 right, 48 left, 54 right, 69 left, 84 left, 87 right, 91 left, 93 right, 101 right, 102 right, 103 left, 103 right, 104 left, 104 right, 105 left, 109 left, 112 left, 112 right, 113 right, 119 right, 124 right, 125 right, 129 right, 132 right, 136 top right, 141 left, 141 right, 152 left, 152 right, 153 left, 153 right, 155 right; /**Simon Smith** 11 right; /**Ian Wallace** 12 right, 25 right, 31 right, 33 right, 55 left, 68 left, 83 left, 120 left, 128 left, 136 bottom right, 136 bottom left, 138 right, 143 right, 154 right, 259 left; /**Philip Webb** 11 left.

FORMULA ONE
CIRCUITS FROM ABOVE

First published in 2014
Second Edition 2016
Third Edition 2017
Fourth Edition 2019
Fifth Edition 2020

Welbeck Non-fiction Limited
Welbeck Publishing Group
20 Mortimer Street
London W1T 3JW

Managing Editor: Martin Corteel
Project Editor Ross Hamilton
Design Manager: Luke Griffin
Production Manager: Rachel Burgess

A CIP catalogue for this book is available from the British Library.

ISBN 978-1-78739-510-7

Printed and bound in China

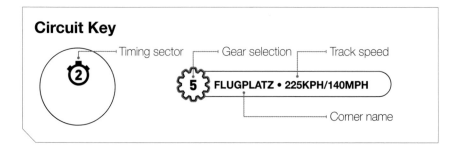

Circuit Key

Timing sector · Gear selection · Track speed

② 5 FLUGPLATZ · 225KPH/140MPH

Corner name

FORMULA ONE
CIRCUITS FROM ABOVE

FIFTH EDITION

BRUCE JONES

WELBECK

Designed with
Google Earth

Contents

Page 3: There's nowhere quite like Singapore at grand prix time, with the circuit marked out in lights in the heart of the city

Opposite: The flow of Sepang's lap through its 15 varied corners was popular in the decades when Malaysia hosted a grand prix, with passing opportunities into the first and last turns.

Introduction

Any fan of motor racing is sure to have a favourite racing circuit. It might be Monza, Monaco or Spa-Francorchamps, favoured because of a mighty corner, a sequence of bends, their special ambience, because their favourite driver or team won there or simply because that was where they first saw and heard a Formula One car being driven at full tilt. The beauty of this is that these and 23 other circuits featured in this book are the greatest circuits raced on since the World Championship began in 1950 and they are all so different, all with very much a character of their own.

In all, the World Championship has held grands prix at 71 circuits across 30 countries through its 66-year history, but the 26 circuits chosen for this book – spread across the planet from Argentina to France, Mexico to the United States of America – represent the cream of the crop. Silverstone, Monaco, Spa-Francorchamps and Monza have stood the test of time from that inaugural World Championship, so it's intriguing to look at how they compare with the very latest additions to the roster in Bahrain, Singapore, Abu Dhabi, the United States, Sochi and Baku. Their histories could not be more different, as the long-standing circuits have been raced on by all of the sport's top names, from Juan Manuel Fangio to Jim Clark and Ayrton Senna to Michael Schumacher, each adding their own layer of history, while the newer circuits have been the domain thus far of Sebastian Vettel, Fernando Alonso and Lewis Hamilton.

Working in conjunction with Google's amazing Google Earth photography, this book shows these circuits as never before, with its pin-sharp satellite photography picking out the details that are seldom or never seen on television, showing clearly from above not only every twist and turn of the circuit but how each circuit sits in its landscape or weaves through a town, as with Adelaide, Monaco and Singapore. You can pick out the F1 pitlane and paddock, the control tower and grandstands and, by adding corner names, gears and speeds, you will have a fantastic viewing guide for when the World Championship next visits, hopefully adding to your enjoyment of the world's fastest moving and most cosmopolitan sport. To give you an even better understanding of what it must be like for the drivers, I've highlighted the eight key corners from each of the selected circuits and explained the particular challenge that each of them provides. The Becketts sweeper at Silverstone stands out, as does Parabolica at Monza, the first two corners at Sepang and the esses at the Circuit of the Americas.

For a number of the circuits, I've also picked out a quartet of the great races held there and highlighted the four drivers who have reaped the greatest results there across the decades. With a record 91 wins to his name, Michael Schumacher has, as you would imagine, an entry alongside many of the circuits.

The passage of the decades, but more importantly the continual progress in building ever faster cars, has led to circuits being modified to ensure the safety of the spectators as well as the drivers, with straw bales being replaced by crash barriers and debris fencing, chicanes being inserted and gravel traps or asphalt run-off areas added over the years. Corners have been altered too or the circuit cut and reshaped, as happened so comprehensively at Hockenheim when its forest loop was truncated in 2002.

The face of the World Championship began to change after being taken over by Liberty Media in 2017, always with a raft of potential new venues waiting in the wings as discussions are held with both old and new.

The Brazilian GP continues to be in jeopardy, even though the grandstands at Interlagos remain packed, as the organizers can't afford to continue paying the hosting rights, so the country's hope is that a circuit in Rio de Janeiro can be readied for when Interlagos stands down. Even the home of the British GP, Silverstone – the venue for the first race of the inaugural World Championship in 1950 – was on shaky ground until a new deal to keep the race until 2024.

Liberty Media's plan is that the new races will be spread F1 more evenly around the globe, with Holland's Zandvoort circuit making a return in 2020 after a 35-year break and Vietnam making its championship bow, while Miami is doing its best to be next in line, using considerable public desire for a race to quell local opposition. If Miami fails to land a deal, then Las Vegas is next in line, while New York is always on the list and South Africa is pushing to make a return.

Below: Lewis Hamilton has already broken clear as Valtteri Bottas leads the chasing pack of Charles Leclerc, Max Verstappen and the McLarens of Lando Norris and Carlos Sainz Jr out of Turn 5 on the opening lap of the 2019 French GP.

Spectators on luxury motor yachts
and balconies line the track at
Tabac during the 2013 Monaco GP.

Chapter 1
Europe

■■■Spa-Francorchamps

This amazing road circuit, rising and falling through the hills of the Ardennes forests, has been part of the World Championship since its inauguration in 1950 and continues to provide one of the sternest challenges that the drivers face all year.

❝ I've had lots of great times at Spa. It's been the place virtually every highlight of my career took place: my first race, my first win and my seventh world title. **❞**

Michael Schumacher

There can be no escaping the fact that Spa-Francorchamps is a proper circuit, one that has a character of its own, shaped by the landscape rather than by a circuit designer's hand. It is very much part of the hills and forests that it bisects, a hugely challenging stretch of blacktop that offers one of the most distinctive settings visited by the World Championship each year. Add to that its rich and occasionally tragic history, and it has a character very much of its own; even today it is a place that needs to be shown respect.

Two-time World Champion Jim Clark was a driver who appeared to have the measure of every track that he raced on, but he would famously fear and hate the place, something that was reinforced on his first outing there by the death of compatriot Archie Scott-Brown in a sportscar race they were contesting in 1958. This was Clark's first brush with death and it affected him deeply.

The circuit started life in 1921, when a triangular course laid out to the south of the village of Francorchamps was used for the first time in a race for motorbikes. The riders had to race over the hill into the next valley to Malmedy before travelling along the valley floor, then turn right near Stavelot and start the climb back to complete the 15km (9.2 mile) lap at what is now the La Source hairpin. A year later, car racers had their first crack at it and, with long straights and many

sections threaded through the forest, it was no place for the timid because there were no barriers to contain the cars. Making matters all the more potentially dangerous, rain would often sweep in, with the added difficulty that it would frequently hit only one part of this spread-out circuit so that the track might be bone dry around the pits but soaking wet over by the fearsome Masta Kink, where drivers had to stay as hard on the throttle as they dared while the track flicked left, then right between some houses.

Over the years, little changed other than the reprofiling of some of the corners to make them less severe. What made the place all the more awesome was the hugely high speeds that were maintained around much of the lap, with BRM driver Pedro Rodriguez's winning average speed in the 1970 Belgian GP being a fraction under 240kph (150mph). Worried by this, the organizers relocated the grand prix to Nivelles and then Zolder, both bland but infinitely safer circuits.

The only way back for Spa-Francorchamps was to cut its lap length, axing the entire section in the next valley and to join the outward leg with the inward one via a new section of circuit that turned right at Les Combes and then dropped down the hill to rejoin the original course again before Blanchimont.

That was in 1979, with the lap being reduced to 6.9km (4.3 miles), and the grand prix returned in

1983. The changes reduced Alain Prost's winning average lap speed in his Renault to 191kph (119mph). Since then, there have been some tweaks to the circuit, most frequently at the Bus Stop chicane at the end of the lap, but the essence of Spa remains the same. Speeds have crept up again and Sebastian Vettel's winning average for Red Bull in 2013 was 220kph (137mph).

The stand-out corners are the sharply rising and twisting Eau Rouge, the long straight for slipstreaming that follows it up to Les Combes, then the downhill, double-apex Pouhon and the flat-out uphill lefthander on the return leg called Blanchimont. It's a circuit that offers a fabulous flow for the drivers, with enough width for them to attempt to overtake.

Spa-Francorchamps is vital for its place in F1's long and varied history, as one of only four circuits used in that first World Championship in 1950 and still on F1's calendar today, along with Silverstone, Monaco and Monza. However, it's also vital to F1 because it proves that modern F1 cars can still go racing, and race well, on a circuit that was not designed on a computer. For photographers, of course, with its spectacular, natural backdrops, it's also a rare joy. ■

Opposite: Spa-Francorchamps' majestic descent from La Source past the old pits and then into the compression at Eau Rouge.

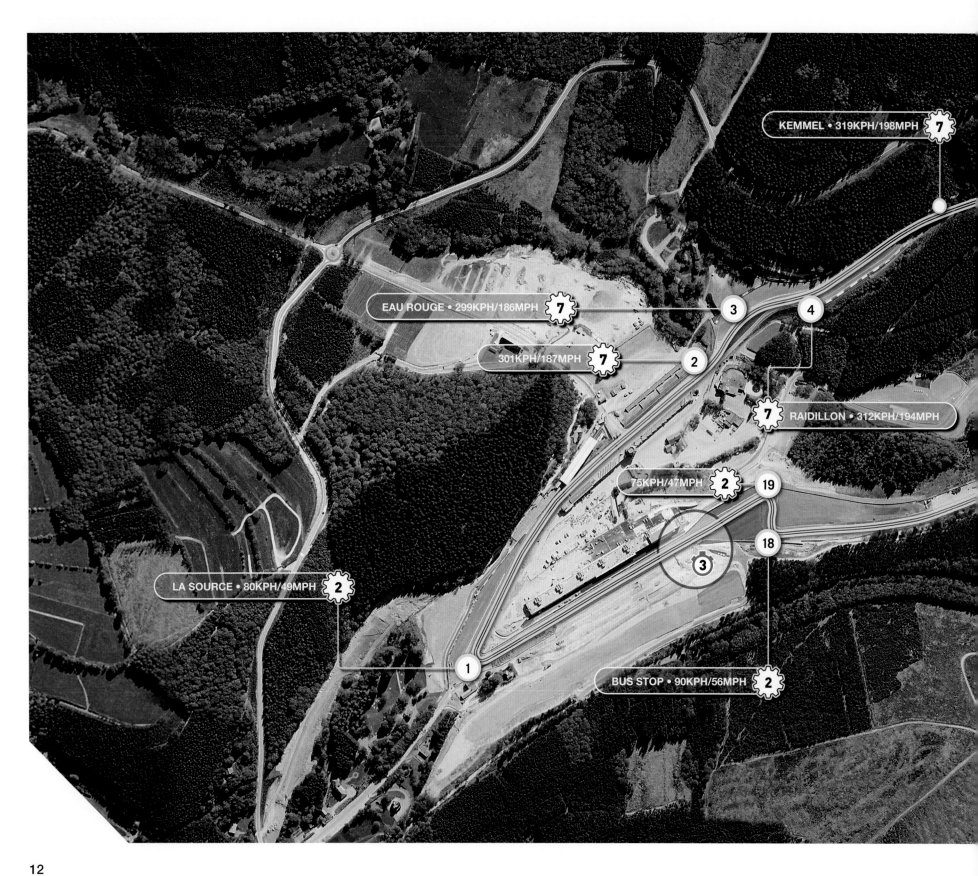

KEMMEL • 319KPH/198MPH **7**

EAU ROUGE • 299KPH/186MPH **7** ③ ④

301KPH/187MPH **7** ②

7 RAIDILLON • 312KPH/194MPH

75KPH/47MPH **2** ⑲

⑱

③

LA SOURCE • 80KPH/49MPH **2**

①

BUS STOP • 90KPH/56MPH **2**

5

(1)

7 4 MALMEDY • 180KPH/112MPH

6

LES COMBES • 138KPH/86MPH 3

2 RIVAGE • 100KPH/62MPH

140KPH/87MPH 3

9

POUHON • 230KPH/143MPH 5 10 A

150KPH/93MPH 3

8

6 APPROACH • 290KPH/180MPH

250KPH/155MPH 5 11

7 APPROACH • 311KPH/193MPH

17 A

12 4 FAGNES • 177KPH/110MPH

16 7 315KPH/195MPH

13

5 CAMPUS • 250KPH/155MPH

180KPH/112MPH 4

14

7 BLANCHIMONT • 314KPH/195MPH

(2)

CURVE PAUL FRERE • 241KPH/150MPH 5 15

Google Earth

Circuit Guide

Belgium's Spa-Francorchamps is a wonderfully organic mix of everything that a racing circuit needs. It has high-speed corners, medium-speed corners and tight ones. It has incline, camber and long straights for trying to pull off a passing move, all with a beautiful backdrop.

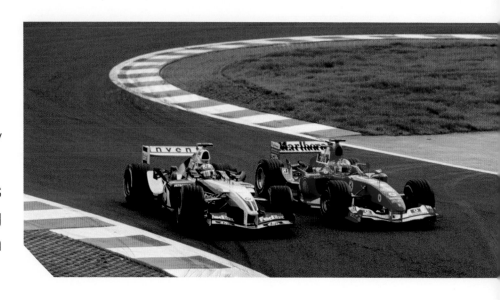

Turn 1 • La Source
Gear: **2**
Speed: **80kph (49mph)**

Having a hairpin as the opening corner of the lap, which has been the case since 1984, when it was moved there from its original position on the downhill slope to Eau Rouge, means that Spa-Francorchamps has had its share of incident over the years. After the short sprint to reach it from the starting grid, drivers have to decide whether to be fast in on the inside line or go in wide and be fast out for the blast towards Eau Rouge. There's an escape road straight ahead.

Turn 2/3 • Eau Rouge
Gear: **7**
Speed: **299kph (186mph)**

This right/left flick is renowned throughout the racing world because it's made a corner to reckon with by its dipping approach being followed immediately by the steepest of inclines, compressing the cars' suspension. Once fabled as a turn that only the brave would take flat-out, it's now less of a challenge due to superior aerodynamics and levels of grip, but it remains a tough corner because it's taken in seventh and momentum out of here is magnified up the long straight that follows.

Turn 5 • Les Combes
Gear: **3**
Speed: **138kph (86mph)**

This is the point at which the circuit was made to turn right when it was almost halved in length in 1979. It now marks the end of a long uphill straight from Raidillon and drivers can attempt a passing manoeuvre here if they can get a good enough tow up the hill. Braking hard from almost 320kph (200mph), the drivers then have to get their car into the righthander and position it almost immediately for a sharp left that follows on the brow of the hillside.

Turn 8 • Rivage
Gear: **2**
Speed: **100kph (62mph)**

The circuit dips gently from Les Combes towards the righthander called Malmedy and then the slope steepens noticeably as it tips the cars down the hill towards Rivage. This is a second-gear, double-apex righthander with trees running down its outer flank on the way in and a steep earth bank on the inside. Drivers have to balance their cars on the way in so that they can accelerate as soon as possible and continue their descent through the faster left flick that follows.

Opposite: Juan Pablo Montoya noses his Williams inside Michael Schumacher's Ferrari at the Bus Stop in 2004. *Above left:* Schumacher leads Jarno Trulli's Renault and Felipe Massa's Sauber out of La Source, also in 2004.
Above right: A view down through the trees to the pitlane, with the La Source hairpin visible in the background.

Turn 10 • Pouhon
Gear: **6**
Speed: **230kph (143mph)**

Continuing down the slope from Rivage, the drivers gain a feeling of space down this wide stretch of track as they look back towards the control tower above the pits that lie straight ahead to the north. What they can see in front of them is the first part of a two-part corner, and it's a great place to see an Formula one car and its driver really put to work as they attempt to carry their speed through its broad, double-apex format.

Turn 15 • Curve Paul Frere
Gear: **5**
Speed: **241kph (150mph)**

This righthander marks the lowest point of the lap and it's the point at which the infield loop inserted in 1979 feeds the cars back on to what was previously the long, flat-out blast from Stavelot to the completion of the lap. The turn is taken in fifth gear after the short dash from Campus, and it's essential that drivers don't scrub off any of this speed because they will be able to carry any momentum up the hill. The corner is named after 1950s racer journalist Paul Frere.

Turn 17 • Blanchimont
Gear: **7**
Speed: **314kph (195mph)**

Most of the flat-out straights which F1 drivers fly along these days are wide open in nature. Not so this uphill stretch of track. It has a bank of trees on the slope rising behind the barriers on the drivers' left and just thin air beyond the barriers to the right as the ground drops away towards the river that runs down the valley. Pushing on at 314kph (195mph) through this lefthand kink, drivers know that they have to balance their turn-in, or they might run wide with horrible consequences.

Turn 18/19 • Bus Stop
Gear: **2**
Speed: **90kph (56mph)**

Introduced in 1980 to slow the cars before they complete their flat-out blast back up the hill to the La Source hairpin, this strangely named corner has generally been a sequence of lefts and rights, and drivers bouncing across the kerbs of these has been the norm. Most recently, it has been simplified into a one-part corner, with just a tight right followed by a left whereas it was for years a left/right followed by a short straight and then a right/left.

Great Drivers & Great Moments

Spa-Francorchamps is a circuit that has always been a considerable challenge to both man and machine. Throw in the added difficulty of the often unpredictable weather, and you have a recipe for thrills, spills and excitement. It's a place that yields only to the very best drivers and seldom fails to add a twist to the tail.

Great Drivers

Michael **Schumacher**
Spa wins – 6

Ayrton **Senna**
Spa wins – 5

Jim **Clark**
Spa wins – 4

Kimi **Raikkonen**
Spa wins – 4

Schumacher's record number of wins at Spa-Francorchamps started with his first grand prix victory. This was in 1992, one year precisely after his F1 debut and he read changing conditions best to win for Benetton. He then added three wins in a row from 1995, the first with Benetton, then the next two for Ferrari before crashing into the rear of David Coulthard's McLaren in atrociously wet conditions in 1998 when way in the lead. Two more wins for Ferrari, in 2001 and 2002, complete his haul.

Delayed by a broken-up track in 1985, the Belgian grand prix was run duly moved to later in the year and Ayrton Senna won for Lotus on a drying track. It then became a very happy hunting ground for the Brazilian: he won at Spa four years in succession for McLaren from 1988. This run could have been longer still because he'd been taken out of the lead by a clash with Nigel Mansell in 1987, then gambled wrongly on staying on slicks in the rain in 1992.

The most remarkable thing about the Scot's four wins here is that he loathed the place, considering it to be unacceptably dangerous, as proved by the 1960 Belgian GP when two drivers were injured in practice and two killed in the race. However, Jim Clark put his fears aside to win four years in a row for Lotus from 1962 to 1965. He would have won again in 1967, but it was only the second race for the new Ford DFV and he had to pit because the spark plugs needed changing.

History relates that only the very best drivers win at Spa-Francorchamps and Kimi's record of four victories bears this out. The Finn first won here for McLaren in 2004 in a chaotic race of six leaders and three safety car periods and then added another the following year, by almost 30 seconds. He then changed teams to Ferrari yet kept on winning on F1's next visit in 2007. His final win, also for Ferrari, came in 2009, but only by less than 1 second from Giancarlo Fisichella's Force India.

Great Moments

1952 Alberto **Ascari** starts a nine-race winning run

1968 Bruce **McLaren** gives his team its first win

2008 Felipe **Massa** given win as **Hamilton** disqualified

2018 Sebastian **Vettel** wins as **Alonso** is taken out

Alberto Ascari missed the opening round of the 1952 World Championship because he was preparing for the Indianapolis 500. However, he made his first outing in Ferrari's new F2-based challenger count and, after getting past Jean Behra's fast-starting Gordini on the opening lap, led all the way in heavy rain. He then won the next eight grands prix in a sequence that included the five remaining races of the 1952 season and the first three of the next to net him both drivers' titles.

Bruce McLaren's eponymous team began building its own cars in 1964 and tried F1 from 1966, but its real success had been in entering cars in the CanAm sportscar series. In the 1960s, races at Spa usually had a sting in the tail and cars were fragile, with many frontrunners failing. This included Denny Hulme, who was leading in the second McLaren and then Jackie Stewart, but he ran out of fuel. So McLaren led onto the final lap and hung on to beat BRM's Pedro Rodriguez.

Lewis Hamilton held a six-point lead over Ferrari's Felipe Massa, then drove a blinder at Spa, coming out on top of a frantic battle with Kimi Raikkonen in the other Ferrari, until the Finn spun off. However, the stewards then penalized the McLaren driver 25 seconds for cutting the Bus Stop chicane when fighting for the lead. Although he immediately relinquished the position to Raikkonen, he outbraked the Ferrari into the next corner and this is what earned him the penalty and handed victory to Massa.

Sebastian Vettel's name is in the record books as the winner of the 2018 Belgian GP. He drove well for Ferrari to do so, overcoming a challenge not just from Lewis Hamilton's Mercedes but from both Force India drivers as they ran four abreast on the opening lap. However, what will be remembered more is the incident that happened behind them at the first corner when Nico Hulkenberg got his braking wrong and crashed his Renault into Fernando Alonso's McLaren, launching it over the top of Charles Leclerc's Sauber.

🇫🇷 Paul Ricard

The pet project of drinks tycoon Paul Ricard, his eponymous circuit was the most modern of its era when opened in 1970. Times, however, moved on and it was dropped after hosting the 1990 French GP. Made safer by the introduction of huge run-off areas, it was back on the F1 calendar in 2018.

> ❝ The place is beautiful. There are a lot of different lines that you can take and it can be tricky to find reference points as, apart from the coloured lines, it's difficult to tell where you are. ❞
>
> *Lewis Hamilton*

The French GP is the oldest grand prix of all, dating all the way back to 1906. Unlike Italy, whose grands prix have almost always been held at Monza, France's grands prix have been constantly on the move.

After the flat-out blast around the triangle of public roads outside Reims was no longer considered safe, the race moved to Rouen-les-Essarts and Clermont-Ferrand and even had a one-off visit to the lacklustre Bugatti circuit on the infield at Le Mans. Both Rouen-les-Essarts and Clermont-Ferrand were fantastic, difficult circuits, but they offered more than a few possible locations for major accidents. Then along came Paul Ricard, and ancient was swapped for modern.

Financed by pastis manufacturer Paul Ricard, the circuit was built on a pine-dotted plateau inland from Toulon. As everything was done from scratch, this was a circuit built without compromise. With a purpose-built pit building and modern safety features, it felt space age. Add to this the fact that its location in the South of France generally meant fine weather, it was an immediate hit.

Paul Ricard's lap felt different from many of its rivals as it was open in nature, with a flat-out sprint down the slope towards a series of low-speed corners before the mile-long blast up the Mistral Straight to flat-out Signes, a corner to test any driver. From there, the corners tightened up again to complete its 3.61-mile course. An extra feature of the circuit was that it was generally wide enough for drivers to attempt different lines into many of the slower corners, making overtaking less of a challenge than it was on older, narrower tracks.

The first World Championship GP was held there in 1971, with Jackie Stewart the first to take the top step of the podium, followed home at a distance by his Tyrrell team-mate Francois Cevert. Although Clermont-Ferrand hosted the race for one last time in 1972, it was back at Paul Ricard in 1973 when Ronnie Peterson inherited victory for Lotus. Then along came the Dijon-Prenois circuit at the other end of France, and the French GP alternated this venue and Paul Ricard from 1974 until 1984.

In 1986, Paul Ricard's safety was called into question after Elio de Angelis died there after crashing his Brabham at Signes during a test. For the next four years, the grand prix was held on a considerably truncated version of the circuit, with a 2.353-mile lap that turned sharp right after the pit exit and then right again to join the original circuit around halfway up the Mistral Straight, thus reducing the entry speed to Signes.

Political pressure led to the French GP moving on in 1991, heading north again after President Mitterand agreed to finance the upgrade of the Magny-Cours club circuit to help boost the economy of the Nevers region. This cast Paul Ricard into decline, but in 1999 F1 ringmaster Bernie Ecclestone bought the circuit and set about turning it into a high-tech testing facility.

Chief among the upgrades was a transformation of the circuit to make it safer by dint of moving the banks beyond the edges of the track way further back. However, the trademark of Paul Ricard isn't the extra space this provided, per se, but the coloured bands that start beyond the marked edge of the track, with the bands being marked in an increasingly abrasive asphalt/tungsten mix as they change from blue stripes to red the further off the track a driver might stray. The idea is that a driver can spin safely on tarmac and so gravel traps are not required. Furthermore, a driver doesn't want to short-cut a corner if they can help it.

The revised Paul Ricard also found its way back onto the international scene as top single-seater, sportscar and touring car series returned.

It took until 2018, though, for F1 to return and although the circuit suited the latest F1 cars, the traffic plans failed in major fashion. F1's new owner, Liberty Media, was not impressed. ■

Opposite: The vivid track markings and rolling French countryside surrounding the track make Paul Ricard one of F1's most distinctive venues.

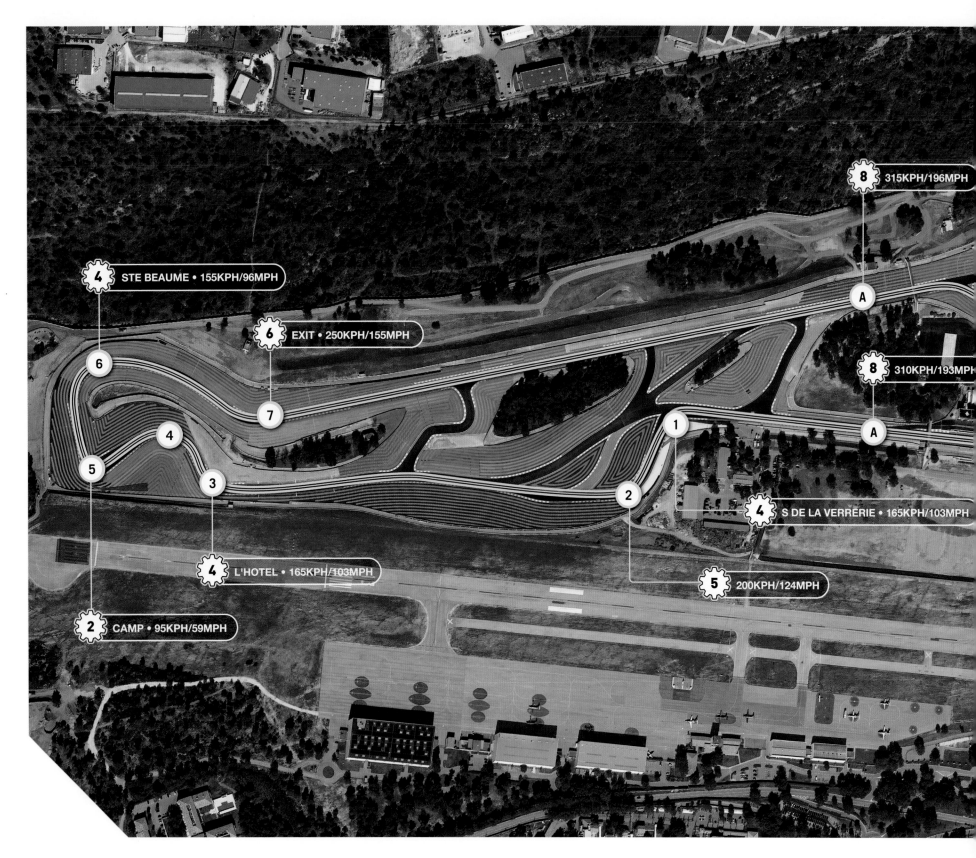

8 315KPH/196MPH

4 STE BEAUME • 155KPH/96MPH

6 EXIT • 250KPH/155MPH

A

6

8 310KPH/193MPH

7

A

4

1

5

3

2

4 S DE LA VERRERIE • 165KPH/103MPH

4 L'HOTEL • 165KPH/103MPH

5 200KPH/124MPH

2 CAMP • 95KPH/59MPH

8 SIGNES • 270KPH/168MPH

10

9

BENDOR • 115KPH/71MPH **3**

12

3 CHICANE NORD • 145KPH/90MPH

13

14

3 LAC • 145KPH/90MPH

15 **2** PONT • 85KPH/53MPH

11

BEAUSSET • 175KPH/109MPH **4**

Google Earth

Circuit Guide

Although the circuit keeps fairly much to the layout of the original circuit that hosted F1 between 1971 and 1990, it now has a vast curtilage of painted tarmac beyond the track limits, giving the drivers an unusual feeling of safety.

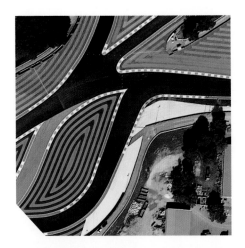

Turn 1 • S de la Verrerie
Gear: **4**
Speed: **165kph (103mph)**

Having blasted down the pit straight, drivers find themselves in a far more enclosed-feeling environment as they approach the first corner in top gear, as trees line both sides of the track. It's hard for them to see the corner until they are almost into it, but they can be reassured by a huge expanse of painted run-off ahead of them as they commit to the high-speed flick to the left and aim to get across to the left for the dipping righthander that follows.

Turn 3 • L'Hotel
Gear: **4**
Speed: **165kph (103mph)**

The downhill approach to L'Hotel feels expansive, as the track runs through the middle of an immense area of painted run-off that makes it tricky for drivers to see the entry to this tight right. In many ways, it's a two-part corner, as the track almost immediately snaps to the left through an even tighter corner. The camber also means that a driver carrying in too much speed will struggle to keep on line. On the opening lap, it can get extremely busy and drivers often get caught out in another's ambitious move.

Turn 6 • Ste Baume
Gear: **4**
Speed: **155kph (96mph)**

This is the lowest point of the lap and the drivers should now be starting to open up after the L'Hotel and Camp corners and begin to consider the Mistral Straight. This simple righthander offers drivers a feeling of safety that they seldom experience at any other circuit thanks to the vast run-off area, but getting their car to turn in so that they can floor the throttle for the lefthand flick that follows is imperative to either a quick lap or to getting a tow from a rival in the race.

Turn 8 • Chicane Nord
Gear: **3**
Speed: **145kph (90mph)**

The Mistral Straight doesn't have the same magic as it did in the circuit's pre-facelift guise. Sloping from the exit of Turn 7 for more than a mile all the way up the hill to Signes, it used to be a flat-out blast long enough for drivers to both check their gauges and to consider the challenge of Signes beyond. As it was considered that the approach to Signes would simply be too fast, this left/right/left flick was inserted, with a more complicated right/left/right/left combination used by other racing categories.

Opposite: Lewis Hamilton keeps the blue lines to the right of his Mercedes as he races to victory in 2018. ***Above left:*** Esteban Ocon hoped for glory on home ground in 2018, but his Force India was out on the opening lap after he clashed with compatriot Pierre Gasly. ***Above right:*** Romain Grosjean qualified 10th for Haas in 2018, but ended up 11th in the race, just out of the points.

Turn 10 • Signes
Gear: **8**
Speed: **207kph (168mph)**

This has always been the signature corner of the Paul Ricard lap. Even with the chicane inserted halfway along the Mistral Straight, it's still a fearsome, top-gear corner. The big change since the circuit was given its considerable overhaul in 2000 has been the addition of a huge area of run-off on the outside of the corner, which is a good thing too as the corner has always been made extra tricky by occasional strong gusts of wind, something that certainly doesn't help when trying to hold your line.

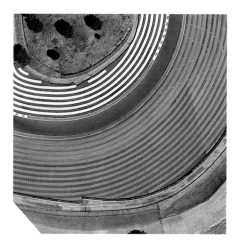

Turn 11 • Beausset
Gear: **4**
Speed: **175kph (109mph)**

The corner's full name of Double Droite du Beausset gives lie to the fact that this is in some ways two corners rolled into one. There's a flat approach, taken at considerable speed as the cars fire out of Signes, then a slightly sloping entry taken in fourth gear. As with the entire track, there is a huge painted area of run-off, but what interests the drivers is getting the car to turn in sufficiently and efficiently not to run wide through the second part of the turn.

Turn 12 • Bendor
Gear: **3**
Speed: **115kph (71mph)**

This lefthander is the point at which the fast middle section of the lap truly comes to an end and the technical final sector begins. The track slopes gently from entry to the exit and then carries on down the mild slope all the way past the pits to Ste Beaume. Taken in third gear, Bendor is a longish lefthander and the open sweep of the following corner, Garlaban, is broad enough for drivers to at least challenge a rival into Lac if that rival has slipped wide here.

Turn 15 • Pont
Gear: **2**
Speed: **85kph (53mph)**

Called Pont because it is positioned above the road entry into the circuit infield, it's hard to get excited about a corner taken in second gear at little over 50mph. However, a good exit from the final corner of the lap is vital if a driver wants to get into position to perhaps attempt an overtaking manoeuvre into the first corner. Because it follows soon after the exit from Lac, a poor exit from the latter means that a driver will be compromised for Pont, with the obvious disadvantages that brings.

Great Drivers & Great Moments

With the Paul Ricard circuit only regaining its World Championship status in 2018, a look back at its history means looking at the 1970s and 1980s when Niki Lauda and Nigel Mansell were in their pomp and Alain Prost proved to be the best of all by winning his home race in the south of France four times.

Great Drivers

Alain **Prost**
Paul Ricard wins – 4

Alain had a wonderful hit rate in his home grand prix. In all, he won the French GP six times in his 13-year F1 career, with the first of these coming at Dijon-Prenois in 1981 and the last at Magny-Cours in 1993. The other four were all achieved at Paul Ricard, starting with success for Renault in 1983 when he won by 30s from Brabham's Nelson Piquet. Then came three wins in three years, with the first two for McLaren in 1988 and 1989 and the last once he'd moved to Ferrari in 1990.

Niki **Lauda**
Paul Ricard wins – 2

When the great Austrian was in brilliant form for Ferrari in his first title-winning season in 1975, he made winning at Paul Ricard look easy as he built on wins in Monaco, Belgium and Sweden in the previous three races, leading every lap to beat James Hunt's Hesketh. Amazingly, he didn't win here again until 1984 when he responded to the form of rapid new McLaren team-mate Alain Prost to catch and pass Patrick Tambay's Renault victory on a day when Prost's race was scuppered by a loose wheel.

Nigel **Mansell**
Paul Ricard wins – 2

After Nigel Mansell discovered the winning touch in the closing races of 1985, he enjoyed more frontrunning for Williams in 1986 and his win here helped defeat team-mate Nelson Piquet. Notably, they shared the podium with McLaren's Alain Prost, whose points for second helped him sneak past the pair to land that year's title. They were still at each other's throats the following year, but again it was the British bulldog who won here in 1987 as their Honda-powered FW11Bs were the class of the field.

Lewis **Hamilton**
Paul Ricard wins – 2

By winning both grands prix since the French GP returned to Paul Ricard, Lewis Hamilton has made the place his own. The first of these successes came in 2018 when he kept clear of a lunging Sebastian Vettel's Ferrari on arrival at the first corner, unlike his unfortunate Mercedes team-mate Valtteri Bottas. Lewis then controlled the proceedings to win by 7s from Max Verstappen. In 2019, Lewis needed no help and this time led every lap to beat Bottas by 18s in a four-race-winning streak.

Great Moments

1973 — Lead battle clash denies **Scheckter**

McLaren's Jody Scheckter made a major impact on F1 when he hit the sport's top level and looked set to take victory in only his third World Championship outing, but it wasn't to be. The South African qualified on the front row and got the jump on Jackie Stewart's Tyrrell at the start then looked very comfortable in the lead. However, when delayed in lapping a backmarker, Emerson Fittipaldi closed in and made a dive into the final corner. They touched and were both out, handing victory to the other Lotus driver, Ronnie Peterson.

1982 — Double delight for **Renault** at home

Jean-Pierre Jabouille delighted Renault when he won the French GP at Dijon-Prenois in 1979, and Rene Arnoux nearly made it a one-two. Three years later, Renault did fill the top two positions, with Arnoux topping the podium at Paul Ricard ahead of team-mate Alain Prost. Arnoux led away, but was soon pushed back by the Brabhams of Riccardo Patrese and Nelson Piquet before returning to a lead he would keep. It was such a competitive year that he became the ninth winner in the first 11 rounds.

1990 — **Capelli** three laps from shock win

The final grand prix at Paul Ricard before its rerun in 2018 very nearly produced a shock result as the Leyton House made a discovery that suddenly propelled its cars to the front of the grid. Nigel Mansell and Gerhard Berger locked out the front row for McLaren but, by mid-distance, Ivan Capelli had guided one of the Adrian Newey-designed CG901s into the lead. And there he stayed, until, agonisingly, with just three laps to go, Alain Prost went past in his Ferrari to squash a fairytale result.

2018 — **Vettel** crashes to help **Hamilton** take victory

Lewis Hamilton was feeling the pressure of a stern challenge from Ferrari's Sebastian Vettel who arrived at Paul Ricard with three wins to his name to Hamilton's two. Yet, the pressure was shifted to Vettel when Hamilton took pole and the German qualified only third as Mercedes filled the front row. Anxious to get past, he clipped Valtteri Bottas's Mercedes at the first corner then clashed with Romain Grosjean's Haas easy for Hamilton as he led Max Verstappen home with ease, with Vettel making it back to fifth.

Hockenheim

This long-time home of the German GP is a circuit that has undergone a considerable transformation over the decades. As a result, its races feel so different that they fall into the ages either before or after the change, thus either with the forest loop or without it.

> ❝ Arriving back into the stadium and seeing all the people there feels good because all the way to the Ostkurve there are no spectators and it feels very lonely. ❞
>
> *Damon Hill*

Like rival German circuit the Nürburgring, Hockenheim dates back to the 1920s, opening for racing in 1929. They couldn't have been more contrasting, though, as their only similarity was that they both ran through forests and Hockenheim was flat and simple in lay-out, with effectively two arcing straights joined by a curve at either end. Mercedes-Benz was its most frequent customer, using the circuit for testing purposes.

After the Second World War, Hockenheim had a quiet life, running national race meetings while the Nürburgring hosted the German GP and international sportscar races. The first major change followed in 1966, when it was shortened by the construction of an autobahn between the circuit and the town of Hockenheim, slicing off its western end. Large grandstands were built at this curtailed end and the track made to run in a small loop in front of them at the end of the lap.

Tragically, what made the circuit famous was when the ultimate driver of the day, Jim Clark, already a two-time World Champion, turned up to race for Lotus in a Formula Two race in the spring of 1968 and was killed when his car speared off into the trees.

Aware that speeds down the straights needed to be kept in check, the organizers inserted two chicanes on the loop through the forest in 1970, with one on the outward leg past the point where Clark had crashed and the other on the return run.

After the one-off German GP held here in 1970, Hockenheim had to wait until 1977 to take over the German GP once Niki Lauda had shown once and for all that the Nürburgring was no longer safe enough for F1 (see page 43). Even though it was nine years on from Clark's death, his presence still lingered here, but this gradually dissipated over the following years as Hockenheim hosted some thrilling grands prix.

Yet Hockenheim continued to present dangers of its own and Patrick Depailler crashed his Alfa Romeo at the Ostkurve during a test in 1980, and was killed. As a result of this, a third chicane was inserted, at the Ostkurve, thus making the circuit safer but removing the one long, fast corner. Yet, one of the drivers' perpetual fears about the place remained. This was a fear of running in the rain, since they would be flat-out on the back section, topping 320kph (200mph), with any spray contained by the trees flanking the track and thus incredibly limiting visibility. It was in just such a scenario that Didier Pironi's F1 career was brought to an end in 1982 during practice when he was unsighted by spray and went to overtake Derek Daly's Williams, only to find another car – Alain Prost's Renault – travelling slowly alongside. He slammed his Ferrari into it as they approached the stadium, suffering awful injuries to his feet and ankles.

The racing here was typified by furious dicing for position on the run to the first corner on the opening lap, then more late braking and occasional place-changing on arrival at the first chicane. Thereafter, overtaking tended to happen only at the three chicanes, but the slipstreaming groups certainly looked spectacular as they raced flat-out through the forest. Finally, in 1995, Michael Schumacher gave the crowds the result they so craved, a first home win for a German driver.

Then, partly to pander to environmentalists, the circuit was forced to make radical alterations in 2002. At a stroke, half of its lap was pared away, the forest section axed and a revised lay-out created by ubiquitous circuit architect Hermann Tilke. Instead of accelerating up to maximum speed and remaining there for the blast from the Nordkurve all the way to the first chicane, drivers soon had to start braking hard when not even halfway along this flat-out stretch and turn sharply right. A kilometre-long arcing run to a hairpin follows before bringing the cars back to the entry point to the stadium via a sequence of twisting curves that are dull but undeniably safer. Thus the very nature of the place was transformed, but the plus side was that the cars would come past the grandstands more often, with the grand prix changing from 45 laps to 67. ∎

Opposite: Michael Schumacher leads the dash down to Nordkurve in 2002, trailed by brother Ralf and Rubens Barrichello.

27

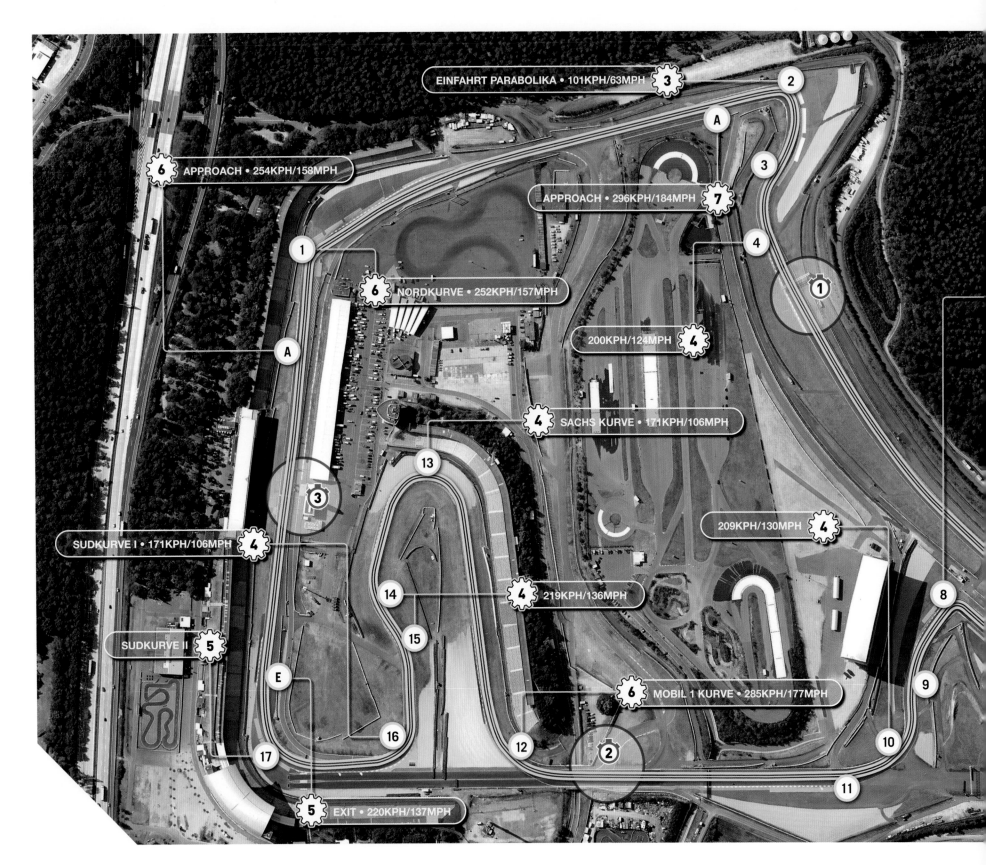

EINFAHRT PARABOLIKA • 101KPH/63MPH 3
2
A
3
6 APPROACH • 254KPH/158MPH
APPROACH • 296KPH/184MPH 7
4
1
6 NORDKURVE • 252KPH/157MPH
200KPH/124MPH 4
A
4 SACHS KURVE • 171KPH/106MPH
13
209KPH/130MPH 4
8
3
SUDKURVE I • 171KPH/106MPH 4
14 4 219KPH/136MPH
15
SUDKURVE II 5
E
6 MOBIL 1 KURVE • 285KPH/177MPH
9
16
12 2
10
17
11
5 EXIT • 220KPH/137MPH

3 MERCEDES ARENA • 106KPH/66MPH

APPROACH • 304KPH/189MPH 7

6 270KPH/168MPH

2 SPITZKEHRE • 64KPH/40MPH

5

A

7

6

Google Earth

Circuit Guide

Hockenheim's lap can be split into two parts. The division comes after the first corner when the cars leave the stadium section and head out to quieter zones, only to move back in front of grandstands full of noisy fans when they reach Mobil 1 Kurve.

Turn 1 • Nordkurve
Gear: **6**
Speed: **254kph (158mph)**

This can be an explosive corner on the opening lap of a grand prix as drivers jostle for position, which has been shown numerous times. Luciano Burti's aerobatic accident in 2001, when he hit Michael Schumacher's faltering Ferrari, offers proof of what can happen when cars come together. On regular racing laps, drivers want to be as far to the left as possible to give them the widest possible line to help them carry the most speed through the corner onto the straight beyond.

Turn 2/3/4 • Einfahrt Parabolika
Gear: **3**
Speed: **101kph (63mph)**

The first corner of what many still consider to be the "new" part of the circuit is a corner that is largely alien to the nature of the previous layout. It's a tight one, almost a hairpin, with drivers again needing to turn in from wide out (unless moving to the inside line to block a passing attempt), to get through not only the corner but the tightening angle immediately after that and the lefthander onto the back "straight" that follows.

Turn 5 • Parabolika
Gear: **6**
Speed: **280kph (174mph)**

Hockenheim, both old and new, is always thought of as somewhere with plenty of lengthy straights for flat-out motoring, but the truth is that they were usually anything but straight, all arcing one direction or the other. Whereas the ones on the old circuit arced to the right, Parabolika arcs the other way. Trees are set back from the lefthand side of the track and these angle back as the run to the Spitzkehre straightens out, giving drivers warning that they will soon need to brake.

Turn 6 • Spitzkehre
Gear: **2**
Speed: **304kph (40mph)**

Overtaking action can almost always be guaranteed if there's a long straight leading into a hairpin, and this is just the formula for Spitzkehre, with drivers needing to brake from 320kph (189mph) in sixth gear to slow all the way down to 64kph (40mph) for this sharp right. The trouble is, the corner onto Parabolika is so tight that cars usually come out line astern, thus making it hard for cars racing rather than lapping to find the performance advantage to catch a tow and pull off a move.

Opposite: Emerson Fittipaldi gets a little sideways at the Sackskurve in 1970 en route to fourth on his second outing for Lotus. *Above left:* Alan Jones, shown at the third chicane, remembers the 1979 German GP fondly because it was his first win for Williams. *Above right:* Ferrari's René Arnoux leads Andrea de Cesaris' Alfa Romeo, Nelson Piquet's Brabham and the Renaults into Sudkurve in 1983.

Turn 8 • Mercedes Arena
Gear: **3**
Speed: **106kph (66mph)**

Having looked straight ahead to the old circuit as they turn in to Spitzkehre, drivers then scrabble for traction as they get the power down on the hairpin's exit to run through the sixth gear kink at Turn 7 and look to make a move in front of the Mercedes grandstand. The corner changes the flow again as drivers have to drop to third gear, again staying out wide on the right as late as possible because they know they'll have to change direction again almost immediately.

Turn 12 • Mobil 1 Kurve
Gear: **6**
Speed: **285kph (177mph)**

This fast righthander used to mark the end of the forest section on the old circuit, giving the drivers something of a shock as they burst out in front of the spectators filling the giant grandstands in the stadium section. Now, the contrast isn't as great, but the drivers still notice a sudden increase in noise as they come out of this easy righthander, trying not to run too far over the flat kerbs on the exit because this would spin their cars around.

Turn 13 • Sachs Kurve
Gear: **4**
Speed: **71kph (106mph)**

Ever since this corner was inserted in 1966, it has been frustratingly slow and technical. Right at the foot of the grandstands, it looks simple enough, if slow, but this fourth gear lefthander is made more interesting by there being a drop down to the apex and then an equivalent incline on the way out again, with the bend usefully lightly banked to help get the cars around it. Overtaking is hard to do here, but not impossible if the driver ahead makes a mistake.

Turn 17 • Sudkurve
Gear: **4**
Speed: **171kph (106mph)**

The corner preceding any straight is clearly worthy of considerable study because momentum lost will never be regained. In many ways, the Sudkurve can be treated as two different corners, with the first a righthander over a slight brow, then a brief drop before the track cuts right again, this time dropping away slightly between turn in and exit, with a small degree of banking enabling drivers to find more grip that helps them to get the power down for the blast past the pits.

Great Drivers & Great Moments

The long straights and chicanes used to provide extremely dramatic races, but throw in fist fights, a pit fire, a track invasion and the suggestion of team orders, and it's not surprising that racing at Hockenheim has always been considered exciting with the outcome frequently changing late in the race.

Great Drivers

 Michael **Schumacher**
Hockenheim wins – 4

Fittingly, as it's his home grand prix, Michael Schumacher holds the record for the most German GP wins at Hockenheim. He managed this for the first time in 1995 for Benetton, reaching the finish 30 seconds clear of Damon Hill's Williams, and then had the embarrassment of stalling his engine as he waved to his fans and so had to be towed in. He then repeated this success for Ferrari in 2002, 2004 and 2006, with team-mate Felipe Massa running obligingly on his heels in the last of these.

 Nelson **Piquet**
Hockenheim wins – 3

Nelson Piquet managed to win three times at Hockenheim, so there's a certain irony that, to many, the most famous thing that he did here was to punch Eliseo Salazar in 1982 after they clashed when he came up to lap the ATS driver. The Brazilian's three wins came in 1981, 1986 and 1987, with the last being extremely fortunate: it was gifted to him when Alain Prost's McLaren suffered alternator failure with five laps to go, leaving Nelson to win easily for Williams.

 Ayrton **Senna**
Hockenheim wins – 3

Ayrton Senna failed to finish higher than second at Hockenheim for Lotus, but won here three times for McLaren. The first came in his first year with the team, in 1998, when he started from pole and led every lap. He repeated the feat in 1989, albeit with team-mate Alain Prost heading him through the middle of the race, then made it three in a row in 1990, when he again had to regain the lead, this time from Benetton's Alessandro Nannini who got ahead by not pitting.

 Lewis **Hamilton**
Hockenheim wins – 3

There was no race at Hockenheim in Hamilton's maiden season, so his first F1 visit there came in 2008 and he won after starting from pole in his McLaren, ahead of Renault's Nelson Piquet Jr. Eight years later, he had an easy run after Mercedes team-mate Nico Rosberg fluffed the start and couldn't make it back any higher than fourth, as Daniel Ricciardo claimed second for Red Bull. In 2018, Hamilton was gifted victory when Sebastian Vettel slid his Ferrari into the gravel after rain swept in.

Great Moments

1970 Jochen **Rindt** pips Jacky **Ickx** to win by 0.7 secs

In 1970, the German GP was moved to Hockenheim because the owners of the Nürburgring had failed to carry out required safety modifications to the Nordschleife. So the F1 teams turned up to this circuit that was the polar opposite to the Nordschleife. The race was between front row starters Jacky Ickx and Jochen Rindt, with the former leading from pole in his Ferrari, but the lead changed between them 12 times before the Austrian edged ahead in his Lotus to win by 0.7 seconds.

1994 Jos **Verstappen** survives a dramatic pit fire

The 1994 season had already claimed the lives of both Ayrton Senna and Roland Ratzenberger at Imola, and left Karl Wendlinger in an induced coma, so it certainly didn't need any more injuries, yet trouble reared its head at the German GP when Benetton rookie Jos Verstappen and his pitcrew were engulfed in flame after a dramatic fire during a pitstop. Fortunately, they all escaped with relatively minor burns, but the team was later found to have tampered with its refuelling rig.

2000 Rubens **Barrichello** helped by a track invasion

F1 can be shaped by bizarre events, and this was definitely the case in 2000, when a former Mercedes employee staged a protest by running along the grass verges before the first chicane. This brought out the safety car and the race soon turned from one of McLaren domination to one that fell into Rubens Barrichello's hands as Mika Hakkinen pitted for wet weather tyres when it started to rain, losing a 30-second lead. Barrichello stayed out to score his first F1 win for Ferrari.

2014 Lewis **Hamilton** advances from the tail

Nico Rosberg made it nine wins from the first 10 rounds for Mercedes, crossing the finish line almost 20 seconds clear of Valtteri Bottas's Williams. Yet the drive of the race came from his team-mate Lewis Hamilton, for the English ace crashed in qualifying and started from 20th on the grid. That he was able to tiger his way up to third place, less than 2 seconds down on Bottas impressed all who watched it, and showed how much he wanted that second F1 title that he'd go on to claim.

Nürburgring

Built in the 1980s to keep the Nürburgring on the international stage, this was criticized at first for being a homogenized, safety-first sort of circuit – as it obviously is in comparison to the original Nordschleife with which it shared the start/finish area – but it has become accepted as one of the homes of the German GP.

❝ The current circuit may be less epic than the original 14-mile [22.5km] layout, but it can still bite you and the weather can turn in a matter of moments. ❞

Lewis Hamilton

The rumblings had gone on for years that the Nürburgring Nordschleife was becoming too dangerous for F1 – or, looked at another way, the cars too fast for the circuit. Indeed, the drivers had campaigned for safety improvements in 1969, with Jackie Stewart leading the crusade that led to the track being widened in places, crash barriers added, crests flattened and trees felled. Yet, within a few years, the rumblings were just as strong again. Then Niki Lauda's near-fatal accident in the 1976 German GP showed that the end was nigh. Hockenheim had taken over and there appeared to be no comeback.

However, the circuit owners elected to do what many fans considered to be "the unthinkable": they built a new circuit on the site. This shared the same start/finish line and the same name, but the Nordschleife was merely an anachronism disappearing into the trees in the background. The new circuit was seen by its promoters as the brave new world, a safe place to go racing and one on which fans could see the cars for much of the lap and get to see them 67 times per grand prix – a contrast to the 14 laps allocated to grands prix held on the Nordschleife.

Many fans were stunned when they saw it for the first time in the autumn of 1984, pointing out that this facility looked as though it had been designed for a different sport. Some said that the gravel traps surrounding almost the entire lap were so large that the fans in the grandstands could scarcely make out the cars. It certainly wasn't love as first sight. Not that Alain Prost cared: he won that first race – run as the European GP – for McLaren after leading every lap.

Brand-new pit buildings gave the new circuit an entirely new feel, all but masking the one part of the track that was shared with the Nordschleife, with a modern hotel nestled into the banks on the far side of the track. The new track then dipped and twisted its way down a gentle slope to the Dunlop Kehre, a hairpin, without a single tree in sight, save for those poking over the tops of the grandstands for the climb back up that slope to what is now Michelin-Kurve. From here, at least, the circuit opened out a little, with a fabulous, dropping sweep from Warsteiner-Kurve allowing the drivers to really let their cars run, and offering the feel of the old circuit again as they were freed from running in front of grandstands and had the backdrop of the Eifel forest across a grassy expanse to their left. After an uphill chicane, the drivers could see the point at which the Nordschleife arced away to the left and off into the forest, but their lap was coming to an end rather than just starting. It was nothing like its full-blood predecessor, but actually not a bad circuit in the modern idiom. It just took years before F1 insiders and racing romantics were prepared to accept this.

Like the Nordschleife, this new circuit also was prone to the arrival of race-shaping downpours, and yet they were never as life-threatening due to the expanses of space either side of the track. There were no hedges running up to the edge of the track here… Indeed, one of the most fondly remembered races was in 1999, when constantly changing conditions not only produced an enthralling race but a surprise winner in Johnny Herbert for Stewart GP.

The circuit changed again in 2002, when the first corner was transformed, being made to double back on itself before feeding into a three-corner loop that brings the cars back to the previous layout where it had exited the first corner esse.

Financial troubles have beset the Nürburgring recently and the heady days in the first decade of the twenty-first century, when Schumachermania encouraged the FIA to allocate Germany two grands prix per year, with the one at the Nürburgring running as the European GP, seem long gone. Indeed, the financial situation of both here and Hockenheim have deteriorated so much that they now alternate the grand prix, with only a local government bail-out enabling the Nürburgring to host the race in 2013. ∎

Opposite: Red Bull Racing's Sebastian Vettel leads the way through the Yokohama-S from Lotus duo Romain Grosjean and Kimi Raikkonen in 2013.

WARSTEINER-KURVE • 201KPH/125MPH **4** 11

MICHELIN-KURVE • 163KPH/101MPH **4**

AUDI-S • 270KPH/168MPH **6**

APPROACH • 299KPH/186MPH **7** A

10

DUNLOP KEHRE • 103KPH/64MPH **3**

258KPH/160MPH **6**

9

7

A

5

200KPH/125MPH **5**

A

8

6 APPROACH • 266KPH/165MPH

1

A

6 APPROACH • 282KPH/175MPH

6

A

5 APPROACH • 201KPH/125MPH

FORD KURVE • 120KPH/75MPH **3**

12 6 ADVAN-BOGEN • 285KPH/177MPH

2 NGK SCHIKANE • 105KPH/65MPH

3 2 MERCEDES ARENA II • 89KPH/55MPH

3 152KPH/94MPH

APPROACH • 240KPH/149MPH 5

4 3 MERCEDES ARENA I 129KPH/80MPH

2 14

13

1 2 YOKOHAMA-S • 76KPH/47MPH

A

A 15

7 APPROACH • 301KPH/187MPH 3

3 COCA-COLA KURVE • 129KPH/80MPH 3

Google Earth

Image © 2014 DigitalGlobe © Google 2014

37

Circuit Guide

The Nürburgring is very much a contemporary circuit, with plenty of run-off space and huge gravel traps around its lap, thus lacking the intimacy of its forebears, but it provides the drivers with a worthwhile challenge as it traverses the rolling terrain.

Turn 1 • Yokohama-S
Gear: **2**
Speed: **76kph (47mph)**

The opening corner of the Nürburgring started life as a right/left esse in the 1980s, with many a scrap between drivers ending up with one or other of the cars marooned in the gravel trap. However, it was changed comprehensively for 2002 and now requires drivers to brake hard for a righthand hairpin, with a gently dipping entry, wary that they have to position themselves for the exit, often with a driver trying to pass them, thus forcing them to drive defensively and cover the inside line.

Turn 6 • Ford Kurve
Gear: **3**
Speed: **120kph (75mph)**

This righthander has remained unchanged since the new circuit was built and it's the tightest corner on the descent that runs from the exit of the Mercedes Arena to the Dunlop Kehre at the foot of the hill. The corner before is fast, taken in fifth gear, but then drivers have only a short distance to haul their cars across the track to the left side to get into position to take this much tighter right, wary that the track drops away on its exit.

Turn 7 • Dunlop Kehre
Gear: **3**
Speed: **103kph (64mph)**

This is a difficult corner because drivers have to slow from around 280kph (175mph) on the downhill approach to get down to third gear for this broad hairpin. In fact, it's a two-apex corner and drivers need to get balanced as soon as possible so that they can get back on the throttle to accelerate back up the hill. One of the best moves here was by Juan Pablo Montoya in 2003, when he drove his Williams around the outside of Michael Schumacher's Ferrari.

Turn 10 • Michelin Kurve
Gear: **4**
Speed: **163kph (101mph)**

Known until recently as the RTL-Kurve, this lefthander at the crest of the hill is a seemingly simple corner, but it requires precision; keeping momentum going is vital because drivers approach in seventh gear and need to drop three cogs. Going in to the corner a shade too fast, though – especially on the often greasy track surface that prevails in the mornings when the circuit hosted the grand prix in the autumn – can lead to a trip across the grass on the exit.

Opposite: A view of Dunlop Kehre, from inside the track near the Audi-S in 1996. *Above left:* Sebastian Vettel's continued stunning form for Red Bull Racing meant that he had plenty of fans supporting him in 2013, like this one at Dunlop Kehre. *Above right:* Job done, as Vettel delivers and takes the chequered flag in front in 2013.

Turn 11 • **Warsteiner-Kurve**
Gear: **4**
Speed: **201kph (125mph)**

Warsteiner-Kurve is another fourth-gear corner that is perhaps even more key to a fast lap than the Michelin-Kurve that precedes it, because it's the way onto the fast back section of the circuit. Drivers need to move from the right of the track at the exit of Michelin to get hard left for the turn-in point and resist the desire to take in too much speed, because traction on the exit is vital for accelerating as soon as possible for the straight onto which it leads.

Turn 12 • **Advan-Bogen**
Gear: **6**
Speed: **285kph (177mph)**

This is yet another corner that has been renamed recently as the Nürburgring struggles to keep its head above water financially. Formerly known as the ITT-Bogen, it's an open righthand kink taken in top gear with a good view to the forest beyond. Drivers enjoy the supportive feeling of their cars sitting extra low as they take the compression here and consider how they might pass any rivals into the uphill chicane that follows, whether to try on the left or the right.

Turn 13/14 • **NGK Schikane**
Gear: **2**
Speed: **105kph (65mph)**

This chicane offers a passing opportunity, with its high-speed approach after the flat-out blast down from Warsteiner-Kurve, bottoming at Advan-Bogen, then the climb to the entry point beneath the spectators sitting in the grandstands. Drivers have to haul their cars down from 280kph (175mph) in top gear to 105kph (65mph) in second, then find the shortest line through this left/right sequence, remembering to stay off the kerbs if it has been raining. Accelerating out too soon can lead to a spin.

Turn 15 • **Coca-Cola Kurve**
Gear: **3**
Speed: **129kph (80mph)**

The Coca-Cola Kurve is the final corner of the lap and the highest point of the circuit and because of this is approached up a gentle incline via the short run from the chicane, with the slope levelling off at the entry point. When running without a pursuer, drivers need to place their car as far to the left as they can, then take the shallowest angle to the apex and use the full width of the exit to get the fastest exit onto the start/finish straight.

Great Drivers & Great Moments

Michael Schumacher is way clear on the number of wins achieved at the Nürburgring, but history shows that others have had a look-in too and that changing weather has shaped more than a few of the grands prix held here.

Great Drivers

Michael **Schumacher**
Nürburgring wins – 4

Michael Schumacher undoubtedly enjoyed winning the German GP at Hockenheim, but the Nürburgring was far more local to his hometown of Kerpen and so he delighted family and friends by winning four grands prix here. The first came in 1995 as he chased after his second drivers' title. He then joined Ferrari for 1996 but had to wait until 2000 for his next Nürburgring win. But he promptly added another in 2001 and a fourth in 2004, when his and Ferrari's dominance enabled him to cruise home.

Fernando **Alonso**
Nürburgring wins – 2

Kimi Raikkonen must curse the Nürburgring, for he should have won here in 2003 and then again in 2005, when his car broke on the final lap. The driver who benefited in the latter, Fernando Alonso, would go on to become only the second driver thus far to score multiple wins here. The Renault racer looked confined to second place when he spotted Raikkonen's McLaren spinning at the first corner and motored past. The Spaniard then won again here two years later, this time for McLaren.

Ralf **Schumacher**
Nürburgring wins – 1

Ralf Schumacher's six grand prix wins are way short of his brother Michael's tally of 91, but he had a fine campaign for Williams in 2003 and this included victory in the European GP at the Nürburgring. Key to this was the fact that the Michelin tyres his team used were superior to the Bridgestones fitted to brother Michael's Ferrari. Stung by criticism that he'd shown little attack following Michael home in Canada, he pressed harder and was rewarded when Kimi Raikkonen's leading McLaren expired.

Mark **Webber**
Nürburgring wins – 1

There are drivers through F1 history who stand out for being good enough to win a grand prix but being denied their chance to do so. Red Bull's Mark Webber looked as though this might include him, but it finally all came right at the Nürburgring in 2009. It had seemed as though another win had got away from him when he was made to pit for a drive-through penalty after clashing with Rubens Barrichello at the start, but he served that and was still fast enough to win.

Great Moments

1984 German GP – Alain **Prost** draws first F1 blood

The praise for the new circuit was thin on the ground during F1's first visit, but Alain Prost found reason to like the place because he closed the gap on his McLaren team-mate and title rival Niki Lauda by winning the inaugural grand prix here after getting the jump on polesitter Nelson Piquet's Brabham on the run to the first corner, then leading all the way. By contrast, Lauda qualified only 15th and spun passing a backmarker, so he had to make do with fourth place.

1998 Luxembourg GP – Mika **Hakkinen** edges title rival

Run as the Luxembourg GP in 1998, this looked set to be a poor meeting for title challengers McLaren when Ferrari outqualified both of its cars. However, Mika Hakkinen overcame his car's lack of pace to pick off early leader Eddie Irvine, then catch Michael Schumacher. By running the four laps between Schumacher's pitstop and his own as if they were qualifying laps, he emerged in front and thereafter kept pressing to pull clear and so take a four-point lead to the final round.

1999 European GP – Johnny **Herbert** wins for Stewart

This remains the Nürburgring's greatest race yet, because it never stopped surprising from start to finish. Heinz-Harald Frentzen led the first half of the race as others changed to rain tyres with varying degrees of success. Then his Jordan's electrics failed and David Coulthard took over, but it rained again and he slid off, letting Ralf Schumacher hit the front. But he picked up a puncture and Giancarlo Fisichella moved in front, then spun and so Johnny Herbert came through to give Stewart GP its only win.

2013 German GP – Sebastian **Vettel's** first home win

The 2013 German GP was Sebastian Vettel's sixth on home soil, but it holds a special place in his heart because it was the first time that he managed to win it, after winning 29 grands prix in other countries. Even then, he was kept on tenterhooks all the way to the chequered flag because Kimi Raikkonen gave chase and was just a second behind at the finish after his Lotus showed far less of an appetite for its tyres than Sebastian Vettel's Red Bull did.

Red Bull Ring

This stunning Austrian circuit began life as the Österreichring, one of the world's most flowing stretches of tarmac. Considered too fast to be safe, it was cut back considerably to become the A1-Ring in 1996, then shut shop after 2003 before being given its third lease of life in 2014 thanks to Red Bull investment.

> **"**I always enjoy driving here, not only as it's my home race, but because it has overtaking opportunities due to the three long straights that begin and end with slow corners.**"**
>
> *Alexander Wurz*

Neighbouring Switzerland was involved in the Formula One World Championship from the outset, with its testing Bremgarten circuit outside Bern. Then came the Le Mans disaster of 1955 in which more than 80 spectators were killed. This led to Switzerland banning racing within its borders. So, Austria took up the challenge of keeping F1 in the Alps. It took years of planning and the development of various facilities in the rural region of Styria north-west of Graz.

The first of these was at Zeltweg, on a simple circuit laid out on a military airfield in 1958. Used at first for club racing, it hosted a non-championship F1 race in 1963, won by Jack Brabham. Granted a World Championship round in 1964, its short length (1.998 miles) and extremely bumpy surface made it extremely unpopular.

Fortunately, just up the slope at Spielberg, a purpose-built circuit opened its doors in 1969 as the nation's excitement about Jochen Rindt grew by the week and attracted 100,000 fans through the turnstiles. This was the Österreichring, and it couldn't have been more different. Almost twice the length, at 3.673 miles, it traversed the mountainside in artistic, flowing straights and parabolas. It was fast, very fast, and the lap record before it was dropped by F1 after the 1987 Austrian GP was just over 150mph. It was also made tricky by its mountainous location being prone to summer storms.

Sadly, Rindt was killed at Monza in 1970 and it took until 1984 for Austrian fans to get to cheer a home win, when Niki Lauda triumphed for McLaren. As F1 was insisting on ever more stringent circuit safety, and the Österreichring didn't have the money to make the required modifications, it dropped out of the World Championship after Nigel Mansell's win for Williams in 1987. Furthermore, its narrow start straight was perhaps the cause of the shunts that required several starts that year.

Austrian fans were thus left without a race of their own, but investment from the country's A1 mobile telecommunications group led to racing's return to the circuit, albeit in severely truncated form. The A1-Ring used much of the old layout, but the track was shorn of one mile of its old lap, with the track turning sharply right before the old first corner and rejoining the Österreichring layout a quarter of the way along the old top straight. Other parts to be trimmed included the old Bosch Kurve, a corner considered to be its most fearsome, and the sweeping Jochen Rindt Kurve that concluded the lap, was squared off and made into two, slower turns. The magical flow of old was gone and long-time F1 fans felt shortchanged, but it still produced great moments, though many weren't aggrieved when it was dropped after the 2003 race.

Lauda seemed to be eternally disappointed at his home race, with the Österreichring producing three

first-time winners in the 1970s in Vittorio Brambilla (1975), John Watson (1976) and Alan Jones (1977). Gerhard Berger hoped to buck the trend but, like Lauda, his home race was to thwart him from 1984 through until 1997. Alexander Wurz's family was involved in the shaping of the A1-Ring, but he too was empty-handed when the race lost its slot.

In the summer of 2011, racing returned to a track with new pits, main grandstand and media centre. Now known as the Red Bull Ring, in deference to the source of its revival budget from the Red Bull energy drink company co-founded by Austrian enthusiast Dietrich Mateschitz, it hosted rounds of the DTM touring car series and Formula Renault 3.5 series. When it returned to the World Championship calendar, for 2014, people spoke more favourably of the place, not just because it was a greatly improved place to work, but because it brought back the old school feel that F1 has been shedding in its pursuit of global spread. It's as hard as ever to locate hotel accommodation in the surrounding area, but the vibe is welcome as a counterbalance to the increasing number of flyaway races. Nico Rosberg loves it, though, as he won for Mercedes in both 2014 and 2015. ∎

Opposite: Nico Rosberg leads Mercedes team-mate Lewis Hamilton into Remus at the first lap of the 2015 Austrian GP on his way to victory.

REMUS • 75KPH/47MPH

RAUCH • 175KPH/109MPH

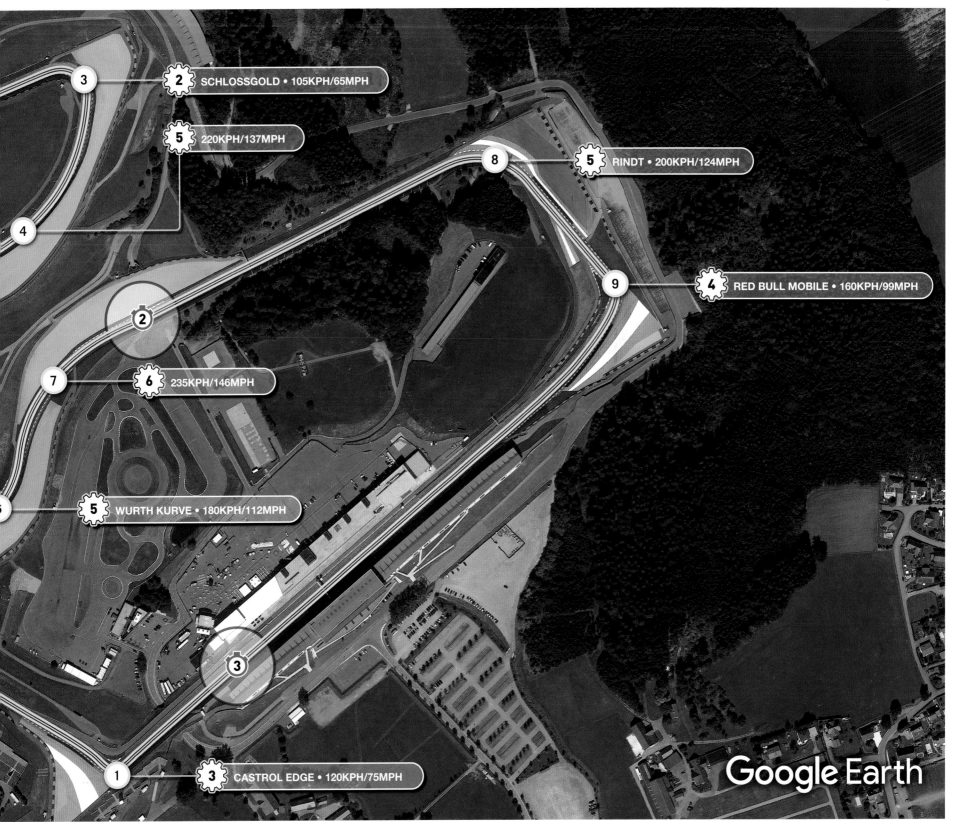

3

2 SCHLOSSGOLD • 105KPH/65MPH

5 220KPH/137MPH

4

8

5 RINDT • 200KPH/124MPH

9 **4** RED BULL MOBILE • 160KPH/99MPH

2

7 **6** 235KPH/146MPH

5 WURTH KURVE • 180KPH/112MPH

3

1 **3** CASTROL EDGE • 120KPH/75MPH

Google Earth

Circuit Guide

The scenery is truly magnificent around the Red Bull Ring, but the drivers have little time to enjoy it as they navigate their way around the mountainside, with an almost constant flow of medium-speed corners and changes of gradient to keep them busy in the cockpit.

Turn 1 • Castrol Edge
Gear: **3**
Speed: **120kph (75mph)**

Braking has to be heavy into this uphill righthander, as drivers approach it at 190mph. Caution is required, as the exit isn't visible as drivers on approach. Having crested the brow, to see trees straight ahead rather than just the sky, there's plenty of run-off, but drivers need to turn sharply to the right, something that isn't always easy in the busy traffic of the opening lap. Some chose second gear, some third, at what is one of the best spots for passing.

Turn 2 • Remus
Gear: **2**
Speed: **75kph (47mph)**

After the long, kinked run up from the first corner, the drivers have climbed appreciably to reach Remus. This is another tight corner that conceals its exit until drivers have reached the apex. This righthander is the tightest corner of the lap and its restricted nature frequently leads to contact as those who made a better exit out of the first corner then got a tow up the hill look to strike. Getting braking right here is critical, and many don't, adding to the fun.

Turn 3 • Schlossgold
Gear: **2**
Speed: **105kph (65mph)**

After another kinked straight, this time across the hillside, the drivers start a gentle drop into the third corner, Schlossgold. With the track continuing to drop away from the entry of the corner to the exit, drivers find this long second gear turn a challenging one as they struggle to keep their car balanced. The old grandstand that used to have the fearsome Bosche Kurve right at the fans' feet, is a more sensible distance back behind a gravel trap.

Turn 5 • Rauch
Gear: **5**
Speed: **175kph (109mph)**

After running through a stretch of track flanked Turn 4 is a kink to the right as the descent from Schlossghold turns into a run across the hillside again. Then, as drivers hit 165mph, they have to consider the first part of a pair of right-handers. Rauch can be taken in fourth, but is generally a fifth-gear turn, pitching the drivers down the hill and offering them a clear view of the paddock, grandstands and valley below. When a driver gets Turns 4 to 6 right, there's a wonderful flow.

Opposite: Mika Hakkinen leads into Turn 1 for McLaren in 1998, after deposing Benetton's poleman Giancarlo Fisichella. ***Above left:*** Takuma Sato's Jordan takes a hit from Nick Heidfeld's Sauber at Remus midway through the race in 2002. Sato had to be cut out of his car but, luckily, wasn't badly injured. ***Above right:*** The montains were still snow-capped when F1 visited in 2003, providing a stunning backdrop as Michael Schumacher raced to victory.

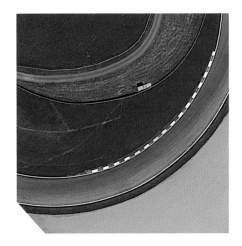

Turn 6 • **Wurth Kurve**
Gear: **5**
Speed: **180kph (112mph)**

This second consecutive left-hand turn echoes the shape of Rauch, but differs in that it cups the cars slightly as it arrests their descent and turns them back across the hillside again. Entry is important, but a good exit is vital, as Wurth Kurve feeds almost immediately into a slight ascent up to the following corner. In many ways, they're close enough to be treated as a pair. A glance to the left gives drivers a clear view of the giant Red Bull sculpture above them.

Turn 7
Gear: **6**
Speed: **235kph (146mph)**

The quick left flick out of Wurth Kurve into a righthander up over a crest at this seventh turn puts the drivers' bodies through heavy G-loading. However, it's considered fairly easy by the drivers as they start to focus on the final two corners that await them. The nature of the track changes here as the track leaves the open meadows of the first part of the lap and enters a short stretch through a patch of woodland.

Turn 8 • **Rindt**
Gear: **5**
Speed: **200kph (124mph)**

Where once there was simply one long, long downhill right-hand corner to complete the lap, there have been two since the Österreichring was transformed to its current format in 1996. Named after Austria's first World Champion, Jochen Rindt Kurve is taken in fifth gear, plunging the drivers down the final slope. There's plenty of space on the exit if drivers should get it wrong, suitably painted in patriotic red-and-white stripes, but a clean line here is required to get the last turn right.

Turn 9 • **Red Bull Mobile**
Gear: **4**
Speed: **160kph (99mph)**

The final corner is tighter than the one before it and it's made extra tricky by a compression that is right next to the apex. It's tempting for drivers to try to negotiate it, but if should they get it wrong, their cars can be spat out towards the outside of the track, with the result than many of them are then spinning back across towards the pit wall. However, a good exit can give drivers a clear opportunity to get a run on the car ahead on the 190mph approach to the first corner.

Great Drivers & Great Moments

Alain Prost won three times at the Österreichring, but no driver has yet managed to equal that tally in the nine grands prix that have been held to date on its shortened successor and Nico Rosberg is the only driver to win twice on this new layout. Outcomes have included Ferrari asking its drivers to swap positions.

Great Drivers

 Mika **Hakkinen**
Red Bull Ring wins – 2

 Nico **Rosberg**
Red Bull Ring wins – 2

 Michael **Schumacher**
Red Bull Ring wins – 2

 Gerhard **Berger**
Red Bull Ring wins – 0

The Finn seemed to take forever to score his first F1 win. That came in the last race of 1997. In 1998, his McLaren–Mercedes was the car to have and Mika made the most of it. His win here came from third on the grid after he took the lead from pole-man Giancarlo Fisichella's Benetton on lap 1. Michael Schumacher put him under pressure, but slid off. In 2000, victory came more easily as he led all the way to win easily from McLaren team-mate David Coulthard.

Two wins in two years reflect a tidy return for Keke Rosberg's son after the reopening of the circuit as the Red Bull Ring. The first came in 2014 after Williams locked out the front row, but had no answer to Mercedes' pace in the race, with Nico's task made easier as team-mate Lewis Hamilton started ninth after a spin in qualifying. The Mercedes duo finished one–two again in 2015 after Hamilton had too much wheel-spin at the start and so wasted his pole position.

It was Michael's sixth full season before he got to contest an Austrian GP, but it took him a further five years before he'd win there. This was in 2002 when the race should have been won by team-mate Rubens Barrichello, but Ferrari told him to let Michael by, even though this was only round five and it left him with double the points of his closest rival. Michael's second win came in 2003, and this one was more legitimate, with only McLaren's Kimi Raikkonen able to get close.

Gerhard never won his home grand prix, and was hampered by its nine-year absence from 1988 to 1996, but he was a huge draw for the fans. His greatest chance of victory came at his third attempt, in 1986 when Benetton had BMW turbo power. Team-mate Teo Fabi took pole but Gerhard grabbed the lead on the opening lap, only to drop back at mid-distance after his battery had been replaced, leaving him to seventh. Records show that his remained his best finish here.

Great Moments

 **1997** Jacques **Villeneuve** moves past **Trulli** to win

1999 **McLaren** clash helps Ferrari's Eddie **Irvine**

 **2002** Jean **Todt** triggers fury with team orders

2019 Max **Verstappen** gives Red Bull back-to-back home wins

Austria's first grand prix for since 1987 offered a surprise. Jarno Trulli had replaced injured Olivier Panis at Prost and come fourth in Germany. He leapt from third on the grid into the lead, but the shock couldn't last as Jacques Villeneuve moved ahead for Williams. Then, late in the race, the Prost retired from second with engine failure, leaving Villeneuve to win easily from David Coulthard's McLaren and close to within a point of championship leader Michael Schumacher who could finish only sixth after a stop-go penalty.

It should have been a McLaren victory, but Ferrari triumphed thanks to a clash between the silver-grey cars at Remus on the opening lap. Mika Hakkinen led away from David Coulthard, but the Scot dived up the inside and they collided, dropping Hakkinen to the tail of the field. Coulthard was able to claim the lead, but Ferrari timed Eddie Irvine's pitstop better to put him in front, with Coulthard unable to usurp him. Hakkinen produced the drive of the race to get back to third.

Ferrari was so dominant in 2002 that Michael Schumacher really didn't need any help. However, team boss Jean Todt brought shame on F1 when he insisted that Rubens Barrichello, who'd led all the way from pole, pull over to let him win, despite Schumacher having already won four of the first five rounds. It's better to remember the day for Takuma Sato the good fortune of escaping with light injuries from a car-shattering shunt when his Jordan was T-boned at Remus by Nick Heidfeld's Sauber.

The Red Bull energy drink company has pumped millions into upgrading this circuit and finally got a first Red Bull Racing win there in 2018 when Max Verstappen was first to finish after both Mercedes failed. The Dutch star did it again in 2019, but this time it was a real scrap in the closing laps of the race as he and Ferrari's Charles Leclerc locked wheels on several occasions in their quest for glory on a day when the Mercedes challenge was unusually muted.

Silverstone

Dubbed the home of British motor racing, Silverstone is far more than that – it's very much one of the great tracks of the world. Indeed, it's the venue that hosted the opening round of the inaugural World Championship back in 1950.

❝ The new loop offers some challenging corners as well as overtaking opportunities. What's important is that we have a circuit to test the world. ❞

Damon Hill

Silverstone is undoubtedly one of the world's great racing circuits. Not only does it offer drivers a real challenge to get their teeth into, but it's steeped in history and has hosted more top international race meetings than almost any other, with world-class sportscar and touring car events alongside its 47 grands prix hosted to date.

After the Second World War, Britain was dotted with airfields with little purpose. The village of Silverstone had one of these and it wasn't long before it was identified by the Royal Automobile Club as a place where a racing circuit might be created around its perimeter roads and up and down its runways. The Air Ministry agreed to a lease and things moved so fast that it hosted the first British GP in its opening year, 1948, with Luigi Villoresi winning for Maserati.

With the dynamic Jimmy Brown as circuit manager, modifications were made for 1949, the stretches along the runways being removed and replaced by the classic Silverstone silhouette that has largely remained to this day, with plenty of sky, plenty of space and plenty of pace. It was then and always has been a place for fast motor racing, offering open corners and room to race as opposed to the strictures offered by many of its rivals.

For 1950, it was given the honour of hosting the first round of the first ever World Championship, with Alfa Romeo showing British fans the levels that could be attained. In 1952, the temporary pits were moved from after Abbey to between Woodcote and Copse, but then little changed until 1975, when a chicane was inserted at Woodcote – no doubt to prevent a repeat of the massed accident triggered by Jody Scheckter when he'd run wide there in 1973. That 1975 British GP proved equally disastrous, though, as torrential rain hit half of the circuit, with car after car sliding off at Club.

Unlike quite a few of the circuits hosting grands prix, Silverstone is a circuit that is in use most weekends from spring to autumn, running events on its full and its national layouts for everything from international level meetings to club events.

As speeds continued to rise and the FIA asked for improved safety, changes were made, with the straight from Abbey to Woodcote given a chicane called Luffield in 1987 before a far more comprehensive alteration – to the same straight – in 1991, this time making the track go into a dip halfway along its length and turn to the right in a corner called Bridge. This fearsome corner was then followed by a loop made by lefthanders at Priory and Brooklands before returning to Luffield. Stowe was also tightened, with the track dropping into a dip called the Vale, this also making Club a much slower corner. The best change of all, though, was when straight after the high-speed left kink at Maggotts, the track was made to run through a new sequence of esses at Becketts, a world-class run of corners.

What marks the British GP out is not just the size of the crowd – always a sell-out, with the spectator banking also packed on the Friday and Saturday as well – but its knowledge and passion. Occasionally, this has overflowed, such as in the height of Mansellmania when the crowds flowed onto the track in support of a new national hero as F1 brought in fans new to racing.

Silverstone has been ever-changing since, with a chicane added at Abbey in 1994 and then its most comprehensive alterations in the past five years. These came at the behest of F1 ringmaster Bernie Ecclestone, who was perpetually sniping that Silverstone was lagging behind the facilities that new, government-funded circuits in the Far East were offering. So, in order to secure its long-term future as a grand prix circuit, Silverstone built a giant pit building between Club and Abbey in 2010, with an extra loop added that curled around the infield and then used the old club straight down to Brooklands. The layout has changed and the startline moved, but the nature has not, as Silverstone still has plenty of sky, plenty of space and plenty of pace. ∎

Opposite: The opening of The Wing pit buildings brought Silverstone into the twenty-first century, along with an extended track layout.

CLUB CORNER • 215KPH/134MPH **5**

APPROACH • 295KPH/183MPH **6**

18

215KPH/134MPH **5** **E**

3

125KPH/77MPH **3** **17**

A

16

1

ABBEY • 295KPH/183MPH **7**

5 STOWE • 240KPH/149MPH

3 VALE • 102KPH/63MPH

2

FARM • 292KPH/181MPH **7**

15

CHAPEL • 250KPH/155MPH **6**

A

2

7 APPROACH • 302KPH/187MPH

14

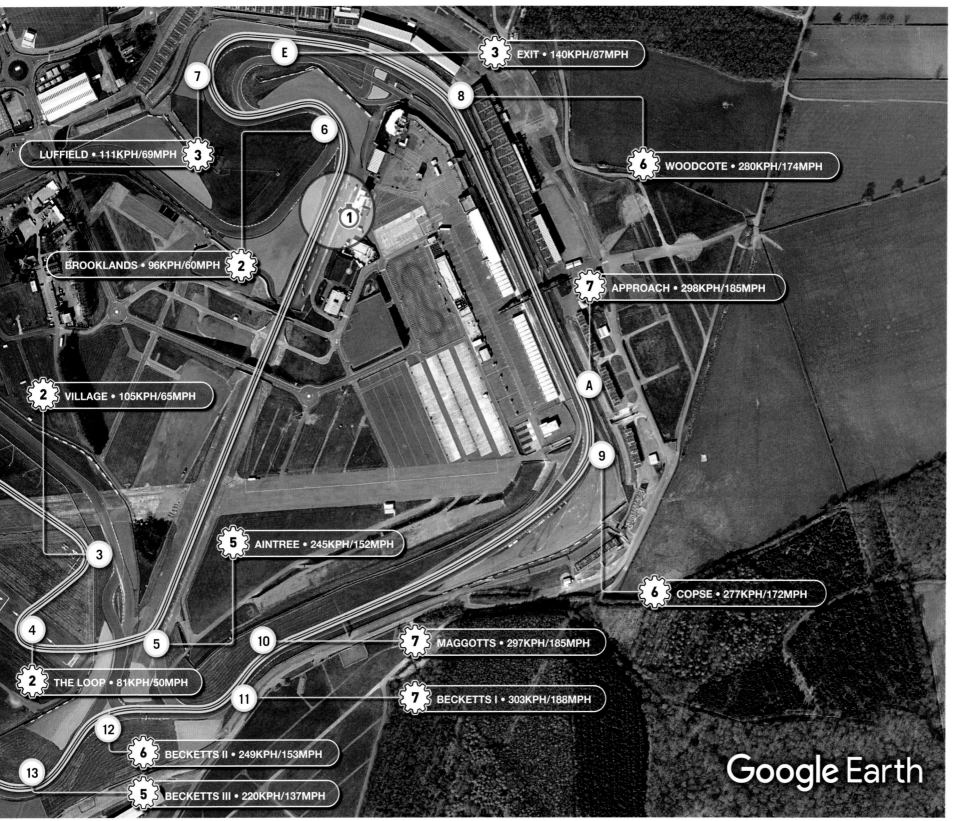

EXIT • 140KPH/87MPH

LUFFIELD • 111KPH/69MPH

WOODCOTE • 280KPH/174MPH

BROOKLANDS • 96KPH/60MPH

APPROACH • 298KPH/185MPH

VILLAGE • 105KPH/65MPH

AINTREE • 245KPH/152MPH

COPSE • 277KPH/172MPH

THE LOOP • 81KPH/50MPH

MAGGOTTS • 297KPH/185MPH

BECKETTS I • 303KPH/188MPH

BECKETTS II • 249KPH/153MPH

BECKETTS III • 220KPH/137MPH

Google Earth

Circuit Guide

Its flat, wide open spaces have always been used to make a track full of high-speed corners and, even though its layout has changed on numerous occasions, the spirit of the track that hosted the first British GP back in 1948 still prevails.

Turn 1 • Abbey
Gear: **7**
Speed: **295kph (183mph)**

Until 2010, this was a rapid corner two-thirds of the way around the lap, but since 2011 it has become the first corner, the point at which the track turns into the infield loop. In its initial incarnation, it was a very fast lefthander, where Tony Brooks rolled his BRM in 1956 when its throttle stuck open. In the mid-1990s, it was slowed by the insertion of a chicane, but at last Abbey is a quick corner again, with a bump before entry making drivers exercise caution.

Turn 6 • Brooklands
Gear: **2**
Speed: **96kph (60mph)**

This long left is a tricky corner in its own right, because it's approached in top gear and requires drivers to lose two-thirds of their speed. Ideally, drivers will be hugging the righthand kerb, ready to take the least severe line around the corner. However, this is a popular overtaking point, so many drivers find themselves having to take a less ideal line as they defend their position, with the consequences of a poor exit line being magnified at the next corner, Luffield.

Turn 7 • Luffield
Gear: **3**
Speed: **111kph (69mph)**

This is a tricky corner because drivers are often out of position after exiting Brooklands, and need to get over to the left side of the track before arriving at Luffield so that they can take the widest entry for the optimum line through the righthander. To compound their problems, Luffield is really a two-part corner and those who miss the first apex will be way off the ideal line at the exit, thus delaying them getting the power down for the blast towards Copse.

Turn 9 • Copse
Gear: **6**
Speed: **277kph (172mph)**

The changing layouts used at Silverstone mean that this corner – the first corner of the lap from 1950 until 2010, before that changed to Abbey – is now found halfway around the lap. This doesn't stop it from being a daunting bend all the same, but no longer are drivers arriving for this sixth-gear corner with a turn-in made blind by the end of the pitwall in a pack of jostling cars. It's a corner that requires precision to keep the flow going.

Opposite: The sign says it all as Felipe Massa guides his Ferrari into Becketts in 2007. *Above left:* This aerial view shows Copse in 2001, when it was still the first corner of the lap. *Above right:* Abbey is now the opening corner, and Red Bull Racing's Sebastian Vettel and Mark Webber are shown leading away at the start in 2011.

Turn 11/13 • **Becketts II**
Gear: **6**
Speed: **249kph (153mph)**

There is scarcely a driver who doesn't rank the Becketts esses as one of their greatest challenges of the season. They are approached at speed, with the added difficulty that drivers have just veered left through Maggotts before they have to turn right, then left, then right again, bringing their speed down from 290kph (180mph) or so in seventh at the first part to not much over 220kph (137mph) by the last, taken in fifth, turning as they do so. A great run through here offers immense satisfaction.

Turn 15 • **Stowe**
Gear: **5**
Speed: **240kph (149mph)**

For decades, this fast righthander at the end of the Hangar Straight was the circuit's signature corner, a place where the bold would be rewarded if they carried more speed in. However, since 1991, it has been less of a challenge because it was made to turn back on itself to feed the cars into the Vale. As a consequence, there is less chance of overtaking here, which has sadly reduced the desire for drivers to work themselves into a slipstreaming position down the straight.

Turn 16 • **Vale**
Gear: **3**
Speed: **102kph (62mph)**

Drivers have to really hit the anchors for this righthander, approached down the dipping and increasingly enclosed straight from Stowe. A wide line through the corner is achieved by entering the sharp lefthander from the righthand side of the track, but this can be scuppered if a rival then dives down the inside to take the corner. Their exit speed will then invariably be affected, but to some it's a risk worth taking. Acceleration up the short slope towards Club corner is vital to finish off the lap.

Turn 18 • **Club Corner**
Gear: **5**
Speed: **215kph (134mph)**

The last corner of the lap was another corner that was slowed in the 1991 redevelopment and, like Stowe, was changed from a high-speed corner through which drivers kept their flow going to a corner that is arrived at slowly. Drivers have to hit the brakes and turn sharply left out of the Vale, then start turning right and turning significantly more as they climb a small rise, then wait for the moment to plant the throttle to accelerate onto the start/finish straight.

Great Drivers & Great Moments

The high-speed nature of the circuit and its wide open corners have led to some remarkable races since Silverstone hosted the first ever World Championship race in 1950, and the selection of names and events chosen here is just the tip of the iceberg of the great names who have triumphed here.

Great Drivers

Lewis **Hamilton**
Silverstone wins – 6

British fans are extremely knowledgeable about their racing. If they are cheering for a British driver then the passion is all the more fervent. In the case of Lewis Hamilton, he put on a masterclass in wet/dry conditions for McLaren in 2008 to take his first Silverstone F1 win. In 2014, his second year with Mercedes, he again won on home ground. Since then, perhaps finding an extra ounce of pace to impress the home fans, he has enjoyed success 2015, 2016, 2017 and 2019.

Alain **Prost**
Silverstone wins – 5

Not only did Alain win the British GP at Silverstone five times, twice more than any other driver, but he did so with four teams and achieved this feat over a span of 11 years. His first success here was in 1983, when he was racing for Renault. He then won again in 1985 on F1's next visit, this time for McLaren, and took a third in 1989 after team-mate Ayrton Senna spun out. He completed his tally by winning for Ferrari in 1991 and Williams in 1993.

Nigel **Mansell**
Silverstone wins – 3

Nigel Mansell had won the European GP at Brands Hatch in 1985 and then the British GP there in 1986, but Mansellmania was in its infancy then. By 1987, though, it was in full swing and the way with which Nigel hunted down his Williams team-mate Nelson Piquet at Silverstone in 1987 had the fans on their toes. When he dived down the inside into Stowe with three laps to go, they went wild. He'd win again at Silverstone in 1992.

Michael **Schumacher**
Silverstone wins – 3

This seven-time World Champion ended his career with multiple wins at most grands prix, and he collected three here. After being denied in 1995 when his Benetton was taken out by Damon Hill, he triumphed for Ferrari in 1998 in a finish that was notable because he took the unusual step of serving his stop-go penalty at the end of his final lap. He also won at Silverstone in 2002 and 2004. Michael probably recalls the 1999 race with the least affection, as he crashed at Stowe and broke a leg.

Great Moments

1950 | **Alfa Romeo** domination in first WC round

When the World Championship arrived for its first ever round in May 1950, it was clear that the Alfa Romeo team would supply the winner, especially when its 158s filled the first four places on the grid. Not even Prince Bira in a Maserati could challenge them and so Giuseppe Farina swapped the lead with team-mates Luigi Fagioli and Jean Manuel Fangio before storming home at the head of an Alfa 1-2-3, with the next finisher – Yves Giraud-Cabantous in a Lago-Talbot – two laps adrift.

1969 | Jackie **Stewart** wins by a whole lap

Only 17 grands prix have ended up with the winner finishing a lap clear, but this happened in 1969, when Jackie Stewart won an enthralling duel with Jochen Rindt. The Austrian had led away in his Lotus, the pair immediately dropping the rest, but the Scot went past on lap 6 in his Matra, only to be repassed 10 laps later. They stayed glued together for the next 46 laps until Rindt pitted with a loose wing endplate, and this left Stewart to win as he pleased.

1973 | Jody **Scheckter** triggers chaos on lap 1

It's safe to say that Jody Scheckter made a massive impact when he broke into F1 as a 22-year-old. The British GP was his third outing of 1973 in McLaren's third car and the South African was pressing hard at the end of the opening lap when he ran wide coming out of Woodcote onto the start/finish straight. In an instant, his M23 spun off the grass and came back across the track, scattering those behind and triggering an eight-car pile-up that stopped the race.

2008 | Lewis **Hamilton** dominates in the wet

Lewis Hamilton had come so close to taking the drivers' title at his first attempt in 2007, so was determined to make amends in 2008 and drove a beautiful race to prove the master of ever-changing conditions for McLaren. Kimi Raikkonen was the only driver to offer even a slight challenge, but Ferrari guessed wrong on tyre choice and Hamilton was left to control proceedings. At the end, he was a minute clear of Sauber's Nick Heidfeld, with Honda's Rubens Barrichello the only other unlapped runner.

Hungaroring

This was a landmark circuit when it was built to host a round of the World Championship in 1986. It took Formula One to a new region, into still-communist Eastern Europe, showing how the sport was opening up and embracing new areas in its desire for a truly global reach.

> ❝ The Hungaroring is a circuit where drivers are busy all around the lap, so it's really demanding and there are barely any opportunities to catch your breath. ❞
>
> *Michael Schumacher*

The World Championship had an established pattern through the 1970s. The vast majority of the grands prix continued to be held in Europe, but after 1980 Watkins Glen was deemed no longer to be safe for the increasing speed of the cars and the search began for a permanent home for the United States GP. Then, in 1985, Australia finally landed a round. With that country's strong racing pedigree, this came as no surprise. What followed in 1986, though, most certainly did.

The shock was the addition of a Hungarian GP: not only had the country's limited racing pedigree faded decades earlier, with its only grand prix being held in Budapest's Nepliget Park in 1936, but the country was behind the Iron Curtain, its government communist and thus opposed to such capitalist pursuits as motor racing. However, when attempts to place a World Championship event in the Soviet Union faltered, the government sanctioned the building of a circuit for the express purpose of hosting a grand prix.

The Hungaroring has a spectacular location in rolling hills to the north-east of Budapest, with its layout (designed by Istvan Papp) taking the drivers along one side of the valley and down the dip across it before traversing the far side, then making the return leg back across the valley again. Because of this, the circuit is one of only a handful of grand prix circuits built over a river. This is found, naturally, at its lowest point, being crossed when the drivers head down into the dip after Turn 3 and then again when they head back towards the pits before Turn 12. This led to a change of track format in 1989, when a chicane immediately after Turn 3 was bypassed, enabling the drivers to carry more speed down into the dip.

This is a circuit where drivers need to set their cars up on soft suspension settings and can run a medium degree of wing because there are many more corners than straights. It's also a track on which drivers need to be alert to the way its surface changes markedly from their opening laps in first practice on the Friday morning of a grand prix meeting through the course of the weekend. Dust is a problem, but it gets grippier as rubber is laid down, although that degree of extra traction can come at a cost to the tyres as temperatures are often sky high here in summer.

The most remarkable thing about the inaugural Hungarian GP was the size of the crowd, with around 200,000 people turning out to witness this novelty, thus dwarfing the turn-out at many of the other European events. It was thus adjudged a hit as Nelson Piquet romped to victory for Williams, but there was one problem then that has affected every grand prix there since: a lack of places to overtake.

With its bowl-like location, viewing from the grandstands on either side of the valley is great but, sadly, the racing is not. While the circuit provides an interesting challenge for drivers attempting to set the fastest lap in qualifying, with the corners coming thick and fast, there's precious little space for overtaking, leading to processional races where the main chance for passing the car ahead comes from a tactically timed pitstop. Nigel Mansell bucked this trend in 1989, when he muscled his way from 12th on the grid to win for Ferrari, but more often than not the race order is static. This was proved comprehensively the following year, when Thierry Boutsen won for Williams, holding back Ayrton Senna's clearly faster McLaren.

Despite the fact that Hungarian driver Ferenc Szisz won the first ever grand prix, the French GP of 1906, Hungarian fans are still waiting for one of their own to run at the front. In the history of the World Championship, there has thus far been just one Hungarian driver. This was Zsolt Baumgartner, who had two races for Jordan in 2003, then a full season for Minardi in 2004, peaking with eighth, three laps down, in a crash-hit US GP. ∎

Opposite: Fernando Alonso accelerates his Ferrari F2012 out of the third gear Turn 6/7 chicane in 2012.

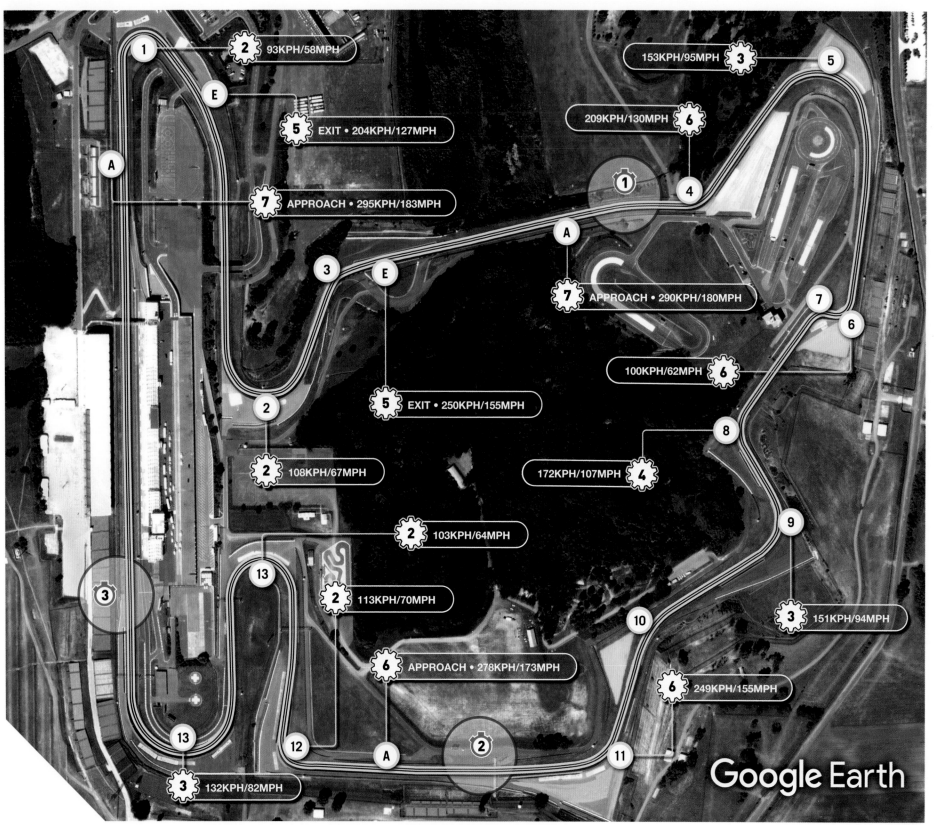

1
2   93KPH/58MPH
3   153KPH/95MPH   5
E
5   EXIT • 204KPH/127MPH
209KPH/130MPH   6
7   APPROACH • 295KPH/183MPH
4
A
A
7   APPROACH • 290KPH/180MPH
3   E
7
6
5   EXIT • 250KPH/155MPH
100KPH/62MPH   6
2
8
2   108KPH/67MPH
172KPH/107MPH   4
2   103KPH/64MPH
9
3
13
3
2   113KPH/70MPH
3   151KPH/94MPH
10
6   APPROACH • 278KPH/173MPH
13
6   249KPH/155MPH
12   A   2
11
3   132KPH/82MPH

Google Earth

Red Bull Racing's Daniel Ricciardo took the lead with just three laps to go to take his second F1 win at the 2014 Hungarian GP.

Circuit Guide

This is a circuit where drivers seem to be turning almost constantly, with only two straights and a host of twisting corners in between. Overtaking is nigh on impossible and the challenge comes from finding the perfect line in qualifying.

Turn 1 •

Gear: **2**
Speed: **93kph (58mph)**

The approach to this corner is down a gentle incline and it represents the only point on the circuit where a driver might realistically think about how best to overtake a car in front. Drivers have to brake as late as they dare, aware that they might have to hamper their exit speed simply to resist an attack from behind. Turn 1 is a two-part corner. It dips from entry to exit as it doubles back and drivers start to position themselves for Turn 2.

Turn 2 •

Gear: **2**
Speed: **108kph (67mph)**

Having arrived down a gentle slope, this lefthander is made all the more interesting because it drops away sharply from the apex. Drivers try to arrive on the far right of the circuit to get the most open and thus fastest run through the corner, but cars tend to dive in from all angles on the opening lap according to the line they occupied when they came out of Turn 1. Contact is not unknown here, but a good move can pay real dividends.

Turn 4 •

Gear: **6**
Speed: **209kph (130mph)**

This is a real rarity at the Hungaroring, a truly fast corner. Drivers arrive after the track has bottomed out at the foot of the valley and hit 290kph (180mph) up the start of the ascent of the opposite slope before dropping down a gear to take this lefthand kink. It's hard for drivers to get a clear view around this corner, especially because the angle of the slope flattens out midway around it, and this makes it extra difficult for balancing the car too.

Turn 6/7 •

Gear: **2**
Speed: **100kph (62mph)**

Having turned through uphill Turn 5 onto the first flat stretch of the circuit since leaving the starting grid, drivers immediately have to get busy through this sequence of fiddly corners set at the foot of natural spectator banking. This right/left chicane is the start of a twisting section of the circuit and forces drivers to run in single file, with numerous clashes over the years when some have tried not to do so, especially if being delayed by a backmarker.

Opposite: Mark Webber brakes hard as he chases Felipe Massa into Turn 1 in 2013. *Above left:* A panoramic view of the Turn 2, with the far side of the track from Turn 5 in the background. *Above right:* There is always jostling for position on the approach to Turn 2 on lap 1, as shown in 2013.

Turn 11 •

Gear: **6**
Speed: **249kph (155mph)**

Having swerved their way along the far side of the valley to the pits, drivers start building up speed after coming out of Turn 9 before carrying it through the sweep of Turn 10. They ought to be hitting 249kph (155mph) when they reach Turn 11, a righthander. With the circuit dropping away at its exit and a short straight following, it's essential that drivers manage to turn in from the lefthand side of the track, clip the apex and then run up to the kerb on the exit.

Turn 12 •

Gear: **2**
Speed: **113kph (70mph)**

This is one of the few corners that have been modified since the circuit opened. Originally a fairly open righthand kink, it was changed in 2003 to a tighter corner by the downhill straight from Turn 11 being extended and then this extra stretch of track taking drivers to a 90-degree righthander. At a stroke, it changed it from a third-gear bend to a second gear one and reduced the chances of a chasing driver being able to line up a move into Turn 13.

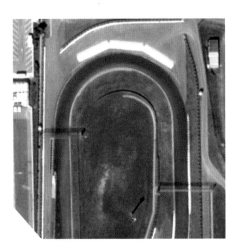

Turn 13 •

Gear: **2**
Speed: **103kph (64mph)**

The penultimate corner of the lap offers drivers a view of the rear of the paddock high above them as they arrive down the short straight from Turn 12. Drivers must resist the urge to carry too much speed into this upward-turning corner because it's imperative to get the power on as soon as possible once they have passed the apex and can see the exit to get right onto the tail of a rival if they want to be close enough to line up a pass into Turn 1.

Turn 14 •

Gear: **3**
Speed: **132kph (82mph)**

Still climbing as they leave Turn 13, drivers need to move from the righthand side of the track to the left so that they can take the widest line through this uphill corner. Any extra fraction of momentum that can be built up through this long righthander is vital, because the track flattens out on exit and, providing a chasing driver doesn't lose control over the exit kerbs, they then ought to be able to get into the slipstream of the car ahead.

Great Drivers & Great Moments

Such is the narrow and twisting nature of the Hungaroring that drivers really need to qualify on pole position, then survive attacks through the first two corners to stand a chance of winning, but there have also been some remarkable drivers coming through the field among those on the victory roll.

Great Drivers

 Lewis **Hamilton**
Hungaroring wins – 6

 Michael **Schumacher**
Hungaroring wins – 4

 Ayrton **Senna**
Hungaroring wins – 3

 Mika **Hakkinen**
Hungaroring wins – 2

Lewis Hamilton's hit rate at the Hungaroring is remarkable. Having won here in his first year of F1, 2007, he added a second victory with McLaren in 2012. Since moving to Mercedes after that season, he won at his first attempt with his new team, then weathered a fierce challenge from team-mate Nico Rosberg in 2016. He has added further wins in 2018 and 2019, the former thanks to grabbing pole position, the latter after outwitting Red Bull with an inspired strategy call.

Michael spread his wins here across 11 years, from his victory for Benetton in 1994 to his win for Ferrari in 2004. That first win cheered Benetton after its German GP pitfire, then his second for Ferrari in 1998 was achieved by a three-stop tactic to get him ahead of the McLarens. He'd win twice more for Ferrari – in 2001, when a one-two ahead of team-mate Rubens Barrichello clinched his fourth F1 title; and again in 2004, when the season's 13th race brought his 12th win.

After a pair of second place finishes on his first two visits to the Hungaroring, Ayrton struck gold when he moved from Lotus to McLaren for 1988, leading every lap after starting from pole. Second in both 1989 and 1990, Ayrton won again in 1991 and then completed his Hungaroring hat trick in 1992, when he resisted the otherwise dominant Nigel Mansell's pace-setting Williams to win and so prevent the Englishman from claiming his long-awaited drivers' title with a victory.

This fast Finn first raced at the Hungaroring in 1991, for Lotus, but didn't take his first win there until eight years later. His success in 1999 came on the second occasion he qualified on pole on this hard-to-pass circuit, and his McLaren team-mate David Coulthard was able to get close only after getting past fast-starting Giancarlo Fisichella and Heinz-Harald Frentzen. Hakkinen made it two in a row in 2000, when a repeat finish was scuppered by Coulthard being delayed by the Minardis.

Great Moments

1986 Nelson **Piquet** wins in front of a huge crowd

1997 Damon **Hill** just loses out for Arrows

2006 Jenson **Button** gives Honda its only win

2014 Daniel **Ricciardo** leaves it late for Red Bull

Ayrton Senna took pole for the inaugural Hungarian GP, then led away as Nigel Mansell powered past Williams team-mate Nelson Piquet and Alain Prost's McLaren to grab second. Two laps later, Piquet demoted Mansell. While he chased Senna, Prost passed Mansell too. Then, on lap 12 of 76, Piquet hit the front. Electrical problems forced Prost to pit and then Senna did enough to emerge from his tyre-change ahead of Piquet, but the Williams driver then overtook him to win as he pleased.

Jacques Villeneuve winning for Williams in 1997 came as no surprise but, had the race been just one lap shorter, Damon Hill winning for Arrows certainly would have been. Hill qualified third, his best grid position by six places, then moved straight into second behind Michael Schumacher's Ferrari, and then hit the front on lap 11 as Michael struggled on the harder tyres. He built a 35-second cushion, only for a hydraulic glitch to hit on lap 75 of 77. Villeneuve swept past on the final lap.

Honda Racing scored its first win here in 2006, and Jenson Button did too, yet this twin triumph was made all the more epic by the fact that they achieved it in a race made unpredictable by wet weather. Kimi Raikkonen led from pole for McLaren, but Fernando Alonso rose from 15th after a qualifying penalty to take over. Then Raikkonen crashed and Alonso's lead was negated by a safety car period. But Alonso later lost a wheel and so Button and Honda got to celebrate.

With Mercedes dominating, F1 needed variety and the fans were treated to plenty of that. Nico Rosberg took pole for Mercedes, but Hamilton's car caught fire and he lined up last. While Hamilton echoed his feat of the previous race by making it up to third, victory went to a car of a different hue as Daniel Ricciardo benefitted as the first four runners passed the pit entrance before a safety car period was announced. The Australian overtook Alonso's Ferrari with three laps to go.

Zandvoort

It's not often that a circuit is given a second lease of life by the Formula One roadshow. Yet, the truly massive popularity of Max Verstappen has been enough for this popular circuit in the Dutch sand dunes to be dusted down, modernised a little and reintroduced to the World Championship after a 35-year break.

> ❝ Zandvoort is an historic track, where the foundation of our sport lies. We like the balance of continuing to grow Formula One in new markets and continuing to find opportunities in historic markets. ❞
>
> *Chase Carey*

It had seemed that Zandvoort's F1 days were far behind it and that its most recent Dutch GP in 1985 was definitely the last. This was hard for the local fans, but they could see that its safety facilities had fallen far below the accepted norm. Worse still, the track had been hacked back in 1989. Yet, people power is a wonderful thing, the orange army of Max Verstappen fans who would fill entire grandstands at grands prix around Europe proved that there was a desire that needed to be met.

New ownership led by Prince Bernhard van Oranje combined with inspired management has brought Holland's time in the F1 wilderness to an end with a revamped version of the track that has filled the gap for the past three decades with a diet of national and minor international race meetings.

The circuit came into being in 1948 when German-built access roads tucked into the sand dunes on the North Sea coast were utilised. These were combined with a flowing layout designed by John Hugenholtz to make a circuit that would host a hugely popular round of the World Championship with just a few breaks between 1952 and 1985.

The layout had a real flow to it, as the track rose and fell through the dunes, inevitably past tens of thousands of fans who would nestle into the sand for

protection on windy days when sand blowing across the circuit was often a peril.

It was Ferrari all the way in the first two visits, with Alberto Ascari winning both. Then Juan Manuel Fangio won for Mercedes in 1955 and Stirling Moss for Vanwall three years later. In 1959, BRM finally claimed its first win thanks to Jo Bonnier. Sixteen years later, another British team would make a breakthrough. This was Hesketh, with James Hunt beating Ferrari's Niki Lauda. These wins apart, the winners at Zandvoort have predominantly been the drivers who would be World Champion at year's end. The list makes remarkable reading: Jack Brabham (Cooper then Brabham) in 1960 and 1966, Graham Hill (BRM) in 1962, Jim Clark (Lotus) in 1963 and 1965, Jackie Stewart (Matra then Tyrrell) in 1969 and 1973, Jochen Rindt (Lotus) in 1970, Hunt (McLaren) in 1976, Niki Lauda (Ferrari) in 1977 and Mario Andretti (Lotus) in 1978.

One feature that always stood out is the battles into, through and out of Tarzan, the lightly-banked tight right at the end of the start/finish straight. It has frequently proved too tempting for a chasing driver not to have a go, with the sight of Rene Arnoux's Renault firing off the tyre wall into the air after his front suspension failed in 1982 still vivid.

Another race that encapsulates Zandvoort's place in history is the 1967 Dutch GP when Lotus gave the Ford Cosworth DFV engine its debut. At a stroke, it enriched F1, as this soon-to-be-customer engine was a major step forward.

Sadly, the circuit had dark days too, with Piers Courage being killed in 1970 when he crashed his de Tomaso and a wheel hit him on the head, killing him. Three years later, compatriot Roger Williamson met a similar fate when his March overturned.

When F1 moved on after 1985, the circuit began to struggle financially. Three years later, it was taken over by the town council and noise pollution laws led to a dune being built between a new track layout and the town in 1989. A decade later, the lap was restored from 1.569 miles to 2.672 miles thanks to the addition of a section that rejoined the original loop with a newly-positioned final corner. Although close to the length of the original, its wonderful flow was lost and the slipstreaming packs that used to burst into a flurry of attempted overtaking manoeuvres into Tarzan were not as frequent. ■

Opposite: Lotus's Elio de Angelis leads Marc Surer's Brabham in the early laps of the 1985 Dutch GP, the last before a 35-year hiatus

TARZAN • 130KPH/81MPH **3** 1

APPROACH • 310KPH/193MPH **8** Ⓐ

Ⓐ

GERLACHBOCHT • 140KPH/87MPH **4**

①

2

HUGENHOLTZBOCHT • 80KPH /50MPH **2**

4

3

12

ARIE LUYENDYK BOCHT OUT • 250KPH /155MPH **7** 14B

11

2 HANS ERNST BOCHT 1 • 85KPH/53MPH

3 HANS ERNST BOCHT 2 • 95KPH/57MPH

ARIE LUYENDYK BOCHT IN • 220KPH/137MPH **6** 14

13

KUMHO BOCHT • 140KPH/87MPH **5**

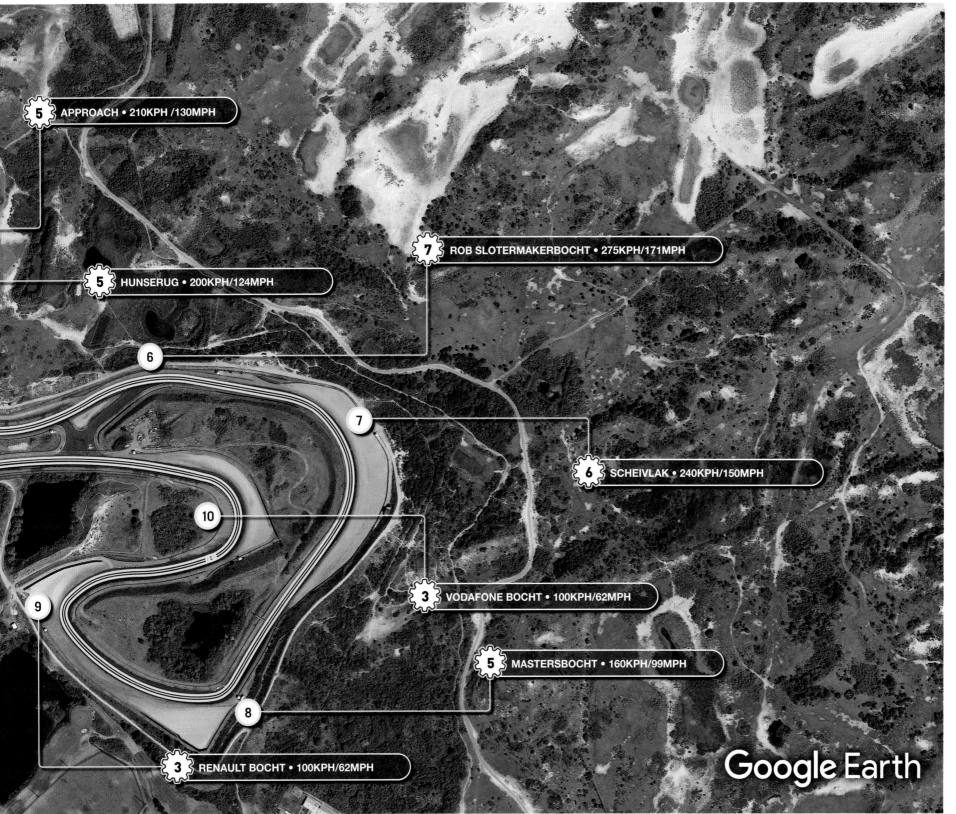

5 APPROACH • 210KPH /130MPH

7 ROB SLOTERMAKERBOCHT • 275KPH/171MPH

5 HUNSERUG • 200KPH/124MPH

6

7

6 SCHEIVLAK • 240KPH/150MPH

10

3 VODAFONE BOCHT • 100KPH/62MPH

9

5 MASTERSBOCHT • 160KPH/99MPH

8

3 RENAULT BOCHT • 100KPH/62MPH

Google Earth

Image © 2019 Landsat/Copernicus © Google 2019

69

Circuit Guide

This classic Dutch circuit offers something very different as its challenge as it follows its course up, over and around the North Sea coast sand dunes is made extra difficult as sand blowing over the racing surface can make its grip levels very changeable indeed, even from one lap to the next.

Turn 1 • Tarzan
Gear: **3**
Speed: **130kph (81mph)**

The blast past the pits has one obvious conclusion: a tall sand dune dead ahead, fortunately with a large gravel trap between it and the track. The circuit turns sharply to the right and is lightly banked to help the cars around after they have braked from their peak velocity. Tarzan is a double-apex corner, with the second turn slightly the sharper. The first part of the turn provides an obvious overtaking spot, but drivers can duck underneath on the way out of the second part.

Turn 2 • Gerlachbocht
Gear: **4**
Speed: **140kph (87mph)**

After accelerating hard out of Tarzan, the cars have to negotiate a left kink behind the back of the tiny paddock and then a slight rise into this righthander. It's on a crest and is relatively tight, cutting to the right through about 80 degrees. What makes Gerlachbocht so tricky is mainly the lack of width but also the fact that the track drops almost immediately into one of the lap's most crucial corners: Hugenholzbocht. It can get very crowded on lap 1.

Turn 3 • Hugenholtzbocht
Gear: **2**
Speed: **80kph (50mph)**

This lefthand hairpin would be tricky if it was on level ground, but it's made much harder to negotiate by being in an appreciable dip, with drivers dropping their cars into the corner, with barriers flanking the track on their right, gaining some traction from its slight banking, before trying to get on the power as soon as possible, often too soon, so that they can accelerate up the slope that rises immediately after the apex to build speed for the stretch that follows.

Turn 6 • Rob Slotermaker Bocht
Gear: **7**
Speed: **275kph (171mph)**

One of the greatest sights in motor racing is a Formula One car in full flow and this left/right swerve offers one of the best places to see this. The swerve is approached after the climb from Hugenholtzbocht clears a crest at Hunserug and then rises again as the track begins to arc left and continues to rise through the righthand element too as the track climbs to the high point in the dunes where crosswinds add to the drivers' experience.

Opposite: Lotus dominated in 1978, with Mario Andretti leading Ronnie Peterson as they enjoyed the benefits of ground-effects. *Above left:* Nelson Piquet's Brabham comes under pressure from Williams' Keke Rosberg in 1985 in the final Dutch GP before the circuit's 35-year break. *Above right:* Rene Arnoux led home a Ferrari one-two in 1983.

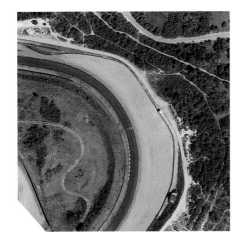

Turn 7 • Scheivlak
Gear: **6**
Speed: **240kph (150mph)**

Formula One cars are far from their most difficult to drive in their current form, especially compared to the savagely turbocharged form they were in when F1 last visited in 1985, but this corner is still a mighty challenge. The track arcs right as it comes off the crest after Rob Slotermaker Bocht, then dips all the way through this long bend, plummeting between huge dunes, with entry concealed until drivers are committed to their turn-in. Fortunately, there is a giant gravel trap.

Turn 8 • Mastersbocht
Gear: **5**
Speed: **160kph (100mph)**

Down the slope from Scheivlak, it's then a short sprint across the first level stretch of track since the start/finish straight before the drivers have to get hard on the brakes for this sharp righthander into which, for some reason, many drivers tend to arrive too fast and spin. Sand blowing from the dunes onto the circuit is their regular excuse. There's then a short straight to an even sharper corner into which overtaking is a definite possibility as the track is wide there.

Turn 11/12 • Hans Ernst Bocht
Gear: **2/3**
Speed: **85kph (53mph))**

Hans Ernst Bocht is a scratchy and uninspiring pair of corners that was inserted when Zandvoort was cut in 1989. It's a 90-degree right behind the circuit's outer paddock then a long 180-degree left, with the first feeding almost immediately into the second and the consequences of going too deep into the first becoming apparent when a driver then fails to turn in sufficiently for the second part. Overtaking is possible but very tricky.

Turn 14 • Arie Luyendyk Bocht
Gear: **6**
Speed: **220kph (137mph)**

After a short straight from Nissan Bocht and then the high-speed right at Kumhobocht, the track is then situated low between dunes for the final and vital sweep onto the start/finish straight. The track runs through a banked constant radius turn, with drivers again attempting to get their cars balanced so that they can be hard on the throttle for the lap's longest straight that follows and, best of all, get close enough to grab a tow off a rival.

Great Drivers & Great Moments

Zandvoort's lengthy main straight followed by the broad hairpin at its end, Tarzan, allows for overtaking opportunities aplenty and the most memorable of its races have been great to watch across the decades, with the atmosphere bolstered by enthusiastic fans lining the sand dunes.

Great Drivers

 Jim **Clark**
Zandvoort wins – 4

Jim Clark and Lotus formed one of F1's great partnerships and the Dutch GP was a happy hunting ground as he won it four times. The first of these was in 1963 when the Scot and his revolutionary Lotus 25 romped home a lap clear en route to his first title. In 1964, he finished 54s clear of John Surtees' Ferrari, then made it three in a row in 1965 and took his fourth win in 1967 when he suppressed dominant Brabham.

 Niki **Lauda**
Zandvoort wins – 3

When he won at Zandvoort in 1974, it was only Lauda's second F1 win and marked a great day for Ferrari as the Austrian led home team-mate Clay Regazzoni. Lauda won again in 1977 when only he and Ligier's Jacques Laffite's finished on the lead lap as his season with Ferrari picked up the momentum needed to land his second F1 title. In his third win, in 1985, he kept McLaren team-mate Alain Prost behind him by 0.222s.

 Jackie **Stewart**
Zandvoort wins – 3

Lotus had been setting the pace in 1968, then Jim Clark was killed and Jackie Stewart began to shine for Matra, winning at Zandvoort ahead of team-mate Jean-Pierre Beltoise. He was passed by Jochen Rindt in 1969, but took the lead again when the Austrian's Lotus broke. In 1973, Ronnie Peterson led the first 63 laps, but his Lotus failed and it was then all Tyrrell as Stewart led Francois Cevert home.

 Alberto **Ascari**
Zandvoort wins – 2

A change of regulations so that the World Championship was run for F2 cars in 1952 suited Ferrari well and Alberto Ascari starred. He missed the first round, won by team-mate Piero Taruffi, then won every other race, with his success at Zandvoort his fifth in a row. This winning streak continued through 1953, of which the Dutch GP was round two. On this occasion, Ferrari filled the first three places until Luigi Villoresi retired.

Great Moments

1959 BRM breaks its duck as **Bonnier** romps home

Jo Bonnier had his day of days to record his one and only F1 win when he qualified on pole and resisted the challenge of the Coopers of Jack Brabham and Masten Gregory to run second with just 13 laps to the chequered flag. Then things changed dramatically with a few laps to go as Stirling Moss's Rob Walker Racing Cooper retired from the lead with gearbox trouble and so Bonnier was surprised to be first to the finish.

1967 Ford **Cosworth** DFV makes a winning debut

This was the dawning of a new age in F1 with the introduction of the Ford Cosworth DFV. Lotus was the chosen team and the engine was one that would revolutionise F1 by providing a powerful yet cost-effective unit that would enable more teams to have a chance of winning. It was the standard-setter from the start. Graham Hill qualified on pole position, but team-mate Jim Clark who won by 23s from Jack Brabham.

1975 James **Hunt** puts the Hesketh team on the map

Lord Hesketh made a splash when he entered a team in F1 in 1973, the aristocrat leading the way in partying. On track, James Hunt impressed, including third place at Zandvoort. In 1975, he kicked off with second in Argentina then took the team's one and only win when he mastered wet but drying conditions here to resist Ferrari's championship-leading Niki Lauda. James would win at Zandvoort again in 1976, for McLaren.

1985 Niki **Lauda** wins on the Dutch track's swansong

World Champion for a third time in 1984, Niki Lauda was having a poor season as his McLaren team-mate Alain Prost dominated. However, the Austrian came good on what would be Zandvoort's last F1 race for 35 years. He qualified only 10th, but polesitter Nelson Piquet stalled at the start and he was fifth at the end of lap 1. From there, Niki had a better strategy than Prost, pitting earlier, then held on to beat Prost by 0.2s.

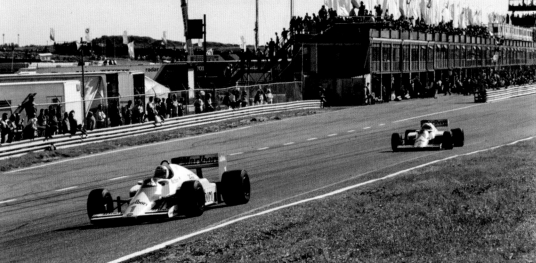

Monza

This fine Italian circuit is the oldest European circuit still in use, making it drip with history, and it continues to offer a distinctive driving challenge. Monza also has the added advantage that the racing here is often riveting, offering scope for drivers to challenge one another down the straights into the chicanes.

> **"**Monza is a circuit I like very much. Having good brakes and traction are important factors here and crucial for a good race.**"**
> *Rubens Barrichello*

Most dedicated race fans will tell you that some circuits offer great racing while others offer a special aura. Monza, or the Autodromo Nazionale di Monza to give it its full name, offers both. It really is an exceptionally special place. Certainly, its facilities are increasingly rough around the edges, despite constant updates, but it offers so much more than almost all of the recently built, tailor-made circuits that have been commissioned around the world. You don't even have to spot the fabled banked circuit of old lurking in the infield to appreciate that this is a serious temple to motorsport.

As long ago as 1922, urged by the nascent Italian automotive industry's desire to show off its sporting aspirations, the Automobile Club of Milan selected a site in a walled park adjoining the Villa Reale estate outside the town of Monza as the ideal place to build a racing circuit. The project was completed in only 110 days thanks to 3,500 people labouring on the project and so Italy had a circuit of which to be proud. It gave rise to a nation that really worshipped motor racing, becoming in time the home of the *tifosi*, the Ferrari-worshipping fans who have eyes for no other cars. Even in recent years when Ferrari hasn't offered its drivers a competitive car, the huge grandstand opposite the pits has been packed with fans clad in Ferrari's red colours. Over the years, *tifosi* without seats in that main grandstand have

even climbed trees or scaled advertising hoardings in order to get a better view of the action, famously booing any driver from a rival team should their car retire from the race.

One notable feature of the original circuit was that it had two main components: the circuit outline that is little changed today and a second element, a banked oval that could either be run as just that or be included as the second half of each lap. If both parts were used, Monza's full lap distance was 10km (6.214 miles).

In 1955, the last corner of the lap, Curva Vedano, was transformed from two asymmetric corners, with the first sharper than the second, into one, long righthander that was, fittingly, named Curva Parabolica, and this is perhaps the least changed corner of the lap, a real slingshot of a corner if a driver gets it right. As the circuit has such a fast layout, though, cars are generally sent out with a low downforce set-up. This means that they have minimal wing angle – they're fast down the straights but struggle through the corners – making it a real balancing act to keep turning right through the Parabolica without running wide into the gravel trap.

The banked circuit was used until 1961 and remains as a reminder of wilder days, decaying gradually as it arcs to the right at around the point of the first chicane.

The other main change to the circuit came in 1972, when the drivers were confronted for the first time with three chicanes that had been inserted around the lap to slow the cars. More than that, they were aimed to break up the packs of slipstreaming cars and thus eliminate the high-speed collisions that had given the circuit such a black name. Indeed, the list of drivers who have perished racing at Monza is way too long. Among the fallen are Giuseppe Campari, who went over the banking at the old South Curve in 1933; Wolfgang von Trips, who cartwheeled into the crowd on the approach to Parabolica in 1961, killing 13; Jochen Rindt, who crashed to his death at the same corner in 1970 and became the sport's only posthumous world champion; and Ronnie Peterson, who was involved in a massed collision on the blast to the first chicane in 1978 and died from his injuries.

Yet, despite the occasional tinkering with the outline of the circuit, Monza's nature remains much as it has always been: a high-speed lap on a ribbon of tarmac cutting through wooded parkland. It has a magic made by a heady mix of its immense history, the challenge of its greatest corners, the passion of its fans and its beautiful setting. ∎

Opposite: Jean Alesi exits the Parabolica onto the pit straight in his Benetton in 1996.

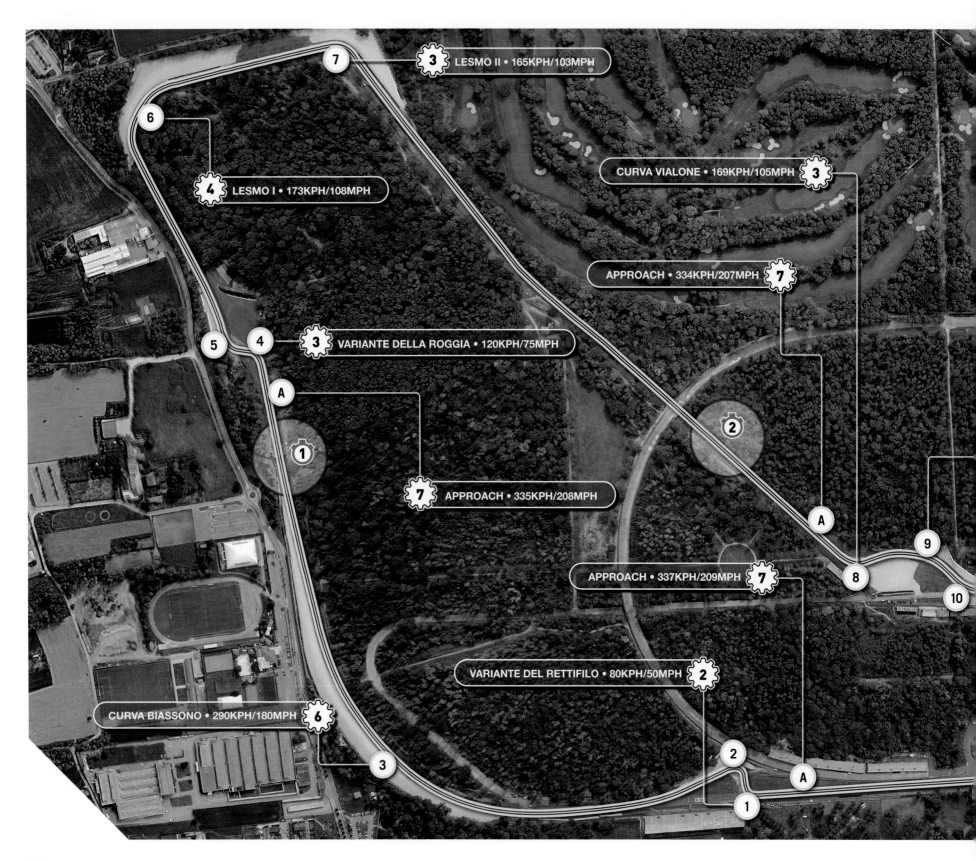

LESMO II • 165KPH/103MPH **3** **7**

CURVA VIALONE • 169KPH/105MPH **3**

6

4 LESMO I • 173KPH/108MPH

APPROACH • 334KPH/207MPH **7**

5 **4** **3** VARIANTE DELLA ROGGIA • 120KPH/75MPH

A

2

1

7 APPROACH • 335KPH/208MPH

A

9

APPROACH • 337KPH/209MPH **7**

8

10

VARIANTE DEL RETTIFILO • 80KPH/50MPH **2**

CURVA BIASSONO • 290KPH/180MPH **6**

3

2

A

1

APPROACH • 336KPH/208MPH **7**

4 VARIANTE ASCARI • 200KPH/124MPH

A

CURVA PARABOLICA • 187KPH/116MPH **4** **11**

3

Google Earth

Circuit Guide

This is a circuit with a flow to it, one that allows drivers to build up speed and offers the space in which to try to overtake. There are slow parts too, but the overall nature is high-speed with the Parabolica a masterpiece.

Turn 1 • **Variante del Rettifilo**
Gear: **2**
Speed: **80kph (50mph)**

This was merely part of the start/finish straight until 1972, when a chicane was inserted to break up the slipstreaming packs of cars and cut speeds through Curva Grande. First a double right/left combination, it was altered in 2000 to a single right/left chicane, with a far tighter first turn. This invariably catches out several cars on the opening lap; there is fortunately an escape road should they need to take evasive action, with drivers then having to weave through giant blocks before rejoining.

Turn 3 • **Curva Biassono**
Gear: **6**
Speed: **290kph (180mph)**

Despite the trees having been moved back from the outside edge of this corner to improve safety, this righthand sweep formerly known as Curva Grande remains a fine bend. Taken in sixth gear, it's not as challenging as it was long ago, because this once majestic but fairly scary bend now has a far shorter approach following the insertion of the Variante del Rettifilo in 1972. Yet it remains a corner that is essential to master to build speed for the run to the second chicane.

Turn 4/5 • **Variante della Roggia**
Gear: **3**
Speed: **120kph (75mph)**

Like the Variante del Rettifilo, this was inserted in 1972 to cut speeds and break up the packs of cars. This second chicane is the opposite of the first: it's a left/right combination, with an approach that offers even less of a view of what follows. With trees still not far from the track on the righthand side, this chicane is often shaded, adding a level of difficulty on bright days. Like the first chicane, it can provide drama, especially on the opening lap.

Turn 6 • **Lesmo I**
Gear: **4**
Speed: **173kph (108mph)**

The Lesmos are often combined in descriptions of the circuit, but they are two, distinct corners. Reached at the furthest point away from the pits, they are both righthanders, but both offer a different challenge. This first one is the faster of the pair and offers drivers little view other than of trees as they approach, but a broader one as they hit the apex because the run to the second Lesmo offers plenty of open space to the drivers' left.

Opposite: Monza's banked section was last used in a grand prix in 1961 and now lies decaying in the infield. ***Above left:*** Jacky Ickx's Ferrari leads the field away from the grid in 1970 on the long, pre-chicane, blast to what was then known as Curva Grande. ***Above right:*** Valtteri Bottas' Williams FW35 Renault leads Charles Pic's Caterham CT03 Renault into Curva Parabolica in 2013.

Turn 7 • Lesmo II
Gear: **3**
Speed: **165kph (103mph)**

The second Lesmo was tightened in 1995, meaning that drivers could carry less speed through the corner but offering greater safety as it left more run-off space for any driver who had gone into the corner too fast. Like most corners at this still classically flowing circuit, speed out of the corner is the aim of every driver, especially because here it feeds the cars onto the kinked straight that takes the cars under the bridge carrying the banked section of the old circuit towards Curva Vialone.

Turn 8 • Curva Vialone
Gear: **3**
Speed: **169kph (105mph)**

Drivers arrive at this third gear lefthander after a dipping and shaded straight that drives under the banked oval, with a rapid exit from Lesmo II offering a chance to try to line up a passing move here. This is the first point at which the drivers can see the sky clearly again because it's where the track emerges from its loop through the woods that started before the second chicane. Dropping four gears, they have to be on the right line or risk arriving at the next corner out of shape.

Turn 9/10 • Variante Ascari
Gear: **4**
Speed: **200kph (124mph)**

Straight out of Curva Vialone, the drivers have to tackle the lap's third chicane, turning right and then almost immediately left again. One of the best recent improvements, from the drivers' point-of-view, is the lowering of the kerbs, allowing them to thump their way across them to take a more direct line through the corner without as much risk of unsettling their cars or, even worse, damaging them. Race engineers have the cars set up on a soft suspension to cope with them.

Turn 11 • Curva Parabolica
Gear: **4**
Speed: **187kph (116mph)**

Accelerating hard out of the third chicane, the drivers accelerate from fourth gear to seventh and can hit 336kph (208mph) before they have to think about slowing for the final corner of the lap. This is one of the few untouched corners, having remained in the same format since 1955. Braking later than a rival here can be an advantage, but momentum out of this corner onto the long and wide start/finish straight is the absolute key for a passing manoeuvre into the first chicane.

Great Drivers & Great Moments

With a history of close and enthralling races filled with overtaking and counter-overtaking, Monza has hosted some epic grands prix over the decades. Unfortunately, though, its high-speed layout has also resulted in numerous accidents and, tragically, many fatalities between the 1950s to 1970s.

Opposite top: Charles Leclerc laps up the adulation of the tifosi after giving what they wanted in 2019: a home victory at Monza.

Opposite bottom left: Phil Hill guides his sharknose Ferrari around the banking in 1961 in a race that claimed the life of team-mate and title rival Wolfgang von Trips and helped him become world champion.

Opposite bottom right: F1's closest group finish came in 1971, when Peter Gethin edged his BRM ahead of Ronnie Peterson's March with three rivals right behind.

Great Drivers

 Michael **Schumacher**
Monza wins – 5

 Lewis **Hamilton**
Monza wins – 5

 Juan Manuel **Fangio**
Monza – 3

 Stirling **Moss**
Monza wins – 3

Not only did Michael Schumacher race to a record five wins at Monza, but he made them doubly valuable to the fans there by claiming all of these while leading Ferrari's F1 attack. His first Monza success came in 1996, in his first year with the Prancing Horse, when he headed home former Ferrari favourite Jean Alesi. He'd win again in 1998 after both McLarens faltered, then dominated proceedings in 2000, 2003 and 2006, with the team announcing his retirement after the last of these.

In terms of prestige, drivers want to win their home grand prix and the Monaco GP, but after that wins in the long-standing races are especially valued, thus Lewis Hamilton's delight at winning at Monza in 2012 when he turned pole position into victory for McLaren. He won again in 2014, catching Nico Rosberg after a bad start and pressuring his Mercedes teammate into making a mistake. Victory came easily in 2015 and 2017, but was more of a challenge in 2018 as he had to fight his way past the Ferraris.

Fangio scored a hat-trick at Monza. His first win here was in 1953, when he won a race-long scrap with Ferrari's Alberto Ascari and Giuseppe Farina plus Maserati team-mate Onofre Marimon, going through when Ascari and Farina clashed at the final corner after a race that had had 19 changes of the lead. He followed this up by winning by a lap in his Mercedes in 1954 after wrapping up his second F1 title in the previous round. He made it three in a row in 1955.

Having played understudy to Fangio when they were together at Mercedes-Benz, this English ace claimed the first of his three Monza wins when he triumphed in 1956 after running out of fuel. Fortunately, he was pushed to the pits by team-mate Luigi Piotti and benefited when Luigi Musso retired his Lancia with steering failure. Stirling would also win in 1957 for Vanwall, well clear of Fangio's Maserati, and again in 1959, when he managed the tyres of his Rob Walker-entered Cooper better than Ferrari did theirs.

Great Moments

 1961 Phil **Hill** scores sad win for Ferrari

1967 Jim **Clark** fights back from a lap down

1971 Peter **Gethin** heads a five-way finish

2019 Charles **Leclerc** sends the *tifosi* wild with delight

Held as the penultimate race of the 1961 season, it was effectively a shoot-out to decide which Ferrari driver would become World Champion. Wolfgang von Trips qualified on pole while rival Phil Hill was only fourth fastest. Hill worked his way into the lead after they reached the banking on the opening lap, but von Trips and Jim Clark's Lotus collided as they approached Parabolica on lap 2, spearing off and killing the German and 13 spectators. Victory for Hill was enough to make him World Champion.

Jim Clark had dark memories of Monza, as he'd been involved in Wolfgang von Trips's fatal accident in 1961. However, he won in 1963 and ought to have added victory four years later. Having qualified on pole, he was leading when his Lotus picked up a puncture on lap 13. The pitstop left him a lap down, but he powered his way back into the lead, only to be slowed by a fuel pump problem, leaving him to be passed by John Surtees and Jack Brabham.

The open nature of Monza that lent itself to slipstreaming was never shown more clearly. As the race entered its final five laps, a pack consisting of five drivers who'd never won a grand prix broke clear. They were Ronnie Peterson (March), Francois Cevert (Tyrrell), Howden Ganley and Peter Gethin (both BRM) and Mike Hailwood (Surtees). Into the final corner, Cevert and Peterson were ahead, but Gethin carried more momentum out of Parabolica and edged in front on the line to win by just 0.01 seconds.

Having claimed his first F1 win at Spa-Francorchamps the previous weekend, Ferrari sophomore Charles Leclerc arrived at Monza with high hopes of matching that in front of the tifosi. They were not to be disappointed, as he not only found a way to win the race but also did so after taking on and beating points leader Lewis Hamilton's Mercedes. The fans went wild when Hamilton slipped up at the first chicane and they knew that their driver had got the job done.

Monaco

Walk the streets of Monte Carlo and there's no obvious space for a grand prix, but the street circuit that climbs high through the town before dicing down to the harbourside is Formula One's most iconic venue, the scene of an annual dose of glamour and drama since 1929.

> **❝** Monaco presents you with everything that you find along a public road: lamp posts, trees, kerbs, gutters, night clubs… It's a road race in the true meaning of the term. **❞**
>
> *Graham Hill*

Most modern F1 circuits are tailor-made, their every turn and undulation crafted by architects, turning a blank piece of land into a state-of-the-art facility. Monaco could not be more different, its limitations obvious from the moment that the royal family gave cigarette manufacturer Antony Noghes permission to run a grand prix around the streets of its principality. That was back in 1929 and even people not interested in motor racing can conjure images of F1's annual visits. In short, there's no track like Monaco's and no grand prix that fans would rather attend, even though almost all overtaking is completed by the first corner of the opening lap because the track is too narrow and twisting to allow for passing moves.

That the World Championship has been happy to visit this restrictive venue ever since its inaugural season in 1950, when Juan Manuel Fangio won for Alfa Romeo, is proof that the appeal of all that happens beyond the racing outweighs its narrow track, tiny pitlane and cramped paddock. The patrons and later the teams' sponsors have always loved Monaco for being able to entertain their friends and business associates on a yacht in the harbour, on a balcony in the Hôtel de Paris or in the casino that it overlooks. It is a venue like no other.

The circuit itself makes for fabulous TV footage, a forward-facing on-board camera showing how even the smallest slip by a driver will cause their car to clang into the crash barriers, as rookie Johnny Servoz-Gavin discovered in 1968, when his race-leading Matra brushed a barrier as he sprinted clear and he went from hero to zero. There is ever-present excitement on this circuit: the spectacle of cars climbing the steep ascent from Ste Dévote to Massenet, diving into the black hole of the tunnel under the Grand Hotel and bursting back out into the sunlight for the slope down to the harbourside chicane – Monaco is unique.

Add to this the rich and lengthy history of the event and the fact that it's in the heart of a vibrant and exciting city, and its appeal is all the more obvious. That many of the drivers live in Monaco because of its generous tax laws makes it a home race for them, adding to their delight if they should win there. Jenson Button summed it up well in 2009, when he finished first for Brawn GP. "Before the weekend, I said that this grand prix isn't different to any other," commented the Englishman, "but that was a bit of a lie, as I was just trying to take the pressure off myself. Winning here is very special."

While the friends and families of all involved join the fans in enjoying this extraordinary venue, the teams and drivers have to work extra hard. Racing at Monaco used to be physically tiring when drivers had to change gear with a lever, the palm of their right hand often raw by the end of the race. Since the advent of semi-automatic gearboxes in the late 1980s, though, it has become less of a test.

Furthermore, the drivers don't suffer the strain of heavy g-force loading that they do at circuits with faster corners. The major strain these days is to get the race tactics right, to chose which compound of tyres to start on and guess when it would be best to pit; getting the timing wrong could lead to a pace-setting driver emerging back onto the track behind a backmarker and being stuck there for laps, losing time as he tries to find a place to overtake. Indeed, the gambling is as great on the track as in the casino, and that's before taking into account how the sudden arrival of a safety car period could alter the order and so scupper all best-laid plans. ■

Opposite: This view, from high above the start/finish straight, shows Ste Dévote on the left plus the run from Tabac to Piscine and the harbour beyond.

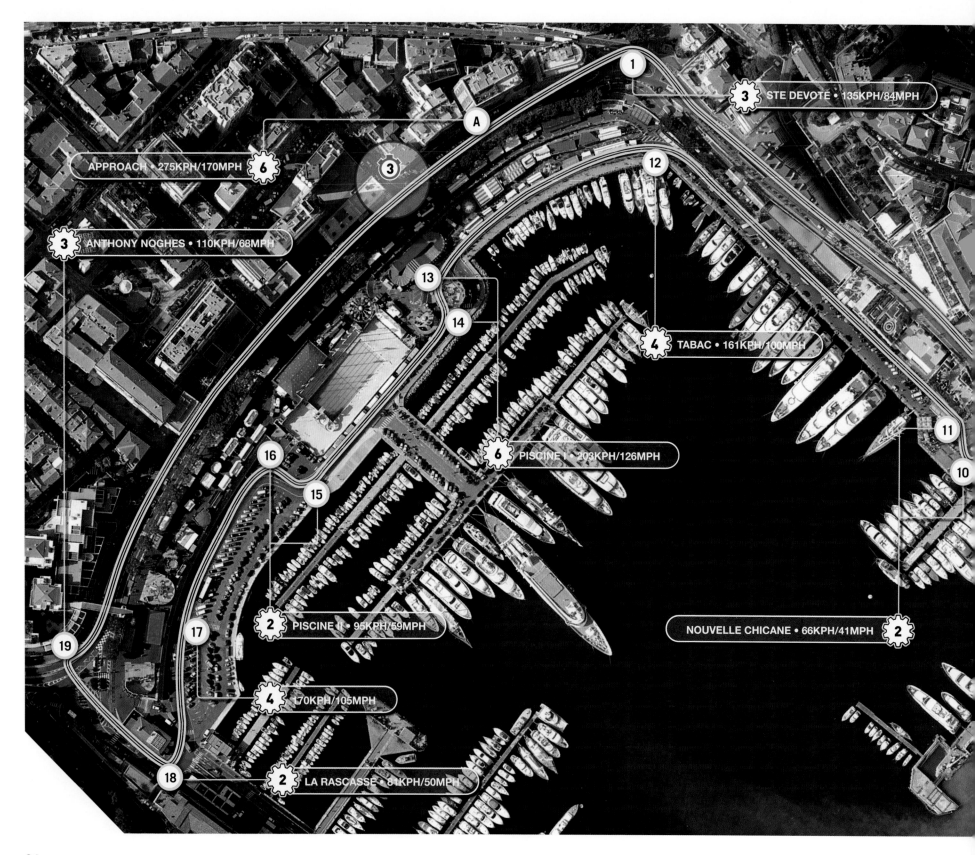

1

3 STE DEVOTE • 135KPH/84MPH

A

APPROACH • 275KPH/170MPH 6

12

3 ANTHONY NOGHES • 110KPH/68MPH

13

14

4 TABAC • 161KPH/100MPH

11

6 PISCINE I • 203KPH/126MPH

10

16

15

2 PISCINE II • 95KPH/59MPH

NOUVELLE CHICANE • 66KPH/41MPH 2

17

19

4 170KPH/105MPH

18

2 LA RASCASSE • 81KPH/50MPH

Circuit Guide

Monaco is a circuit unlike even other street circuits and the corners that make up its undulating lap are a mixture of low- and medium-speed, with only short straights and a curving tunnel in between.

Turn 1 • Ste Dévote
Gear: **3**
Speed: **135kph (84mph)**

A 135kph (84mph) corner would be considered slow on almost any F1 circuit, but this righthander is one of the quicker ones at Monaco. Its approach down the curving start/finish straight is made more daunting by the buildings that rise sheer from behind the barriers on the left and by the burning desire for drivers to make a move into here on the opening lap. Fortunately there's an escape road for when those desperate moves go wrong and drivers have to pull out of their manoeuvre.

Turn 3 • Massenet
Gear: **4**
Speed: **158kph (98mph)**

The blast up the hill from Ste Dévote is thought of as a straight but, being Monaco, even this contains a swerve in it. Arriving at the crest of the hill at 273kph (170mph) and with the shape of Monte Carlo's Casino looming ahead of them, the drivers have to drop down to fourth gear and commit to turning into this lefthander. The track is narrow and the turn-in blind, and drivers have to get into position immediately for the following corner.

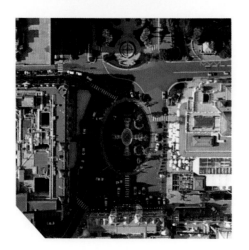

Turn 4 • Casino
Gear: **4**
Speed: **166kph (103mph)**

This is one of the most famous parts of the circuit, but the drivers have no time to admire the casino and gardens to their right in the centre of the square. They have to master the change in the gradient as the track turns left and starts to drop gently downhill in order to stop their cars from drifting towards the barriers while they attempt to keep them on a tight line. On exit they run out towards the left as they start their descent from the highest point on the circuit.

Turn 6 • Grand Hotel Hairpin
Gear: **2**
Speed: **63kph (39mph)**

After negotiating the righthand hairpin at Mirabeau, the drivers reach the second downhill hairpin in succession, this one an even tighter left. Drivers sometimes try to overtake here, especially if the driver they are chasing makes a poor exit from Mirabeau, but there's precious little space. Those gazing from the roof terraces of the Grand Hotel witness many collisions here, with drivers becoming delayed further by their cars being stuck together, their wheels interlocked.

Opposite: There's a stark change from daylight to darkness when the cars power away from Portier into the tunnel, but lighting helps to reduce the transition. *Above left:* Felipe Massa tackles the downhill hairpin in front of the Grand Hotel. *Above right:* The view down from the balconies of the apartments overlooking the start/finish straight, the sweep to Piscine and the harbour beyond is unrivalled.

Turn 8 • **Portier**
Gear: **2**
Speed: **81kph (50mph)**

After the track dives under a flyover, it turns sharply right here as it hits the seafront for the first time in its lap, with drivers having to be exceedingly cautious not to glance the outside barrier, which Ayrton Senna did in 1988. Early acceleration out of here is vital to carry extra speed into the tunnel that follows. Ayrton Senna famously clipped the barrier when in a dominant lead here in 1988, the damage forcing him into a retirement.

Turn 10/11 • **Nouvelle Chicane**
Gear: **2**
Speed: **66kph (41mph)**

Still accelerating as they exit the tunnel back into the sunlight, the cars hit 281kph (175mph) before drivers have to brake hard as the gentle downward slope levels out and steer left, then immediately right. Fortunately, there is an escape road directly ahead for those who fail to slow enough to turn into the chicane. The kerbs are low and drivers try to avoid hitting them too hard, which might delay their acceleration onto the short straight to Tabac.

Turn 12 • **Tabac**
Gear: **4**
Speed: **161kph (100mph)**

Flanked by yachts on its left and a grandstand crammed into the narrow space inside Ste Dévote on its right, this fourth-gear lefthander is named after a tobacconist's kiosk that used to stand there. The corner is made extra tricky because drivers can't see around it. Until 1972, this was the final corner of the lap because the start/finish line was then on the harbourfront. Martin Brundle famously got it wrong while qualifying in 1984, when he arrived here with his Tyrrell on its side.

Turn 13/14 • **Piscine**
Gear: **6**
Speed: **203kph (126mph)**

The construction of a public swimming pool on the harbourfront in 1972 meant the insertion of a pair of esses around it, with a left/right flick, followed by a short straight and then a right/left one at its far end. To make matters trickier still for the drivers, the turn-in is all but blind for each esse, making the 257kph (160mph) approach seem all the more excessive due to the complete lack of run-off there. The cars look extra dynamic here.

Great Drivers & Great Moments

A circuit as out of the ordinary as Monaco's has produced some staggering drives and some equally unexpected results across the decades. Here are a selection of the drivers and the grands prix that have stood out on a circuit where even a slight brush with the surrounding crash barriers can lead to embarrassed retirement.

Great Drivers

Ayrton **Senna**
Monaco wins – 6

Graham **Hill**
Monaco wins – 5

Stirling **Moss**
Monaco wins – 3

Lewis **Hamilton**
Monaco wins – 3

This exceptional Brazilian holds the record of six Monaco wins, but it could easily have been eight – he was denied victory when the 1984 race was red-flagged early because of wet conditions just as he moved his Toleman past Alain Prost's McLaren for the lead. Four years later, having won in 1987, he clipped the barrier at Portier and was out escaping to hide his disappointment. Having learnt his lesson, he then won this most prestigious grand prix every year from 1989 to 1993.

This moustachioed Englishman made the streets of Monaco pretty much his own in the 1960s, starting in 1963, when he won for BRM after Jim Clark hit gearbox trouble. He then added wins in 1964 and 1965, also for BRM, before winning for Lotus in 1968 and 1969 to earn the nickname of Mr Monaco. Sadly, his 1975 outing was hit by engine troubles and resulted in non-qualification of his Hill GH1 and so he elected to retire from racing there and then.

Victory at Monaco in 1956 marked Stirling's first grand prix win and he added to this victory for Maserati with another in 1960, when entrant Rob Walker decided he ought to change from a Cooper to a Lotus. Moss fought his way to the front after a poor start, only for rain to interject. Brabham then took the lead in his works Cooper then spun, but it took a chase back after a plug lead change for Moss to make it two victories. He won again for Rob Walker in 1961.

By Lewis Hamilton's standards, his 23% wins to starts ratio – three in 13 – here is relatively poor. Frustrated not to win in Monaco in his rookie year of F1, 2007, Lewis came good in the rain in 2008. He didn't win again until 2016 when he benefitted from Red Bull not having tyres ready for Daniel Ricciardo. Lewis was unusually emotional in dedicating his 2019 win to his mentor at Mercedes, triple World Champion Niki Lauda, who had died a few days before the race.

Great Moments

1955 Alberto **Ascari** survives a dip in the harbour

1970 Jack **Brabham** throws it away on the last lap

1992 Nigel **Mansell** just fails to pass Ayrton **Senna**

2018 **Ricciardo** is the master of disguise

One of the most dramatic images of Monaco in the 1950s was provided by the 1952 and 1953 World Champion when he was distracted by smoke from Stirling Moss's Mercedes as it expired and so lost concentration at the chicane – his Lancia Ferrari flying into the harbour. He survived the dunking with nothing more than a loss of pride and minor facial injuries, but his luck was to run out just four days later when he was killed testing a Ferrari sportscar at Monza.

Jackie Stewart led away from pole in his March from Chris Amon's similar car, but a misfire delayed him and Brabham took the lead. Jochen Rindt moved his Lotus to 9 seconds behind with four laps to go, amazingly catching Brabham as they started the final lap; the pressure told, and Brabham braked too late for the Gasworks Hairpin and slid into the bales, letting Rindt dive by for victory before he could reverse out to finish second, 23 seconds behind.

Nigel Mansell had won the first five grands prix of the season, so when he claimed pole it was expected that he'd make it six in a row in his Williams. However, with seven laps to go and a healthy lead over Ayrton Senna's McLaren, the rear of his car felt strange and so he pitted. A corner weight had come loose. By the time he rejoined, Senna was in the lead. Mansell then did everything except drive over the McLaren to get back in front, but still failed.

Drivers will tell you that any grand prix win is great, but a Monaco GP win is just that extra bit special. Daniel Ricciardo's success in 2018 was especially so, as his Red Bull had a mechanical problem that struck shortly into the race and deprived it of 160bhp. Fortunately, Monaco is such a tight circuit that it is more about track position than outright power. By adapting his driving style, the Australian managed not only to overcome, but to disguise the fault from his chief pursuer, Ferrari's Sebastian Vettel.

Baku

Azerbaijan stretched the boundaries when it was granted its first F1 race under the courtesy title of the Grand Prix of Europe in 2016. However, this little-known nation on the shore of the Caspian Sea – in Asia – provided a distinctive backdrop in its capital Baku and so provided the championship with welcome novelty.

> "It's a heavy-braking circuit, a bit like Montreal mixed with a bit of Monaco, mixed with a bit of Valencia and a bit of Sochi. It's a challenge to be on the limit."
>
> *Lewis Hamilton*

Once a state in the old Soviet Union, Azerbaijan now is a country that wants to boost its image beyond the accepted one of simply being an oil-rich nation. So, after hosting a handful of sporting and musical events, it plumped for a grand prix as its best option to shine the spotlight on its grandest features. A street race around its capital, Baku, was what it wanted and, once it had been given the courtesy title of Grand Prix of Europe (the date was one of those allocated to a race in Europe), that's what it got, starting in 2016. To most, the definition of Europe had to be stretched considerably, but its efforts have been appreciated, as it offers the World Championship something new and exciting.

Rather than another tailor-made circuit being built to yet another design by F1 architect Hermann Tilke, F1 fans benefitted by the circuit being laid out around Baku's UNESCO-protected old citadel, Icheri Sheher. Space is usually at a premium on street circuits, but Tilke was allowed plenty of room in which to work in the newer, more wide open parts of the city, and duly produced a layout with the World Championship's second-longest lap distance that toured past Baku's most important buildings.

Of course, street circuits have their restrictions and Baku has a few narrow pinch-points. There were even a couple of cobbled areas that were temporarily relaid with asphalt.

Landmark buildings are passed along the way, which is important as the government paid to host the race so that it could promote its image worldwide. For example, both the grandiose National Academy of Sciences and the Azerbaijan State Philharmonic Hall are passed at Turn 15 and the Maiden Tower at Turn 18.

The Baku City Circuit was dubbed the fastest street circuit in the world before the World Championship circus flew into town in June 2016. Pre-event advertising had boasted, "The speed is higher in the land of fire", and so it was. Indeed, F1's first visit to Baku proved them right as it offered a blast down the 1.5km main straight along Baku's Neftchilar Avenue long enough for Valtteri Bottas's Williams to do 378.0kph (234.9mph) in qualifying. To put the unusual length of the straight into perspective, drivers are flat-out from Turn 19 and – on a clear day – can only see the end of it once they have negotiated the kink at Turn 20, after which it's still as long as the back straight at the Shanghai International Circuit.

This really is a circuit of two halves, with the testing section around the citadel requiring heavy braking and downforce, suggesting a real compromise to keep the engineers on their toes.

The teams and drivers really didn't know what to expect when they turned up for their first visit. This is always the case with any new circuit, but doubly so when public roads are used. This is because bumps that drivers wouldn't get on a purpose-built circuit can be found all over the place.

One question that the sport's most purist fans will ask will be whether this will be an event that lasts many years – a reasonable one in a country that has zero motorsport culture. After all, Turkey had a similar paucity of motor racing history, with only a smattering of rallying being held within its borders, but it made its debut in the World Championship with a fabulous circuit outside Istanbul in 2005, only to be dropped after 2011 – and the circuit is no longer in use. Azerbaijan's only driver on the international racing scene is Gulhuseyn Abdullayev, who raced in the Spanish-based Euroformula Open F3 series in 2016.

With traditional European-based grands prix having fallen by the wayside, there was considerable negativity surrounding the awarding of the Grand Prix of Europe title for Baku's first F1 race before it was retitled as the Azerbaijan GP for 2017. Yet, people thought it a worthy addition to the calendar and they can feel less aggrieved with the announcement that France, the country that hosted the first ever grand prix, in 1906, will be back on the calendar from 2018. ∎

Opposite: There are battlements on the headland behind the circuit in Monaco, but this wall around Baku's citadel is next to the track.

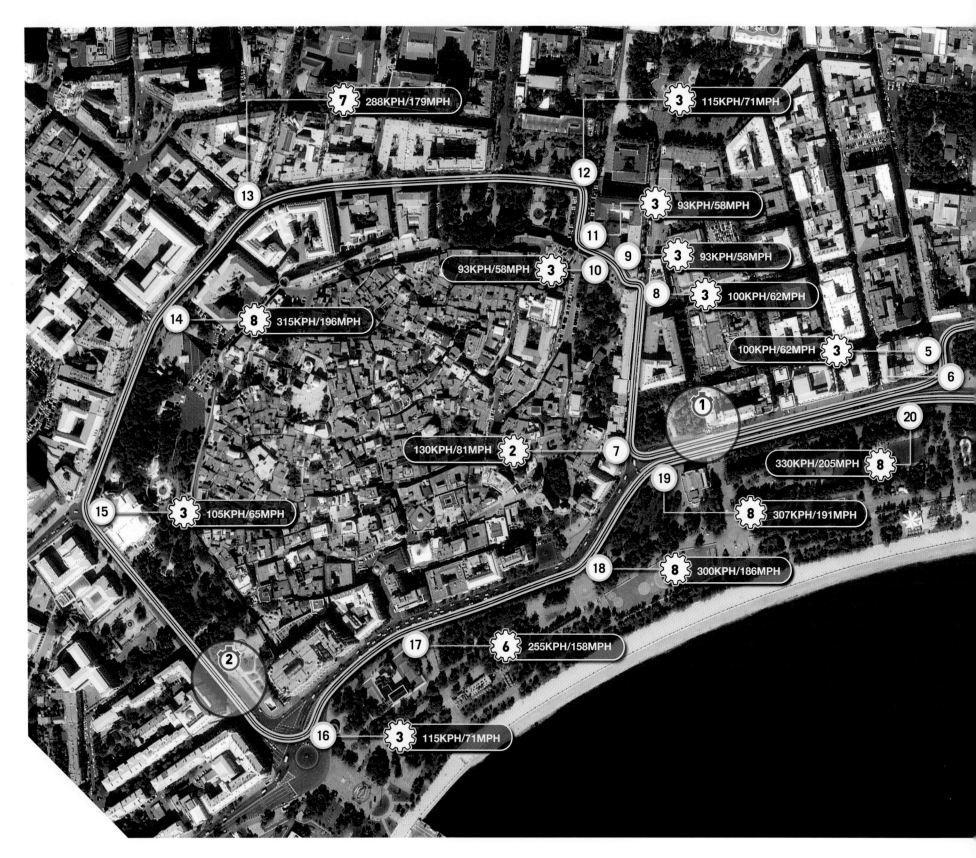

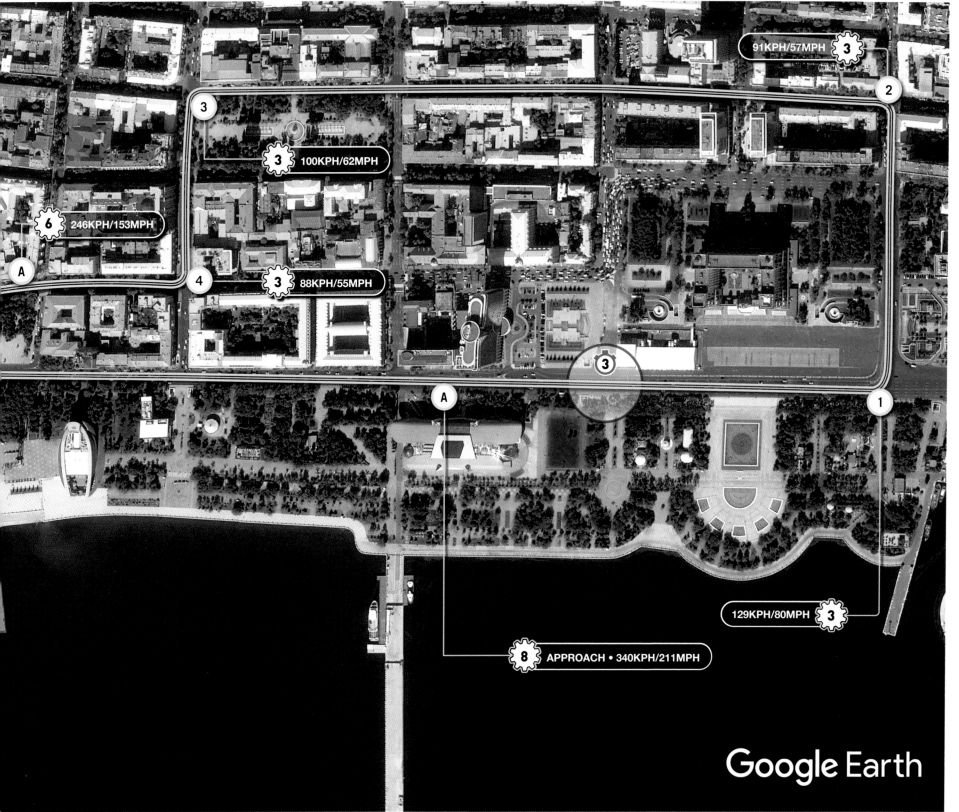

91KPH/57MPH **3**

2

3 100KPH/62MPH

6 246KPH/153MPH

A

4 **3** 88KPH/55MPH

3

A

1

3 129KPH/80MPH

8 APPROACH • 340KPH/211MPH

Google Earth

Circuit Guide

The Baku circuit was a challenge for teams and drivers alike when they had their first sighting of it in 2016. It's a track of diverse character, with fast sections as well as tight and slow ones and bumps everywhere.

Turn 1

Gear: **3**
Speed: **129kph (80mph)**

There's no time for the drivers to admire the views to their right, out across the Caspian Sea, as they blast past the pits at 340kph. Their focus, sensibly, is squarely on what lies at the end of the straight, namely a 90-degreee lefthander. The track is acceptably wide here, which is a relief as not only do they need to haul their cars down to around 129kph, but also they must be wary of resisting any driver who has gained a tow past the pits and might want to pass.

Turn 4

Gear: **3**
Speed: **88kph (55mph)**

Following on from the first three corners – all 90-degree lefthanders onto straights lined with buildings and trees – Turn 4, does things differently: it turns to the right. On its own, it's not particularly complicated, but as it's approached from almost the moment drivers have exited Turn 3 they quickly need to cross the track to get into position for this fourth change of direction. With another shortish straight on its exit, drivers must get their line just right so they can build as much speed as possible.

Turn 5–6

Gear: **3**
Speed: **100kph (62mph)**

Approached after a slight left kink on the short run from Turn 4, these are very much two corners as one, with the left/right combination a definite chicane. There's a sizeable blockade to focus the drivers' mind right in front of them at the turn-in point to the first part: a five-storey hotel. Snap to the left, then sharply to the right, and it's hard on the power again as drivers start changing their mindset for the different section of circuit they are about to enter.

Turn 7

Gear: **2**
Speed: **130kph (81mph)**

This is the tightest corner – to this point – of the lap, a righthander that requires heavy braking and precise application of the throttle. Then, with the barriers seeming as though they are starting to hem in the cars, and the buildings behind them noticeably closer to the drivers, so starts the anti-clockwise journey around Baku's citadel. There's a slight rise out of Turn 7 and only the shortest of straights before drivers reach the most testing part of the lap and the "embrace of the old city walls".

Opposite: Valtteri Bottas hauls his Williams down from top speed past the pits to negotiate the tight left at the end of the main straight. *Above left:* Sebastian Vettel brakes hard to slow sufficiently for Turn 8 and make sure that his Ferrari is on the one line to take the corner. *Above right:* This is the narrowest stretch of track used in F1, as Turn 8 flicks the cars hard left around the end of the citadel's wall and then twists directly through Turns 9 and 10.

Turn 8–12
Gear: **3**
Speed: **93kph (56mph)**

Noticeably tighter at the turn-in point to Turn 8, at 7.6m it is the narrowest part of the lap, the drivers are presented with what looks like an ever diminishing return as the track is now almost lined with the walls of buildings on the narrow road around the citadel. Fortunately, after flashing past the castellated tower at Turn 9 and starting to climb more steeply, the righthander over a brow at Turn 10 feeds the cars past a grandstand into a more open tree-lined curve all the way through to Turn 12.

Turn 13
Gear: **7**
Speed: **258kph (179mph)**

Having heaved a sigh of relief in getting through the Turns 8–12 sector of the lap with their car unscathed, drivers then get to use their higher gears and enjoy the first high-speed turn of the lap. The buildings are more generously spaced here as the drivers lean to the left, then do so again at Turn 14 and carry as much momentum as they can along this highest point of the circuit before turning more tightly through the lefthander at Turn 15 and start dropping down the slope again.

Turn 16
Gear: **3**
Speed: **115kph (71mph)**

This ninety-degree corner at the foot of the slope appears wide on entry, but it turns through enough degrees to the left to make drivers really focus on their entry line, as exit speed and balance from here is critical. This is because the section of circuit that follows encourages no use of the brakes all the way to the end of the start/finish straight. To offer a little visual respite, the righthand flank of the track has parkland beyond it rather than yet more buildings, making it feel less oppressive.

Turn 18
Gear: **8**
Speed: **300kph (186mph)**

This left-hand kink, and the right-hand kink that follows, are really the final hurrah of the lap, as they require precision to get the best line through this combination of swerves. As the final corner of the lap, Turn 20, is nothing more than a flat-out kink, this stretch is one through which any driver considering a DRS-assisted passing move past the pits really needs to position their car as close as possible to the one they're hunting. They need to get a preliminary tow before trying to make the most of the artificial assist.

Great Drivers & Great Moments

The very nature of Baku's street circuit, with its combination of fast and open balanced by tight and bumpy makes unplanned incidents a considerable possibility and winning extra difficult. Yet, after its first three grands prix, the moment most remembered is when Sebastian Vettel drove into Lewis Hamilton in 2017.

Great Drivers

Nico **Rosberg**
Baku wins – 1

With the 2014 and 2015 drivers' titles under his belt, Lewis Hamilton was seen as the lead driver at Mercedes, but he was challenged by a "new" Nico Rosberg in 2016, one who was determined to topple him. The change in the German was clear when he won the first four races. This race at Baku was the eighth of the season and Hamilton was fighting back, but F1's first visit here belonged to Rosberg after his team-mate clipped a wall in qualifying and started from 10th.

Daniel **Ricciardo**
Baku wins – 1

The smiling Australian was a popular winner of the first Azerbaijan GP – the event had been the European GP 12 months earlier. Having advanced from 10th on the grid in his Red Bull, Ricciardo looked set for third place, but ended up as the 2017 winner when Ferrari's Sebastian Vettel picked up a 10s penalty for sideswiping Lewis Hamilton. The Mercedes driver lost ground as he pitted to have a loose headrest fixed and Ricciardo drove away to claim the fifth F1 win of his career.

Lewis **Hamilton**
Baku wins – 1

As Lewis Hamilton continues his pursuit of Michael Schumacher's record of 91 grands prix wins, it felt inevitable that he would add one on this unusual street circuit. Surprisingly, a self-inflicted setback in 2016 and a delay for a car problem in 2017 meant it took until the third time of asking for him to finish in front. It required a little luck, as his Mercedes team-mate Valtteri Bottas was heading for victory until he suffered a blow-out after running over debris.

Valtteri **Bottas**
Baku wins – 1

Valtteri Bottas appeared to have had no option except to be Lewis Hamilton's understudy at Mercedes at the start of 2017. Occasionally, there were glimpses of superior speed, but this was more usually over one lap. However, his form in the opening four races of 2019 was different, better than before. Polesitter in Baku, Bottas was slow away, letting Hamilton take the lead. However, buoyed by confidence, he snatched back the lad and was still narrowly in front at the chequered flag.

Great Moments

2016 **F1** finds somewhere discernibly different

At the start of the 21st century, most circuits introduced to F1 were designed by Hermann Tilke. Singapore's street circuit was different and so was this one at Baku. It was with great delight that F1 revelled in the all-new and clearly different backdrop as the field raced along the Azerbaijan capital city's waterfront before snaking around the walls of the citadel. It was expected that concrete walls around the lap would claim victims, but the first race here ran off almost without any damage.

2017 **Vettel** hits **Hamilton** behind the safety car

History records that Daniel Ricciardo won the second grand prix held here. What gets lost is that he was given a helping hand when Sebastian Vettel had a moment of madness behind the safety car. Vettel had been caught out when leader Lewis Hamilton backed up the pack at an earlier restart and tried to anticipate the second release. He got too close and clipped Hamilton, believing this slow release also had been deliberate. Vettel swerved into the Mercedes and was lucky to be given only a 10s penalty.

2018 It's third time lucky for **Hamilton**

Having been moved forward to the end of April, the circuit felt very different for F1's third visit, because less grip was to be found. That couldn't be used as an excuse for the retirement of the two Red Bulls. Daniel Ricciardo challenged Max Verstappen in a battle over fourth and made a dive to pass him into Turn 1. It seemed doomed to failure from the moment that he thought about it and both men crashed out. Sebastien Vettel then ran off and Valterri Bottas suffered a puncture, leaving Hamilton to win.

2019 **Russell** has a near miss with a manhole cover

Watching George Russell spend his rookie F1 season in a back-of-the-pack Williams didn't make you think he was lucky. Getting away with hitting a loose manhole cover in the first practice session in Baku most certainly did. Always a hazard on street circuits, all manhole covers should be firmly secured before cars are allowed to go out for their annual visit, but this one wasn't. It damaged the floor of his car as well as setting off the fire extinguisher in his cockpit.

Sochi

Russia had long wanted to hold a round of the World Championship and proposed several venues, none of which came to anything. Then President Putin got involved and his push for the Black Sea resort of Sochi, home of the 2014 Olympic Winter Games, to have a second sporting event in the city hit gold.

> ❝ It's really so much about the fine details at this track. The steering input, releasing the brakes and turning in all count for so much at Sochi. ❞
>
> *Valtteri Bottas*

Moscow had tried several times to land a Russian GP. They had proposed races either at a purpose-built circuit, outside the city, or around a temporary street circuit right in its very centre. These proposals had come to naught, as did St Petersburg's bid. Then, propelled into the "this must happen" category, President Putin's decision for the government to bankroll the transformation of the Olympic Park section of his favoured Sochi resort on the coast of the Black Sea finally propelled Russia to become part of the Formula 1 World Championship. At a stroke, he ended the long-standing conundrum and also did something that has long proved a problem around the world: creating a secondary use for a one-off event facility.

The Russian GP debuted in autumn 2014, and it put considerable pressure on the event organisers, because they had around seven months to make the track and its facilities ready after this Black Sea resort had hosted the Olympic Winter Games and Winter Paralympic Games. So, after all the years of dashed expectations, it seemed unfortunate that Russia's entry to F1 was going to be a rushed one.

Certainly, in the race against time, time very nearly won, but team personnel were impressed when they arrived at the start of October 2014, albeit with most having their thoughts occupied by the dreadful head injuries that Marussia driver Jules Bianchi had suffered at the Japanese GP the previous weekend. Not only was the track finished, but its infrastructure was good too. Better still, the grandstands were packed with spectators.

One unusual feature of this circuit laid out around the area that had been the dedicated centre for the Olympic Winter Games was that its lap length was generously the third longest in use at the time by the World Championship, with 3.634 miles (5.848 kilometres) included in each tour. The Baku City Circuit – longer by a tenth of a mile (0.155km) – made its bow two years later, and they are both a combination of fast and slow. A further benefit of being in an established year-round resort – summer by the lake, winters skiing in the mountains behind – is that there are plenty of hotels, even if they typically send their prices rocketing at grand prix time.

The lap of the Sochi Autodrom is all on the level, so viewing tends to be limited to what lies immediately in front of the particular grandstands, that's to say a corner and two straights or two corners and a straight according to grandstand position, but there's generally a good degree of width that helps with seeing more of the track.

For Russia's first F1 racer, Vitaly Petrov, the establishment of his home grand prix came too late as he had lost his F1 ride at the end of the 2012 season. However, the timing was perfect for the country's second F1 racer, as Daniil Kvyat had just made his breakthrough that spring with Scuderia Toro Rosso, affording him a great shop window for his talents.

Emphasising the change in the times, there is a whole host of young Russian talent working its way up through the junior single-seater categories with the aim of reaching F1, so this alone ought to ensure the long-term future of this race. Many of the circuits introduced in the past two decades have withered on the vine because none of their young local stars made it up racing's ladder to F1 to give home fans one of their own to cheer, but this clearly won't be a problem in Russia's case, with patriotic companies being urged from the very top of the government to back their progress through the junior single-seater categories..

The very nature of the blast from the grid to the first real corner of the lap, Turn 2, lends itself to drivers attempting to make a passing manoeuvre and not always getting it right. This has been the case in each of the three grand prix run to date and adds sure-fire excitement. ∎

Opposite: Turn 2 can be seen in the background before the track arcs anti-clockwise past the Iceberg Skating Palace up to this the midpoint of Turn 3.

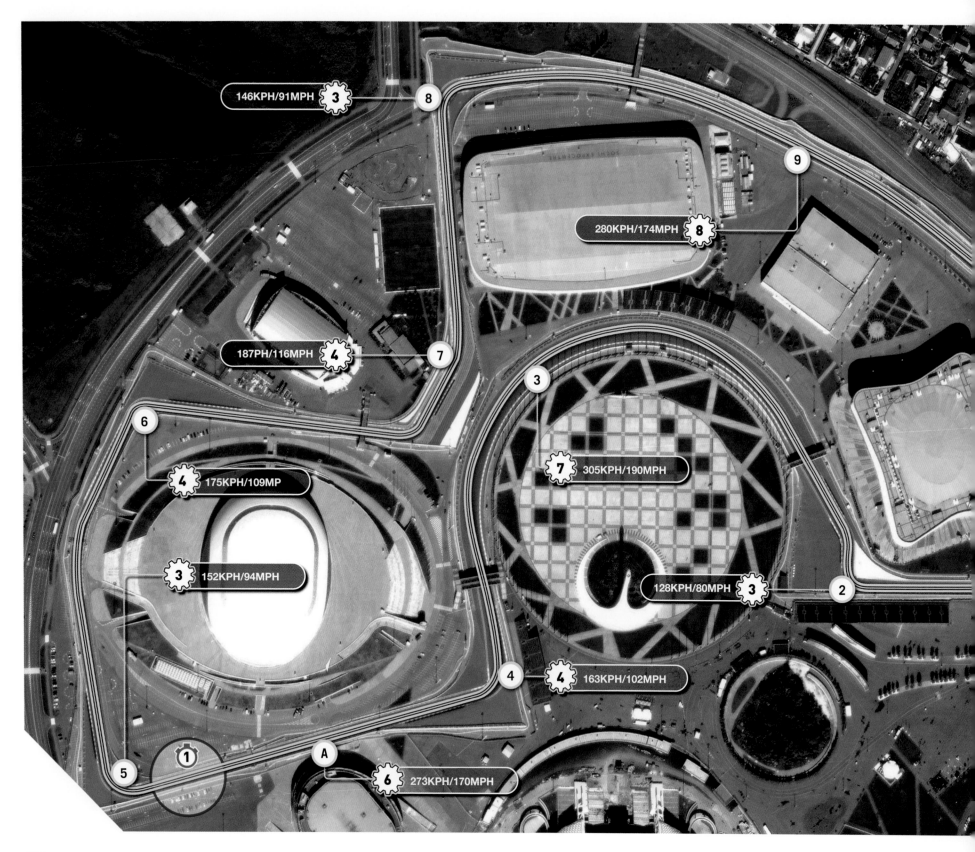

146KPH/91MPH **3** 8

280KPH/174MPH **8** 9

187PH/116MPH **4** 7

3

6

4 175KPH/109MP

7 305KPH/190MPH

3 152KPH/94MPH

128KPH/80MPH **3** 2

4 **4** 163KPH/102MPH

1

5

A

6 273KPH/170MPH

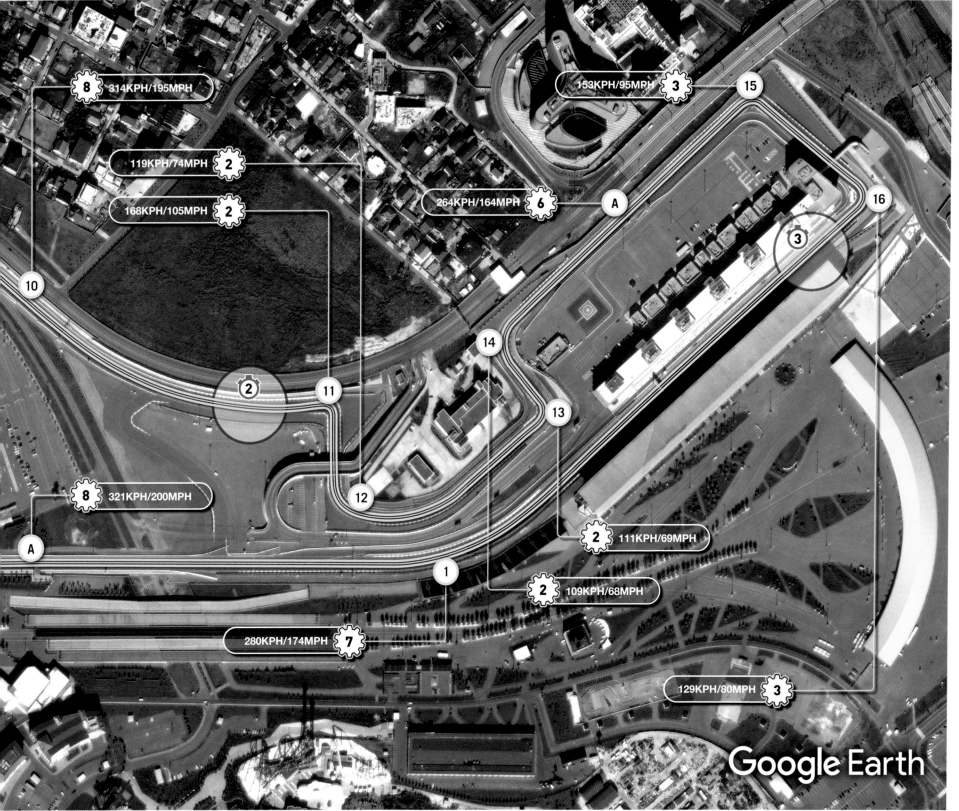

Circuit Guide

There's the Black Sea to one side and the Caucasus mountains behind, but this circuit is based around man-made structures as it snakes its way around the sporting complex used as the base for the 2014 Olympic Winter Games.

Turn 2

Gear: **3**
Speed: **128kph (80mph)**

Thanks to the kinked start/finish straight, the drivers can't see the first true corner from the grid on the opening lap of the race and so have to get through a flat-out righthander before they can see what lies ahead. It's a near 90-degree right with a wide track width between the concrete walls at the point of turn-in. There's also generous run-off straight ahead to allow those who have left their braking that fraction too late to have somewhere to go after they've got it wrong without ending their race.

Turn 3

Gear: **7**
Speed: **305kph (190mph)**

There's plenty of track width here, but it can't be used for much as the drivers are halfway around the Sochi Autodrom's signature corner. It's a 180-degree parabola around a garden. With its constantly turning nature, it's hard for drivers to change their line, as Romain Grosjean found out in Jenson Button's wake in 2015. If the afternoon is sunny, drivers also have to contend with the stroboscopic effect of the shadows of the flagpoles that line the park as they power from Turn 2 to Turn 3.

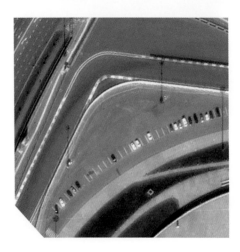

Turn 6

Gear: **4**
Speed: **175kph (109mph)**

After the righthand 90-degree corners at Turn 4 and Turn 5, the drivers have to negotiate a sixth-gear kink to the right before they can get clear sight of Turn 6. Then it comes as not much of a surprise to the drivers, as it is yet another tightish corner after yet another short straight as they blast part the dome-roofed Olympic skating venue. Variety, however, is not a feature of the Sochi Autodrom, so they pretty much can guess that Turn 6 will be followed by another short straight and be correct.

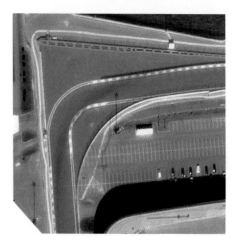

Turn 8

Gear: **3**
Speed: **146kph (91mph)**

Tighter than the preceeding couple of corners, this third-gear righthander has added interest as it opens onto the lap's only fast stretch – other than the start/finish straight. As a result, corner exit strategy is critical as drivers get their cars balanced and put the power down as early as possible in an attempt to get close to 200mph on the swerving run alongside Triumfalnaya Street that follows. Drivers need to get out of Turn 7 well enough to be able to get to the far left of the circuit on turn in.

Opposite: Nico Rosberg locks up as he fights Mercedes team-mate Lewis Hamilton for the lead into Turn 2 on the opening lap of the race in the inaugural Russian GP in 2014. *Above left:* Sergio Perez wears the obligatory Russian fur hat on the podium as he celebrates his third place finish for Force India in 2015. *Above right:* Turn 2 is always a place of incident, and 2016 proved no different, as Red Bull's Daniil Kvyat hit Sebastian Vettel's Ferrari.

Turn 10

Gear: **8**

Speed: **314kph (195mph)**

After passing the Iceberg Skating Palace on the drivers' right, not that they can see it from their lowdown position flanked by crash barriers, they know from their track walk on the Thursday that this little kink to the left following the flat-out kink to the right (Turn 9) requires some all-but instant action: braking, They ought to be travelling at up to 195mph, possibly in a rival's slipstream, and have to hit the brakes hard for Turn 11, which they can only see once they are through Turn 10.

Turn 11

Gear: **2**

Speed: **168kph (105mph)**

After their second chance to really get motoring, the 90-degree righthander at Turn 11 comes as something of a shock, leaving the drivers in no doubt that they are entering a run of corners in which precision is more important than flow as they turn right followed by a pair of lefts and a right before the track reunites itself with Triumfalnaya Street. Adding to the difficulty, as the drivers slow to get around this second-gear corner, is that a rival might be trying to pass after the lap's second DRS zone.

Turn 14

Gear: **2**

Speed: **109kph (68mph)**

The second righthand turn in this fiddly stretch has little to mark it out as the backdrop is similar to so many points around the lap, being one of crash barriers, debris fencing and grandstands behind. Taken in second gear, after the faster, more open lefthander that leads into it, the corner is tight. Drivers planning to make a visit to the pits need move quickly to the right after exiting the corner, as the pit entry is on the right on the approach to Turn 15.

Turn 16

Gear: **3**

Speed: **128kph (80mph)**

Like so many corners at the Sochi Autodrom, this final one of the lap can only be spotted by the drivers moments before they reach it. Furthermore, the features around this third-gear righthander just before the block of pit buildings don't mark it out like, say, Eau Rouge at Spa-Francorchamps, making selection of a turning-in point all the more difficult. As with Turn 8, the last corner of the lap is all about getting back onto the power as early as possible for the blast past the pits.

Great Drivers & Great Moments

To win in Sochi it appears that you need one thing: a Mercedes. Indeed, the silver arrows have triumphed in all five F1 of the World Championship's visits to date, with Lewis Hamilton taking the lion's share of the glory. Almost as important is taking pole position, because passing is far from easy.

Opposite top: Lewis Hamilton started a burst of late-season form in 2019 that helped propel him to victory at Sochi and then on to the title.

Opposite bottom left: Valtteri Bottas was all smiles in Sochi in 2017 after scoring his maiden grand prix victory.

Opposite bottom right: Nico Rosberg locks up spectacularly as he dives past Mercedes team-mate Lewis Hamilton on the opening lap in 2014.

Great Drivers

 Lewis **Hamilton**
Sochi wins – 4

 Nico **Rosberg**
Sochi wins – 1

 Valtteri **Bottas**
Sochi wins – 1

 Daniil **Kvyat**
Sochi wins – 0

Mercedes' Lewis Hamilton weathered an attack from team-mate Nico Rosberg to win Sochi's debut race in 2014, and made it two from two in 2015, although he was fortunate this time as Rosberg led until suffering a throttle pedal problem. Lewis added a third win in Sochi in 2018 when team-mate Valtteri Bottas obeyed team orders to let him through. Lewis' most recent win, in 2019, was made possible partly becauze Ferrari's Sebastian Vettel refused to obey team orders to let team-mate Charles Leclerc to pass.

The 2016 season was the one when former World Champion Keke Rosberg's son applied himself like never before to topple his Mercedes team-mate Lewis Hamilton who was in commanding form. Hamilton's car, unluckily, had an engine management problem, leaving him 10th on the grid. Nico started from pole positions made a good enough start to stay just clear of a first lap incident and led all the way, as Hamilton fought his way through to second.

Signed by Mercedes for 2017 in a late move after 2016 World Champion Nico Rosberg suddenly retired, the Finn settled in to Lewis Hamilton's team so well that he arrived in Russia for round four looking settled. Ferrari's drivers filled the front row and Bottas was third, faster than Hamilton. Impressively, he blasted past both Ferraris by the first corner. The closing stages had Sebastian Vettel close in on fresher tyres, but Bottas held firm for his first win.

There had been no Russian F1 drivers before 2010, when Vitaly Petrov took his bow. Since then, there have been two more, with Daniil Kvyat making the bigger impression. In 2016, however, it was not in the way he wished, because he braked too late into Turn 2 on the first lap, thumped into the back of Sebastian Vettel's Ferrari to put it out of the race – but not before it his side of Kvyat's Red Bull team-mate Daniel Ricciardo, slowing it for the rest of the race.

Great Moments

2014 **F1** experiences something very different

2015 **Perez** shines brightly for Force India

2017 **Ferraris** fill the front row, but still can't win

2018 **Leclerc** strikes for the little teams

F1's visit to the first ever Russian GP at its new Sochi home was one of exploration. A half-year after hosting the Winter Olympics, some facilities were still being converted for F1 use when everyone arrived. As for the track, it was clear that the entry to Turn 2 offered an overtaking chance, so Nico Rosberg tried it. He locked up as he passed Mercedes team-mate Lewis Hamilton, leaving him with flatspotted tyres that needed changing. This allowed Hamilton to win as he pleased.

While Mercedes and Ferrari competed for the outright honours in 2015 – they won all 19 races – the odd top result for a less fancied team is often remembered for longer, simply for being out of the ordinary. One such result was when Sergio Perez built on an upswing of form for Force India to reach the podium. Lewis Hamilton beat Sebastian Vettel, but the Mexican started seventh, benefitted from a well-timed pitstop during a safety car period and finished third.

Mercedes remained the dominant force in 2017, and it was seen as a pleasant change when another team made it onto the front row. There was double delight when both cars on the front row at Sochi were Ferrari red, with Ferrari's Sebastian Vettel taking pole ahead of Kimi Raikkonen. Any thoughts of victory were snatched away almost immediately as they were passed by Valtteri Bottas, but it at least provided the TV cameras with a less common sight.

The 14 drivers representing seven of the 10 teams in 2018 knew they were likely to be fighting over scraps rather than for the main prize, such was their performance deficit to the top three teams. Indeed, to finish above seventh place usually required a retirement from Mercedes, Ferrari or Red Bull. In 2018, "best of the rest" plaudits at Sochi went to Sauber's rising star Charles Leclerc, the last unlapped driver, who claimed seventh place. No wonder Ferrari wanted his signature.

Barcelona

Spain had hosted its grand prix at four other circuits before the Circuit de Catalunya was built at Montmelo outside Barcelona, but this has been the race's home ever since its debut in 1991 and the rise of Fernando Alonso has done something that had happened at no Spanish GP before – filled the grandstands.

> ❝ It's a very enjoyable circuit, with Turns 3 and 9 a real test, but it's also hard to set the car up for, as there are high-speed, medium-speed and low-speed corners. ❞
>
> *Pastor Malonado*

Formula One hasn't always enjoyed its current popularity in Spain, with Fernando Alonso a national hero, but only those with longer memories will recall the times when grands prix would be held there with no Spanish involvement and thus only part-filled grandstands.

Had Alfonso de Portago not been killed during the 1957 Mille Miglia sportscar road race, it's quite possible that he would have gone on to win grands prix for Ferrari and so Spain would have had more reason to love and support F1. Unfortunately, he did meet his end and Spanish drivers were absent from the pinnacle of the sport through the 1960s and 1970s. The nation's motorsporting success was instead driven by its motorbike racers, with tens of thousands turning out to watch the likes of 13-time World Champion Angel Nieto, Ricardo Tormo and Sito Pons but largely ignoring their four-wheeled racers.

Despite this lack of popularity, the Spanish GPs held at Pedralbes in Barcelona's western suburbs in 1951 and 1954 were finally followed by the country's World Championship return in 1968, using the Jarama circuit that had been built outside Madrid. This then alternated with the Montjuich Park circuit in Barcelona until 1975, when spectators were killed at the latter. However, meagre crowds, due to the fans having no national hero to cheer, led

to a lack of investment and Jarama lost its race after 1981. Fortunately for Spanish fans, the mayor of Jerez de la Frontera in the south-west of the country wanted to promote his sherry-producing region and so financed the building of a circuit that would host the Spanish GP from 1986 to 1990.

But then Barcelona struck back with a tailor-made circuit of its own: the Circuit de Catalunya. Financed by local and governmental grants, it offered superior facilities and an interesting layout. Better still, it was located far closer to the bulk of Spain's population and offered excellent viewing. It was then treated to a vibrant debut grand prix in 1991, when Nigel Mansell and Ayrton Senna fought wheel-to-wheel.

Like Estoril before it in neighbouring Portugal, this circuit has long been a popular venue for winter testing. Indeed, its weather is more predictable than Estoril's was, although the wind here often swaps direction (blowing as a headwind down the start/finish straight in the morning, and a tailwind in the afternoon), thus hampering the teams' findings. However, the variety of corners and changes of gradient around the lap mean that the engineers can work on all sorts of chassis and aerodynamic set-ups that they will need through the course of the season.

Mansell won the first two Spanish GPs held here, Michael Schumacher added a pair in 1995

and 1996 and Mika Hakkinen won three in a row for McLaren from 1998. Yet Spanish fans still had no one of their own at the sharp end of the field, even though Barcelona-born Pedro de la Rosa was trying his best for assorted midfield teams, including Arrows and then Jaguar Racing.

What it took to interest the Spanish fans was the arrival of former World Kart Champion Fernando Alonso, who burst onto the car racing scene with such aplomb that he was an F1 driver by the start of his third year. His form then took off in 2003, when he started winning races for Renault. The crowd numbers exploded and he sent them home deliriously happy when he won the Spanish GP in 2006, a feat that he repeated with Ferrari in 2013.

Although this was a huge success, the Spanish economy was entering a dip and the circuit then faced a challenge to its supremacy because a street circuit was created in Valencia. This gave Spanish fans a second race, as it was run as the European GP from 2008, but that lasted only until 2012 and it has now been dropped, returning the Circuit de Catalunya to its previous position of supremacy. ∎

Opposite: Sergio Perez steers his McLaren out of the Turn 14/15 chicane ahead of Adrian Sutil, Romain Grosjean, Paul di Resta and Mark Webber in 2013.

APPROACH • 294KPH/184MPH **6**

6 EXIT • 280KPH/175MPH

4 REPSOL • 161KPH/100MPH

A

1

E

4

5 RENAULT • 235KPH/146MPH

3

5

3 SEAT • 121KPH/75MPH

150KPH/93MPH **3**

8

5 254KPH/158MPH

2

6

7

4 200KPH/125MPH

3 ELF • 141KPH/88MPH

WURTH • 145KPH/90MPH **3**

1

5 CAMPSA • 246KPH/153MPH

3 BANC SABADELL • 139KPH/87MPH

6 EXIT • 260KPH/161MPH

CHICANE RACC • 92KPH/57MPH 2

9

E

12

EUROPCAR • 213KPH/133MPH 5

13

11

RACC

Circuit de Catalunya

14

15

2

10

LA CAIXA • 133KPH/83MPH 3

3

NEW HOLLAND • 241KPH/150MPH 6

16

Google Earth

Circuit Guide

The Circuit de Catalunya is a technical circuit that has every type of corner from low-speed to fast sweeper, and the lap is made all the more interesting by near constant changes of gradient, making it great for driving if not for overtaking.

Turn 1 • **Elf**
Gear: **3**
Speed: **141kph (88mph)**

This is always an exciting corner, with its 306kph (190mph) approach along the downward-sloping start/finish straight and then heavy braking before drivers dare to start turning into this near 90-degree righthander. With this being the main place for overtaking, it can get very busy here, not just on the opening lap but throughout the race and there have been numerous clashes here over the years. A tight line in helps drivers to get onto a more open line through Turn 2.

Turn 3 • **Renault**
Gear: **5**
Speed: **235kph (146mph)**

This is a corner that really works the tyres on the outer (lefthand) side of the car as it arcs uphill and around to the right. Drivers pushing too hard risk graining those tyres. Taken in sixth gear, it also tests the strength of drivers' neck muscles. A slow exit from Turn 2 compromises speed through here, but a clean entry not only makes a driver fast through this long, constant radius bend, but boosts speed along the short straight to the following corner.

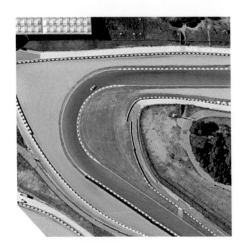

Turn 5 • **Seat**
Gear: **3**
Speed: **121kph (75mph)**

After rounding the double right fourth corner, the track rises again towards the fifth, Seat. This, like the third corner, can be a place where the cars are buffeted by wind, so drivers have to be prepared for that. A late turn into this tight lefthander is essential for a driver to be able to take the widest possible line out. The track drops away on the exit and feeds the drivers onto a brief, kinked straight on which they can hit 254kph (158mph) in fifth.

Turn 7 • **Wurth**
Gear: **3**
Speed: **145kph (90mph)**

As soon as the drivers have run through the kink, their view ahead used to be filled not with sky and clear space but with a tall earth bank, focusing their minds on getting their braking just right for this 90-degree left turn. More recently, the earth bank has been moved back and gravel traps inserted to make it less threatening. Dropping to third gear, drivers need to get the car balanced so that they can accelerate hard as soon as possible to power them up the climb that follows.

Opposite: Ferrari's Felipe Massa leads Kimi Raikkonen's McLaren and the Hondas of Rubens Barrichello and Jenson Button out of Turn 2 in 2006. *Above left:* Mika Hakkinen leads McLaren team-mate David Coulthard, Giancarlo Fisichella's Benetton and Michael Schumacher's Ferrari down to the first corner, Elf, in 1998. *Above right:* This was the moment that Fernando Alonso clinched the win that counted most to him in 2013.

Turn 9 • Campsa
Gear: **5**
Speed: **246kph (153mph)**

Taken over the crest of the slope, this may not look particularly tricky on a circuit map, but it's the most difficult corner of the entire lap because the apex can't be seen until the cars are almost upon it and the exit only when the apex is reached. So, placing the car is best done with experience, but there is at least plenty of run-off should drivers get it wrong, although Heikki Kovalainen's McLaren bounced clean across that after experiencing wheel failure in 2008.

Turn 10 • La Caixa
Gear: **4**
Speed: **133kph (83mph)**

At the end of the interior straight, this corner is approached downhill at 298kph (185mph). Drivers need to place their cars to the far righthand side of the track in order to help them take the least sharp angle around this lefthand turn, dropping from top gear to third as they do so. They must also pay attention to wind direction, which can really affect their optimum braking point, most especially if there's a tailwind. Overtaking is occasionally possible here.

Turn 12 • Banc Sabadell
Gear: **3**
Speed: **139kph (87mph)**

This is tighter in angle than the third corner, Renault, but similar in nature in that it's a long righthander taken uphill. The climb returns the circuit to not far short of the altitude of Campsa, but at least its second apex is visible on approach. Drivers used to really wind their cars up through here because it fed into the fast and open final two corners, but since 2007 it has fed onto a shorter straight and then a sharper righthand turn.

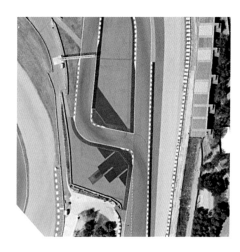

Turn 14/15 • Chicane RACC
Gear: **2**
Speed: **92kph (57mph)**

The realignment of the end of the lap in 2007 has been by far the most major change in the circuit's history. Instead of sloping downhill through a fast right, the track was made to cut right before the penultimate corner and then twist through this left/right chicane halfway down the slope to the final righthander. This was thought to be a good idea to help a chasing driver to get close enough to catch a tow down the start/finish straight, but it has done the opposite.

Great Drivers & Great Moments

The Circuit de Catalunya has always been a circuit on which overtaking is extremely difficult, so victories have often been decided by qualifying on pole position rather than by inspiration during the grand prix, but there have been some stand-out moments and star performances across its 24-year history.

Great Drivers

Michael **Schumacher**
Barcelona wins – 6

Six of Michael's record tally of 91 grand prix wins came in the Spanish GP, making the Circuit de Catalunya his equal second most successful hunting ground (with Suzuka). The victory that stands out is the one he scored in 1996, when he didn't put a wheel wrong in the wet (see below). Michael had already won here for Benetton in 1995 and would go on to win four in a row for Ferrari between 2001 and 2004, with his victory in 1995 his most comprehensive.

Lewis **Hamilton**
Barcelona wins – 4

It took Lewis Hamilton until his eighth year of F1 before he stood on the top step of the Barcelona podium. This was in 2014 when he prevailed over Mercedes team-mate Nico Rosberg, who came on strong after running a different tyre strategy. In 2017, Lewis made a poor start from pole before coming through. The following year, he dominated from the front. Then, in 2019, he failed to match team-mate Valtteri Bottas in qualifying, but got the jump at the start and beat the Finn by 4s.

Mika **Hakkinen**
Barcelona wins – 3

This double World Champion had a great record at the Circuit de Catalunya, following up a dominant first win here in 1998 with two more in 1999 and 2000, all ahead of his McLaren team-mate David Coulthard. Indeed, the Finn was all set to make it four wins in a row here in 2001, when he suffered a last lap clutch failure and arch-rival Michael Schumacher motored past to win for Ferrari by a large margin from Juan Pablo Montoya's Williams.

Fernando **Alonso**
Barcelona wins – 2

When Fernando triumphed here in 2006, it was the win that the Spanish fans had been waiting for all of their lives. Driving for Renault, he qualified on pole and had an answer for everything that Michael Schumacher could throw at him, and so sent 130,000 people wild with delight as they waved their national and Asturican flags. Fernando had finished as runner-up in both 2003 and 2005 and later added a second win here in 2013 for Ferrari, also winning at Valencia in 2012.

Great Moments

1991 Nigel **Mansell** and Ayrton **Senna** do battle

If the fans weren't all convinced that F1 could be spectacular when the circuit opened in 1991, they were certainly so by the end of that year's Spanish GP because they had been treated to some of the decade's closest and most visceral racing. The battling was between Williams racer Nigel Mansell and McLaren's Ayrton Senna, with the pair running almost the length of the start/finish straight, their cars inches apart before a poor tyre choice led to Senna spinning in changing conditions, letting Mansell win.

1996 Michael **Schumacher's** wet weather masterclass

Every now and again, when conditions for racing are terrible, a driver rises above it all to produce a drive of sheer genius. In 1996, Michael's first year with Ferrari, he did just that. The F310 wasn't particularly competitive, but the German came on strong as rain fell and conditions worsened, passing Jacques Villeneuve's Williams for the lead at one-fifth distance and then extending his advantage all the way to the finish as others spun, winning by fully 45.3 seconds from Jean Alesi's Benetton.

2012 Pastor **Maldonado** holds on to win for Williams

No one doubted that Venezuelan racer Pastor Maldonado possessed a good turn of speed. However, he had become known for being infuriatingly erratic and making mistakes. Yet, in 2012, not only did Pastor enjoy hitting the front on the rare day that Williams was able to offer him a competitive car with which he had qualified on pole, but he soaked up intense pressure from local hero Fernando Alonso, keeping ahead all the way to give Williams its first win since 2004.

2016 Max **Verstappen** wins as the Mercedes clash

Four races into 2016, Red Bull Racing, tired of Daniil Kvyat, demoted him to Scuderia Toro Rosso and promoted Max Verstappen. The Dutch teenager qualified fourth and soon was second behind team-mate Daniel Ricciardo when the Mercedes front row starters Lewis Hamilton and Nico Rosberg clashed on the opening lap. However, Red Bull changed Ricciardo to a three-stop strategy to counter Ferrari. It didn't work, as he fell to fourth, allowing Verstappen to win first time out.

Chapter 2
Asia and the Middle East

Felipe Massa guides his Ferrari through Turn 22 of Marina Bay, Singapore, passing the giant Ferris Wheel.

▮▬ Yas Marina

With money no object, this oil-rich country decided to host a round of the World Championship to boost its identity and so built a circuit of staggering grandiosity. It immediately impressed the teams when they first visited in 2009, but it is yet to produce a great race.

❝This track has a bit of everything, with high-speed and low-speed corners, positive and negative camber, and the walls are pretty close most of the way around.❞

Jenson Button

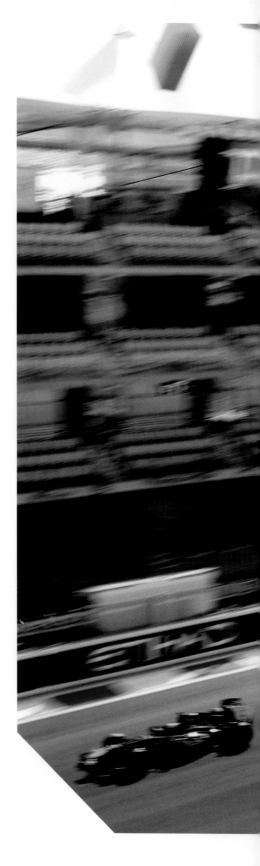

As the senior member of the United Arab Emirates, and the one with the greatest oil reserves, Abu Dhabi hasn't had to trumpet its wealth in the past. However, the rampant promotion of flashier junior emirate Dubai seems to have changed Abu Dhabi's approach, and the creation of the Abu Dhabi GP in 2009 was proof of this.

Like all other countries on the Arabian Peninsula, Abu Dhabi has no motorsport history, nothing to build on and no fan base to lure to the racing. Yet, this was seen as no impediment, because it was reckoned from the outset that the bulk of the spectators would be drawn from the tens of thousands of expatriate workers in the Gulf region. Indeed, one of the reasons for hosting a grand prix was to attract tourists to Abu Dhabi. To this end, it created the Yas Marina development that would offer far more than just a state-of-the-art racing facility. As well as the circuit, it would have a marina, a golf course, top-end hotels and even a Ferrari theme park, making Yas Island a place that people might chose for a holiday rather than just a weekend away.

So it was that Formula One's circuit designer of choice, Hermann Tilke, was given the design brief to create something dramatic. And this he did with a 21-corner stretch of tarmac that combines all the ingredients which an entertaining and challenging circuit should have, from a tightish first corner to

a run of esses, a chicane and a hairpin even before the cars have reached the first straight. The run from Turn 7 to Turn 8 is long enough for cars to hit just under 322kph (200mph) before the drivers have to brake very hard for the hairpin/chicane combination in front of a huge grandstand. With this being followed by a long, arcing straight into another tight corner, overtaking was expected to be rife. The final part of the lap is something of a departure, made up of a run of tighter corners, offering a very different challenge. The Yas Marina circuit even broke new ground, with its pitlane exit dipping into a tunnel under the track before delivering the cars to a safer merging point just after Turn 2.

It would take someone of powerful imagination to liken the Yas Marina circuit with Monaco's, yet it does possess two of the principality's key components: it too runs alongside a yacht-filled marina and also runs under a hotel, with a spectacular arch spanning the track between Turn 18 and Turn 19. However, you simply can't manufacture a setting like Monaco, where circuit melds with town and the glamour is for real.

Compared to the Sakhir circuit in fellow Gulf state Bahrain, though, the Yas Marina really benefits from being part of a sports and leisure complex, those yachts being packed with people in Abu Dhabi to have fun.

One other factor that marked out the Yas Marina as being a little different from other Tilke-designed circuits is that the grand prix has always been held as day turns to night, with the backdrop becoming all the more spectacular as darkness falls and the lights come on all around the circuit, with the hotel under which the circuit passes being a shroud of colour.

When the teams got their first sight of the circuit, they were more than a little impressed by its quality and could easily believe the alleged build cost of $1 billion. Abu Dhabi's inaugural grand prix in 2009 was won by Red Bull Racing's Sebastian Vettel after pole starter Lewis Hamilton's McLaren was slowed by a brake problem.

Sadly, the circuit has yet to provide the truly great racing that was expected of it because, although the racing has been close, overtaking has proved far harder than planned. This was shown most clearly in the final round of the 2010 World Championship when Fernando Alonso's title hopes evaporated; his Ferrari became bottled up behind Vitaly Petrov's Renault after a pitstop and he simply couldn't get past, allowing that evening's winner Vettel to pip him to the title by four points. ∎

Opposite: There's no time to admire the architecture as Toro Rosso's Jean-Eric Vergne brakes hard for Turn 1 in 2013.

APPROACH • 300KPH/186MPH

260KPH/162MPH

100KPH/62MPH

250KPH/155MPH

70KPH/43MPH

APPROACH • 315KPH/196MPH

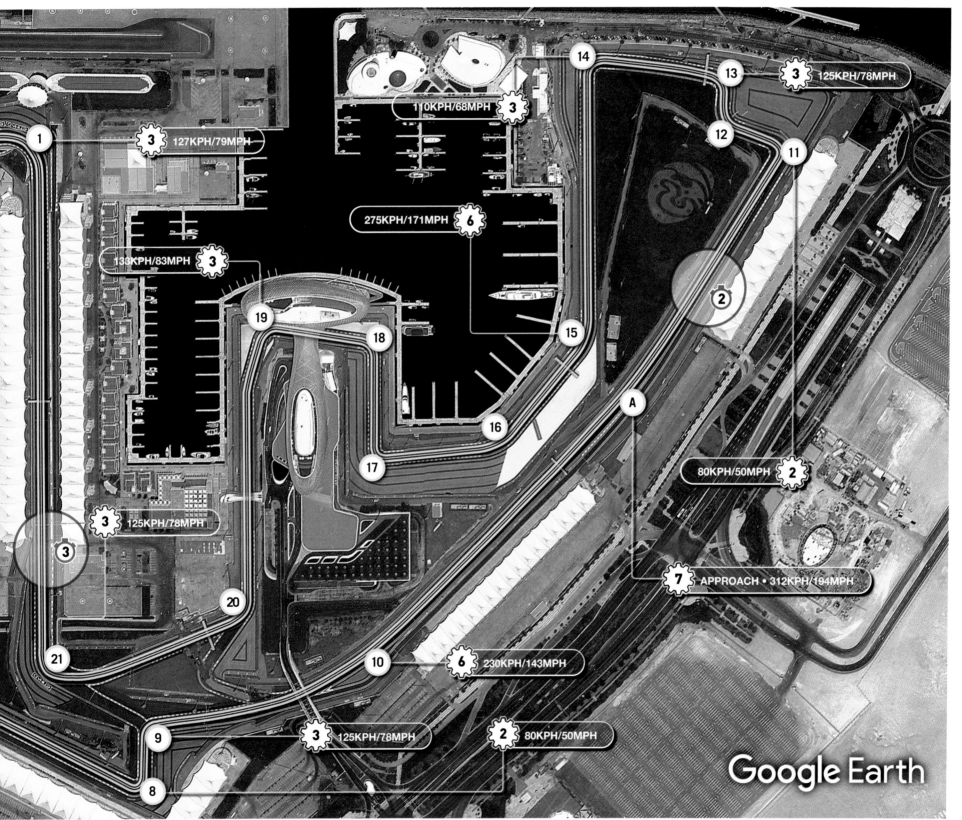

Circuit Guide

The Yas Marina circuit is one that offers a challenge for the drivers, its starkly different sectors presenting them with everything from very fast to very slow plus the unusual experience of driving through fading light and then under floodlights.

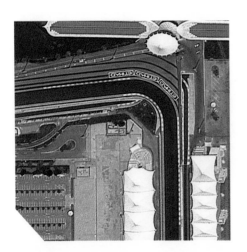

Turn 1 ●

Gear: **3**
Speed: **127kph (79mph)**

The flat-out blast from the starting grid to the first corner is one of the shortest the F1 drivers face and it has an unusual feel because it's hemmed in by lofty grandstands on either flank. It can get crowded on arrival at this third-gear 90-degree lefthander, with the potential reward of making a passing move not always outweighing the risk, as Rubens Barrichello discovered in Abu Dhabi's inaugural grand prix in 2009, when he bent one of his Brawn's front wing endplates against Mark Webber's Red Bull.

Turn 5 ●

Gear: **3**
Speed: **100kph (62mph)**

After the fast, serpentine sequence of twists through Turns 2, 3 and 4, the drivers have to hit the brakes hard for Turn 5. They might wish to make a passing move into this tight lefthander, but being fast into this corner can compromise the ability to tackle Turn 6 that follows immediately beyond it. To make matters more complicated, the most important part of the corner is making a good exit in order to be in position for the Turn 7 hairpin.

Turn 8 ●

Gear: **2**
Speed: **80kph (50mph)**

The sooner a driver can get the power down out of the Turn 7 hairpin, the more speed a car can build down the back straight. If all has gone well, and a slipstream tow has been achieved, then the entry to this tight left is a potential passing point. It's an unusual corner, because the drivers can see little other than a huge grandstand straight ahead of them. Balancing braking and exit speed is critical because it feeds straight into a chicane.

Turn 10 ●

Gear: **6**
Speed: **230kph (143mph)**

Accelerating hard out of the righthand second part of the Turn 8/9 chicane, drivers then keep their foot planted on the throttle as the track starts to arc away to the left; they change up to sixth gear, looking to get close enough to the car in front to be able to catch a tow down the remainder of the straight towards Turn 11. With grandstands along the righthand flank, the drivers' view is largely of the hotel and marina complex further around the lap.

Opposite: Jenson Button rockets past the marina as he heads for Turn 15 in his McLaren in 2011. **Above left:** The setting of the sun, as shown here over the pit straight grandstands in 2013, adds to the spectacle.
Above right: The floodlights are on as Lewis Hamilton negotiates the twisting entry to Turn 4 in his Mercedes in 2013.

Turn 11 ●
Gear: **2**
Speed: **80kph (50mph)**

Not dissimilar to Turn 8 in that it's a tight lefthander at the end of a long straight, Turn 11 differs chiefly in that its grandstand is to the righthand side of the track rather than in front of it, making it feel less imposing to the drivers. Entry to the corner is far from simple: like Turn 8, it feeds directly into another, and drivers looking to pull off an overtaking move must be aware that their work could be undone if they drift wide on exit.

Turn 13 ●
Gear: **3**
Speed: **125kph (78mph)**

This sharp lefthand turn out of the third chicane complex feels like the point at which the circuit exits its second sector and enters its third. From here, the sweeping and then fast sectors feed into slower, tighter corners that run around the marina; drivers have to accept that they will be running in line astern because there's little opportunity to pass another car. Acceleration, balance when cutting across the kerbs and precision under braking are now the key for the remainder of the lap.

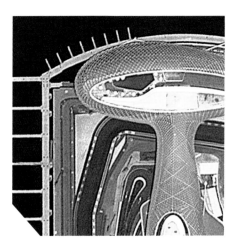

Turn 19 ●
Gear: **3**
Speed: **133kph (83mph)**

Three corners from the completion of the lap, this 80-degree lefthander feels to drivers as though it is releasing them into a more open world again because they tackle it seconds after running under the elaborate, architectural span of the Yas Viceroy Hotel. Back into full light, in daylight conditions at least, they are best advised to let their cars run towards the outside of the track on the exit but immediately consider pulling across to the other side, the left, for the approach to the following corner.

Turn 21 ●
Gear: **3**
Speed: **125kph (78mph)**

After negotiating quick Turn 20, drivers have to brake and change down to third gear for the final corner of the lap. This is a righthander of around 100 degrees, which is tucked in quite close to the inside of the Turn 8/9 complex at the end of the back straight. Feeding the cars back into view of the fans in the grandstands lining the start/finish straight, this corner is more critical in qualifying than it is in the race because it's not a spot for overtaking.

Great Drivers & Great Moments

It seems amazing that there have already been 10 grands prix held at Abu Dhabi's ultra-modern tailor-made circuit, but Sebastian Vettel and Lewis Hamilton in particular have reason to savour those races as they have proven themselves to be multiple winners at glitzy Yas Marina.

Great Drivers

Lewis **Hamilton**
Yas Marina wins – 5

Lewis improved a mediocre 2011 season by winning here, helped by poleman Sebastian Vettel having a puncture. Since joining Mercedes in 2013, Yas Marina has been a happy hunting ground, with wins coming in 2014, 2016, 2018 and 2019, with the first of these helping him claim his second F1 title. Two years later, he had mixed feelings, as second was enough for team-mate Nico Rosberg to be crowned. In 2018 he won a battle with Vettel's Ferrari, then he led every lap in 2019.

Sebastian **Vettel**
Yas Marina wins – 3

Winning the inaugural Abu Dhabi GP was special for Sebastian – a first win anywhere is a landmark – but it was doubly enjoyable as it was his only second win of the Jenson Button and Brawn dominated 2009 season. Victory was better still in 2010, as he passed both his Red Bull team-mate Mark Webber and Ferrari's Fernando Alonso to clinch his first world title. His third win at Yas Marina, in 2013, was so dominant that he won by half a minute.

Kimi **Raikkonen**
Yas Marina wins – 1

Red Bull Racing, Ferrari and McLaren were the top three teams in 2012, so it was expected that F1's fourth visit to Yas Marina would result in a win for one of their drivers. McLaren's Lewis Hamilton had everything under control until his car stopped and Championship leader Sebastian Vettel had started from the back of the grid, and this allowed Lotus's Kimi to triumph. His surprise win helped him to finish third in the standings, showing his merit.

Valtteri **Bottas**
Yas Marina wins – 1

Valterri's main task in 2017, his first year with Mercedes, was to support team leader Lewis Hamilton's championship charge. Having stepped up from the less competitive Williams, he was happy to find himself at the sharp end of the field. With wins in Russia and Austria to his name, Valtteri came on strong in the last few races. At Yas Marina he not only outqualified Hamilton, but also started better and took a thoroughly deserved victory.

Great Moments

2009 Red Bull wins after **Hamilton** retires

Polesetter Lewis Hamilton should have won the first Abu Dhabi GP for McLaren, but twice ran wide off the circuit and then parked his MP4-24 back in its garage after 20 laps with a brake problem. This allowed the Red Bulls to take control, Sebastian Vettel winning easily from team-mate Mark Webber and Brawn's Jenson Button. This result took Vettel past Brawn's Rubens Barrichello in the points table to end the year as runner-up to Button.

2010 Outside chance **Vettel** takes the title

Ferrari's Fernando Alonso topped the World Championship going the final round, with Red Bull pair Mark Webber eight points behind and Sebastian Vettel another seven adrift. Vettel, qualified on pole, while Alonso third and Webber fifth. Webber and Alonso mistimed their pitstops and found drivers like Vitaly Petrov unwilling to let them pass. With the circuit offering few passing places, Vettel won by 10 seconds, with Alonso seventh and Webber eighth, so the German became World Champion.

2015 **Rosberg** masters team-mate **Hamilton**

Nico Rosberg had spent most of the year playing second fiddle to his Mercedes team-mate Lewis Hamilton, who had clinched his third drivers' title with three races to go. Rosberg took pole position and won the next two races, in Mexico and Brazil, before the Abu Dhabi finale. The German driver then made it a pole-win hat-trick, once again making a good start. Hamilton changed his tactics as he tried to find a way past, but Rosberg had all the answers.

2016 **Hamilton** elicits help from **Vettel**

Lewis Hamilton knew that even if he won the 2016 finale at Yas Marina, his Mercedes team-mate Nico Rosberg would be crowned World Champion with a podium finish. Hamilton led away from pole, with Rosberg in second, but knew that he needed outside help. He slowed in the final laps, allowing Rosberg to close up, and Sebastian Vettel and Max Verstappen to get on Rosberg's tail. The quartet finished covered by 1.6s, but Rosberg stayed second to become champion.

Sakhir

Countries in the Middle East had long wanted to attract F1 to their shores, and Bahrain won the race to do so. This was in 2004 and they built a new circuit in the desert to do this. It has yet to fill its grandstands and missed its 2011 slot due to political unrest, but it now has the attraction of being a night race.

❝ The layout is tricky and there are some interesting corners with good sequences that you have to time perfectly in order to get them right. ❞

Juan Pablo Montoya

With considerable backing from the Bahraini royal family, led by Crown Prince Shaikh Salman bin Hamad Al Khalifa, the Bahrain International Circuit was opened on the site of a former camel farm and oasis at Sakhir, roughly 32km (20 miles) to the south of capital city Manama in 2004. Designed by Hermann Tilke, it immediately gave the World Championship a different flavour, offering something far removed from tree-lined Spa-Francorchamps, Montreal's island-based Circuit Gilles Villeneuve, Melbourne's suburban Albert Park or the streets of Monaco.

To give the circuit visual appeal, which isn't easy in this rocky stretch of desert, Tilke decided to split the circuit into two, making the area around the pits and paddock the "oasis" sector denoted by lush green grass verges. Then, as the track moves away from the circuit's hub, it enters its "desert" sector ,where all is as arid as the landscape around it, with a craggy, rocky feel rather than the rolling sand dunes that most people imagine when conjuring the image of a desert. Despite this concept, the circuit's most distinctive feature is the VIP Tower, a 10-storey edifice with a definite Arabic style that stands high above the first and second turns and Turn 10, offering the lucky VIPs fabulous views across the entire circuit. At the opposite end of the pitlane, there's a further nod to local style with a three-storey race control building in the style of a desert pavilion.

The layout of the Bahrain International Circuit has an opening section that bunches the cars together and makes overtaking possible not only on the opening lap. There follows a good length of a straight to a hairpin, before a middle section dotted with sweepers and some tight corners; then it all starts to open out again to end the lap with a good long stretch of top gear motoring. With not much of a backdrop to draw the eye, Tilke added to its interest by using what gradient was available, with Turns 4 and 13 the highest points.

The circuit was admired by the teams on their first visit in 2004 because it exceeded their expectations and the facilities were excellent. What was remarkable too, was the way that the project management team had had to cope with the date of Bahrain's inaugural grand prix being brought forward by six months at F1 supremo Bernie Ecclestone's insistence, cutting their schedule from two years to 18 months – they managed this in style. It was a definite accolade for Bahrain, and the finished project looked like $150m well spent.

Concerns that racing in the desert would be made farcical by sand blowing across the track and catching the drivers out were abated by glue being sprayed onto the verges of the desert section of the track.

In 2010, in a bid to boost the chance for more overtaking, an extra loop of track was added, turning left from the straight after Turn 4 and then swerving right, then tight left before doubling back through three more turns and rejoining the straight further down towards the start of the Turn 5/6/7 sweeper sequence. This wasn't adjudged to be a success, though, as it was too tight and merely reduced the number of times that the cars came past the grandstands without adding any extra overtaking.

One factor that the race organizers must hope is now behind them is the political unrest that hung over this event for several years, which included rioting in the streets and led to the cancellation of its grand prix in 2011. Fortunately, this appears to have calmed down and the teams' fears were allayed as they enjoyed successful races from 2012 to 2014. Yet, even in years when there were no threats of terrorism, the circuit's capacity of 70,000 grandstand seats seemed excessive and they have yet to be filled at any of the grands prix – a problem exacerbated by the grand prix being held on a Sunday, a working day in Islamic countries. Unfortunately for the circuit's management, the arrival of the Abu Dhabi GP in 2009 with its more attractive Yas Marina circuit and all of its tourist attractions have certainly reduced this race's appeal. ∎

Opposite: With Nico Rosberg already pulling clear, fifth-placed Felipe Massa heads Mark Webber, Kimi Raikkonen, Jenson Button, Sergio Perez et al out of Turn 10 in 2013.

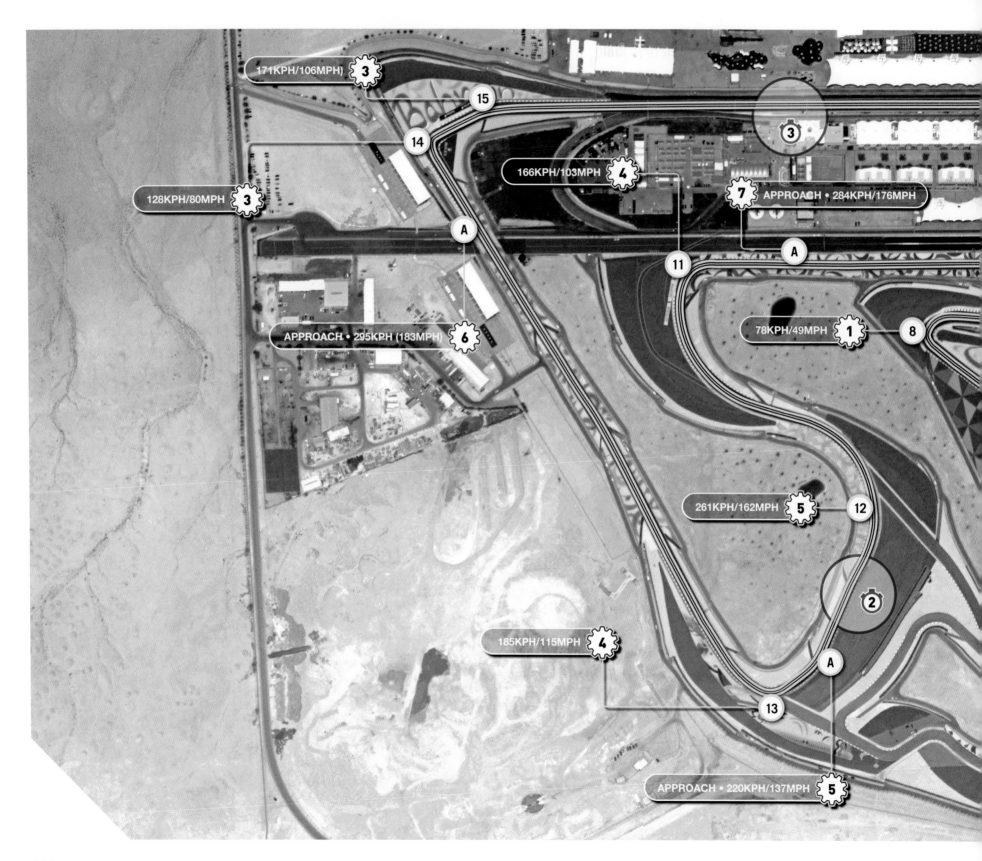

171KPH/106MPH) **3**

15

14

128KPH/80MPH **3**

166KPH/103MPH **4**

7 APPROACH • 284KPH/176MPH

A

3

11

A

APPROACH • 295KPH (183MPH) **6**

78KPH/49MPH **1**

8

261KPH/162MPH **5**

12

2

185KPH/115MPH **4**

A

13

APPROACH • 220KPH/137MPH **5**

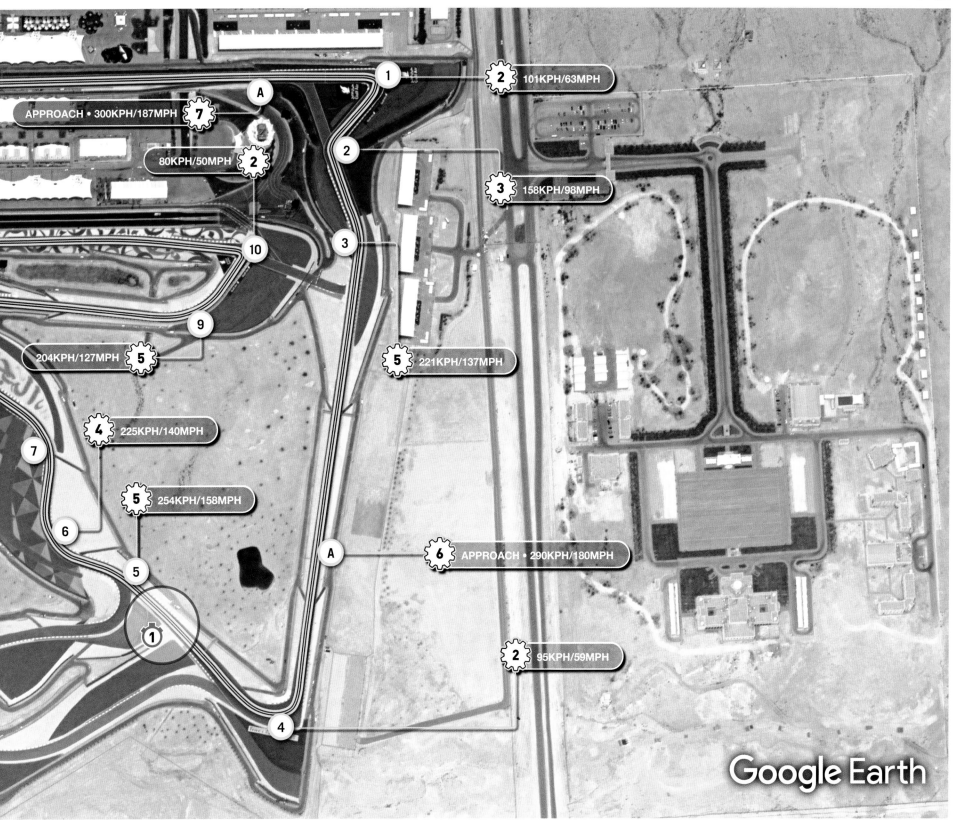

127

Circuit Guide

Designed to have two different-feeling sectors, the lap of Sakhir is split into oasis and desert: the track in the area around the pits and paddock is the oasis, with grass verges, which contrast with the desert sand and rock to the rear.

Turn 1 •

Gear: **2**
Speed: **101kph (63mph)**

This is a great opening corner, being a tight right approached down the circuit's longest straight with a wide entry to offer any attacking driver a clear opportunity to overtake. Similar to the first corner at Sepang, but not as acute a corner, it feeds back on itself and directly into Turn 2, and so drivers have to ensure that their bold moment into Turn 1 doesn't push them too far to the outside for them to get back onto line for Turn 2.

Turn 2 •

Gear: **3**
Speed: **158kph (98mph)**

Taken one gear higher than the first corner, Turn 2 is where drivers who were able to grab the inside line into the first corner, and thus have the shorter approach, are now on the outside line. They must resist being pushed too wide out of this lefthander; getting edged out onto the kerbs could cause them to lift off the throttle and thus lose vital momentum onto the lap's second straight. Accelerating hard, the right kink of Turn 3 follows almost immediately.

Turn 4 •

Gear: **2**
Speed: **95kph (59mph)**

Having hit close to 306kph (190mph) on this blast deep into the desert section of the lap, drivers are faced with almost uninterrupted views into the rocky desert beyond. They must focus on identifying their braking point, though, as well as checking for errant sand, as they brake and change down to second gear, ready to double back to the right. Luckily, there's a wide exit and the kerbs are not too vicious, so they don't have to hold it tight as they put the power down.

Turn 5 •

Gear: **5**
Speed: **254kph (158mph)**

Possibly the most spectacular stretch of circuit as far as the TV cameras are concerned is this trio of downhill sweepers located midway down the long approach to Turn 8. Turn 5 whips cars away to the left, then Turn 6 back to the right and Turn 7 back left again to complete the deviation from the course. Cars can be seen teetering for grip as they negotiate this, with drivers hoping to keep their throttle pedal planted. A failure to carry speed can ruin a qualifying lap.

Opposite: Ferrari's Felipe Massa leads a pack of points-chasers into Turn 13 early in the 2013 Bahrain GP. *Above left:* A few palm trees and an artificial pond don't make an oasis, but this ornamental oasis at least brightens the infield by Turn 12. *Above right:* Fernando Alonso leads fellow frontrunners Nico Rosberg, Paul di Resta, Felipe Massa, Mark Webber and Jenson Button out of Turn 1 into Turn 2 in 2013.

Turn 8 •

Gear: **1**

Speed: **78kph (49mph)**

Fast approaching the rear of the paddock, this is the point at which the drivers have to arrest their speed again, hauling their cars down to first gear and less than 80kph (50mph) for this ultra-tight right. The ideal attacking line into here is to be fully on the left side of the track in order to turn in from the widest angle and thus be able to carry the greatest amount of speed into the corner. If being attacked, a driver might need to hold a middle line to defend their position.

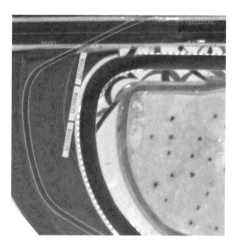

Turn 11 •

Gear: **4**

Speed: **166kph (103mph)**

This marks the return to the desert section of the circuit, with the lefthander approached along the grass-lined straight behind the paddock. An open corner, it tightens halfway around its arc as the drivers hit the throttle again and the track starts to rise for the gentle climb all the way up the slope to Turn 13. There's a slight camber to help cradle cars through the turn, enabling drivers to really throw their cars into the corner and yet still get around it, with run-off aplenty if they get it wrong.

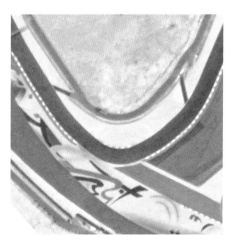

Turn 13 •

Gear: **4**

Speed: **185kph (115mph)**

Like Turn 4, this is a double-back corner that turns the cars back towards the oasis sector that completes the lap. A curving, slightly uphill approach is followed by a righthander that tightens on itself halfway around. There's plenty of space on the exit to run a little wide if necessary, but the drivers' main concern is getting hard onto the power as soon as possible because the track starts to dip away for the descent that follows down a straight to the final two corners.

Turn 14 •

Gear: **3**

Speed: **128kph (80mph)**

Turns 14 and 15 are really one corner, with Turn 15 simply being a swerve on the exit of Turn 14. Approached down the lap's second longest straight, it could be seen as a possible passing place, but this works only for a leader coming up on a backmarker; drivers of cars lapping at similar speeds tend to concentrate more on getting the perfect exit so they can be in position to complete the passing move at the end of the start/finish straight into Turn 1 after flashing past the pits.

Great Drivers & Great Moments

Since 2004, the Bahrain GP at Sakhir has provided something a little different to the World Championship thanks to the circuit's desert setting and the occasional scattering of sand on the racing line. However, it was the transition to a race that ran into the night that made it really stand out.

Opposite top: Brawn GP, formed after Honda quit F1, shocked everyone with a technical advantage that gave Jenson Button a winning start to 2009.

Opposite bottom left: Fernando Alonso is flanked by his engineers and mechanics after scoring the first win of his 2006 title-winning season with Renault.

Opposite bottom right: Sebastian Vettel heads clear of the pack on the opening lap in 2018, putting his Ferrari into a lead lost only when he pitted for new tyres.

Great Drivers

 Sebastian **Vettel**
Sakhir wins – 4

 Fernando **Alonso**
Sakhir wins – 3

 Lewis **Hamilton**
Sakhir wins – 3

 Felipe **Massa**
Sakhir wins – 2

Sebastian was the fourth different winner – for four different teams – when he won for Red Bull Racing in 2012, leading home the Lotus pair of Kimi Raikkonen and Romain Grosjean. Tyre problems affected almost everyone else that year, and in 2013, when the finishing order was identical. Sebastian's third Sakhir win came in 2017, this time for Ferrari, after a fumble by Mercedes. Twelve months later, Sebastian again won courtesy of better tyre strategy.

Renault had won the first two races of 2005 and arrived in Bahrain full of optimism, Fernando didn't disappoint, winning by 25s from Toyota's Jarno Trulli. He won again in 2006 by beating a revitalized Ferrari challenge headed by Michael Schumacher. In 2010, Bahrain was the season-opener and Fernando made it a dream debut for his new team Ferrari by rising from third to lead home a one-two for the Italian team after leader Sebastian Vettel's Red Bull lost power.

Mercedes was on a roll by 2014, arriving in Bahrain with one win each for Nico Rosberg and Lewis Hamilton, so it was key for one of them to find an advantage. Rosberg took pole, but Hamilton beat him to the first corner and held on to win. Hamilton won again in 2015 after Rosberg qualified badly. There was a third Hamilton third win at Sakhir in 2019, though this race would have gone to Ferrari's new boy Charles Leclerc but for a faltering engine.

Felipe's new Ferrari team-mate Kimi Raikkonen had won the 2007 season-opener, so the Brazilian needed to win at Sakhir to lose the No.2 tag he had gained as Michael Schumacher's partner. Starting from pole, he resisted a challenge from McLaren's Lewis Hamilton to win. Despite two disappointing races to start the 2008 season, Felipe made amends by winning back-to-back Bahrain GPs, though he was gifted the lead when poleman Robert Kubica made a poor start.

Great Moments

2004 **Schumacher** lays down marker in the desert

2009 **Button** makes it three wins from four

2016 **Grosjean** shows Haas form is no fluke

2018 Ferrari outthinks Mercedes for **Vettel** victory

It really was uncharted territory when F1 first arrived at Sakhir. Everyone was impressed by the facility but concerned about the sand blowing across the track. A potential problem was avoided by coat of glue, but drivers running wide kicked small stones back on to the circuit. Ferrari dominated proceedings and Michael Schumacher easily won the inaugural Bahrain GP from team-mate Rubens Barrichello, with third-placed Jenson Button's BAR Honda 25s further back in third.

The Brawn team – resurrected from Honda's withdrawal at the end of 2008 – was a revelation early in 2009 as it exploited a loophole in the rules to run a double-decker diffuser. Jenson Button reaped the rewards and, starting from fourth on the grid he passed the two Toyotas on the front-row – driven by Jarno Trulli and Timo Glock – then stretched clear of Sebastian Vettel's Red Bull to record his third win in four rounds on the way to his title-winning season.

No one expected much of Haas when it debuted in F1 in 2016. The Americans were a made-up team of no pedigree and so everyone was shocked when Romain Grosjean – despite starting 19th on the grid – snatched sixth place in the opening race of the season in Australia. When he qualified ninth next time out at Sakhir, people paid more attention, and the interest grew significantly as the French driver went one place better and crossed the finish line fifth overall.

The most recent of Sebastian Vettel's four Sakhir wins came in 2018 when Ferrari outthought Mercedes in pitstop strategy. They decided not to bring in Vettel for a second stop and he hung on, under increasing pressure from Valtteri Bottas's Mercedes as his tyres deteriorated, to make it two wins from two. Lewis Hamilton, who started ninth after a grid penalty, rose to fourth, which became third when Kimi Raikkonen left his pitstop too soon and hit a mechanic.

Shanghai

Built on marshy land to the north of fast-expanding Shanghai, this circuit wows everyone who has visited it since 2004 because of its sheer scale. Everything about the Shanghai International Circuit is huge, except for the crowds who have resolutely not yet taken to F1, perhaps needing a Chinese driver to cheer.

> **"**This track has high-speed and low-speed corners, good rhythm, even a bit of a banked corner. The layout is more like the old tracks, just with the walls pushed out.**"**
>
> *Jacques Villeneuve*

The thing that excited the Formula One circus the most when talks of a possible grand prix in China were first discussed, was the fact that it would offer the teams and their sponsors a way into the gargantuan and fast-expanding Chinese market. F1 management and teams alike dreamed of this gateway to massively enhanced sales in the world's most populous country. It was a no-brainer to make sure that it happened. And so, with Chinese governmental backing, it did, with the Shanghai International Circuit opening in 2004.

Thus, in one fell swoop, China had a world class racing facility, having previously had only minimal contact with motor racing. This had come in several forms – a street circuit in Portuguese enclave Macau since the mid-1950s, then a street circuit in nearby Zhuhai from 1993, followed by China's first permanent racing circuit being built just outside Zhuhai in 1996. This had been built with the hope of landing a grand prix, even making its way onto the provisional World Championship calendar for 1998, but it was then dropped because of "infrastructure problems" and so it remained not fully finished, although operational for lower level racing.

The Chinese then became more focused on its bid for the 2008 Olympic Games, but Shanghai wanted something to counter Beijing's Games

and so the circuit was commissioned in 2001, with a deal clinched the following year for a grand prix from 2004.

Circuit designer Hermann Tilke described this circuit as his "toughest project" because he had to build the circuit and all the associated facilities on land that was "really very swampy, 300 metres [984ft] deep." What he had to do to solve this problem was to sink huge polystyrene blocks 14 metres (46ft) deep to stabilize the ground and then construct all the buildings on concrete piles. In all, 40,000 piles were driven into the ground to increase rigidity for what was to be built on top.

The lap starts with an intriguing uphill righthander that feeds directly into a further right on the crest of the rise; this in turn feeds directly into a sharp left as the track levels out again at the foot of the rise. The turning doesn't stop there, either, as Turn 3 leads straight into Turn 4, where drivers try to get onto the throttle as early as possible for the straight that follows. The circuit then opens up and, after a hairpin at Turn 6, follows a meandering course until it reaches Turn 11, where it starts a sequence of tight twists not dissimilar to Turns 1 to 3, albeit on the level. Then it really opens out with an incredibly long straight down to a hairpin before an open kink leads the cars back on to the start/finish straight.

In addition to the sheer size of the gigantic pit straight grandstand, the feature that marks the circuit out as unique is what is to be found behind the giant paddock. Offering a rare element of national identity among the endless concrete are individual two-storey villas for each of the teams to use as their headquarters while at the grand prix, built in a Chinese style, approached over bridges and surrounded by lakes and gardens.

Since the first Chinese GP, won by Rubens Barrichello for Ferrari in 2004, there have been some great races at the Shanghai International Circuit, with many a change of position into the first corner, into Turn 6 and, mostly, into the hairpin at the end of the back straight. However, it's not a circuit to which the sport has warmed, because it is so large that it dwarfs the people there, making it feel empty. In fact, much of it is empty, with the huge grandstands encircling the Turn 11–13 complex never being used and now being covered in advertising banners to mask this fact. Add the smog that often obscures the sun, and the circuit can feel characterless. ∎

Opposite: The view from the top of the giant grandstand opposite the pits towards Turn 6 is amazing, unless smog sets in.

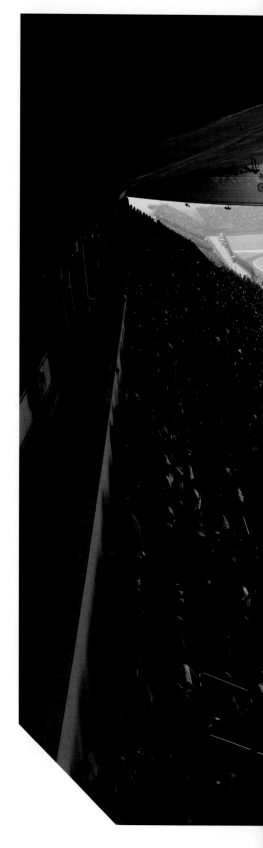

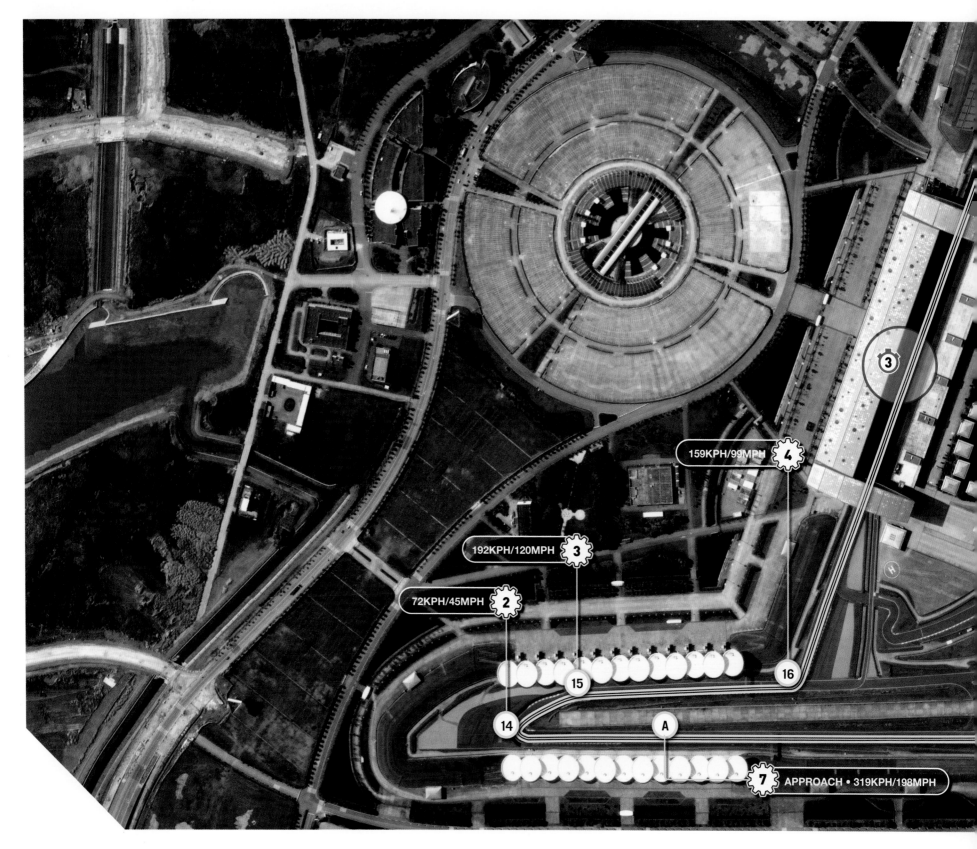

159KPH/99MPH **4**

192KPH/120MPH **3**

72KPH/45MPH **2**

3

16

15

14

A

7 APPROACH • 319KPH/198MPH

1

4 175KPH/109MPH

6 APPROACH • 298KPH/185MPH

3

2

5

2 76KPH/47MPH

4

A

1

3 110KPH/68MPH

6

2 85KPH/53MPH

A

5 APPROACH • 220KPH/137MPH

7

6 270KPH/168MPH

A

3 108KPH/67MPH

6 APPROACH • 270KPH/168MPH

9

8

12

2 85KPH/53MPH

3 185KPH/115MPH

10

11

2

13

4 187KPH/116MPH

E

EXIT TO TURN • 249KPH/155MPH **5**

Google Earth

Circuit Guide

From the seemingly never-straightening first four corners up and over a ridge to the wicked sweepers around the back of the paddock and the wide and incredibly open back straight into a hairpin, this track provides the drivers with a real ride.

Turn 1 •

Gear: **4**
Speed: **175kph (109mph)**

The track is broad as the cars pass under the second "wing" over the start/finish straight and arrive in the braking area for the first corner. The view ahead is open across a large concrete apron, but a driver's eyes must be focused on how the track narrows and rises to the right. Dropping from top gear to fourth, drivers have to pick their line according to whether they are attacking or defending, with a line around the outside often proving the best if attacking.

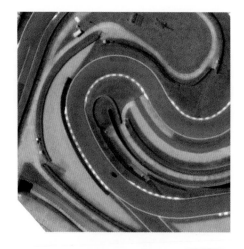

Turn 3 •

Gear: **2**
Speed: **85kph (53mph)**

Dropping sharply into a compression as the track reaches the level of the start/finish line again, drivers have to change down to second gear and, on the opening lap in particular, be wary of wing-bending attacks from either side because the traffic can become very heavy at this squeeze point. This is the first really sharp corner of the lap and is very physical simply because of the simultaneous change in both direction and gradient. A tight line out of the turn can pay dividends.

Turn 6 •

Gear: **2**
Speed: **76kph (47mph)**

Drivers arrive at this turning point having built up some decent speed along the kinked straight from Turn 4. Braking from 298kph (185mph), they then have to drop down from sixth gear to second. With low grass banks set back some way on either side, it feels wide open, but the righthander is relatively tight, albeit with its angle relaxing after the apex; drivers use the kerbs on the way out so that they can start getting the power down again as soon as possible.

Turn 7 •

Gear: **6**
Speed: **270kph (168mph)**

This little considered stretch of the Shanghai circuit at the rear edge of the paddock is actually one of the most exciting, because both the cars and the drivers are really made to work through this pair of sweepers. Drivers don't have time to really appreciate the view of the lofty grandstand ahead of them as they turn in on as smooth an arc as possible through this sixth-gear lefthander, knowing that they must achieve the balance to be on line for Turn 8.

Opposite: The pit entry can be tricky, as Lewis Hamilton discovered in 2007, when he didn't get this far... *Above left:* Braking hard, Sebastian Vettel leads Romain Grosjean and Jenson Button into Turn 14 in 2013.
Above right: The giant main grandstand is in the background as Jean-Eric Vergne negotiates Turn 4 in his Toro Rosso in 2013.

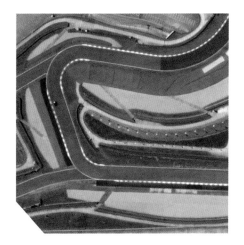

Turn 10 •

Gear: **3**
Speed: **185kph (115mph)**

After decelerating for third gear Turn 9, drivers have to turn left again almost immediately, accelerating as they do so. To take as much speed as they can onto the straight that follows, many cut across the kerbs on the inside then use those on the outside as they head off towards the furthest end of the track. Back in 2005, Juan Pablo Montoya triggered a safety car period when he ran over a drain cover here in his McLaren and dislodged it.

Turn 13 •

Gear: **4**
Speed: **187kph (116mph)**

Passing the giant but empty grandstands encircling this section of the track (which is shaped like the head of a hockey stick), this is the point at which the drivers can get on the throttle again after negotiating the sharp lefthander of Turn 11 followed immediately by a long right. More open in angle than Turn 12, exit speed from this constant radius righthander is vital because it feeds onto the incredibly long back straight. Cars look slower than they are here because of the scale of the place.

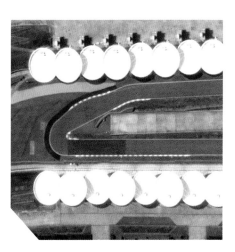

Turn 14 •

Gear: **2**
Speed: **72kph (45mph)**

Few drivers arrive at this righthand hairpin without needing either to attack the car in front or to defend their position from a rival. Having hit more than 322kph (200mph) on a good lap down the back straight, they are offered plenty of space to try their move, because the track is wide here when they start braking as they pass the grandstand on their left. They change down to second or even first gear, hoping that they won't need to use the run-off space ahead of them.

Turn 16 •

Gear: **4**
Speed: **159kph (99mph)**

The final turn is reached through a slight kink and then a gentle rise. With a lofty grandstand on the drivers' left side and open space on their right, drivers are naturally drawn towards the more open side of the track; this is the correct place to be because this is the line they need to tackle this fourth-gear lefthander. The corner will be forever remembered as the place where it went wrong for Lewis Hamilton when he slid into the gravel trap in 2007.

Great Drivers & Great Moments

Victories in China matter a lot to the teams because of the shop window that this race provides their sponsors in this burgeoning economic powerhouse, but the drivers are more than happy to win here too, and there have been some epic scraps since the Shanghai International Circuit's World Championship debut in 2004.

Great Drivers

 Lewis **Hamilton**
Shanghai wins – 5

 Fernando **Alonso**
Shanghai wins – 2

 Nico **Rosberg**
Shanghai wins – 2

 Kimi **Raikkonen**
Shanghai wins – 1

Victory at Shanghai in 2008 set up Hamilton for his second bid for the title as he won from Ferrari's Felipe Massa. His next win in China came in 2014, leading every lap and making it three wins from the first four rounds. Lewis repeated in 2015, though he had team-mate Nico Rosberg hot on his heels and Ferrari's Sebastian Vettel close behind. In 2017, Hamilton added a fourth win, again chased by Vettel. Then, in 2019, Lewis and team-mate Valtteri Bottas outran the Ferraris.

The Chinese GP was the final race of the 2005 World Championship and Fernando triumphed for Renault by 4 seconds from Kimi Raikkonen's McLaren in an event spoiled by a safety car deployment to move a dislodged drain cover. At the time it seemed unlikely that Alonso would have to wait another eight years for his next win here, but he did. Driving for Ferrari in 2013, he won what was likened to high-speed chess as drivers found their tyres going off markedly.

Having a world champion for a father can make a young driver's life difficult. Not so in the case of Keke Rosberg's son Nico, as the 1982 World Champion stays in the background. He had reason to be delighted when everything went Nico's way in the race here in 2012, allowing him to score his first F1 win at the 111th attempt. It was also the first for Mercedes since the 1950s. Five years later, Nico had an easy run as Mercedes team-mate Lewis Hamilton had to start from the back of the grid.

Ferrari claimed its third win in Shanghai in 2007 on F1's fourth visit and the driver at the wheel for this one was Kimi Raikkonen. The race was see-sawing between him and McLaren's Lewis Hamilton as the conditions kept changing with rain blowing in and out, when Hamilton slid into a gravel trap. Ferrari's Finn then motored on untroubled to win easily. Raikkonen headed to the final round in Brazil seven points behind, and an outside title shot but, famously, he won.

Great Moments

 2004 Rubens **Barrichello** wins inaugural GP for Ferrari

2007 Lewis **Hamilton** slides off and blows it

2010 Jenson **Button** reads the condition right to win

2012 Nico **Rosberg** takes Mercedes' first win

Michael Schumacher was the main man for Ferrari when the teams visited Shanghai. However, it was team-mate Rubens Barrichello who came away with the spoils because the German, who seemed to have relaxed from his usual focus, had an extraordinary weekend. Already World Champion, Schumacher slid off on his qualifying run and ended up 18th, then started from the pits with a new engine but could climb only to 12th, while Barrichello held off Jenson Button's BAR.

McLaren's rookie Lewis Hamilton looked set to claim the drivers' title. He started the race with a 12-point lead over Fernando Alonso and was leading from Ferrari's Kimi Raikkonen, but his rain tyres were going off. McLaren waited to see if more rain would come and Raikkonen went past to lead. Then, when Lewis finally peeled off to change to dry tyres, he slid into the gravel trap at pit entry and was beached there. Thus Raikkonen was able to win for Ferrari and keep the title race open.

Jenson had an inspired 2009 season in which he and Brawn GP stormed to their first and only F1 titles, and the start of the 2010 season with McLaren gave him victory on only his second outing, in Australia. Then, when he came to Shanghai for the fourth round, he won again, followed home by his more highly rated team-mate Lewis Hamilton; Jenson profited from an early-race decision to stay on dry tyres as rain began to fall, before it dried again.

Created from Brawn GP, which had dominated in 2009, this Ross Brawn-led team took time to find its feet again, but its third year as Mercedes GP gave the squad reason to cheer. Its breakthrough came at Shanghai, when Nico Rosberg started from pole and saw off the challenge of team-mate Michael Schumacher, who retired with a loose wheel. Jenson Button looked to have the pace to beat him due to three-stopping his McLaren, but a pitstop blunder allowed Rosberg to stay in front and win.

● Suzuka

Built as long ago as 1962, Suzuka has always been a considerable challenge and few places show a Formula One car being put through its paces to the same extent. It's a magnificent combination of high-speed corners, changing gradient and camber, which really makes the drivers work for their living.

❝ Suzuka's the most beautiful race track along with Nürburgring's Nordschleife and Macau, and it's a dream to drive, but overtaking is harder than it looks. ❞

Sebastian Vettel

Many of the world's greatest racing circuits are the result of local topography rather than clever design work. Take Spa-Francorchamps or the Nürburgring Nordschleife, both twisting their way around rolling landscape. Suzuka has a foot partly in this camp, because its raw ingredient of an open hillside in Japan was a great starting point, although the circuit was designed for purpose rather than simply taking over public roads as happened at Spa-Francorchamps.

This great circuit was shaped in 1962 at the behest of Honda by John Hugenholtz, the circuit manager who had interpreted the ideas of Sammy Davis, the Le Mans 24 Hours winner, for the creation of fast, flowing Zandvoort in his native Holland in the late 1940s. The result is such a gem that Suzuka is all but unchanged more than 50 years later, and very few circuits of similar vintage can match that.

The basic shape of the layout that was draped over the hillside near the city of Nagoya is a figure of eight, making it one of only a handful of circuits that crosses over itself. Suzuka was intended to be simply a test circuit on which Honda could test its motorbikes and the cars from its new automotive division. However, it was too good to be restricted to this and soon races started to be held, with future Lotus F1 boss Peter Warr winning the Japanese GP for sportscars in 1963. It was a further 24 years before it landed a grand prix date, though.

Not only was its lap an intense challenge, but it also produced some great racing, with the drama kept high by it often being the penultimate or final round of the World Championship. Few will forget the shoot-outs between Ayrton Senna and Alain Prost in 1989 and 1990, when they came into contact each time, helping neither of them. Michael Schumacher's attempts to keep McLaren's Mika Hakkinen from the 1998 drivers' title was incident-filled too, from the moment that he stalled his Ferrari on the starting grid.

What helped to make the racing so exciting is that this circuit, built in the grounds of an amusement park, offers more than a few places at which drivers have a reasonable chance of making a passing move stick. The downhill blast to the fast first turn is the main one of these, but there's also scope to try to overtake into the hairpin, and again at the Casio Triangle right at the end of the lap if a driver has been brave enough to get into a slipstreaming tow down the back straight and through mighty 130R.

In between this trio of points, the track uses the gradient well to make the drivers and their cars really work hard, and the photographers love the opportunities it offers them, with the amusement park's lofty Ferris wheel or monorail providing an unusual backdrop. On a bright day, which is far from guaranteed in the grand prix's traditional autumnal

date, fans in the main grandstand can see all the way past the first corner and on down to the sea. On many an occasion, though, they have been fortunate to see even the far side of the track because, when the rain comes down, it really comes down. This was topped in 2004, though, when a typhoon blew through and came close to forcing the cancellation of the race.

The Japanese fans also give the grand prix a sense of occasion because they are unbelievably passionate in the way that they support their heroes, sitting all day long festooned in face paint, scarves and flags.

Despite being ready to host a grand prix from the outset, it took a quarter of a century before the circuit made its Formula One bow; Japan stayed on F1's sidelines despite Fuji Speedway hosting two grand prix in 1976 and 1977. Then, in 1987, with the Casio Triangle having been inserted a few years earlier to slope the cars' passage through the final corner, it landed its place on the World Championship calendar. That first race was deprived of the main excitement when Nigel Mansell crashed in qualifying and so couldn't race, leaving the way clear for his Williams team-mate Nelson Piquet to take the drivers' crown. ■

Opposite: Felipe Massa (right) and Fernando Alonso guide their Ferraris through the Casio Triangle in 2013, with the funfair in the background.

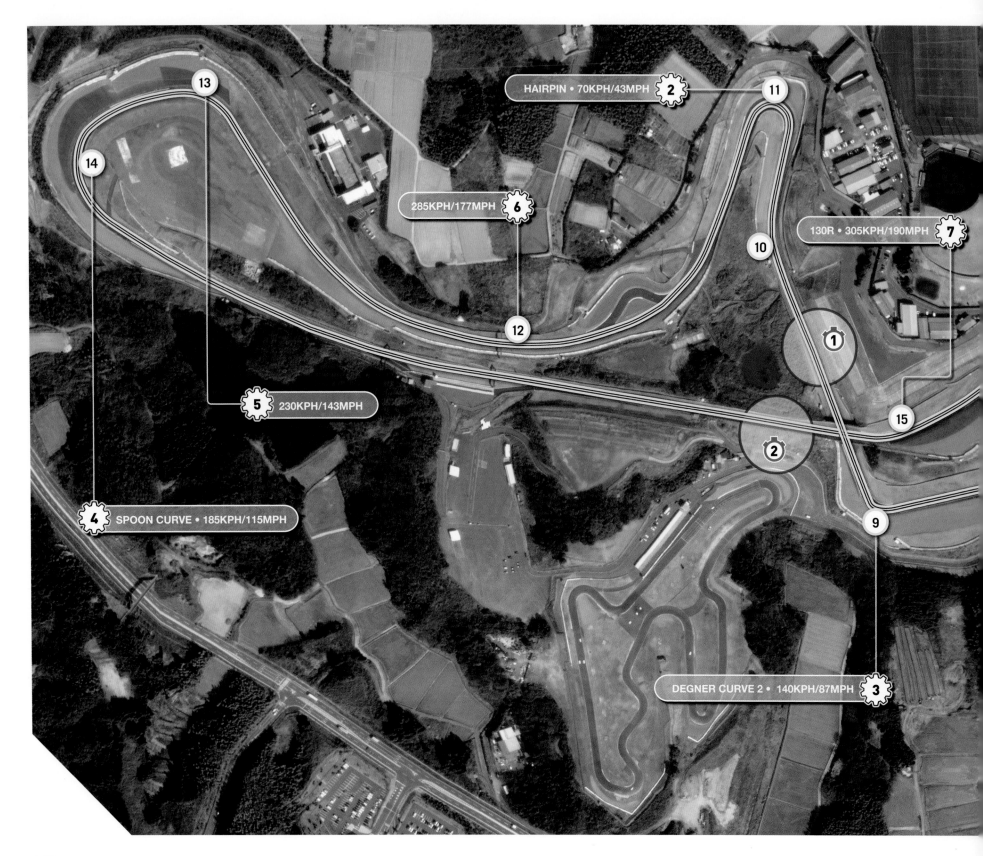

HAIRPIN • 70KPH/43MPH **2**

285KPH/177MPH **6**

130R • 305KPH/190MPH **7**

5 230KPH/143MPH

SPOON CURVE • 185KPH/115MPH **4**

DEGNER CURVE 2 • 140KPH/87MPH **3**

CASIO TRIANGLE • 95KPH/59MPH

260KPH/162MPH

FIRST CORNER • 260KPH/162MPH

APPROACH • 303KPH/188MPH

DUNLOP CURVE • 193KPH/120MPH

DEGNER CURVE 1 • 260KPH/162MPH

S-CURVES • 210KPH/130MPH

S-CURVES • 245KPH/152MPH

160KPH/99MPH

Google Earth

Image © 2014 DigitalGlobe © Google 2014

Circuit Guide

The S Curves are there to be attacked, the Degners for carrying as much momentum as possible, the Spoon Curve for picking the perfect exit and 130R simply for the brave to hang on through, meaning that every lap is a challenge.

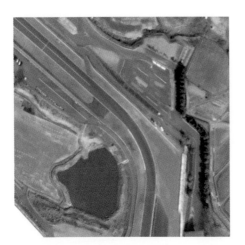

Turn 1 • First Corner
Gear: **6**
Speed: **260kph (162mph)**

Approaching this first corner down a gentle slope, drivers are travelling at 314kph (195mph) and the corner appears open, with a wide gravel trap straight ahead for a feeling of safety. A dab of the brakes is all that's required as they carry as much momentum as possible through this gently angled righthander and then attempt to ensure that they remain to the outside for the much tighter second turn, something that isn't always easy in traffic on the opening lap. This is where Senna and Prost collided in 1990.

Turn 3–6 • S-Curves
Gear: **5**
Speed: **210kph (130mph)**

130R is perhaps Suzuka's most famous corner, but this uphill sweep of esses is by far its hardest sequence. In fact, many reckon that it's F1's toughest challenge, harder to get right even than Silverstone's Becketts sweepers. The approach looks simple enough, but the first left is followed almost immediately by a right, then a left and then a second right (this tighter than any of the three before it, and steeper too), with speeds dropping with each turn. Any mistake is magnified in each subsequent turn.

Turn 7 • Dunlop Curve
Gear: **4**
Speed: **193kph (120mph)**

The drivers are on the lefthand side of the track when they exit the last of the S-Curves, but need to pull directly to the opposite side to be in position to tackle what follows as the slope flattens out behind the top end of the paddock. This is a corner that seems to keep on turning and turning some more, and drivers really have to hang on through here; not surprisingly, many are sometimes afflicted by understeer as they try to get the power down before the exit.

Turn 8 • Degner Curve 1
Gear: **6**
Speed: **260kph (162mph)**

There are two Degner Curves and they could not be more different in nature. This first one is approached at great speed in sixth gear as the track dips slightly, with drivers immediately being presented with the more enclosed approach to the second Degner. With the earth bank topped by the return leg of the track looming on the right, drivers have to drop down to third gear to be slow enough to negotiate this tighter right and then get on the power under the bridge.

Opposite: A critical moment at the chicane in 1993 as Ayrton Senna comes up to lap an obstructive Eddie Irvine's Jordan. *Above left:* Romain Grosjean pushes Sebastian Vettel out of the final uphill S-Curve towards Dunlop Curve in 2013. *Above right:* Putting his Mercedes's power down out of Turn 2 in 2013, Lewis Hamilton prepares to attack the S-Curves.

Turn 11 • **Hairpin**
Gear: **2**
Speed: **70kph (43mph)**

After powering their way under the bridge carrying the return leg of the lap, there's a righthand flick and then, suddenly, full view of one of the few obvious places to overtake. This lefthand hairpin is a tight one and drivers have to drop to second gear, taking very different lines in according to whether they're attacking a car ahead or defending from one behind. With a rising exit, drivers can get on the power early and the gradient change helps to cradle the car.

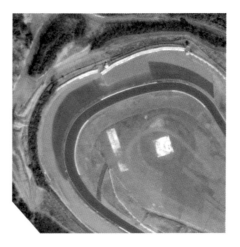

Turn 13/14 • **Spoon Curve**
Gear: **4**
Speed: **185kph (115mph)**

After the incredibly long, sweeping righthand bend that runs up the slope from shortly after the hairpin, and then a longish left that it switches into over the crest of a gentle incline, the drivers reach this, the furthest point of the track. Called Spoon because of its shape, it's a vital corner to get right because it feeds the cars onto the long back straight. With the second part dropping and tightening, a dab on the brakes is required to steady the car before accelerating out.

Turn 15 • **130R**
Gear: **7**
Speed: **305kph (190mph)**

The straight from Spoon Curve is long, with the separate club circuit down the bank to the right. Then, having reached 314kph (195mph), the drivers arrive at what was once the most feared corner. It's described as a flat-out bend, but 130R (so called for its 130-degree radius) is only flat-out for the brave, with most having a slight lift off the throttle. The earth bank on the exit was moved back a few years ago to provide more run-off for any who run wide.

Turn 16/17 • **Casio Triangle**
Gear: **2**
Speed: **95kph (59mph)**

In complete contrast to the blast through 130R, drivers have to hit the brakes and hit them hard for this right/left chicane. As they approach and consider possible passing manoeuvres, the second part of the corner is out of their sight, and it's made all the more difficult by the fact this second part of the sequence is even sharper. Then, as the track falls away on the exit, drivers have to start accelerating hard through the dropping righthander that feeds them onto the start/finish straight.

Great Drivers & Great Moments

Such is the difficulty of this magnificent circuit – the challenge of its mix of corners and the often torrential rain which can hit it – that a win here feels like two at most other circuits, and Suzuka has enjoyed some epic races across the decades, especially as it used to host the final Grand Prix when titles were often still at stake.

Opposite top: Mika Hakkinen begins his celebrations by locking up to show off to his McLaren crew after victory in 1998 gave him his first drivers' title.

Opposite bottom left: The wreckage of Ayrton Senna's McLaren after the Brazilian collided with Alain Prost's Ferrari at the first corner in 1990.

Opposite bottom right: Typhoon Hagibis had threatened to wipe out the 2019 Japanese GP, but it blew past. Qualifying and the race were held on the Sunday, with Valtteri Bottas winning for Mercedes.

Great Drivers

 Michael **Schumacher**
Suzuka wins – 6

 Sebastian **Vettel**
Suzuka wins – 4

 Lewis **Hamilton**
Suzuka wins – 4

 Ayrton **Senna**
Suzuka wins – 2

Second in 1994, Michael Schumacher went one better for Benetton in 1995. He then finished second on his first outing here for Ferrari in 1996 before taking a second Suzuka win in 1997, showing his affinity for this circuit. The home fans really respected his skills and, once Ferrari hit form in 2000, there was no stopping him: Michael rattled off further wins in 2001, 2002 and 2004. He was all set for a seventh win in 2006, his last year before quitting for the first time, when his engine failed.

Despite having contested just over a third of the grands prix that Michael Schumacher did, Vettel picked up wins in Japan for Red Bull Racing in 2009, 2010, 2012 and 2013 in a run broken only in 2011, when Jenson Button won for McLaren and he was third, 2 seconds adrift. The best of his four wins was in 2012, when he started on pole and led every lap to beat Ferrari's Felipe Massa by 20 seconds, with title rival Fernando Alonso being taken out at the first corner.

Lewis took until 2014 to win at Suzuka, mastering terribly wet conditions in an event overshadowed by an accident that left Marussia racer Jules Bianchi with terrible head injuries. Twelve months later, dry weather made life easier and Lewis passed Mercedes team-mate Nico Rosberg on the opening lap then pulled away to win. His third win at Suzuka came in 2017 when chief challenger Sebastian Vettel's Ferrari suffered with a misfire. In 2018, it was Mercedes all the way.

No overseas driver has ever been as celebrated in Japan as Ayrton Senna. Perhaps it was because he scored so many wins around the world for cars powered by Honda engines. Perhaps it was because they saw something of the warrior in him. However, he also earned their appreciation by winning here in 1988 to beat his McLaren team-mate Alain Prost to the title. He would win again at Suzuka in 1993 with a masterful drive in which he saw off Prost's more competitive Williams.

Great Moments

1990 Alain **Prost** meets Ayrton **Senna**

1994 Damon **Hill's** wet weather masterclass

1998 Mika **Hakkinen** clinches his first world title

2019 Valtteri **Bottas** wins to give Mercedes sixth title

They had clashed at Suzuka in 1989, when racing for McLaren and fighting over who'd become champion, and Alain Prost and Ayrton Senna would fight again in 1990 when in a similar position, but with Prost now with Ferrari. Angered by the FIA's refusal to move pole position away from the dirty side of the track, Senna dropped behind Prost on the run to Turn 1 and ducked up the inside, and they collided. He'd later admit that this was in revenge for being hit by the Frenchman in 1989.

Michael Schumacher held the upper hand in the 1994 title battle when they arrived in Japan, but Damon Hill for Williams wasn't going to give up without a fight. In atrociously wet conditions, he produced a drive that's considered by many as his finest moment. The race was stopped early on as cars aquaplaned off the track, then restarted and Benetton's Schumacher pressured Hill, but he never put a wheel wrong and closed the gap between them to just one point before the Adelaide finale.

Victory in the penultimate round at the Nürburgring had given McLaren's Mika Hakkinen a four-point lead over Ferrari's Michael Schumacher, so the stage was set for a shoot-out at Suzuka. The German wasted his pole position by stalling at the beginning of the parade lap, forcing him to start from the back. He made strong progress as Hakkinen led, climbing to third, but then hit debris and had a blow-out, forcing him to retire. Thus Hakkinen was able to cruise and collect his first F1 title.

Typhoon Hagibis looked set to hit the 2019 Japanese GP, but it blew past allowing the race to go ahead, albeit with qualifying on raceday. Ferrari dominated this, with Sebastian Vettel taking pole ahead of team-mate Charles Leclerc. Vettel appeared to anticipate the race start, backed off and was passed as the lights changed to green. Leclerc overtook him, but Mercedes's Valtteri Bottas passed both on lap 1 and controlled the race to revitalise his season.

Sepang

Circuit architect Hermann Tilke is accused by some race fans of designing bland circuits, but this early work remains one of his best because it offers drivers not just a sinuous lap to get their teeth into, but plenty of space for them to line up and execute overtaking manoeuvres.

❝ You feel very safe on this circuit, with wide run-off areas and the possibility of overtaking. The only difficult point is to handle the temperature and humidity. **❞**

Jean Alesi

Some F1 fans might presume that Malaysia's involvement with motor racing dates back only to 1999, when it hosted a grand prix for the first time, but they are out by several decades if they believe this. Led by expatriates working there, the first motorsport in Malaysia was in the 1960s, using temporary street circuits at Penang and Johore Batu, with many drivers heading down to neighbouring Singapore for races there.

Malaysia's first permanent circuit was built at Johore Batu in 1968. Also known as Selangor after a palace that overlooked it, it gave Malaysian drivers a place to race until 1977, when it was closed after an accident in which six children were hit by a car and killed. Modified and reopened as Shah Alam, it went on to host a round of the World Endurance Championship in 1985. However, conditions were too hot and humid for the comfort of the drivers and the track was considered way too bumpy, which is typical for tracks in the tropics because of the extreme weather to which they are exposed. Worse still, the World Championship event attracted only 3,000 spectators.

It was time for a rethink and, after several false starts as the country's motorsport movers hatched plans for Asia to host its first grand prix beyond Japan, a brand new circuit was built in a tree-fringed depression alongside Kuala Lumpur's international

airport in 1999. This was Sepang, and the ample budget used for the programme was clearly money well spent because circuit designer Hermann Tilke produced a design that set new standards. Even a cursory glance at the plans that he had concocted with former F1 racer Marc Surer revealed that this was a circuit designed from scratch to really allow drivers to race. For example, there were two 900m (half-mile) straights into hairpins. Also, to ensure that chasing drivers had a chance to pull off a passing move, the track at the entry to these corners was wide; the value of this has been proved ever since, as it allows drivers to defend and those behind them to attack.

The lap is augmented by some wonderful, sweeping sections where the cars are able to be shown at their most dynamic, with the runs through Turns 5 and 6, then through Turns 12 and 13 of particular merit. Many a circuit can be a challenge to a driver, but this one was designed so that it could be challenging as well as a place where they could actually race each other. No small part in this was the fact that the circuit's management team showed plans to Michael Schumacher and took heed of the suggestions that he made. History relates that it was wise to stick with the design for the opening hairpin and the way it feeds into Turn 2, as Michael had wanted the hairpin

tightened, but the reason that it works and provides such great racing is that they retained the width that Tilke had recommended.

One of Sepang's key features is the double-sided grandstand. This gives 50,000 spectators views of the pits and start/finish straight, much of the track from Turn 1 to Turn 6 and also, for those sitting on the reverse face, of the return straight to the final corner as well most of the run of the circuit from Turn 8 to Turn 14. Topped by a huge integral canopy, this provides essential shelter for the fans, not only from the intense sun but the tropical rain that comes quick and heavy when it hits. The drivers simply have to suffer in the heat and humidity.

Rain has played a role in many of the grands prix held at Sepang since its debut in 1999, notably in 2009, but what stands out is how Tilke got it right from the outset: the facilities still look great and the circuit hasn't needed a single amendment since it opened. It's that rare thing, a drivers' circuit where they can race as well, which is fantastic because the Malaysian GP usually follows the opening round in Melbourne and so offers a first chance to see the cars flat-out. ∎

Opposite: Sebastian Vettel powers his Red Bull RB9 down the main straight past Sepang's trademark canopied grandstands in 2013.

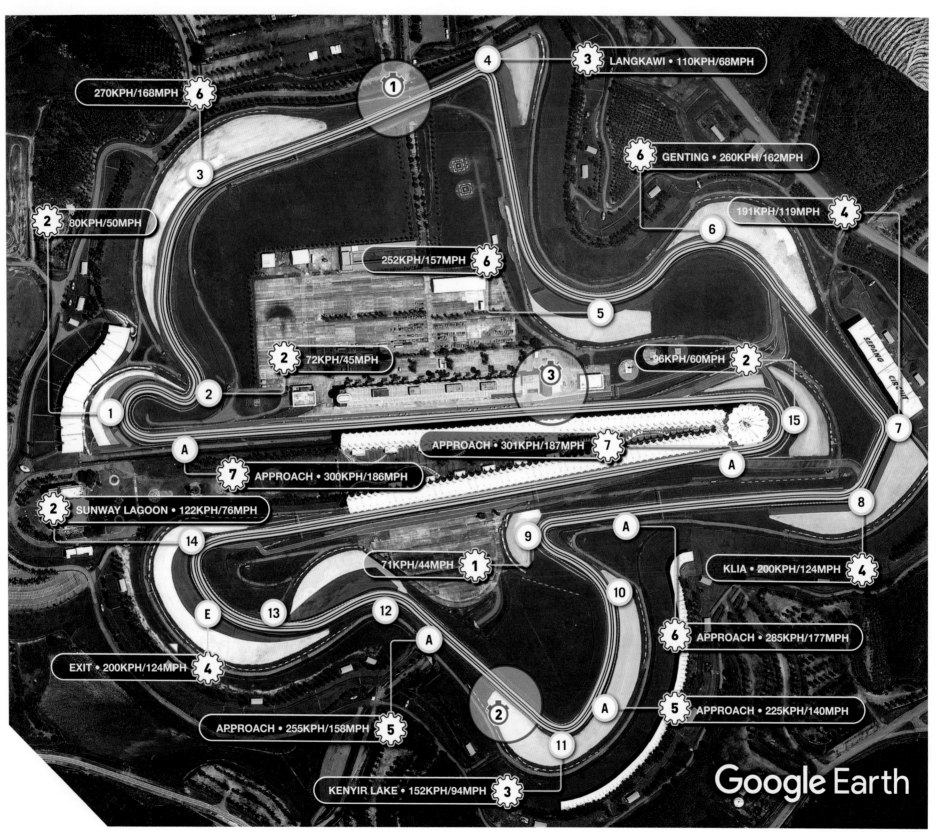

LANGKAWI • 110KPH/68MPH

270KPH/168MPH

GENTING • 260KPH/162MPH

191KPH/119MPH

80KPH/50MPH

252KPH/157MPH

72KPH/45MPH

96KPH/60MPH

APPROACH • 301KPH/187MPH

APPROACH • 300KPH/186MPH

SUNWAY LAGOON • 122KPH/76MPH

71KPH/44MPH

KLIA • 200KPH/124MPH

APPROACH • 285KPH/177MPH

EXIT • 200KPH/124MPH

APPROACH • 225KPH/140MPH

APPROACH • 255KPH/158MPH

KENYIR LAKE • 152KPH/94MPH

Google Earth

Image © 2014 DigitalGlobe © Google 2014

Fernando Alonso's Ferrari F138 leads
Mark Webber's Red Bull, Lewis Hamilton's
Mercedes and the rest of the field into
Turn 9, on the opening lap of the 2013
Malaysian grand prix.

Circuit Guide

From the wide straight leading down to the first hairpin via the sweepers midway around the lap to the high-speed sweepers at the back of the circuit, this is a track that has a fabulous flow and, better still, allows for racing with plenty of overtaking.

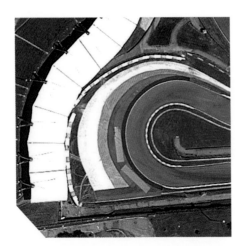

Turn 1 •

Gear: **2**
Speed: **80kph (50mph)**

The track is wide here and feels wider still because the spectator banking is some way back on the drivers' left; the feeling of space is augmented by the grandstand beyond the corner being way back behind an enormous gravel trap. The drivers have to brake heavily down from near on 306kph (190mph) to around 80kph (50mph) in second. As this righthander turns through around 200 degrees before feeding almost straight into Turn 2, drivers choose their line according to traffic around them.

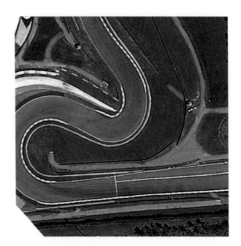

Turn 2 •

Gear: **2**
Speed: **72kph (45mph)**

If a driver gets through Turn 1 without contact on the opening lap, they then have to get on the power quickly before braking hard for even tighter Turn 2. Ideally, they'd attack this from the righthand side of the track, in order to be quicker on the dipping exit, but this isn't always possible if a driver has run wide coming out of Turn 1. On occasion, a driver can make a bold passing move here, like the one produced by McLaren's David Coulthard on Michael Schumacher's Ferrari in 1999.

Turn 4 • **Langkawi**

Gear: **3**
Speed: **110kph (68mph)**

After accelerating all the way from Turn 2 through the arc of Turn 3 and up the gentle slope from there, hitting 290kph (180mph), the drivers have to brake hard because the slope suddenly flicks up before the corner, meaning that they arrive over a crest. Taken in third gear, drivers must try to prevent their cars from understeering as soon as possible on the exit of the corner because the track now opens up into a sweeping run all the way to Turn 9.

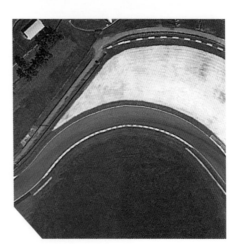

Turn 6 • **Genting**

Gear: **6**
Speed: **260kph (162mph)**

The Sepang circuit is really finding its flow by this point, a third of the way around the lap, and this righthand sweep, taken in sixth, is the counterbalance to the lefthand sweep that precedes it. A driver will know for sure whether his car is handling well if it can run through here with a good balance. At this point, the driver will be trying to maintain as much speed as possible for the short straight that follows, and any loss of momentum will cost him.

Opposite: Sebastian Vettel leads the pack into the first corner in 2013, with the 21 other runners jostling for position on a damp track. ***Above left:*** There's no escaping the country you're in – as shown by Lewis Hamilton flashing past a Malaysian flag in his Mercedes in 2013. ***Above right:*** Mark Webber arrives at the end of the back straight in his Red Bull in 2013, braking hard to slow for Turn 15.

Turn 9 •

Gear: **1**
Speed: **71kph (44mph)**

The sweeping back section of the circuit is brought to a near halt at this lefthand hairpin, drivers dropping from seventh gear to first. It's possible to make a passing move into here if the driver ahead has clipped a kerb or run wide through the close-together combination of Turns 7 and 8. Yet, there can be contact too, because the entry is wide enough but the hairpin's rising exit is incredibly cramped and traction is not always easy to come by, especially if the circuit is wet.

Turn 12 •

Gear: **6**
Speed: **257kph (160mph)**

After climbing to Turn 11 and accelerating out of the third gear righthander, the track now drops away again gently, with drivers getting a great view of the back of the lofty covered grandstand that runs along most of the start/finish straight. They need to ignore that, though. The sixth-gear lefthander ahead of them needs to be got exactly right to carry vital momentum through it – it takes an esse-like course because the track almost immediately starts turning to the right again.

Turn 14 • **Sunway Lagoon**

Gear: **2**
Speed: **122kph (76mph)**

Heavy braking is required as the drivers arrive at the penultimate corner of the lap at the end of a long and tightening arc from Turn 12 to Turn 13. Changing down to second gear, drivers have to ensure that they don't carry too much speed when they arrive at the apex of this tight right because it's more important to get turned in cleanly and get back onto the throttle so that they can accelerate out down the circuit's second longest straight.

Turn 15 •

Gear: **2**
Speed: **96kph (60mph)**

The cars hit 306kph (190mph) in top gear in the shadow of the giant grandstand and drivers file towards the righthand side of the track as they line up their approach to the final corner. This is a lefthand hairpin that works best with a "wide in, wide out" line, but many an overtaking driver is presented only with the option of trying their passing move down the inside and then trying to sort out their exit, with many moves seeing the passed driver emerge in front again.

Great Drivers & Great Moments

With plenty of space for slipstreaming and overtaking, there have been some classic races at Sepang since its debut in 1999. The often extreme weather here has also played its role in creating the excitement when tropical storms have struck during the grand prix.

Great Drivers

 Michael **Schumacher**
Sepang wins – 3

 Fernando **Alonso**
Sepang wins – 3

 Sebastian **Vettel**
Sepang wins – 3

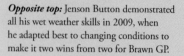 Kimi **Raikkonen**
Sepang wins – 2

This seven-time World Champion could have claimed the honour of winning Sepang's inaugural grand prix at the end of 1999, but he handed that instead to his title-chasing Ferrari team-mate Eddie Irvine. As if to prove the point, he triumphed in 2000, when he was chased all the way by McLaren's David Coulthard, then won again in 2001 in a monsoon ahead of team-mate Rubens Barrichello. In 2004, he added a third when he was chased all of the way by Williams racer Juan Pablo Montoya.

Fernando has not only won the Malaysian GP three times but has the distinction of having done so for three teams. His first, with Renault, came in 2005 in a race that he led all the way to win by 25 seconds from Jarno Trulli. Then, having just moved to McLaren, he won again in 2007 after getting ahead of Ferrari's poleman Felipe Massa at the first corner. The Spaniard's most recent victory came in 2012 with Ferrari when he hit the front in the wet and resisted an attack from Sergio Perez.

Having scored his maiden F1 win in 2008, then added four more after moving to Red Bull Racing in 2009, Sebastian got his 2010 campaign off to a good start by winning here in the third of that year's 19 rounds. This gave him the momentum that resulted in his first drivers' title. He won at Sepang again in 2011 as he set off towards title number two, lost out with a puncture in 2012 and then won once more in 2013 as Red Bull again controlled proceedings.

Kimi's second ever grand prix was here in 2001, and it ended in disappointment when his Sauber failed on the opening lap. However, he gave his second season with McLaren some momentum when he won here in 2003. This was his first F1 win and, after failing to land the drivers' title in 2005, he joined Ferrari in 2007 and won here for a second time in 2008 in a race that gave the Italian team a boost after a disastrous showing in Australia.

Great Moments

1999 Ferrari assists
Eddie **Irvine**

2001 **Ferrari** falls off then picks the right tyres to win

2009 Jenson **Button** splashes to victory

2012 Sergio **Perez** hounds Fernando **Alonso**

F1's first visit to Sepang was made dramatic by it being the penultimate race of the 1999 season, with McLaren's Mika Hakkinen holding only a two-point lead over Ferrari's Eddie Irvine. After missing six races with a broken leg, Michael Schumacher returned to action to support Irvine and led from pole, but let the Ulsterman go past, then delayed Hakkinen to help Irvine win. The Ferrari one-two was later rescinded because the cars' bargeboards exceeded the limits, but both drivers were reinstated on appeal.

This was the first time the Malaysian GP was held near the start of the season and it slotted in behind Australia and produced the same winner. However, it came the hard way after Michael Schumacher and team-mate Rubens Barrichello spun off on oil at Turn 5 on lap 3. Rain had just started and the safety car was deployed. Opting for intermediates when others went for rain tyres was a masterstroke as they roared up the order and by lap 16 Michael was back in front, where he stayed.

In the opening races of 2009, it seemed that Jenson Button really could walk on water because he won five of the first seven rounds. At Sepang, he really did walk on water: although Nico Rosberg led early on, the way that Button adapted to the rain in his Brawn put him in front and he was still in front when it got too wet to continue. The cars sat on the grid, but there was to be no restart because it got too late and light was fading, thus handing victory to Button.

Every now and again a performance from a young driver stands out. One such drive happened in 2012, when second season F1 racer Sergio Perez came close to winning for Sauber. Lewis Hamilton had led away for McLaren in the wet, but the race had to be stopped until conditions dried out. He led away again, but he overshot his pit and Ferrari's Fernando Alonso took over. Late in the race, Perez caught Alonso, shaped up to pass him, but slid wide and so missed his chance.

Marina Bay

This circuit was like a breath of fresh air when it made its bow in the World Championship in 2008. Not only was it the sort of city-centre circuit that F1 had sought for years, but it had the added attraction of its race being held after nightfall, making F1 look more spectacular than ever.

> **"** It's a very physical circuit and so you need to put a lot of work into the car to get a good lap. I'd say it requires double the effort of Monaco. **"**
>
> *Lewis Hamilton*

With the World Championship swinging its attention towards having an ever-increasing number of grands prix beyond Europe, the plans for what would become the Singapore GP surfaced in 2006, presenting drivers not only with the concept of racing on a street circuit other than Monaco but also of racing after nightfall. These dreams were realized when the Marina Bay Street Circuit was opened in time for the 15th round of the 2008 World Championship.

This was far from the country's first taste of motor racing, though, as there had been racing in Singapore since 1961, when the Orient Year GP for sportscars was run on a temporary circuit. This was laid out on the Upper Thomson Road with a slower, twistier return leg completing the 4.8km (3-mile) lap, and the race was won by Ian Barnwell in an Aston Martin DB3S. The event would become the Malaysian GP, then Singapore gained independence in 1965 and it hosted its own grand prix from 1966. Single-seaters gradually took over and the race was run until 1973, when Vern Schuppan won in an F2 March. Plans to build a permanent circuit in the mid-1980s came to nothing, so it was to be another 35 years until powerful single-seaters raced in Singapore again.

With government backing, a route for a temporary circuit was plotted with the city's most iconic buildings as a backdrop. This was important because the money was being spent not just to appease sports

fans but to market Singapore globally. When F1 fans got their first look at the Marina Bay circuit, the first thing that made it stand out wasn't, in fact, its city centre location. Instead, it was the fact that almost all of the action was run after dark as F1 experienced its first night race. The images were amazing and Singapore looked stunning in the backdrop, a city lit up to emphasize that this was no race tucked away in a rural backwater. This was racing where perhaps a whole new audience could enjoy its thrilling spectacle and sound. Any concerns felt by the drivers beforehand, that they might have trouble in the dark, were dispelled: there were 1,500 lights shining onto the track and the floodlighting for the braking zones and corners in particular was more than good enough for them to pick out their markers.

The setting also afforded some incredible viewing points, with 1982 World Champion Keke Rosberg doing some TV commentary work from high above the circuit on the Singapore Flyer, a giant Ferris wheel.

What marks the circuit out from other street circuits, apart from being used after nightfall, is the fact that it has plenty of long straights rather than the usual twists and turns. Indeed, Kimi Raikkonen set the race's fastest lap for Ferrari at over 172kph (107mph), making it 16kph (10mph) faster on aggregate than Monaco.

As well as its combination of long straights, tight corners, crossing a bridge and handful of fast

bends in its 23-corner lap, the circuit also offered the novel experience of the track running right underneath a giant grandstand between Turns 19 and 20 before feeding back onto Raffles Avenue.

Drivers liked the concept of the race and its location. Some even found racing after dark to be pretty special, but they were unanimous after their first visit that something had to be done about the bumps, especially on the straight down Raffles Boulevard between Turns 5 and 7. What the teams did like, though, was that although the circuit is temporary, the pit buildings are impressive and permanent, ensuring a high standard. The people who loved the Marina Bay circuit the most, though, were the TV camera crews and the photographers, who could combine cars racing, night skies and buildings illuminating the backdrop.

In 2011, it was mooted that the grand prix might relocate to a circuit away from the middle of the city, but this wasn't realized. Other plans discussed included changing Turn 10, with Sebastian Vettel one of a handful of drivers requesting that this tight lefthander be modified to improve its safety because they reckoned its kerbs were too high and the surface too bumpy at this narrow point. ∎

Opposite: F1 cars racing after dark has been a revelation since Singapore joined the world championship. This is Romain Grosjean leading Mark Webber in 2013.

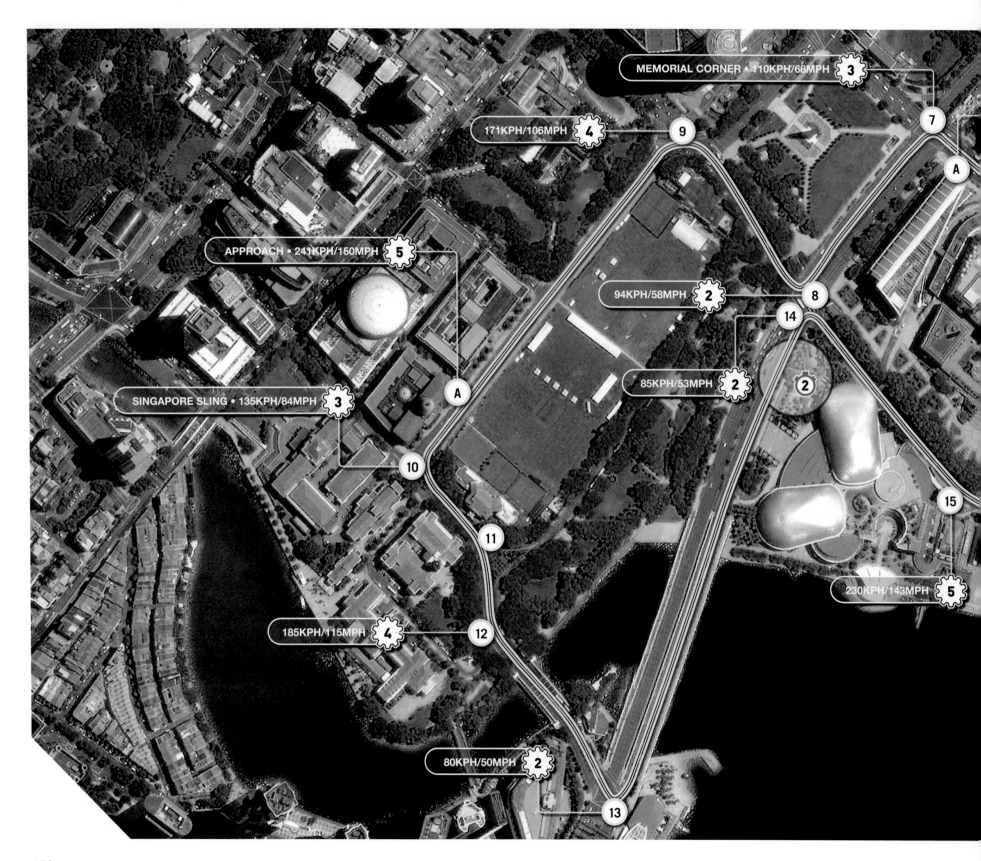

MEMORIAL CORNER • 110KPH/68MPH **3**

171KPH/106MPH **4** — **9**

7

A

APPROACH • 241KPH/150MPH **5**

94KPH/58MPH **2** — **8**

14

85KPH/53MPH **2** — **2**

SINGAPORE SLING • 135KPH/84MPH **3**

A

10

15

11

230KPH/143MPH **5**

185KPH/115MPH **4** — **12**

80KPH/50MPH **2**

13

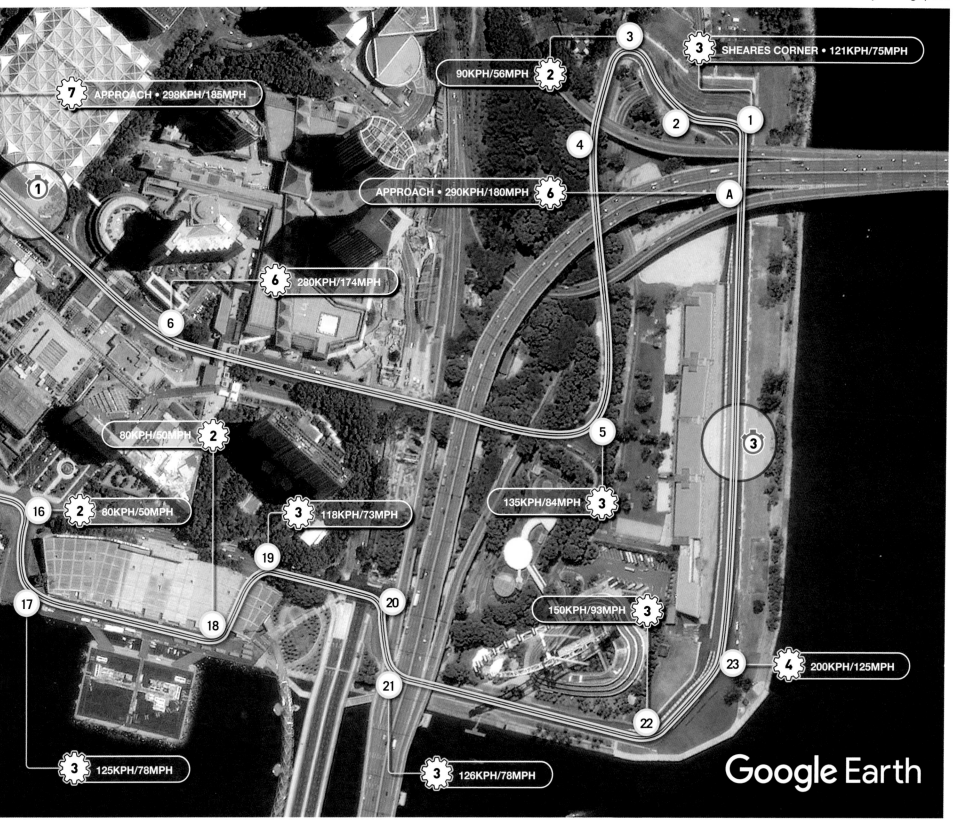

SHEARES CORNER • 121KPH/75MPH

90KPH/56MPH

APPROACH • 298KPH/185MPH

APPROACH • 290KPH/180MPH

280KPH/174MPH

80KPH/50MPH

80KPH/50MPH

118KPH/73MPH

135KPH/84MPH

150KPH/93MPH

200KPH/125MPH

125KPH/78MPH

126KPH/78MPH

Google Earth

Circuit Guide

With concrete barriers lining the route and 90-degree corners more prevalent than open sweepers, this is a circuit on which drivers can't afford to relax for an instant. Throw in the difficulties of racing under floodlights, and it's definitely a test.

Turn 1 • Sheares Corner
Gear: **3**
Speed: **121kph (75mph)**

Purpose-built rather than converted from a public road, this part of the track is smoother than the rest, but the first corner is made difficult by being the first part of a three-corner sequence: it feeds directly into Turn 2 and that, in turn, into Turn 3. Passing the pits at 290kph (180mph), drivers have to brake hard under a road bridge for this lefthander and try to stay off the kerbs. On the opening lap, it's extra busy, and drivers are aware that avoiding contact is imperative.

Turn 3 •
Gear: **2**
Speed: **90kph (56mph)**

This is the lap's first slow corner and the drivers have to drop to second gear to slow sufficiently for this tight left onto Republic Boulevard. Getting into position to take the apex isn't always easy after their jousting through the first two corners. If they look up, they have the strange sight of running under the curving flyovers that carry Singapore's main roads as they open up for the blast down to Turn 5 and then all the way on down to Turn 7.

Turn 7 • Memorial Corner
Gear: **3**
Speed: **110kph (68mph)**

The kinked straight before this 90-degree lefthander offers a rare chance for the engines to breathe, with drivers topping 298kph (185mph) when they flash past the city views that are revealed as the track runs past Singapore's top hotels and prime shopping malls, before having to drop to third gear in order to turn off Raffles Boulevard and onto the Nicoll Highway. This is where Lewis Hamilton clashed with Mark Webber as he tried to pass the Australian's Red Bull after a safety car restart in 2010.

Turn 10 • Singapore Sling
Gear: **3**
Speed: **135kph (84mph)**

The drivers race down St Andrew's Road with City Hall and Singapore's Supreme Court on their right and the Padang playing fields, home to the Singapore Cricket Club, on their left. Then it's time to get hard on the brakes and drop from fifth gear to third as the circuit feels like a typical street circuit again with a left/right/left chicance. Kimi Raikkonen got it wrong here in a late charge in 2008, when he hit the kerbs and fired his Ferrari into the wall.

Opposite: The start lights are out and Sebastian Vettel and Nico Rosberg lead the charge down towards the first corner in 2013. *Above left:* Felipe Massa leads Jenson Button into tight Turn 3 in 2013. *Above right:* There are numerous high vantage points for photographers to capture out-of-the-ordinary shots of F1 cars in action.

Turn 13 ●

Gear: **2**
Speed: **80kph (50mph)**

After taking a sinuous route past the old colonial parliament buildings on Connaught Drive and across the century-old, steel-framed Anderson Bridge, drivers have to jink right and then brake heavily for this tight lefthander in front of the Fullerton Hotel. As with so many tight corners, exit speed is everything, especially with the long blast that follows, along which drivers accelerate hard over the much longer and wider Esplanade Bridge, rising over its crest and then dropping towards Turn 14.

Turn 14 ●

Gear: **2**
Speed: **85kph (53mph)**

Any aerial view of the circuit shows just how close this righthander, where the drivers turn off Esplanade Drive onto Raffles Avenue by the Esplanade Theatre, comes to Turn 8, where the cars also turn sharp right before starting their circumnavigation of Padang park. They appear to be just metres apart, albeit separated by the barriers that run up the middle of this dual-carriageway. Like at the lap's other tight corners, good traction out of this corner is what a driver will be looking for.

Turn 17 ●

Gear: **3**
Speed: **125kph (78mph)**

For the fastest line through the run of six medium-speed corners that start at Turn 16, drivers need to use the kerbs to take the most direct route through this serpentine sequence. Infamously, this lefthander is where Nelson Piquet Jr gyrated his Renault into the wall in 2008 and brought out the safety car that immediately helped team-mate Fernando Alonso, who had just pitted, to move to the front and win. (It was discovered the following year that Piquet Jr had been instructed to crash.)

Turn 22 ●

Gear: **3**
Speed: **150kph (93mph)**

Having weaved their way under the grandstand between Turns 19 and 20, the corners open out a little. This penultimate corner is one through which drivers will have no time to admire the Singapore Flyer Ferris wheel to their left. Instead they will be focusing on taking the smoothest line through this left kink and the fourth gear kink that follows straight after it as they accelerate hard towards the start/finish straight and hopefully hit 290kph (180mph) before having to brake for Turn 1.

Great Drivers & Great Moments

Street circuits can lead to processional races, but Singapore's Marina Bay circuit has two key ingredients to keep the action interesting. First is the generous width of the track, which helps to make overtaking moves worthy of consideration. The other element that adds to the spectacle is the race being held in the dark.

Great Drivers

Sebastian **Vettel**
Marina Bay wins – 5

Sebastian Vettel and Red Bull Racing were masterful at Marina Bay, winning every year from 2011 to 2013. He beat Jenson Button in 2011, then benefitted when Lewis Hamilton's gearbox failed in 2012. In 2013, he won by 32s from Ferrari's Fernando Alonso. Two years later, now with Ferrari, he got a helping hand when the safety car was deployed after a spectator got onto the track. Win number five came in 2019 when his tyre strategy moved him past team-mate Charles Leclerc.

Lewis **Hamilton**
Marina Bay wins – 4

Brawn caught its rivals on the hop in 2009, but when Lewis dominated from pole for McLaren it suggested that the balance might be turning. Hamilton, now with Mercedes, came good again in 2014. moving ahead of team-mate Nico Rosberg to lead the World Championship standings after the German retired. A third win came in 2017 when Sebastian Vettel triggered an accident at the start and Hamilton won again in 2018, this time easily.

Fernando **Alonso**
Marina Bay wins – 2

The Spaniard's two wins on the streets of Singapore couldn't be more different. The one in 2008 was later discovered to have been the result of chicanery from his Renault team (see below). His 2010 victory, for Ferrari, was a masterclass though, as he edged out Sebastian Vettel's Red Bull for pole and stayed in front throughout the race's 61 laps to win ahead of Red Bull's Sebastian Vettel. This win kept alive his hopes for a third drivers' title, but it wasn't to be.

Nico **Rosberg**
Marina Bay wins – 1

The 2016 Singapore GP was pivotal for Rosberg, as he threw down the gauntlet to Mercedes team-mate Lewis Hamilton and proved he was serious about chasing the title. He took pole position with a remarkable lap that was more than 0.5s faster than Red Bull's Daniel Ricciardo, with Hamilton third. In the race, Rosberg resisted Ricciardo's pressure and so earned the 25 points that moved him to the top of the championship table ahead of Hamilton.

Great Moments

2008 **Piquet Jr** helps **Alonso** by spinning off

The inaugural Singapore GP was a hit, until it was revealed the result was fixed. Fernando Alonso started 15th and pitted just before Renault team-mate Nelson Piquet Jr spun into the wall, apparently on team orders. Alonso had reached fifth place when the safety car withdrew. Polesetter Felipe Massa pulled away from his pitstop with a fuel hose still attached and others were given stop-go penalties, which allowed Alonso to win, from Nico Rosberg and Lewis Hamilton.

2015 Spectator on the circuit scares drivers

Any number of permutations can affect a driver's race, from rain to a puncture but a spectator deciding to go for a stroll on the circuit during the race cannot be predicted. This occurred in 2015 and, naturally, the safety car was scrambled while the spectator was removed to safety. The driver most affected was Red Bull's Daniel Ricciardo, who had been catching race leader Sebastian Vettel before falling just a fraction short in his pursuit of the winning Ferrari.

2017 **Vettel** eliminates two by first corner

Sebastian Vettel will want to forget his desperate opening-lap move which took out three frontrunners. He made a poor start from pole, while Ferrari team-mate Kimi Raikkonen made a scorching one from fourth and passed him. Fearing that Max Verstappen also would overtake, he moved across on the Red Bull, which clipped Raikkonen, causing his car to snap right and hit Vettel, taking out all three. It left the way clear for Lewis Hamilton to win.

2018 **Perez** fumble costs Force India points

Lewis Hamilton won without problem for Mercedes, but a driver using Mercedes power angered his team by taking out his team-mate on the opening lap, probably costing them points. Force India's Sergio Perez appeared to resume the hostilities of 2017 when he clashed with Esteban Ocon and put him into the wall at Turn 3. The Mexican told his team he hadn't even noticed Ocon as he had been busy battling with Haas's Romain Grosjean.

The view down from the Circuit of the America's observation tower across Turn 17 towards the run of sweeps from Turn 3 to Turn 6.

Chapter 3
The Americas

Buenos Aires

Brazilian drivers hold far more titles than Argentinian ones, but it was Argentina that led the way for South America in the 1950s, with their attack spearheaded by Juan Manuel Fangio and Buenos Aires – then the continent's leading circuit. Its third stint of hosting a grand prix ended after Michael Schumacher won in 1998.

> ❝ The track is a little bit Mickey Mouse in terms of layout, but it's good fun to drive on, as the corners are slow, so you can slip and slide. ❞
>
> *Eddie Irvine*

Argentina's first love in motor racing was the Temporada races that roared across the country from town to town, but there were fatalities, including Juan Manuel Fangio's co-driver Daniel Urrutia as well as spectators, and this led to a push for the building of permanent circuits. The most important of these was built in 1951 in Buenos Aires' Parc Almirante Brown on a flat piece of swampy land with the city skyline as a backdrop. Finance came from the government, with a clue to its backer President Perón's being given by its name, the Autodromo 17 Octobre, commemorating the date he came to power.

It opened for racing in 1952, the scale of Perón's ambition shown by the fact that it had 12 different circuit layouts, putting it very much ahead of its time. The reason that Perón was happy to spend so much money was that he saw motor racing as a way of building Argentina's reputation abroad. And, in Fangio, he had the perfect ambassador. The sport's organizers took heed and Argentina was granted the opening grand prix of 1953, making it the first country outside Europe to host a round of the World Championship. This inaugural race was spoiled, however, by the death of 15 spectators when Giuseppe Farina crashed his Ferrari into the crowd in avoidance of a spectator who had run across the track. Despite this horrendous start, the European visitors loved the circuit and, especially, the cosmopolitan city. The racing wasn't bad, either, and

the race's January date offered them welcome respite from the European winter. For the tens of thousands of Argentinian fans, matters improved in 1954, when Fangio scored the first of four consecutive wins here, and history was made in 1958, when Stirling Moss scored the first World Championship win for a rear-engined car on a day when Fangio and the others had to pit for fresh tyres while his nimble Cooper made its tyres last the full distance.

When Perón was deposed in 1955, the circuit was renamed as the Autodromo Oscar Alfredo Galvez after the country's leading touring car driver.

The lap started with a long righthander that fed the cars onto a back straight down to high-speed Ascari corner. Next up was a hairpin, an esse and then a looping infield section before a straight down to a hairpin, with the lap ending with a left kink. Known as Circuit No 2, this was used when F1 first visited. When sportscar races were held, a longer layout was used: Circuit No 15. This veered left midway through the first corner and turned it into a right/left sweep before opening out onto a straight over a lake down to a long, double-apex righthander that led onto the back straight. This was fast, open territory where drivers could hit top speed before reaching a tighter, twistier section starting just before Ascari, which included some mid-speed corners and two hairpins to take it out to 5.9km (3.7 miles) in length.

Despite this strong start, Argentina was dropped from the World Championship after 1960 because the organizers were short of money, and F1 didn't go back until 1972, after a trial return for a non-championship race in 1971. This time, it used Circuit No 9, which was like Circuit No 2, except that the run down to the final hairpin close to the landmark arch at the circuit's entrance was truncated. Then, from 1974, the F1 drivers were allowed to cut loose on Circuit No 15, with Jody Scheckter's victory on the Wolf team's first outing in 1977 standing out and Ligier's Jacques Laffite beating pre-season favouites Lotus two years later, sending a similar shockwave through F1. However, as a result of political unrest because of the Falklands War in 1982, the Argentinian GP was dropped again.

The circuit's final spell hosting a grand prix began in 1995 and lasted for four years, with drivers using yet another track derivation, Circuit No 6. This was effectively Circuit No 9 with 0.8km (half a mile) of infield loop added to it. This was done by the track cutting sharp right through the first corner and then following this with a pair of lefts and another righthander before hitting the back straight. ∎

Opposite: Damon Hill powers his Williams away from pole position in 1996, followed by Michael Schumacher, Jean Alesi and Gerhard Berger.

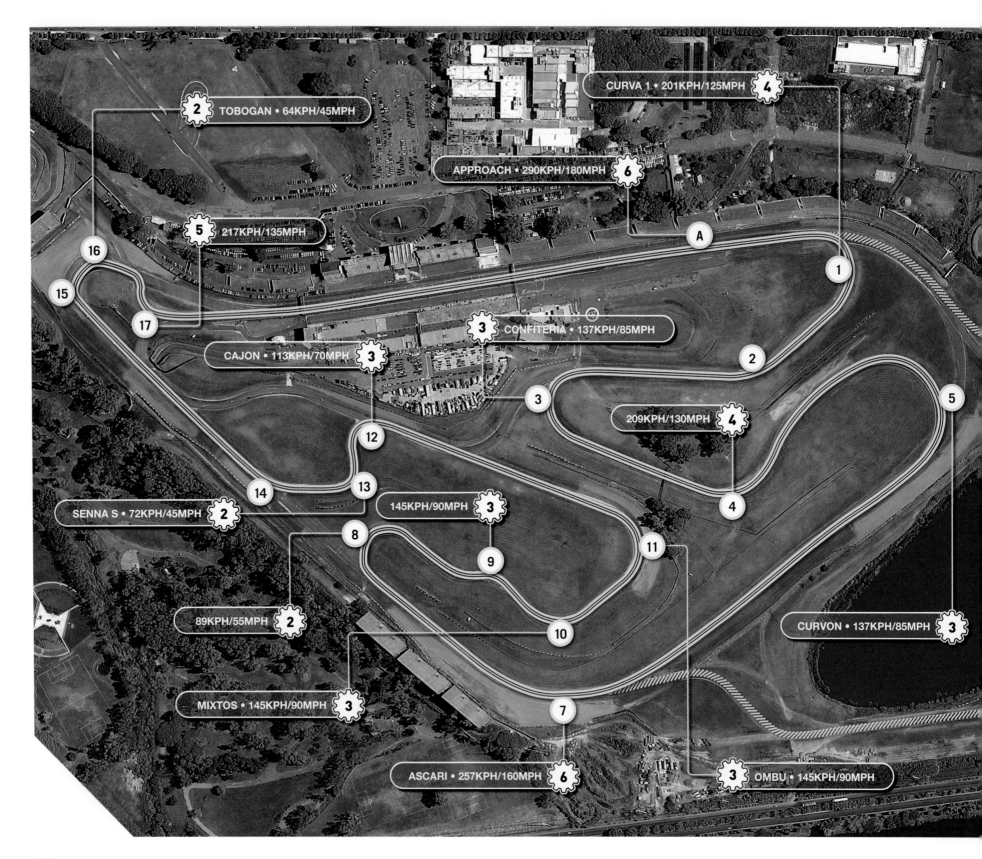

CURVA 1 • 201KPH/125MPH **4**

TOBOGAN • 64KPH/45MPH **2**

APPROACH • 290KPH/180MPH **6**

217KPH/135MPH **5**

A

1

CONFITERIA • 137KPH/85MPH **3**

CAJON • 113KPH/70MPH **3**

2

3

209KPH/130MPH **4**

5

12

4

14

13

SENNA S • 72KPH/45MPH **2**

145KPH/90MPH **3**

8

9

11

89KPH/55MPH **2**

10

CURVON • 137KPH/85MPH **3**

MIXTOS • 145KPH/90MPH **3**

7

ASCARI • 257KPH/160MPH **6**

OMBU • 145KPH/90MPH **3**

16

15

17

Image © 2014 DigitalGlobe © Google 2014

Circuit Guide

Once famed for its long straights, the circuit layout that F1 used for its last four visits in the 1990s was very different, being made up almost entirely of medium-speed corners and hairpins that did little to excite drivers or fans.

Turn 1 • Curva 1
Gear: **4**
Speed: **201kph (125mph)**

Approaching the first corner in fifth gear, drivers have to brake in front of the array of grandstands to their left, then use the broad sweep of the track to turn in to the righthander at 201kph (125mph) in fourth gear. It's a popular spot for overtaking, so drivers have to defend the inside line if under attack, but a wider entry line is preferable, with drivers then usually holding a middle line around the corner so they can cope when it tightens halfway around its arc.

Turn 3 • Confitería
Gear: **3**
Speed: **137kph (85mph)**

After the drivers have accelerated through the kink at Turn 2, and on down the short straight after it, they brake hard for this tight, double-apex lefthander behind the paddock. One of the most spectacular incidents that occurred here came in 1996, when Pedro Diniz's Ligier pulled off on fire. He'd only just rejoined the race following a refuelling stop in which the fuel valve jammed open; fuel ignited on the exhausts after it sloshed out when he braked for the first corner.

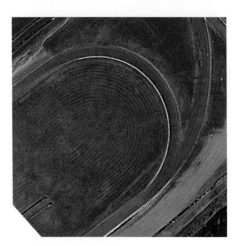

Turn 5 • Curvon
Gear: **3**
Speed: **137kph (85mph)**

A real feature of this circuit is long, double-apex corners and this one feeds the drivers onto the back straight, with drivers having to brake hard and drop from fifth gear to third before getting back onto the throttle as early as possible in order to power through the second apex and carry as much speed as they can out of the corner. Embarrassingly for the Jordan team, Ralf Schumacher barged team-mate Giancarlo Fisichella out of second place here in 1997 before finishing third himself.

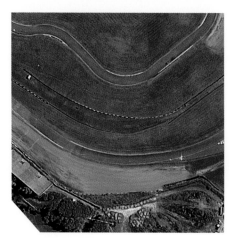

Turn 7 • Ascari
Gear: **6**
Speed: **257kph (160mph)**

The entry to this high-speed corner used to be made extra tricky by a bump right on the apex where the loop of the longer Circuit 15 rejoined the grand prix circuit, and it would make cars go light at this critical point. A further problem was the lack of kerb on the exit, meaning that anyone running wide could be in for a scary run across the grass beyond. So, for two reasons, the lines through here were limited and caution had to be employed.

Opposite: Francois Cevert accelerates his Tyrrell 006 through the final corner onto the start/finish straight, with the landmark arch down by the main entrance. *Above left:* The same corner, Turn 17, seen from the opposite direction, with the pit buildings in the background. *Above right:* Ralf Schumacher turns his Jordan into Turn 3 in 1997 after accelerating up the slope from Turn 1.

Turn 8 •

Gear: **2**
Speed: **89kph (55mph)**

Having accelerated out of Ascari, the drivers then have to scrub speed quickly for the tightest hairpin of the lap, dropping from fourth gear to second. If superior momentum has been achieved through Ascari, this is a possible overtaking point. Providing no rivals are attacking from behind, drivers turn in from the extreme left to take the widest line through this tight right, aware that the most important part of the corner is getting the power down early to build speed for the esses that follow.

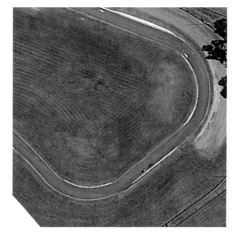

Turn 9/10 • **Mixtos & Ombu**

Gear: **3**
Speed: **145kph (90mph)**

This quick pair of corners, turning left and then right, is no place for overtaking because drivers try to straightline the corners as much as possible, using the kerbs to do so. Coming so soon after tight Turn 8, the drivers are accelerating hard here, but hold on to third gear rather than changing up to fourth because the esses are followed almost immediately by the first of a pair of medium-speed lefthanders, where taking the wrong line into the first can have ramifications into the second.

Turn 14 • **Senna S**

Gear: **2**
Speed: **72kph (45mph)**

Much tighter than the esses that went before it – Viborita – this left/right combination introduced in 1995 for F1's return really slows the flow down: the opening lefthander tightens partway around before the track veers off to the right. It was here that Luca Badoer rolled his Forti Corse without injury in 1996 after clashing with Pedro Diniz when the Ligier driver tried to lap him. There's then a right kink leading onto a short straight down to the second hairpin.

Turn 16 • **Tobogan**

Gear: **2**
Speed: **64kph (45mph)**

The penultimate corner is a righthand hairpin with drivers thankful that at least the second part of the corner is less extreme than the first. It is possible to overtake on the way in, but drivers are aware that good exit speed is more important. Accelerating hard out of here, the drivers then keep fully on the power as they flick left onto the start/finish straight. James Hunt spun his Hesketh out of the lead here in 1975 and had to make do with second place.

Great Drivers & Great Moments

Opposite top: Alan Jones in action in Williams FW06-Cosworth during the 1978 Argentinian Grand Prix.

Opposite bottom left: Despite being slowed by an errant plastic bag blocking one of his radiators, Alan Jones still came through to open his 1980 account with victory.

Opposite bottom right: McLaren's David Coulthard and Mika Hakkinen lead away in 1998, but Ferrari's Michael Schumacher took the fight to them and emerged triumphant.

The Argentinian fans had to wait only until the second Argentinian GP for a home win, thanks to Juan Manuel Fangio. Sadly, compatriot Carlos Reutemann wasn't able to match this when he carried their hopes through the 1970s into the 1980s.

Great Drivers

 Juan Manuel **Fangio**
Buenos Aires wins – 4

 Emerson **Fittipaldi**
Buenos Aires wins – 2

 Damon **Hill**
Buenos Aires wins – 2

 Denny **Hulme**
Buenos Aires wins – 1

Argentina's government believed so much in Juan Manuel Fangio's remarkable talents that it financed his forays to Europe in 1948, understanding see how his successes would boost the country's image abroad. Having retired from its inaugural grand prix in 1953, Fangio then didn't put a wheel wrong, winning the race for the next four years. In 1956, though, his Lancia-Ferrari had its fuel pump fail, so team-mate Luigi Musso was ordered to pit and Fangio then took over his car and raced to victory.

Perhaps as revenge for Argentinian ace Carlos Reutemann winning the first Brazilian GP, Brazilian ace Emerson Fittipaldi made successful cross-border raids in the other direction to win the season-opening races in 1973 and 1975. He won the first of these for Lotus after getting past Jackie Stewart when his Tyrrell hit tyre problems. Two years later, now with McLaren, Emmo did it again, this time getting past first Reutemann and then overhauling James Hunt's Hesketh.

In being first to the chequered flag in both 1995 and 1996, Damon Hill managed to win a grand prix that his father Graham never did. The first of these came in an event that marked F1's first visit to Argentina since 1981. Damon had to wait while his Williams team-mate David Coulthard led away, then Benetton's Michael Schumacher had a spell in front before he took over for good. The following year, he won again, leading all the way from pole position.

The dogged Kiwi's victory was down to determination combined with the failure of his rivals' machinery. Ronnie Peterson led away, but his Lotus was passed on lap 3 by local hero Carlos Reutemann's Brabham. Peterson then slowed with a brake problem, yet there was to be no home win, as Reutemann's air scoop broke loose with a few laps to go, his engine lost power and McLaren's Hulme motored past for his eighth and final grand prix win before retiring at the end of the year.

Great Moments

1954 Juan Manuel **Fangio** sends the crowd wild

1958 Stirling **Moss** scores first rear-engined win

1980 Alan **Jones** lays out his stall for a Williams year

1998 Michael **Schumacher** muscles his way through

The opening round of the 1954 World Championship was a great one for Argentina's F1 fans because Juan Manuel Fangio came out on top of the first race for the new 2.5-litre F1. His works Maserati was the only non-Ferrari on the front row of the gird, and he had no answer to the pace of Giuseppe Farina's in particular. Yet he stayed close to them and finally made progress when rain fell mid-race, using his wet weather skill to keep his car straight while his rivals went spinning.

The opening race of 1958 has a place in F1 history because it was the first grand prix won by a rear-engined car. The man who achieved this was Stirling Moss after running non-stop in his Rob Walker Racing Cooper on a day when his rivals all had to change tyres. Mike Hawthorn led off for Ferrari, then Juan Manuel Fangio took over in his Maserati. However, this developed a misfire and Ferrari's Luigi Musso backed off, thinking Moss was going to have to pit, which he didn't.

Alan Jones ended the 1979 season in style for Williams. In 1980, he hit the ground running and qualified on pole here for the opening round. He led away, but a plastic bag covered one of his radiators and he had to pit for it to be removed, falling to fourth. From there, he picked his way past Gilles Villeneuve, Nelson Piquet and Jacques Laffite to beat Piquet by 24.6 seconds. It was a sign of things to come: Jones raced on to the drivers' title.

This was the third round of the season and McLaren had dominated the first two races and then looked set to do the same, but Ferrari's Michael Schumacher had other ideas. He passed Mika Hakkinen early on, then barged David Coulthard out of the lead. The German opted for a two-stop strategy, so his car was lighter than Hakkinen's and this helped him pull clear, make his extra pitstop and still come home first. Coulthard's recovery from sixth was thwarted when he clashed with Jacques Villeneuve's Williams.

Interlagos

This circuit may be rough around the edges, in need of investment to bring it up to contemporary standards, but it remains one of the sport's great venues, with its dipping and swerving lap made all the more exciting by the passion of the crowd and the bonus that it often hosts the championship decider.

« Interlagos has some great corners such as the Curva do Laranja and there are real overtaking opportunities into the Senna S at the start of the lap and under-braking for Descida do Lago. »

Rubens Barrichello

Brazilians seem always to have loved motor racing: plans made for this neighbourhood of São Paolo as long ago as 1920 by British engineer Louis Romero included a circuit along with the houses in a "satellite city". It was at this point that the name Interlagos, meaning "between the lakes", was suggested by a Frenchman who said it reminded him of Interlaken in Switzerland. The land was then found to be unsuitable for housing, so the plot lay empty.

Nothing happened for years, until São Paulo hosted a street race in 1936. This had a disastrous outcome, though, as French racer Hellé Nice crashed and killed six spectators, although she escaped with her life. This certainly sped up the process of building a permanent circuit. The Sanson construction company decided in 1938 to buy a sloping site that formed a natural bowl on the outskirts of the city and Brazil's first purpose-built racing circuit was ready for racing in 1940. It has been a much-loved facility ever since, where spectators are able to enjoy some of the world's most panoramic views over a circuit. Throw in their effervescent passion for F1, and Interlagos is a riotous place to go racing. Undoubtedly, its facilities are tired by contemporary standards, and team personnel have been held up at gunpoint while stuck in traffic jams outside the circuit gates, but

the fact that it's currently F1's only South American venue means that the country that produced Ayrton Senna will remain a key part of the World Championship until somewhere more modern comes along.

Unusually, the lap runs in an anti-clockwise direction, and the first corner is an immediate test for whether the less used muscles on the right side of the drivers' necks can cope with a rapid change of direction. The circuit then drops away and pours the drivers down the face of the slope to Descida do Lago before turning left and coming back up the slope again to Ferradura. The stretch that follows has the cars rising and falling across the slope, with next to no chance of overtaking. Instead, drivers get as close as they can to the car in front and focus on getting the best possible exit from Juncao so that they can accelerate harder and faster than the car they're chasing up the arcing stretch of track past the pits from there.

This 4.3km (2.7-mile) lap is entertaining for drivers and fans alike, but it's a shadow of its original self because the circuit that was used until 1979 was just a fraction under 8km (5 miles) long; all of this additional length came from an extra loop that headed straight on at the first corner, then ran deeper into the valley around a lake before coming

back up the slope and then dipping down and rising again to meet the current circuit at Ferradura.

Neighbouring Argentina had hosted a World Championship round in Buenos Aires since 1953, but Brazil had to wait until 20 years after that. Interlagos held a non-championship race in 1972, won by Carlos Reutemann, and this showed that the circuit could cope with F1, so it became the home of the Brazilian GP from 1973, when Emerson Fittipaldi gave the fans a hometown winner. The race then transferred to Rio de Janiero's Jacarepagua circuit, after a trial race there in 1978, and it wasn't until 1990 that Interlagos got it back for good, using the current circuit layout for the first time to bring the cars past the grandstands more often.

The circuit's full name is the Autodromo José Carlos Pace after the popular Brazilian Brabham driver who won here in 1975 but was killed in a light plane crash two years later, although it continues to be known universally as Interlagos.

São Paulo is often hit by rain and the torrents that run across the track have been known to affect the outcome of more than one race. There's never anything predictable about Interlagos. ∎

Opposite: The sprawling suburbs of Sao Paulo are the backdrop as Felipe Massa descends towards Pinheirinho in his final outing for Ferrari in 2013.

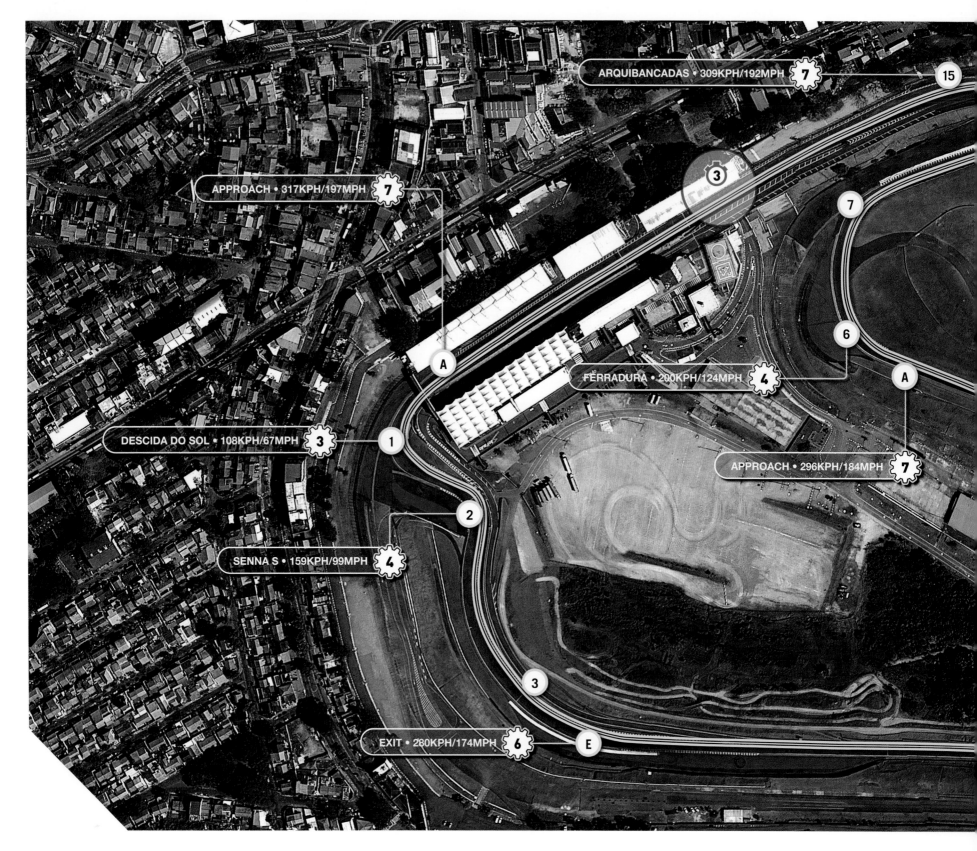

ARQUIBANCADAS • 309KPH/192MPH **7** **15**

APPROACH • 317KPH/197MPH **7**

3

7

6

A

FERRADURA • 200KPH/124MPH **4**

A

DESCIDA DO SOL • 108KPH/67MPH **3** **1**

APPROACH • 296KPH/184MPH **7**

2

SENNA S • 159KPH/99MPH **4**

3

EXIT • 280KPH/174MPH **6** **E**

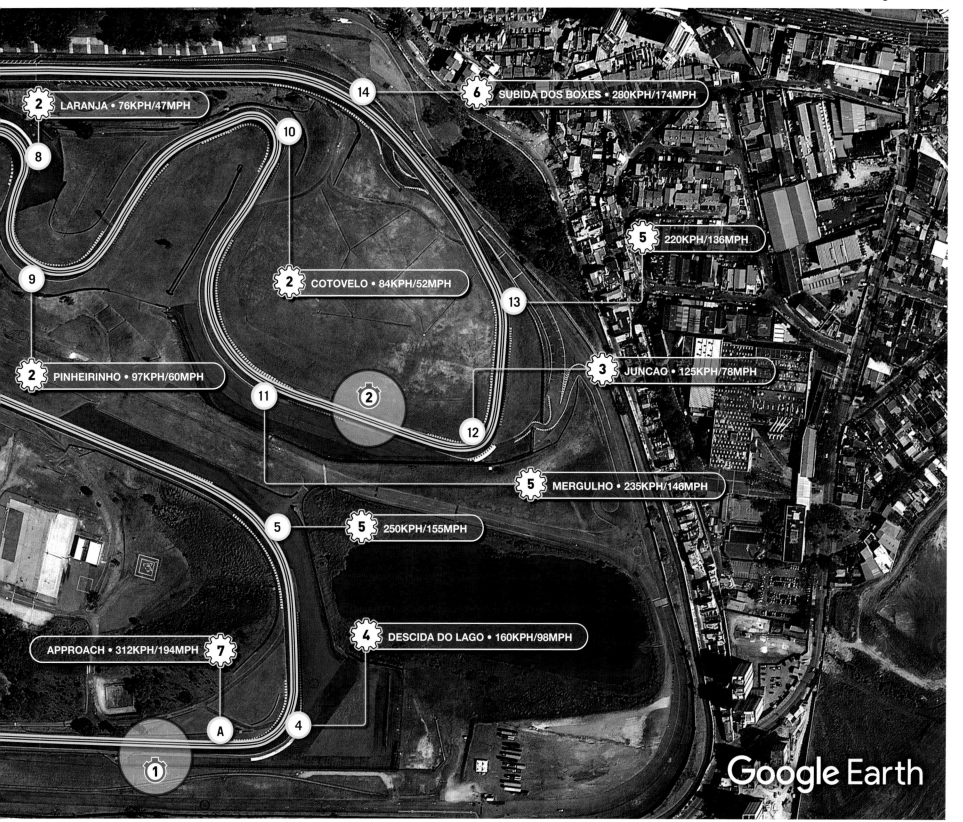

2 LARANJA • 76KPH/47MPH

6 SUBIDA DOS BOXES • 280KPH/174MPH

5 220KPH/136MPH

2 COTOVELO • 84KPH/52MPH

3 JUNCAO • 125KPH/78MPH

2 PINHEIRINHO • 97KPH/60MPH

5 MERGULHO • 235KPH/146MPH

5 250KPH/155MPH

4 DESCIDA DO LAGO • 160KPH/98MPH

7 APPROACH • 312KPH/194MPH

Google Earth

Circuit Guide

From the blind entry to the first corner through the compression at Senna S, then the drop out of Laranja and the need to make the perfect exit from Juncao, a lap of Interlagos is something very special.

Turn 1 • Descida do Sol
Gear: **3**
Speed: **108kph (67mph)**

The approach to this corner is scary enough for the drivers because they are enclosed by high walls on either side as they run flat-out up the rising and curving start/finish straight. The turn is blind on entry, hidden by the end of the pitwall, and the corner requires heavy braking from 322kph (200mph) in top gear to third. The track drops away sharply to the left and drivers must try to avoid running too wide onto the grass bank beyond, because Turn 2 follows immediately.

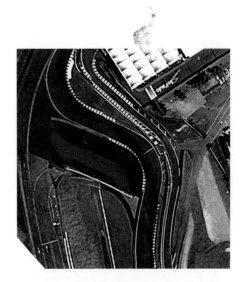

Turn 2 • Senna S
Gear: **4**
Speed: **159kph (99mph)**

If a driver can hold a tight exit line from Descida do Sol, they will be well placed for the Senna S that follows straight after it. With the track dropping into a compression, the drivers need to take the widest line they can manage because the track swings right. They want to be hard on the power once their car is settled because this corner then feeds via an arcing lefthander onto the lap's second longest straight, down the hill to Descida do Lago.

Turn 4 • Descida do Lago
Gear: **4**
Speed: **160kph (98mph)**

This is a definite overtaking point because the track is broad as they arrive, the drivers often looking to pull out of another's slipstream to make a move into this fast lefthander. Braking from almost 322kph (200mph), they have to change down to fourth gear. It can go wrong, though, as shown in 1994, when Jos Verstappen's Benetton was pitched off on the approach, then veered back into the path of Eddie Irvine, who then clipped Martin Brundle and Eric Bernard after Verstappen was sent rolling.

Turn 6 • Ferradura
Gear: **4**
Speed: **200kph (124mph)**

From the lowest point on the hillside at Descida do Lago, the drivers power through open Turn 5, then on up the hill to this, the first of three righthand corners that make up a sweep over a crest before the track drops down again. With a view largely of the earth bank behind the corner, drivers have to drop to fourth gear and find a balance for their car through this and the next corner before having to brake and drop to second for the final part of the complex.

Opposite: Vitaly Petrov keeps his Caterham at the head of the midfield pack on the climb from Pinheirinho to Cotovelo on lap 1 in 2012. *Above left:* Rain strikes often and Fernando Alonso is shown kicking up spray on the pit straight in 2012. *Above right:* The first corner is always fraught on the opening lap, so Lewis Hamilton is best placed by leading into the blind lefthander in 2012.

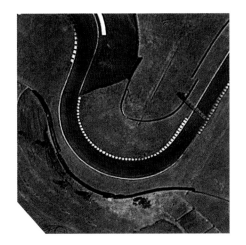

Turn 9 • **Pinheirinho**
Gear: **2**
Speed: **97kph (60mph)**

With the circuit now taking a serpentine course across the face of the hillside, Pinheirinho is the first bend of the passage with a downhill entry, and it's a long lefthander that simply turns the cars around and sends them up the slope again. Traction is quite difficult here and drivers risk losing momentum if they try to get onto the power too soon for the short, kinked straight that leads them to the following corner. There's no scope for overtaking here.

Turn 10 • **Cotovelo**
Gear: **2**
Speed: **84kph (52mph)**

This is the slowest point on the circuit, a tight righthand hairpin. The first part of the corner looks relatively open as the drivers come up the climbing approach, but then it reaches an apex and tightens noticeably, and requires drivers to drop to second gear or even first. The drivers accelerate hard down the slope and on through the long lefthander that follows, taken in fifth gear with a feathered throttle because a lack of traction can be a problem.

Turn 12 • **Junção**
Gear: **3**
Speed: **125kph (78mph)**

Junção is the one that drivers consider to be the most important corner of the lap. The reason that this innocuous third-gear lefthander is so vital is that it leads onto the start of the start/finish straight. The sooner that a driver can get his braking done, get the car balanced and start accelerating, the better, for this advantage will then be carried all the way to the first corner and a quick exit will give a driver a chance to pick up a slipstreaming tow.

Turn 14 • **Subida dos Boxes**
Gear: **6**
Speed: **280kph (174mph)**

Most drivers don't really consider this to be a corner, but rather the second of three kinked points in the run from Junção to the first corner, Descida do Sol. However, it was here that Lewis Hamilton moved into the fifth place that he needed to become World Champion in 2008, when he had just blasted his McLaren past Timo Glock, who was struggling in a dry-tyred Toyota on a wet track on the final lap. In doing so, he pipped Ferrari's Felipe Massa to the title in the most dramatic fashion.

Great Drivers & Great Moments

Some circuits deliver wins that can seem straightforward, yet there is almost always a twist at or two in any grand prix held at Interlagos, whether through contact, mechanical failure or, most often, through the arrival of rain. So, any driver who has won here can take special satisfaction in his work.

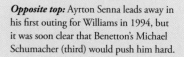

Opposite top: Ayrton Senna leads away in his first outing for Williams in 1994, but it was soon clear that Benetton's Michael Schumacher (third) would push him hard.

Opposite bottom left: Local hero Emerson Fittipaldi leads away from Lotus team-mate Ronnie Peterson and Jackie Stewart's Tyrrell at the start in 1973.

Opposite bottom right: Max Verstappen was extra keen to win in 2019 after his disappointment in 2018 and led away from Hamilton and Vettel.

Great Drivers

Michael **Schumacher**
Interlagos wins – 4

Michael scored his first Interlagos win in 1994 with Benetton, opening his campaign with victory by a full lap over Damon Hill after passing Ayrton Senna, who later spun out. He won again here in 1995 after Hill led but retired and he was chased home by David Coulthard in the other Williams. Michael then doubled this tally after moving to Ferrari by winning in 2000 after Mika Hakkinen's McLaren failed and again in 2002 by a nose from his brother Ralf's Williams.

Sebastian **Vettel**
Interlagos wins – 3

Sebastian Vettel was an outside bet for the title in 2010, but his season was gaining momentum and victory put him into the mix as he finished in front of his championship rivals, team-mate Mark Webber and Ferrari's Fernando Alonso. Three years later, he struck again, which came as no surprise as this win was his ninth in a row. The German's third win in Brazil came in 2017, and it was made easier by Lewis Hamilton having to start from the pits before racing through to fourth.

Emerson **Fittipaldi**
Interlagos wins – 2

Emerson was a driver who was almost brought up at the circuit, with his father being a radio commentator, so it's fitting that he should win the first grand prix held here. Racing for Lotus in 1973, he moved past pole-sitting team-mate Ronnie Peterson and led every lap. He won again in 1974 for McLaren after passing Peterson, before finishing second behind compatriot Carlos Pace's Brabham in 1975. He then finished fourth for the family team in 1977 before the race moved to Jacarepaguá.

Felipe **Massa**
Interlagos wins – 2

When he had made it to F1, Felipe said the only time he'd worked at Interlagos before was as a pizza delivery boy... So, imagine his delight in 2006 when he scored his second win to round out his first year with Ferrari. This was Brazil's first home win since Ayrton Senna in 1993. He scored a second win in the dramatic 1998 finale when it looked as though this would land him the title, only for Lewis Hamilton to gain the place he needed on the last lap.

Great Moments

1991 Ayrton **Senna** finally wins at home

Ayrton was the pre-eminent driver of his age, but his record in Brazil was one of frustration, with second place his best result in six visits to Jacarepaguá. After placing third on F1's return to Interlagos in 1990, he achieved his longed-for home win in 1991, when he not only resisted the challenge of Williams drivers Nigel Mansell and Riccardo Patrese but managed a gearbox problem through the closing laps. The crowd went wild, but Ayrton was so exhausted he had to be lifted from the car.

2003 Giancarlo **Fisichella** comes out on top

Through the history of the World Championship, there have been a handful of races where not everyone present has been sure of the identity of the winner. The 2003 Brazilian GP was one such race. Run in wet conditions, the race was red-flagged after Fernando Alonso had a huge crash. Kimi Raikkonen was adjudged to have won the restarted race for McLaren, but so confused were the timekeepers that it took several days before it could be confirmed that Giancarlo Fisichella had won for Jordan.

2008 Lewis **Hamilton** wins his second shoot-out

For the second year in a row, Interlagos hosted a last round title shoot-out. As in 2007, this involved Lewis Hamilton and it appeared as though he'd been pipped at the last by Ferrari's Felipe Massa after losing ground with poor tyre strategy and having to watch the Brazilian win the race and, apparently, the title. But the Toyotas were still on regular tyres as rain fell ever more heavily and so Lewis was able to pass Timo Glock on the climb to the finish line and deny Massa.

2019 **Verstappen** avenges his 2018 Brazilian disaster

Twelve months after losing a first Brazilian win when his Red Bull was hit as Force India's Esteban Ocon tried to unlap himself, it came right in 2019. This time, as he was controlling the race, all the action was behind him, with the Ferrari drivers clashing and then Lewis Hamilton fumbling an attempt to deprive Red Bull's Alex Albon, of second, pitching the latter down the order. A five-place penalty left Hamilton seventh and surprised Toro Rosso racer Pierre Gasly second.

⭐ Montreal

This is a circuit on which it's hard to overtake, the cars take a physical battering and the pit and paddock facilities are cramped, yet the Circuit Gilles Villeneuve was a hit from its introduction in the late 1970s and remains popular today because it has a great atmosphere and everyone loves visiting Montreal.

> ❝The track has a great history and it's like a street circuit, as it's quite bumpy. It's like a go-kart track too, as we have to take the kerbs to achieve a quick lap. ❞
>
> *Lewis Hamilton*

By the mid-1970s, as the push for improved driver safety was gaining momentum, it became clear that Mosport Park's days of hosting the Canadian GP were numbered. The picturesque circuit in the wooded hills of Ontario had hosted a Canadian GP for sportscars from 1961, with F1 taking over the slot in 1967. However, few upgrades had been done and the lack of run-off was starting to spook the drivers, something that was emphasized by Ian Ashley, who suffered leg injuries when he crashed his Hesketh in practice in 1977.

So, for 1978, the Canadian GP had a new home, in Montreal, financed by Labatt's brewery. Not only did this take racing to the people rather than expecting them to drive 72km (45 miles) from the closest city, which was Toronto in Mosport Park's case, but it offered an exciting circuit with brand new facilities and the city's skyline as an attractive backdrop.

Built on the Ile de Notre Dame in the St Lawrence River, but connected to the city centre by both road bridges and metro line, the site was certainly easy to get to. The island is narrow, though, so finding a route for the circuit took some planning; it has to weave its way around the futuristic pavilions left there after Expo World Fair in 1967, a large casino, and the rowing lake used when Montreal hosted the Olympic Games in 1976. The result is a long,

thin circuit that runs down one side of the rowing lake, extends at its southern point to the edge of the river before it doubles back and threads through a wooded section on its run to the hairpin. The overall feeling is of alternating between sections that seem fairly cramped for the drivers and those where it seems very cramped, as there are concrete walls and trees close in on either side of the track, with the blast from the hairpin to the pits the only truly open stretch. Yet, there's scope for plenty of flat-out motoring. Combine this with the heavy braking required at several points around the lap, and it's easy to understand why it's so punishing on both cars and drivers.

Ferrari's Gilles Villeneuve was Canada's new racing hero in 1978, so the timing of the opening of this circuit in his native Quebec could not have been better. When he then rewarded the home fans with victory first time out, it was the dream start for the race organizers and why they immediately renamed the track as the Circuit Gilles Villeneuve. His death in 1982 hit the Canadian fans hard, especially because there was no rising Canadian star to take his place. Almost a quarter of a century later, though, they finally had another reason to wave their Canadian and Quebecois flags as they came out in their thousands to support Gilles' son

Jacques, but sadly he never managed to land them the win that they craved.

Perhaps the greatest draw of all for the circuit is that it's located just a short ride from downtown Montreal, making it an enormously fun and cosmopolitan place to stay for teams, drivers and fans alike, also giving the television crews considerably more chance to put F1 into context than they get at a circuit deep in the countryside such as Silverstone or Hockenheim.

Due to the width restrictions around the wall-lined route of the circuit, there have been many race-ending accidents since the circuit's debut in 1978. The worst of all, though, came in 1982, when Didier Pironi stalled his Ferrari and Riccardo Paletti was unable to avoid slamming his Osella into the back of it. The Italian rookie would die later in hospital.

One of the greatest developments in Montreal's history of hosting the grand prix came in 1982, when its race date was brought forward to early summer. Thus, the risk of cold snaps was eliminated, although rain remains an occasional threat. ∎

Opposite: Montreal has always produced a big crowd. Here, they get to see Romain Grosjean run wide at L'Epingle behind Mark Webber and Giedo van der Garde in 2013.

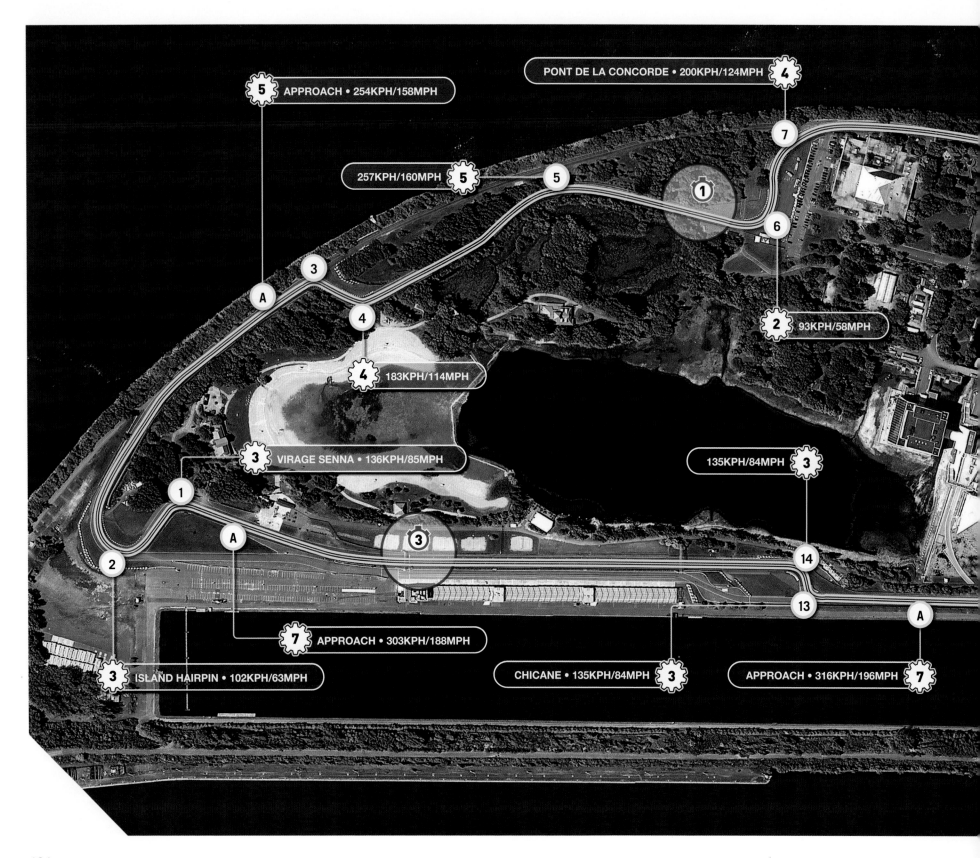

PONT DE LA CONCORDE • 200KPH/124MPH **4**

7

5 APPROACH • 254KPH/158MPH

257KPH/160MPH **5**   5

1

6

3

2 93KPH/58MPH

4

4 183KPH/114MPH

3 VIRAGE SENNA • 136KPH/85MPH

135KPH/84MPH **3**

1

A

3

14

2

13

7 APPROACH • 303KPH/188MPH

A

3 ISLAND HAIRPIN • 102KPH/63MPH

CHICANE • 135KPH/84MPH **3**

APPROACH • 316KPH/196MPH **7**

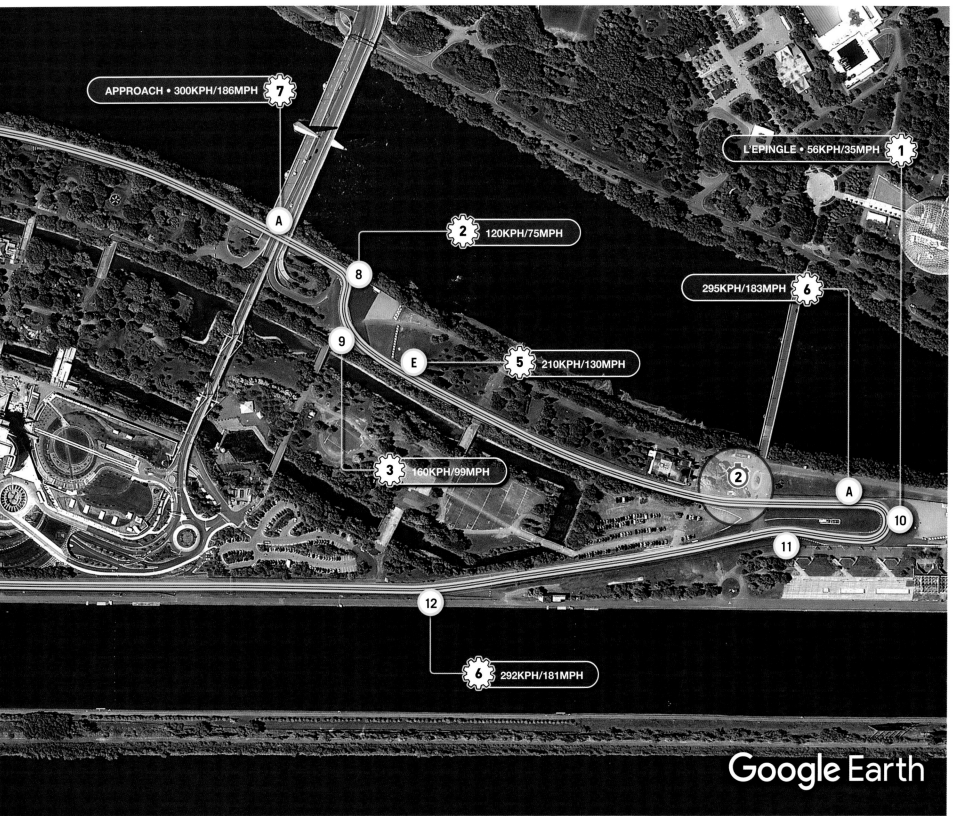

APPROACH • 300KPH/186MPH **7**

L'EPINGLE • 56KPH/35MPH **1**

A

2 120KPH/75MPH

8

295KPH/183MPH **6**

9

E **5** 210KPH/130MPH

3 160KPH/99MPH

2

A

10

11

12

6 292KPH/181MPH

Google Earth

Circuit Guide

Built on an island and hemmed in by trees and a lake, this strip of a track feels alternately enclosed, tight and twisty, and open and flat-out for the return leg. It's a car-breaker, working the cars' engines and brakes harder than most.

Turn 1 • Virage Senna
Gear: **3**
Speed: **136kph (85mph)**

The drivers arrive through a right kink, then almost immediately have to hit the brakes hard for the first corner. They have to halve their speed from almost 306kph (190mph). On lap 1, fortunately, they arrive at a slightly reduced velocity after their standing start, which is fortunate because the cars inevitably bunch for this tight left, and Benetton's Alexander Wurz was famously sent rolling here in 1998, when Jean Alesi's Sauber cut across its path. This doesn't stop drivers trying moves on lap 1, though.

Turn 2 • Island Hairpin
Gear: **3**
Speed: **102kph (63mph)**

Any driver who has run wide coming out of the first corner will have to pay the price when they get to this corner into which it immediately feeds. Arriving at the feet of the people in the grandstand here, they will then find themselves running out of room to get around this wide righthand hairpin, because the ideal entry line is from the left side of the track, not the right. Inevitably, this is also the scene of many a first lap collision as drivers jostle for position.

Turn 4 •
Gear: **4**
Speed: **183kph (114mph)**

The drivers have just relaxed into accelerating hard along this stretch of track from the Island Hairpin with a bank of trees on their right and distant views across the river to the city on their left when they have to slow again as this chicane comes suddenly into view. Dropping down the gearbox, they have to flick right, then left and the exit is critical because there's a wall right on the edge of the track with which drivers make contact if they get it wrong.

Turn 6 •
Gear: **2**
Speed: **93kph (58mph)**

This back section of the circuit offers pretty much only one line through its constant twists, the drivers feeling channelled by the concrete walls that line either flank of the track. At Turn 6, though, they enjoy the "luxury" of having a grass verge ahead of them, as they turn hard left into the first part of a wider-spaced chicane. This is where Sebastian Vettel slid wide in his Red Bull in 2011 and Jenson Button powered past for a famous win for McLaren.

Opposite: Force India's Adrian Sutil leads a train of cars through the sweeper past the pits and enters third-gear Virage Senna in 2013. *Above left:* Nico Rosberg leads Mark Webber and Fernando Alonso at the 2013 Canadian Grand Prix. *Above right:* Nico Rosberg resists the challenge of Red Bull's Mark Webber out of Island Hairpin early in the 2013 Canadian GP.

Turn 7 • Pont de la Concorde
Gear: **4**
Speed: **200kph (124mph)**

A less extreme corner than the one before it, Pont de la Concorde is where the drivers have to get through the corner and then get hard back on to the power; good exit speed from this third gear righthander is vital because the track starts to open out from here and the run to the hairpin is an appreciable one. As elsewhere, the walls aren't far from the racing line and it was here that Olivier Panis crashed his Ligier in 1997, breaking his legs.

Turn 9 • Pont des Iles
Gear: **3**
Speed: **160kph (99mph)**

The third chicane of the back section, this right/left flick presents the drivers with an extra challenge as they brake hard and shave more than 130kph (80mph) off their speed. They drop to second gear because the track is bumpy here – a legacy of Montreal's long, freezing winters – and this can upset the cars. The second part of the chicane is less tight and drivers enjoy having rare run-off to their right as they power out onto the short straight to the hairpin.

Turn 10 • L'Epingle
Gear: **1**
Speed: **56kph (35mph)**

With a grass verge on either side and a rare feeling of space – the drivers can see the return leg as they approach this ultra-tight righthander – drivers have to focus on the fact that this is one of only a handful of places at which it is possible to overtake. Many prefer, though, not to risk a move into here but to concentrate on exiting the hairpin right on the tail of the car ahead so that they can line up a passing manoeuvre down the circuit's main straight that follows.

Turn 14 • Chicane
Gear: **3**
Speed: **135kph (84mph)**

The straight runs alongside the 1976 Olympic rowing lake and drivers are finally able to hit top speed and stay there for more than a few seconds, catching a tow down towards this right/left flick onto the start/finish straight and plot their move. The lefthand exit isn't visible until the drivers are turning into the first part of the chicane and drivers are advised to stay off the kerbs on the exit; many have run over them and then clattered the wall beyond.

Great Drivers & Great Moments

On a circuit that is notorious for being a car-breaker thanks to its flat-out blasts and frequent heavy braking, a modicum of mechanical sympathy can pay dividends, and Michael Schumacher clearly found the right formula because he won here seven times. Collisions or glancing the walls have scuppered others.

Great Drivers

 Lewis **Hamilton**
Montreal wins – 7

 Michael **Schumacher**
Montreal wins – 7

 Nelson **Piquet**
Montreal wins – 3

 Ayrton **Senna**
Montreal wins – 2

Lewis landed his first career F1 win at Montreal, the first of three for McLaren, in 2007, a race notable for three safety car periods. Three years later, he resisted the burgeoning Red Bull attack and, in 2012, McLaren's two-stop strategy proved superior to Ferrari's plan. Wins four, five and six were for Mercedes in 2015, 2016 and 2017. In 2019, he joined Michael Schumacher on seven Montreal wins after Vettel beat him to the finish but was penalised for rejoining the track in a dangerous manner.

Schumacher's career really lifted off in 1994 and he won here in dominant fashion for Benetton. With the exception of his eight wins at Magny-Cours, Montreal proved to be one of his most successful stamping grounds (equal only to Imola), for Michael would win here in 1997 after joining Ferrari, then again in 1998, 2000, 2002, 2003 and 2004. The highlight among these was the one in 2004, when he managed to get to the front from sixth on the grid.

Once Nelson got BMW turbo power for his Brabham, the wins in Montreal began to flow. The first came in 1982, when he had to work his way to the front. Two years later, he didn't even have to pass anybody because he started on pole and led from lights to flag. Nelson would have to wait until 1991 for his next Montreal victory, when he was racing for Benetton. Nigel Mansell had been set to win for Williams until he stalled at L'Epingle on the final lap.

Hampered by a turbo problem when well placed in 1985, Ayrton only started winning in Montreal three years later in his first season with McLaren, 1988. He qualified on pole and had to sit behind team-mate Alain Prost for 19 laps until he found a way past. He led in 1989 until his engine blew with three laps to go, but had more luck in 1990, when he was beaten to the finish by team-mate Gerhard Berger before the Austrian dropped to fourth with a 1-minute jump-start penalty.

Great Moments

1978 Gilles **Villeneuve** gives circuit dream debut

1995 Jean **Alesi** sheds tears of joy for his first win

2008 Robert **Kubica** makes his breakthrough

2011 Jenson **Button** hunts down Sebastian Vettel

The timing of Gilles' arrival in F1 couldn't have been better for the people behind this circuit because he had had an increasingly good first full season for Ferrari. Montreal's first race was the season-closer and, having qualified third, he could only watch as Lotus stand-in Jean-Pierre Jarier stormed off into the lead. He passed his team-mate Jody Scheckter for second place, but Jarier was 30 seconds in the lead. Then the Frenchman pulled off the circuit with no brakes and so Gilles was able to delight the local fans.

There have been few more emotional drivers than Jean. So, you can imagine the tears of joy that he shed in 1995 when he approached the chequered flag in front of the field for the very first time. He was in his fifth year with Ferrari and looked to finish this race second behind Michael Schumacher but, with 11 laps to go, the Benetton called at the pits with a gearbox problem. This left Jean way out front and he duly won by half a minute from the two Jordans.

Sauber had never won a grand prix. Working in partnership with BMW in 2008, it appeared to have a car good enough to score points but not to win. Then came Montreal and the team not only won but took a one-two finish. Robert Kubica benefited when leader Lewis Hamilton hit Kimi Raikkonen's Ferrari that was stationary at pit exit during a safety car period. Early race leader Nick Heidfeld had a great chance to win in the other Sauber, but Kubica's two-stop strategy proved superior.

This race had the ending of a Hollywood movie. Sebastian Vettel led away on a wet track, McLaren's Jenson Button and Lewis Hamilton clashed, Button was given a drivethrough penalty, then the race was stopped because of standing water. Fernando Alonso and Button collided after the restart and Button got a puncture. The safety car came out and then Button passed car after car, finally catching Vettel, who cracked under the pressure halfway around the final lap for Button to take a famous win.

Circuit of the Americas

The United States of America has been a tough market for Formula One to crack, and its spasmodic passage around the country doesn't make for good reading. However, with the construction of this magnificent circuit outside Austin in Texas, it finally has a circuit admired by people the world over.

> **"** The track is tricky and very challenging, and mixed too, with high-speed and low-speed corners. Possibly the best place for overtaking is at the end of the DRS zone into Turn 12. **"**
>
> *Sebastian Vettel*

When the teams turned up at the brand new Circuit of the Americas in November 2012, with its lofty grandstands, plunging slopes and sweeping esses, they knew immediately that the USA had finally produced a worthy home for its grand prix for the first time since Watkins Glen took over the honours of hosting the race from Riverside in 1961. For here was a giant among road circuits, a track that had been designed and built without compromise, a track that has world class facilities and, best of all, a layout that is blessed with considerable gradient change that tests the drivers and shows the cars at their best.

The most experienced F1 racer of all time, Rubens Barrichello, was immediately excited by the prospect of the new circuit, telling *F1 Racing,* "Hills make it more interesting. Look at the best corners at Spa: Eau Rouge is steep uphill and Pouhon is downhill. The slopes require increased commitment in the cockpit."

The anti-clockwise layout was filled with corners echoing the best of the best from the leading circuits around the world, with some sequences proving an intense challenge for the drivers, which is just how it should be when a designer has been afforded a clean sheet plus the benefit of a plot with 40.5m (133ft) of gradient. After decades of F1 losing ground in the USA, Hermann Tilke and

his team had to get it right to entice the fans back and the Circuit of the Americas has done just that.

The first thing that strikes anyone about the Circuit of the Americas is its rise and fall. The second thing is the sheer variety of corners, from long straights into tight corners, to a testing run of esses and corners where a driver can really carry some speed, offering American fans a real opportunity to see F1 cars at their best. Furthermore, with so much gradient built into the lap, spectators are treated to panoramic views of much of the track.

The circuit's location in Texas works in its favour too, as the race can be held in autumn, when the F1 season is coming to a climax, without fear of the chill and rain that used to hit Watkins Glen in upstate New York even when its race was held a whole month earlier. Not only is Austin a city looking to boost its global image, but it truly wants the race rather than putting up with it – as Phoenix seemed to do when hosting the US GP between 1989 and 1991 – and it embraces the race, making it part of a festival of events. Having the drivers wear Stetsons on the podium adds a welcome American flavour too.

The teams and drivers like the buzz of the city too. Perhaps best of all, the circuit's proximity to the border brings with it a large influx of Mexican F1 fans, adding an international flavour to proceedings.

With plans for the re-establishment of the Mexican GP in the pipeline, the excitement of a three-race sweep starting here, then going to Mexico City and on for a finale in Brazil makes great sense.

Yet, it would be remiss to fail to point out that the circuit had a bumpy ride through construction, with original front man Tavo Hellmund being eased aside and the race, fleetingly, having its original championship slot taken away from it. The thought of this opportunity being missed was almost too much for American F1 fans to bear, so there was relief when all was settled and construction was able to start again and continue to completion.

The United States really needed to have an F1 circuit of its own, to show American fans that not all racing needs to be held on a banked oval, and so the Circuit of the Americas has taken its place at the head of the country's road racing tree above Road Atlanta, Road America and Mid-Ohio and looks set to be the race's home for years to come, much to the relief of the FIA that has been pushing so hard for the grand prix to establish a permanent base. ■

Opposite: Red Bull Racing's Sebastian Vettel leads Romain Grosjean, Lewis Hamilton and the pack down the hill into Turn 2 on the opening lap in 2013.

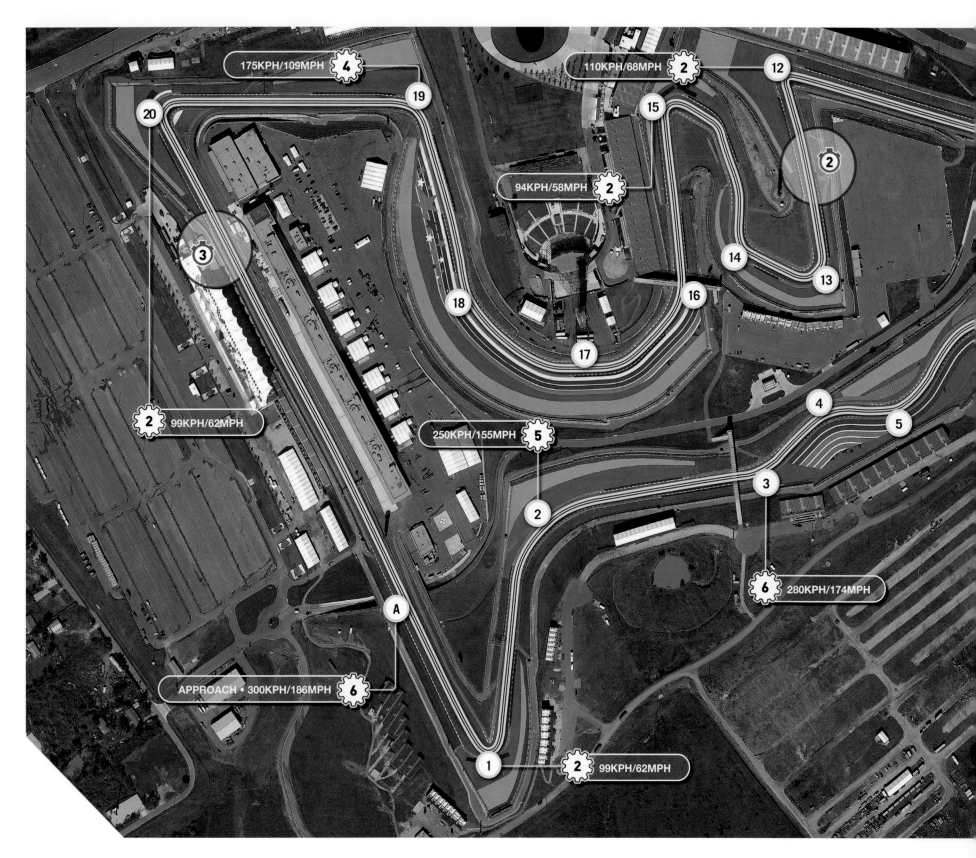

175KPH/109MPH **4**

110KPH/68MPH **2** 12

19

20

15

2

94KPH/58MPH **2**

3

14

13

18

16

17

2 99KPH/62MPH

4

5

250KPH/155MPH **5**

3

2

6 280KPH/174MPH

A

APPROACH • 300KPH/186MPH **6**

1 **2** 99KPH/62MPH

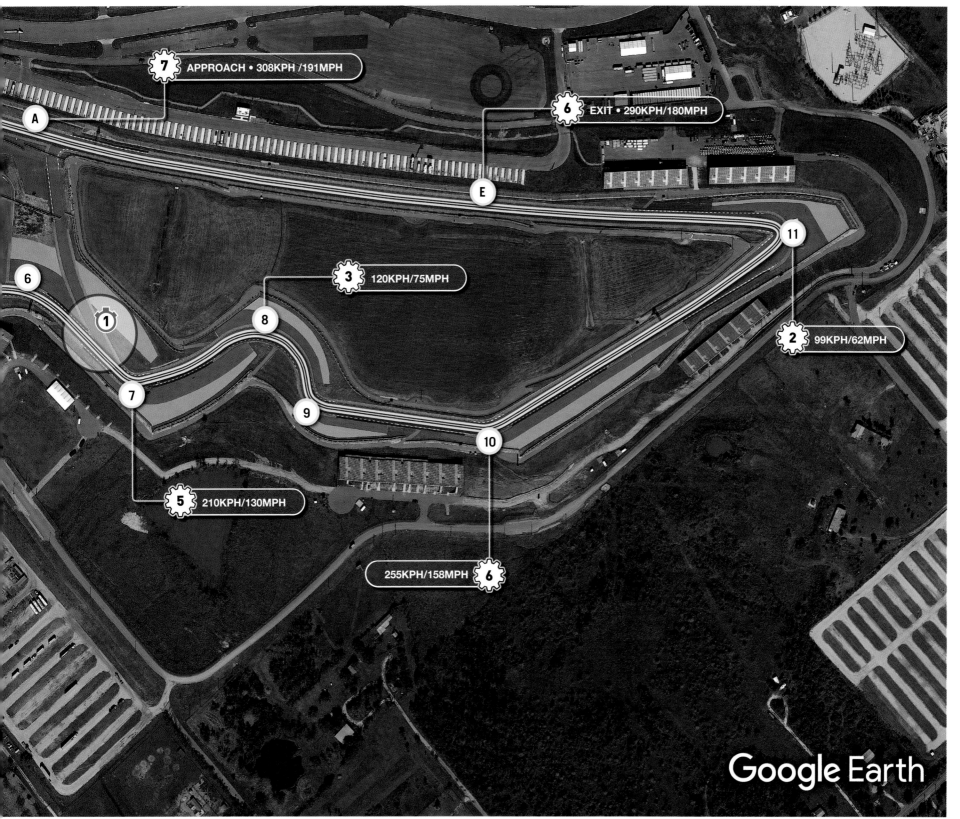

7 APPROACH • 308KPH /191MPH

6 EXIT • 290KPH/180MPH

A

E

11

6

3 120KPH/75MPH

8

1

2 99KPH/62MPH

7

9

10

5 210KPH/130MPH

255KPH/158MPH 6

Google Earth

Circuit Guide

Hermann Tilke gave the Circuit of the Americas a wonderful flow to its lap. He used the rolling terrain to include corners not dissimilar to the very best turns from the best of Formula One's outstanding circuits around the world.

Turn 1 •

Gear: **2**
Speed: **99kph (62mph)**

Approached by one of the steepest climbs tackled in F1, matched only by Eau Rouge at Spa-Francorchamps and the climb to the first corner at the Red Bull Ring, this lefthander is reached at the crest of the hill, with the track flattening out where the drivers are braking hardest. There is plenty of track width to allow different entry lines, but a driver's work isn't completed on turn-in, because the exit is then made tricky by the way that the track drops away.

Turn 2 •

Gear: **5**
Speed: **250kph (155mph)**

Having accelerated down the descent from the first corner, the drivers get a fantastic view of the distinctive viewing tower and the return leg from Turn 12 to Turn 19 in the distance as they accelerate hard and plunge down the slope past grandstands and hospitality balconies; but they must focus immediately on pulling across from the righthand side of the track to the left so that they can sweep down through the fifth-gear righthand kink at Turn 2.

Turn 3 •

Gear: **6**
Speed: **280kph (174mph)**

This is the start of one of the greatest stretches of track in F1, offering rapid changes of direction as experienced only through Becketts at Silverstone and the S Curves at Suzuka. Turn 3 makes the first of a run of four corners in esse formation. The most impressive thing for people watching here is the fact that the drivers take these in sixth gear, at around 280kph (175mph), and the way the cars stick to the track is testament to the downforce they generate.

Turn 7 •

Gear: **5**
Speed: **210kph (130mph)**

After the shortest of straights, Turn 7 is sharper than the four-corner esses that preceded it and so requires drivers to drop down a gear from sixth to fifth. The cars are still travelling at 210kph (130mph), though, as they start this second run of, admittedly slower, esses before the track drops away out of Turn 10. Precision continues to be everything here where drivers are free to concentrate on their lines because there's no chance of either passing or being passed.

Opposite: Lewis Hamilton's Mercedes W04 leads Mark Webber's Red Bull RB9 Renault out and away from Turn 1 in their battle over third place in 2013. *Above left:* Fernando Alonso guides his Ferrari through those sweepers in 2013, with the tower in the background. *Above right:* The drivers are shown off to the crowds in the main grandstand before the start in 2013.

Turn 11 ●

Gear: **2**
Speed: **99kph (62mph)**

The furthest point of the lap from the paddock is this lefthand hairpin. The drivers arrive at the foot of the slope down from Turn 10 in sixth gear, and this is a definite overtaking opportunity because they have to brake heavily and drop to second gear. As with so many hairpins, especially those where passing is possible on the entry, the exit line can be compromised by others, but a driver arriving alone will turn in from the right and get straight back onto the throttle.

Turn 12 ●

Gear: **2**
Speed: **110kph (68mph)**

This tight lefthander is a definite overtaking point, as proved by Mark Webber in 2013, when he pulled off a great passing move on Lewis Hamilton's Mercedes after using the slipstreaming tow that he had been able to harness through the DRS zone down the lengthy straight from Turn 11. Having to trim around 200kph (124mph) from their approach speed means that braking is heavy here, and it's made all the more exciting when drivers' tyres are worn late in the race.

Turn 19 ●

Gear: **4**
Speed: **175kph (109mph)**

At the end of the slower section that began at Turn 12, this fast lefthander is approached down a gentle incline behind the paddock, and traction is made hard to come by because the corner has a dipping exit. The sheer diversity of corners around this 20-corner lap shows how the race engineers have to work every bit as hard as the drivers in order to be able to send them out with a car that is set up to manage every type of corner.

Turn 20 ●

Gear: **2**
Speed: **99kph (62mph)**

The final corner of the lap is a slow lefthander that is reached just after the cars have negotiated the lowest point of the circuit on the blast from Turn 19, rising up again before the corner. From here, exit speed is everything as strong acceleration onto the start/finish straight can then be carried all the way up the hill towards Turn 1, perhaps enabling a driver to get a tow and thus put them into a position to try a passing move on a car ahead of them.

Great Drivers & Great Moments

The design of the purpose-built Circuit of the Americas works well in that not only do its dips and rises and especially its run of esses make the cars look spectacular, but the layout offers more than a few possible passing places, with Turn 1 on the opening lap almost guaranteed to supply fireworks.

Great Drivers

 Lewis **Hamilton**
COTA wins – 5

 Sebastian **Vettel**
COTA wins – 1

 Kimi **Raikkonen**
COTA wins – 1

 Valtteri **Bottas**
COTA wins – 1

Lewis Hamilton has a growing collection of cowboy hats – one for each his five F1 wins in the seven races since COTA first welcomed Formula One. His first, for McLaren, came when he caught and passed Sebastian Vettel's Red Bull. The wins in 2014, 2015, 2016 and 2017 were for Mercedes, the first two requiring bold moves to pass team-mate Nico Rosberg. In 2016, engine failure fears proved false and, in 2017, he hunted down and caught Ferrari's Vettel.

The World Championship's second visit to COTA was a celebration for Red Bull's Sebastian Vettel, who had claimed the 2013 drivers' title at the previous round. With victories in each of the previous seven races, he was a clear favourite to add to this impressive run. From pole position, the German ace was never challenged and finished 6s clear of Romain Grosjean's Lotus. A clash with Daniel Ricciardo's Red Bull in 2018 denied Vettel a possible second COTA win.

Kimi Raikkonen hasn't been known to smile a lot; he dislikes attention when out of the car. He wants to race and everthing else, for him, is a waste of time. "The Ice Man" has his fans and so his success at the Circuit of the Americas in 2018 was greeted with delight by many. He made a brilliant start to pass Lewis Hamilton's polesitting Mercedes, then controlled the event for his first win since the opening round of the 2013 World Championship.

Although 2019 yielded a sixth F1 World Championship for Lewis Hamilton, his Mercedes team-mate Valtteri Bottas put up his best challenge yet. His fourth win of the year here proved he could, on his very best days, not just equal Hamilton's pace but beat it. He controlled the race from pole and rebuffed not just Red Bull's Max Verstappen, but also Hamilton's different – one-stop – strategy. Unlike Lewis's successful similar plan in Mexico, this didn't quite work and the Finn was able to drive to victory.

Great Moments

 2012 Great race marks impressive debut

2015 **Hamilton** muscles **Rosberg** off the track

2017 Turn 12 continues to be **Hamilton**'s place

2018 From near the back to near the front

The first grand prix held at the Circuit of the Americas enjoyed a fabulous scrap for the lead as McLaren's Lewis Hamilton chased Sebastian Vettel. When the Red Bull was slowed momentarily by Narain Karthikeyan's HRT approaching Turn 12, Hamilton dived up the inside to take the lead and the win. For American fans, it proved they had a circuit that was good enough to host the US GP after decades of being a peripatetic event.

Lewis Hamilton's COTA victory in 2015 gave him his third F1 title, so naturally he was delighted with the result. On the other side of the Mercedes garage, though there were certainly no smiles as Nico Rosberg was angry about Hamilton's opening lap move, one he felt cost him a potential victory. Rosberg was slow away from pole, so Hamilton dived up the inside into Turn 1 and pushed him wide on the exit. It dropped Rosberg to fourth behind both Red Bulls.

If a driver can get a good exit from the lefthand hairpin at Turn 11, they might get a tow from a rival down the circuit's longest straight to the tightish left at Turn 12. It is Lewis Hamilton's favourite place for overtaking and he provided a masterclass of an example of this vital skill in 2017. Hamilton got close enough to Sebastian Vettel's leading Ferrari on the straight to employ his car's DRS, lining up a successful, and spectacular, passing move into Turn 12.

Max Verstappen can't have expected much when he failed to set a time in Q2 and then took a five-place penalty for a gearbox change at COTA in 2018. He lined up 18th, but was up to ninth place by the end of the opening lap. He then picked off car after car as he ascended the order. Sebastian Vettel's spin helped, but the young Dutchman deserves credit for finishing 1.281s behind Kimi Raikkonen's winning Ferrari in second place, after such a disastrous start.

Mexico City

Mexico has been in love with Formula One since the early 1960s, when the Rodriguez brothers broke onto the scene. Its grand prix has come and gone since, and Mexico City is now set for its third spell in the World Championship with this high-speed circuit modified to meet contemporary standards.

❝ I don't think we should be coming here until the track is resurfaced and the run-off areas improved. We go to street circuits with a better surface than we have here. ❞

Ayrton Senna

Mexico used to be famous for its crazy road race, the Carrera Panamericana. However, it wanted circuit racing too and so this circuit was built in 1962 in the Magdalena Mixhuca area of the capital city. The timing was perfect, as this corresponded with its greatest racing hopes, the Rodriguez brothers, starting to make a splash.

The younger of the Rodriguez brothers, Ricardo, was a Ferrari driver by the age of 19 and he alone filled the grandstands for the first Mexican GP in 1962. This was a non-championship event and Ferrari declined to come, so he was entered in a Rob Walker Racing Lotus. Tragically, he crashed to his death in practice at the slightly banked Peraltada sweeper that concludes the lap.

This was a blow, but the event gained World Championship status for 1963, by which time Ricardo's older brother Pedro had reached F1. Jim Clark won that first one for Lotus and would win again in 1967. It was held as the final round each year from 1964, and there was often extra drama, none more so than in 1964 when BRM's Graham Hill arrived in the championship lead, five points clear of Ferrari's John Surtees. Surtees's team-mate Lorenzo Bandini ran into Hill and damaged his exhausts. Clark now looked set to take victory and title, but an oil leak slowed him and his engine seized on the final lap, allowing Surtees through to grab the crown.

In 1970, 200,000 spectators turned up hoping that local hero Rodriguez could win for BRM. Climbing over the barriers they sat on the grass verges right alongside the track. Despite Rodriguez and Jackie Stewart pleading with them to withdraw, they refused and the race had to go ahead like that. Fortunately, no driver crashed into them as Jacky Ickx motored to victory for Ferrari, but the World Championship decided that enough was enough and would stay away until 1986.

When F1 returned, drivers said that they liked the track, although the bumps that dotted its length were less welcome. The trickiest point, or the one that presented the greatest potential consequences, was the Peraltada, a corner taken flat in fifth gear by those who dared. Naturally, Ayrton Senna was one such driver and he came unstuck at this fearsome righthander in 1991 when he hit the bump towards the exit, lost control and inverted his McLaren in practice. A year later, Senna was caught out by the bumps again, this time going off at the Eses.

Bumps aside, the other main factor that the engineers always had to consider was the thinner air because of the track's altitude of 7350 feet (2,240m) – comfortably the highest elevation out of all the circuits. This meant that the engines struggled to suck in enough oxygen to work efficiently, although turbocharged engines didn't fare as badly.

Gerhard Berger had every reason to like the place, though, as he won on F1's return in 1986, marking not only his but Benetton's first win too.

A decade after F1's last visit in 1992, won by Nigel Mansell for Williams, top level racing returned in 2002 when the ChampCar series headed south of the border, with the Peraltada neutered by the track being fed instead through a baseball stadium that had been built inside the old banked corner. Then, in 2007, the A1GP series made the first of two visits.

For F1's return in 2015, the track has been extended from 4.421km to 4.580km, the extra length being added with a twisting section through the baseball stadium, bisecting the grandstands there before rejoining the old layout halfway around the Peraltada. The main grandstand has been replaced with a new one offering space for hospitality suites and 33 new pit garages. There's also a new control tower by pit entry. Larger temporary grandstands have been erected at the first corner complex, and also at Horquilla, helping to boost the number of grandstand seats to 120,000, with capacity for 30,000 more fans around the circuit perimeter. ∎

Opposite: It's Williams in front on Formula One's last but one visit, in 1992, with Nigel Mansell (5) leading the way from Riccardo Patrese as Ferrari's Ivan Capelli crashes in the background.

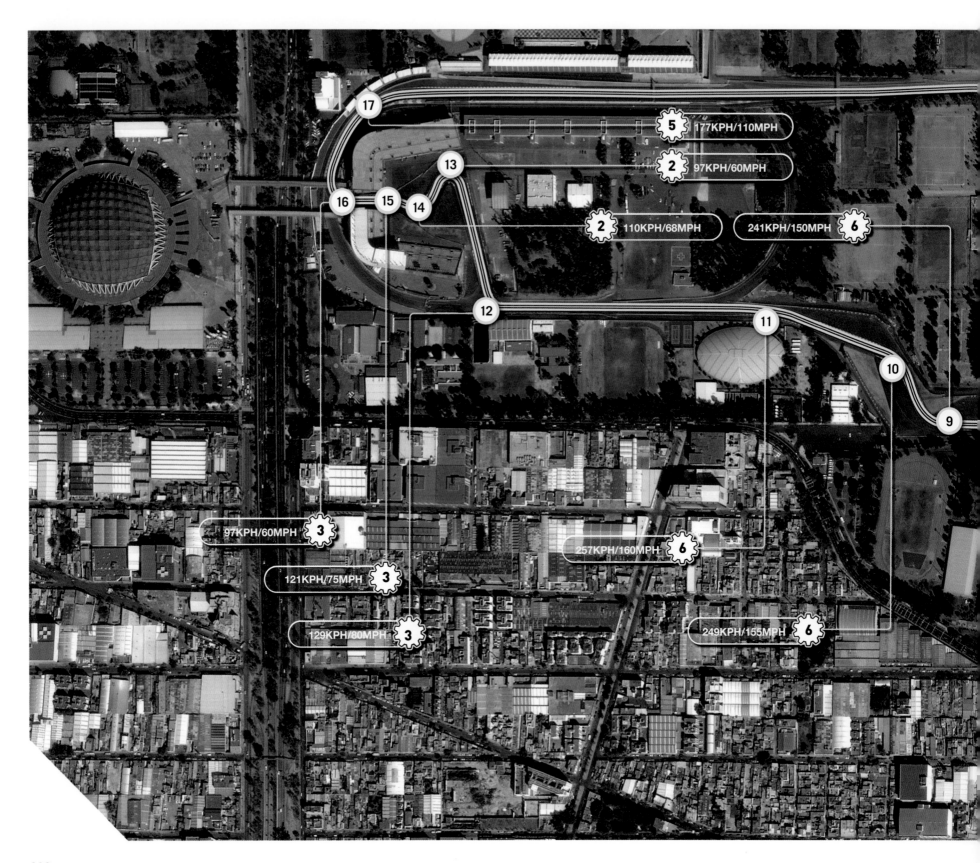

A

1

2 ESPIRAL • 129KPH/80MPH

8 314KPH/195MPH

2

3

4 209KPH/130MPH

3 ESE MOISES SOLANA • 169KPH/105MPH

6 ESES • 233KPH/145MPH

5 217KPH/135MPH

8

A

6 257KPH/160MPH

7

4

5

3 ESE DEL LAGO • 143KPH/90MPH

3 110KPH/68MPH

6

2 HORQUILLA • 97KPH/60MPH

Google Earth

Circuit Guide

Set in parkland, this 4.580 kilometre circuit mixes the high-speed with the sinuous and throws in a stadium section to enhance the drivers' feeling of being in an arena. Hopefully, the bumps for which it became synonymous, will have been flattened.

Turn 1 • Espiral
Gear: **2**
Speed: **129kph (80mph)**

The tree-lined run from the starting grid to the first corner seems to go on and on. It's wide, too, but then it suddenly seems to tighten on the drivers who brake hard and drop down from top gear to perhaps as low as second gear for this 90-degree righthander. Not only is exit speed crucial here, but track position too because it feeds directly into a set of esses, so a passing move not completed out of Turn 1 has every chance of being so by Turn 2.

Turn 2 • Ese Moises Solana
Gear: **3**
Speed: **169kph (105mph)**

The trees are now far from the sides of the track and everything feels more open for the drivers as they position their cars not just for this lefthander but for the righthander that follows directly after it. Unusually for the Autodromo Hermanos Rodriguez, there is a decent amount of run-off here, so drivers are enticed into attempting passing moves, but any loss of momentum out of Turn 3 as a consequence of going off line then costs them down the straight that follows.

Turn 4 • Ese del Lago
Gear: **3**
Speed: **143kph (90mph)**

Having accelerated past a running track, tennis courts and a park, and under two spectator bridges, the drivers see the grandstands surrounding Horquilla ahead of them, but their course veers to the left first. This requires a drop to third gear and then, almost immediately, drivers must slow further for the even tighter righthander that follows. At the turn-in point there is a sense of space, before a shorter track layout turns right to feed into the famous esses.

Turn 6 • Horquilla
Gear: **2**
Speed: **97kph (60mph)**

This is the furthest point from the pits and has been given an increased identity of its own by increasing the capacity of the grandstands. There will be plenty for fans to see as they can watch the action all the way from Ese del Lago to Turn 7. Immediately in front of them, though, the drivers have to brake hard for a pair of tight righthanders, the second of which is slightly more open, then accelerate up a slight incline towards the esses that run from Turn 7 all the way to Turn 13.

Opposite: Jack Brabham is chased through the Eses by Lotus' Mike Spence in 1964, with the mountains that ring Mexico City as a backdrop. *Above left:* This great shot shows the bewinged cars of 1968 as they run through Ese del Lago on the run to Horquilla. *Above right:* Jacky Ickx leads the way for Ferrari in 1970 followed by Tyrrell's Jackie Stewart and his team-mate Clay Regazzoni, with the crowd overflowing onto the surrounding grass verges

Turn 8 • Eses
Gear: **6**
Speed: **233kph (145mph)**

By this midpoint of the esses, a driver will know clearly whether their car is handling well or not, as the track continues almost relentlessly through a sinuous passage of five twists, going left, right, left, right, left. Making life slightly easier for them, the track is inclined gently towards the apex of each bend to "cup" their cars as the drivers continue to accelerate as hard as they dare. It's a fearsome stretch of track, so drivers will be comforted by the run-off area on either side having been increased.

Turn 11 • Eses
Gear: **6**
Speed: **257kph (160mph)**

The key to this fifth and final swerve through this lengthy run of esses that started back at Turn 8 is for a driver to have their car fully balanced through the right swerve at Turn 10 so that they can skim the apex where the circuit turns left in Turn 11. The short straight that follows down to Turn 12 has the drivers hard on the power as they accelerate past the point where the autodrome's oval circuit feeds onto what would be its back straight.

Turn 12 • Recta del Ovalo
Gear: **3**
Speed: **129kph (80mph)**

When F1 last visited the circuit in 1992, the drivers would have been flat-out at this point, gritting their teeth for the challenge of their sweep into the lap's most daunting corner, the Peraltada. However, it has long been considered too dangerous, with too many bumps and too little run-off. So, the drivers now have to focus instead on braking hard and dropping to third gear for the 90-degree right here which takes them into the baseball stadium, giving them an immediate change of pace and change of feel.

Turn 17 • Peraltada
Gear: **5**
Speed: **177kph (110mph)**

The last corner of the lap is certainly not what it once was. Instead of being taken one gear down from top, as in the 1990s, it's now a much slower bend, through which drivers are hard on the power as they continue accelerating out of the penultimate corner. Every fraction of speed that can be squeezed out by the drivers planting their throttle as they burst from the shade of the grandstand into the full sun of the pit straight is then magnified all the way down the straight.

Great Drivers & Great Moments

Mexico has a huge passion for Formula One. Enthralled by the Rodriguez brothers in the 1960s, fans have had Sergio Perez to cheer in the Mexican GP's third F1 stint in the 21st century, but the already raucous and excitable fans are still waiting for a first home win and will go wild when it happens.

Great Drivers

 Jim **Clark**
Mexico City wins – 2

Clark shared victory with Lotus team-mate Trevor Taylor in 1962 when the Mexican GP was held as a non-championship event. He repeated his win in Mexico's first World Championship race in 1963 and was denied by engine failure when leading in 1964. There was confusion at the start in 1967, with Clark being rear-ended, but he was able to continue, took the lead from team-mate Graham Hill after two laps and went to win by more than a minute.

 Nigel **Mansell**
Mexico City wins – 2

Nigel was trailing Williams team-mate Nelson Piquet by 18 points – the equivalent of two wins – with three rounds remaining in 1987, so had to win. He took pole, but was jumped at the start by Ferrari's Gerhard Berger and Benetton's Thierry Boutsen. Mansell regained the lead when they retired, and comfortably beat Piquet. In 1992, Mansell and Williams were the pick of the pack and he dominated for the second of his five wins to start the season.

 Alain **Prost**
Mexico City wins – 2

Prost, a two-time World Champion, had a big challenge in 1988, his new McLaren team-mate Ayrton Senna. The Brazilian regularly outstripped him in qualifying and it was no different in Mexico City. However, Alain made a brilliant start and, despite a visor tear-off entering a radiator, led all the way to the finish. Racing for Ferrari in 1990, he qualified only 13th but rose to second and then inherited victory when Senna had a tyre blow-out.

 Max **Verstappen**
Mexico City wins – 2

Lewis Hamilton had the F1 title almost in the bag in 2017, but all eyes soon swung to Verstappen as the Red Bull racer passed poleman Sebastian Vettel and kept Hamilton behind into the first sequence of corners. Hamilton and Vettel touched, leaving Hamilton to lose time with a puncture and Max to win as he pleased. In 2018, it was Red Bull team-mate Daniel Ricciardo who was bogged down starting from pole, the Dutch star sped past and went on to dominate the race.

Great Moments

1965 **Ginther** gives Honda its first F1 win

Honda did things differently to the other F1 teams when it brought a Japanese approach to F1 in 1964 and claimed its first grand prix win in 1965, courtesy of Richie Ginther. He leapt from third to first, with Jackie Stewart up from eighth to second as poleman Jim Clark was hampered by a failing engine. Stewart's BRM was slowed by a clutch problem, letting Dan Gurney's Brabham through to second, but Ginther was in control and had 2s in hand over his compatriot.

1991 **Senna** flips but is able to race

The lap's last corner, the Peraltada, was fearsome before being modified in the 21st century and is now entered only halfway around what was a wonderful if scary 180-degree sweep. The corner had a small degree of banking, but required bravery and a well-balanced car to take in sixth gear. In 1991, Ayrton Senna was flying in qualifying, but the tail came around and he hit a tyre barrier before flipping. Although shaken, Senna raced and finished third.

2018 **Hamilton** secures his fifth F1 crown

Equalling Juan Manuel Fangio's tally of five World Championship titles was massive to Lewis Hamilton, and he wanted to do so with a lights-to-flag victory, but it wasn't to be. Indeed, the British driver's Mercedes struggled to find any grip throughout the race and he could only play a supporting role behind Red Bull's Max Verstappen. With Ferrari finding form again, there was no podium for Hamilton, but any frustration disappeared when the paddock celebrations began.

2019 **Hamilton** makes tyres work to close in on title

Being struck by Max Verstappen's Red Bull going through the first two corners of the opening lap was a setback for Lewis Hamilton, but he set about making up his lost positions and got up to fourth place in short order. Verstappen was not so lucky though, as he had a tyre blow a few laps after their contact. Hamilton went on to hard compound tyres and stayed on them for the rest of the race. He pitted once, unlike the two visits made by most of his rivals.

Melbourne's daytime road traffic seems oblivious to Red Bull's Mark Webber leading Lewis Hamilton in the 2010 Australian Grand Prix.

Chapter 4
Australia

⚑ Adelaide

Australia is a country with a rich motor racing pedigree and it had long deserved a grand prix before it finally joined the World Championship in 1985. Adelaide's end-of-season race on its city centre circuit proved to be an instant hit.

> ❝You sit on the starting grid with fighters roaring overhead and the crowds cheering and you really can't help but be drawn into Adelaide's very special event.❞
>
> *Damon Hill*

For a country that takes on and beats the best at various sports, not having a round of the World Championship was galling to its motorsport fans. There was a lively and well-supported national racing scene and there had been an Australian GP since 1928, but this had been a national event held for and largely won by Australian drivers. Run to Formula 5000 regulations in the 1970s, it updated itself to Formula Pacific in the 1980s, but the grids were poor and international interest limited. Yet, with the decision to build a circuit in Adelaide, the nation that had given Formula One three-time World Champion Jack Brabham and, more recently, 1980 champion Alan Jones, was finally granted a seat at motor racing's top table.

Australia's first World Championship round was the final race of the 1985 campaign, and Adelaide landed the right to host this. Having risen from the seed of an idea planted by local businessman Bill O'Gorman, which was then supported by state premier John Bannon, this was something of a coup, as the capital of the state of South Australia had long felt overlooked, with Sydney and Melbourne attracting international recognition for their sights and sporting events. The circuit was laid out in the city's Victoria Park. It was centred on the horse racing course there, and the temporary circuit crossed its layout twice going to and coming back from the section where the F1

cars used the streets on the perimeter of the park, from Wakefield Street to Dequetteville Terrace.

As soon as the teams and drivers saw it for the first time, they loved it, as there was space for their equipment, a great flow to the lap and a relaxed feel to proceedings. The weather wasn't bad, either. Better still, Adelaide is a small enough city to embrace an event like a grand prix and treated F1's visit as the key ingredient in its annual "Streets Ahead" festival. With the race being the last one of the year, the teams were also more than happy to party once the chequered flag had fallen, with top level concerts adding to the festival feel.

The inaugural grand prix in 1985 was won by Keke Rosberg after a great battle with Ayrton Senna. He had dropped back after the Brazilian damaged his Lotus's front wing against the Finn's Williams before retiring with engine failure. Niki Lauda also led in his final grand prix but wasn't destined to make the finish either, as his McLaren developed a brake problem and he clipped a wall. The following year's race was more famous, though, as its outcome and the championship's, was decided by an incident that is still considered one of F1's iconic moments. Nigel Mansell was in control, all set to become World Champion for the first time when he had a tyre blow at full speed at the end of Dequetteville Terrace, and he did well to wrestle his Williams to a halt in the escape road.

Rain isn't something that one tends to associate with Australia, but it proved a particular problem at Adelaide in the two events that it hit, in 1989 and 1991, as drainage from the circuit was inadequate. This was shown in 1989, when Martin Brundle had spun his Brabham in practice and was immediately hit by Senna, who had been completely unsighted by the hanging spray.

For all the memories of sunshine and rain, plus some great racing, many think of Mika Hakkinen when they think of Adelaide because the Finn had a huge accident in qualifying in 1995 and was fortunate that rapid attention from F1 doctor Prof Watkins kept him alive. That year's race also sticks in the mind, because David Coulthard led but crashed on pit entry, leaving his Williams team-mate Damon Hill free to win, with second-placed Olivier Panis's Ligier fully two laps behind.

However, the party came to an end when Melbourne grabbed the race from them in 1996 and although Adelaide's street circuit continues to be used, its last international event was when the American Le Mans Series hosted a race that started on 31 December 2000 and carried on to New Year's Day 2001. ∎

Opposite: Racing in Adelaide was invariably conducted in a colourful, party atmosphere. This is Ferrari's Gerhard Berger in 1994.

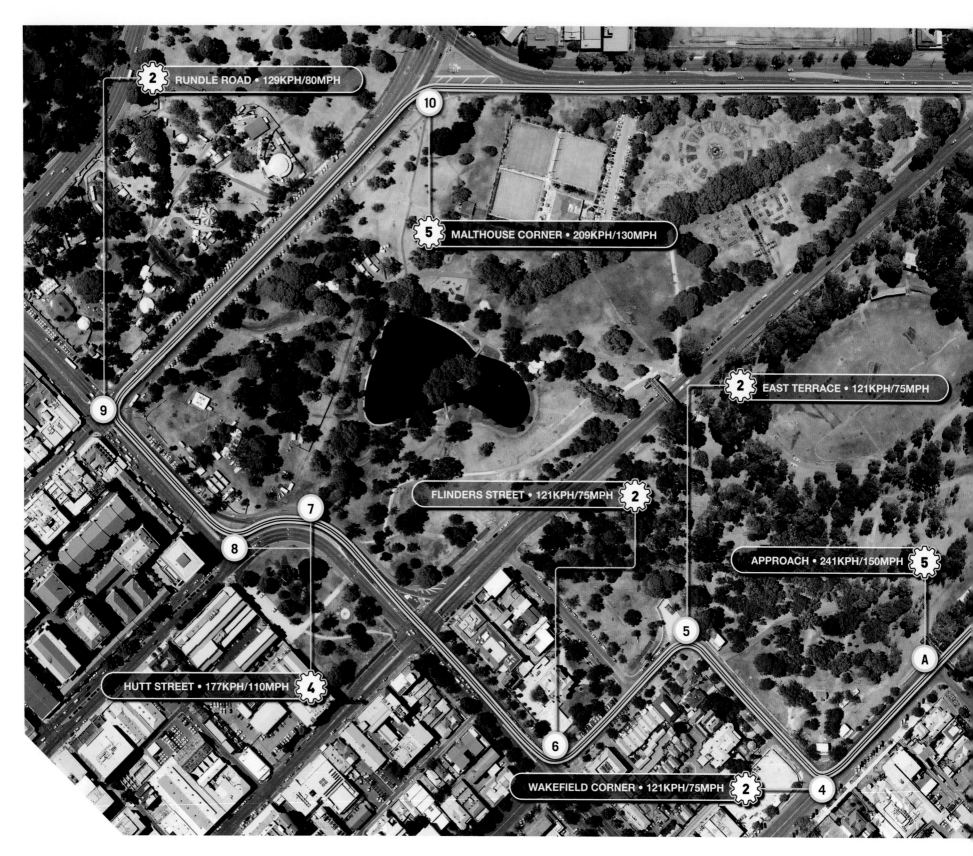

RUNDLE ROAD • 129KPH/80MPH

MALTHOUSE CORNER • 209KPH/130MPH

EAST TERRACE • 121KPH/75MPH

FLINDERS STREET • 121KPH/75MPH

APPROACH • 241KPH/150MPH

HUTT STREET • 177KPH/110MPH

WAKEFIELD CORNER • 121KPH/75MPH

210

DEQUETTEVILLE HAIRPIN • 80KPH/50MPH

APPROACH • 310KPH/193MPH

177KPH/110MPH

209KPH/130MPH

APPROACH • 225KPH/140MPH

SENNA CHICANE • 177KPH/110MPH

FOSTER'S CORNER • 97KPH/60MPH

Google Earth

Image © 2014 Aerometrex © Google 2014

Circuit Guide

This is a circuit of two halves, with its series of 90-degree bends on street junctions contrasting totally with the flat-out blasts and sweeps that follow. It will forever be remembered, though, for Nigel Mansell's blow-out and dive up the escape road.

Turn 1–3 • Senna Chicane
Gear: **3**
Speed: **177kph (110mph)**

Starting in the middle of the city's Victoria Park, the circuit certainly doesn't have the feel of the street circuit it becomes and the tree-lined opening esse bend offers a fine flow through its left/right/left sequence. Usually negotiated side-by-side on the opening lap of the race, the key is not so much about achieving optimum exit speed onto the short straight beyond it but simply to avoid any wing-bending contact. Getting to the front on the first lap can be key to making an escape.

Turn 4 • Wakefield Corner
Gear: **2**
Speed: **121kph (75mph)**

The whole feel of the circuit has changed by the time that the drivers reach this, the first of three consecutive 90-degree bends as the lap ventures out of Victoria Park. The park is still on the drivers' right, but there are now shops and houses on their left. Naturally, the drivers' aim is to brake as late as possible for this righthander, but it is very bumpy on the approach, making getting this just right and not sliding onwards extremely difficult.

Turn 5 • East Terrace
Gear: **2**
Speed: **121kph (75mph)**

Finding a flow through the three 90-degree corners is hard and any driver who has failed to pull across to the righthand side of the circuit after rounding Wakefield Corner will struggle to negotiate this lefthander because the straight between them is only short. Going in off line scrubs off what little momentum the drivers have. This was where Michael Schumacher damaged his Benetton when leading in 1994, doing so just out of sight of Damon Hill, who was chasing hard in his Williams.

Turn 6 • Flinders Street
Gear: **2**
Speed: **121kph (75mph)**

The last of the run of 90-degree bends is much the same as the pair that preceded it, with the blast up Flinders Street from East Terrace another short one. Grip is hard to find and the walls surrounding the circuit are there to damage the cars of those who try to go into the corner too fast and get it wrong. This is where Michael Schumacher controversially turned across on Damon Hill in 1994 and settled the outcome of the drivers' title.

Opposite: The circuit's downtown setting is abundantly clear as Nigel Mansell flashes past in his Williams in 1992 ***Above left:*** The moment of truth approaches at Turn 6 in the 1994 finale as Michael Schumacher is about to swerve his damaged Benetton across into Damon Hill's Williams. ***Above right:*** Street racing ace Ayrton Senna picks the fastest line through Turn 9 to claim pole for McLaren in 1991.

Turn 7/8 • Hutt Street
Gear: **4**
Speed: **177kph (110mph)**

At last, a chance for the drivers to take a corner at speed after the run of 90-degree bends. This left/right sweeper is taken in fourth gear and drivers are naturally keen to start building a flow as the circuit opens out again. However, this corner is made difficult by the camber being adverse. With a concrete wall there to greet them should they get it wrong, it is what Mike Hakkinen once described as a "confidence corner". There's then a short straight to yet another 90-degree bend.

Turn 10 • Malthouse Corner
Gear: **5**
Speed: **209kph (130mph)**

The circuit opens up after Turn 9 and this fast right kink leads on to the only appreciable straight of the lap, so it's vital for a driver to get a clean run through this fifth gear corner. However, the kerbs are high on the inside and Mika Hakkinen was fortunate to survive a huge impact here in qualifying in 1995, when his McLaren suffered a rear tyre deflation, vaulted the inside kerbs and hit the outside wall hard. An emergency tracheotomy saved his life.

Turn 11 • Dequetteville Hairpin
Gear: **1**
Speed: **80kph (50mph)**

The savage change from flat-out in top gear to heavy braking and dropping down the gearbox to first is required for this righthand hairpin. It offers undoubtedly the main opportunity for overtaking if a driver has worked a tow down the straight. Nigel Mansell, though, discovered in 1986 that it's impossible to turn in to the corner if one of your rear tyres has exploded. He was forced to wrestle his Williams to a halt, along with his world title hopes.

Turn 15 • Foster's Corner
Gear: **2**
Speed: **97kph (60mph)**

After a tight left and a sweeping esse behind the paddock, the drivers reach the final corner of the lap. It's another hairpin, but it's way less extreme than the Dequetteville Hairpin and can be taken a gear higher. The bumpy nature of the circuit both on the way in and the way out make braking and acceleration difficult as drivers try to get themselves into a good position to make an attacking run past the pits towards the sweepers that open the lap.

Melbourne

Racing in Melbourne has proved a hit since the Australian GP was moved there in 1996, with the city proving a fun place to be and the grandstands and spectator banking filled to capacity on each of the meetings' three days.

❝I love Melbourne, but not only the track, as the atmosphere around the grand prix is fantastic and all the people here enjoy the whole weekend.❞

Fernando Alonso

Adelaide was distraught when its deal to host the Australian GP came to a close at the end of 1995 and the race was moved to Melbourne's Albert Park, and even pushed to host a second Australian race under the convenience title of the Pacific GP. This never happened and Melbourne has been Australia's home of F1 ever since, with its sports-mad citizens having New South Wales premier Jeff Kennett to thank for this.

Kennett negotiated a deal with Bernie Ecclestone and the site he chose for the temporary circuit was in Albert Park, a municipal park to the south of the city centre. Albert Park had hosted racing before, hosting the Australian GP on a temporary layout around the park's lake in 1953 and 1956, when it was a non-championship event largely for driver from Australia and New Zealand. The winner of the second of these, though, was a young British driver by the name of Stirling Moss in a works Maserati, who also won the Tourist Trophy sportscar race at the same event. Local opposition then led to its closure and eventually to the opening of two circuits on the outskirts of Melbourne, at Calder and Sandown Park.

There was strong opposition from a handful of locals, who felt that putting a grand prix circuit in Albert Park again would be environmentally unsound and would lead to the despoiling of the park. Consequently, considerable steps were taken to minimize its impact, with the organizers agreeing to dredge the lake and upgrade the somewhat rundown park's sports facilities as recompense.

The lap they laid out is a mixture of slow and medium-speed corners as it runs in a clockwise direction around the lake in the middle of the park, with the only truly fast corners being Turns 11 and 12, where the circuit swerves left and then right on the far side of the lake. Otherwise, there are a predominance of medium-speed corners, yet the lap still has a good flow. Furthermore, the fans enjoy excellent viewing from grandstands and hospitality decks that line much of the route. Those who choose to sit in the stands overlooking the first three corners are almost invariably treated to some extremely close racing, peppered with incident on the opening lap.

Australians are accustomed to an extremely high level of sporting event, so the grand prix programme is more packed here than anywhere else to keep them entertained, with almost continuous support races whenever the F1 cars are not on track through the three days. In turn, the teams enjoy the city's high quality of hotels and restaurants, while they also appreciate the ease of access to the circuit, because thousands of fans eschew arriving by car and come in by tram, thus reducing the car parking queues that can be such a hassle at other venues.

The city's inaugural World Championship event kicked off the 1996 World Championship, just four months after F1 left Adelaide for good, and was won by Damon Hill for Williams. He was beaten to pole position by team-mate Jacques Villeneuve, and after Martin Brundle had an aerial shunt in his Jordan and necessitated a restart, Hill and Villeneuve traded the lead until debutant Villeneuve was told to slow because his Renault engine was blowing out oil. Having let Hill by, he slowed his pace and yet was still able to finish second. The way that Melburnians supported the event, packing out the grandstands, showed that they loved F1's visit every bit as much as their neighbours in Adelaide had. Since that first race, Melbourne's grand prix boss Ron Walker has driven the event forward, made it very much a key part of the World Championship, as a vibrant place to open the season, with capacity crowds helping to show F1 in its rudest health.

Well attended, with the added twist of being the first time each year that the fans get to see how the new cars compare with each other, Melbourne's grand prix is now very much part of the establishment. It's one of Melbourne's sporting crown jewels, along with its hosting of the Australian Open tennis tournament, Test matches at The Melbourne Cricket Ground and the best-attended Australian Rules Football matches. ∎

Opposite: Nico Rosberg runs flat-out around the far side of Albert Park's lake in his Mercedes in 2013, with the city centre as his backdrop.

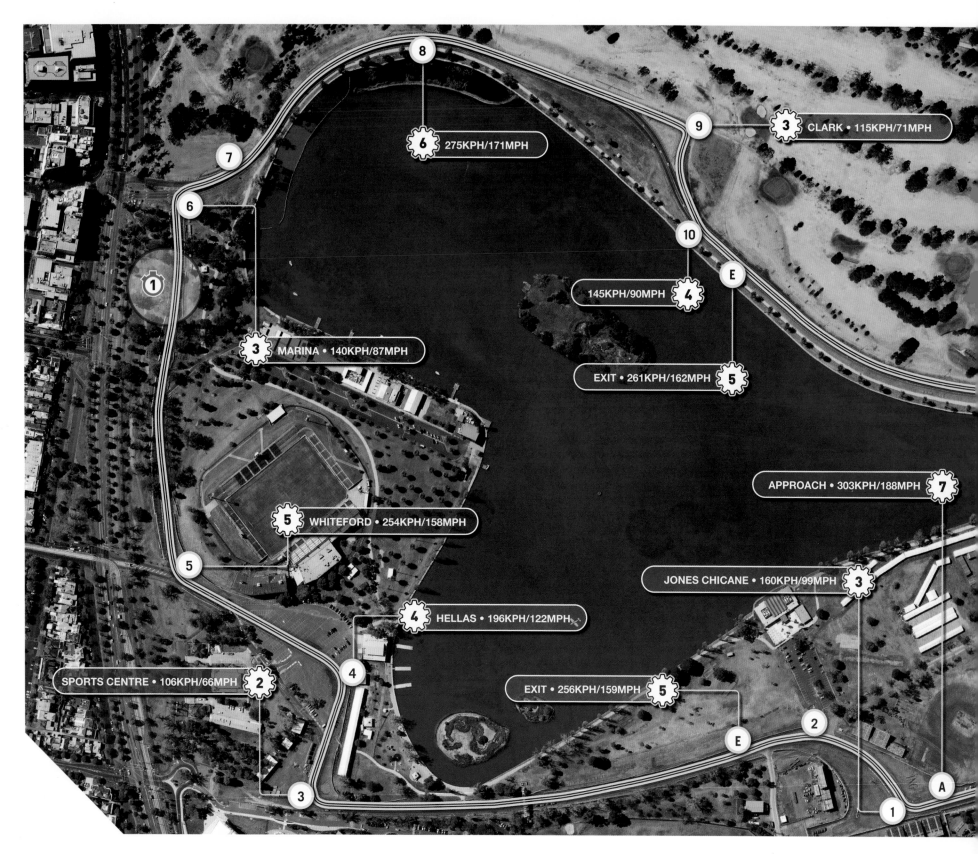

CLARK • 115KPH/71MPH

6 275KPH/171MPH

145KPH/90MPH **4**

3 MARINA • 140KPH/87MPH

EXIT • 261KPH/162MPH **5**

APPROACH • 303KPH/188MPH **7**

5 WHITEFORD • 254KPH/158MPH

JONES CHICANE • 160KPH/99MPH **3**

4 HELLAS • 196KPH/122MPH

SPORTS CENTRE • 106KPH/66MPH **2**

EXIT • 256KPH/159MPH **5**

ASCARI • 143KPH/89MPH **3**

WAITE • 248KPH/154MPH **5**

12

A

13

APPROACH • 282KPH/175MPH **6**

11

2

2 SENNA • 89KPH/55MPH

5 226KPH/140MPH

15

14

STEWART• 166KPH/103MPH **3**

16

3

PROST • 180KPH/112MPH **4**

Google Earth

Circuit Guide

This has always been a difficult circuit for teams to launch their new cars on at the start of the season, because it's a real mixture, with every type of corner except for any really high-speed ones.

Turn 1 • **Jones Chicane**
Gear: **3**
Speed: **160kph (99mph)**

This opening corner has been the scene of more clashes between cars than almost any other used by F1. The nature of the corner, as it folds back through 90 degrees to channel the cars to the right and almost straight into Turn 2, explains why many an opening lap move goes wrong here, with drivers lured to make rash passing moves by the feeling of space. Famously, Ralf Schumacher got it wrong here in 2002, when his Williams was launched off Rubens Barrichello's Ferrari.

Turn 3 • **Sports Centre**
Gear: **2**
Speed: **106kph (66mph)**

The drivers must feel as though the walls are closing in on them as they exit Turn 2 and the track becomes flanked by walls and the trees behind as they accelerate down the straight to Turn 3. Martin Brundle will certainly recall the bunching that can happen as the cars brake heavily for this 100-degree righthander, because his Jordan clipped another car in the braking zone in 1996 and flew straight on into the mercifully large run-off area that opens out ahead of them.

Turn 5 • **Whiteford**
Gear: **5**
Speed: **254kph (158mph)**

After fleetingly enjoying the feeling of space through Turn 4 as it feeds the cars to their left through the car parking area of the Lakeside Stadium, the track immediately narrows down again as it enters its second run funnelled between temporary concrete walls. This right flick is fast, taken in fifth gear, and drivers tend to ride over the inside kerb here as they attempt to take the straightest line onto the short straight that follows.

Turn 6 • **Marina**
Gear: **3**
Speed: **140kph (87mph)**

Running in the shade of the trees that line either flank of the approach to this corner alongside Albert Road, with drivers arriving at 290kph (180mph), Turn 6 requires heavy braking because it's a second-gear corner with an exit that needs to be taken with accuracy. The track then immediately starts to swerve to the left again as the drivers advance to the "lakeside" section of the lap. Many drivers have attempted to go in too fast here and slid off into the vast gravel trap.

Opposite: Sebastian Vettel leads the field through Turn 4 on the opening lap in 2013, but victory would be taken by Lotus's Kimi Raikkonen. ***Above left:*** Spectators line almost the full length of the circuit. Here, they watch Williams's Pastor Maldonado brake hard for Turn 13. ***Above right:*** Fernando Alonso heads Adrian Sutil as they accelerate through Turn 2.

Turn 9 • Clark
Gear: **3**
Speed: **115kph (71mph)**

Just as the drivers start to get into a flow through the sweeping corners around the far side of Albert Park's lake, they're hauled back by this tight righthander. If taken right, riding the kerbs a little but not too much, this is a simple chicane. If got wrong, it can waste momentum, so exerting a little caution here is wise because good exit speed is vital for a driver to attain the highest speed their car can manage for a blast that will take them all the way to Turn 13.

Turn 12 • Waite
Gear: **5**
Speed: **248kph (154mph)**

Taken in fifth gear, drivers gain sight of this sweeper only after they have come around the sloping spectator banking that blocks their view until they're hitting the apex at high-speed Turn 11. They have to balance their cars as they fleetingly get a view of the tall buildings on Queens Road and haul their cars to the right through what is effectively a very rapid chicane. There's a great feeling of space again because there are wide grass verges on either side of the track.

Turn 13 • Ascari
Gear: **3**
Speed: **143kph (89mph)**

The high-speed lakeside section of the lap comes to an end here as the track tightens up again at this near 90-degree righthander that turns around the end of the lake. The flow reverts more to how it was through the first few corners of the lap, with a run of similar corners to follow. The track dips under the shade of the trees again on its exit and, providing a driver has resisted any attack into Turn 13, they should stay ahead for the rest of the lap.

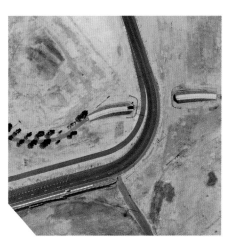

Turn 16 • Prost
Gear: **4**
Speed: **180kph (112mph)**

After tight Turn 15, this final corner looks rather simpler to negotiate, but there's not a lot of space on the outside of the righthander and the desire to carry as much speed as possible out of this corner to perhaps build towards a passing move into Turn 1 has led to drivers running wide over the kerbs. The most famous of these incidents came when Michael Schumacher did just that in 2003 before hitting the outside wall with his Ferrari and spinning across the track.

Great Drivers & Great Moments

As Melbourne has, more often than not, hosted the opening round of the season, the pack has usually been given a shuffle, so the world's eyes are always fixed on Albert Park to see who will be the first to lay down a marker for the season ahead. None has been as surprising as when newly reformed team Brawn GP turned up and took victory in the 2009 season-opener.

Great Drivers

 Michael **Schumacher**
Melbourne wins – 4

By Michael Schumacher's lofty standards, four wins from his 14 outings in Melbourne was a poor haul. However, his victories were all important because they marked the start of a campaign, setting the tone for the rest of the year. The first of these was lucky; the McLarens led but broke down in 2000. After that, he was trailed home by David Coulthard in 2001, then won as he pleased after his rivals were caught up in a first corner shunt in 2002 and dominated in 2004.

 Jenson **Button**
Melbourne wins – 3

The collapse of Honda Racing left Jenson without a drive for 2009. Fortunately, not only was it resurrected as Brawn GP, but its car was the class of the field, allowing him to win the season's opening race in Australia then win five more to become a dominant champion. Following on from that incredible year, many thought that his move to McLaren for 2010 would see him playing second fiddle to Lewis Hamilton, but Jenson came here for the second round and won to confirm his credentials.

 David **Coulthard**
Melbourne wins – 2

In becoming the second winner in Melbourne, in 1997 at the start of his second year with McLaren, David was able to put behind him the embarrassment of crashing into the pitwall at the final race in Adelaide in 1995. He was helped by three factors: Eddie Irvine taking favourite Jacques Villeneuve out at the first corner, Heinz-Harald Frentzen's Williams hitting brake problems, and by pitting just once. The Scot would win again in 2003, rising from 11th in a race of changing fortunes.

 Kimi **Raikkonen**
Melbourne wins – 2

This flying Finn achieved a dream start to his first spell at Ferrari when he won in 2007 after starting from pole. He controlled the race from the front, beating Fernando Alonso's McLaren easily. Then, having returned from his years away in rallying in 2012, Kimi marked the start of his second year back with Lotus by winning in 2013. This was a surprise because everyone thought that a Red Bull would win, but Kimi worked his way forward from seventh through better tyre preservation than his rivals.

Great Moments

1998 David **Coulthard** lets Mika Hakkinen through to win

The outcome of 1998's opening race remains one of the oddest in F1 history. It was clear from the start of practice that McLaren had the best car. Mika Hakkinen and David Coulthard duly filled the front row and raced away untroubled but, midway through the race, Hakkinen thought he'd been called to the pits. He hadn't, so this detour dropped him behind Coulthard. Then, late in the race, the Scot let him past, honouring a pre-race agreement that whichever led into the first corner would win.

2005 Giancarlo **Fisichella** makes a winning return

Giancarlo's return to the team he'd raced for when it was Benetton kicked off in the best way possible when he grabbed pole for the first race of 2005 after benefiting from rain that arrived before his leading rivals had made their runs. Giancarlo then started his Renault with a heavy fuel load and this enabled him to run a long opening stint and it set him up for victory, although the drive of the day came from team-mate Fernando Alonso who rose from 13th to third.

2009 Jenson **Button** gives Brawn its first win

The collapse of Honda Racing and the subsequent reinvention of the team as Brawn GP left few expecting this midfield team to shine, but it very much did just that at the opening race of 2009. Helped by its use of double diffusers, the team's BGP 001s were the class of the field and Jenson Button not only qualified on pole ahead of team-mate Rubens Barrichello but then led every lap to lead home an extraordinary one-two finish for the team ahead of Jarno Trulli's Toyota.

2019 **Bottas** shows renewed form after winter break

Valtteri Bottas displayed new-found form for the 2019 season by dominating the opening race of the campaign. This came as a surprise, not only because he beat Mercedes team-mate Lewis Hamilton but also that he left the Ferraris in his wake despite the Italian team having dominated pre-season testing. Hamilton was on pole, but Bottas jumped him and, four laps in, Hamilton damaged his car's floor. He was still able to finish second, while the Ferraris fell behind Max Verstappen's Red Bull.

Index

222

Left: The sun goes down on the Yas Marina Circuit, Abu Dhabi, in November 2013.

Credits

The publishers would like to thank the following sources for their kind permission to reproduce the pictures in this book.

All Formula One Grand Prix Action Photography: © Motorsport Images

Special thanks to Zoë Schafer, Kevin Wood and Tim Clarke for their expert knowledge and assistance researching the photography for this project.

Every effort has been made to acknowledge correctly and contact the source and/or copyright holder of each picture any unintentional errors or omissions will be corrected in future editions of this book.

Bibliography

From Brands Hatch to Indianapolis, Tommaso Tommasi, Hamlyn, 0 600 33557 7
Grand Prix Battlegrounds, Christopher Hilton, Haynes Publishing, 978 1 84425 694 5
The International Motor Racing Guide, Peter Higham, David Bull, 1 893618 20 X
The World Atlas of Motor Racing, Joe Saward, Hamlyn, 0 600 564053
World Motor Racing Circuits, Peter Higham & Bruce Jones, Andre Deutsch, 0 233 99619 2
Plus articles from *Autosport*, *F1 Racing* and *Motor Sport* magazines